Lincoln and the Decision for War

CIVIL WAR AMERICA

Gary W. Gallagher, editor

Lincoln

and the Decision for War ✳ The Northern Response to Secession ✳

Russell McClintock

The University of North Carolina Press

Chapel Hill

This book was published with the assistance of
the William R. Kenan Jr. Fund of the University of
North Carolina Press.

A Caravan book.
For more information, visit www.caravanbooks.org.

Manufactured in the United States of America
Set in Monticello and The Serif types by Keystone Typesetting, Inc.

The paper in this book meets the guidelines for permanence
and durability of the Committee on Production Guidelines for
Book Longevity of the Council on Library Resources.

Library of Congress Cataloging-in-Publication Data
McClintock, Russell.
Lincoln and the decision for war : the northern response to
secession / Russell McClintock.
    p. cm. — (Civil War America)
Includes bibliographical references and index.
ISBN 978-0-8078-3188-5 (cloth: alk. paper)
1. United States—Politics and government—1861–1865—Decision
making. 2. United States—Politics and government—1857–1861—
Decision making. 3. United States—History—Civil War, 1861–
1865—Causes. 4. Lincoln, Abraham, 1809–1865—Political and
social views. 5. Secession—Southern States—Public opinion.
6. Northeastern States—Politics and government—19th century.
7. Nationalism—Northeastern States—History—19th century.
8. Political culture—Northeastern States—History—19th century.
9. Public opinion—Northeastern States—History—19th century.
I. Title.
E456.M26   2008
973.7—dc22   2007029356

cloth   12 11 10 09 08   5 4 3 2 1

for my mother,
who has devoted
her life to giving her
children a better life
and succeeded

Contents

Preface

Like a lot of people, I have an absorbing interest in the Civil War. In particular, it is the idea of the war that enthralls me—it is so out of keeping with the rest of U.S. history. Although scholars today generally dismiss the notion that there is such a thing as a national character, I think anyone would agree that armies of Americans marching through the fields and towns of the United States engaging in brutal, bloody battle with armies of other Americans must be considered out of character, to say the least. How did it happen, then? It is a question that has preoccupied generations of historians.

In my deep fascination for the war and its causes lie this book's broad origins, but like the war, it, too, has a more specific, immediate story. It began one day in the kitchen of a friend's house, back in my younger, undergraduate history-major days—back when I was first discovering how the mere mention of my studies in history, and especially the Civil War, elicited in most people a powerful response: in some, the startling fervor of the history lover, in others, a horrified shudder produced by the half-repressed memory of a tyrannical teacher and long lists of names and dates. My friend's father is of the former class. A Civil War buff, he was wild about my chosen field of study and each time I visited had a new book to show me or story to tell. On this particular day, Mr. Maxfield was relating a conversation he had had with a client or coworker who insisted that slavery was the cause of the Civil War. I remember vividly the conviction with which he exclaimed to me, "It wasn't slavery that started the war—it was secession!" Deferential young man that I was, I nodded in agreement, keeping to myself my initial thought that as an explanation this raised more questions than it answered. Without slavery, I knew, there would have been no secession.

That is all I remember of the conversation, but remember it I did. I found myself going back to it, turning it over in my mind. I began reading up on secession. And over time I came to realize the significance of my friend's father's observation. Without slavery, there would have been no secession, certainly, and thus no war—but slavery itself did not spark the Civil War. Secession did. It was my first discovery of the concept of proximate versus remote causation, my first recognition of the commonsense notion that the roots of any historical event involve both short-term, immediate factors and long-term, underlying forces. But still I didn't fully agree with Mr. Maxfield's argument. (Numerous historians have focused on secession in explaining the origins of the Civil War, but to me it was—and still is—his idea.) Another thought nagged: secession did not actually cause the war either. What if the North had let the South go? No war. For one looking to identify that final, most direct cause, I realized, that was the key.

This book, then, tells the story of America's last, irrevocable step into civil war. It is intended to be my own small contribution to a generations-long discussion of how the war happened. If along the way it also implies something about the American character, then so be it.

✴ Considering what lonely work research and writing is, producing this book has brought me into contact with a remarkable number of people and led me to incur a large number of debts. I hope that expressing my gratitude here is sufficient payment.

I will begin by thanking those who helped nurture this study in its embryonic stages: Ronald J. Maxfield, who unknowingly inspired my early interest in the topic, and at Providence College, Robert Deasy and Mario DiNunzio.

Since that time I have received generous financial support from several sources, without which the scope of my research could not have approached that which the topic requires. I would like to thank the Gilder Lehrman Institute of American History for a Gilder Lehrman Fellowship, the Illinois Historic Preservation Agency and the Illinois State Historical Society for a King V. Hostick Prize, and the Clark University History Department for both a five-year teaching assistantship (apparently I was a slow learner) and critical travel funding. I would also like to thank the staff members at the Illinois State Historical Library (now the Abraham Lincoln Presidential Library), the Chicago Historical Society, the Library of Congress, the Pierpont Morgan Library, the New York Public Library, the New-York Historical Society, the New York State Library (where they were kind enough to remember an undergraduate intern from long before), the Massachusetts Historical Society, and the American Antiquarian Society. I was met at each and every one of these institutions by individuals who were enormously helpful and unfailingly welcoming. Thanks also to the reference staff at Clark University's Goddard Library, Mary Hartman, Irene Walch, and Rachael Shea, who always went out of their way for me.

And special thanks go to Christie Guppy and Mike and Mona Murphy, old friends who in putting me up made a couple of research trips a lot more fun than research trips are supposed to be.

I am grateful to the administration, faculty, and students at St. John's High School, whose enthusiastic encouragement has greatly facilitated the final stages of this book. I am fortunate to find myself in a community that epitomizes generosity, faith, class, and true professionalism. My thanks to Steve Gregory in particular for taking the time to read and critique the manuscript, and to Kyle Deming, who read just one line but made an important suggestion nevertheless.

In this limited space I cannot possibly express the debts I owe to the warm and supportive members of the History Department at Clark University, who nurtured me through seven thoroughly enjoyable years. Special thanks go to Diane Fenner, a wonderful help and a friend. Several of my graduate colleagues read and offered valuable advice on various parts of the manuscript: Tony Connors, Carol Cullen, Lisa Connelly-Cook, and Terry Delaney all challenged or encouraged my thinking in important ways. This book is better history for their unflinching honesty, and I am a better historian for having been trained with them. In addition to offering valuable insight regarding the manuscript, Janette Greenwood always went out of her way for me, from providing a model of classroom excellence to searching doggedly for additional funding. Amy Richter was a fierce supporter, relentless critic, and good friend. Her rigid standards were all the more effective for her tempering them with patience, humor, and affection. Finally, Drew McCoy continues to be my rock throughout this long process. He knew enough to let me find my own way, yet displayed a remarkable sense of when to give a word of encouragement or a gentle push in the right direction. At a few critical times, not all of them related to this project, his unblinking trust in me shored up my faith in myself.

At the University of North Carolina Press, my work has been improved dramatically by the criticism of Daniel W. Crofts, whose suggestions forced me to sharpen both my thinking and my prose, and saved me from some embarrassing errors. Thanks as well to my second anonymous reader, who chose to remain so, and to David Perry, David Hines, Kathleen Ketterman, and Mary Caviness, who has been all one could want in an editor.

At various times and in various ways David, Dan, Denise, and Greg McClintock have all adjusted their lives to accommodate my studies, even as they kept me sane (and humble) by having not the slightest interest in history. Thank you. I also owe special thanks for critical help in a variety of personal ways to Barbara and Glen Martin, Tammy Nadeau, Beverly and Fran Garafoli, and Ron and LuAnn Pichierri.

My greatest debt is to my mother and father, Roberta and Dave McClintock, for their unquestioning sacrifices, unbounded faith, and unconditional love. As if that were not enough, my mother has been a vital part of the book itself, painstakingly transcribing hundreds of letters and proofreading several drafts of the manuscript. She can deny it all she wants, but I mean it literally when I say I could not have produced this book without her, in so many ways. I love you, Mom. This is for you.

My debt to Rylee, Morgan, and Martin for their incredible patience with Daddy's never-ending work is profound, and can never be repaid. But I will try. Finally, it is impossible to express my gratitude to Jennifer, who has been picking up the slack for me, without complaint, since the day we were married. Yet for all the extra work she has taken on, the arranging of her schedule around mine, and the countless days when she saw me only at mealtimes—without any of which this book would not exist—her greatest contribution has been simply to be there. If not for her, I would likely have given this up years ago (and probably wound up in a better-paying profession, but we try not to think about that). This book is a giant step on the road to our dream, the dream that over the years has kept both of us going. I continue to be awed at her devotion to it, and to our children, and to me. Thank you, my lovely wife.

Introduction

The outlines of the story are easily enough told. In the presidential election of 1860, a long history of sectional strife culminated in victory for the Republican Party. Not surprisingly, given the Republicans' anti-South, antislavery message, the voting that year was remarkably lopsided with regard to geography. In the eighteen free states—generally speaking, those states from Pennsylvania to Iowa, north—Republican candidate Abraham Lincoln won 54 percent of the popular vote and nearly every electoral vote. In the fifteen slave states— roughly from Maryland, Kentucky, and Missouri, south—Lincoln received just 2 percent of the popular vote and captured a total of two counties; his name did not even appear on the ballot in the Deep South cotton belt. To a great many Southerners, the election's results exposed their powerlessness before a hostile enemy. The seven states of the Deep South formally withdrew from the United States and met in early February to form a new government. Secessionists and unionists in the other eight slave states spent the next months debating whether to join the new Southern Confederacy.

The remainder of the country was left with the stunned realization that America's unique experiment in self-government, whose example was to have inspired the overthrow of monarchy and the spread of republican principles throughout the world, was imploding. The outgoing administration of President James Buchanan, fearful of initiating war, hesitated to act. The incoming Lincoln administration, powerless until the inauguration, maintained an official silence. Congress quickly deadlocked between members who wished to entice the Southern states with concessions to slavery and those who refused to bow to the threat of disunion. And throughout the free states, citizens spent the winter arguing, petitioning, pleading, haranguing, accusing, and, above all, anxiously pondering a suddenly uncertain future as abstract questions regarding the nature of their national Union abruptly became all too real and immediate.

The paralysis lasted from early November until April, when military forces from the seceded states attacked federal troops stationed at Fort Sumter in South Carolina. The recently inaugurated Republican president, Abraham Lincoln, called for volunteers to suppress the Southern rebellion, and an instantly united North responded vigorously. Debate ceased and war began, a horrific civil war that would last four long years, cost over 600,000 lives, and transform the American republic forever.

Even in its broad outlines, then, the significance of this story is plainly seen; it tells of the opening of a great and terrible war. But the Great Secession Winter, as it has been called,[1] was a defining period in U.S. history not merely because it climaxed in war. During those five months, Southern actions forced Northerners not only to discuss but to decide questions with momentous implications for their country's future, in both the short and the long terms. Those discussions and decisions offer historians an unparalleled glimpse not only into the war's immediate causes but also into the thoughts and attitudes of antebellum Northerners. It was during this crisis that citizens of the free states finally defined the fundamental nature of the American Union, a task at which their Revolutionary forebears had deliberately and tragically balked.

When we look a bit closer at the story, what strikes us first is that in the weeks and months following the 1860 election, the North had been sharply divided in its response to secession. In the face of national rupture, keen political rivalries and widely divergent attitudes and beliefs polarized residents of the free states. Throughout the winter and into the spring partisans argued passionately over the North's proper course, particularly with regard to the two critical issues that secession brought to the fore: whether to compromise with the South in hopes of preventing disunion and, that failing, whether to use force to maintain national authority. Their discussion seldom took the form of rational, enlightened debate. Since each side was convinced that the other's proposals could end only in ruin, advocates of both sides raged at what seemed the other's willful blindness, if not outright treason. Much of the energy expended during the crisis was spent in a rancorous display of finger-pointing as Northerners tried to come to terms with the implications of disunion.

Hidden to them but apparent to the historian is that the same cyclonic forces that divided Northerners simultaneously transformed the very questions they were debating, stripping away partisan differences and laying bare the powerful bonds that lay beneath. Eventually, both sides came to understand that regardless of their very real differences as to means, all sought a single end: preservation of the Union. Once secession had rendered the integrity of the Union the only truly meaningful question, the underlying Northern consensus on that vital issue made war all but inevitable. With the Confederate attack on Fort Sumter, which early on in the crisis had become a concrete focal point for Northern unionism, any remaining alternatives vanished. Northerners of all parties reacted with fury to what they perceived as aggression against the flag, and a suddenly united region rallied to the president's call to arms. And, in Lincoln's words, the war came.

✳ Examining the secession crisis for insight into why and how the American Civil War began is not an original idea. Most studies of the period have focused on the South; in recent decades especially, an explosion of local, state, and regional surveys has tremendously increased historians' understandings of the origins of Southern sectionalism and secession.[2] Tracing the war's origins is not so simple, however; as Eric Foner has pointed out, "the decision for civil war in 1860–61 can be resolved into two questions— why did the South secede, and why did the North refuse to let the South secede?"[3] Just as historians have often neglected the latter query, so would many Northerners at the time have been confused by it. Most Republicans, in particular, did not consider that they had a choice but saw themselves as merely reacting to Southern aggression. Thus Lincoln's attitude toward the South: "In your hands, my dissatisfied fellow countrymen, and not in mine, is the momentous issue of civil war. . . . With you, and not with me, is the solemn question of 'Shall it be peace, or a sword?'"[4] Yet secession was not inherently violent. In actuality, the Civil War began not when the Southern states seceded but when the Northern states acted forcibly to stop them. In the end it was Northerners who decided whether it was to be peace or a sword. Settling that question, in fact, lay at the heart of Northern debates.

Despite the profound significance of the North's reaction, Kenneth M. Stampp's *And the War Came* remains, over half a century after its initial publication, the only comprehensive study of the North during the secession crisis.[5] Before Stampp and since, the considerable literature on this aspect of the crisis has tended to focus on a few specific areas. A number of books and articles have addressed the response of particular Northern regions or localities to the crisis, but few have done so with an eye to any larger significance.[6] The few broad accounts of that fateful winter have tended to be popular histories that gloss over deeper issues in favor of drama and action.[7] From the 1920s to the 1960s, some of America's greatest twentieth-century historians, including James G. Randall, David M. Potter, and Stampp, conducted a lively and valuable debate on the role of Abraham Lincoln, exploring his actions and motivations with such thor oughness that more recent historians of the crisis have tended to avoid this perspective.[8] Finally, a handful of works have focused on particular elements of the federal government's response, such as congressional debates over compromise, events at the Southern forts, and the 1861 Washington Peace Conference.[9]

Stampp's work, then, is the only real precursor to the present account. That his work has held up as well as it has for over fifty years is impressive; that it has held up over the last fifty years in particular is incredible. The decades since his book's publication in 1950 have witnessed a revolution in historical study, as changing cultural values and an astounding shift in the gender, class, and ethnic and racial composition of academia have sparked a fundamental reconceptualization of the past, even as a breaking down of disciplinary walls has sparked a massive rethinking of how we go about studying the past. Although it is still of great scholarly value, then, it is inevitable that Stampp's study shows its age. For example, it reflects the author's own moral concerns in focusing primarily—almost solely—on the attitudes of not just the Republican Party but the radical antislavery wing of that party in particular; it was natural that a historian who in the 1950s and 1960s would be instrumental in overhauling racist interpretations of the Civil War era would dismiss the views of the Republicans' opponents, and even the party's moderates and conservatives, as less than legitimate.[10] As a result, in its analysis, *And the War Came* overlooks a major portion of the Northern public. Redressing that imbalance is among my foremost goals.

In addition, Stampp leans toward a form of economic determinism, a legacy of the Progressive school that had been so dominant in the years of his graduate training, in explaining the historical basis of both the sectional conflict and Northern attitudes. As a result, his answers to the two fundamental questions raised by the crisis—why did so many Northerners oppose slavery's westward expansion so strongly that they would risk disunion rather than compromise on it, and why did almost all Northerners oppose disunion so strongly that they would go to war to prevent it?—are severely outdated. Writing well before Bernard Bailyn's seminal work on the American Revolution turned the attention of historians to the importance of ideology in public perception and discourse, Stampp dismisses the inflamed rhetoric of the crisis as "word juggling," "hairsplitting," and even deliberately "fraudulent." Hence he misses a wonderful opportunity to examine Northerners' cultural attachment to such important symbolic issues as the West, enforcement of the laws, and the Union itself, and to analyze the role of such ideas and assumptions in their responses to secession.

Plainly there is a crying need to incorporate a general account of the North into our picture of the secession crisis. This study is intended to be a first step toward that goal. In it I hope to provide a broad analysis of the Northern response to secession, as well as a possible framework for future local- and state-level studies that speak to a broader context.

✳ In approaching the secession crisis, I have, like scholars before me, placed politics at the center of the story. That was not my original intention; this project was not always conceived as a purely political history. In fact, when I began this project, the working subtitle was "Northern Society, the Crisis of the Union, and the Coming of the Civil War"; I thought I would best understand Northerners' responses to disunion by examining their social structure and conflicts. The change in approach reflects two realizations on my part.

First was a recognition that the secession crisis was essentially a political crisis, both in its nature and in its treatment. It began in direct response to the outcome of a national election, specifically to the triumph of a particular party. Thus it not only represented the breakdown of constitutional government—the failure of the federal system instituted by the Revolutionary generation some seventy years earlier—but was also intimately tied to the structure and operation of the antebellum party system. Equally important is that the crisis was linked with politics in the minds of Northerners. This is made immediately apparent by their frequent use of the phrases "as to politics" and "in political news" when introducing the topic of secession in letters and diaries. More to the point, though, they never questioned that this was a crisis that should be resolved by their government representatives, particularly those at the federal level. Ordinary and elite alike looked to Washington for a solution. This is not to say that nonofficeholders abstained from the decision-making process—far from it—but it is telling that the many citizens who sought to influence government policy did so through traditional political channels: writing letters to political leaders and the overwhelmingly partisan press, circulating and signing petitions, attending rallies and speeches, voting in state and local elections. In many ways, the Northern debate over disunion resembled nothing so much as it did a political campaign.

My second realization was that the field of political history has become remarkably inclusive over the last several decades. When Kenneth Stampp wrote his account, the genre still focused almost entirely on the speeches, acts, and backroom dealings of party leaders. However, in exploring why Northerners' reactions to Southern secession were so tied up with party politics and how those ties influenced the crisis, today's political historian has the resources to examine each party's social and economic makeup, cultural expectations, and electoral motivations, as well as the relationship among party leaders and ordinary voters.

Given this roundabout path to the political approach I eventually adopted, social and cultural historians will be surprised (and no doubt dismayed) to see how much of this book is given to the same kind of speeches, acts, and backroom dealings of party leaders that informed the writings of Stampp's generation. My attention to the words and actions of powerful men like Stephen Douglas, William Seward, and above all Abraham Lincoln reflects another discovery on my part: that for all its accomplishments, political history has moved too far from the traditional approach.

Advances in political history in the 1960s and 1970s revolutionized the discipline by applying statistical analysis to an untapped wealth of empirical information, primarily census data and voting rolls. Practitioners of this new method told us, for the first time, exactly who was voting for what party, which enabled them to write with greater authority than anyone before them about why people voted the way they did. It was they who first established the remarkable connection between voting behavior and so-called ethnocultural factors such as ethnicity and religion, leading some to characterize antebellum politics as "tribal"—an invaluable insight, even if exaggerated.[11] In the 1980s and 1990s, historians unsatisfied with this approach worked with the concept of political culture, a useful (if amorphous) idea that enabled scholars to uncover broadly accepted, often unspoken attitudes and assumptions toward politics, thereby providing meaningful context for both traditional and quantitative political history. These historians have employed a wide range of methods to flesh out the culture that governed political beliefs and behavior, with impressive results.[12]

Such approaches have taught us a tremendous amount about why people in the past thought and acted as they did. I found it impossible, however, to rely primarily on either of these methods of research and analysis while telling a story, at least the kind of story I wanted to tell.[13] Nevertheless, it is impossible to write political history today without relying on the findings of those who have used them over the past four decades; their insights inform every page of the present volume.

I also found a more important problem with abandoning the traditional, "elitist" approach to politics than just difficulty telling a story: the much-maligned "great white men" in power really did lie at the center of events. Recent historians are right to point out that the rank and file had considerable influence over party leaders, that continuous negotiation between elites and masses impelled politics more than the top-down dictation that earlier generations of historians often assumed. Shared ideology, loyalty, traditions, and ethnic and religious background provided the foundation for unity and action within parties, giving ordinary voters reason to follow party leaders while restricting how much leaders could deviate from their constituents' expectations. The Northern response to secession cannot be understood without taking into account these considerations. Yet the older political history—the high-politics, narrative approach—remains necessary. Not just useful, but necessary.[14]

There are two reasons historians must pay close attention to high politics. The first is that the electorate paid close attention to it, and acted in response to it. Party organizers gave structure to the negotiations and the shared values on which modern political historians have focused, and the words and actions of trusted party leaders swayed popular opinion profoundly. The second is that American democracy is not direct but representative; the influence of the people is often critical, but it is leaders, acting in their dual capacity as elected officials and party managers, who make final decisions. Thus, to comprehend the process by which Northerners decided to oppose disunion through force of arms—the decision most immediately responsible for the Civil War—one must examine the views and motives of political actors in their respective roles as principals, activists, and plebeians, and the relationship among actors at these various levels. To do that requires the integration of newer findings with traditional narrative; neither is complete without the other.

✳ By applying the concept of political culture and the conclusions of statistical analysts to the story of the Northern decision for war, this study makes significant contributions to our understanding of mid-nineteenth-century America in three areas: the immediate origins of the Civil War, the antebellum political system, and the early presidential career of Abraham Lincoln.

What was the impact of antebellum political culture on Northerners' response to secession? First, as I have pointed out, it dictated that their response would be political—that is, that they would delegate to a few elected officials the ultimate decision of what course they would take, and that talk of resisting this decision, even among those who vehemently disagreed with it, was minimal. Northerners believed that the essence of the American republic was representative government and that the sine qua non of representative government was the rule of law. They believed that this combination—self-government and the rule of law, institutionalized in the constitutional system—sustained a nation destined to alter human history by spreading the ideals of freedom throughout an oppressed world. Moreover, they saw the republic and its Constitution as the precious legacy of the Founding Fathers, whose achievements and sacrifices they spoke of with a reverence bordering on awe. Their devotion to the Founders' legacy was not only ideological; they saw it as the cornerstone of the stability, prosperity, and rapid progress that underlay both their national pride and their own sense of personal liberty. As a result, while politics may have been only tangential to the private lives of most free-state citizens, it was central to their public culture and their national identity.

And parties were central to politics. By midcentury, well-organized parties had become an integral part of the American political tradition, a key element of most political rituals, especially the most sacred: voting. Many Americans professed a contempt for partisan behavior, but because the parties represented values, beliefs, and assumptions about what America meant and how it was supposed to work, it was inevitable that Northerners viewed what they considered to be a political crisis through the lens of partisanship. Parties were so fundamentally a part of Northern political culture by 1860 that to approach a political crisis without their being front and center was as inconceivable as viewing secession as anything other than a political question.

That the North reacted politically—and through partisan politics in particular—had profound consequences. Where voters did influence the course of the crisis, it was by expressing their views to party leaders. The most important examples of this occurred in late December, when rank-and-file Republicans helped to convince congressional moderates to back away from compromise, and in March, when Republican opposition to evacuating Fort Sumter was an important factor in Lincoln's policy toward the garrison there. It is significant that in both cases it was Republicans whose voices mattered; in an important sense, the greatest impact of ordinary Northerners on the crisis lay in their electing Lincoln in early November, which not only provoked the crisis but guaranteed that his party would control its outcome.

Meanwhile, party organizers dictated the issues under discussion and established the range of available options; it is telling that what was otherwise a torrent of public meetings and letters from constituents was merely a trickle when Congress was out of session in November and March and people had nothing firm to react to. In addition, by giving the people a sense that they had a voice in the process, party leaders effectively minimized the risk of extralegal activity, such as the organization of private militia companies by radical hard-liners or the sabotage of government installations by radical conciliationists. This ensured that the final decision would be in the hands of the individuals who held the reins of power: those such as Douglas and Seward who led important party factions, but ultimately the one person who controlled first the Republican Party and later the executive branch of the federal government, Lincoln.

Conversely, what does the crisis tell us about antebellum political culture? Although the debates of the secession winter changed little—in some ways *because* they changed little—they provide the historian a fascinating window into the era. For one thing, as I have noted, the response to secession confirms the conclusions of a number of historians regarding the centrality of politics to public life, and of parties to politics and government. For another, the written record contains the outlines of two very different conceptions of American nationalism, conceptions that were intimately linked to partisan ideology in ways that historians of nationalism generally overlook. Conciliationists—Democrats, primarily—emphasized federalism and the voluntary nature of the Union. The problem, in their eyes, was the Republicans' moralistic efforts to impose their views on the South, which threatened to undermine the federal system the Founders had created. To coerce the seceded states back into the Union through force of arms would destroy republican government, they said; the border slave states must be enticed into remaining so that the Deep South states could be persuaded to return peacefully. Hard-liners—that is, most Republicans—grounded their opposition to compromise and support for the possible use of force in the sanctity of both the rule of law and the Union itself. To give in to Southern demands, they believed, would set a precedent that would subvert the electoral process and render republican government impossible; to permit secession to occur would set a precedent that would make any kind of government impossible.

Taking a step back from the debates reveals the limits of those differences. For one thing, as I discussed earlier, the attempts of members of all parties to influence the decision-making process occurred through traditional political means. This helped to set crucial boundaries for the debates; for example, rather than even consider taking drastic action outside of the political system when stalwart Republicans prevented meaningful compromise, conciliationists tended to retreat in despair. Of even more significance was the near-universal outcry against South Carolina's aggression in early January and again in mid-April. Together these reveal that despite genuine, passionate conflict, faith in and commitment to the constitutional system provided the basis for a broad-based, Northern brand of nationalism.[15]

Finally, what does the crisis reveal about Abraham Lincoln, that most admired and studied of American presidents? Most underappreciated by historians of the crisis has been the complex humanity he displayed throughout the trial: his early blindness to the true danger of Southern disunionism; his tentative, almost timid first steps toward leadership; his fascinating capacity for both rigid partisan dogmatism and nuanced understandings of Southern motives and perceptions; the intense strain that paralyzed him for three critical weeks and nearly laid him low; and the strength that enabled him somehow to maintain his grip on power and eventually engineer a clear policy. Also of great significance was Lincoln's political skill, most notably in shepherding his divided party through a supremely trying crisis and in resolving that crisis in such a way as to unify a polarized North behind a war that neither he nor they had wanted. Vital in that regard was the remarkable representativeness of Lincoln's views— that his opinions on the expansion of slavery, secession, and the use of force were so typical of the mass of Republican voters was essential to his sustaining party unity and thereby maintaining control of the crisis.

Historical debate surrounding Lincoln and secession has centered on two topics: his relationship with Senator and later Secretary of State William Henry Seward, and his decision to send provisions and reinforcements to Fort Sumter. Seward has traditionally been presented as either a scheming, ambitious villain or a naive idealist (or both), who in any case is outfoxed at every turn by the wiser, more far-seeing Lincoln until he eventually gives up his tricks and becomes the president's most loyal follower. My reading of the evidence leads me to embrace the more sympathetic portrait drawn by Patrick Sowle and Daniel W. Crofts.[16] Seward did quite a bit of scheming and he was certainly ambitious, but his goal was not to make himself "premier" of Lincoln's administration but rather to save the Union from both disunion and war. I see Lincoln and Seward as both leaders and representative figures of the hard-line and conciliationist factions, respectively, among moderate Republicans. That Lincoln did win at every turn serves as a valuable illustration of the political system's structure and operation: both individuals were master politicians, but Lincoln's control of the patronage and later the executive branch left Seward with no choice but to engage in increasingly desperate attempts to convert Lincoln to his thinking.

With regard to Fort Sumter, the attempted reinforcement of which led Confederate forces to attack the fort and trigger war, the primary question has been whether to interpret Lincoln's course as peaceful or manipulative: was Lincoln trying to avoid war or provoke the Confederacy into aggression? I conclude that Lincoln acted as peacefully as he could given the political circumstances and his own ideological constraints. He acted only when all other options that he was willing to consider—and that is the key phrase—were exhausted. I am unconvinced by David M. Potter's argument that Lincoln's strategy could have avoided war in 1861, or, more to the point, that the president himself had any hope that it could. More persuasive is Kenneth Stampp's position—as he refined it three decades after publication of *And the War Came*—that once Lincoln realized war was inevitable, he acted to make its commencement somehow advantageous to the central government. Whether his strategy was devious simply depends on one's perspective. In the view of the Confederates, it certainly was. In Lincoln's eyes, though, once Sumter's loss was imminent, his duty was to unite the North, retain as much of the Upper South as possible, and maximize his chances of winning a war that by then was inescapable. The best way to do that was to spotlight the Southern aggression that he believed had induced the crisis in the first place.[17]

✳ In this study, I use "the North" to mean the free states. As this encompassed a huge expanse and a sizable population, I have attempted to balance depth and comprehensiveness by focusing my research on three Northern states: Massachusetts, New York, and Illinois. In addition to meaningfully representing the main regions of the antebellum North— New England, the Mid-Atlantic, and the Northwest, respectively—these states demand particular attention for the central roles their major political figures played, the considerable influence their public commentators exerted, their economic importance, and their diversity of political conditions. However, I have endeavored to maintain a broad perspective: my emphasis is not on these three states but on the Northern attitudes they reveal. Where regional distinctions were significant, which I found to be surprisingly rare, I have delved more deeply into local conditions; otherwise I have used the data to form general conclusions.[18]

Trying to gauge public opinion in an era that precedes scientific polling is a tricky proposition at best. Given the limited temporal scope of this study, it is possible to deal with this problem by engaging as broad a range of sources as possible, most productively the letters and diaries of both political insiders and outsiders (and especially the wealth of letters written by constituents to political leaders); petitions; political pamphlets and broadsides; the records of the U.S. Congress and the Massachusetts, New York, and Illinois state legislatures; and partisan and independent newspapers.

In order to manage a topic that tempted me with endless paths into antebellum culture, I have limited myself to tracing the decision for war itself—that is, the process by which the North came to unite behind an effort to prevent disunion. I note this not only to give the reader a sense of the book's scope and purpose but also to make two more specific points as well. First, the process of decision-making tended to become sharper and narrower as the crisis wore on. It grew sharper in that while the questions under discussion were, early on, numerous, and their significance uncertain, as the winter months passed, they became fewer and their larger importance more plain. It grew narrower in that while the number of people involved in the decision appeared to be quite large through January and even into February, as congressmen, state legislators, editors, and untold thousands of others sought to influence events, power was gradually revealed to rest with just an elite few, and finally in the hands only of the president. Thus in the early chapters of this study, Lincoln is one of many individuals whom we follow through the labyrinth of Northern politics; at times, he even seems to drop out of the picture as he deliberately maintained a low profile far from the center of action in Washington. By the final chapters, though, his presence is dominating; by March, the story of the Northern decision for war was very much the story of Abraham Lincoln.

Second, the political system through which that process occurred was, although the most open and democratic in the world at that time, fundamentally inequitable. African American men could vote in only a handful of states, and even there they were subject to discriminatory restrictions;

women could not participate formally at all. That does not mean that they had no impact whatever; historians have documented a host of means by which blacks and women participated in politics informally.[19] But with regard to the present topic, I found no evidence that either group significantly influenced the Northern decision-making process in the winter of 1860–61. Moreover, the opinions of blacks and women that appear in the written records do not differ substantially from those of white men with similar politics. Therefore I found it inappropriate and unproductive in this instance to analyze sources according to distinct categories of race or gender.

Autobiographies and reminiscences are even more problematic for this study than they are in general due to the shifting perceptions and loyalties of the war that followed. Since contemporary sources are more than adequate in most cases, I avoided retrospective accounts whenever possible, and always when I could not corroborate their claims.

✳ In regard to quoted material in this book, I have retained original spelling and punctuation wherever possible. Only where it is necessary for clarity have I used "*sic*" or adjusted spelling or punctuation, and I have made it clear when I have done the latter.

Chapter 1 ✳ On the Brink of the Precipice ✳ The Election of 1860

The dramatic confrontation of 1860–61 forced Northerners to make any number of momentous decisions, including, in the end, whether to engage in a civil war to prevent secession. It is ironic, then, that the conflict's roots could be said to lie in a nondecision: the refusal of the 1787 Constitutional Convention to specify who within the new government would have final authority to decide constitutional disputes. Of course, it could be argued that the true origins of the crisis lie a century before that in an "unthinking decision": colonial planters' switch from white indentured servants to black slaves as their chief labor force.[1] Or perhaps its causes lie further back still, in the Spanish conquerors' importation of African slaves to their New World sugar plantations—but that would draw us to Portuguese sugar growers' first use of African slaves in the eastern Atlantic islands, or even to late-medieval traders' introduction of sugar, and the coffee and tea it was meant to sweeten, to a new western market to begin with.

Whether or not the crucial decisions had been avoided or unthinking or lay (as a romantic nineteenth-century writer might phrase it) shrouded in the mists of history, their outcomes left Americans of 1860 to harvest the fruit of their forebears' labor—or more accurately, of their reliance on slave labor. Slavery had profited the young republic greatly, had fattened the purses of Southern planters and Northern merchants, bankers, and manufacturers, but now the bill had come due, and fresh decisions must be made about paying it. The Deep South made its choice quickly. It had been a true slave society (both economic well-being and social order relying on the "peculiar institution") for twice as long as it had belonged to the union of states; it would depart that union if remaining in it threatened its way of life. The Upper South was torn, slavery's claws being dug not quite so deeply there as in the cotton states. Many of its residents strove to sever ties with the Union, but others struggled mightily to maintain them. Most huddled between, eyes northward, waiting to see whether the new government was indeed the menace that disunionists claimed.

It was with the citizens of the Northern free states, then, that the future of the republic lay. It would be a long, cheerless winter of decision for them, a time in which alternatives were hazy and vague, all roads looked evil, and resolving one dilemma generally only produced another.

Perhaps the first individual to appreciate the magnitude and maddening complexity of what was happening in 1860 was an obscure federal artillery officer named Truman Seymour, who on a mild Southern evening in early November faced the first great decision of the crisis. Somehow this son of a poor Vermont preacher found himself on a dimly lit wharf in Charleston, South Carolina, with his country's future in his hands. Lieutenant Seymour had not gone to the wharf insensible of risk; before setting out on his mission—to load arms and ammunition from the city's federal arsenal into a boat and carry them across the harbor—he and his handful of soldiers had dressed in civilian clothing and waited until nightfall. Their precautions had failed. A prosperous-looking man who claimed to own the wharf now stood before them threatening, if loading continued, to whip a sullen and growing crowd of onlookers into a violent mob.

Seymour was not new to danger; he had distinguished himself for bravery on the battlefields of Mexico. But no situation he had faced in Mexico could have prepared him for the devil's choice that lay before him. If he defied the wharf's owner and carried out his charge, the crowd was likely to attack, not only injuring and maybe killing some of his men, but in doing so sparking an incident that could easily escalate into civil war. But if he backed down and returned his cargo to the arsenal, the small garrison of troops across the harbor might be left dangerously weak and vulnerable to attack by zealous secessionists.[2]

It is unlikely that the unfortunate Lieutenant Seymour bothered to consider what forces had conspired to produce this moment, but if he did his thoughts would have been with neither the Constitutional Convention nor seventeenth-century planters, and certainly not with the late-medieval sugar trade. He would have known exactly what caused his encounter on the Charleston wharf: the national election the day before. Throughout election night the telegraph had hummed with reports from around the country, and news of Abraham Lincoln's victory was confirmed by the time Charleston residents awoke. They greeted it with flag-waving, fireworks, and parades as enthusiastic as those in any Northern city. "The tea has been thrown overboard, the revolution of 1860 has been initiated," prominent fire-eater R. Barnwell Rhett proclaimed grandly.[3] The city's U.S. District Court judge, district attorney, and customs officer all resigned their posts that day, the judge announcing, to the delight of the masses and the envy of the politicians, "So far as I am concerned, the Temple of Justice raised under the Constitution of the United States is now closed. If it shall never again be opened I thank God that its doors have been closed before its altar has been desecrated with sacrifices to tyranny."

That same day, South Carolina's state legislature called a special convention to meet in mid-January for the purpose of seceding; three days later, under force of public pressure and an ardent desire to force the hands of other, more cautious slave states, it would move the date of the convention up a month to December 17. Thus would the exhilaration that followed the election's outcome lead to the assembling of the first secession convention just six weeks later, a full two and a half months before Lincoln was even inaugurated. What was more, the legislators began preparing for the possibility of war by adding 10,000 volunteers to the state's defenses.

As Seymour would soon discover, though, it was not certain that fighting, if it occurred, would be done by organized forces. City and state leaders feared that the furious celebrations of coming independence could spin out of control. The likely flashpoint was obvious: a garrison of seventy-odd U.S. troops was stationed at Fort Moultrie, foremost among Charleston harbor's four coastal fortifications, to guard the port from foreign threat and to recondition its worn and outdated defenses. With the U.S. courts and the customhouse shut down, that garrison was now the only remaining federal presence outside of the local postmaster. To city inhabitants intent on casting off their old allegiance and founding a new nation, the soldiers took on the alarming aspect of foreign occupiers.

Moultrie's officers recognized the danger and had already urged their commander, Col. John Gardner, to safeguard the forts. The engineers in charge of renovations, particularly conscious of the fortifications' weakness, requested that Gardner provide arms for the most loyal laborers working under them before they were overrun by a mob—an eventuality that seemed imminent after the previous Saturday, when a number of civilians sporting blue secession cockades boldly toured the construction area at Fort Moultrie to assess the progress of repairs. At first Gardner had rejected the request for more arms, thinking such a move unwise given the emotional state of Charleston and the questionable loyalty of the workmen. However, the jubilation that followed the election convinced him that inaction held more peril than action. He ordered Seymour's small party to the arsenal to withdraw additional weapons and ammunition. But both Moultrie and the arsenal were under watch; before the nervous soldiers could finish loading their small boat, a hostile crowd had gathered and Seymour faced his lonely decision.

The lieutenant sensibly opted for discretion over valor. He ordered the crates back into the arsenal and returned to the fort empty-handed. In doing so he averted an ugly incident that would have roused Northern public outrage and placed enormous pressure on the lame-duck administration in Washington to respond with force. What impact his choice would have on the fort's long-term safety remained to be seen.

The following day Seymour returned to Charleston to call on the city's mayor, who, recognizing that he had no legal right to interfere, agreed that the arms could be transported. But now, perversely, Colonel Gardner refused to take the weapons. Officially, he protested that he needed no permission from local authorities to transfer federal arms from a federal arsenal to a federal fort, but in fact he feared—again, quite sensibly—the consequences of attempting to withdraw them. In any event, the weapons and ammunition remained in the arsenal, and the soldiers returned to their coastal stronghold.

That decision made, a new dilemma developed. Charleston authorities, fearful lest another such episode not end so happily, wired to Washington that unless the War Department revoked Gardner's authority to procure arms, "collision was inevitable." Upon being handed the message, Secretary of War John B. Floyd replied without hesitation, "Telegraph back at once, say you have seen me, that no such orders have been issued and none such will be issued under any circumstances." (In fact, Floyd himself had absently authorized the withdrawal, but that was conveniently forgotten.)[4]

Thanks to Lieutenant Seymour's judgment and Colonel Gardner's decision to follow his subordinate's lead, the immediate danger had passed by the time Floyd's response reached South Carolina. Still, the results of the episode were significant. In Charleston, South Carolina militia now guarded the arsenal, city leaders warned Gardner that they would resist any attempt at reinforcement, and the garrison, for its part, no longer permitted any civilian presence in the forts. In Washington, forging a viable policy for the forts became the administration's foremost concern and its most troublesome challenge. The ease with which Charleston harbor almost slid into violence engendered in President James Buchanan and several of his cabinet ministers an attitude of supreme caution and deference to Southern caveats, while stirring in others an intolerance for secessionists' defiance of federal authority. Over the following weeks a similar rift would develop among all Northerners, coloring every option and shaping every debate for the next five months and eventually forcing a decision over war.

✳ President Buchanan and others inclined to optimism had reason to hope that, provided open conflict were avoided, the crisis would be compromised away: it was far from the first sectional conflict, and all had somehow been resolved before. The history of sectional crises and compromises was as old as the Constitution, whose existence had itself required intense negotiation over the tender subject of slavery—and that at a time when most Northern states still allowed the controversial institution within their own borders. Through a series of crises since that time, two common threads ran: all arose out of Southern concerns that the federal government might somehow be able to interfere with slavery, and all were resolved through some arrangement whereby Northern leaders agreed to squelch any movement against what soon became a distinctly Southern institution. For both sides, the costs of antislavery action were simply too high: by the 1820s slavery had become so vital to the South's economy and so central to its society and its culture that white residents could not afford to ignore any possible threat, while the vast majority of Northerners, for their part, believed that maintaining peace between the sections was far more important than ending slavery.

So it would seem reasonable that a solution would present itself in 1860 as well. But the new crisis would prove different from any that had come before; the constant threat of armed conflict at the Southern forts, so quick to emerge, showed that clearly enough. Only once before had violence loomed so near. In 1833, President Andrew Jackson had responded to South Carolina's "nullification" of federal law by threatening to march an army into the Palmetto State and hang whom he considered the traitorous nullifiers. But the risk then had revolved around the unlikely prospect of an outside federal force invading a state; even had a rapid compromise not been worked out in Congress, the legal and logistical problems alone, never mind the utter lack of support from Jackson's native South, would have delayed any action until cooler heads could prevail. In 1860, however, political negotiations would have to take place while a weak federal force was already positioned in the heart of Southern radicalism, in a situation in which hostilities could break out at any time.

What also boded ill for resolving this crisis was the objection most Northerners had to mollifying Southern concerns over the forts. Particularly unpromising was that the newly elected president shared their disgust with his predecessor's policy of appeasement. In mid-December Lincoln would respond to rumors that Buchanan intended to evacuate the Charleston outposts by snapping angrily, "If that is true, they ought to hang him," and then notifying the general in chief of the army and key Republican leaders that upon taking office he would immediately order the forts' recapture.[5] The rumors turned out to be false, and the Charleston forts were duly transferred to Lincoln's authority two and a half months later, but if Northern leaders were so averse to conciliation, preserving the peace long enough for some resolution to develop would plainly be a difficult proposition.

This unique risk of conflict stemmed from a more basic difference from previous crises: Southerners had threatened to break up the Union before, but never had a state actually plunged into secession without waiting for its fellows—a wait that always before had delayed disunionism long enough to kill it. It was South Carolina's unprecedented declaration of independence, formalized in mid-December but already real in the public mind in early November, that made the federal presence on its soil such a burning issue. At the same time, that act pushed the national debate beyond more traditional—and more negotiable slavery related matters and forced Northerners to confront the question of the perpetuity of the Union itself, a matter not open to any middle-ground solution or parliamentary sleight-of-hand.

In the final analysis, as Lieutenant Seymour and his contemporaries well knew, what led to his confrontation on November 7 was secession, and what provoked secession was Lincoln's election on November 6. That, then, is where our story begins.

✳ On a beautiful fall Saturday in the small lakeside city of Oswego, New York, twenty-four-year-old Gus Frey penned a letter to his brother Lud in Palatine Bridge. With just three days remaining before the election, he fairly bubbled, "Politics is about the only topic of Conversation just now." Brimming with enthusiasm, he listed the speakers at the large Republican rally he had attended at nearby Pevirs Hollow the night before and at the one to be held in Oswego that night. He bragged about the large majority that local party officials expected to give Lincoln on Tuesday and expressed his hope that Lud and his colleagues would be equally successful down in Montgomery County. He scoffed at the possibility that a Republican victory might have dangerous consequences: "We shall carry old Abe the Rail Splitter triumphantly into the White House. And immediately after this I suffer we must expect to see a 'wery large army,' of fierce big whiskered Southerners, to carry fire and Slaughter into our peaceful homes over the list. I doubt very much whether any one is very much scared by all the raw head and bloody bones stories of the Democratic papers." "But," Gus concluded, "you probably dont care to hear any more about Politics and so I will say no more about it, till after next Tuesday, and on the night of that day could you see me you would doubtless think me a fit subject for the insane asylum, when you saw me giving three times three, throwing up my hat and turning four somersaults backwards."[6]

Not all of Oswego's residents were so sanguine. Although politics was considerably more peripheral to Sarah Woolsey Johnson's life than it was to young Gus Frey's, on Sunday, November 4, the day after her fellow-townsman wrote so enthusiastically to his brother, Sarah Johnson expressed her own strong feelings about the result of the impending contest. In the midst of the news of family and neighbors that dominated her private journal, she wrote, with no elaboration, "Very gloomy about election. God help this distracted country." Two days later her fears were confirmed. On the evening of the sixth, she observed simply, "Election. Mr Lincoln of course elected." Then, no doubt thinking of the likes of Gus Frey and his compatriots, she added in a rush, "Again I say God help the country the Republican party here are radical in the extreme."[7]

In such private writings can we see the attitude toward politics of (for lack of a better term) ordinary Northerners: here, an excited young man eagerly involved in one of his first campaigns and an older, less politically engaged woman, unable to vote and more concerned with the issues of daily life. Two features of these brief snapshots stand out: the deep interest of both individuals in the outcome of the election, and their diametrically opposed views of what that outcome would mean. In these our two writers were profoundly typical of participants and observers across the North. Everyone knew the election of 1860 was momentous; by election day everyone knew the Republicans would win; and nobody agreed on what would happen next.

In its pageantry and excitement the election of 1860 rivaled any campaign in living memory. Throughout the North, huge rallies, fireworks displays, and torchlight processions were the order of the day. New York City lawyer George Templeton Strong described one such parade of the Wide Awakes, the organization of militant young Republicans, as "imposing and splendid": "The clubs marched in good order, each man with his torch or lamp of kerosene oil on a pole, with a flag below the light; and the line was further illuminated by the most lavish pyrotechnics. Every file had its rockets and its Roman candles, and the procession moved along under a galaxy of fire balls. I have never seen so beautiful a spectacle on any political turnout." The city being a Democratic stronghold, a few weeks later Strong and tens of thousands of his fellow New Yorkers witnessed an anti-Republican exhibition that dwarfed the previous one, a torchlight parade "more numerous than any political demonstration I have ever witnessed." Being unsympathetic to the cause, he and a friend left early, but hours later, as he was writing in his diary, he could still hear the parade going by outside his window.[8]

Across the country and throughout the months leading up to the election, multitudes of Americans witnessed and participated in similar displays as the parties pulled out all the stops to attract voters. And it seemed they succeeded. On election day, November 6, over 82 percent of eligible Northerners showed up at the polls to cast a ballot, some waiting in line for hours or leaving and returning later in order to do so.[9] The turnout was all the more impressive when one considers that the contest's result was no longer in doubt. After state and local Republican triumphs in the key states of Pennsylvania, Indiana, and Ohio in early October, most leaders and many supporters of all three anti-Republican parties—Northern Democrats, Southern Democrats, and Constitutional Unionists—acknowledged that Abraham Lincoln would be the next president.[10] They were correct: Lincoln captured the electoral votes of every free state save New Jersey (which he divided with Democrat Stephen Douglas), giving the Republicans an easy electoral majority.

Despite the foregone conclusion, voters turned out for any number of reasons: they felt strongly about the potential consequences of Republican victory; they wanted to be a part of something important; control of Congress and several state governments was still up for grabs; or simply because they were drawn by the spectacle—or by promises of party activists to "treat" them with alcohol or cash. Republicans like Gus Frey hoped to run up the score on their despised opponents. Many of their opponents simply refused to bow to the inevitable, like the Illinois Democrat who acknowledged that the state was probably lost but demanded nevertheless, "Will the democracy now falter in this contest that may save or rend our grand confederacy[?]"[11] His words reflected as neatly as any the voters' belief that more than usual was at stake in this particular election. The upheaval that had rocked the political world for the past decade—that had destroyed the Whig Party, divided the Democracy, and ratcheted up sectional animosity to an unprecedented and unsustainable level—was finally coming to a head. A New York City dry-goods merchant captured the prevailing mood when he noted in his diary on the evening of the election, "If we do not misinterpret the signs of the times, this day the 6th of Nov 1860, is one of the most important ever known in our history."[12]

The election did indeed have immediate and radical consequences in several slave states, most notably, as we have seen, in that longtime hotbed of secessionism, South Carolina. The tidal wave of disunionism that began in Charleston quickly swept through the rest of the cotton belt, and if secessionist fervor was not as unanimous in the rest of the Deep South as it was in the Palmetto State, it was easily powerful enough to sweep away unionist resistance. By the end of November, four more states—Alabama, Florida, Georgia, and Mississippi—had scheduled secession conventions, and another—Louisiana—had called its legislature for that purpose. In Texas, only the resistance of unionist governor Sam Houston briefly delayed similar action. The rush of events left many bewildered Northerners feeling, as one correspondent wrote, that "our Union is on the brink of the precipice."[13]

The anxiety of that precarious position showed in the stock markets even before the election. Fearful of the consequences in the South, merchants in New York, especially, reacted nervously to the impending Republican victory. In late October stock prices took an ominous dip. Republican commercial and financial elites tried to convince their colleagues that the crisis was minor and would pass quickly once Southerners realized that the Republican menace was not real. They argued that a Republican victory at the polls would be less disruptive than the most likely alternative, a bitter and prolonged struggle in the House of Representatives. Their efforts availed nothing. The port of New York was the clearinghouse for virtually the entire Southern cotton crop; New York factors sold the South's cotton; New York insurance companies insured the crop and the ships that carried it; New York banks held the planters' debts; New York factories and merchants supplied a significant portion of the South's manufactured goods. When rumors circulated after the election that a Southern confederacy would repudiate the region's debts and institute export taxes, the stock market plummeted. Since the city was also the hub of Northern commerce, the effects rippled outward through the region's urban centers. Smaller banks and dry-goods traders began to fail. In some industries factories began laying off workers. Whatever Northerners thought or said or wrote about secession during what was quickly becoming a national crisis, they would be doing it in the midst of a major financial panic.[14]

✳ Neither the outcome of the election nor its immediate consequences should have been surprising: four years earlier, in their first national campaign, Republicans had almost captured the executive branch by winning all but five Northern states. All they needed to do to win this election was keep the states they had and pick up Pennsylvania and one other state that had eluded them in 1856. Adding to their optimism was that in their first election they had polled better in the North than the Democrats had. The difference between defeat and victory had been the 14 percent of Northerners who voted for former Whig president Millard Fillmore, candidate of the anti-immigrant American Party. Should the Republicans win over a sizable portion of the nativist Fillmore voters, they would take the White House in 1860.[15]

Only a few years before that, the success of a political party openly dedicated to restricting slavery and the power of the South had been unthinkable. For decades the existence of two competitive, national parties had channeled politics away from the kind of North-South antagonism the Republican Party represented. Northern politics in the 1830s and 1840s had revolved around popular concerns about major social and cultural changes that accompanied the rapid rise of a modern capitalist economy. Thus the old Whig and Democratic parties had rallied voters around economic issues such as a national bank, a protective federal tariff, and federal subsidies for "internal improvements" such as roads, canals, and railroads. In fact, Whig and Democratic leaders had carefully steered clear of slavery-related issues after the traumatic Missouri Crisis of 1819–20, when Congress had deadlocked over admitting Missouri into the Union as a slave state and a number of Southerners spoke of seceding.

But as time passed, two things happened. For one, sectional antagonisms worsened. Southern planters had consciously avoided much of the economic development occurring in the North. They were fearful of the effect the accompanying dislocation would have on slave discipline; besides, with cotton booming they had little incentive to try anything new. As a result, North and South drifted further apart economically and culturally. The ramifications of this were enormous. By 1860, Northerners controlled the nation's manufacturing, banking, and shipping, even of cotton. Southerners often resented what many perceived as an essentially colonial relationship in which they remained in debt (planters' wealth being tied up in land and slaves) while Northern factors, insurance agents, and textile manufacturers reaped cotton's great rewards. Many Northerners, on the other hand, were coming to see the South as economically backward and, even though by the late 1850s cotton exports exceeded in value all other exports combined, stagnant.

The anxious imaginations of each section exacerbated these tensions. By the 1850s, Southern defensiveness regarding slavery and Northern anxiety toward modernization led each region to mask its own internal worries by associating itself with the revered Founding Fathers of the Revolutionary era and using the other as a negative reference. To emphasize the purity of their own traditional, chivalrous society, Southern writers and spokesmen painted the North as decadent, a land dominated by greedy, exploitative industrialists whose values undermined the virtuous agrarian republic America's Founders had envisioned. Spokesmen for the North, on the other hand, extolled their region's unlimited opportunity for economic independence and social respectability. Any man could rise, they said, who lived according to "free-labor" (as opposed to slave-labor) principles: hard work, thrift, and self-control. To them the South was the antithesis of that ideal, a place where slaveholding degraded honest labor and aristocratic planters dominated society and government in a mockery of the Founders' egalitarianism.[16]

Growing cultural antagonism placed a great burden on the national parties, as Northern and Southern partisans found less and less on which they could agree. Adding to that problem by the late 1840s was a second result of the North's economic evolution: in the free states, to a new generation who had grown up with the new ways, the old partisan quarrels seemed less important. Old national issues like the Bank of the United States and government-supported internal improvements had largely been settled. Free-labor ideals, originally a Whig value, were now embraced by almost all Northerners. Earlier Democrats had successfully cast Whig industrialists and financiers as would-be aristocrats, but now anti-aristocracy had taken on a more general appeal. As a result, voters turned to new concerns —and when they did, the early-nineteenth-century sweep of evangelical Christianity through culturally war-torn areas of the North ensured that the new issues would be morally rather than economically based. Among them was a rising objection to slavery.[17]

In the late 1840s and early 1850s, as the old party system foundered on the rocks of obsolescence and slavery, the wind that drove it to its doom was westward expansion. The United States' swift growth in population, prosperity, and economic might fueled a surge in national pride that found its most aggressive expression in the rise of "manifest destiny," a faith that the country was destined to spread across the continent. Ironically, in this display of national unity lay the groundwork for horrific civil war. Touchy Southerners, sensitive to the slightest threat to their fundamental institution or stain on their honor, insisted on carrying slavery with them into new territories whether the climate or soil would support it or no. A growing number of Northerners were equally adamant that slavery not expand.[18]

Since slavery's expansion into the West was the chief point of contention between North and South in the 1850s and between Northern Democrats and Republicans in 1860, the reasons "free-soil" Northerners had for objecting to it bear examining. For one, a popular notion held that slavery would gradually die out if contained within its present boundaries. Thus expansion threatened to give new life to the South's peculiar institution, upsetting antislavery Northerners' best hope for an eventual end to the national blight. For another, growing antislavery sentiment led Northerners to reinterpret a powerful Jeffersonian vision that portrayed the West not only as an "Empire of Liberty" where American ideals of freedom and self-government could spread, but also as a vital outlet for the growing body of laborers in Northern cities who, despite free-labor claims, were already beginning to form a permanent underclass of poor wage workers. Thus to many Northerners, the spread of slavery would corrupt the West. First, the taint of its oppression would debauch the noble vision of an Empire of Liberty. Second, slavery would bring with it the undemocratic, planter-dominated society of the South, thereby preventing ambitious wage workers from moving West and becoming productive, landowning yeomen a myth anxious Northerners clung to regardless of its increasingly questionable authenticity. Finally, an important factor for many Northerners was their desire to keep the West open not just for free labor but for free white labor; racism was deeply rooted in the North as well as the South.[19]

The clash of Southern proslavery values and Northern "free-soil" principles resulted in a cycle of escalating tensions. As Northern criticism of slavery grew, Southerners became increasingly defensive. In response, they acted aggressively to protect what they considered their equal rights, using the federal government to force slavery westward. The result was a self-fulfilling prophecy: the more forcefully the South defended slavery's rights against perceived Northern attacks, the more Northerners came to resent Southern power and speak out against slavery. Radicals on both sides—Northern abolitionists and Southern secessionists—fed the fire. Initially, they were the only ones who believed their claims that haughty Southern planter-aristocrats were conspiring to spread their power throughout a Caribbean slave empire and even into the free states themselves or, alternatively, that a frenzied antislavery North was trying to destroy slavery in the Southern states. But the more Southern leaders fought to extend slavery through federal legislation and ultimately the Supreme Court, the more Northerners were convinced of the reality of a Slave Power conspiracy and acted to limit its might; and the more Northerners tried to restrict slavery and the influence of Southern planters, the more Southerners were convinced of the reality of an abolitionist conspiracy.

By 1860, this conflict had persisted for much of the previous dozen years. That seems a brief span in the long view—for the historian grappling with the coming of a cataclysmic civil war, for example—but for a young man voting in his first election, friction between North and South had dominated politics since his earliest memory. Given the nature of those sectional battles, it is not surprising that in 1860 young Northern voters in particular were overwhelming in casting their ballots for a new anti-Southern Republican Party.

The rise of the Republicans illustrates a critical aspect of Northern public culture, one that played a key role in the Northern response to secession in 1860–61: Northerners understood sectional conflict in political terms. Almost all of the events leading up to the crisis were political actions. Most of the Southern aggressions that energized Northerners were acts of Congress: the Fugitive Slave Law of 1850, which allowed for agents of the federal government to track runaway slaves through Northern states and even force ordinary citizens to help them; the Kansas-Nebraska Act of 1854, which opened up to slavery a vast expanse of western territory from which it had been barred for decades; and support for the Lecompton Constitution, the proslavery constitution under which Kansas applied for admission as a state in 1857, despite the well-known fraud and violence in which it had been born. Capping these off was the Supreme Court's *Dred Scott* ruling, which established the radical Southern position on westward expansion as the law of the land: neither Congress nor territorial legislatures, the Court decreed, had any authority whatever to keep slavery out of any western territory.

What provoked widespread Northern ire, then, was neither the immorality of slavery nor the plight of the slaves but whether the national government would support and encourage slavery and how that support and encouragement might affect Northern society. The rise of evangelical Christian reform in the North had raised public awareness of slavery's evils, certainly, but what drove large numbers of people in the free states to action was the belief that despotic planter-aristocrats were controlling the federal government in order to extend their dominion and destroy the Northern way of life. And the action those people took, overwhelmingly, was the quintessentially political one of forming a party and trying to win elections. Few antislavery Northerners became abolitionists; at the height of their popularity, those who advocated an immediate end to slavery never comprised more than a small minority of the population. Instead, the vast majority of antislavery Northerners became Republicans.

That pattern is best revealed in their responses to those Southern provocations that did not involve formal acts of government. In May 1856, for example, Congressman Preston Brooks of South Carolina responded to a radical antislavery speech by Massachusetts senator Charles Sumner by striding into the Senate chamber the next day and beating Sumner about the head with a cane until he was half dead. Northerners were outraged. "Has it come to this, that we must speak with bated breath in the presence of our Southern masters?" demanded the *New York Evening Post*, reflecting the popular reaction. "Are we too, slaves, slaves for life, a target for their brutal blows, when we do not comport ourselves to please them?"[20] This, perhaps the single most influential event in the rise of anti-Southern feeling in the North, was an act of personal violence—but again, the reaction to it was political: many who had not previously been won over by Republican agitation against the South now joined the new party.[21]

The most glaring divergence from this commitment to politics is the exception that underscores the rule. In 1859, antislavery zealot John Brown spectacularly rejected political means by seizing the federal arsenal at Harpers Ferry, Virginia, in an effort to spark a massive slave revolt. Southern spokesmen (like most subsequent historians) dwelled on Northern demonstrations of support for Brown, but in reality his actions were much more widely condemned in the free states than supported. Moreover, what support he did garner outside of abolitionist circles was largely due to his success in downplaying the violence of his scheme to newspaper reporters, among whom he created an image of himself not as a radical, a terrorist, but as a simple man of courage and conviction. Although he did win sympathy, it must be remembered that even among Brown's sympathizers none seriously considered imitating his course.[22]

As the primary cause of Southern conservatism and the chief target of

Northern condemnation, the ultimate source of sectional difference was the institution of slavery. It was, therefore, on that issue that the great sectional conflicts of the 1850s rested. Yet even in 1860 few Northerners proposed to interfere with slavery in the Southern states. The chief reason for this was the same imperative that dictated their political response to apparent Southern aggression: their firm commitment to the system of government created by the Founders. To them, as we shall see, that system was institutionalized by the Constitution and embodied in the Union. Specifically, the Constitution permitted neither the general government nor the free states to interfere in the domestic affairs of the slave states, and even those who felt an ethical or moral aversion to slavery believed the Union would be threatened by antislavery agitation. To the vast majority of Northerners, commitment to the Constitution and the Union were simply higher priorities than any antislavery feelings they might hold. Radical abolitionists, who reversed those priorities by condemning the Constitution as "a covenant with death and an agreement with Hell," were vilified.[23]

And so the mounting hostilities between North and South took the form not of widespread raids on Southern plantations or plots to inspire slave revolts but of a struggle for power over the federal government. That struggle climaxed with the election of 1860, a bizarre contest that, with the rise of the purely Northern Republican Party and the splitting of the Northern and Southern wings of the Democratic Party, developed into two separate campaigns. In the South, Democratic candidate John C. Breckinridge battled John Bell and the Constitutional Union Party, an ad hoc organization comprised of sectional conservatives who favored any policy that would restore national harmony. In the North, competition lay between Democratic candidate Stephen A. Douglas, the Illinois senator who had opened the territories to slavery with his controversial Kansas-Nebraska Act and then spent the next six years struggling to maintain what he had meant to be a moderate, compromise stance, and Abraham Lincoln, a relative unknown whose moderate positions on slavery and nativism and leadership of a key state, Illinois, had won him the Republican nomination.

Due to the North's advantage in population and number of states, the latter race was the one that mattered in the all-important electoral college. There, as we have seen, the Republicans triumphed. Although Lincoln won only 39 percent of the nation's electorate and was outpolled by almost a million votes, he captured almost every Northern electoral vote. The Republicans improved on their 1856 results by attracting most young, first-time voters, a significant number of Fillmore nativists, and oddly enough, a great many Protestant German immigrants.[24] The newcomers meshed uncomfortably with each other and with the free-soilers and radical antislavery agitators who formed the party's core; nevertheless, it was with this awkward coalition behind him that the new president-elect would deal with the threats of disunion that neither he nor most of his colleagues took any more seriously than did young Gus Frey.

✳ Back in the 1830s and 1840s, Whigs and Democrats alike had embraced a political party system that gave them access to the workings of their government, made sense of dramatic economic and social changes that were transforming their world, and channeled political strife away from potentially threatening sectional issues arising from Southern slavery. When that party system fractured and collapsed, voters felt disenchanted with and alienated from a politics that no longer seemed to represent their views. They embraced new parties that promised to restore accountability to government by emphasizing the issues about which voters cared, moral questions such as temperance, nativism, and especially slavery. That the new party system did not channel conflict away from sectional differences but was built around them troubled a great many Northerners, but in the national campaign of 1860 those concerns merely strengthened new party loyalties, pitting those who feared the consequences of sectional agitation against those who saw a Southern Slave Power as the more dangerous threat to liberty and self-government.

As we shall see, though, once the campaign had concluded, how the two parties would deal with its bitter fruit was determined not only by their ideological views prior to the election but also by their particular political circumstances. Democrats' and Republicans' attitudes toward the South were chief among their differences and would produce contrasting responses to secession, but of equal importance were deep internal divisions that plagued each party.

Chapter 2 ✳ I Would Not Endanger the Perpetuity of This Union ✳ November

Uncertain of what was going on in the South, Northerners experienced a state of anxious bewilderment during the weeks immediately following the election. Compounding that feeling was an absence of active political leadership, as Stephen Douglas, James Buchanan, and Abraham Lincoln, each for his own reasons, largely refrained from making public statements. In ordinary times their silence would have been neither significant nor unusual: although party organization and leadership drove antebellum politics, it was the organizations and leaders in the various states that provided the central element. In the face of a growing national crisis, however, the lack of direction from national party leaders proved critical. Left to their own devices, state and local leaders, particularly editors, spewed forth a jumbled confusion of assessments and strategies that exacerbated tensions within both the Republican and the anti-Republican camps. That both sides blamed the other for this threat to the Union and predicted that the other's policies, if continued, would lead to destruction served to bind each group together. Yet the centrifugal force of these mutual recriminations is clearer in hindsight than it was at the time. More apparent to participants was the instability of their embryonic new political order, the genuine possibility that the turmoil of party realignment would resume—or more accurately, continue.

Unsure of what was going on, never mind what might be done about it, ordinary Northerners tended to remain passive during this initial stage of the crisis, opting to watch and await developments. While party managers debated their course, among the public an expectant and rather ominous silence prevailed.

✳ As a prominent lawyer and party sage, Samuel J. Tilden was not a typical Northern Democrat; having all but retired from active politics a decade earlier, he was not even a typical party leader. Nevertheless, his view of disunion and the crisis it threatened to produce was remarkably representative of the anti-Republican position in the period just before and after the election. Because of this, Tilden's widely read tract on the crisis and the circumstances under which he came to write it bear close examination.

Perhaps the most disheartening moment of Tilden's early political life occurred on the stage of New York's famed Cooper Union Institute in October 1860. Earlier in the campaign, convinced of the profound danger of a Republican victory, Tilden had come out of his decade-long semiretirement to help lead a "fusion" movement to unite New York's various anti-Republican forces. He had little hope that fusion efforts would result in a national electoral victory, but if the Republicans were denied New York they could not command an electoral majority and the election would be decided in the House of Representatives. There, it was thought, anything might happen.[1] Given the long-standing animosity between Democrats and the old-line Whigs of the Constitutional Union Party, and between rival factions of the Democracy itself, the process of fusion had been slow and halting. By early October, however, a complicated agreement had been reached among the three anti-Republican groups.[2]

Tilden hoped that fear of Republicans' manipulating and distorting the federal system in order to impose their own values onto the rest of the nation would be enough to unite Democrats and Constitutional Unionists. The latter, though comprised mainly of former Whigs and Know-Nothings, had actually been the least problematic. The real challenge lay with the state's two Democratic factions and their history of internecine squabbling. The rift dated back to the early 1840s, but the real blow had come in 1848, when a splinter group known as the Barnburners, Samuel Tilden among them, had joined the new Free-Soil Party. Headed by former Democratic president Martin Van Buren and Whig antislavery editor Charles Francis Adams, the Free-Soil ticket was organized to protest Southern attempts to spread slavery into the vast new territory recently acquired in the Mexican War.[3] Party ties soon pulled most of the Barnburners back into the Democratic fold, but only after the rupture had given the state to the Whigs and helped them win the White House. Resentment smoldered for years between so-called Hardshells, who supported Southern rights and resisted the Free-Soilers' return, and Softshells, who included both the Barnburners themselves and those who had been more tolerant of their wayward brethren. During the 1850s, the two factions had gone so far as to put rival candidates into the field.

In 1860, that quarrel fed into the national party schism, which stemmed from the long-standing feud between Southern Democrats, who demanded that the party support a radical proslavery position, and Northern Democrats, who sought a more moderate course. At the heart of the rift was Illinois senator Stephen A. Douglas, whose 1854 Kansas-Nebraska Act had established a territorial policy he called popular sovereignty, a quintessentially Democratic notion designed to remove the explosive issue of slavery in the territories from national politics by replacing centralized authority with local control. That is, the entire question was to become the responsibility not of Congress but of the people who actually settled in the territories. Trouble arose three years later when Douglas rejected both the fraudulent proslavery Lecompton Constitution, calling it a mockery of popular sovereignty, and Southern demands for a federal slave code to prevent antislavery settlers from really barring slavery. The party's 1860 national convention had fallen apart when Northerners refused to endorse a slave code and Southerners refused to tolerate Douglas's nomination. As we have seen, the organization split into two, nominating rival presidential candidates and drafting rival platforms.

In New York, the Softshell majority advocated popular sovereignty in the territories and supported Douglas, while the Hardshell minority maintained a strong pro-Southern stance, favored President Buchanan in his long patronage war with Douglas, and backed Southern Democrat John C. Breckinridge. The division alarmed those like Tilden who wanted to overlook past differences in order to prevent the potentially calamitous consequences of a Republican victory—thus sparking the fusion movement. But Tilden felt his hopes of genuine cooperation dashed at a fusion rally at the Cooper Institute, when the mixed crowd hissed the former Barnburner off the stage shortly after his speech began, demanding instead to hear from the city's radical mayor, Fernando Wood.[4] Plainly the anti-Republican alliance was a fragile one, at least in New York City.

Mortifying as it was, the Cooper Institute episode only fortified Tilden's determination to strengthen the fusion movement. Tilden had been associated with the staff of the *New York Evening Post* back in their Barnburner days. Unlike him they had never abandoned their free-soil position, and the *Post* was now a radical Republican paper. So when a co-editor of the *Post* publicly, and somewhat mockingly, offered to print whatever it was Tilden had tried to say that night, he was doubtless surprised when his old friend accepted. Tilden chose to paint this further embarrassment as an opportunity to educate Republicans about the consequences of their campaign, but in fact it was a desperate attempt at a bold gesture that might invigorate his fusionist colleagues.[5] Over the next two weeks he expanded the notes of his abortive speech, eventually submitting almost 13,000 words of closely reasoned argument for his conviction that a Republican victory would be a disaster from which the nation might not recover. The *Post* printed it, and according to the practice of the day, it was subsequently published in pamphlet form.[6]

Tilden opened his tract with an assault on Republican claims to political legitimacy, charging that a party with no support at all in almost half the country was "a phenomenon, new and startling," that violated the very idea of self-government. By granting the Southern minority no role in government whatsoever, the Republican Party assumed an attitude toward the South comparable to that of a foreign conqueror. Far milder forms of sectionalism had terrified Washington, Jefferson, and Jackson, he wrote, but the wise and brave Republican "scoffs at the danger" of disunion "and scoffs at all who see it as insincere and timid!"[7] Republicans might protest that Southerners misunderstood their intentions and feared them only because demagogic, authoritarian political leaders misrepresented their party's views, but Tilden insisted that even moderate Republican policies were genuinely threatening to the South. What Republicans did not seem to realize was that imposing their own ideals on the South was "moral coercion." Northerners must recognize that slavery defined Southern race relations, that "a shock to [slavery] is associated in the mind of the dominant race, with a pervading sense of danger to the life of every human being and the honor of every woman." Under constant threat of servile insurrection, Southerners could not afford to distinguish between abolitionist pledges to end slavery immediately and moderate Republicans' gradual, indirect approach; to them, antislavery federal appointees in the South or an antislavery Supreme Court were as lethal in the long run as the violence of John Brown. When observed objectively, he concluded, Republicans' sectionalism was a dangerous perversion of the federal system that the revered Founders had constructed.[8]

Tilden presented two arguments against the effort to halt the spread of slavery. First, echoing conservatives throughout the country, he pointed out that no existing territories possessed the climate and geography needed to sustain a slave society—and even if any did, an excess of land in the existing slave states made slavery's extension unnecessary for at least another generation. Why cause a stir now, "more especially at the hazard of scattering in ruins the glorious fabric of civil liberty reared by our fathers?"[9] Second, destroying slavery by containing it geographically would force masters to overwork and underfeed slaves as resources became scant, surely not the result reformers desired. Moreover, was it not logical that as white men fled the worsening conditions, "at last, when the system culminates in emancipation, must not the result be communities almost exclusively of blacks? . . . Should we not, in the ultimate effects of the restrictive policy, convert our sister states into negro governments? Will we then allow them equality in our Union?"[10]

Tilden acknowledged that a Republican reversal of policy would destroy the organization, but he pleaded with Republicans to recognize the inevitable consequences and utter needlessness of their goals. Not comprehending the nature of a federal system, they were seeking to use constitutional means to subvert constitutional government. In defense of a mere abstraction they threatened the very foundation of Southern society, provoking secession and risking civil war.[11] The fate of the Union came down to one question: "Elect Lincoln, and we invite those perils which we cannot measure. . . . Defeat Lincoln, and all our great interests and hopes are, unquestionably, safe."[12] On the result of the presidential canvass rested nothing less than national survival.

Of course, Samuel Tilden was not the only Cassandra crying his warning to a heedless North. The prediction that Lincoln's election would provoke disunion and war was the central feature in each of the anti-Republican campaigns—indeed, it was the raison d'être for the Constitutional Union Party. But his appeal is especially valuable to the historian both because he captured so well those lines of reasoning most frequently shared by anti-Republicans of all stripes, and because his motivation for doing so—and it was undeniably a conscious, deliberate strategy—so clearly reveals the nature of the Republicans' opposition.

Next to the warnings of secession and civil war that lay at the heart of his essay, Tilden's emphasis on Republicans' moral aggression and their violation of federalism represented their enemies' most popular argument. He wisely grounded his appeal in a traditional Democratic call to empower local rather than centralized government and to resist puritanical attempts to legislate morality—in other words, to mind one's own business and leave other people's to them, as the framers of the Constitution had intended. In that way Tilden brought his point home to Northern Democrats, who would associate the South's rejection of Republican moralism with their own local resistance to such policies as temperance and public schools. That argument provided a common ground for Douglas and Breckinridge supporters. The Hardshell *New York Journal of Commerce* spelled the argument out powerfully:

> The fundamental mistake of the people of the North, the fatal error which has led to most of the troubles now pressing like an incubus upon the country, consists in that meddlesome spirit which prompts [Republicans] to interfere with the affairs of other communities, and to seek to regulate and control them as they rightfully do their own. They seem to consider it their mission to dictate to the people of the South what shall be the character of their domestic institutions, what the relation of master and servant, and how all their matters shall be regulated, precisely as they act upon the same questions at home within their own proper jurisdiction.[13]

Moreover, this was a sentiment to which the old-line Whigs of the Constitutional Union Party could also subscribe. After all, these were generally the same "Cotton" Whigs who had found it impossible to remain allied with their high-minded "Conscience" brethren who insisted on attacking the South. "Why not permit each State, as by the original compact, and it was thought was secured by the great instrument under which we have grown great and prospered, to hew out its destiny in its own way, and with its own institutions, without interference from its sister States?" pleaded one pro-Bell editor. "Why seek to meddle with that which concerns us not?"[14]

Yet while Tilden's pamphlet emphasized local control and resistance to moral imperialism, it failed to exploit the third principal aspect of Democratic ideology: race. Antipathy to blacks was an integral part of Democratic thinking throughout the late 1850s. Fairly typical was an Illinois editor's charge that the Republicans were "a nigger-stealing, stinking, putrid, abolition party, [which] has for its prime object the repeal of the Fugitive Slave law, and the placing of niggers above white men in legal rights, intelligence and everything else."[15]

Stephen Douglas himself exemplified the centrality of race in his famous 1858 reelection campaign against Abraham Lincoln. In response to Lincoln's charge that popular sovereignty violated the Founders' vision of the ultimate extinction of slavery, Douglas maintained that the government "was made by white men, for the benefit of white men and their posterity forever." The status of blacks "is a question which the [white] people of each state must decide for themselves." The real issue was not the morality of slavery at all but the future of the American republic, which Republican antislavery agitation was threatening. "I care more for the great principle of self-government, the right of the people to rule, than I do for all the negroes in Christendom," he railed. "I would not endanger the perpetuity of this Union. I would not blot out the great inalienable rights of the white man for all the negroes that ever existed." In such arguments the Democrats' antireformism, emphasis on local control, fears for the republic, and deep-seated racism combined to present a powerful indictment of Republicanism.[16]

Douglas's argument occupied the same middle ground that Tilden claimed: under a federal system of government, only Southerners could decide the basis for their race relations, and any attempt to govern otherwise would end in tragedy. Unlike Douglas, though, Tilden did not press the favorite Democratic tactic of painting Republicans as wild-eyed abolitionists who sought to equalize the races politically and socially. He did not challenge New Yorkers, as Douglas had Illinoisans, "If you desire negro citizenship, if you desire to allow them to come into the State and settle with the white man, if you desire them to vote on an equality with yourself, and to make them eligible to office, to serve on juries, and to adjudge your rights, then support Mr. Lincoln and the Black Republican party."[17]

Such appeals were popular among Democrats of both factions in 1860,[18] so Tilden's decision to avoid this cardinal point almost entirely seems odd. No doubt it stemmed partly from his initially directing his appeal to the *Post*'s Republican audience, and perhaps from his own Barnburner history. Of greater significance, though, is that he was trying not to alienate Bell-Everett supporters, those conservative former Whigs who feared Republican antislavery agitation yet frowned on Democratic race-baiting.[19] Tilden's virtual silence on race reminds us that it was no accident that few other tracts captured the heart of the anti-Republican argument so neatly; this pamphlet had been born of the desperation of one who had witnessed, from the stage of the Cooper Institute, just how deeply divided the republic's defenders were. His mission was to provide a common platform for the two Democratic factions and the Constitutional Unionists.

Tilden's effort to reduce the anti-Republican argument to its lowest common denominator is apparent throughout the essay, in his affirming the validity of Southern anxieties; stressing the genuine danger of disunion; accusing the Republicans of departing dramatically from the ideas and values of the Founders; arguing the illegitimacy of a sectional party in a federal system of government; and demonstrating the short-sightedness of the free-soil position. Each argument rested on values common among anti-Republicans, and all were brought together in the heartfelt plea for Republicans to continue the hallowed American tradition of subordinating partisan concerns to the survival of that embodiment of the Founders' vision, the Union.[20]

Despite Tilden's success in basing his argument in such widely held ideals, he and the others who tried to unite against the Republicans failed signally, particularly in their efforts to piece together the fractured Democracy. Too many of their colleagues felt too much animosity toward their rivals. Across the North, Douglas and Breckinridge partisans breathed fire, often appearing more antagonistic toward each other than toward the Republicans. Douglas's managers charged the pro-Breckinridge "conspirators" at the Democratic convention with carrying out a deliberate plot to break up the Union; after Lincoln's election, the Douglas press was quick to blame the Breckinridge faction for the result. Northern Breckinridge Democrats, decisively outnumbered though they were, returned blow for blow, accusing Douglas of selfishly destroying the party and waging a sectional campaign in order to gain access to federal spoils.[21]

There was more behind the hostility than bitterness and resentment: control of the Northern wing of the party was at stake. The factions had been openly vying for power since 1857, when Buchanan had snubbed Douglas and his allies in patronage distribution and Douglas had defied the administration over the admission of Kansas under the Lecompton Constitution. During the 1860 campaign Douglas counseled his followers to reject fusion with the Breckinridge minority but to support the Bell-Everett ticket, virtually ceding defeat to the Republicans in order to cement his power over the Northern Democracy and attract additional conservative support. In that way he hoped to fashion a coalition that would win back Southern conservatives and moderates and successfully challenge the Republicans in the North four years later. When anxious fusionists warned him that a Democratic schism would only strengthen Republican prospects, Douglas shrugged, "Let it. It will give us the organization in 1864."[22]

Finally, the Democratic rift was rooted also in important ideological disputes. Fusionists such as Tilden may have wanted to avoid contentious issues and focus on the Republican peril, but other Democrats did not hesitate to express strong opinions on the question most responsible for dividing their party: federal protection of slavery in the territories. Douglas's supporters took as an article of faith his outspoken conviction that only congressional nonintervention—that is, popular sovereignty—could save the Union.[23] On the other hand, Breckinridge supporters in the North held a slave code to be the only means of protecting Southern rights in the territories and considered Douglas's popular sovereignty to be as discriminatory as any Republican proposal.[24]

On its own, the question of a slave code was controversial enough to make fusion's success unlikely. But as Southern indignation assumed an air of resolve, it was the twin volcanoes of secession and federal coercion that precluded any real chance of the Northern Democracy's reunification. The focal point was Douglas's categorical rejection of disunion and espousal of force in an August speech at Norfolk, Virginia. While the right of revolution was "inherent and unalienable," he argued, the election of a Republican president by constitutional means would in no way justify such a course on the part of the South. Asked how he would respond to secession, he declared, "I think the President of the United States, whoever he may be, should treat all attempts to break up the Union, by resistance to its laws, as Old Hickory treated the Nullifiers in 1832"—a reference to President Jackson's famous threat to lead an army into South Carolina. Douglas would use Breckinridge Democrats' failure to uphold that position as rationale for his fierce denunciation of fusion, declaring at a New York rally, "I am utterly opposed to any union or any fusion with any man or party who will not enforce the laws, maintain the constitution, and preserve the Union in all contingencies." His conclusion left no doubt as to his views on secession: "I wish to God we had an Old Hickory now alive," he thundered, "in order that he might hang Northern and Southern traitors on the same gallows."[25]

Southerners denounced Douglas for such talk, of course, and the Breckinridge Democrats of the North echoed their condemnation of his "coercive threat." Typical of the argument against Douglas's stance was that of Caleb Cushing of Massachusetts, former attorney general and respected constitutionalist. In a widely read speech in late November, Cushing asserted that the Constitutional Convention had deliberately refused to grant the general government authority to use force against a disobedient state; James Madison himself had argued that such action would be equivalent to a declaration of war and would instantly absolve the states from their constitutional ties. Any attempt by the federal government to coerce a seceding state "will thus itself produce the legal dissolution of the Union."[26]

In one sense the Northern Democracy's division between Hardshell and

Softshell factions was relatively unimportant: the overwhelming majority of Northern Democrats were Douglas supporters. Even in the eastern cities, where Hardshell support was strongest, its potency was exaggerated by its overrepresentation in the partisan press. Yet as Democratic speakers and editors wrestled with the growing crisis, it became plain that the Breckinridge faction represented not so much a distinct view as one end of a spectrum. With few exceptions, Northern Democrats, and anti-Republicans generally, blamed Republican antislavery agitation for the crisis and believed substantial Northern concessions to the South to be the only realistic resolution, even if they continued to disagree on what form such concessions should take. Moreover, despite Douglas's unequivocal position prior to the election, in the early weeks of the crisis most of the pro-Douglas majority either stood against coercion or, more often, studiously avoided any public declaration on the subject.[27]

In the month after the election, in fact, Douglas himself maintained a near-total silence. His only public statement before Congress convened was a widely printed open letter to prominent New Orleans supporters. In it he reiterated his belief that Lincoln's election, while deplorable, was no justification for secession: the new president would be powerless against a hostile Congress and Supreme Court and in four years would be voted out of office with no harm done. If Lincoln should violate Southern rights in the meantime, a united North would join the South in resisting him. But with disunionism changing from threat to reality and his own followers chary of his Norfolk doctrine, Douglas made no mention of coercion.[28] He was wise to back off and check the direction of the wind, for the situation was shifting. Once the crisis began in earnest, and especially after the public realized that conflict at the Southern forts was a real possibility, the topic would become paramount in Northern debates; if he was going to help resolve this crisis—and perhaps even make it work to his advantage—Douglas needed to know not only what was going on in the South but also where his Northern allies and constituents stood.

✳ Neither was leadership coming from the other source of Democratic authority, the White House. There, Secretary of War Floyd's reassurance to South Carolina regarding the forts was an early indication of the cautious, tentative nature of the administration's Southern policy. Unlike Douglas, who had the luxury of another month to observe the situation before Congress met, the president and his ministers had to face developments as they arose. As they did, Buchanan—a Northerner selected for his Southern sympathies back when the Democracy was still a national institution—found himself and his closest advisers profoundly divided.

Although the president had always been something of a micromanager, more apt to dictate to his ministers than ask their opinion, the current situation found him at a loss. In the wake of the election, he put to his cabinet two questions: what course should the administration take toward disunion, and should he announce a policy immediately or wait until his December 3 annual address to Congress?[29] His own inclination was to call a convention to consider compromise measures. Since a Northern rejection of compromise would cast the South in a positive light, a convention would put the onus of making concessions on the North—where, Buchanan was convinced, it belonged. The three Northern members of his cabinet—Secretary of State Lewis Cass of Michigan, Attorney General Jeremiah S. Black of Pennsylvania, and Secretary of the Navy Isaac Toucey of Connecticut—all approved of a convention. However, reflecting the discordance of the Northern Democracy as a whole, they agreed on little else. Cass and Black firmly rejected the right of secession and favored reinforcing the Southern forts, including Moultrie, against attack. Toucey tended to follow Buchanan in thinking that although Northern agitation was at fault for the current state of affairs, disunion was unlikely outside of South Carolina.

The Southern members, too, were as divided as their native section. Secretary of the Treasury Howell Cobb of Georgia and Secretary of the Interior Jacob Thompson of Mississippi held secession to be a constitutional right; they were ready to follow their states should they choose to secede and set as their task facilitating a peaceful separation. Thompson supported a convention; Cobb saw it as useless. Floyd, a Virginian, did not object to a convention but thought it unnecessary since the incoming administration would be too weak to pose any real threat to the South. Yet he did believe secession to be constitutional, and was anxious to maintain peace in any event. Postmaster General Joseph Holt of Kentucky, who remained in the background at this early stage, was the only cabinet minister to reject the idea of a convention outright, arguing that its failure would accelerate secession, which he opposed.

Debate raged over the next weeks, both in and out of formal cabinet meetings. Pressure from all sides was intense. Buchanan wavered on the critical issue of reinforcing the Southern forts, influenced on the one hand by events at Charleston and on the other by Cobb's and Floyd's threats to resign should strong action be taken. On one thing only was the cabinet united: desiring more time to work on Buchanan, all rejected a proclamation and advocated waiting on a statement of policy until his address to Congress. This the president agreed to do.[30]

Amid the uncertainty following the election, and given Douglas's relative silence, a strong statement or action from Buchanan might have provided the guidance that the Northern public was lacking. True, the administration was reviled throughout the North, despised by Republicans and Douglas Democrats alike for its taint of corruption and its pro-Southern leanings, and the well-publicized rancor within the cabinet eroded confidence even further. Yet Buchanan's reticence only increased the general level of contempt and fueled rumors that he was planning to turn federal property over to the secessionists.

With the organization divided and no guidance coming from the leaders of either wing, the party line slipped into chaos. Party managers, particularly newspaper editors, propounded a muddled hodgepodge of views, leaving confused voters to maintain their own watchful silence; at no other point before Lincoln's inauguration in March would the mailbags of Democratic leaders be so empty. Like Douglas, Democrats waited for Congress to assemble before settling on any definite course.

✳ In spite of the gathering momentum of secession and the earnest warnings of Democrats and Constitutional Unionists, Republicans showed no anxiety about disunion before the election and remarkably little after it. Their unconcern was perhaps best illustrated by the course of election night in Lincoln's hometown of Springfield, Illinois. The day had been wild and raucous and grew more so as the results of the canvass became clear. Bands played, cannons were fired, and crowds gathered at various points throughout the city to celebrate the expected Republican triumph, roaring at the promising reports that issued occasionally from the busy telegraph office. The largest and rowdiest of these crowds milled around the statehouse, which dominated the town square. Upon hearing preliminary results from the critical state of New York, wrote one reporter, "men pushed each other, threw up their hats, hurrahed, cheered for Lincoln, . . . cheered for New York, cheered for everybody; and some actually laid down on the carpeted floor, and rolled over and over." And when the Empire State was officially placed into the Republican column, signaling Lincoln's victory, "Springfield went off like one immense cannon report, with shouting from houses, shouting from the stores, shouting from house tops, and shouting everywhere. Parties ran through the streets singing, 'Ain't I glad I joined the Republicans,' till they were too hoarse to speak."[31] No one in the streets of Springfield appeared to be worried about Southern threats.

Nor did the candidate himself. Earlier that night Lincoln had left his temporary office upstairs in the statehouse to join an assemblage of politicos inside the telegraph office. There he sprawled on a couch to observe the returns as they came in. His companions greeted each fresh bit of good news enthusiastically, but Lincoln was more subdued—no doubt conscious of his many observers, and perhaps beginning to feel as no one else could the sobering press of victory. Shortly after midnight he ventured out briefly to meet with a group of Springfield ladies, among them his wife, who had arranged some refreshments. Though he "came as near being killed by kindness as man can be without serious results" by the crush of well-wishers, he smiled affably, drank coffee, and shook hands all around. Within half an hour, though, he had ducked back inside the telegraph room. There he stayed until his triumph was certain and the throng outside had dispersed to carry the merriment through the streets, where they celebrated until dawn.[32]

At about two in the morning, Lincoln finally made his way home. He found himself exhausted but incapable of sleep. "I then felt, as never before, the responsibility that was upon me," he later recalled. Unable to shake his somber mood, he sat down at a table, took up a pen, and began to write. It was not the Southern electoral returns or the possibility of secession they suggested that was on his mind, however. What he labored over for the next several hours was a list of names. Lincoln's first act as president-elect was to begin the process of cabinet selection.[33]

The reason he offered later for undertaking such a task in the early-morning hours after election day was that he "began at once to feel that I needed support—others to share with me the burden."[34] Yet, weighted down with the magnitude of his new responsibilities, Lincoln did not choose to confer with a few of the friends and colleagues with whom he had spent the night at the telegraph office, nor did he talk matters over with his wife, who had long been an important political adviser and had waited up until he came home. Instead he sought relief from his sudden sense of isolation by sitting down alone to mull the composition of his official cabinet. The list he eventually compiled included only one person whom he knew well and trusted, Chicago political boss Norman B. Judd.[35] Despite his recollection, Lincoln was concerned with more than just sharing his burden.

The selection of official presidential advisers was also something more than a few hours' labor by any single individual could resolve. The composition of Lincoln's cabinet would dominate the thinking of Republicans for the next five months, frequently taking priority even over the national crisis. As Lincoln recognized in the cold small hours of that wakeful first night, this was a choice that would shape his entire administration, coloring every decision of both party politics and national statesmanship that he would make in the coming months and years. The task he began that night was nothing less than defining the Republican Party—the new party in power, as it had never before existed in its brief life as a party in opposition.

The cabinet was the topmost level of federal patronage, the center of a vast web of political ties that radiated outward to encompass over 35,000 civilian positions in the federal government and influence tens of thousands more throughout the states. The strands of that web bound together party members in the different branches of the federal government, bridged the national and state organizations, and united the distinct and largely autonomous state parties into a reasonably coherent whole. Lincoln's choice of advisers would affect the entire network. He must select men who would represent the party geographically, leaving no region or critical state feeling snubbed, and he must satisfy the demands of rival factions both nationally and in the states. This required extensive consultation with state party elites to be sure his choices matched their wishes. Acting unilaterally would alienate influential party leaders, weakening party unity and undermining the cooperation needed to govern under a system of checks and balances. Encouraging input, on the other hand, would permit state party leaders to expand their own influence through access to federal patronage, thus forging for Lincoln necessary alliances in Congress and the state governments. Given his inexperience in national politics, this was even more critical for him than for many other chief executives.

On the other hand, accepting too much advice would promote the suspicion that Lincoln was weak and easily dominated. There was at this time widespread concern—more pronounced the farther one was from Illinois—regarding Lincoln's character. Before his nomination in May, he was largely unknown outside of the Northwest, an Illinois lawyer whose career in public office consisted of four terms in the Illinois legislature and a single, unremarkable term in the U.S. House of Representatives—and even that had ended over a decade earlier. Despite their embrace of the homespun image of the self-made rail-splitter, Republicans were uncertain how Lincoln's moderate views would play out in this moment of decision.

Although they tended to speak of him as they wished him to be—radicals assuring themselves and others of his firmness, conservatives, of his prudence and restraint—there was also apprehension that he would fall under the influence of the rival faction. As a result, partisans would lobby Lincoln and other party leaders doggedly over the cabinet.

As Democratic presidents Pierce and Buchanan had discovered before him, distributing federal offices and contracts could be a harrowing task even within a well-established party organization. The Republicans were far from that, and if their newness to national power created a rare opportunity for Lincoln to mold his party, it also generated tremendous challenges. Foremost among these was the prospect that the former Whigs who comprised the large majority of Republicans would take advantage of the party's success and snub the former Democrats. Salmon P. Chase, long a leading light of antislavery politics and now newly elected senator from Ohio, explained the danger to a fellow former Democrat, Illinois senator Lyman Trumbull: "If, as is given out confidently in some quarters, an attempt shall be made to convert the Republican into the old Whig Party, it will signally fail & the Democratic Party will return to power in a majority of the states next year." Chase concluded, "No disunion need create alarm except the disunion of the Republican Party"—a common sentiment in the fall of 1860.[36] The party was indeed vulnerable, faced with the possibility of a major crisis in the immediate wake of its first national victory. Republicans had yet to prove that their organization could be more than an opposition coalition, an alliance of convenience between previously antagonistic factions brought together only by an aversion to slavery's westward expansion.

Nor were prior hostilities among its member groups all that threatened to divide the party once it had achieved power: like Tilden and the fusionists, Lincoln had broad ideological differences to overcome. As historian Eric Foner has elaborated, Republicans held a wide range of antislavery views. Conservatives such as Illinois judge David Davis and Massachusetts businessman John Murray Forbes generally opposed slavery not so much as a moral wrong as an inefficient and dangerous labor system. Once control of the federal government had been wrested from the Slave Power, they believed the party should concentrate on important economic issues such as the tariff and internal improvements. Most conservatives were former Whigs who had joined the new party late and with reluctance and felt little loyalty to the young Republican organization.[37] At the opposite end of the spectrum, radical Republicans such as Chase and Massachusetts governor-elect John Andrew viewed slavery as a moral evil. To them, abolition was the party's primary goal, and they rejected outright any compromise involving slavery and especially its expansion. Like conservatives, many radicals felt little loyalty to the party; it was merely a means to their end, and when it was no longer useful many of them would have little trouble abandoning it.[38] Former Democrats were disproportionately represented among the radical wing, since moderate and many conservative Whigs moved into and dominated the new Republican Party, whereas moderate and conservative Democrats had generally stayed put. As a result, former Democrats often dominated radical factions at the state level, linking the party's Democrat-Whig and radical-conservative divisions.[39]

Moderate Republicans such as New York senator William H. Seward and Lincoln himself constituted a majority in the party and thus held the balance of power between the two extreme positions. Moderates held a broad range of views, but in general they shared both the conservatives' emphasis on nonslavery issues and the radicals' zealous opposition to slavery's expansion. Though often opposing slavery chiefly as a system of labor and a source of power for planter-aristocrats, many moderates also viewed the institution as a moral wrong.[40]

Efforts to increase commonalities among these factions had backfired, largely because they had coincided with the contradictory goal of broadening the party's constituency. In trying to bring in the conservatives who had voted for Fillmore in 1856, the Republicans toned down their party's antislavery image and expanded its platform to include various Whiggish economic planks. In addition, in choosing their presidential nominee, delegates to the national convention at Chicago bypassed Seward, far and away the party's leading figure, due to his pro-immigrant, antinativist record and radical antislavery reputation.[41] This strategy proved critical to their success,[42] but by bringing in voters too conservative to have embraced Republicanism earlier, it also blurred the party's focus and exacerbated its rivalries. Conservative minorities in most Northern states were now strong enough to balance the older, more radical influences, creating tremendous tension.

Lincoln's own state of Illinois is instructive regarding both this situation and the president-elect's ability to handle it. Personal and ideological friction affected party dynamics there from the beginning. In the northern Third Congressional District, for example, conservatives David Davis and Leonard Swett sought in 1856 and again in 1858 to block the renomination of abolitionist congressman Owen Lovejoy. Only the judicious intervention of Lincoln, a respected elder statesman who was tightening his hold on state party leadership at that time, prevented the young organization from self-destructing. But this local quarrel soon melded with another in Chicago between former mayor "Long John" Wentworth, editor of the *Chicago Democrat*, and Norman B. Judd, chairman of the powerful state central committee. Between 1857 and 1860 fierce personal attacks and bitter accusations of double-dealing pulled more and more party leaders into the fray.

Soon the Illinois party was arrayed into a radical faction led by former Democrats Judd, Ebenezer Peck, and (more loosely) Lyman Trumbull and represented by the *Chicago Tribune*, and a conservative alliance dominated by former Whigs Davis and Swett and represented by Wentworth's *Democrat*. The schism almost erupted into war in 1860 when Judd, in the midst of a battle with Swett for the party's gubernatorial nomination, sued Wentworth for libel. Lincoln, who had successfully remained above the fray, interceded again, mediating the libel suit and engineering the nomination of the moderate Richard Yates, a former antislavery Whig, for governor. His actions not only united the state organization but also established Lincoln as its unrivaled leader; coupled with Illinois's critical importance in Republican electoral strategy (as well as a moderate reputation on slavery and immigration and some skillful maneuvering at the convention), that leadership won Lincoln the party's nomination.[43]

Every Northern state had a similar story. Despite his success in Illinois, then, it is little wonder that Lincoln could not sleep after being elected to lead the nation with this patchwork opposition coalition behind him. And he soon had cause to be grateful for having so early gotten his own thoughts in order regarding his cabinet, for he was quickly inundated with advice and appeals from all over the free states. A dizzying stream of names was brought to his attention, all with some claim to official recognition and most opposed by rival local factions.

✳ Cabinet controversies were inevitably and inextricably entwined with the party's response to secession: the individuals Lincoln chose as his advisers would strongly suggest which way he was leaning in his attitude toward the gathering storm in the South and would have great influence over his policy. Thus Republicans were convinced that in dealing with the Southern problem, "the first great difficulty will be the formation of the Cabinet. *That* will be looked to as indicating the *policy* of the administration."[44] What made this even more challenging for Lincoln was that extremists on each side announced themselves ready to cast off extremists on the other, leaving moderate Republicans fearful (and anti-Republicans hopeful) that the party would come undone under the weight of victory.[45]

The schism had not yet reached crisis proportion, however. So far support for a realignment of parties was limited to the ideological margins; most Republicans wanted to maintain the alliance of conservatives, radicals, and moderates, of former Whigs, Democrats, and Free-Soilers, that had so successfully attracted Northern voters. With that in mind, at a five-day meeting with vice president elect Hannibal Hamlin and other party leaders in late November, Lincoln made clear his intention to balance the two factions in his cabinet.[46] It would be in December that the fight would really heat up; until then, he merely sent out feelers and tried to make sense of a barrage of advice and demands that only increased with the passing weeks.[47]

In the meantime, Lincoln also kept his eye on the potential threat to party unity posed by disgruntled Southerners and their inevitable demands for concessions. For the moment, a significant Republican division over compromise seemed unlikely. Prior to the election, Republicans from young Gus Frey to Lincoln himself had exhibited blatant skepticism toward Southern warnings of disunion. As political satirist James Russell Lowell noted pointedly, "The old Mumbo-Jumbo is occasionally paraded at the North, but . . . the old cry of Disunion has lost its terrors, if it ever had any." Horace Greeley's *New York Tribune* mocked, "The south could no more unite upon a scheme of secession than a company of lunatics could conspire to break out of bedlam." And when Seward demanded of an audience in St. Paul, "Who's afraid?" a thunder of voices replied, "Nobody." "Nobody's afraid," repeated Seward with satisfaction.[48]

Preelection jeering might be written off as a necessary campaign tactic; to do otherwise than deny disunion threats would play into the most powerful weapon available to the party's Northern rivals. But with the election past, Republicans continued to treat secession lightly, both publicly and privately. On November 10, as the South Carolina legislature was moving up the date of its secession convention, the *Chicago Tribune* dismissed the Palmetto State's bluster: "South Carolina may fume and fulminate, and call conventions and pass resolutions till the crack of doom. . . . Up to this writing nobody is scared that we know of." Editor William Cullen Bryant phrased it more simply when he reported to his brother, "As to disunion, nobody but silly people expect it will happen."[49] Several writers suggested cynically that federal patronage, if nothing else, would keep Southern politicians loyal. "Many foolish and rash things are yet to be done," one businessman wrote from New York, "but I think it safe to conclude that when Congress assembles, every Southern member will be in his Seat, and every Southern *office occupied*."[50]

A Boston editor summarized the prevailing attitude when he noted, "Almost the only topic of political interest just now, is the rumored insane attempt of a few hot-headed fanatics, to induce the people of a few slave states to secede from the American Union. There is in this nothing new, unexpected, or alarming."[51] Indeed, to most Republicans there was not. Southern threats of disunion could trace their roots as far back as the Kentucky Resolutions of 1798, the Missouri Crisis of 1819–20, and the Nullification Crisis of 1832–33. They had been a regular feature of national politics since 1850. To most Republicans, dealings with the South had developed into a tiresome routine: Southerners demanded political advantages, Northerners balked, Southerners threatened to secede, and Northern Democrats gave in and voted with the Southerners. Warnings of disunion had become especially common during and after the Republicans' first national campaign in 1856, and now John Brown's raid and another sectional Republican campaign had guaranteed that Southerners would break out their tired threats yet again. Charles Sumner, returned from a long convalescence after his 1856 beating at the hands of Congressman Brooks, reflected the dominant mood of his party when he argued, "Since this is not the first time such cries are heard,—since, indeed, they have been long-sounding in our ears, so that their exact value is perfectly understood from the very beginning,—there seems no longer excuse or apology for hearkening to them. They are to be treated as threats, and nothing more."[52]

Given their history, Republicans generally considered those threats to be "the fruit of timidity in the North," a tool for extorting further concessions on slavery. A strong fear existed that the war with the Slave Power could still be lost—that displaying a willingness to bargain might indicate weakness and encourage secessionists. They were determined, now that they stood on the brink of victory, not to be intimidated.[53] Most Republicans were in agreement with the Indiana writer who declared, "The question of slavery must now be met and settled. I do not believe that it will result in anything more than an attempt to grab another *compromise*." An Ohioan added an important and highly popular variation: "Allow me to express the hope that, while the men of the South be met with calmness and kindness, they be made to understand at once that the day of compromises has passed away."[54]

Urging "calmness and kindness" was more than a high-minded expression of generosity. Most Republicans believed it was vital to strike a delicate balance between firmness and conciliation, to, as one put it, "consent to no secession, and yet . . . avoid any collision with the chivalry if possible." They took it as an article of faith that secession was the result of a deliberate plot among a relatively small group of Southern radicals, and that the mass of the Southern people would, if not provoked, exhibit a strong Union spirit. When the *New York Tribune* declared flatly, "The secession strength in the South is overrated," the overwhelming preponderance of Republicans agreed. Therefore, as an Indiana adviser suggested to Lincoln, "Prudence, (or what is called a 'masterly inactivity,') on our part, at present, will bring all right in the end." Or, as Gus Frey's elderly cousin Henry wrote more colorfully, "If let alone they will be like Pats Skunk — they will stink themselves to death."[55]

Therefore, few Republicans wanted Lincoln to make any public statement of his Southern policy prior to his inauguration. Conservatives, including some Republicans, counseled the president-elect that a word from him would strengthen the hands of Southern unionists immeasurably,[56] but most Republicans were dead set against the idea. Their chief concern was that issuing a statement would make Lincoln appear weak, thus strengthening rather than undermining secessionism. From Columbus, Ohio, came the outraged, and typical, cry, "For Heaven's sake do not be guilty of such a piece of flunkeism! The North would despise such an act, and by it the South become more rampant in its foolish disunion threats. People love and respect a bold, a just, a courageous man! They despise a coward. . . . Nothing could be more humiliating to us and disastrous to our cause, than to see you, the chosen leader of a bold and noble party, crawl upon your belly before a hand full of traitors in the South." Party leaders across the North concurred; as New York governor Edwin Morgan predicted, if Lincoln were to declare his policy, "instead of *appeasing*—it would only create an appetite for *more*."[57]

Such thoughts echoed Lincoln's own. To most requests for a statement he replied with a polite form letter directing the writer to his past speeches.[58] To a few correspondents, though, Lincoln explained that breaking his silence could do no good and might do harm. Promising yet again to respect the constitutional rights of Southern states would be "but mockery, bearing an appearance of weakness, and cowardice," with the result that "the secessionists, believing they had alarmed me, would clamor all the louder." The bottom line: "I should have no objection to make . . . if there were no danger of encouraging bold bad men to believe they are dealing with one who can be scared into anything."[59]

That attitude illustrates the perilous gap that divided Northern views from Southern. Lincoln believed that a review of his earlier speeches with their oft-repeated pledges to respect the Constitution and its clear restrictions upon federal interference with slavery in the states would reassure anxious Southern unionists. Like most Republicans, he saw no legitimate reason for Southerners' anxieties toward his administration. In reality, a review of Lincoln's speeches could do nothing to mollify those who feared his election. In them, his denials of either ability or desire to interfere with slavery in the Southern states were consistently coupled with an insistence that the institution must be placed in the "course of ultimate extinction." Again and again he condemned slavery as a "great moral, social and political evil"; by treating humans as property, he argued, the institution was "calculated to break down the very idea of a free government, even for white men, and to undermine the very foundations of free society." He accused slaveholders and leading Northern Democrats of a conspiracy to nationalize slavery by forcing even the free states to protect slave property within their borders. Finally, he firmly rejected secession as unconstitutional and charged that Southern aggression, not Republican agitation, was responsible for the disunion movement.[60]

To Lincoln, like most Republicans, these views represented a reasonable middle ground that upheld minimum Northern principles while sharply curbing the radical wing of his party. To his opponents, however, the president-elect embodied the Republican stance that Samuel Tilden described in his pamphlet: an ostensible moderation that in fact threatened the institution of slavery just as much as radical abolitionism and that was now driving the Deep South from the Union and might do worse before it was through.

By the middle of November, Lincoln was reconsidering his reticence. It was true that he had clearly stated his position on the rights of the Southern states many times, and it was true that during the campaign his views had been reprinted in many of the major newspapers, as well as collected and published. But perhaps conservatives had a point when they argued that the election had fundamentally altered the situation, that Southern unionists needed more assurance from Lincoln the president-elect than they could get from the speeches of Lincoln the private citizen.[61] Some suggested that a speech or public letter from a close adviser like Senator Lyman Trumbull might be just as useful but more palatable than a direct statement from Lincoln himself.[62] Though still doubtful, Lincoln decided to give that plan a try. He asked Trumbull to incorporate a brief passage into his speech at Springfield's "Grand Republican Jubilee" in mid-November, leaked word to the press, and positioned himself conspicuously on stage with the evening's speakers.[63]

The Jubilee, held on a clear autumn evening two weeks after the election, was one of numerous Republican celebrations held throughout the North. Like others, it was indistinguishable from a campaign rally in form, featuring banners, bonfires, a "grand illumination" of window lights, cannons, "martial bands," fireworks, and a parade of 1,200 uniformed Wide Awakes. The Springfield festival differed from the rest only in Lincoln's brief, blandly phrased address, delivered from his front porch, appealing for a magnanimous attitude from Northerners—his first public words since the election—and in the special attention given the formal speeches later in the evening. Lincoln's presence on stage was widely noted, and Senator Trumbull's words, in particular, were closely heeded.[64]

Trumbull was one of the first speakers.[65] He opened with an expression of his party's conservatism, repeating Republicans' oft-stated intention to "bring the government back to the policies of the fathers"; with the victory, he said, "the spirit of liberty, which, with our rulers, was dead, is alive again; and the Constitution, ordained to secure its blessings, which was lost sight of, is found." He insisted that Republicans were not the fanatical "advocates of negro-equality or amalgamation, with which political demagogues have so often charged them." Then Trumbull began to silently mingle the president-elect's words with his own. The next passage of his speech reiterated Lincoln's frequent pledge to respect the constitutional rights of the Southern states; since Republicans fully acknowledged that the federal government had "no more right to meddle with slavery in a State, than it has to interfere with serfdom in Russia," Trumbull declared, there was every reason to believe that the states' domestic affairs would be as safe under Lincoln's administration as under any other.[66]

Though hesitant to threaten force against seceding states directly, especially since none had yet taken any concrete, irrevocable step, Lincoln and Trumbull nevertheless agreed that they needed to address the issue. In doing so, they expressed the common belief that secessionism had been gotten up by political agitators who were determined to exploit the Republican victory for their own selfish motives. Lincoln's contribution to the speech continued, "Disunionists, per se, are now in hot haste to get out of the Union, precisely because they perceive they cannot much longer maintain an apprehension among the Southern people that their homes and firesides and lives are to be endangered by the action of the Federal Government. With such, '*now or never!*' is the maxim." In fact, it concluded confidently, "I regard it as extremely fortunate for the peace of the whole country that this point, upon which the Republicans have been so long and so persistently misrepresented, is now to be brought to a practical test, and placed beyond the possibility of doubt." Unless the secessionist cabal succeeded before the unionist masses had time to rally, such a test would put an end to all Southern anxiety.

That marked the end of Lincoln's passage, as Trumbull eliminated from it a sentence about Southern unionists' using the secessionists' own military preparations to put them down. With no indication that the foregoing words had been Lincoln's, he went on, insisting that there was no cause for secession and denying the constitutionality of secession under any circumstances. To this point Trumbull had been careful to temper both his own words and, by skipping over the passage about military preparations, Lincoln's. Now he felt obliged to offer a brief but stern warning to secessionists. Should the conspirators succeed in keeping down the unionist majority and carrying out their rebellion, he predicted, "there will be but one sentiment among the great mass of the people of all parties, and in all parts of the country, and that will be that 'the Union—it must and shall be preserved,' and woe to the traitors who are marshaled against it." But Trumbull's hard tone vanished as quickly as it had appeared; with his next breath he explained that once the "full effect" of Republican measures had been felt, Americans would be united, "the cry of disunion [would] be hushed," and Republican principles would bring lasting prosperity to the nation.

For those who examined Trumbull's words for hints of Lincoln's policy, the message was clear. The incoming administration would follow the Chicago convention's platform: that is, it would refrain from direct action against slavery in the states and enforce those aspects of the Constitution that protected slavery but would permit no further extension of the peculiar institution. Regarding any attempt at secession, Lincoln would neither make concessions to appease disunionists nor take preemptive action but would await the inevitable unionist reaction from the Southern people. Secession was an act of aggression for which the new administration would not stand, but there was neither need for it nor expectation that it would happen.[67]

Reaction to the speech was mixed and predictable. Republican newspapers praised its blend of moderation and firmness; moderate anti-Republicans perceived in it a welcome abandonment of hard-line party principles; and radical anti-Republicans and Southern disunionists interpreted it as a virtual declaration of war. A disgusted Lincoln considered the whole experiment a failure, just as he had thought it would be, and swore not to repeat his mistake. "Has a single newspaper, heretofore against us, urged that speech with a purpose to quiet public anxiety?" he demanded privately. With exasperation he noted the tendency of his opponents to interpret it as best suited them. "This is just as I expected, and just what would happen with any declaration I could make. These political fiends are not half sick enough yet. 'Party malice' and not 'public good' possesses them entirely. 'They seek a sign and no sign shall be given them.'" Thenceforth Lincoln, like Douglas and Buchanan, would maintain public silence.[68]

✳ Trumbull's was the speech for which observers were waiting, but he was not the only one to discuss the party's stance on the developing crisis that night. Governor-elect Richard Yates repeated many of Trumbull's specific points, but it was significant that he brought a considerably less muted tone to his arguments. Similar as they were in many respects, the differences between the two speeches were suggestive of a wider, if still undeveloped, division among Republicans over the proper attitude toward disunion.[69]

Yates, too, began by insisting that the ideals espoused by Republicans were those of the nation's Founders; indeed, he hammered at this point, charging that Southern actions violated both the Founders' antislavery ideals and the rule of law upon which they had constructed the republic. As for threats of disunion, Yates agreed that the proper response was to "keep cool." Echoing Trumbull in what was perhaps the most typical Republican refrain of those first weeks, he insisted that disunion had no popular support: "I take the bluster of a few hotspurs of the South as but little indication of Southern sentiment."

From there the two speeches diverged as Yates next declared that Northerners had been humiliated enough. Republicans must call the fire-eaters' bluff: "It is time the question was tested. Whether the South really intends to dissolve the Union or not, the result of the late election has informed her that the independent judgment of the American people cannot be coerced by insolent threats of secession or disunion. . . . Let us know once and forever whether a majority or minority shall rule. Let us know whether the millions of freemen of this nation are to get on their knees to Slavery at every Presidential election." With this brief passage, Yates not only tapped the very heart of the Republicans' mass appeal—the need to defend American liberty and self-government from the dominance of the Slave Power— but also dismissed the notion that the Union was in any real danger and appealed to Northerners' manly pride to resist Southern intimidation. It was a formula that was repeated ad nauseam, but to great effect, in those early weeks and throughout the crisis. It also went much further than anything Trumbull had said.

Nor was the governor-elect finished. Appealing simultaneously to his listeners' courage and devotion to principle, their support for the Union, and their commitment to the spirit of the Founders, Yates roared, to "tremendous applause,"

> I know that every desire of [Lincoln's] heart is for peace, but, if occasion demands, South Carolina will find in him the true metal, the fire and flint, the pluck of Old Hickory himself. . . . The election of a President by a majority of the people is no excuse for treason, and . . . all the power of the Government should be brought to bear to crush it out wherever it shall rear its unsightly head. . . . Before [the dissolution of the Union] shall be consummated South Carolina and the politicians who have trifled, and blustered, and threatened, will find out the spirit of '76 is not finally extinct, and that there is an awful, frightening majesty in an uprisen people.

In many ways the speeches of Yates and Trumbull were remarkably similar. Both contradicted the charges of Tilden and others by equating Republican principles with the ideals of the Founding Fathers and insisting that the South would soon praise Lincoln's benevolent administration. Both sought to balance conciliation and resolve. However, by closing with sword rather than olive branch and by doing so in considerably harsher language, Yates revealed his center of gravity to be noticeably farther North. For those looking beyond Trumbull's address for an indication of the party's attitude toward the South, Yates's combative tone was significant. What made it even more so was that Yates had a more moderate reputation than Trumbull. A former Whig, he had initially favored the candidacy of conservative Missourian Edward Bates over that of Lincoln, and as we have seen, his own candidacy in 1860 had been a compromise between the rival Illinois factions. Yates was no radical, no Charles Sumner or Owen Lovejoy. Yet he saw fit to utilize the national spotlight not to reassure Southerners but to warn them.

There was another problem, perhaps more ominous even than Yates's words and the crowd's obvious approval. The popular strategy of mingling magnanimity and resolve while sitting quietly and waiting for the inevitable unionist reaction was precisely what Lincoln was attempting to follow with his mild public remarks and his minimal suggestions to Trumbull. Theoretically, maintaining a passive posture should have been an easy task—but as the speeches at the Springfield Jubilee revealed, in practice it was not so simple. If two moderates like Trumbull and Yates could not present a united front while standing on the same stage, how could the entire party, divided as it was by background, ideology, and geography, maintain the necessary low-key manner? Already the deep divisions beneath the surface of Republican unity threatened to mar the party's moment of glory.

Throughout the free states, in fact, radical and conservative Republicans were beginning to display attitudes more widely divergent than those displayed at Springfield. Casting aside any consideration of a "masterly inactivity," a number of radicals deliberately taunted the Southern fire-eaters, as when Massachusetts senator Henry Wilson jeered, to thunderous cheers, "Tonight, thanks be to God, we stand with the Slave Power beneath our feet. That haughty power which corrupted the Whig party, strangled the American party, and used the Democratic party as a tool, lies crushed to the dust tonight, and our heel is upon it." In Chicago, Long John Wentworth's *Democrat* sneered, "Will they eat dirt? Will they take back all they said about disunion, a Southern confederacy, the rights of the South, the blood of their enemies, and all that sort of thing? . . . The chivalry *will* eat dirt. They will back out. They never had any spunk anyhow. The best they could do was bully, and brag and bluster." Michigan senator Zachariah Chandler concurred gleefully, "This disunion howl . . . is almost musick to my ears. *Let them howl*, it will do them good."[70]

Like Yates, some moderates could not resist warning secessionists that the North would not stand for treason. But even at this early date a few went further, talking openly of suppressing insurrection. A New York bank president wrote, "I hope to hear that Mr. Lincoln has ordered some good hemp to hang—although opposed to hanging—these infamous political agitators & disunionists." An Illinois constituent instructed Trumbull to "tell Mr. Lincoln that little Boone [County] can be relied upon for 500, wide awakes, well armed and equipped, if needed." An Indiana editor asserted belligerently, "We are heartily tired of having the threat stare us in the face evermore. If nothing but blood will prevent it, let it flow."[71]

The party line was muddled further by unexpected advice from Horace Greeley, a leader of the New York radicals and editor of the most widely read Republican paper in the country. Just three days after the election, Greeley startled readers of his *New York Tribune* by declaring, "If the Cotton States shall become satisfied they can do better out of the Union than in it, we insist on letting them go in peace. The right to secede may be a revolutionary one but it exists nevertheless. . . . And whenever a considerable section of our Union shall deliberately resolve to go out, we shall resist all coercive measures to keep it in. We hope never to reside in a republic whereof one section is pinned to the residue by bayonets."[72] This introduced a major new variable into the equation. It is true, as David M. Potter has argued, that the eccentric editor was not advocating peaceable secession so much as taking a drastic stance against compromise. But readers at the time did not appreciate the subtlety. Greeley's stance shocked most Republicans and struck a chord among some radicals. A few other editors took up Greeley's cry, and a handful of Republicans, such as Ohio's radical senator Ben Wade, expressed similar notions privately. "The day of Compromises has past," wrote Wade, "and that Government which is moved to temporize by the threats of Traitors is not worth preserving." Such expressions would increase with the approach of South Carolina's secession convention in mid-December.[73]

While Greeley and other radicals were so passionately opposed to compromise as to profess to prefer secession, a growing number of conservative Republicans took the opposite stance, venturing the idea that a judicious compromise might be necessary to prevent disunion. Boston editor Edgar Littell, worried by letters he was receiving from the South, proposed a grand meeting to announce the party's conservative intentions. In Washington, Ohio representative Thomas Corwin spread false rumors that Lincoln had assured him that his Southern policy would be conciliatory and that he would appoint a number of prominent conservatives to his cabinet.[74] The first major figure to advocate compromise openly was Henry J. Raymond, conservative editor of the *New York Times* and longtime ally of Seward and Thurlow Weed, bosses of the state party's old Whig faction. In a November 14 editorial, Raymond proposed an amendment to the Fugitive Slave Law designed to placate Southerners without violating the Republican platform: he suggested that the free states simply pay the value of fugitive slaves rather than return them.[75]

As a basis for compromise, Raymond's proposal did not begin to sound the depths of the sectional dispute, but its publication did mark a breach in the wall of Republican unanimity against conciliation. Perhaps because of its author's prestige, the *Times* proposal seemed to open the eyes of Republican conservatives to the possibility of making concessions without violating party principle. Particularly popular was the notion of repealing the so-called personal liberty laws, Northern state laws designed to impede enforcement of the federal Fugitive Slave Law. By late November, Democratic and Constitutional Unionist demands that the states with such laws repeal them were winning supporters among Republicans—especially in New York and other cities, where the effects of the financial panic were being felt most strongly.[76]

Since most Republicans believed that a masterly inactivity was the only way to uphold their party's principles without provoking Southerners, they found troubling both radicals' taunting of secessionists and advocacy of peaceable secession and conservatives' openness to compromise and condemnation of the personal liberty laws. But the earthquake that truly shook party confidence came from an entirely unexpected quarter: Thurlow Weed, the undisputed ruler of the New York State organization and alter ego of Senator William H. Seward. On November 24, Weed's *Albany Evening Journal* flouted Republican dogma by proposing not just a strengthening of the Fugitive Slave Law but also a re-extension of the old Missouri Compromise line, the line of 36°30' north latitude that for over thirty years had demarcated slavery and freedom in the western territories. Although it had been the Kansas-Nebraska Act's repeal of that line six years earlier that had led to the founding of the Republican coalition, from early on the party had rejected its reinstitution, insisting on nothing less than barring slavery from all federal territories. But now, Weed explained, the Republicans' accession to the White House marked the end of the controversy over slavery in the territories. There was no need to legislate against slavery in federal territories because the lands remaining would not support a slave-based economy anyway. The executive branch could easily keep slavery out through regulation; in the meantime, reestablishing the line would assist the cause of union while granting a meaningless concession.[77]

The abandonment of the party's central plank by the boss of its most important state organization and political manager of the party's most powerful national leader, came as a shock to Republicans across the country. It sparked a vehement reaction against the idea of concessions—especially concessions like Weed's, which struck at the very heart of Republicanism. "We dont take the Evening Journal or Times for our guide," a local party activist from western New York insisted. "We are here utterly opposed to have the principles of the Republican Party compromised away." Junior New York senator Preston King protested to Weed, "It cannot be done. You must abandon your position. . . . You and Seward should be among the foremost to brandish the lance and shout for war."[78]

Nevertheless, by early December an increasing number of Republican supporters found themselves torn between, on the one hand, firmly held principles and an aversion to backing down before Southern ultimatums, and on the other, a growing fear that if nothing were done this crisis might actually tear the country apart. The question that already began to haunt moderates like Lincoln was whether the party could be held together long enough to meet the emergency and fulfill its victory.[79]

✳ To most Republicans the national election of 1860 had been a golden opportunity to cast off the oppressive rule of the arrogant and aggressive Southern Slave Power that had dominated the national government for decades. To their opponents in the Northern states it had been a desperate attempt to prevent the ascendancy of a sectional party of Puritanical zealots, fanatics whose hatred of Southern domestic institutions would pervert constitutional government and provoke disunion. Each group's perception of events following the election was similar. Northern Democrats and Constitutional Unionists blamed the burgeoning crisis on antislavery agitation and insisted that only a Republican retreat from its discriminatory anti-Southern doctrines would save the Union. Republicans countered that it was Democrats' toadying and submissiveness that encouraged the South's empty threats to secede; a firm adherence to their principles would call the disunionists' bluff and finally settle the divisive question of slavery's place in the republic.

But as the drive toward secession gained momentum in the Deep South and a financial panic disrupted the Northern economy, rifts within the parties grew. The Democratic schism had been painfully obvious during the campaign when state organizations split between rival presidential candidates, despite largely ineffectual efforts to create fusion tickets. Cracks in Republican unity began to show only after the party's victory, once their coalition against the slave lords had to deal with the pressures of impending power.

The crisis over secession would dramatically increase these strains. Just as the irrelevance of old issues and the rise of new ones had dashed the previous party system by the mid-1850s, so the reality of disunion raised newer questions still, questions that might well threaten the partisan coalitions that had vied for power in 1860. At several points in the months to come, the issues of compromise and coercion would stand poised to cross party lines and encourage new combinations, suggesting that the partisan realignment of the 1850s had yet to run its course and that party loyalties, especially among Republicans, were not yet cemented. Throughout the crisis, a crucial determinant of the Northern response to disunion would be the ability of the existing organizations first to rally their followers around a particular secession policy and then to maintain unity despite the maelstrom of conflicting pressures that followed.

For the moment, the few Northern leaders who sensed the unsteadiness and its potential ramifications did so only dimly. In the early weeks of the crisis an absence of active leadership produced uncertainty and hesitation. Unsure of what was actually happening in the South and receiving conflicting messages from party spokesmen, far fewer Northerners took an active role in the decision-making process than would do so in the following months, once specific policies had been proposed and distinct party lines formulated. About all that was clear as November passed into December was that such questions as a Union-saving compromise versus a Union-saving rejection of compromise, or a Union-saving show of force versus a war-averting acceptance of disunion, would rest, like so much else, on the actions of congressional party leaders. As Congress prepared to reconvene, all eyes were on Washington.

Chapter 3 ✳ Proportions of Which I Had but a Faint Conception
✳ Early December

When they considered most national issues, Northerners thought in terms of politics and looked to the words and actions of their political leaders—elected officials, editors, and the like—for direction. Whether the public chose to follow or reject that guidance, leaders set the initial terms and tone of debate and made the final decisions. In the weeks after the election, a lack of guidance from key party leaders and uncertainty regarding the true course of events in the South produced an air of anxious waiting throughout the North. More confused than enlightened by a cacophony of contradictory speeches and editorials, the Northern public held its collective tongue. Once Congress met in early December, however, the crisis began to assume greater definition. Congressional proposals and debates provided Northerners with concrete ideas to draw upon and respond to. At the same time, the impending secession convention in South Carolina gave a more tangible quality to disunion, an immediacy that was heightened still more by the steadily worsening economic panic. As public opinion became more distinct, the vast machinery of Northern popular politics began to roll into motion. A growing number of constituents wrote to ask their elected representatives' advice and make their own views known. Before long some segments of Northern society began to move beyond letter-writing to engage in the next level of popular politics: petitions and mass demonstrations.

Since most Northerners perceived the crisis through the lens of partisanship, popular opinion was fairly predictable. Democrats blamed the crisis on Republican fanaticism and sympathized with Southern fears; Republicans blamed the crisis on Democratic subservience and scoffed at Southern bluster. There was inconsistency, though: already some Republicans—especially conservatives, many of whom had joined the party late and with reluctance—had displayed a willingness to offer the South substantive concessions. In Congress, the pressure of responsibility and a greater realization of the crisis's complexity forced congressmen's views to either harden or yield, increasing party irregularity and tension. As the larger question of whether to compromise at all overshadowed specific proposals, party lines began to crack. Moderate Republicans were affected most; the rigid resolve that reigned in their districts had ill prepared them for the complicated realities they faced in the capital. As many adopted the conciliatory attitude of the conservatives, it seemed likely that they would combine with Northern Democrats and Southern unionists to form a pro-compromise majority. Radicals, anticompromise moderates, and outraged constituents fought to close ranks. As early as mid-December, the Republican Party, like the Union itself, seemed in danger of disintegration.

✳ Due to his unique circumstances—his official position, of course, but more specifically the ongoing problem of the Charleston forts and the fast-approaching deadline for his annual message to Congress—James Buchanan was the first Northerner to comprehend the full scope of the dilemma that secession posed. Like most Northern Democrats, Buchanan was deeply committed to both the constitutional rights of the states and the perpetuity of the Union. In early December he found himself under intense pressure to choose between them. As chief executive, Buchanan had to report to Congress on the condition of the country, thereby presenting the first official assessment of and policy toward the developing crisis. He was also responsible for U.S. property in South Carolina—of all the issues raised by secession, the one least open to delay or compromise. Already the presence of a federal garrison at Fort Moultrie had almost led to blows with zealous Charlestonians, and in the weeks following the election the touchy situation there had continued to bedevil the administration. In composing his annual message, then, the president faced the unenviable task of plotting a course that upheld federal authority without triggering violent Southern reaction.

In formulating his policy Buchanan was torn between the opposing arguments of Attorney General Jeremiah Black and Secretary of the Interior Jacob Thompson and pressured by several of his Southern advisers' threats to resign should he order any kind of direct action against secession. Desperate to find solid ground, in mid-November he asked the attorney general to compose a brief outlining the extent of the president's constitutional authority regarding secession. Black replied that Buchanan had every right to defend federal property from attack or to recapture it once lost. However, he could use the army to enforce federal law only if local federal officers requested assistance. South Carolina's federal officials had all resigned, so unless Congress gave him additional authority, using military power in this case "would be simply making war." The Union would cease to exist the moment the federal government committed such an act, Black concluded—just as Caleb Cushing would in his Newburyport speech a few days later. Finally, in Black's judgment the president had no authority to recognize secession, whatever his own thoughts on the matter; that, too, was solely up to Congress.[1]

Armed with this opinion—that the president had the right to defend federal property from attack but could neither coerce a state into remaining in the Union nor recognize secession—Buchanan sought an increasingly elusive balance between remaining within his limited constitutional authority and rescuing his imperiled country from both dissolution and war. He decided that his role was to mediate between North and South: he intended, he said, "to come between the factions as a daysman, with one hand on the head of each, counseling peace."[2] Yet there was no doubt where his sympathies lay. A group of secessionists who met with him in the White House reported that although Buchanan denied the right of secession and condemned any attempt to exercise it "without resorting first to conciliatory measures," he also assured them "emphatically" that he would "first appeal to the North for justice to the South, and if it was denied them, 'then . . . I am with them.' "[3]

Meanwhile, the situation in Charleston was still explosive. Since Colonel Gardner's abortive attempt to withdraw arms from the arsenal, the administration—at least those members of it not committed to secession—had struggled with the problem of maintaining peace without sacrificing federal authority. The first order of business was to prevent hostilities in the short run, and to this end the administration adopted a policy of conciliation. A few days after Secretary of War Floyd reassured South Carolina officials that Colonel Gardner neither had nor would receive orders that would upset the status quo, he further placated the touchy Carolinians by replacing Gardner, a Boston native, with a Southerner, Maj. Robert Anderson of Kentucky.[4]

As November faded, debate over the forts continued to rage in the cabinet. The two sides now supported their cases with recent communications from Charleston. Secretary of the Treasury Howell Cobb and Secretary Thompson backed up their insistence that sending reinforcements would lead to war with a letter from South Carolina governor William H. Gist. Though asserting that his state desired a peaceful and dignified transition to independence and would take no offensive action toward the forts, Gist warned that he would not be able to restrain the people of

Charleston should the general government send additional troops or arms. In effect, the governor was offering the president a deal: peace in return for maintenance of the status quo, at least until South Carolina seceded and sent delegates to Washington to negotiate a formal separation. Equally adamant that Buchanan was obligated to defend the forts by strengthening the Charleston garrison, Black and Secretary of State Lewis Cass offered the assessment of the new commander, Major Anderson, that Fort Moultrie was so rundown and vulnerable that should it be attacked—a likely occurrence, from what he could tell—it would be overrun easily. Anderson requested immediate reinforcements as well as permission to transfer his garrison to Fort Sumter, which, situated on a small island in the middle of the harbor, was far more defensible.[5]

It seemed the time had come for Buchanan to decide between maintaining peace and enforcing federal authority. On Sunday, December 2, the day before his address was due before Congress, he made his choice. Reluctantly, he agreed that honoring Anderson's request was necessary if he were to maintain the government in the face of disunion. That evening he called Floyd to the White House to issue an order for reinforcements.

Had Floyd given that order, the entire course of the crisis, and possibly U.S. history, would have been radically different in ways impossible to know. South Carolina forces surely would have attacked the forts some four months sooner than they did—four crucial months of escalating tension, of debate and negotiation, and ultimately of the crystallization of ideas, emotions, and political alliances. Had the attack occurred in early December, a Democratic president with strong Southern sympathies and a profoundly divided cabinet would have been in charge of the national response, and Northern and Southern publics still unsure of what was going on, much less how they felt about it, would have been forced into hasty decisions. An attack may have rallied a united South and forced a divided North reluctantly to acknowledge South Carolina's independence, or it may have alienated the other Southern states, rallied the North, and led to a quick campaign that would have settled the issue of secession for good but left underlying sectional issues—read: slavery—unaffected. Or, as would happen several months later, an attack may have rallied both sides and sparked a long and horrific civil war that, no matter which side won, would have left deep and lasting scars that would forever transform the American republic.

But in early December 1860, none of those things happened. The moment passed. Floyd, who opposed secession but was equally averse to coercion, advised the president that such a momentous decision should not be made without consulting the general in chief of the army, Winfield Scott. It was a laughable suggestion. Shortly before the election, Scott, a brilliant military commander and insufferable political busybody, had forfeited what little influence he had with the administration when he submitted to Buchanan and Floyd a rambling, disjointed, and utterly unsolicited paper with the ponderous title, "Views suggested by the imminent danger of a disruption of the Union by the Secession of one or more of the Southern States."[6] In it he presented a muddled opinion on the right of secession, tried to predict the new confederacies that would result from disunion, and assured his native South (he was a Virginian by birth) of the harmlessness of the Republicans. The central point of his essay was a recommendation that the Southern forts be reinforced, but he failed to suggest how that might be accomplished given that all but fifteen of the army's 198 companies were scattered across the West, and his own admission that just five companies, about 150 men, were available to be transferred to the South. Obviously intending the document to be public, Scott sent copies to various men of influence in the North and South, including newspaper editors.

At the time, Buchanan had dismissed even the military advice contained in Scott's "Views" as impractical and simplistic; throwing the handful of available reinforcements into the various Southern forts, he thought, would, if anything, encourage secessionists by drawing attention to federal weakness. But now, hesitant to risk a confrontation, he allowed himself to be persuaded and sent for the general, whose constant squabbling with his superiors had led him years before to transfer his headquarters to New York. Floyd's delay tactic turned out to be even more successful than he had thought: the aged hero was confined to his bed and would, for the time being at least, be unable to make the trip to Washington. As it turned out, more than a month would pass before the troops Anderson requested were sent. Over that time, circumstances in both Washington and Charleston would change significantly.[7]

The next day, with his decision on the Charleston forts still hanging, Buchanan dispatched a clerk to deliver his annual message to Congress.[8] Its contents reflected his own long-held views, as well as the recent cabinet debates. He began with his most basic belief regarding sectional conflict: the blame lay entirely with Northern abolitionists. Their agitation had "inspired [the slaves] with vague notions of freedom," he charged, with the result that "a sense of security no longer exists around the family altar. . . . Many a matron throughout the South retires at night in dread of what may befall herself and her children before morning." Should those fears continue to spread through the Southern masses, he predicted, self-defense would become necessary and "disunion will become inevitable." The solution was obvious to someone of Buchanan's Democratic sensibilities. In a passage reminiscent of Samuel Tilden, he asserted, "All that is necessary . . . to settle the slavery question forever and to restore peace and harmony to this distracted country . . . all for which the slave States have ever contended, is to be let alone and permitted to manage their domestic institutions in their own way."[9]

On the other hand, echoing Douglas's New Orleans letter and Democratic editors across the North, Buchanan insisted that the South must recognize that a legal election was no legitimate cause for dissolving the Union. The federal government had no power to act against slavery. Should Southern rights be violated, then "the injured States, after having first used all peaceful and constitutional mean to obtain redress, would be justified in revolutionary resistance." He reiterated the point: secession was "neither more nor less than revolution. It may or it may not be a justifiable revolution; but still it is revolution."[10]

Concerning the practical matters arising from secession, Buchanan followed the opinion of his attorney general almost to the letter. There being no federal officers in South Carolina, he announced, unless Congress expanded his authority, he was powerless to execute the laws there. Beyond collecting customs duties and defending federal property, "it is . . . my duty to submit to Congress the whole question in all its bearings." Nevertheless, he added, "I should feel myself recreant to my duty were I not to express an opinion on this important subject." Here the influence of Buchanan's Southern advisers, notably Thompson, became evident. Not even Congress had the power to authorize the use of military force against a seceding state, he asserted. Even if it did, it would be unwise to use that authority. Coercion would pervert and demolish the very thing it was intended to save: "War would not only present the most effectual means of destroying [the Union], but would vanish all hope of its peaceable reconstruction. . . . Our Union rests upon public opinion, and can never be cemented by the blood of its citizens shed in civil war."[11]

Buchanan closed by proposing that Congress recommend compromise measures to the state legislatures. Since it was constitutional restrictions and silences that created the awkward position he and the country now occupied, only amending the Constitution could resolve the crisis. The amendment the president proposed addressed what he considered to be the three main points of sectional difference: it explicitly recognized the property rights of slaveowners in the Southern states, provided federal protection for slavery in the territories, and made an unambiguous declaration against Northern personal liberty laws.[12]

The first formal compromise proposal was now on the table.

✳ Predictably, Northern response to the president's message broke upon party and factional lines. Pro-administration partisans praised what the *New York Herald* called its "calm, patriotic, consistent and convincing views."[13] The Republican press objected to its blatant partisanship as a "gross perversion of facts" and dismissed its crisis proposals as "a melancholy exhibition of servility and incompetency" and a "last wail in behalf of the Cotton Lords."[14] Douglas Democrats were ambivalent. They welcomed Buchanan's assessment of the crisis's roots but condemned his proposal to incorporate federal protection of slavery in the territories into the Constitution. They generally concurred with his denial of the right of secession but criticized his "ill-timed confession of weakness" regarding the government's ability to preserve itself. "The present crisis in National affairs requires great prudence and forbearance on the part of the Executive," concluded a Buffalo editor, "but it does not demand the virtual abdication of executive power by the President."[15]

Historian Kenneth Stampp concludes that Buchanan was "out of touch with the main currents of Northern opinion."[16] He is both wrong and right. On one hand, Stampp makes the common error of associating public opinion too strongly with Republican opinion and thus relies too heavily on Republican sources. Certainly a majority of Northern voters had supported that party, but the anti-Republican minority was quite large, comprising about nine voters in twenty. And much of Buchanan's message reflected long-revered and widely held doctrines of the Democratic Party: like Tilden, Buchanan blamed sectional conflict on Northern antislavery fanaticism, expressed sympathy with the plight of white Southerners, and displayed a traditional Democratic emphasis on local government. Moreover, the line between partisan positions on the issues raised by secession were not firm. Public support for compromise was growing even among Republicans; in neither party was there a consensus on coercion. Indeed, Buchanan's assertion that to hold the Union together by force would be to destroy it reflected not only the opinion of many anti-Republicans but also the argument of Horace Greeley and other radical Republicans. To a significant degree, then, the president's message was well within the main currents of public opinion.

On the other hand, few Northerners agreed with Buchanan on either the key question of slavery in the territories or the issue that would soon displace it in importance: the federal government's authority to enforce the laws within a seceded state. A number of factors colored Northerners' perception of Buchanan's policy on the latter, which was the most controversial point of his message. First, his rejection of coercion was viewed alongside his failure to reinforce the Southern forts, fostering a popular belief that he denied not only the government's right to bring force against secession but also its right to defend itself from assault. That was not true, but it made his rejection of secession seem worthless rhetoric nonetheless. Second, a deep contempt for Buchanan himself encouraged disparagement of his position. To many, his middle-of-the-road stance merely confirmed his status as lackey to the arrogant, radical proslavery Southerners despised by Republicans and Douglas Democrats alike. "Oh my soul what a disgrace has Jas Buchanan brought upon himself and his country," was a typical refrain among both groups. "Infamy & shame must forever cover his name."[17]

Finally, at that early stage in the crisis, few people saw the need for choosing between stark options. Like Buchanan, most Northerners desired to maintain federal authority while resolving the crisis fairly and peaceably. Unlike him, they had not faced a situation in which they had to choose between those goals. As a result, the Northern public had yet even to identify all of the options that faced them, never mind consider their ramifications. In order to give compromise a chance, Buchanan had subordinated federal authority to the preservation of at least a short-term peace, then placated disunionists by denying the government's ability to take forcible action. Most Northerners were still unsure how they felt about the use of federal force, but they believed that the crisis could and would be resolved peacefully without its coming to that. Hence they rejected what appeared to be the president's choice of disunion over coercion.

Thus it was Buchanan's denial of the general government's authority to act against secession that drew the deepest scorn from the broadest cross section of Northerners. William Seward neatly captured the sweeping popular disdain for the president's legalistic hairsplitting when he mocked, in an oft-repeated phrase, that the message "shows conclusively that it is the duty of the President to execute the laws—unless somebody opposes him; and that no state has a right to go out of the Union—unless it wants to."[18] Try though Buchanan might to repress it, the controversy over the forts transformed a thorny abstraction into a concrete problem, and a public relations nightmare.

The trouble was not so much that the president was out of touch with Northern public opinion, though in crucial ways he was, as it was that he was more in touch than his fellow Northerners with the daunting complexity of the situation and the profound inadequacy of the Constitution to meet the crisis. If the corrective measures he proposed had little chance of mending the sectional rift, neither would anything anyone else suggested that winter.

✳ The reaction to Buchanan's message illustrates the profound interconnection between the public and its political leaders, a facet of antebellum political culture central to the North's response to the crisis. As the first official statement on secession, it provided a much-needed focal point for Northern response. A few voices—Trumbull's, Greeley's, Weed's—had risen above November's buzz of speculation and proposals and sparked widespread comment, but none was able to shape the substance of Northern public discourse the way the president's could. As soon as Buchanan's address and the reconvening of Congress gave them something concrete and official to respond to, Northerners abandoned the passive, wait-and-see attitude that had prevailed throughout November. The volume of correspondence addressed to the president and other national leaders increased dramatically. The letters, though usually polite, formal, and even deferential in tone, were very much intended to convey constituents' views; Northerners relied on their representatives to take political action, but they were not shy about inserting their opinions into the debate. In the coming weeks, their letters would exert a critical influence on the actions of Congress, to which attention now turned.

On the face of it, the odds were poor that the Thirty-sixth Congress would create even a temporary sectional truce. A product of the political turmoil of the 1850s, it was deeply divided by both party and section. Although Democrats controlled the Senate with thirty-eight of the sixty-six seats, all but ten of them (and every major committee chair) belonged to Southerners. The Douglas supporters who comprised the vast majority of Northern anti-Republicans were represented by only two senators, including Douglas himself. In the lower chamber, Republicans controlled the House, but with a plurality, not a majority. In the first session, this had led to a two-month battle over the speakership, at the end of which Republicans had been forced to lay aside Ohio moderate John Sherman for New Jersey conservative William Pennington.[19] Prospects for compromise in this second session were further hobbled by resentment over the bitter, sectional election that had just concluded and by the fact that this Congress was now a lame duck—the one that had just been elected was not due to take office for another year.

A final problem was that after four weeks of rudderless drift, neither party entered the session with a clear strategy for meeting disunion.

✳ Despite the deepening gloom brought on by political instability and financial panic, anti-Buchanan Democrats were optimistic: Stephen Douglas, the Little Giant, was ready to take charge of matters in Washington and set the ship aright. Just as heartening as this prospect of clear and active leadership was the opposition's disarray. If Buchanan had ever possessed an opportunity to rally support among Northern anti-Republicans by announcing a bold policy, it had clearly passed with his address. On the other side, the Republican coalition appeared to be unraveling. Douglas supporters looked with glee upon the growing split among their rivals, sure that they detected behind it a widespread conservative rejection of Republican ideas. The observation that "the Linkin men hear is sorry they voted for him, as they now see troubal a head" was frequently accompanied by a prediction that "were the Election to take place today . . . [Douglas] would carry 9/10 of the vote. The Masses are looking back and carefully taking a retrospect of the principles advocated by their leaders in this last Lincoln frizzle." These claims found confirmation in the results of early-December municipal elections in Massachusetts. There Unionists won or made great gains in towns that just a month earlier had given large majorities to the Republicans, evidence that a reaction among that party's voters was indeed occurring.[20]

That left Douglas to take a bold stand for compromise and Union. Throughout the opening days of Congress, supporters from all over the North and Upper South expressed confidence that he, and he alone, could save the Union in this time of need. Only his principle of popular sovereignty could rally the support of both Southern and Republican conservatives, resolve the crisis, and settle the slavery issue once and for all. Looking ahead, many suggested that such a triumph would be sure to win Douglas his rightful place in the White House four years hence.[21]

The object of such admiration arrived in Washington determined to do whatever was necessary to patch together a compromise, but he was considerably less hopeful about the immediate prospects. "I regret to say that our country is now in imminent danger," Douglas wrote privately. "I know not that the Union can be saved."[22] With the Democracy hopelessly divided, Douglas saw little chance of accomplishing anything constructive in the next three months—unless, as his supporters suggested, he could somehow unite with Southern and Republican conservatives behind a compromise. Such a development not only would save the Union (his overriding goal) but also would gut Republicanism and revitalize his own party.

On the first day of the session, Douglas began deliberating with Kentucky senator John J. Crittenden, conservative elder statesman and heir to legendary compromiser Henry Clay, to come up with a solution acceptable to Northern and Southern conservatives. At the same time, he worked to lay the groundwork for interparty cooperation by both publicly and privately denouncing party labels. "I am ready to make any reasonable sacrifice of party tenets to save the country," he announced. It was a wise move; as the crisis deepened a latent antiparty spirit inherited from the Founders would become increasingly apparent.[23]

The session did not begin well for Douglas's strategy, due largely to his own weakness in Congress. In the Senate, Republicans and radical Southerners delayed formation of a committee to consider compromise proposals, where Crittenden had planned to unveil his grand plan. The House did create such a committee, but Speaker Pennington excluded all Northern Democrats from membership, effectively cutting off Douglas from compromise negotiations there. Another factor was Douglas's outspoken antisecessionism. Trying to present himself as the voice of moderation and reason, as he had done during the election, he painted both disunionists and Republicans as radicals and warned that the nation's only alternatives were "conciliation and concession, or civil war." Attacking disunion might have been necessary to retain his Northern supporters, but most Southerners not only held to the constitutional right of secession but were already suspicious of Douglas for his opposition to federal slave codes and the Lecompton Constitution and especially for his coercionist "Norfolk doctrine." Moreover, some northwestern Democrats, including John McClernand of Illinois, Douglas's top lieutenant, went further than he in their rhetoric, not only speaking harshly against disunion but threatening war to prevent it.

Then, on the second day of the House committee's deliberations, thirty Southern congressmen issued a manifesto advising their states to secede.

With this the true depth of both Deep South secessionism and the Democratic schism was revealed; Douglas and Crittenden knew for sure that no support was forthcoming from that direction. Without cooperation from both Republican and Upper South conservatives, their cause was lost.[24]

✳ If Northern Democrats lacked a clear strategy, they at least had a clear leader. With Lincoln steadfastly maintaining his silence, Republicans in Congress were left to sort out an official party line for themselves. How difficult that task would be became apparent early on: in the first days of December, Washington press correspondents reported simultaneously that at an informal Republican caucus "the unanimous sentiment was in favor of compromise" and that "the consultations among the republicans result in the almost unanimous conclusion that they will offer no compromise."[25] Many congressmen agreed with Senator Trumbull, who wrote his wife that "the feeling among Republican members is uniform, so far as I have observed in condemnation of the newspaper articles which talk of new compromises & concessions, & of probable secession,"[26] but events soon revealed a much wider variety of opinion.

In the absence of guidance from Springfield, many assumed that Senator Seward would step into the breach. The New Yorker was, along with Stephen Douglas, one of the two most powerful individuals in Northern politics, and he was widely expected to be the controlling force in the new administration. Charming and perpetually cheerful, not a brilliant orator but peerless in backroom meetings and private dinners, he controlled the Republican organization in the Union's most populous and prosperous state, had for years been the party's premier spokesperson, and until Lincoln's last-minute upset in Chicago, had been the clear front-runner for the Republican presidential nomination.

Seward also had the great advantage of broad-based appeal and influence. Though he had long been an outspoken critic of slavery, in many ways his views were quite conservative. He genuinely hated slavery as both a moral wrong and an inefficient and unfair labor system, but unlike radicals such as Chase and Greeley he placed less faith in political action as the best means to end it than in the historical force of human progress. Since he believed, in the words of historian Phillip S. Paludan, that "it was impossible to bargain away freedom's ultimate victory," he was willing to compromise almost any point and felt no qualms about altering his rhetoric or even his policy to suit different situations. He also cultivated a remarkable range of personal and political connections, including members of all parties and factions. These qualities gained him a significant number of enemies as well, for many considered him an unprincipled opportunist. In his home state, *Evening Post* editor William Cullen Bryant and Seward's former ally Horace Greeley had led the radical faction that had helped to defeat him at the Chicago convention.[27]

Like all Republicans, during the campaign Seward had dismissed threats of secession. By mid-November, however, reports from his Southern contacts had convinced him that the disunion movement was much stronger than Republicans thought. He knew that suggesting the necessity of concessions would challenge party orthodoxy and probably reduce his influence both in Congress and with the new administration. Therefore, he and Thurlow Weed, his close friend and partner, decided that Weed would publish a compromise proposal as a sort of trial balloon, permitting Seward to judge party opinion before committing himself. When, as we have seen, Republicans reacted harshly to Weed's editorials, the partners quickly distanced Seward from them.[28] The deception was the first of many ruses the wily statesman would employ over the coming months. For now, it led Seward to arrive in Washington with two immediate goals: to play his own cards close to the vest while he worked out a plan, and in the meantime, to keep congressional Republicans from doing or saying anything to exacerbate Southern fears.

Confronted immediately over Weed's controversial editorials, Seward denied that he had had any part in them and assured his anxious colleagues that they "would know what I think and what I propose when I do myself."[29] Privately, he reported to Weed that "the Republican party to-day is as uncompromising as the Secessionists in South Carolina" but predicted grimly, "A month hence, each may come to think that moderation is wiser."[30] In an effort to keep the radicals from provoking Southern delegates until that happened, Seward set to work persuading every Republican he could that the party must maintain a "respectful and fraternal" silence.

He was largely successful: numerous observers noted that the Republicans "are quiet, say nothing, promise nothing, threaten nothing," and several explicitly linked this policy with Seward.[31] When New Hampshire radical John P. Hale delivered a fiery rebuttal to the boasts and taunts of Deep South fire-eaters, his colleagues repudiated his rashness (privately, of course), and a reasonably respectful and fraternal silence was preserved. In fact, not willing to be maneuvered into taking a stance, Republican senators went so far as to join Deep South radicals in delaying the appointment of a committee to consider resolutions to the crisis. That may not have been Seward's goal, but inaction was better than listening to party hardliners alienate the South by trading insults with secessionists.[32]

In the House, meanwhile, Republican representatives were already moving toward conciliation. On the second day of the session, House Republicans did what their Senate brethren refused, voting by more than three to two to create a special committee to consider compromise proposals; composed of one member from each state, it came to be called the Committee of Thirty-three.[33] As Seward had predicted, many were already discovering that the disunion movement appeared far more formidable up close than it had from the safe distance of their districts. As Illinois representative Elihu Washburne wrote to Lincoln, "The secession feeling has assumed proportions of which I had but a faint conception when I saw you at Springfield, and I think our friends generally in the west are not fully apprised of the imminent peril which now environs us." Not that the resourceful New Yorker had left that to chance: while he was encouraging a fraternal silence among his compatriots, he was also urging Southern unionists to convince the Republicans of the danger of disunion in their states. They needed little prompting: momentum for secession was strong even in the Upper South, and to combat it unionists needed hard evidence that the Republicans were not as malevolent as disunionists were painting them.[34]

Republican support for the House committee puzzled and angered hard-liners, who bitterly resented Southern threats and feared that even discussing concessions would only encourage disunion.[35] Yet several Republicans went even further and presented compromise proposals for the committee's consideration. The most influential of these was offered by John Sherman, the prominent Ohio moderate who had been the party's first choice for Speaker the previous winter: in order to eliminate the issue of slavery in the territories from national politics, he said, Congress should simply divide all existing territories and admit them as states, with the status of slavery to be determined in their constitutions.[36]

More was to come. On just the second day of the House committee's deliberations—Thursday, December 13—Indiana Republican William McKee Dunn submitted a resolution stating boldly that regardless of whether Southern "discontents" had any legitimacy, "any reasonable, proper, and constitutional remedies . . . necessary to preserve the peace of the country and the perpetuation of the Union, should be promptly and cheerfully granted." This was strong language, but with South Carolina's secession convention just four days away, elections for convention delegates in several other Deep South states looming, and Upper South unionists pleading for some kind of goodwill gesture to halt disunion in their states, Republicans on the committee felt tremendous pressure not to appear hostile to compromise. Fully half of them supported the resolution, and it passed easily.[37]

It began to appear that Douglas and Crittenden's hope for Republican compromise support—and Douglas's less high-minded dreams of a Republican schism—would not be disappointed.

✳ Anxious Northerners followed the developments in Washington closely in letters, in both local papers and the widely distributed New York press, and surprisingly often in the pages of the *Congressional Globe*. The compromise effort in Congress was nourished by a groundswell of conciliatory public opinion. As in the capital, anti-Republicans led the charge. From the southernmost area of the Northwest, a backwoods region of Southern transplants and a longtime bastion of Democracy, came particularly strong demands for compromise and echoes of the president's condemnation of Northern radicalism. But it was in the other traditional stronghold of the Democracy, the eastern cities, that the procompromise movement first transcended the level of correspondence and broke into action. There, both elements of an awkward but powerful alliance between elite merchants and poor immigrant workers mobilized against a crisis that they, too, saw as the product of moralistic Republican extremism. In Boston, a largely Irish mob took control of an abolitionist meeting commemorating the execution of John Brown, damning Brown and threatening to hang the city's African Americans and suppress its abolitionists if the crisis continued. In the melee that followed, the famous abolitionist orator Frederick Douglass himself was shouted down and hauled off the stage. In Philadelphia, the Republican mayor moved an abolitionist speaker twenty miles out of town for fear of similar mob violence, and the city council chose instead to hold a mass "Union meeting" that called for Northern concessions.[38]

The largest and most influential demonstration took place on the evening of Saturday, December 15, when more than 2,000 New York City merchants gathered at business offices on Pine Street. There they endorsed an appeal to the South, composed by a committee of twenty-four leading men, that captured many of the concerns of anti-Republicans across the North. The address begged Southerners for time, for a suspension of disunion until the budding conservative reaction in the North had a chance to blossom. It appealed, as did so many pleas for Union in those troubled days, to "the memory of that fraternal friendship which bound our forefathers together through the perils of the Revolution" and which had since produced a country unrivaled in its wealth and power. And it reminded Southerners of the unswerving loyalty Northern conservatives had displayed over the years, arguing that, since "we have asserted your rights as earnestly as though they had been our own[,] you cannot refuse, therefore, to listen to us."[39] What the assembly, and Northern anti-Republicans in general, most wanted Southerners to hear was exactly what Stephen Douglas (and Winfield Scott, for that matter) had assured them earlier: that there was no real danger. Not only had the election added several seats to anti-Republican strength in Congress, but the Republican Party could not long survive in power; already its leadership was splintering over a Southern policy. Moreover, a great many conservatives had voted Republican for reasons entirely unrelated to slavery; both the recent elections in Massachusetts and the numerous campaigns to repeal personal liberty laws proved that they and other Northerners rejected radical Republicanism.[40]

Beneath these expressions of conciliation lay a reluctant sense of resignation. If anti-Republican assurances should prove false, the appeal concluded, if Southern rights were violated and constitutional equality among states destroyed, then, as a last resort, separation would be in order. But if it should come to that, the Pine Street demonstrators implored, at least let the separation be peaceful, that the republic might be saved "the horrors of civil war and the degradation of financial discredit."[41]

Typical of early demonstrations, those in Boston, Philadelphia, and New York were conservative affairs organized by anti-Republicans and dedicated to compromise. That is not surprising, as anticompromise Republicans still felt that their best strategy was to remain silent and wait for the inevitable Southern unionist reaction. But that the early Union meetings also took place in large cities and were organized by workers, businessmen, or political interests associated with them points to another, deeper factor: the severe and steadily worsening financial panic that Lincoln's election had triggered. By December every aspect of the economy had been affected. For six weeks all of the major stock exchanges had spiraled steadily downward, injuring investors, companies, and banks alike. New York and Boston banks, mindful of the disastrous consequences when they had suspended specie payments during the recent panic of

1857, struggled to find creative ways to continue payments, but banks elsewhere gave up and suspended. Merchants throughout the North suffered as the Southern trade stagnated.

New York, where that trade was estimated at $200 million a year, was hit hardest. There, local newspapers were filled with the advertisements of desperate retailers trying to stay afloat by unloading their stock at fire-sale prices. By year's end over 850 of them would fail. Manufacturers responded to the resulting decline in orders by slashing production, and by the end of November an estimated 15,000 city workers had been laid off. In Boston, the Irish workers who hijacked the abolitionist meeting were facing similar circumstances.[42]

The most frustrating feature of the recession was its artificiality. The fall harvest had been good and the economy was strong; were it not for the political crisis brought on by secession, this would have been, by all accounts, a banner year. Shortsighted, selfish politicians were to blame, many felt. Yet the panic's political origin was also its most hopeful feature: an artificial crisis could be corrected. In the weeks after the election, businessmen were prominent among those who called for calmness and reason. Many wrote anxious letters to Southerners and Republicans alike, pleading with them to find some reasonable adjustment of their differences. By mid-December, private letters having availed nothing, the business community was ripe for communal action. The organizers of the Pine Street meeting and other rallies had tapped into a deep and powerful current.[43]

✳ What anti-Republican letter-writers, demonstrators, and editors demanded, naturally, were Republican concessions. More surprising was the growing number of Republican constituents and editors who also supported compromise. In New York, the pro-Seward *Courier and Enquirer* came out in favor of compromise soon after Weed's *Albany Evening Journal* did, while the *Times* continued to press for concessions. Major party papers in Indianapolis, Detroit, Cincinnati, Pittsburgh, and Springfield, Massachusetts, followed suit.[44] Political correspondents from all parties reported procompromise sentiment rising among conservative Republicans, the latecomers whom the Republicans had exerted so much effort to attract between 1856 and 1860. Having been wooed by such additions to the platform as a protective tariff and homestead legislation, they comprised the segment of the party least committed to the core Republican doctrine of opposition to slavery's expansion, so it made sense that they would be the first to question it when faced with the genuine possibility of disunion.[45]

Like that of their rivals, the Republican movement for compromise was led by urban businessmen. However, contrary to the claims of party hardliners that businessmen were mercenaries whose politics were dictated by their pocketbooks, the views of most Republican businessmen toward the crisis placed them firmly within the mainstream of party conservatism. As New York dry-goods merchant and prominent radical George Opdyke reported, "In my intercourse with the merchants of this city, which is quite general, I have yet to meet with the first republican, in any branch of business, who favors a *compromise of principle*."[46] As we shall see, a dispute over just what constituted a compromise of principle lay at the heart of the growing split between conciliationist and stalwart Republicans.[47]

There is a danger of overgeneralizing. That there were urban businessmen who supported the Republicans indicates a range of outlooks within that group, and Opdyke's own radical views demonstrate how far that range could extend. Moreover, even individual attitudes could fluctuate wildly. That Republican businessmen were particularly inconsistent in their stance should not surprise us; maintaining political principles in the face of personal ruin could be agonizing.

The profound ambivalence that many felt can be seen in the letters of New York importer George D. Morgan, cousin and business partner of Governor Edwin D. Morgan. Like many Republican merchants—like many Republicans in general—Morgan had predicted in October that the economy would improve once the election was over, condemning the fearmongering of the Southern traders as "sheer selfishness on the part of most and hypocrisy on the part of some." By the end of November, however, he was calling for compromise, praising Weed's "very manly sensible and just proposal" and urging his cousin to support any course that would undercut South Carolina's legitimacy and strengthen border-state unionism. Just a week later, however, Morgan noted that it appeared that force would be necessary to prevent disunion. By mid-December, he had backed away from coercion and was leaning toward Greeley's position on the necessity of peaceable secession: North and South hated each other and were united only by "commercial purposes and material interest," he observed, and "no Union was ever formed or can be maintained but by concession and compromise." Nevertheless, a few weeks later Morgan was still exhibiting the desire to maintain both peace and political principle that marked most Republicans: "I fear that if we do not conciliate the Border Slave States now in agreeing to some plan of compromise it will be harder to do it a while hence, but we must all stand firm."[48]

Not all Republican businessmen passed through the same progression of attitudes, but Morgan's letters illustrate the emotional vacillation to which they were prone. They also remind us of how bewildering and volatile the crisis seemed at the time—and of the inherent weakness of our sources in tracing Northerners' responses; the expression of any individual's ideas presents not a definitive, undeviating view but a mere snapshot of a particular moment.

We can safely say, though, that on the whole, Republican urban businessmen tended to maintain conservative views, and what was more, many took advantage of financial, social, and political connections to try to further compromise. In New York, for example, leading merchants such as Moses Grinnell, Robert B. Minturn, and A. T. Stewart appear to have influenced Weed and Seward's proposal to extend the 36°30' Missouri Compromise line, and many others added their support in the weeks that followed.[49] A number of Republican businessmen were even willing to cooperate with their political enemies in the cause of compromise. In Boston, the conservative social and business elite, several Republicans among them, assembled in mid-December to publish the so-called Shaw memorial, a widely hailed call for the repeal of Massachusetts's personal liberty law.[50] At the same time in New York, a similarly bipartisan group, including about thirty leading Republicans, agreed that "the first steps would have to be taken by the North." Over the next two weeks they composed two memorials to Congress, one aimed at Republicans and the other at anti-Republicans. The Republican petition urged that all states be treated with respect and equality and suggested a compromise involving the passage of a fair and effective fugitive slave law, the "readjustment" of personal liberty laws, and a territorial resolution based on Sherman's proposal to admit all the territories as states.[51]

The development of a procompromise movement outside of Washington in mid-December marked the beginning of large-scale public involvement in the crisis, but it was only the first stage. Although highly publicized in the anti-Republican press, mass meetings would be relatively few before the new year. Not until mid-January would pro- and anticompromise "Union meetings," petition drives, and other means of popular political participation explode across the North. Nevertheless, those initial steps in the middle weeks of December represented an important turning point in the Northern response to secession, another step up in the public's involvement in the decision-making process.

✳ In Washington, procompromise sentiment among Republicans had advanced so far that it seemed to some members of the House Committee of Thirty-three that the only impediment to compromise was Lincoln's continuing silence. "Should he lead off on some reasonable and practical plan," New York Republican E. G. Spaulding fretted, "it would have great weight and decide the course of many who are now passive and in doubt as to what should be done."[52] Unknown to Spaulding, Lincoln had already involved himself in the congressional debate over compromise, but not in the way that the conciliatory congressman envisioned. Concerned over reports of a breakdown in party orthodoxy, the president-elect was working behind the scenes to prop up listing Republican devotion and nip disloyalty in the bud. Beginning on December 10, he wrote a series of confidential letters, first to Republican members of the Illinois congressional delegation and then to various state party leaders, all with the same theme: "Let there be no compromise on the question of *extending* slavery. If there be, all our labor is lost, and, ere long, must be done again." Territorial concessions, whether they be popular sovereignty or an extension of the 36°30′ Missouri line, were "all the same. Let either be done, & immediately . . . extending slavery recommences. On that point hold firm, as with a chain of steel."[53]

Lincoln's disapproval of the compromise movement in Congress was typical of Republicans outside of Washington. By the middle of December, the muddle of views that Republicans had expressed in the wake of the election was beginning to settle into two broad categories: support for and opposition to compromise. When the congressional session opened, the moderate Republican majority had generally agreed that the secession movement did not reflect the will of the Southern masses, that it was a plot by a few radical demagogues. Given time, they thought, an inevitable conservative reaction would swing the region back into line. Now the moderates disagreed over whether the unionist backlash could occur without Republican assistance. Some, like Seward and John Sherman, joined conservatives in the belief that Republican intransigence was crippling the Southern unionist effort; others, including Lincoln and Trumbull, agreed with the radicals that concessions would encourage secessionism and destroy the Republican Party.

As soon as the congressional session commenced, rank-and-file Republicans inundated their representatives with letters expressing their opinion of what should be done. Their tone ranged from concerned to outraged, but the message was consistent: the party must not abandon its principles. The difficulty, especially for the politician trying to discern the will of his constituents, was that upholding party principle was interpreted in an astonishing variety of ways. Conservatives agreed with Thurlow Weed that Lincoln's election itself signaled the demise of the Slave Power. To be anything but generous would play into the hands of the disunionists, who were gaining Southern support due to Republican inflexibility. From their perspective, a conciliatory policy would "place the disunionists on the defensive at every point" and would "disarm S. Carolina & cut her off from the sympathy & countenance of the other Southern States." They insisted that compromising even the territorial question would be "no concession, no yielding, no lowering of our standard, no giving up of principle."[54]

The fact was that few Republican leaders, even among the radicals, objected to granting any concessions whatever. Lincoln himself informed William Kellogg, Illinois's representative on the Committee of Thirty-three, "You know I think the fugitive slave clause of the constitution ought to be enforced—to put it in the mildest form, ought not to be resisted."[55] Far from being a violation of the party's Chicago platform, this was in keeping with the party's long-stated commitment to upholding all aspects of the Constitution. Connecticut radical Gideon Welles explained, "I think the [fugitive slave] law itself obnoxious in many particulars and susceptible of great and beneficent improvements. But a law-abiding citizen cannot do otherwise than submit to it, however repulsive may be its details, and a public officer must obey and faithfully execute it." Salmon Chase was even willing to go so far as to join the *Times* in granting compensation for fugitives. And most hard-line politicians were also willing to grant the South a cabinet seat, provided the appointee was a sound unionist.[56]

But as a Cincinnati writer observed to Lincoln, "The *politicians* are one and the *people* are another entirely different class."[57] From the party's geographical core—a belt running from the rural and small-town East across the upper Northwest—the mass of rank-and-file Republicans declared themselves firmly opposed to any concession at all. Their reasoning varied. Like Lincoln, many felt what one writer expressed as the conviction that "if we yield one [point], we are conquered and our hard won victory is a cheat—a delusion." Numerous others wrote in the same vein as the correspondent who was determined that "them of the South see and understand, that *blustering* and *threatening* wont *win* this time."[58] A great many

Republicans feared for their party's future, like the New Hampshire party leader who warned that "were the Republican leaders, in Congress or out, to favor such a compromise as Weed suggests, we would be deader than ever the Whig party was."[59] That was not just narrow-minded partisanship (though partly so, of course). Their concern was unfailingly tied to apprehension for the Union itself. For Republicans, their party principles and the continued existence of American self-government were intimately linked: they believed, as one constituent wrote, that "the perpetuity of free institutions depend upon the firmness of the Republican party & its representatives now assembled at Washington."[60]

The argument expressed most frequently was that concessions in the face of Southern threats would reveal weakness and submission. Countless correspondents urged their leaders not to be "weak-kneed" or "weak in the back," not to degrade the North. Treating the South with forbearance was one thing, but agreeing to dishonorable concessions was something else. "I cannot conceive of a more humiliating position than the great Republican party after a most signal triumph cowering before the insane threats and ravings of a few negro owners, and cotton growers," noted one writer. Insisted another, "The bravado and insolence of the South has been borne with long enough. It is time now that *we stand upon our rights*."[61]

A surprising number of writers did not bother to explain why they opposed compromise at all; for many, it was enough merely to declare, as an Ohio man did, "There is only one feeling in this section of the country amongst your constituents . . . stand to the Chicago Platform, don't give away not for a thousand part of an inch, no compromise, stand to the Union and the Constitution and the people is with you."[62] If the South was bent on pushing the issue, they were determined to ride out the storm. Like Lincoln, who wrote sternly, "The tug has to come & better now than later," and Richard Yates, who had avowed at the Springfield Jubilee, "It is time the question was tested," a great many Republicans expressed the belief that once they had overcome this crisis, disunionism would no longer be a threat. An Illinois writer summarized the prevailing sentiment in the party when he wrote, "I am satisfied we will have to face the music of Secession sooner or later, & may we not just as well face it now as at any other time."[63] If a growing number of Republicans in Washington were beginning to move toward compromise, most party members outside of the capital were determined to stand their ground.

In Washington, the combination of Lincoln's behind-the-scenes intervention and the rank-and-file backlash against conciliation had a swift effect, as hard-liners used it as a base from which to mount an aggressive campaign against compromise. Armed with written evidence of the president-elect's anticompromise views, the stalwarts worked to stabilize the party line.[64] By December 18, Congressman Washburne was reporting to Lincoln that although compromise was still a danger, "I think there is now a firmer feeling among our Republicans here." Republican members on the Committee of Thirty-three in particular felt the pressure. Massachusetts representative Charles Francis Adams noted of his colleagues, "Several who had recorded their votes in favor of Mr. Dunn's resolution, including the author of it himself, had received so many and such sharp remonstrances from their constituents as very materially to reinforce their energies and perseverance. They were now among the stiffest and most uncompromising." A short time later he added, "The declarations coming almost openly from Mr. Lincoln have had the effect of perfectly consolidating the republicans." Democrats observed the phenomenon as well: "Lincoln's belicose demonstrations has brought the republicans here up to the war point," John McClernand observed with disgust.[65]

One important consequence of House Republicans' open movement for conciliation was that it freed stalwarts from Seward's policy of fraternal silence, and the hard-line reaction took public form as well. On the seventeenth, Ohio radical Ben Wade vented his ire on the Senate floor, and in so doing expressed in clear and vigorous terms the stalwarts' case against concessions. To begin with, he said, the Democrats could not be trusted; after their cavalier repeal of the venerable Missouri Compromise six years earlier, Wade scoffed, "I should hardly think any two of the Democratic party would look each other in the face and say 'compromise' without a smile." What was more, the Republicans had nothing to concede, as the only complaint against them was that they had won an election. Articulating the powerful dual appeal to honor and self-government that was swiftly becoming central to the anticonciliation argument, he railed, "Sir, it would be humiliating and dishonorable to us if we were to listen to a compromise by which he who has the verdict of the people in his pocket, should make his way to the presidential chair. When it comes to that, you have no Government; anarchy intervenes."

Secession, Wade continued, was utterly without justification; the real issue was simply the South's unwillingness to relinquish the power they had held for so long: "You intend either to rule or ruin this Government. That is what your complaint comes to; nothing else." He concluded by vowing that the federal government would defend itself; he did not desire to make war upon a state, but he would insist on enforcing federal law and defending federal authority. If war resulted, it would be on the head of the disunionists.[66] That view of force, not as coercion, but as enforcing the law, held great appeal for rank-and-file Republicans, who saw secession as a gross violation of the law and order on which self-government rested. Wade's speech captured the basis of stalwart Republicanism as well as any single source; these points would form the core of hard-liners' arguments for the next four months.

The response of congressional Republicans revealed the effectiveness of the hard-line campaign: unlike Hale's speech, which had been met with censure, Wade's was lauded. The veneer of unity that Republicans had tried to maintain when the session began just two weeks earlier was gone. The party was clearly headed toward confrontation.[67]

✳ For the first time since the election, the president's message and the early congressional deliberations gave a semblance of form to the confusion generated by secession. Given something to respond to, Northerners did so eagerly, writing thousands of letters to their representatives and organizing the first public demonstrations. Already their participation had an impact on the process of decision-making as the outrage of Republican constituents was helping to push key moderate congressmen away from a movement toward compromise.

These early weeks of the session revealed three other trends that would significantly influence the government's course that winter. First, the disjunction between the crisis in Washington and that perceived by Northerners back home was tremendous, especially for Republicans. The situation appeared much different on the ground, and later comers to the capital, including the president-elect himself, would also be surprised at the moderating effect that exposure to Southern unionists tended to have. It is not surprising that Republicans—including, we shall see, some stalwarts—found themselves torn between following the demands of their constituents and offering what suddenly seemed to be necessary, even critical concessions. Second, the response of congressional Republicans to Lincoln's subtle intervention was the first indication of the tremendous power at his disposal. Even national leaders reacted to leadership, and the coming months would reveal that if he was willing to hold onto and use his authority, Lincoln held the Northern response to secession in his hands. Finally, the tug of war within the Republican Party would only grow fiercer as debate over compromise continued. As the hard-liners persisted in holding firm, conciliationists would face a choice: back away from the response they believed the crisis demanded, or risk tearing the party apart on the eve of triumph.

Still to be seen was the impact that these developments would have as South Carolina's secession convention convened, economic conditions worsened, and the danger of a conflict at the Southern forts loomed ever closer. The crisis was still young, and circumstances were shifting almost day by day.

Chapter 4 ✳ **The Issues of the Late Campaign Are Obsolete** ✳ Late December

Although arguments in Washington and the partisan press continued to revolve around the traditional points of contention between North and South—slavery in the territories and fugitive slaves—below the surface a fundamental shift was taking place in the nature of the debate. Already the specter of impending disunion had transformed the question by framing the old issues as compromise proposals; now it was shifting the primary concern from the place of slavery in the Union to the survival of the Union itself. Lyman Trumbull spoke for Republicans across the North when he observed, "The question is no longer about African slavery, but whether we have a government capable of maintaining itself." The awesome scale of that query put incredible pressure on political leaders and, as procompromise sentiment grew among conservative and moderate Republicans, increasingly blurred party lines.[1]

So far the entire discussion had been theoretical. Nothing definite having yet occurred, Northerners were still free to argue abstractly about whether the secessionists were sincere or merely bluffing; whether, if they were sincere, any states would actually go, and how many; and whether, if any states did go, they would come back, and how long it would take. Now South Carolina's convention was at hand, and a growing host of Northerners was realizing, as President Buchanan had weeks earlier, that federal property in the South—particularly the coastal forts—constituted an all-too-tangible point of conflict between union and disunion. With a collision there, a worrisome future possibility could become a fearsome present reality. The president faced mounting demands for some kind of action.

✳ Taking action on the Charleston forts was precisely what Buchanan had decided he could not afford to do—not yet, at least. On December 8 and 10, still waiting for General Scott to arrive from New York, Buchanan met with South Carolina's congressional delegates. They assured him that the forts would be perfectly safe until official representatives from South Carolina arrived to negotiate a transfer of ownership—provided that Anderson's garrison at Fort Moultrie was neither reinforced nor shifted to Fort Sumter. The president reminded them that although he wanted peace as much as they did, he was bound by oath to obey the laws; moreover, he could make no formal pledge of inaction, as the disposition of federal property was entirely up to Congress. Nevertheless, the Southerners left convinced that Buchanan had unofficially consented to their conditions. They reported later that as the second meeting was breaking up, he told them, "This is a matter of honor among gentlemen. . . . We understand each other."[2]

Whether he had pledged his honor or not, Buchanan had indeed concluded that a maintenance of the status quo was now the best policy. With congressional negotiations just getting under way, he was convinced that any attempt to strengthen the forts—especially with the scant number of troops at his disposal—could do nothing but trigger hostilities and undermine the peace process. It is also likely that his strategy was influenced by the December 8 resignation of Secretary of the Treasury Howell Cobb. Although Cobb was an open secessionist, his continued presence in the cabinet allowed Buchanan to persuade himself that Georgia would not secede and South Carolina would be isolated in disunion. Cobb's resignation undercut his confidence that he was dealing with South Carolina from a position of strength. As the crisis continued to evolve, the president felt what little control he had slipping away.[3]

Even as Buchanan's determination to maintain his own masterly inactivity hardened, pressure to take action on the forts came from inside the government. Shortly after Cobb left the cabinet, Secretary of State Cass also resigned, explaining that the administration's narrow interpretation of federal power and failure to properly garrison the forts damaged national authority.[4] Convinced that he must maintain a balanced policy, neither yielding to disunion nor risking the fragile peace, Buchanan used his cabinet replacements to gratify both sides in the conflict, making Attorney General Jeremiah Black, a strong unionist, the new secretary of state and the pro-Southern Philip Thomas of Maryland the new secretary of the treasury. To fill Black's place he promoted Assistant Attorney General Edwin Stanton, another ardent unionist.

Cass's departure called the attention of the administration's many enemies to the forts, triggering a hail of public condemnation, but the criticism that followed his resignation was nothing compared to what was coming. Over the next three weeks, public censure of Buchanan would reach a crescendo, and a major reason for that arrived in the capital on Wednesday, the twelfth. Secretary of War Floyd had suggested bringing in Winfield Scott primarily to delay action on the forts, but also because, given the inconsistency of the general's "Views," he felt confident he could persuade the old soldier of the folly of sending reinforcements.[5] In the former objective he was wildly successful; over the intervening ten days Buchanan had indefinitely postponed his decision to increase the Charleston garrison. In the latter, however, he failed utterly. Weeks of frustrated, indignant marginalization since the election had only strengthened Scott's judgment that the public property must be defended and that inaction would have disastrous consequences.[6] Once in Washington, the general urged upon Floyd and Buchanan the necessity of reinforcing all of the Southern forts as soon as possible. Angered at what he felt were Cass's and Scott's blatant attempts to sabotage his administration, Buchanan dismissed the advice out of hand. Undeterred, Scott followed up his interview with a note comparing Buchanan's policy unfavorably with that of Andrew Jackson during the nullification crisis. Buchanan was unimpressed.[7]

Though he did not sway the president, Scott's arrival in Washington had a pronounced effect on the Northern public. Between Cass's resignation, the general's well-publicized dispute with the administration, and the December 17 convening of South Carolina's secession convention, Northern attention was irresistibly drawn to the Charleston forts. For a great many Northerners—mainly Republicans but also a growing number of Douglas Democrats—Winfield Scott became a rallying point for antisecession sentiment, his seemingly bold and manly stance contrasting sharply with Buchanan's weak vacillation. The dichotomy became even more pronounced when, a few days after South Carolina's formal secession, the telegraph wires carried rumors throughout the Northern press that the president was preparing to order the forts' evacuation. Outraged cries of treason erupted. "Our disgraceful executive has been playing into the hands of traitors," fumed New York lawyer George T. Strong, a Republican. A Douglas supporter from Massachusetts offered the creative suggestion that "the best thing that could *now* be done for the Country would be to Send down to Washington a delegation of Old Women, armed with Six pieces of . . . diaper to *clout* Mr Buchannan, double and triplicate and to pin them on his posteriors with a wooden skure instead of a diaper pin for he has evidently got the *bowel complaint*." Northerners were losing patience with the president's delicate handling of secession.[8]

✳ Buchanan was not the only one feeling the strain of leadership. "The appearance of Mr. Lincoln has somewhat changed to the worse within the last week," observed a reporter on Friday, the fourteenth. "He does not complain of any direct ailment, but that he looks more pale and careworn than heretofore is evident to the daily observer."[9] As might be expected—Lincoln more than had his hands full juggling his back-channel campaign against Republican backsliding, the painstaking process of cabinet selection, and a never-ending parade of office-seekers and well-wishers who jammed his office every day.

In the midst of all this, more disturbing reports arrived from the capital. Despite having argued his position to the top of his chain of command, General Scott was not yet ready to admit defeat. Following his abortive interview with Buchanan, he had several meetings with prominent Republicans for the twofold purpose of sounding out Lincoln's intentions toward the forts and conveying to the president-elect his own conviction that they must be reinforced. Scott showed no compunction about criticizing the current administration's disregard of his counsel. "He talked to me very freely in regard to the present state of affairs, and his differences between himself and the President and the Secretary of War," Congressman Washburne informed Lincoln. "His recommendations to that end were made in October and had they been regarded he thinks a vast deal would have been accomplished towards averting the impending trouble." Through a different intermediary the general also sent Lincoln a copy of his note to Buchanan about Jackson and the nullification crisis.[10]

Lincoln asked his correspondents to assure General Scott of his resolve; they should respond, he said, that "I shall be obliged to him to be as well prepared as he can to either *hold*, or *retake*, the forts, as the case may require, at, and after, the inaugeration."[11] The very next morning, the issue of the forts was thrust on Lincoln more forcefully when he arrived in his office to a telegraph report that Buchanan had ordered Anderson to surrender if attacked. "If that is true," Lincoln snapped indignantly, "they ought to hang him." Over the following days he wrote several party leaders of his intention to either defend or, if necessary, recapture the forts.[12]

Yet it was not secession but factional maneuvering that occupied most of Lincoln's time and energy. The central issue remained the cabinet. Republican leaders bandied about dozens of names in conversation and in correspondence, but at the center of almost everyone's attention was William H. Seward. It may have been assumed that Seward would seek to control Lincoln's administration, but that did not mean that his radical rivals would acquiesce—at stake was nothing less than control of the party. Wary of alienating Lincoln with a purely negative campaign, the anti-

Seward movement quickly settled on one of its own as a substitute candidate to head the powerful state department: Lincoln's other major rival for the party's nomination, longtime radical leader and former Democrat Salmon Chase. The various radical groups began to campaign. Key members of the powerful Bryant-Greeley faction in New York accosted Trumbull, who not only was widely considered Lincoln's closest adviser but also was a former Democrat; they also made plans for a pilgrimage to Springfield. Abolitionist elder statesmen Joshua Giddings of Ohio and central committee secretary George G. Fogg of New Hampshire, among others, met with Lincoln to urge Chase. Closer to home, the Judd faction took up the cause in Illinois. A stream of correspondents from across the North wrote the president-elect for the same purpose.[13]

Despite the strength of this effort against Seward and for Chase, the campaign probably did little more than confirm Lincoln's long conviction that party unity required both in the cabinet. It was increasingly obvious to him that these two, more than anyone else, not only represented the warring factions but commanded their loyalty.[14]

His first move was to secure Seward—as the rumor mill had reported, Lincoln did indeed intend to offer his chief rival the principal place in his cabinet. He moved cautiously. Conscious that both his party's unity and his own leadership were tenuous, Lincoln had no intention of having his first cabinet offer thrown back in his face, and rumors abounded that Seward was unwilling to subordinate himself to Lincoln. As a result, the president-elect's course toward the first major decision of his administration was tentative and halting, even amateurish. At a late-November conference in Chicago, he had directed vice president elect Hannibal Hamlin, a Maine senator, to find out whether Seward would accept an offer. Hamlin, a former Democrat who did not favor Seward's appointment, proceeded to the Senate, sounded out Seward's New York colleague Preston King with no success, and wrote Lincoln for permission to approach Seward directly. "*My* impression is he will not desire a place in your Cabinet," he added, "but he may."[15]

Since Lincoln knew that Hamlin's broaching the subject with Seward directly would be equivalent to making the offer, he saw no choice but to go ahead. On December 8, he addressed two letters to Seward: one a formal offer of the State Department and the other a personal assurance that, contrary to rumor, the proposition was not an empty courtesy but a genuine desire for Seward's services. But at the last moment he balked, probably worried by Hamlin's negative prediction. Rather than send the missives directly, Lincoln enclosed them with a note to Hamlin in which, remarkably, he left to him and Trumbull the ultimate decision of whether to present them to Seward. The two old Democrats delayed until the thirteenth, when, finding no compelling reason to withhold the offer, Hamlin finally delivered it. Pleading a desire to consult with friends (that is, Weed) about the offer, Seward immediately left Washington for New York.[16]

While he waited for Seward's reply, Lincoln moved ahead with the selection process. According to an oft-repeated policy of "justice for all," he should have focused next on choosing a radical former Democrat, most likely Chase. Despite his protestations, though, Lincoln had more on his mind than fairness. For one thing he was anxious about the growing rift in the party and feared that announcing the selection of a radical would alienate conservatives and moderates. With that in mind he made inquiries to determine just how radical Chase and Gideon Welles of Connecticut were, but he contacted neither directly.[17]

A second, closely related concern was the effect that his cabinet selections would have in the South. Holding the party together and maintaining a firm commitment to party principles were vital to achieving a complete and permanent victory over the Slave Power. But with South Carolina's convention looming, the financial panic worsening, and a potentially disastrous conciliation movement gathering steam among congressional Republicans, he also realized that firmness alone was not enough. He also had to take care of the other aspect of the party's dual policy: fairness and generosity. Projecting an image of narrow-minded intransigence would alienate conservatives of both sections and could, as Southern unionists warned, drive more Southern states into secession. In mid-December, moving cautiously as always, Lincoln sent out carefully phrased replies to the anxious letters of two prominent Southern unionists, Representative John A. Gilmer of North Carolina and former representative Alexander Stephens of Georgia. In both he emphasized his moderate attitude toward slavery and the South, insisting that there was no substantive difference between their views and his.[18]

Lincoln also examined the names of dozens of Southern unionists that correspondents and editors had been recommending for inclusion in the cabinet. He thought including one or more loyal Southerners a good idea, but it raised difficult questions regarding his struggle to balance resolve and magnanimity. Frustrated at the flood of suggestions and the difficulty of determining the fine line between conciliation and appeasement, he had a short, unsigned notice placed in Springfield's Republican newspaper. Was it known, the note inquired, "that any [Southern] gentleman of character, would accept a place in the cabinet," and if so, "on what terms? Does he surrender to Mr. Lincoln, or Mr. Lincoln to him, on the political differences between them? Or do they enter upon the administration in open opposition to each other?"[19]

Despite his public misgivings, Lincoln already had two Southerners in mind. He sent an emissary to sound out former treasury secretary James Guthrie, a Kentucky unionist, but Guthrie demurred.[20] His next effort yielded more success. Just a few days after the notice questioning the feasibility of a Southern cabinet member appeared in the paper, Lincoln offered a post—attorney-general or, if Seward proved unavailable, secretary of state—to conservative former Whig Edward Bates of Missouri, another popular rival for the presidential nomination and the closest thing to a universally acclaimed cabinet contender there was. Bates accepted, and on his urging, the selection was made public a few days later.[21] Due largely to his own inflexibility on territorial compromise, Lincoln's cabinet was taking on a decidedly conservative, old-Whig tone.

For Lincoln, the various elements of the crisis were coming together. He was willing to placate Southern concerns with gestures toward conciliation: the repeal of unconstitutional personal liberty laws, private letters to prominent unionists, even the appointment of Southern cabinet members —but beyond that he was unwilling to go and determined that his party would not go. There would be no compromise on slavery's expansion into the federal territories and no backing down on the protection of federal property.

✳ Although Seward had expected Lincoln to tender him the State Department eventually, the offer put him into a difficult position. He could not reject the post and let the opportunity to shape the new administration pass, but to accept it would risk having his hands tied. At that point Lincoln's congressional maneuverings had not yet been disclosed, and the senator desperately needed to know his views on secession. "I wish indeed that a conference with you . . . were possible," he wrote Lincoln as he left Washington.[22] Two days later he arrived in Albany to discover that his wish, or the next best thing to it, had been granted: Illinois conservatives David Davis and Leonard Swett had sent word to Weed that Lincoln wished to discuss the cabinet with him. The New Yorkers debated the best means to lure Lincoln out without tipping Seward's hand and once more turned to the trial-balloon tactic. Weed published his most conciliatory editorial yet, then set out for Springfield.[23]

By the time he returned, the grizzled editor had discovered that for all his shrewdness and guile, in the president-elect he had more than met his match. According to Weed's later account, his last-minute editorial worked, nicely raising the topic of secession, which Lincoln had seemed unwilling at first to discuss. Weed explained his thoughts on the crisis: with a Republican in control of the executive branch, he argued, slavery was effectively barred from the territories. Thus, to grant concessions now would assuage the South without actually surrendering principle. At the same time it would draw attention away from the morass of compromise and rally a united North behind the issue of Union: if the Republicans showed themselves willing to concede on such an apparently vital question, reasonable Northerners could not but condemn continued Southern obstinacy.[24]

It appeared to Weed that Lincoln was impressed with the idea. The meeting seemed to go well in a number of ways, in fact. Although Lincoln resisted the editor's attempt to stack the cabinet with conservative former Whigs, Weed did elicit from him an agreement that at least two Southerners should be appointed. By the time he left, he even had a letter from Lincoln to Congressman John Gilmer, sounding out the North Carolinian's views on a cabinet position. This was a double triumph, since Lincoln implied that should Gilmer be offered and accept an appointment, he would take the place currently earmarked for Montgomery Blair, a radical former Democrat from Maryland whose influential family was staunchly opposed to Seward. Finally, Lincoln went so far as to give Weed a compromise proposal that he wanted Seward to present to the Senate's committee on the crisis, which had just been organized at long last.[25]

In reality, Lincoln had outmaneuvered Weed at every turn. The latter returned to New York apparently unaware that Lincoln completely disagreed with his ideas on territorial compromise; that he had already offered cabinet positions to two former Whigs, including one Southerner (Bates), and was considering more Southern names; and that he was already in correspondence with Gilmer, albeit not about the cabinet. What Weed did know as he boarded the train was bad enough: Lincoln's "compromise," on its face a coup, actually revealed in stark terms the limits of the editor's influence. It consisted of three resolutions. The first two dealt with the Fugitive Slave Law, weakening it so that no private citizen could be forced to assist in the apprehension of fugitives but urging its enforcement and advocating the repeal of state personal liberty laws. The third resolved simply "that the Federal Union must be preserved." In a letter to Trumbull written as soon as Weed left, Lincoln noted the resolutions' deliberate silence on the critical issue of the day: "They do not touch the territorial question."[26]

Seward met Weed's train at Syracuse and the two discussed the interview and resolutions on the ride to Albany. What Seward heard intensified his predicament, especially now that South Carolina's secession on December 20 dramatically increased the pressure on Congress to resolve the crisis quickly, before other states followed suit or some kind of clash precipitated armed conflict. Ideally, Lincoln's cabinet offer would have left Seward with not only the stature of being the new administration's representative in Washington but also the freedom to act on his own initiative. Lincoln's resolutions eliminated that possibility. Proposing them to the committee would not only render Seward an agent of the president-elect, a mere errand boy, but would damage his standing among Southern unionists and the other contacts he needed to forge a compromise. Yet he could not reject Lincoln's resolutions and still accept the State Department, without which he had no real prospect of influencing administration policy and would lack the additional weight in Congress that being Lincoln's chief adviser would bring. Finally, now that he knew Lincoln's narrow views on the crucial territorial question, Seward's rejecting a cabinet post and continuing to work for compromise was likely to inaugurate open warfare between the factions and shatter the party.

Lincoln had indeed tied Seward's hands adroitly. Historian David Potter writes of this episode, with much truth, "It is scarcely too much to say that, somewhere along the route [from Syracuse to Albany], the active leadership of the Republican party passed from Seward to Lincoln, and the cause of territorial compromise received a blow from which there was no recovery."[27]

It is doubtful that that was his intention—that is, that the resolutions were conceived as a ploy to restrict the senator's campaign for conciliation. Beyond Weed's open stance in favor of compromise there is no evidence to indicate that Lincoln was even aware yet of Seward's views on the crisis, never mind his congressional maneuverings. All that Lincoln's correspondents in Washington had reported about Seward were his efforts to maintain Republican silence, which Lincoln supported wholeheartedly; most of his influence had been exerted behind the scenes, through his Upper

South friends. What seems most likely is that Lincoln's resolutions, like his letters to Stephens and Gilmer and his efforts to find Southern cabinet advisers, represented a genuine attempt at concession. What neither man had truly grasped before was how widely their ideas of realistic conciliation measures differed—a divergence that was coming to characterize Republican national leaders more generally, and that reached to the heart of the dilemma that secession presented the party.

The distinction arose from the two leaders' access to different sources of information and especially their contrasting priorities. What Seward realized, and Lincoln did not, was that the Southern unionism on which hard-line Republicans had built their strategy did not exist—at least not the way they conceived of it. No matter their commitment or aversion to actual secession, most Americans living south of the Mason-Dixon line wholeheartedly accepted the *right* of a state to withdraw from the Union. Though Upper South unionists denied that the Republican threat to slavery was severe or imminent enough to justify immediate secession, most could sympathize with the constitutional principles and the fears that motivated secessionists. Southern unionism, then, was highly conditional. It was true that most Southerners, especially in the border states, did not intend or even desire to leave the Union—but if secessionist predictions proved true and Republicans did reveal an intention to act against slavery, their views would change. Thus, pleaded unionist leaders, without significant guarantees of Republican goodwill, they would be powerless to combat disunion in their states.[28]

Like most Republicans, Lincoln did not understand why repeated assurances that the North had neither authority nor inclination to interfere with slavery were not enough to satisfy the South. On at least three occasions in December, including in his letters to Gilmer and Stephens, he clumsily attempted to placate Southerners by affirming, "You think slavery is right and ought to be extended; we think slavery is wrong and ought to be restricted. For this, neither has any just occasion to be angry with the other." Despite his own Southern roots and connections, Lincoln simply did not grasp slavery's centrality to Southern society and culture.[29]

What Lincoln realized, and Seward did not, was that despite the recent infusion of conservative voters, the core of Republican strength lay in its dual commitment to restricting the reach of the Slave Power and maintaining the purity of the West. Lincoln may not have comprehended the true nature of Southern unionism, but he did recognize that unionists demanded nothing less than a full reversal of Republican policy on the territories. He knew that such a concession would destroy the party, thereby ceding victory to the Slave Power and leading inevitably, as far as he could see, to the nationalization of slavery and the perversion of the American republic. "The republican party is utterly powerless everywhere," he had written long before the election, "if it will, by any means, drive from it all those who came to it from the democracy for the sole object of preventing the spread, and nationalization of slavery. Whenever this object is waived by the organization, they will drop the organization; and the organization itself will dissolve into thin air."[30] Lincoln's resolutions represented as much of a compromise as he thought the party could safely offer. He could not have believed they would mollify the committed secessionists of the Deep South, but he seems to have thought they might bolster Southern unionists and offer a rallying point for his own dangerously divided party—thus his observation to Trumbull that they "would do much good, if introduced, and unanimously supported by our friends."[31]

That, in essence, was the dilemma that the Republican Party faced in settling on a compromise policy. Refusal to concede on the territorial issue risked driving the entire South into disunion, while concession would likely destroy the party and admit defeat to the republic's enemies. Whether it was possible to keep the party together to achieve its national vision without acquiescing in secession or engaging in war was the question that perplexed and haunted moderate Republicans on both sides of the compromise question.

✳ Although it was precisely what Stephen Douglas had hoped would occur, the Republican conflict that placed Seward into so awkward a position also created unforeseen difficulties for the Illinois senator and his supporters. For them the essential problem was a growing realization of their irrelevance: because secession was a direct reaction to the triumph of Republican principles among Northern voters, no compromise that did not have that party's support would satisfy secessionists. Thus the initiative in responding to secession lay entirely with the Republicans. As a result, although signs were hopeful of the party's collapse, until that happened the most immediate effect of the split was to place Republicans in control of both the procompromise and the anticompromise movements. Northern Democrats were left in a purely defensive posture, subject to being co-opted no matter what stance they took.

As Illinois editor Charles Lanphier explained to Congressman John McClernand, the Republicans' lack of authority until the inauguration left them without any responsibility, free to pander to public resentment of the South. In Illinois, at least, they were taking full advantage: "Evidently their game is to put us in the attitude of acquiescing in peaceable secession," he wrote bitterly, "while they are the rampant, belligerent, fighting, warring, *bellicose* party, *but can't do anything until after 4th March*." The danger, Lanphier emphasized, was of Republicans' painting the Democrats as secession sympathizers: "We must not be put in the fix of antagonism to the Union in any shape." From Washington, McClernand agreed that the Democracy, especially in the West, could not be perceived as weak on preserving the Union: "The Northwest cannot afford to submit to disunion except as an unavoidable necessity. Rally our friends to that point. The State ought to *hasten* to arm herself." Such defensive measures, he predicted, not only would prepare Illinois to resist disunion if necessary but would "open the eyes of the people to the effects of Lincoln's election," thereby pinning responsibility for the crisis right where it belonged.[32]

Their concerns were insightful. The Northern Democracy was indeed vulnerable to accusations that its desire for compromise translated into sympathy for disunion; Republicans hammered at that point in the following months. The defensive strategy that Lanphier and McClernand proposed, to seize the initiative by presenting both secessionists and Republicans as anti-Union extremists, was precisely the course that Douglas and other moderate Democrats would follow. The problem that party leaders faced was their constituents' wide disagreement on the use of force.

A great many Northern Democrats concurred with Lanphier and McClernand, condemning disunion and vowing to prevent it with armed might if necessary: "When all reasonable concessions should be unfortunately rejected, then coercion might, as all the power of this nation should be employed to prevent a few fanatics in the North & ambitious & unprincipled leaders in the South from destroying this fair heritage!" exclaimed one correspondent. Others were more explicit: "I cannot be made to believe there can be any peaceable secession—The whole of this City & State [New York] will go in for a 7 years fight—before they will yield to a break of this union," wrote another. A third: "Your friends [here], (and there is a large majority) think the union must be preserved at all hazards, if 100,000 of them fier eaters must bee hung or Subjugatet by the Sord."[33]

However, a significant portion of the party sharply opposed maintaining the Union through force. Chicago editor James Sheahan warned Douglas of a popular rejection of his Norfolk doctrine: "Should disunion take place,

I am free to confess there is a wide spread defection from the proper principle. Thousands upon thousands are utterly opposed to any force being employed to subjugate the seceding states. Civil War is horrible to contemplate, and the feeling is, that if the south must go, let them go in peace." Many of Douglas's constituents confirmed that assessment: "Secession is a dissolution of the government. Secession and coercion by the government is dissolution of the government and war in addition." "God forbid that we should ever draw the sword upon our own countrymen." "Let blood once be shed where will it stop?"[34] As the Illinois leaders feared, that attitude left the Democracy open to aspersions on its patriotism, especially in the face of growing militarism among Republican hard-liners.

If the issue came down to coercion, then, the party would find itself deeply divided. In the meantime, what Northern Democrats did agree on was that every effort should be made to resolve the crisis peacefully.[35] Nowhere was that outlook more clear than in the actions of Stephen Douglas himself, who labored desperately to construct a workable compromise even while he maintained his determination to defend the Union through force "as a last resort." "I will not consider the question of force & war until all efforts at peaceful adjustment have been made & have failed," he wrote Lanphier. Although he remained convinced that a peaceful resolution was possible only if the issue of slavery was removed from the reach of Congress, Douglas vowed to support any plan that looked as if it might satisfy the South. Patching together a resolution to the crisis, he believed, would simultaneously save the Union without war and, by unifying Northern and Southern conservatives, resurrect the national Democracy.[36]

So far, though, Douglas had had no vehicle through which to work. Republican leadership in the House had snubbed Northern Democrats in appointing the Committee of Thirty-three, while opposition from Deep South and Republican hard-liners had delayed the creation of any similar body in the Senate. It was not until December 18 that the upper house finally managed to create a select committee—the Committee of Thirteen— to consider proposals for resolving the crisis. Unlike the House committee, whose composition was generally unremarkable, the Committee of Thirteen included luminaries from all parties, including Douglas, Crittenden, and Seward, as well as Jefferson Davis of Mississippi and Robert Toombs of Georgia, soon to be the president and secretary of state, respectively, for the Southern Confederacy. Given such celebrity, the Senate committee attracted considerably more public attention.

On the day the Committee of Thirteen was authorized, Crittenden unveiled his much-anticipated grand compromise proposal. His plan immediately captured the hopes of compromise supporters North and South, and became the particular focus of Upper South unionists. It offered protection for slavery in all areas where federal law could reach it, including the Fugitive Slave Law, slavery in the District of Columbia, and the interstate slave trade. Its centerpiece, however, was an extension of the Missouri Compromise line westward, with slavery federally protected south of the line and prohibited north of it. In order to make that sacrifice of the *Dred Scott* doctrine more palatable to the South, the plan stated explicitly that the north-south division would pertain to all future territorial gains—a provision that Republicans, including Lincoln, had long since declared their principal objection to any territorial compromise, believing that it would encourage Southern dreams of a Central American slave empire. Finally, in order to ensure that the resolution of sectional conflict was permanent, Crittenden offered all of his propositions in the form of constitutional amendments, the last of which provided that none could be altered or abolished. Slavery would be permanently written into the Constitution.[37]

Despite the plan's rejection of his cherished popular sovereignty, Douglas was true to his pledge to support any proposal that promised to settle the crisis, and he pushed hard for it on the committee. But when the Crittenden plan came up for discussion on December 22, the committee rejected the extension of the Missouri line that lay at its heart. The six Northern Democratic and Upper South senators on the committee were in favor, and even the two Deep South delegates reluctantly agreed to recommend it, but only if the Republicans went along. All four Republicans present—Seward was still in New York meeting with Weed—voted against it. As a result, the two cotton-state representatives added their nays, and just like that it was dead.[38]

Two days later, on Christmas Eve, Douglas presented his own proposal. His plan echoed much of Crittenden's but, not surprisingly, addressed the territorial problem with a complex formula for popular sovereignty.[39] Like Seward, though, Douglas was rowing against the current. The anticonciliation campaign of Republican hard-liners was having its effect, and it was becoming apparent that the secession of South Carolina had pushed the crisis in a new and dangerous direction. The prospect of a compromise was growing dim, and with it Douglas's hopes for both the Union and the Democracy. It was difficult to foresee how either could survive if Republican stalwarts succeeded, as their rivals felt was likely, in bringing on a collision.

✳ Charles Francis Adams spent the evening of Saturday, December 22, at the home of William Pennington. Although Adams was a freshman representative, it was hardly remarkable that the longtime antislavery editor, former vice presidential candidate for the Free-Soil Party, and son and grandson of presidents would be among the dinner guests of the Speaker of the House. Adams was long accustomed to moving among the highest circles.

Among the other guests was Senator John J. Crittenden, the most visible force for compromise in Washington. Crittenden was in low spirits; that afternoon his carefully composed plan to resolve the sectional crisis—the plan that he had introduced to the Senate with such high expectations just four days earlier, that was the talk of the nation and the toast of conservative unionists North and South—had been killed in committee. His hopes for the survival of the Union, Crittenden noted sadly during dinner, had never been lower. Just after the meal, as Adams was passing out of the room, he overheard Crittenden speaking with another guest. The Kentucky senator noted glumly that he had done all he could, then added, "The decision is in his hands." Curious to know to whom Crittenden was referring, Adams glanced around—and was startled to find himself the object of their attention. "This is the man," Crittenden said solemnly, placing his hand on the astonished congressman's shoulder.[40]

A bewildered Adams passed off the remark. Much as he opposed the principle behind Crittenden's plan, for a freshman congressman, even one of Adams's unique background and extensive connections, to be singled out by one of the most respected and venerable members of the Senate must have been intimidating indeed. "I laughed as if enjoying the joke, and went out, home," he recorded that night in his diary. Yet he could tell that Crittenden had been quite serious. Adams surmised that the Kentucky senator attributed the suddenly unified Republican front that had defeated his proposal to an angry speech Adams had made before the Committee of Thirty-three two days earlier, a speech that, despite the supposed secrecy of committee sessions, had inspired considerable talk and earned enthusiastic congratulations from Adams's colleagues. Mulling the matter over that evening, he dismissed the idea that his speech had anything to do with the growing movement against compromise. To him it was obvious that the real cause was the recent spate of communications from Lincoln in Springfield.[41]

The incident was small and, in the larger course of events, insignificant. But the dinner exchange between Adams and Crittenden illustrates the tremendous pressures to which moderate Republicans were subjected as the forces of conciliation and anticompromise battled for their support. It also offers an early indication of the central role Adams would play in determining the course they would take in the coming weeks.

Strategically, moderate Republicans were the most important group in Congress. Since they not only balanced the radical and conservative extremes but comprised a sizable majority of the party, ultimately it must be they who decided the Republican response to secession. And since all but the most committed Southern disunionists were looking to congressional Republicans as a gauge of the threat to their society, in effect the entire issue of compromise lay in the hands of party moderates. However, the label referred to individuals not with a fixed, narrow set of principles but holding a broad range of views. As we have seen, many maintained a staunch opposition to substantive concessions while others advocated a more flexible response.

If the stances taken by Lincoln and Seward exemplified key differences among moderate Republican leaders, the actions of Charles Francis Adams in late December and January represent a third type of moderate response, and perhaps the most common one: wavering. Although the uncertainty of some moderates stemmed merely from weak-minded indecision, in most it reflected the impossible position in which they found themselves: searching with inadequate information for solutions that might not exist; struggling to satisfy the conflicting demands of ideology, party, and nationalism; knowing all the while that a misstep could lead to war. On one side they faced hard-line colleagues, unyielding and often bellicose constituents, an aversion to a humiliating surrender to the arrogant Southerners, and the long-held conviction that Northern concessions merely fueled Southern arrogance. From the other side came tremendous pressure from conciliatory colleagues, the pleadings of desperate Southern unionists, and a growing fear that Northern intransigence was playing into the hands of the secessionists. It was no wonder that many Republicans vacillated between firmness and magnanimity, the two qualities whose balance had been so easy to call for in November but now proved so elusive.

In recording the incident at the dinner party, Adams noted that although he had not had "the remotest communication" with Lincoln, their views were quite similar. He was right. Both were typical of the many moderates who resisted the rising Republican conciliationism, fearing its effects. Like Lincoln, Adams had not taken secessionist rhetoric seriously at first—he thought the South had "no true grounds of complaint" and considered disunionism to consist of mere threats "to deter the Republican party from using their triumph." He thought his party should cede "every doubtful point" to stave off a national crisis, but he would not agree to any sacrifice of principle. Like most of his Republican colleagues, Adams came to Washington convinced that given time and the absence of overt provocation from the North, the Southern unionist majority would reassert itself and the crisis would pass.[42]

It was no accident that the heated outburst to which Crittenden attributed the strengthening of Republican resolve had occurred on the same day that South Carolina had announced its secession from the Union. For Adams, Massachusetts's representative on the Committee of Thirty-three, South Carolina's declaration capped a series of developments that, as far as he was concerned, pushed the North too far. First, several of the Deep South delegates to the committee either had refused to fill their posts or had withdrawn from its deliberations. Then the Arkansas delegate had threatened that the rest of the Southerners on the committee would also leave if the Republicans would not agree to his impossible demand for federal slave codes in all territories, present and future, south of 36°30'. And then, on the twentieth, South Carolina seceded—without consulting its own citizens, without waiting for other states, and certainly without waiting to see whether the North was willing to redress any of its supposed grievances.[43]

So Adams was already irate when, on that same day, he encountered yet another example of Southerners' refusal to engage in practical discussion. It began when Maryland unionist Henry Winter Davis suggested a plan similar to the one John Sherman had presented the previous week: since the controversy over slavery in the territories could obviously not be resolved, it should be sidestepped by eliminating the territories. Specifically, Congress should admit New Mexico, a nominally slave territory encompassing the entire territorial region south of 36°30', to statehood. The territorial question would thereby be removed from national politics without violating Republican principles. The other Southern members immediately announced that they could not support Davis's proposition and demanded instead a vote on the territorial slave code.[44]

To Adams, preventing even the discussion of a moderate proposal by hiding behind a ridiculous ultimatum displayed an utter disregard for his party's views, let alone the principle of rational debate. Coming as it did on the heels of South Carolina's secession, it was simply too much. Rising, Adams blasted secession as treason, sneered at the notion that Republicans should trust the South to abide by another compromise line, and flatly refused to condone the Southern attempt to pervert the Constitution into "a mere guaranty" for the security of slavery. Permitting the expansion of slavery "in this, the nineteenth century, in the face of the civilized world" would constitute "moral degradation," and he, for one, would see the Union destroyed before acquiescing in their scheme. That evening he concluded in his journal, "The critical moment has arrived in which our Institutions must be rescued from this moral and social disease. . . . A retreat would only bring the necessity for other trials still more difficult and dangerous at a later moment."[45]

Yet by the time Crittenden charged him with causing the defeat of his compromise plan two days later, Adams had already had something of a change of heart. The cause was a less confrontational interview with another border-state unionist. On the morning of the twenty-first, as Adams walked to the Capitol, Henry Winter Davis offered him a ride in his carriage. Inside, Davis got Adams's attention by confirming his suspicion that radical Southerners had no genuine interest in compromise but were merely trying to maneuver the Republicans into rejecting their terms, thereby strengthening their hand against Southern unionists. What the Republicans needed to do, Davis urged, was make an offer of their own. Giving their support to his New Mexico statehood plan would assure frightened Southern unionists of Republicans' good intentions and reveal the "hollowness" of secessionist arguments. That, in turn, would divide the South, splitting the generally conservative border states from the more radical cotton states and halting the spread of secession.[46]

When Adams related Davis's argument to a caucus of the Republican committee members, he found most willing to support the measure. It seemed to be the only compromise they could offer without precipitating a major split in the party. Indeed, it was as far as most committee members would consent to go themselves. Several who had earlier supported the liberal Dunn resolution, which had pledged the committee to support a peace-saving compromise regardless of the legitimacy or illegitimacy of Southern grievances, had since been severely upbraided by their constituents. Here at last was a concession that did not seem to violate party principle. Even if New Mexico did submit a proslavery constitution, which would have the same practical effect as protecting slave property south of the Missouri line, it would not be the federal protection that Southern Democrats demanded for the territories. Moreover, Republicans would neither have admitted Congress's powerlessness to ban slavery from the territories nor extended federal slave codes to territories acquired in the future, two core problems underlying any plan yet proposed.[47]

The caucus agreed to the New Mexico statehood plan, and even added a proposal that a recently arrived Seward had just made in the Senate committee: a constitutional amendment that guaranteed the security of slavery in the states, a relatively harmless gesture that would formalize what Republicans believed the Constitution already implied. Committee chairman Thomas Corwin, an Ohio conservative, assigned Adams to present the official proposal. Adams was convinced that it would be the ruin of his career, but he agreed.[48] The Committee of Thirty-three accepted both Republican measures, voting to recommend them to the full House even after two radical Southerners withdrew in protest of what they viewed as a fraudulent pretense of compromise.[49] Despite the surge of hard-line pressure, conciliation was moving forward, if only cautiously, among the Republicans.

But caution was indeed the watchword. Adams had met with his party colleagues on Christmas Eve, a Monday; by that Friday, the more eminent Committee of Thirteen had effectively failed after rejecting a similar plan. Adams's good friend William Seward had returned to Washington on Monday to find that Republican committee members had already rejected the Crittenden plan. To break party lines now would needlessly alienate Lincoln and divide the Republicans, so he entered his own belated nay and focused on damage control. The committee rejected the liberalized version of Lincoln's resolutions that he offered (afterward he pretended to Lincoln that he had not actually seen the real resolutions but was acting on Weed's description of them), but even his offering them, he calculated, meant that Senate Republicans had at least proposed something.[50]

Three days later two other Republicans joined Seward in supporting a variation of the New Mexico plan, raising brief hope of a genuine compromise proposal. However, negotiations collapsed when the Republicans insisted on that old bone of contention, the admission of Kansas as a free state. At that point the committee adjourned, all possibilities exhausted.

On Monday, the thirty-first, it officially dissolved itself, reporting to the Senate that it had no recommendations for resolving the crisis.[51]

✳ "Practically," Thurlow Weed recognized astutely in mid-December, "the issues of the late campaign are obsolete."[52] By the time the South Carolina convention announced its formal secession, the crisis had gone far toward polarizing Northern public opinion and disrupting the fragile party alignment that had produced Lincoln's election. Congressional Republicans flirted with a genuine schism over the necessity for compromise, while Democrats were divided on the question of enforcing federal authority in seceding states. It is possible that a majority of Northerners favored compromise, and indisputable that a majority throughout the still-loyal states did, but with the hard-liners controlling the Republican Party, little was being accomplished in Congress. The presentation of a modest concession by the lower house committee was largely overlooked. What the Northern public focused on was the failure of the Committee of Thirteen to accomplish anything at all—and even that was pushed into the background when the long-feared outbreak of hostilities at Charleston harbor threatened once more.

On December 20, after three days of deliberation, South Carolina formally withdrew from the United States. The event marked a significant shift in the national crisis. No longer was disunion an abstraction, a frightening but as-yet-speculative prospect. Now South Carolina would assert its independence, and there were countless ways in which doing so was likely to bring it into conflict with federal authority. What was more, the event found President Buchanan nearly exhausted, his administration falling apart and popularly reviled due to its efforts to avoid open hostilities with the proud Palmetto State. His chances of continuing success seemed hopeless.

In fact, it took less than a week for Buchanan's delicate peace to collapse. Beginning in the final days of 1860, a series of stunning incidents in Charleston harbor brought the country to the brink of civil war, challenging Northerners' priorities, threatening to recast the party system, and transforming the very nature of the crisis. Northerners of all parties displayed a remarkable and previously unsuspected accord on the need to defend federal property and federal authority. The fragile Republican effort at conciliation was forced into wholesale retreat, and even Northern Democrats, although they remained united behind the need for compromise, revealed themselves to be nearly as solid behind the need to defend the government. Within the collective value system that shaped Northern political culture, national preservation and pride clearly trumped devotion to states' rights among all but the most extreme Democrats.

However, the same widespread commitment to the rule of law that underlay so much of Northerners' aversion to secession also dictated that the decision on how to respond to Southern aggression rested with one man. Barring further violence at Charleston, whether the outburst of patriotic zeal would translate into civil war would depend entirely on James Buchanan.

✳ Northern reaction to South Carolina's declaration of independence was remarkably subdued; after six weeks of anticipation, the act itself seemed anticlimactic. In New York, for example, George T. Strong recorded in his diary, "This proceeding surprises nobody and makes no sensation. That its foolish inhabitants want to be called an Empire or a Herzogthum or a Tribe makes no difference."[1] But whether such expressions were sincere or represented a sort of verbal whistling past the graveyard, the first formal act of secession had ramifications that materially altered the crisis. The most immediate of those concerned the Charleston harbor forts. On that front, as much as Secretary Cass and General Scott had intensified public pressure, it was Maj. Robert Anderson, the new commander of Fort Moultrie, who proved to be the true thorn in Buchanan's side.

Since his arrival in Charleston, Anderson had been issuing regular warnings about the unstable political condition of Charleston and the vulnerability of his garrison. Every sign pointed to an immediate movement against the forts once South Carolina seceded, an assessment confirmed by explicit statements by the mayor and a number of prominent Charleston citizens. "I hear that the attention of the South Carolinians appears to be turned more toward Fort Sumter than it was," Anderson reported, "and it is deemed probable that their first act will be to take possession of that work." Once they did, he stated emphatically, delivery of reinforcements would be impossible and his own position at Fort Moultrie would be untenable. "Fort Sumter is a tempting prize," he explained, "the value of which is well known to the Charlestonians, and once in their possession, with its ammunition and armament and walls uninjured and garrisoned properly, it would set our Navy at defiance, compel me to abandon this work, and give them the perfect command of this harbor."[2] It was these reports that Cass and Scott used to support their position and that—as Northern editors began to sift them out of the mass of telegraphic reports from Washington and place them into more prominent positions— led growing numbers of Northerners to question the administration's commitment to Union.

In response to Anderson's repeated requests for a clarification of his orders, Floyd dispatched an emissary, Maj. Don Carlos Buell, to Charleston. Arriving on the tenth, Buell reminded Anderson that his first priority was to avoid a collision and informed him that, as a result of that concern, the War Department would not be sending additional troops or taking any other action that might disturb the situation. However, should the forts be attacked, or should Anderson "have tangible evidence of a design to proceed to a hostile act," he was to defend himself—to include transferring his garrison into whatever fort he deemed most advantageous. Buchanan subsequently approved these instructions, and on December 21 had them reissued as a formal order.[3] Meanwhile, he and Floyd arranged for the warship *Brooklyn* to remain stationed off Fort Monroe, Virginia, ready to transport reinforcements to Fort Moultrie should they become necessary.[4]

In the days following South Carolina's secession, as Charleston's attention focused on the forts, Anderson's sense of urgency mounted. Beginning the night of the twentieth, state authorities stationed two boats between Forts Moultrie and Sumter to prevent the garrison's transfer. "I think that I could, however, were I to receive instructions so to do, throw my garrison into that work," he reported on the twenty-second, "but I should have to sacrifice the greater part of my stores, as it is now too late to attempt their removal."[5] There was no time to await an answer. With secession declared, commissioners had been sent to Washington to negotiate for the peaceful transfer of the forts. Anderson was certain that once their mission had failed, the unmanned forts, including Sumter, would be seized and his own surrender demanded. With Sumter's guns aimed at him, he would have no choice but to capitulate. At that moment the orders confirming Buell's verbal instructions arrived from Washington, and Anderson decided to exercise the discretion granted him. Deciding that the armed patrol boats and repeated warnings he had received over the past weeks clearly constituted "tangible evidence of a design to proceed to a hostile act," he determined to move his men to Sumter at his own discretion. Shortly after nightfall on Wednesday, December 26, he ordered the guns at Moultrie spiked to prevent their immediate use and quietly transferred his command to the previously unoccupied island fort.[6]

Predictably, South Carolinians exploded in frustration and outrage. As soon as the movement was discovered, Governor Francis Pickens, who had taken office just a week earlier, sent an aide to demand Anderson's return. Referring to the December 10 meeting between Buchanan and the South Carolina congressional delegation, he insisted that the president had agreed that no reinforcement was to occur, particularly of Sumter. Anderson replied coolly that none had—he had merely shifted his garrison from one of the forts under his command to another. Moreover, he had acted entirely on his own responsibility. Incensed, Pickens ordered the immediate seizure of Fort Moultrie and the harbor's other forts, as well as the Charleston customhouse. The federal arsenal was formally occupied three days later. Whether those acts were the opening maneuvers of a civil war would depend entirely on the response from Washington.[7]

✳ Until now, the president had held tightly to the hope that a diplomatic resolution could be found, and he had done all he could think of to bring one about. He had sent Caleb Cushing to the South Carolina secession convention to make a vain eleventh-hour plea for Union. Desperate to calm rising public passions and convince Southerners of Northern goodwill, he had announced that January 4 would be a day of national fasting and prayer. Despairing of a congressional compromise, he even sent an emissary to Springfield to talk Lincoln into speaking out in favor of a national convention.[8] And through it all, in the face of mounting criticism and the resignation of two key cabinet members, he had struggled mightily to avoid armed conflict without sacrificing federal authority, frantically maintaining hope that Congress would find a way to head off secession peacefully. But his balancing act could not be maintained much longer. In mid-December Buchanan's entire administration began to collapse.

It started with the growing Northern condemnation of his policy toward the forts, to which the stubborn chief executive had refused to bend. Public censure increased dramatically when he permitted Secretary of the Interior Jacob Thompson to act as one of the multitude of state agents crisscrossing the South to discuss secession. Buchanan had agreed to this in the conviction that Thompson was working to forestall, not encourage, disunion, but that distinction mattered little to a public that by now was conditioned to think him capable of promoting disunion. Popular suspicions were encouraged by the outspoken secessionism of the *Washington Constitution*, the administration's longtime mouthpiece. It was not until Christmas Day that the president finally broke with the paper and began withdrawing its lucrative government printing contracts, by which time his already frail reputation had been even further damaged.[9]

Ironically, the worst blow had its roots in a financial scandal entirely unrelated to secession. Years earlier, Secretary Floyd had taken to advancing contractors a sort of promissory note that they could use as collateral to obtain loans until Congress authorized their payment. Since he was careless in his records, eventually over $5 million in unofficial notes was circulating and banks stopped accepting them. One enterprising contractor sidestepped that difficulty by arranging with a clerk in the Department of the Interior, a relative of Floyd's wife, to use the notes to borrow negotiable bonds from an Indian trust fund. On December 19, facing exposure, the clerk publicly confessed to having lent out $870,000 in bonds in return for Floyd's notes. For a brief time the resulting scandal overshadowed even the perilous situation at Charleston harbor.

Floyd had already taken ill under the intense and sustained pressure of the past seven weeks and was confined to his bed when he learned of the scandal. With the addition of this new strain he apparently snapped, for his subsequent actions were not in keeping with the aversion to both secession and coercion he had displayed throughout the crisis. On Thursday, December 20, he ordered a large number of heavy guns to be shipped from the federal foundry at Pittsburgh to some uncompleted forts in Texas. When, on Christmas Day, suspicious citizens in Pittsburgh telegraphed the capital inquiring about the matter, a fresh scandal arose to eclipse the last one.[10] "The news from Pittsburgh has waked up our Citizens, and all who were for peace upon any terms almost are now talking of war," reported an Ohio conservative. The recession played a role as well, he added: "As many of them are out of employment say, they would as soon fight a little as not." The shipment was stopped, but once again, the damage had been done. The administration's credibility lay in tatters.[11]

Such was the situation when news of Anderson's transfer to Sumter reached Washington on the twenty-seventh. With confidence in the chief executive at its nadir and a desire for firm action rampant, "the gallant Anderson" became an instant hero to Northerners of all parties. In cities across the North thirty-three-gun salutes (one gun for every state, including South Carolina) were fired in his honor, and private and public expressions of praise abounded. "These are times to develop one's manhood," one Boston businessman enthused. "We have had none finer since 1776." An editorial in the *Boston Courier*, a Constitutional Union supporter, typified the way even fervent conciliationists spurned disunion and rallied to the defense of federal authority: "We must own that the news of the transaction at Charleston harbor was learned by us yesterday with a prouder beating of the heart. We could not but feel once more that we had a country —a fact which has been to a certain degree in suspense for some weeks past. . . . It is a decisive act, calculated to rally the national heart. . . . Although this intelligence created a good deal of excitement, men felt a sort of relief, as if things were coming to a crisis, or that the beginning of the end was at hand."[12]

Buchanan, on the other hand, was denounced as a "weak and traitorous" scoundrel. Northerners everywhere weighed in on whether the president was, as one put it, an "imbecile, and not competent to the emer gency; or has so far committed himself to the authors of the evils that are now upon us, that he is either tacitly acquiescing, or secretly promoting their aims and ends." A New York City Hardshell noted the contrast: "The President seems to be execrated now by four fifths of the people of all parties," while "Anderson's act is much commended here. It seems to be received with enthusiastic joy in every place north and west of us."[13]

The days following Anderson's move and South Carolina's seizure of the forts were a tempest of commotion, confusion, and fear. Events seemed to be following each other in such rapid succession that the venerable unionist Edward Everett observed from Massachusetts, "It may truly be said, that we know not what a day or two or an hour may bring forth."[14] The greatest anxiety was in Washington, where rumors abounded of secessionist armies forming in Virginia and Maryland and preparing to march on the capital. Henry Adams, the congressman's twenty-two-year-old son, reported, "The terror here among the inhabitants is something wonderful to witness. At least the half of them believe that Washington is to be destroyed by fire and sword. Some are providing a retreat for their families." General Scott ordered the organization of a militia "to repel invasion, suppress insurrection and preserve public property." Seward turned momentarily from his efforts to find a peaceful resolution to the crisis to warn Lincoln of a "plot . . . to seize the capitol," and he recommended to the governors of New York and Massachusetts that they prepare their states' militia forces to defend Washington.[15]

Similar rumors passed quickly through the telegraph wires and filled the newspapers, and from across the North offers of armed support flooded into Lincoln's office in Springfield. Calls went up to prepare for war. "Send out an appeal for a Washington that will rally the freemen of the north if need be into organised and armed cooperation," came the cry. "The rebellion can only be suppressed by the demonstration of active overpowering force ready to crush out all acts of overt treason." In Westchester, Pennsylvania, "members from all parties" called a meeting to enroll volunteers in a militia regiment "to offer their services to the Government to maintain the Constitution and enforce the laws." From Albany, Weed concluded from the unprecedented public demonstrations that "it would require but the slightest intimation of the necessity of combined action to secure millions of volunteers to go anywhere, or do anything to maintain the Union." Even the deeply conservative Everett, who for weeks had condemned the rise of passion and prejudice and despaired of a rational resolution to the crisis, embraced the popular mood so far as to suggest that the president should step down and Congress give General Scott dictatorial powers over the country.[16]

In the excitement and passion, it seemed to some that the parties themselves were breaking apart. Proponents of compromise had been urging their opponents for weeks to rise above party concerns and unite to save the Union. Now, with civil war imminent and the president disgraced, it appeared that a nonpartisan rallying to the Union was indeed under way—but not as conciliationists had envisioned it. "The democrats are all coming over to our side You will soon have but one party in the north," a Detroit supporter assured Lincoln. It seemed to be true everywhere, even in the hub of pro-Southern sentiment: "South Carolina is destroying the influence of all her friends here," wrote a New York conservative. Another reported, "Many men a week or two ago in favor of concession are stiffening a little to resist all conciliation. More than that the *reported* acts of Buchanan and his Cabinet are making coercionists out of democrats." A Buchanan intimate discovered that South Carolina's action left him "but one of two courses to choose from, viz.—to join in with the secessionists or his country. His choice was easily made." A traveling Republican congressman noted, "There has undoubtedly been a tremendous revulsion in public feeling in New England and N. York City within a few days. The events at Charleston are fast making a *united north*. The most conservative in N.Y. now say 'no more compromises,' and that the forts and U.S. property must be returned to the possession of the Government." And from Washington, an Illinois Democrat wrote Lincoln gravely, "Now is the time for party sacrifices and patriotic elevation. . . . Politically I am where I was on the issue of the last canvass, believing non-intervention on the slavery question to be the true doctrine—patriotically I am with all the friends of the Union, and shall look to its preservation as the great paramount consideration."[17]

Thurlow Weed had been predicting since November that if the Republicans could make the Union rather than slavery the central issue of the crisis, a united North would rally behind them. He had focused his energies on formulating a Union-saving compromise, but now he did not hesitate to urge Lincoln to take advantage of the sudden outburst of patriotic fervor. From New York he told the president-elect, "We shall have a *United north*—a condition about which I have been filled with solicitude."[18]

✳ As if the administration's circumstances were not grim enough, the day the Sumter news reached Washington was the same day that the newly arrived South Carolina commissioners were scheduled to meet with the president. The meeting, postponed until the next day, was brief. The three Southerners regretted the aggressions of Major Anderson and asserted that although they understood the major to have acted against the president's orders, no negotiations could take place until all the troops in Charleston harbor were withdrawn.

Buchanan conferred with his cabinet. Thompson, Treasury Secretary Philip Thomas, and Floyd (who refused to submit his resignation) agreed that the move violated Buchanan's agreement and that the forts must be evacuated altogether. The embattled secretary of war, sick as he was, engaged in a shouting match with Secretary of State Black, which culminated in the latter's waving a copy of Anderson's orders and roaring, "There never was a moment in the history of England when a minister of the Crown could have proposed to surrender a military post which might be defended, *without bringing his head to the block*!" The cabinet continued to meet over the next few days—now without Floyd, who finally resigned in protest, he said, of Buchanan's dishonorable course. By Sunday, the thirtieth, Black was so upset about the way discussions were going that he contacted the president privately to remind him of his commitment to defend the public property. He threatened to resign if Anderson's men were withdrawn.[19]

In the midst of these intense debates over the commissioners, the president learned that both the Committee of Thirteen and his overture to Lincoln regarding a national convention had failed. The committee reported to the Senate on the thirty-first that it had no recommendations for resolving the crisis. Duff Green, Buchanan's emissary, met with Lincoln on the twenty-eighth and urged him to speak out in favor of a popular referendum on the Crittenden amendments. The president-elect offered Green the same argument he had conveyed to congressional Republicans: extension of the 36°30′ line would only encourage Southern expansionist schemes, and Republicans could not afford to and would never agree to sacrifice the principles on which they had won the election. Lincoln did not give Green a formal answer, instead promising a written response (which, like Seward's cabinet offer, he forwarded for approval to Trumbull, who later passed it along); nevertheless, Green appears to have wired news of his failure to Buchanan the next morning. It seemed that a diplomatic resolution to the crisis was not forthcoming.[20]

In light of Black's arguments, the rejection of compromise by both the Senate and the incoming administration, and the commissioners' arrogant and impolitic demand, Buchanan's faith that the crisis might end amicably was crushed. His long effort to maintain federal authority while avoiding conflict had failed; he must choose. His reply to the commissioners was stern. In a letter sent December 31, he informed them that his first instinct upon learning of Anderson's transfer had been to order the garrison's return to Moultrie; however, South Carolina authorities, without waiting for or even requesting an explanation, had removed that option by forcibly seizing all of the other forts in the harbor as well as the customhouse and arsenal. And now they insisted that the government abandon the harbor entirely? "This I cannot do; this I will not do," he declared. "Such an idea was never thought of by me in any possible contingency. No allusion had ever been made to it in any communication between myself and any other human being." The commissioners wrote an indignant reply in which they placed the responsibility for inaugurating civil war on Buchanan's head, and left the city in a huff. Negotiations, such as they were, had closed.[21]

Buchanan's response to the latest development in the crisis marked a dramatic shift in policy. Rocked by scandal and intense public criticism and forced to decide between sustaining peace and maintaining the government, he confirmed the ascendancy of the militant pro-Union faction of his cabinet by moving Joseph Holt into the War Department to take Floyd's place and replacing short-lived secretary of the treasury Philip Thomas with outspoken unionist John A. Dix of New York. Then, bowing to the demands of Black, Holt, and General Scott (and perhaps to his own anger at South Carolina's headstrong governor and arrogant commissioners), Buchanan completed his conversion by once more ordering reinforcements for Anderson's garrison. This time the order was issued, and on Saturday, January 5, a ship secretly carrying 250 U.S. soldiers and six months' provisions quietly steamed out of New York harbor, bound for Charleston.[22]

✳ As the new year dawned, prospects for a peaceful resolution of the crisis looked bleak. South Carolina had formally seceded. The Senate's celebrated Committee of Thirteen had adjourned without accomplishing anything. Republicans on the House committee had quietly put together a package of tepid concessions, but although these represented the outer bounds of what most Republicans would agree to, guaranteeing federal noninterference with slavery in the states and admitting New Mexico to statehood were hardly measures to inspire enthusiasm among Southern unionists. Most critically, South Carolina's erection of artillery batteries aimed at Fort Sumter and seizure of federal property in Charleston, and the ensuing rumors of an attack on Washington, had gone far toward uniting Northerners behind a forceful response—which was just what the president, braced by his revamped cabinet, was said to be planning. Then, in the first days of January, Northerners were further enraged when the governors of Georgia, Alabama, and Florida, without even waiting for their states to officially secede, ordered the confiscation of federal forts and arsenals within their borders. Finally, South Carolina's secession was cemented when Mississippi, Florida, and Alabama also resolved themselves out of the Union; Georgia, Louisiana, and Texas were expected to follow shortly.[23]

But if Southern aggression roused a new militancy in most Northerners, the imminence of war stirred a desperation for peace in others. Rather than despair, conciliationist leaders launched another offensive, spearheaded once more by Senators Crittenden and Douglas. Despite Republican opposition, the encouragement they had been receiving from across the North and Upper South convinced them that Northern public sentiment was behind compromise, particularly the Crittenden plan. They had also received "private assurances" from New York that support would be forthcoming from Seward, whose acceptance of Lincoln's State Department was appearing in the newspapers at this time.[24]

With that support in mind, the two senators issued a joint public letter assuring concerned Southerners that their rights could be secured within the Union. "Don't give up the Ship," they pleaded. "Don't despair of the Republic." Meanwhile, they focused their main efforts on reviving Crittenden's popular compromise proposal. On January 3, citing numerous reports of massive public sympathy for a peaceful resolution to the crisis, Crittenden asked the Senate to refer his amendments directly to the people, to be decided upon in a national convention. In that way, he believed, the paralysis of partisanship could be avoided: Senate Republicans who sought a peaceful resolution to the crisis but feared crossing their colleagues or constituents could assist the plan without actually voting for its implementation. He also sought to attract Republican support by adding two propositions drawn from Douglas's failed proposal: a national ban on black voting and officeholding and federal subsidization of black colonization to Africa.[25]

When Crittenden sat down, Douglas rose to speak in support of the unusual proposition, his first major address of the session. The eagerly anticipated speech, delivered before packed galleries, epitomized the aggressiveness with which Northern Democrats opted to combat hard-line Republicans' questioning of their patriotism—a task that South Carolina's actions were making more difficult by the day.

Appealing to the antipartisanship and anti-extremism of Northern and Southern conservatives, Douglas charged the Republicans with "attempt[ing] to manufacture partisan capital out of a question involving the peace and safety of the country." Obviously their objections to Crittenden's plan were not genuine, he said: for six years they had condemned him for violating the "sacred pledge" of the Missouri Compromise, but now that he supported its reinstitution, they attacked it as an ignominious surrender. Worse, they refused to help resolve the horrific crisis even though it was their own actions that had caused it; it was, he claimed, such fanaticism as Abraham Lincoln's "dangerous and revolutionary opinion" that the nation could not exist half slave and half free and Ben Wade's demands for unconditional submission and threats of war that enabled Southern demagogues to play on public fright.[26]

The greatest challenge for the Douglas Democrats, especially during the hysteria following Anderson's transfer, was to support peace without appearing weak. With that in mind, Douglas attacked the Republicans as naive ideologues: for all their talk of upholding the Constitution and enforcing the laws, he stormed, they had to deal with the basic fact that "the revolution is complete." "In my opinion South Carolina had no right to secede," he declared, "*but she has done it.*" The question now was not how to prevent disunion but how to reverse it—by force of arms or by a peaceful resolution of sectional differences? Here Douglas reached the core of the anti-Republican argument. "Are we prepared IN OUR HEARTS for war with our own brethren and kindred?" he demanded. "I confess I am not." He explained, "While I affirm that the Constitution is, and was intended to be, a bond of perpetual Union; while I can do no act and utter no word that will acknowledge or countenance the right of secession; while I affirm the right and duty of the Federal Government to use all legitimate means to enforce the laws, put down rebellion, and suppress insurrection, I will not meditate war, nor tolerate the idea, until every effort at peaceful adjustment shall have been exhausted. . . . War is disunion, certain, inevitable, irrevocable disunion. I am for peace to save the Union."

Yet Douglas also rejected the argument that the use of force was incompatible with free, republican government. "Sir, the word government means coercion. . . . The necessity of government is found to consist in the fact that some men will not do right unless coerced to do so." However, "coercion must always be used in the mode prescribed in the Constitution and laws." Illustrating just how much Northern Democrats had come to appreciate Buchanan's fine distinctions of a month earlier, he avowed that to use force in order to reduce the de facto government of South Carolina, a government whose legitimacy none of its own citizens questioned, would be a perversion of the law, not its enforcement.

The only way to enforce the laws without resorting to blatant conquest, Douglas concluded, was to find a compromise that removed the issue of slavery from national politics. He believed that popular sovereignty would be the most effective policy, but it was clear that the American people overwhelmingly supported Senator Crittenden's proposal to extend the Missouri Compromise line, and he would accede to their wishes. Would the Republicans do the same? Would they trust the people to speak again now that they realized what was at stake? Would they back up their verbal assurances of goodwill toward the South with firm pledges? Closing with a reiteration of the theme of partisanship, Douglas concluded severely, "It seems that party platforms, pride of opinion, personal consistency, fear of political martyrdom, are the only obstacles to a satisfactory adjustment."

By the time he returned to his seat, Douglas had effectively laid out the twofold strategy that he and the Northern Democracy would follow through the rest of the crisis, a strategy that echoed Lanphier and McClernand's ideas but steered a more moderate course with regard to coercion. First, he had tried to regain the initiative by going on the attack, pinning the blame for the crisis on Republicans' fanaticism and partisanship and challenging them to back up their denial of aggressive intent with guarantees. Second, he had attempted to minimize the division in his own party by vigorously upholding the government's right to preserve its integrity while at the same time insisting that it would be irresponsible and counterproductive to exercise that right under the present circumstances and before trying all possible means of resolving the situation peacefully. Not only did that approach play to the Northern Democracy's ideological proclivity to steer a middle ground between Northern and Southern extremists, but given the weak position of the party it was probably the most effective political tactic available.

The speech and the plan to submit Crittenden's amendment to a popular referendum found widespread support among conservatives of both sections.[27] Meanwhile, the two senators tried other means to revive the flagging compromise movement. Crittenden chaired an informal committee of fourteen congressmen, including five Republicans, from the border slave and free states. The committee approved a proposal submitted by James Hale, a Pennsylvania Republican, that was carefully designed to temper those parts of the Crittenden plan that were most offensive to hard-liners in his party. Rather than mandating that territorial governments in the regions south of 36°30′ protect slavery, the border-state plan, as it came to be known, simply barred federal interference with it—in effect, silently dropping Crittenden's slave code and replacing it with popular sovereignty. It dealt with the sticking point of "territory hereafter acquired" in a similar fashion, simply dropping Crittenden's proposal to subject all future territories to the 36°30′ line. Finally, the border-state compromisers did away with Crittenden's multiple constitutional amendments, instead proposing that only a federal guarantee of the rights of slavery in the states—to which Republicans on the House committee had already agreed—be written into the Constitution; the rest would take the form of congressional legislation. Thus, even as Crittenden and Douglas continued to press for the Kentucky senator's original proposal, they were quietly supporting a movement to meet the goodwill gesture of the Republicans on the Committee of Thirty-three.[28]

✳ What might have become of all those efforts had circumstances taken a more favorable turn will never be known. Given moderate Republicans' unwillingness to precipitate a split in the party, it is likely that hard-line opposition to any substantive concession on the territorial issue would have doomed the Crittenden and border-state plans no matter what was going on outside of Washington. As it happened, though, the timing of the latest proposals could not have been worse. In the face of South Carolina's secession and seizure of federal property, several congressional moderates who had been sympathetic with Southern unionism now pulled back in revulsion. As Charles Francis Adams observed with characteristic understatement, "The excitement in the country immediately reacts on the members here."[29]

Once more, Adams himself exemplified the trend. On Wednesday, January 2, just five days after presenting the most conciliatory Republican proposal yet, he reversed course once more. Adams declared to the committee that South Carolina's actions prevented any concessions whatever; Republicans could not risk emboldening disunionists by appearing to cave in to their threats. Until the South became more reasonable, he said, there was nothing to discuss. He "intimated very broadly that if the gentlemen continued to oppose what we had done we might as well give up all further progress."[30]

Withering attacks from his constituents and allies in Massachusetts had played no small part in Adams's decision; a few days later the determination of a full party caucus to reject "any and all compromise whatsoever" confirmed his resolve.[31] Although he was not present at the caucus, Adams understood its central message, the same one that had shackled Seward for weeks: compromise on slavery's expansion, even in as mild a form as the admission of New Mexico, would destroy the party. Since the hard-liners in Washington would not budge and the party faithful throughout the North did not appreciate the complexities that inspired the compromise movement, the conciliationists' choice was to give way or precipitate a split. Adams knew which way he would go: unless the party unambiguously supported New Mexican statehood and the amendment protecting slavery in the states, he would withdraw his support for them.[32]

First, though, he would test Southerners' intentions. Adams added to his proposals an introductory resolution declaring that accepting the results of a constitutional election was "the paramount duty of every good citizen of the United States." It was a succinct statement of hard-liners' most basic objection to compromise: they should not be asked to make concessions to those who threatened treason rather than submit to electoral defeat. If a majority of the committee's Southern representatives could not support this, Adams declared, he would reject his own propositions. With three Deep South members absent (two had never attended) and seven more slave-state delegates abstaining, even a unanimous vote in favor of the new resolution did not mollify him. The crisis, he concluded, had passed the point where Congress was able to resolve it. In fact, the vote suggested that his original plan had succeeded: he had set out to divide the slave states, and now the representatives of the key states of Virginia, Kentucky, and Tennessee declared openly that Lincoln's election provided no legitimate cause for secession. Nevertheless, in a final vote on January 11, Adams joined the majority of Republicans who opposed their own party's proposals. Although they passed anyway, three days later the committee overwhelmingly rejected the report as a whole. Chairman Thomas Corwin barely won permission to present the proposals to the House merely as his own personal recommendation. Adams voted against Corwin and wrote his own minority report suggesting that Southern attitudes made further discussion pointless.[33]

Adams's change of heart was representative of what was going on throughout the party. Indeed, recent events were having a profound effect on Northerners of both parties, as an early-January incident in the House revealed. On Monday, the seventh, Tennessee unionist Emerson Etheridge requested a suspension of the rules, which required two-thirds approval, so that he might offer a compromise proposal that had not been previously scheduled. In the overheated atmosphere produced by the excitement at Charleston—now stoked by rumors that reinforcements were en route to Fort Sumter—the House refused to suspend the rules, thereby preventing the measure from even coming to debate. But immediately following Etheridge's defeat, the rules were successfully suspended for a resolution lauding "the bold and patriotic act of Major Anderson" and pledging to "support the President in all constitutional measures to enforce the laws and preserve the Union."

The way the votes broke down is telling. Although Southerners and Northern Democrats voted almost as a body in favor of permitting Etheridge to make his proposal, only a handful of Republicans joined them.[34] On the other hand, every Republican and all but five Northern Democrats supported suspension for the Anderson resolutions, and among Northerners only three Democrats voted against the resolutions themselves.[35] In the wake of the excitement in the South, Republicans were as solid against substantive compromise as Northern Democrats were for it; however, in the face of a direct challenge to the national government, Northerners of both parties agreed on the need to stand by the flag and enforce the laws.[36]

✳ Such was the state of the compromise movement on January 10 when news of the fate of Anderson's reinforcements reached the North. The long-delayed mission had begun as a farce and ended as a debacle. On January 5, the same day the reinforcements had "secretly" left New York, a dispatch from Major Anderson reported that South Carolina forces were constructing a defensive battery on Morris Island, at the mouth of the harbor. That would not have caused much concern had not General Scott at the last minute convinced Buchanan that a warship like the *Brooklyn*, which for weeks had been waiting off of Fort Monroe, Virginia, for precisely this purpose, was too slow and heavy for the task. Buchanan had acquiesced, and Scott's personal aide had gone to New York and hired a side-wheel merchant steamer, the *Star of the West*, which, it was thought, could load its cargo more quietly, reach Charleston more quickly, and maneuver across the tricky channel bar more easily than the *Brooklyn*.

Now the situation had changed, for unlike the heavily armed *Brooklyn*, the unprotected *Star* would be at the mercy of the Morris Island guns.[37]

Since Anderson's message also asserted confidently that from their new position at Fort Sumter he and his men could "command this harbor as long as our Government wishes to keep it," the expedition's risk suddenly seemed unwarranted. Scott wired New York to stop the ship, but it was too late. Making matters worse, his letter informing the garrison that the ship was coming did not reach its destination in time. When the *Star of the West* steamed into Charleston harbor, Robert Anderson had no idea what was going on.[38]

The authorities at Charleston, on the other hand, were well aware. If the numerous reports from New York (both private and published) had not been enough to convince Governor Pickens of the destination and purpose of the *Star of the West*, an indignant Jacob Thompson had wired news of the mission as soon as he found out about it on the fifth, just before he resigned in protest. The result was predictable: as the ship maneuvered through the channel in the pale first light of Wednesday, January 9, the new Morris Island battery opened fire. The captain pushed on, but when Fort Sumter's guns remained silent he had no choice but to steam out of the harbor and back to New York.[39] Two potentially critical events had just occurred: Buchanan's long-delayed attempt to reinforce the Charleston garrison had failed spectacularly, and South Carolina forces had fired upon a ship bearing the flag of the United States. What significance either would have would depend on Buchanan's response, but to most of the country it was clear that if a state of war did not now exist, a long step in that direction had just been taken.

✳ Even before word of the expedition reached Washington, Crittenden's call for a national convention was getting nowhere. If he had any chance of moderate Republican support in those troubled days, which is doubtful, he had lost it by demanding that a peaceful resolution to the crisis include Republican acknowledgment that "no section of the country, has a right to set up its particular opinion on any subject as the image of orthodoxy, and say those who do not come up to this rule of orthodoxy shall not share with us in anything that belongs to this government." He added, unwisely, "The dogma of my State is that she has as much right to go into the Territories with her slaves as you, who do not choose to hold such property, have to go without them." His remarks confirmed Republican suspicions that Southerners would be satisfied with nothing less than their party's total abandonment of its core principles.[40] Three days later, when reports of the *Star of the West* came in, Republican opposition hardened. When Crittenden again brought his proposal before the Senate, New Hampshire radical Daniel Clark moved to substitute for it a resolution rejecting any need to amend the Constitution and insisting instead that existing laws be enforced. For the next week Republican stalwarts used a series of parliamentary tactics to postpone debate on Crittenden's plan.[41]

In this inflamed atmosphere, with momentum against compromise growing, William Seward finally decided that the time had come to step from behind the curtain and declare himself—at least partially. He announced that on January 12 he would address the Senate on the crisis. It is doubtful that he thought he could inspire renewed support for Republican concessions in Congress; his primary concern was to encourage unionism in the border slave states, where loyalists feared infection from the secession fever that was spreading so rapidly through the Deep South. Given Seward's great stature—further enhanced by the recent news that he would head Lincoln's cabinet—and his public silence to that point, his announcement caused a great stir. On the appointed day the galleries were packed to overflowing.

Most of Seward's address was an eloquent plea for calm and reason, to lay partisan concerns aside and unite in the only objective that mattered: preservation of the Union.[42] Only at the end did he make specific proposals, urging Congress to advocate repeal of the Northern states' personal liberty laws, send to the states a constitutional amendment forbidding any future amendment that gave Congress authority to interfere with slavery in the states, pass a law against invasions of states such as John Brown's, and construct two Pacific railroads, one North and one South. The core of his plan, though, was his recommendation for a constitutional convention to resolve the more substantive grievances between the sections—not immediately but "one, two, or three years hence," after current passions had died.[43]

As compromise proposals went, Seward's were tame. His conciliatory tone was applauded by both Northern and Southern conservatives, but the speech made no apparent impact on his Republican colleagues in the Senate: four days later, they succeeded in quashing the Crittenden plan by voting to substitute Clark's hard-line resolutions.[44] It appeared that a suddenly unanimous Republican opposition had finally defeated the most widely hailed plan of sectional compromise.

The weakness of Seward's proposals offers great insight into the limita tions conciliatory Republicans faced, especially in the wake of events at Charleston harbor, and more specifically, the restrictions placed upon the senator by his undefined relationship with Lincoln. Despite his grave concerns, Seward could do little but plead for time for emotions to cool. A brief line toward the end of his speech reveals his outlook: "We must be content to lead when we can, and to follow when we cannot lead," he noted, "and if we cannot do for our country all the good that we would wish, we must be satisfied with doing for her all the good that we can."[45] Ever the political realist, Seward had identified with great precision the awkward, tenuous, and ultimately helpless position he occupied throughout the crisis, a position that the early-January eruption of militant patriotism had suddenly made all too apparent to him.

✳ Meanwhile, far from the scene of action, the president-elect was still at work composing his cabinet; even in the frenzied days after Anderson's move to Sumter, momentous events in Charleston and Washington could not distract Lincoln from the impossibly tangled party considerations that continued to vex him. As Buchanan's advisers planned their reinforcement expedition and the proponents of compromise mounted their rearguard action in Congress, Lincoln was committing the first major blunder of his administration. It began on Sunday, December 30, the day after he rebuffed Duff Green's overture from the president, when he met with that "greatest of Pennsylvania wirepullers," Simon Cameron, about a place in the cabinet.[46]

Cameron was a natural candidate for an appointment. Pennsylvania, large, wealthy, and crucial to the Republican victory in November, was generally recognized to be entitled to representation on Lincoln's council, and Senator Cameron was generally recognized to be a major force— arguably *the* major force—in the Pennsylvania party. Although a hum of disapproval of the senator buzzed through the national Republican press, since the election Lincoln had received a steady flow of correspondence and visitors in support of him and virtually nothing in opposition. Moreover, although Lincoln's campaign managers, Davis and Swett, denied making any promises at the Chicago convention, Cameron's handlers understood their critical support for Lincoln's nomination to entail reciprocity from the incoming administration. To disappoint their expectations risked alienating a key faction of a powerful state.[47]

Still, Lincoln knew it would be a controversial appointment. For one thing, Cameron's easy movements from the Democracy to the Know-

Nothings to the Republicans had gained him a reputation as an unprincipled opportunist. More damaging was the taint of corruption that surrounded him. Known to his critics as "the Great Winnebago Chief" for his mishandling of Indian funds in the 1830s, Cameron was also charged with manipulating elections and legislatures through bribery. Yet so many recommendations for him poured into Springfield that Lincoln could hardly see how not to appoint him.[48] When Cameron impressed at Sunday's interview, Lincoln offered him a position, in writing, before he departed the next day.[49]

It was one of the first important choices Lincoln had made for himself since the election, and he immediately had cause to regret foregoing his usual practice of passing his decisions by Trumbull and Hamlin. The former, already hearing the rumors that had begun to circulate as soon as Cameron arrived in Springfield, wrote from the Senate chamber on Monday, "The probable appointment of Mr Cameron to the office of Sec. of Treasury, meets with the decided opposition of our truest friends in the Senate. . . . Not a Senator I have spoken with, thinks well of such an appointment."[50] Trumbull's judgment proved correct: word of the selection provoked a flood of outraged letters and visits from Republican leaders.

Displaying an indecision that was characteristic in those early months, Lincoln immediately reversed himself. A leader of Pennsylvania's formidable anti-Cameron faction, Alexander McClure, persuaded Lincoln that the appointment "would utterly demoralize both your administration and our party organization in this State." After speaking with McClure, Lincoln addressed a short, private note to Cameron rescinding his offer, considerately suggesting that the Pennsylvanian officially decline the offer in order to put the weight of public ridicule onto Lincoln's shoulders.[51] But Cameron had no intention of letting Lincoln off that easily. Proud of the plum he had won, and perhaps deliberately trying to make it difficult for Lincoln to retract the offer once the inevitable firestorm began, Cameron had already shown the letter to several friends, as well as to the Washington correspondent of the *New York Herald*; one irate congressman reported to Lincoln that he "has acted the fool completely—showing round your letter offering the place to him to any body and every body as a child would show a toy." Cameron simply ignored the second note. This stymied Lincoln: with the invitation public and its withdrawal confidential, the offer hung in limbo, subject to endless public speculation.[52]

To further complicate the situation, news of Seward's acceptance of the State Department had just begun to circulate. Since he and Cameron were widely considered to be allies and Bates, Lincoln's only other selection to that point, was a former Whig and emphatically conservative, it seemed to the radical/Old Democrat faction that their rivals were taking control of the administration. Thus the Cameron imbroglio immediately exploded into what one historian has called "a mighty battle of republican factions." The pro–Salmon Chase campaign shifted into high gear as radicals across the North sought to salvage what they could. The Seward-Cameron–David Davis forces mobilized in response. Between the two factions, the deluge of correspondence and visitors that fell upon Springfield in January dwarfed earlier efforts. For the next several weeks Republican managers throughout the North appeared considerably more concerned with the patronage than with secession.[53]

Of course, Lincoln had decided long before that Chase must be invited into the cabinet.[54] Now he made his first direct approach, meeting with the Ohioan two days after writing to Cameron. The interview went well; although no formal offer was made (Lincoln had learned that lesson), each was favorably impressed with the other. But the party's delicate condition made the situation exceedingly complex. Lincoln explained his bind in a frank letter to Trumbull. Placing Chase at the head of the Treasury Department, he wrote, seemed "a *necessity*" in order to reconcile William Cullen Bryant and the powerful New York radicals to Seward's appointment. So far, so good. But in order to balance Chase, a former Democrat whose opposition to a protective tariff would alienate Pennsylvania, "Gen. C[ameron] must be brought in to co-operate." Moreover, although Cameron's opponents had actually threatened "to send charges into the Senate to procure his rejection," Lincoln could not help but observe that "he is more amply recommended for a place in the cabinet, than any other man." On top of all that, Chase insisted to Lincoln and everyone else who raised the question that he did not wish a cabinet post at all, but intended to serve out the senatorial term to which he had just been elected. After meeting with him, Lincoln was fairly certain that Chase would accept an invitation, but he hesitated to take that risk, the Cameron fiasco having made both his own position and the party itself even more vulnerable than they had already been.[55]

Adding to his trouble was the long shadow of secession. While immovable on territorial compromise and the defense of federal authority, Lincoln was aware of the predicament of Southern unionists and the damage Republican rigidity might do their cause. Nominating Chase, a long-acknowledged leader of the radicals, would give secessionists a powerful weapon in their fight to convince Southerners of Republican hostility. Therefore, Lincoln also kept a close eye on Seward's efforts to recruit Congressman John Gilmer, whose appointment Seward believed would be of critical importance in defusing secession in the Upper South. But Gilmer was wary, mistrustful of Lincoln and reluctant to ally himself with an administration that might be opposed to the interests of his state and section. He spent several days discussing the situation with friends and colleagues in North Carolina, meanwhile urging Seward to find a more suitable candidate. Seward hid his anxiety and passed along several additional Southern names to Lincoln, but he feared that if Gilmer declined, Lincoln would follow his initial plan and appoint Maryland hard-liner Montgomery Blair. Gilmer refused to be hurried, and January passed without a definite answer.[56]

Still, Seward recognized that with Cameron's invitation he had scored an important win. Lincoln's next move, he knew, would likely involve a nod to the radicals. He was fortunate, then, that the battle soon reached such a pitch that Lincoln had enough. He made it known that he would make no more cabinet decisions until his arrival in Washington in late February.[57]

But even as compromise floundered in Congress and Lincoln labored to keep his party together without discouraging a precarious Southern unionism, another front was opening in the intensifying battle to determine the Northern response to secession: in the midst of the uproar over events at Charleston harbor, almost every Northern state legislature convened. Anxious observers watched closely to see how political leaders farther from Washington and closer to the people would react to disunion, and what kind of pressure the states would exert on Congress.

✳ For residents of Lincoln's hometown, there were more pressing events going on in early January than the endless parade of Republican notables. Since Springfield had been made the state capital in the 1830s, the legislative session was easily the most important time of year, commercially and socially, for the town; even now, when the presence of the president-elect had brought continuous national attention to Springfield, the convening of the legislature created an additional buzz of excitement. As usual at this time of year, the streets of the capital were crowded and the hotels full.[58]

The convening of this particular General Assembly occasioned more than common anxiety among partisans. The central concerns of leaders and activists in both parties were the same as those held in Washington and across the North: compromise, coercion, and party unity. Republicans, who held a relatively slim majority of forty-one to thirty-four in the House and a razor-thin edge of thirteen to twelve in the Senate, were particularly worried about infighting. Rumors swirled that Long John Wentworth was plotting revenge against Norman B. Judd over last summer's gubernatorial nomination fiasco, when Judd had sued Wentworth for libel, derailing both men's ambitions and resulting in the nomination of Richard Yates. Lyman Trumbull, Judd's ally, was up for reelection to the U.S. Senate, which at that time was decided not by popular vote but by the state legislatures. Wentworth was said to be conspiring with the Democrats to have Trumbull replaced.[59]

Leading Democrats, meanwhile, feared that their representatives would split on national affairs, with those from the more extreme southern region of the state resisting Douglas's firm stance against secession. The division was already sharp enough to prevent the Democrats from appearing on opening day, January 7, apparently for a last-minute caucus to try to settle on a common agenda. The chair of the state central committee reported to Douglas that the party was "terribly disorganized" and could not agree on resolutions. Illustrating the close ties that existed between national and state organizations, he desperately urged Douglas to contact "*all* of our leading men. *There must be no delay.*"[60]

The next morning the Democrats took their seats as if nothing had happened, and the first order of business in the House, selection of a Speaker, went smoothly. That, however, was the last thing to go according to schedule. Not waiting for the House to complete its organization, Democrat William Archer proposed adjourning in honor of the anniversary of Andrew Jackson's stirring victory in the Battle of New Orleans. In doing so he stirred up a hornet's nest.

Archer's move had two important goals: to buy more time for his party to align its views, and to establish the Democrats on firm Union ground and hopefully lure conservative Republicans away from their party's hardline position. His resolution deliberately placed Jackson and the battle into a broad national context. The preamble alluded only vaguely to the present state of the country, noting that "proper respect" for "our fathers" was "calculated to inspire the men of the present day with a true spirit of patriotism, and . . . thereby give all a more lively appreciation of the value of our glorious Union." The resolution described the battle merely as "an event memorable to the annals of American history" and recommended adjourning "in honor of the day and its hero."[61]

Jackson Day resolutions were standard practice, but they took on added meaning in the current national crisis. Since Lincoln's election, Andrew Jackson had become far and away the most ubiquitous historical reference in a culture steeped in historical thinking. In the late 1820s and 1830s, Jackson had been the symbolic figure around which the previous party system had first arranged itself, early Democrats and Whigs organizing in support or protest of the controversial leader, respectively. Now the falling away of the old issues and the rise of new, more immediate questions were sufficient to sweep away the partisan rancor of an earlier age and make Jackson accessible to all. As Northerners made the connection between the nullification crisis of 1832–33 and their own national woes, Jackson once more became a household name, celebrated for his angry refusal to countenance South Carolina's defiance of federal law.

Northerners of both parties summoned the memory of Jackson, especially as a standard that their own president was failing miserably to meet. Buchanan's vacillation led Northerners to cry, "Oh, for an hour of Old Hickory!" until that lament challenged Jackson's famous toast—"The Union—it must and shall be preserved!"—as the most oft-repeated sentiment of the crisis. But it was Republicans, especially, who embraced Jackson's strong stand. Party newspapers reprinted Jackson's forceful Nullification Proclamation, a copy of which Lincoln was reported to be reading in formulating his own views on the crisis, while editors, speakers, and correspondents urged their leaders to take "a firm Jackson stand" against secession and hoped that Lincoln would be "another Jackson."[62] And on January 8, all over the North, state and local leaders ordered commemorations of Jackson that made explicit connections to the current crisis. In Massachusetts, for example, newly inaugurated governor John Andrew ordered 100 guns fired on Boston Common in honor of the Battle of New Orleans and Major Anderson. In Chicago, Mayor Wentworth ordered business suspended that people might gather to express their devotion to the Union, with cannons firing and bells tolling throughout the day. Similar displays honored Jackson and Anderson in dozens of cities and towns from Maine to Michigan.[63]

It is impossible that Archer was unaware of the bellicose sectional overtones the memory of Jackson had assumed, but he appears to have underestimated the degree to which stalwart Republicans had co-opted his own party's hero and foremost symbol. Perhaps trying to preempt them, Archer remarked on the connection between Jackson and the current crisis, suggesting that the legislature "devote the rest of the day to recollection of one of our patriots . . . who saved his country from ruin in one of its darkest and most gloomy periods."

If Archer hoped that his oblique reference to the crisis would satisfy his rivals in the House, they quickly set him straight. "All that Gen. Jackson did behind the cotton bales at New Orleans," declared Republican John Y. Scammon, to the applause of his colleagues, "was as nothing compared with what he did in the Presidential chair, to preserve the integrity of the Union and enforce the Constitution and the laws." He immediately moved to amend the resolution so as to make the subtle reference to secession overt. To Archer's suggestion to adjourn "in honor of the day and its hero," Scammon proposed adding, "and of his firmness and devotion, patriotism, and unflinching courage and determination in enforcing the Constitution and laws against all resistance, from whatever quarter it might come."[64]

Scammon's amendment infused the resolution with a strong tinge of coercion, and Democrats remonstrated with him to withdraw it. Archer's "old-fashioned" resolution, pleaded William H. Green, would enable the House to celebrate the day unanimously. Perceiving their rivals' vulnerability, Republicans turned the debate into a question of loyalty versus treason. Harvey Hogg offered his hope that "our Democratic friends" would "stand shoulder to shoulder in maintaining the Union, in upholding the Constitution, and enforcing the laws," while Lawrence Weldon expressed astonishment that the party of Jackson could oppose the amendment. It was patently obvious that "old-fashioned resolutions will not suit today," Weldon exclaimed. "We are now situated with treason, disunion, and civil war stalking through parts of our land." Jackson's "saving us from a domestic foe" was as worthy of celebration as his "saving us from a foreign foe."

Democrat H. M. Vandeveer retorted indignantly that times certainly had changed when patriotism entailed the celebration of triumph over one's brother. He and his colleagues also expressed regret that Republicans had introduced partisanship into the debate. However, given the turn the discussion had taken, no Republican was likely to vote against the amendment. Democrats decided to make the best of it. After registering a final protest, Green offered an amendment to Scammon's amendment, one that pointed out in no uncertain terms what it was that the Republicans insisted upon celebrating in the nation's moment of trial. If the Democrats could not win over any conciliatory Republicans, at least they could make their rivals' belligerence clear to the people—while still going on record as having supported the resolution.

Both amendments were accepted, and the resolution was adopted unanimously. It read as follows (with the amendments indicated in brackets): "*Resolved*, that this day, the 8th day of January, being the anniversary of the battle of New Orleans, an event memorable to the annals of American history, we will adjourn in honor of the day and its hero, [and of his firmness and devotion, patriotism, and unflinching courage and determination in enforcing the Constitution and laws against all resistance, from whatever quarter it might come] [as expressed in his proclamation to the people in 1832; the sentiments of which we heartily endorse] till tomorrow morning at nine o'clock."

The Illinois Assembly's controversy over the Jackson resolutions was indicative of the discord that would prevail in legislatures across the North. Although formal division over such issues generally followed party lines, maintaining unity was a struggle for both parties. Both played to the rising antiparty sentiment, accusing the other of engaging in "political maneuvers" and placing party dogma over the fate of the Union.[65] And over and over again, debate over seemingly innocuous, unrelated matters came back to secession and coercion.[66]

✳ Coercion was the primary source of contention in the legislatures, especially in the wake of the Charleston harbor seizures. Throughout the North it threatened to obscure party lines. In the New York legislature, which convened on January 2, a Republican, Assemblyman Lucius Robinson, wasted no time in declaring for compromise, introducing a set of resolutions recommending that Congress admit Kansas as a free state and divide the remaining territories into two large states, to be admitted under whatever constitutions their residents submitted. Meanwhile, a Democrat, Senator Francis B. Spinola, calling on his colleagues to lay party aside and unite in support of the Union and Constitution, introduced resolutions declaring it the "religious" and "patriotic" duty of all states to preserve the Union, and instructing Governor Morgan to offer the state's military resources to the president for that purpose.[67]

Over the following days a rough pattern emerged. As various legislators offered a steady stream of resolutions relative to the crisis (one overzealous assemblyman went so far as to move that every member who had not already presented Union-saving resolutions must do so),[68] it became apparent that the most vocal Republicans, at least, held to a hard-line position. That was due largely to the impassioned atmosphere of early January, but also to the Democratic caucus's support for Robinson's resolutions; in any case, only a few of Robinson's colleagues followed his lead, at least publicly. The same was true of Spinola's; despite the excitement in South Carolina, most Democrats remained committed to a peaceful resolution of the crisis.[69]

The Robinson and Spinola resolutions drew the most attention, both in and out of the legislature, but for the time being all of the various crisis resolutions were submitted to a select committee in each chamber. However, when the first rumors of the attack on the *Star of the West* reached Albany on January 10, Spinola immediately interrupted the Senate's regular business to urge that his resolutions be taken up in a special session that evening. If the reports should prove true, he exclaimed, "not a moment should be lost in arming the State, and thus demonstrating to the people of the whole country . . . that on the question of preserving the Union and upholding the majesty of our National laws, New York is a unit." His fellow Democrats were less enthusiastic, and debate over his motion quickly sank into an exchange of personal attacks and charges of treason. Finally, Spinola withdrew his motion, cutting off debate.[70]

The next day action in the Assembly precluded the resumption of conflict in the Senate. Speaker of the House Dewitt C. Littlejohn opened the day's session by presenting a set of resolutions that, although careful to express "gratitude and admiration" to Upper South unionists, openly declared Southern seizures of federal property to be "treasonable" and charged that with the attack on the *Star of the West* "the insurgent State of South Carolina" had "virtually declared war." The resolutions directed the governor to offer the president "whatever aid in men and money he may require to enable him to enforce the laws and uphold the authority of the Federal Government." With no debate the House passed the resolutions 101 to 27; remarkably, when the roll was called, the number of assemblymen willing to have their names recorded in opposition dwindled to two, both of them New York City Democrats.[71] The resolutions were conveyed to the Senate, which despite the rancor of the previous day unanimously suspended its own business and adopted them by a vote of twenty-eight to one. The resolutions official, copies were then ordered sent to the president and the other states.[72]

As it did in Congress and among officials and private citizens across the North, news of the *Star of the West* had welded the New York legislature into a virtually unanimous body behind the issue of upholding federal authority. Similar legislative battles across the North produced a spate of such patriotic resolutions, many inspired by New York's. As in Albany, the

Massachusetts General Court and Ohio General Assembly declared secession to be revolution, praised Southern unionists, and offered the president the manpower and financial resources of their states for the maintenance of the Constitution and the laws. Wisconsin lawmakers went further and simply adopted the New York preamble and resolutions as a whole. The Minnesota legislature echoed the prevailing themes in even more forceful language, expressing "astonishment and indignation" at South Carolina's "outrages" and demanding that the federal government make "the strongest and most vigorous effort to assert its supremacy, and to check the work of rebellion and treason." Even conservative Pennsylvania offered military aid to the federal government, denouncing as treasonous "all plots, conspiracies and warlike demonstrations against the United States," calling for their suppression, and quoting Andrew Jackson's characterization of secession as "repugnant" to American principles. Only in New Jersey and Rhode Island did conciliatory forces prevail, and the New Jersey legislature made a point of declaring that the Union was not a mere compact and that "to stand by and sustain" it was "the duty of every good citizen."[73]

✳ The crisis had evolved rapidly in the month and a half since Congress had convened, too rapidly for most Northerners to grasp fully. Still, by the middle of January it appeared that two critical questions had been answered. First, it seemed certain that congressional Republicans would not compromise on the key issue of slavery in the western territories. The furthest they had indicated any willingness to go was admission of the present territories as states, which would not so much settle as sidestep the contested question of slavery's rights. Given Southerners' determination to guarantee their access to the national domain and Republicans' resolve to prevent slavery's extension, that seemed to be the best that could reasonably be hoped for; the strength of feeling on each side of the issue likely made it impossible to resolve the question politically. However, after what virtually all Northerners perceived as South Carolina's aggression at Charleston harbor, Republican ranks closed against even that concession.

Second, with or without such a compromise, it appeared inevitable that the entire Deep South would follow the Palmetto State out of the Union; indeed, by January 20 four more states had already done so. Moreover, the Upper South seemed poised to follow. The potential calamity that threatened to attend large-scale disunion had been starkly prefigured in Charleston harbor, where South Carolina forces had taken the seemingly irrevocable steps of commandeering federal property and firing upon a U.S.

ship. To give additional force to that shocking vision of things to come, secessionist forces were daily seizing more federal property throughout the cotton states, even before their states formally seceded. Those actions roused the Northern people to a fervent commitment to the defense of the Union and placed tremendous pressure on the president to respond boldly. By mid-January, not only had the escalation of tensions swamped the movement for compromise in a rush of pro-Union zeal, but it also threatened to make the entire issue of compromise irrelevant by forcing President Buchanan to respond to actions that many Northerners interpreted as the opening shots of civil war.

The crisis had reached an important crossroads, and the direction it would take next depended entirely upon James Buchanan. If the president chose to interpret the attack on the *Star of the West* as an act of war and called out the military and the militia to put down the Southern rebellion, the emotional climate in the North indicated that Republicans and most Democrats would rally to defend national authority and federal property, and war would result. If he did not—if Buchanan somehow patched together another armistice and the fragile standoff resumed—it was already apparent that conciliationists would press once more for some sort of compromise. The question then would be whether the hard-liners could maintain public fervor as the immediacy of the events at Charleston harbor faded and secession continued to spread.

Chapter 6 ✳ One's Opinions Change Fast in Revolutionary Times ✳ January–February

For several tense days following South Carolina's attack on the *Star of the West*, the country stood poised on the threshold of war. With mass Union rallies, letter-writers, and editors of all parties calling for the defense of the flag, the president would have had no trouble finding popular support for a military response. Once Buchanan chose to acquiesce in a makeshift truce at Charleston harbor, however, the furor passed with surprising rapidity.

As the immediate danger of war receded, conciliationist leaders searched desperately for a peaceful way to salvage the Union. With secession now a reality in the Deep South, they shifted to a new objective: if the border slave states were prevented from seceding, they argued, the Southern confederacy was bound to fail and the cotton states would return. However, any sign of federal belligerence would drive the Upper South out, producing a fifteen-state confederacy far too large and powerful to conquer and rendering disunion irreversible. Such arguments found a receptive audience; popular sympathy for a peaceful settlement of the crisis rose steadily. By late January, a majority of Northerners favored some form of compromise.

January also witnessed a marked change in the manner in which the North responded to secession. Already the convening of Northern state legislatures had opened a new medium for discussion. Although they were not subject to the same level of scrutiny as congressional negotiations, the debates, speeches, and resolutions issuing from the state capitals were closely observed by party leaders and constituents alike. But the focus remained on Washington. There, congressional committee deliberations gave way to floor debates, rendering discussion of the complex issues involved in secession much more open and thus even more subject to public pressure. This public discussion of compromise combined with an emotional reaction to the brush with war to raise the level of concern among Northerners. Popular involvement increased, not only through letter-writing but also through petition drives and mass meetings.

Yet as the weeks passed with no positive action, the passion generated by Fort Sumter and the *Star of the West* largely dissipated amid all the talking, demonstrating once again that although at times the people could wield a powerful influence over their representatives, those at the top controlled the machinery of government and party, and hence the process of decision. It was James Buchanan who decided not to pursue further military action. It was Abraham Lincoln who prevented any substantive concessions. By mid-February, conciliationists were coming to realize their powerlessness. With the congressional session running down and Lincoln's inauguration approaching, long frustration led many into a kind of war-weary lethargy.

✳ Even as Union meetings and state legislatures across the North pledged to support President Buchanan in his defense of federal authority, the administration's new stance faltered as soon as Major Anderson made another unexpected move, this time agreeing to a temporary armistice with the South Carolina forces. The attack on the *Star of the West* had been followed immediately by an exchange of threatening letters between Anderson and Governor Pickens in which each blamed the other for instigating hostilities. Anderson backed down, determined to avoid civil war if possible. He persuaded Pickens to maintain the status quo until the incident had been reviewed in Washington.[1]

Upon hearing of the truce two days later, Buchanan expressed frustration. Anderson, he complained, had tied his hands at a time when, with South Carolina's military preparations incomplete, U.S. forces stood a better chance of repulsing an attack than they would at any time in the future. Despite his protestations, the president was doubtless relieved: still caught in the same dilemma that had paralyzed him for over a month, he realized that any further conflict not only would risk an immediate, all-out war but would probably wreck any possibility of congressional compromise and thereby defeat hopes for a diplomatic resolution to the crisis. Once more his instinct for caution prevailed. The decisive factor, Buchanan concluded, was Anderson's covenant, a gentleman's agreement by which he was bound, for now at least. He would wait until Governor Pickens's messenger arrived with a demand for Fort Sumter's surrender. He would then reject it, ending the armistice honorably and freeing him to proceed with reinforcement plans—if the political situation permitted.[2]

Once more, Buchanan had let his opportunity to take a firm stance slip away. A number of Southern congressional leaders intercepted Pickens's representative, Isaac Hayne, and convinced him to hold onto the governor's belligerent letter for awhile. Meanwhile, they attempted to negotiate a long-term truce whereby South Carolina would agree not to attack the fort if Buchanan pledged not to attempt another reinforcement—the same bargain, in effect, that they thought they had made in early December. Buchanan again refused to commit to any agreement, but it was early February before Hayne presented the letter and gave the president an opportunity to reject its surrender demand. By that time, over three weeks had passed since the *Star of the West* was fired upon, and the forces that surrounded Fort Sumter had been strengthened considerably.[3]

Oddly enough, it was at about that time that the administration did agree to a similar truce at Fort Pickens in Pensacola harbor, Florida, the only other significant Southern fort not yet commandeered by the seceding states. Almost overlooked during the excitement at Charleston, Florida forces had seized the Pensacola Navy Yard and driven Lt. Adam Slemmer and his small garrison into Fort Pickens, which was, like Sumter, an island fortification. Two weeks later, on January 24, the sloop-of-war *Brooklyn*— the same ship that was originally to have carried the reinforcements for Fort Sumter—steamed out of Fort Monroe, Virginia, with a company of troops bound for Pensacola. When it arrived on February 6, though, the soldiers remained on board. While they were en route, Buchanan agreed to the same conditions for Pickens that Anderson had arranged at Sumter: there would be no attempt to reinforce the fort unless it were attacked. Again, the president's primary concern was diplomatic: although congressional attempts at compromise once more seemed to have failed, a national peace conference (which is discussed in the next chapter) was scheduled to commence in Washington on February 4. Hopes for a peaceful conclusion to the crisis now centered on this convention; Buchanan did not wish to undermine it before it began.[4]

The difference between the two forts was that Pickens was positioned in such a way that it could be reinforced at any time from the sea. At Fort Sumter, however, the harbor's geography and the growing strength of the South Carolina forces prevented a naval expedition's getting through to the fort without falling under heavy fire—thus Buchanan's frustration at Anderson's truce, which gave the South Carolinians more time to build up their defenses. Indeed, although Anderson continued to deny any need for reinforcements, his dispatches grew less confident as the weeks went by. On February 6, as the *Brooklyn* was arriving outside Pensacola harbor, he reported to the War Department, "They are, I expect, pretty nearly ready over there. God grant that these people may not make the attack which they have so long threatened." The next day he wrote ominously that the anticipated arrival of three rifled cannon "would make our position much less secure than I have considered it."[5] Nevertheless, despite the daily shrinking of options regarding the fort, the president could not but have been relieved as the days passed and the cries for war ebbed. Regardless of public opinion, he had yet avoided open hostilities.

✳ The assault on the *Star of the West* had rallied Northerners to an impassioned defense of the flag, but as days and then weeks went by with no further action, the powerful combination of a brush with war, the rapid spread of secession throughout the Gulf states, and the widely hailed efforts of Senators Crittenden and Douglas reinvigorated conciliationists' search for some kind of peaceful resolution. Enthusiasm was strengthened among Democrats by their leaders' renewed arguments that Republican radicalism was to blame for both the crisis and the failure to find a compromise, which made them appear as much the aggressors as the secessionists. For it was plain that the question of who had been the aggressor was the operative factor in the patriotic outburst of late December and early January. That brief solidarity revealed that most opponents of coercion would leap to defend federal authority and national honor against Southern attack. Had Buchanan responded vigorously, they would have stood behind him in the resulting war. When he did not, a great many Northerners returned to their opposition to coercion, with the overtone of aggression the word implied.

To hard-liners, on the other hand, South Carolina's actions were a deliberate attack on the national government and deserved immediate reprisal; they were surprised when Northern unanimity in condemning the Southerners did not last. As pressure for compromise grew stronger than ever, not only from the opposition but also within their own party, the result was polarization and growing bitterness over compromise and the use of force.

In Albany, for example, in the wake of the legislature's militant resolutions, Democrats and a handful of conciliatory Republicans redoubled their efforts to map out a clear distinction between supporting disunion and advocating compromise. The day after supporting the Littlejohn resolutions, House Democrats objected to a Republican resolution to honor Major Anderson, which would have included presenting the officer with a sword, a gesture typical of such resolutions across the North. They proposed a substitute resolution approving the major's "bold and patriotic act" and supporting the president "in all constitutional measures to enforce the law & preserve the Union," but argued that for the sake of Upper South unionists, "who, if they stand with us, will secure the safety of the Union," New York should not present "a sword, which looks like an emblem of war." Enough moderate Republicans accepted the argument that the House failed to pass the resolutions.[6]

That kind of Republican sympathy would place tremendous pressure on party integrity over the next weeks. That same day, for example, the Senate found itself mired in debate over whether to agree with the House to form a joint committee on the crisis. Republican radicals objected that the move was merely a scheme to force the Senate to consider the conciliatory Robinson resolutions, which, along with numerous other crisis proposals, were still being considered by the House's crisis committee. (Robinson, it will be recalled, was a Republican himself.) The exchange that followed illustrates the hostility that marked similar debates throughout the North. Even as they jockeyed for political position and accused each other of placing party ahead of country, the two sides differed so widely, so genuinely, that at times each seemed incapable of even understanding the other.

Shocked hard-liners wondered at even discussing compromise: what had happened to the unity of the previous day, when the parties had joined in offering the state's money, resources, and men for the cause of Union? "There was nothing said then of abandoning principles, but a determination was evinced to put down rebellion and punish traitors," noted Senator Samuel Hammond. Republican stalwarts such as Hammond could not see how unionism and compromise could coexist: "I love the Union," the senator avowed, "but if the election of a President in the constitutional way . . . is to be seized upon as a pretext to force us to abandon those principles, then rather than that, let the Union be dissolved." Democrats saw things differently, for both ideological and political reasons. Scandalized by Hammond's extremism and seeing an opportunity to cut conciliatory Republicans from the herd, they were quick to point out the treasonous implications of such views and beg their opponents to denounce them.[7]

Attempting to regain control of the discussion, moderate Republicans followed the strategy of their colleagues all over the North: shying away from Hammond's radical belligerence, they tried to shift the terms of the debate to the need to enforce the laws. At that point Senator Spinola, with his impeccable unionist credentials, explained a crucial distinction that informed most anti-Republicans' opposition to coercion, a distinction that three months later would fundamentally shape the crisis's outcome. He retorted, "Sir, every Democrat in the Empire State is in favor of enforcing the laws, but if it is sought to place them on the abolition and disunion platform of Greeley, then they say to you fight this war of your own seeking yourselves. You will have enough of it, for you will not meet with opposition in the South alone, but all over the country. On the other hand if the object is the high and holy one of saving the country and preserving its unity, then the Democracy will wheel into line and save it, as they have done before."[8]

As in Congress, in Illinois, and around the North, the Democrats' efforts were in vain. Republican tensions were real and obvious; the entire question, after all, arose from the radicals' objecting to a joint committee that they thought endorsed a fellow Republican's compromise resolutions. But in the wake of the clash at Charleston harbor, conciliatory Republicans were unwilling to break with their party. When the hard-liners pressed, they fell into line. In Albany, the conciliationists who had extended a hand across the aisle over a sword for Anderson now backed down. The question of a joint committee was tabled.

✳ Meanwhile, in legislatures across the North, the abstract question of using force against disunion manifested in concrete proposals, usually involving preparation of state militias for the defense of Washington. In Illinois, the issue of coercion had first arisen indirectly through the Jackson Day skirmish, but the real battle raged over the militia bill that Republicans proposed two days later. Publicly, they merely noted that the militia was outdated, inefficient, and falling behind the reforms enacted in other states.[9] Privately, however, they drew an explicit connection to secession: with tensions escalating at Charleston harbor and secession spreading across the Deep South and possibly into the border slave states, the North needed to be prepared militarily.[10]

Moderate Democrats, reluctant to place the party in a seeming anti-Union position, publicly accepted Republican assurances that the militia bill was not aimed at the current crisis and focused their criticism on the more traditional issues it raised, such as the added expense and an expansion of the governor's authority.[11] However, their radical colleagues denounced the bill as an irresponsible act of belligerence. It was clearly intended "to whip South Carolina into submission," and if Republicans tried to use it so, some warned, they would "first . . . have to whip one hundred and forty-six thousand democrats at home."[12]

Similar debates were occurring in several other Northern states. In Massachusetts, where the militia had already been overhauled (and was now serving as a model for other states' efforts), the legislature debated an increase in the size of the volunteer force in response to the crisis. The primary issue for that overwhelmingly Republican body was not whether an increase would be instituted, but how large it would be and whether the new regiments would remain in place until the governor disbanded them or would have to be renewed by the legislature each year.[13] Other, more politically competitive states tended to follow the pattern of the New York Senate's fight over a joint compromise committee: that is, partisan conflict and significant intraparty divisions combined to produce an unstable structure in which both sides maneuvered to exploit each other's very real vulnerability. In Albany itself, for example, a bill authorizing half a million dollars for equipping the militia passed in the Senate but bogged down in the House when Democrats appealed to conservative Republicans not to antagonize Southern unionists.

The mix of vicious partisan warfare and blurring party boundaries that increasingly marked the Northern political landscape can perhaps best be seen in the ongoing melee in Springfield. There, while Republicans and Democrats traded charges of disunionism in the legislature and the pages of the local party newspapers,[14] moderate Democrats struggled to control the deep divisions that the question of coercion was causing. The issue came to a head on January 16 at the state party convention, where the resolutions committee took from midafternoon until almost nine o'clock that night to agree on a set of principles. Through all that time, the delegates waited without the usual orations; organizers feared that speakers "might provoke discussion." When resolutions were finally presented, they were adopted unanimously (as resolutions at political conventions and rallies almost always were), but even after all the hours of negotiation the more radical members of the committee were said not to endorse them.[15]

The radicals' precise grievance is not clear, but it could not have been a waffling on the issue of force—on the contrary, some conservative Democrats were put off by the resolutions' assertion that "the employment of military force by the federal government to coerce the seceding states, will inevitably plunge the country into civil war, and entirely extinguish all hope of a settlement of the fearful issue now pending before the country." Moreover, echoing Douglas's recent embrace of the reviled Buchanan doctrine, the convention denied the federal government's authority to use the military to enforce the law within a state "except in aid of the civil authorities." On the other hand, it may have been the stern denial of any constitutional right of secession that rankled the radicals, or perhaps the anticoercion resolution's failure to advocate resistance to Northern aggression. Or maybe they felt that the resolutions as a whole simply did not put enough emphasis on coercion, for they covered an array of issues. They went on to advocate compromise (Douglas's, Crittenden's, the border-state plan, or any other "by which harmony might be restored"), to affirm the federal government's obligation to protect the property rights of slave-owners, to denounce personal liberty laws as unconstitutional, to urge that a convention of the states discuss the crisis and recommend a settlement, and finally, to recommend that the state legislature ask Congress to call a constitutional convention and press other states to do likewise. Whatever the case, although the party had managed to unite formally on the general ground of conciliation and opposition to coercion, the backroom arguments and lingering resentments reveal a broad range of views and a reluctance to compromise them.[16]

Although Charles Lanphier's *Illinois State Register* lauded the resolutions' "temperate tone, wise counsel and sound constitutional doctrine," Republicans were quick to live up to his and McClernand's prediction that they would label anything smacking of conciliation as unpatriotic. Edward Baker, editor of the rival *Illinois State Journal*, introduced his editorial the next day with bold headlines proclaiming, "Secession justified! Treason aided and comforted! General Jackson's doctrine repudiated!" He demanded caustically, "Will somebody be kind enough to point out to us the difference in sentiment between the South Carolina traitors who are trampling under foot the American flag, violating Federal law, seizing Federal forts, firing upon Federal vessels, and the leaders of the Democratic convention of Illinois who apologise for it all and who say there is no power to prevent it?" "If there is a difference," he concluded, "we are unable to perceive it." Much of this was political posturing, of course, but his incomprehension, like that of Samuel Hammond in the New York Senate, was sincere. To him and other Republican hard-liners, the issue was a clear-cut one of treason versus loyalty. Other stalwarts echoed his righteous anger privately. "The great mass of the Democrats are at heart secessionists," editor Charles H. Ray, another member of the radical Judd faction, raved to Trumbull. "You will see the resolutions. . . . They are portentious indeed."[17]

While Republican stalwarts delighted in exploiting their rival's vulnerability on the loyalty issue, the Democrats' emphasis on the dangers of civil war was taking its toll on Republicans. For all the thunderous indignation of the hard-liners, conciliatory sentiment was growing and their party, too, was having trouble maintaining unity. Judd was troubled by the Democrats' plan to "put themselves in the condition of Union Savers by concession." Republicans in the legislature were dividing, he observed: conciliationists were "raging on the subject of the Republican party standing still when they say it might by some simple concession serve the border Slave States," while "some of our true men [that is, hard-liners] are restless to say the least of it, of our position" of masterly inactivity. As a result, "some of our friends fear a loosening of the ties of party unless there is some action." Others also commented on the resurgence of conciliationism, several predicting that the legislature would endorse the border-state plan "if introduced by any republican," a move that would cause a serious rupture in the party.[18]

It did not take long for the conciliatory reaction to have an impact. As the militia bill stagnated in committee, the Republican caucus continued to wrangle over crisis resolutions like those passed earlier by New York and other Northern states. Anxious conciliationists pushed for the state to speak out in favor of the border-state plan, while stalwarts resisted any concession at all. Moderates tried to find middle ground with resolutions offering to attend a constitutional convention if another state were to call it. However, even after they added clauses denying that Illinois actually wanted to amend the Constitution and, like New York, offering the president aid for the enforcement of the laws, hard-liners continued to object. Inevitably, the caucus's "protracted & warm" debates over compromise spilled into the Assembly: on January 14, Republican Ruben Blades presented resolutions supporting a variation on the so-called Corwin-Adams plan to admit the existing territories as states. It was sent to committee with the other resolutions, but the quarrel was plainly coming to a head.[19]

Both parties were fighting to maintain a fragile unity in the face of a rapidly changing political environment. Struggling to reconcile a wide disparity on the contentious question of force, the Democracy tried to unite on a procompromise position and cast their rivals as fanatical warmongers. The Republicans, who had been universally deaf to Democrats' pleas for "traditional," secession-neutral Jackson Day resolutions just two weeks earlier, now found themselves divided on the far weightier matter of a national compromise, to the point that some feared that conservative members might bolt and join the Democrats.[20]

The Illinois experience was not unique, nor even uncommon: in legis latures throughout the North, procompromise sentiment was gaining momentum even while patriotic commitment to federal authority remained strong. At all levels of government, in fact, the two parties found themselves rocked not only by divisions among elected officials but also by widespread and increasingly strident demands from the rank and file for both firmness and conciliation. In this new, highly charged post-Sumter phase of the crisis, pressure was growing swiftly—the question was, in which direction would the greater force be exerted?

✳ As Northern opinion underwent a dramatic shift in the wake of the war scare, so, too, did the means by which it was expressed. Although state government was still cherished in the mid-nineteenth century as representing the most effective combination of size and accountability to the people, Northerners were not content to let their legislatures be the sole or even the primary means by which their will was communicated to Congress. From the middle of January to the end of February, hundreds of thousands of Northerners acted to influence the federal government's handling of the crisis themselves. We have already seen the direct impact that a rash of hard-line correspondence had on Republican members of the Committee of Thirty-three in late December and early January. In subsequent weeks, ordinary Northerners of both parties sustained the massive volume of correspondence while their demands, whether for compromise or for firmness, grew increasingly shrill and their views more extreme.[21]

That torrent of individual voices was matched by a deluge of petitions and mass-meeting resolutions that inundated Washington over the final six weeks of the congressional session. Determined that their voices be heard, concerned citizens held Union meetings—both sides claiming the label—in cities and towns across the North; almost every day members of Congress presented fresh memorials favoring or opposing compromise, advocating or denouncing the use of force. Republican stalwarts petitioned against the extension of slavery, against repeal of fugitive slave laws, against the Crittenden proposals, or simply against compromise. Most often they simply demanded enforcement of the laws, a vague but powerful cry that had become the position of choice for hard-liners as pressure for compromise grew.

As impressive as they were, however, the offerings of the anticompromise movement were outshone by the surge of petitions, memorials, and resolutions on the other side. Conciliationists, taking care to spotlight the cooperation of local Republicans whenever possible, pleaded for the border-state plan, for the various proposals of Douglas or other senators, or for a national convention to amend the Constitution, and a remarkable number simply begged for a resolution of the disturbed state of the country. But far and away the most favored form of conciliation—the most prevalent subject of petitions and resolutions, period—was the Crittenden plan. Although most popular in the conservative border states of Pennsylvania, New Jersey, and Ohio, it drew support from the citizens of small towns and large cities and from political conventions, Union rallies, municipal governments, workingmen's organizations, and volunteer fire companies from Maine to Wisconsin.[22]

Amid the wild charges and mutual recriminations, the heated threats, heartfelt appeals, and impassioned denunciations of these letters, resolutions, and petitions, a pattern emerged. Under the ever-growing pressure of events—Congress's byzantine tug-of-war over compromise, the Deep South's formal acts of secession and seizures of federal property, South Carolina's attack on the *Star of the West*, and not least, the rising volume of Northern public opinion itself—the confusion, uncertainty, and anxious silence of November evolved into fairly plain and unabashedly outspoken alternatives. In private and public letters, in resolutions and petitions, in editorials, speeches, and sermons, even in diaries, the same basic ideas were being expressed by Northerners in all states and at all levels of public life, from ordinary citizens on up. The vast array of issues being debated in November and December had now settled down, for the most part, to two: compromise—not any one in particular so much as the desirability of compromise itself—and the use of armed force against secession. Any middle ground became more and more untenable. The North had become polarized.

Hard-liners still comprised the overwhelming majority of Republicans, especially outside of Washington. They continued to maintain that their party had nothing to concede, having committed no offense greater than winning a constitutional election. A Minnesota editor explained rhetorically, "What Republican believes the principles enunciated in the Chicago platform to be a violation of the rights of the South? None. What, then, have we done of which we need be ashamed, or from which we should recede? Nothing."[23]

In addition, hard-liners continued to assert resentfully that "concession *now*, is a premium upon treason," for compromise in the face of threats would merely encourage the traitors and ensure similar tactics in the future. "Why don't [the compromisers] see that all our troubles arise from the fact that past concessions have encouraged false constructions of the Constitution & invited new aggressions[?]" one frustrated writer grumbled in a typical complaint. Most agreed with another's assessment that "had the North never made any concession, the South would long since have ceased making demands; and we shall never have any *permanent peace* u[n]til we compel the South to respect us, and look upon us as their equals—which they do not now." The concern with respect was widespread; stalwarts' arguments were frequently undergirded by a sense of threatened honor, a belief that the party's, the North's, and the country's collective manhood could not tolerate a "humiliating surrender" to Southern threats. One irate constituent expressed this common sentiment thus: "Let the Aristocracy of the South understand for once there is some Back bone in the north, and that if there is some *traitors* to their Interest, that they are not all Sycophants and Lick Spittles, ready to do the Behests of the Chivalry even to the destruction of our government and to the annihilation of the constitution."[24]

To most Republicans, the idea of even discussing concessions in the face of armed rebellion was outrageous; they tried to deflect pressure for conciliation with demands that the government enforce the laws. That attitude reflected a powerful strain within popular political thought, for Northerners believed that only the rule of law protected individual liberty and equality of opportunity from the dangers of government tyranny on the one side and social anarchy on the other—hence the widespread belief that, as one correspondent phrased it, "the duty of maintaining just government is as sacred and binding as that of maintaining our hearths and altars; it is the same thing." It also represented a surviving relic of the Revolutionary-era principle that the survival of a republic depended upon the virtue of its citizens—or rather, as this idea was updated by a party activist in Illinois, that "insubordination to law, is the destruction of this or any other Republic."[25]

Given the centrality of the principle of law and order, it stood to reason that no matter how one felt about the legitimacy of Southern grievances or the need for Northern concessions, secession—especially when accompanied by the seizure of federal property—represented a shocking violation of the law, a "torrent of disunion and lawless violence." The notion that secession was a legitimate right was "absurd" not just to Republicans but to most Northerners: it was Democrat John McClernand who predicted that "it would lead to a subversion of all order, government and stability. It would inaugurate a reign of anarchy, confusion and chaos which would ingulf in utter ruin the dearest interests of society." Secession's breach of this deeply cherished value is what led many hard-liners to agree with the Massachusetts Republican who declared that secessionists' even making demands of the North "attack[s] the fundamental principles of republican liberty." "It is not the Union only which is in danger," explained Edward Baker in the *Illinois State Journal*;

> deeper down than that lies the great principle of Constitutional Government, upon which this Union is founded, and without which "the Union cannot permanently endure" . . . the assumption of power by a constitutional majority. Now we insist that any surrender of the nature demanded, to any lawless combination acting in defiance of the Constitution and the laws, can amount to nothing less than a subversion of the very foundation upon which this Government is erected; and those who stand up manfully, refusing to make the surrender, are taking the only course that can surely save the Union from destruction.[26]

That sense of violation also accounted for the rapidity with which Northern resentment more generally had boiled over when South Carolina's secession—enacted, as Charles Francis Adams had noted, without bothering to make any formal grievances, without waiting to see if the North would offer to assuage its concerns, and without formally consulting even its own people—was followed almost immediately by the confiscation of Charleston's arsenal, customhouse, and other forts and the use of armed force against a ship carrying U.S. troops and displaying the U.S. flag. With those actions secessionists went beyond an "empty paper declaration" and committed treason. "All the old questions of slavery in the territories, admission of States or return of fugitives vanish with the smoke of the first gun fired at Charleston," a Connecticut editor wrote. "One issue confronts us: Shall the majority of Law and the authority of government be vindicated, or have we mob-law and anarchy?"[27]

Yet most Northerners, including a growing minority of Republicans, believed that it was possible to uphold government authority and still offer concessions. The most pressing consideration behind the massive resurgence of procompromise support was fear that disunion would spread to the Upper South. Conciliationists argued that the hard-liners' intransigence was playing into the hands of secessionists, for the Union could still be preserved peacefully if the Upper South could be wooed into rejecting secession. The logic behind that sentiment varied: a Philadelphia diarist feared that if Virginia and Maryland left, "the seceders would possess

Washington & would be powerful enough to form a great confederacy"; an official in the Buchanan administration predicted that a check of disunionism in the border slave states "would dampen the ardor of the rebels . . . further South"; a Republican business leader in New York worried that unless Northerners believed every effort had been made to retain the border slave states, there would be no "unanimity in support of the gov't in the event of a civil war." But the most popular expression was of a belief that the Deep South could not survive alone. As George T. Strong observed from New York, "One's opinions change fast in revolutionary times. Three months ago, I thought with horror and incredulity of the chance that poor little South Carolina might be mad enough to 'secede' alone. Now I am content to let her go, and carry all the Gulf States with her to chaos and the devil, if Maryland, Virginia, Kentucky, Tennessee, and Missouri will but be true to themselves and to the Union. . . . We need not attempt to reconquer and retain the territories of the new Southern Confederacy. It cannot sustain itself long. It must soon decompose into anarchy."[28]

Whatever their reasoning, a growing number of Northerners insisted that meaningful Republican concessions, particularly on the critical issue of slavery in the territories, would impede the spread of disunion long enough for Upper South unionists to defeat secessionism in their states. William Jayne, Illinois state senator and brother-in-law of Lyman Trumbull, noted that encouraging such a delay was an important objective of those Republicans in the legislature who supported a national convention: "The [proposed] resolutions amount to this, it gives Union men in the border states something to stand on. . . . It gives time & that is what we want."[29]

The late-coming conservatives had been the difference between Republican defeat in 1856 and victory in 1860; once they and some of the more moderate Republicans gave their support to a peaceful settlement, that left a majority of Northerners favoring compromise of some kind.[30] That did not mean compromise would prevail, however. By late January, with the departure of most Deep South congressmen, the Republicans were left in control of both houses of Congress and thus the decision-making process, and most Republicans continued to reject conciliation. In addition, common ground among Northern conciliationists was limited. On one hand, Upper South unionists, anti-Republicans, and some Republicans declared the border-state plan to be the minimum required to save the Union, and the Crittenden plan preferable. On the other hand, many—probably most—conciliatory Republicans were unwilling to offer any more than the Adams-Corwin proposal: a constitutional amendment guaranteeing the security of slavery in the Southern states and the admission of the present western territories as one or more states. These differences precluded any well-defined, focused campaign, without which there was no real chance of swaying enough moderate Republicans to force a compromise. However, that is much clearer in hindsight than it was at the time; as the outpouring of procompromise sentiment grew, advocates of conciliation were optimistic about the future.

The issue of coercion stirred up even greater emotion. It is significant that when considering the use of force, hard-liners did not speak in terms of coercion, which conjured up antirepublican visions of a powerful central state wielding a large standing army as a weapon of tyranny; instead they spoke of defending the Constitution and enforcing the laws. As far as they were concerned, their rivals' emphasis on coercion was, in the words of Senator Trumbull's brother George, "misleading the ignorant very much," for "if the men in the country who are opposed to coercion, are asked if they are for enforcing the laws [they] say yes." In reality, declared the *Illinois State Journal*, which was widely (and with some truth) believed to be Lincoln's mouthpiece, "this government will never make war upon any portion of its people until such people make war upon the Government—and then it will be a war for defense, not of aggression, and will cease the moment those who are fighting against the Government lay down their arms. . . . Is there anything wrong in this?"[31] In other words, hard-liners saw themselves as acting defensively, preserving the rule of law against Southern rebellion and the Union against Southern treason; it was not they but the secessionists who were the aggressors here.

There was, however, a growing segment of militant Republican hard-liners who, especially after the Charleston seizures and the *Star of the West* episode, were eager for a fight. "I don't think that these fireeaters can be brought to their senses until they have been pretty soundly thrashed," a West Point cadet wrote home. "They are getting altogether too saucy," his cousin agreed. "I don't think it is worthwhile to be too nice about the matter just give them a few loads of grape[shot] and see what virtue there is in that." These arguments, too, were often grounded in defense of national or Northern honor. As one Illinois man expressed a common feeling to his senator, "At home, here, remote from the scene of action, our blood boils to hear that the flag of our Country has been insulted. That our Government is so ineffective in repelling and punishing the offenders, is sufficient to arouse all the latent fight there is in any Man." Another agreed, "The men who without reason hiss Yankee doodle, abolish the 4th of July, & spit on the National Flag are to be pacified. I say, Sir, let them be pacified by the law of arms." A third: "If we perish—let us perish like men & patriots—& not like pattroons and cowards—Compromise if we can without sacrificing our manhood & principles—but never under threats & at the point of the bayonet."[32]

Although they grounded their arguments in typical Republican principles, only a minority went so far; most hard-liners continued to believe that a firm stance against Southern demands would bring a peaceful resolution to the crisis. In fact, one of the few nearly universal sentiments in the North was that "the idea of this Republic, holding conquered Provinces or States by *force*, is utterly repugnant to our feelings, and the spirit and genius of our institutions." An overwhelming majority of Northerners, most stalwarts among them, not only wished to avoid such a prospect but believed they could; they simply disagreed on the best method of doing it.

At the same time, as Douglas himself exemplified, support for the government's *right* to use force went well beyond the hard-liners, well beyond Republican lines even: most Northerners agreed that if all other options were exhausted, or especially if federal property were attacked, a military response would become necessary. Both conservative Democrats and hard-line Republicans agreed with Douglas's view that "government *is* coercion"; as one Massachusetts Republican asserted, "That only is government which can *command* obedience and *enforce* it. The existence of society and social order is possible on no other theory." Or, as a Democratic congressman declared more bluntly, "If a State has a right to throw off her Federal obligations at pleasure, ours is the weakest and most worthless Government that was ever founded." In that regard there was little difference between the sentiments of the conservative Democrat who dismissed criticism of coercion as "a clamor got up, if not to make us all traitors, at least to frighten us out of our propriety" and the conciliatory Republican who expressed faith that Northerners "will go for any Compromise Congress may agree to submit. We don't want to arm[,] but our Country's flag must not be dishonored and trampled upon—This Union must not be disserved and broken up."[33]

Nevertheless, a significant anti-Republican minority supported peaceable disunion. A few of these argued that secession was a valid right of states, but most simply believed coercion to be a greater evil than disunion. Typical were the Ohio constituents of Congressman George Pendleton, who reasoned that "if dissolution is inevitable, they want it in peace. Peace may preserve this Government; peace may reconstruct this Union; peace will preserve friendship."[34]

More extreme was the handful of radical Democrats, especially in the southern regions of the Northwest, who vowed to resist federal coercion by force of arms. For many such, the determination to resist stemmed from a strong suspicion of Republican motives, a conviction that, as one wrote, " 'Northern fanatics,' . . . under the pretense of '*enforcing the law*,['] are anxious to bring on a contest." However, that belief was fairly uncommon, and most who held it would not dream of defying federal authority. Douglas himself wrote privately that "many of the Republican Leaders desire war & Disunion under pretext of saving the Union. The[y] wish to get rid of the Southern Senators in order to have a majority in the Senate to confirm Lincolns appointments; and many of them think they can hold a permanent Republican ascendancy in the northern States, but not in the whole Union."[35] Neither Douglas nor most of his followers thought their suspicions to be incompatible with a commitment to defending the Union against secessionist aggressions. Despite Republicans' frustration at the popular outcry against coercion, most of those who decried—or even threatened to resist—the use of force did recognize the difference between coercion and defense. As the almost universal response to the Charleston harbor incidents demonstrated, most Democrats would support the government as long as they believed it to be fighting for self-preservation and not for any nefarious Republican schemes.

At the other extreme, a few radical Republicans continued to call for disunion not as an alternative to war but as an alternative to compromise. Like Horace Greeley's *Tribune*, however, most ostensible supporters of peaceable secession were not so much advocating disunion as rejecting concessions to the South. The president of Illinois College, for example, asserted, "We would infinitely prefer the Union should be dissolved than, made *such* a Union as the South intends to make it." Put that way, the notion was not so radical; Lincoln himself had once expressed a similar thought when he had urged voters to so save the Union "as to make, and to keep it, forever worthy of the saving." If fighting actually broke out, there could be little doubt that such people would support it eagerly.[36]

What we see by late January, then, is a North profoundly divided over compromise and coercion. A growing minority of Republicans were open to some form of conciliation, but most were not; if few focused anymore on specific party tenets, the stalwart majority nevertheless continued to insist that their representatives stick to the Chicago platform, even as they placed new emphasis on resisting disunion and upholding law and order. Conciliationists, on the other hand, argued the necessity of preventing the further spread of secession; many pointed also to preventing the destruction of the republic that would inevitably accompany war. As to the use of force, while the widespread commitment to defending the Union is apparent to the historian, what impressed Northerners at the time was the great divergence of opinion. Hard-line Republicans despised and feared what seemed conciliationists' sympathy with treason, while the latter felt the same about hard-liners' apparent warmongering. We are right to note their agreement on the ends, but what most concerned them was their passionate dispute over the means.

✳ The outpouring of public opinion and the politicians' reaction to it revealed three related and highly significant tendencies. First, that Northerners continued to rely on traditional channels of political expression despite mounting fears of disunion and war demonstrates not only the degree to which they perceived the crisis as being essentially political in nature, but also the depth to which the political system was ingrained in their public culture. A few extremists might talk of taking matters into their own hands—hanging or shooting secessionists or Northerners who sympathized with the South (or, alternatively, who threatened to use force against secession)—but their actions remained political.

Second, the views of rank-and-file Northerners did not differ appreciably from those of their party leaders or each other. While some officials were excoriated for acting against their constituents' will, it was much more common that leaders were supported by their districts. More striking, whether constituents applauded, attacked, warned, or simply informed their representatives, their ideas and language were remarkably consistent throughout the North. The uniformity should not be surprising. For one thing, the astonishing proliferation of technological advancements such as the telegraph and the railroad made the North a much smaller place than it had ever been before; the pages of America's newspapers were filled with editorial clippings and telegraphic reports from all over the country. On top of that, especially in the wake of the recent partisan realignment, parties were built around shared ideologies. Emphasis might vary from state to state, but it was nonetheless ideas that bound partisans in 1861. Finally—and this became more important as the new issues increasingly crossed party lines—the constant Union petitions and rallies, though certainly genuine and frequently impassioned, were seldom spontaneous: in general they were as ordered and directed as most political actions in antebellum America. Local party activists drew up and circulated the petitions; they organized the meetings, made the speeches, wrote the resolutions and sent them off to their colleagues in Congress, and printed the newspaper accounts. In doing so they expressed views that they held in common with the party rank and file, not manipulating public opinion so much as channeling it in a productive direction—but it was they nonetheless who served as the vehicle by which the people's voices were heard.

The third trend exposed by the explosion of public expression was the Republican Party's continued inflexibility in the face of rising dissent. Under the growing pressure for compromise, most Republicans clung to their party's core doctrines all the more tightly. This was a testament to their devotion to those principles and the party that represented them, and also to their deep-seated distrust of their opponents' motives—integral components of partisanship both. For their part, few Republican conciliationists in Congress or the state legislatures were willing to defy their leadership and constituents by pushing compromise past the point where it might split the party. As a result, the firmness of the hard-line majority— and, as we have seen and shall see again, of the president-elect in particular —continued to dictate the party's response. Such unity proved a source of continual surprise to their opponents, who had been predicting a major break in Republican ranks since before the election.

Taken together, these developments trace a pattern that illustrates quite powerfully the central role of parties in antebellum political culture. Even when the issues changed and the lines separating the parties blurred, the unceasing petition drives and mass meetings confirm that partisan organization and tactics continued unabated. More significantly, although the crisis had been threatening since mid-December to force a continued party realignment, when Lincoln was finally inaugurated in early March the coalition that had elected him would be essentially intact. That much of that loyalty resulted, as we shall see, from the carefully calculated actions of both William Seward and Lincoln himself further demonstrates the power of partisan leaders to control party activity.

Once conciliatory Republicans refused to buck the party line, anti-Republicans were powerless to effect a compromise. No matter how frequently they pointed out that a majority of Northerners desired some kind of peaceful adjustment, the system left them incapable of exploiting that advantage. Consequently, as first January and then February passed and

Congress's adjournment grew near, more and more of them fell prey to demoralization and a kind of fatigued apathy.

For many Northerners these patterns and this process were not distant and abstract but lay at the heart of their crisis experience. Because the stakes were so high—emotionally, politically, and financially—Northerners were personally affected by the party system and its workings more during the crisis than at any other time save for the height of political campaigns. A few examples should serve to demonstrate these points.

✳ In Boston, procompromise activity had continued unabated in the weeks after circulation of the Shaw memorial protesting the state's personal liberty law. After drawing up and signing the memorial, the city's conservative elite, the "Brahmins," began organizing petition drives, utilizing, among other tactics, the inspired idea of recruiting the assistance of clergymen. First they focused on the legislature's repeal of the offensive law, but by January they had also begun directing their efforts toward Congress. By the middle of the month a petition vaguely supporting "a plan of compromise as may be deemed expedient to restore tranquility and peace to our now distracted country" had gathered an estimated 14,000 signatures. Most of them, the organizers claimed, were from legal voters— an astonishing number if true, as there were only 19,000 voters in Boston.[37]

Significantly, however, the petition could boast the support of no prominent Republicans. Whether this was the product of arrogant refusal to court the Republicans or simply inability to attract them—the Massachusetts party being dominated by radicals—it would prove a fatal shortcoming. In any case, to ensure that the impressive document reached Washington in grand style—which was necessary in part to compensate for what one organizer called its "indefinite & feeble" message—the Brahmins looked within their own ranks. It was decided that a committee of five leading citizens headed by Edward Everett—former governor, secretary of state, and U.S. senator, as well as vice presidential candidate of the Constitutional Union Party in the recent election—would conduct the petition to the capital. Former Speaker of the House and senator Robert C. Winthrop and wealthy industrialist and Constitutional Union gubernatorial candidate Amos A. Lawrence lent additional prestige.[38]

Whether the managers were aware of it when making their selections, the combination of Everett and Lawrence offers a revealing example of how broadly views on the crisis could range even within as restrictive a group as the conservative Boston Brahmins. Unlike the younger Lawrence, who had been active in politics throughout the 1850s, Everett had retired from public service in the middle of the decade, alienated, like a great many conservative Whigs of his generation, by the rise of the new morality-driven politics. While Lawrence had been a key figure in the organization of Massachusetts's Constitutional Union Party, Everett had only reluctantly agreed to allow his name on the party's national ticket. Although he was "filled with sorrowful amazement" by the election's consequences and was convinced that his and Bell's election by the House would have averted secession, Everett made no secret of his relief that he did not now have to serve.[39]

After the election, the growing crisis had left Everett despondent. Despite maintaining that it was "the duty of every good citizen, by word & deed to contribute his mite, however small, to rescue the country from the impending peril," Everett repeatedly turned down entreaties to speak in favor of the Union. To one correspondent he explained, "Till developments at Washington and the action of the Northern Legislatures,—to say nothing of the movements at the South,—shall present more definitive issues than exist at present, I do not feel that my voice could be uttered to any purpose. But I shall most anxiously watch the march of events." He confided in his diary, "The time is not far distant when I shall be relieved from all my frailities, burdens & sorrows."[40] When a committee arrived in mid-January to request that he lead the contingent to deliver the compromise petition, Everett saw no way to reject the mission, but he recorded privately, "The affair, I fear, has gone too far for influence."[41]

Lawrence, on the other hand, had gone to work with a will as soon as the gravity of the crisis became apparent. In addition to writing letters to influential figures on both sides of the question, he had been a prime mover in the creation and signing of the Shaw memorial and had spearheaded the petition campaign against the personal liberty law, and he presided over a regular gathering of "Union men" to discuss current developments and possible remedies. He did not hesitate to accept his commission to go to Washington.[42]

The difference in enthusiasm with which Everett and Lawrence met the crisis was linked to a deeper distinction. Everett had come to consider a peaceful resolution impossible and—after briefly flirting with the notion of a military dictatorship during the excitement of early January[43]—to hope instead that the inevitable separation would not lead to war. Lawrence, however, had neither given up on compromise nor accepted the possibility of peaceable secession. He considered disunion treason and favored a strong federal response should one become necessary. He supported Major Anderson and viewed the attack on the *Star of the West* as "the climax of aggression wh[ich] must end in the subjug[atio]n of S. Carolina or in the destruction of the [American] Confederacy." The Republicans were not the only party suffering from deep divisions.[44]

The committee received their invitations on January 21 and were sent off two days later by a cheering throng. They arrived at the capital on the evening of Thursday, the twenty-fourth. There they quickly discovered that their peace mission did not have the support of their state's congressional delegation. For one thing, when they had set themselves up in a hotel suite and issued word that the petition would be available for inspection in their rooms, some of the representatives groused at being expected to call on the committee rather than be called upon. Everett's response reflected his generation's disapproval of modern politics. "In old times the representative called on the constituent," he noted. "There is no one so jealous as a man suddenly lifted out of his Sphere."[45]

But the petition itself was the real source of friction. Upon meeting their train on arrival, Sumner informed them with characteristic bluntness that their mission was "all wind"—prompting Lawrence to retort rather pointedly to the verbose senator that their intention was, rather, "to prick a bag of wind and produce a collapse for their country's good."[46] Charles Francis Adams displayed more tact when he called (without complaint) to pay his respects to the commission, but his opinion did not much differ from Sumner's. After nine weeks' observation of Congress's handling of the crisis, he knew that without Republican support and involvement their effort was wasted. "The peculiarity of it," he noted privately, "is that it comes from every other source than the dominant party. Of course its authority here is correspondingly weakened from that cause."[47]

The committee members spent the next few days calling upon and receiving influential Washingtonians. The reports they received of the condition of the country were not encouraging. President Buchanan "expressed great anxiety in regard to a collision at the South, & conversed freely on the condition of the country, expressing a strong desire to be free from the cares of office." General Scott—looking, Lawrence thought, "20 years older than when I saw him last"—told them of his concerns and frustrations regarding the security of the capital. Senator Seward was remarkably candid in describing his growing distance from Republican doctrine regarding the territories, his efforts to create a national party, and his failure to "obtain the personal co-operation of Mr Lincoln." Although the irrepressible New Yorker offered his usual prediction that all would come out right in the end, his manner suggested less certainty.[48]

On Monday, Congressman Alexander Rice—a Republican, like the entire Massachusetts delegation—presented the petition to the House. Draped in the American flag, with its distinguished entourage seated in the front seat of the diplomatic box, it made an impressive appearance and was greeted with applause from the galleries and from many representatives. In contrast to the inspiring display, however, Rice's presentation was unenthusiastic and brief, and the House quickly moved on to other business. A short trip to the Senate chamber concluded the committee's official business.[49]

After another day of calls, Lawrence left Everett and Winthrop in Washington and headed for home. A few days later he attended a massive compromise rally at Faneuil Hall, which initiated another, broader-based petition drive and led him to conclude hopefully, "The people seem to be waking up at last." Such expressions of optimism were increasingly rare, however; his experience in Washington had sapped Lawrence's customary enthusiasm. To the numerous inquiries about the Union's prospects he faced upon arriving home, he was "obliged to answer that it is very dark at present." Although it was already being surpassed by the new memorial—which, in the space of just a few days and from a broader geographic area, would attract 22,000 signatures, this time in explicit support of the Crittenden plan—from what he had seen, the massive Boston petition, and his own mission to deliver it, had accomplished nothing of any value. For the next few weeks, for the first time since the election, Lawrence recorded in his diary only a few passing references to the crisis, apparently finding comfort instead in more mundane, domestic concerns.[50]

✳ When he read in the local Utica papers that he had been selected as a delegate to the New York State Democratic Convention in Albany, John Munn was not impressed with the honor. Not only was Munn not a Democrat, but as a former Whig he had no desire to associate with that party. If it were a nonpartisan gathering of conservatives, he would have attended gladly, but this tactic of publishing his name without consulting him merely reminded him of past efforts of local partisans to recruit him as a candidate for mayor. He had been somewhat flattered at the time, but he knew that "the mere party men want to avail themselves of any popularity they can command. . . . I have too much contempt for that class to lend myself to their use."[51] A few days later, however, after discussing the matter with some fellow old-line Whigs, Munn changed his mind. The Albany convention, it seemed, was not another attempt to ensnare him in party politics but "was conceived in a proper spirit & is not to be shaped to suit the aspirations of politicians." Feeling strongly that it was "the duty of all men to do all in their power to reconcile the conflicting elements now at work to destroy the best form of Government ever devised," he decided to attend.[52]

Like Edward Everett and Amos Lawrence, John Munn was a former Whig who had viewed the Constitutional Union Party as the only hope for preventing sectional conflict. Like Lawrence, Munn was a successful businessman whose opposition to the Republican Party stemmed from a conservative outlook that extended well beyond financial interest; like Everett, he recoiled in disgust from the North's increasingly professionalized politics. Unlike those two men, however, his prominence was strictly local, and he had never sought a position in public service.[53] In short, although Munn was by no means a "typical" Northerner (if such a person could be said to have existed), in his political background and views he was a typical Northern conservative—one of that significant minority whose support was so eagerly sought by both the Douglas Democrats and the Seward faction of conciliatory Republicans. And like most Northern conservatives in the winter of 1860–61, he would cooperate with the party that spoke most forcefully for compromise. Munn was one of those at whom Douglas and the Democrats directed their increasingly strident calls to place the Union before party considerations. As his decision to go to Albany illustrated, such individuals were proving responsive.

Munn left his home at six A.M. on Thursday, January 31, making his way through lofty snow drifts to the railroad station. After meeting a number of fellow delegates on the train, he arrived in Albany at eleven to find all of the hotels full. Fortunately, he ran into an acquaintance and was able to arrange for "a hard cot in one corner of his room," where he would later spend an uncomfortable and restless night. For now, having secured a place to stay, he proceeded to the "beautiful and spacious" convention hall, where he quickly concluded that his trip was worth whatever unpleasantness accompanied it. Crowded galleries overlooked the "animating scene" of 500 enthusiastic delegates. More important, he was pleased to find numerous old-line Whigs in attendance and "an almost entire absence of party feeling" in the proceedings. Once the convention was organized and a series of prominent, highly respected conservative speakers began to address the gathering, Munn found himself overcome by their patriotic sentiments. "As I looked upon those hundreds of stern & earnest faces, often melted to tears," he recorded, "I felt that we ought to have a common country, when such men came up to its rescue."[54]

Despite Munn's impression of nonpartisanship, the gathering was of necessity dominated by the state Democratic organization. And it was not entirely able to avoid partisan issues; one of the first questions it faced (before Munn arrived at midday, apparently) was the seating of competing delegations from New York City: one from the regular Democratic machine at Tammany Hall and the other from Mayor Fernando Wood's rival Mozart Hall. In an effort to maintain its nonpartisan tone (and avoid alienating either organization), the convention voted to seat both groups. At that the Tammany delegates walked out, not to return until the next day after a committee led by former governor Horatio Seymour hand-delivered resolutions inviting them back.[55]

But as Munn's account indicates, such political maneuverings did not, in the end, detract from the convention's high tone. As Samuel Tilden's influential pamphlet had done three months earlier, the speakers (of whom, not coincidentally, Tilden was one) aimed at finding the broadest possible common ground. The speeches that Munn singled out as particularly inspiring all concurred in their main points: condemnation of Republican fanaticism and obstinacy, sympathy with Southerners' fears, rejection of the practicability of using force against a united South, and a plea for Northerners to encourage Upper South unionism by supporting substantive compromise. Lyman Tremain drew especially loud cheers when he praised the efforts of conciliatory Republicans such as Lucius Robinson and Thurlow Weed who manfully defied their party's "iron rule" for the sake of the Union.[56]

There were, of course, variations in opinion. James S. Thayer's address included a thinly veiled threat to resist any attempt at coercion: "We must now and at all times oppose a resolute and unfaltering resistance. . . . If a revolution of force is to begin, it shall be inaugurated at home (cheering)." Chancellor Walworth compared the South's resistance to that of the American Revolutionaries. However, most speakers denounced secession and recognized the government's right and duty to defend itself.[57] The convention's official resolutions reflected a conservative outlook calculated to attract a wide spectrum of anti-Republican support. They called on Northerners to transcend party politics; urged Congress to support the Crittenden propositions or any other compromise acceptable to the border slave states; rejected coercion as an invitation to civil war (but went no further than that); and called on the New York legislature to submit the Crittenden plan to the people and, if Congress failed to pass any substantive compromise measure, to urge that body to call a constitutional convention.[58]

John Munn returned home Friday evening flush with excitement at what he had witnessed. "It was an assembly worthy of the occasion & could only have been brought together by a common feeling of danger to our country & a desire to do all things possible to save it," he wrote proudly in his diary that night. Nevertheless, he was not hopeful for the future, for he realized that Republican intransigence would negate any effort he and his colleagues might make. "I fear the madness & folly of the South is to be met by the same spirit in those who are in power here & will soon be at Washington," he continued. "I pray that wisdom may yet control the hearts & action of these men & save us from what now seems nothing but ruins." By the next night, his enthusiasm receding, he was consoling himself with the thought that "at any rate we have had the opportunity of putting ourselves on record as having attempted to stay the progress of fanaticism & folly at both ends of the country." Like Amos Lawrence's, John Munn's efforts and the emotional reaction that followed seem to have left him drained and, for a while at least, unresponsive to the crisis; his diary, too, is virtually silent on national affairs for some time after his return home. As the long secession winter dragged on, the relentless press of events and the constant frustration at what they perceived as Republican obduracy taxed the power of even the most committed conciliationists to sustain either their faith in a peaceful outcome or their efforts to achieve it.[59]

✳ Beginning on January 21, ordinary business came to a virtual standstill in the U.S. House of Representatives. Various issues relating to secession had dominated the session since it opened, of course, but once Thomas Corwin formally presented the Committee of Thirty-three's abortive recommendations, the House devoted much of each day to discussion of the crisis. The result was a seemingly endless string of orations. Some congressmen pleaded for one—or any—of the major compromise plans; a few presented new plans, generally some variation on what had already been proposed; others argued for the rejection of all compromise; still more simply wanted to get their views on record for posterity and, of course, the benefit of their constituents. Whatever one's motives, it was a nerve-racking time for all involved; in the earlier weeks, especially, speeches were punctuated frequently with interruptions and bickering over questions of order, questions of intention, and perceived slights.

Despite the widely varying motives of the speakers, despite a range in oratorical ability as great as that in opinion, and despite the fact that, heard in what began to feel like infinite succession, the speeches bored even many of the members themselves—despite all those things, to each congressman his own speech was of central importance, and represented a tremendous personal effort to express his principles, or at least those of his constituents. Although there was a substantial amount of political posturing, many of the representatives took their position of power quite seriously and went to great lengths to say just what they believed—some of them in opposition to their supporters' wishes. John McClernand, for example, speaking in the immediate aftermath of the *Star of the West* attack, delivered an address so forceful in its support of national authority that it proved an embarrassment to his friend Lanphier back in Springfield; Edward Baker trumpeted the Democratic congressman's supposed conversion in the pages of the Republican *Journal*.[60] On the other side of the aisle, radical Republican Roscoe Conkling of New York faced sharp criticism from constituents back in Oneida County after he offered to support most of the Corwin proposal for the sake of Upper South unionism. To a friend he explained earnestly, "Before making the speech which you say is so passionately condemned, I examined, with a care never before observed, myself, my feelings & my motives. I endeavored to lift myself up to the reality that I was an actor in transactions relating to nothing less than the preservation or partition of a great empire, the fate of a nation the greatest in the future, the world has ever seen." Although he was not happy with the way it came out, his address represented "that policy which in my heart I believe most likely to promote a continuance of the Union and the government." He avowed that he would have delivered it even if it meant political death.[61]

Charles Francis Adams also knew as he prepared his speech that he risked political death. Although his political friends had vehemently denounced the conciliatory course he had followed in late December and early January, just a couple of weeks later Adams decided to renew that course. As his indignation and disgust at Southern actions in South Carolina and on the Committee of Thirty-three faded, he found himself once more persuaded by the heartfelt pleas of Upper South unionists like Emerson Etheridge and John Gilmer for a Republican gesture of goodwill. Adams decided again to brave the ire of the Massachusetts radicals and once more endorsed his old proposal, which most people now referred to as the Corwin plan. As far as criticism from home went, he had consoled himself in December with the thought that "if the current of revolution could be slackened by my sacrifice of myself, it would be but gain," and he expressed the same determination now, writing to a friend, "This may be unpopular, but I think it is right."[62]

But if the anger and scorn of one's supporters can be regarded as a measure of honesty and forthrightness, then perhaps no Northern representative was more sincere in his convictions than Illinois Republican William Kellogg. His conciliatory speech in early February made him a pariah to his constituents, sparking outraged mass meetings and leading at least one major newspaper to read him out of the party. In fact, Kellogg's violent fluctuations between the views of Lincoln and Seward and the consequences he faced for finally siding with the latter illustrate as well as any other episode in that long, anxious winter the bewildering complexity the crisis had attained, the means by which the Republican Party retained its unity, and the intricate and far-reaching web that linked congressional factions, Upper South unionists, the president-elect, state legislatures and party leaders, and, not least, ordinary voters.

Like Adams, Kellogg was a moderate Republican who had wrestled all winter with the tension between resolving the crisis peaceably and remaining true to his party's principles. Typical of the moderates, Kellogg found the situation in Washington much more complicated than he had believed it to be, and he was moved by Southern unionists' pleas for Republican concessions. His first act upon being selected as Illinois's representative on the Committee of Thirty-three in early December was to write Lincoln, warning the president-elect of the growing seriousness of the crisis and asking what position he should take. Confident that Lincoln's reply would stress magnanimity over firmness, he became one of the most vocal supporters of compromise in the committee's early days. While waiting for a response from Springfield, he not only implied in a speech before the committee that Lincoln would favor conciliation but went so far as to propose a compromise plan based on popular sovereignty.[63] The ties of party proved stronger than the appeals of Southern unionists, however: after receiving Lincoln's letter sternly opposing any concessions, Kellogg executed an abrupt about-face and thenceforth was as stalwart as any radical. He consistently opposed all compromise measures discussed in caucus or presented to the committee, including Adams's proposals.[64]

But by mid-January, the strain of the crisis had begun to wear and Kellogg returned to his former conciliationist stance. In part, at least, that appears to have resulted from his close ties with Leonard Swett, a leader of the conservative, pro-Seward faction in Illinois. Swett had been in Washington since late December lobbying for compromise and against a cabinet position for Illinois radical Norman B. Judd, and had spent a great deal of time closeted with Seward. Seward either talked with Kellogg himself or had Swett talk to him about traveling to Springfield to convince Lincoln of the Southern unionists' dire need for Republican concessions. By that time Kellogg was convinced of the need for compromise; on the night before he left Washington, in fact, he quarreled over that issue with Joseph Medill, editor of the radical *Chicago Tribune*. "Bill Kellogg has become crazy to have the Republicans back down and compromise with the disunionists," Medill reported to Judd. "He is in favor of some such scheme as Crittenden's slave code." So tight had Kellogg become with Swett and Weed during the latter's frequent trips to Washington that Medill suspected the three of some "d—d conspiracy . . . to entrap Lincoln into an acquiescence in some base surrender of Republican principles."[65]

Kellogg reached Springfield on the nineteenth and spent most of the next two days closeted with Lincoln. A swarm of rumors greeted his arrival and quickly made their way into the telegraphic columns of the major newspapers, most of them speculating that the congressman was in town either to talk Lincoln into supporting a compromise or to oppose Judd's appointment to the cabinet. Kellogg did indeed discuss cabinet matters with the president-elect—he, Swett's partner David Davis, and Governor Yates joined in a meeting with two prominent Pennsylvanians to urge Simon Cameron's appointment—but that was not, of course, his primary purpose. As Lincoln explained it, Kellogg "was here, in a good deal of anxiety, seeking to ascertain to what extent I would be consenting for our friends to go in the way of compromise on the now vexed question."[66] Lincoln's reply appeared to confirm Seward's and Kellogg's worst fears. His words, as Kellogg gave them to a reporter shortly afterward, typified the view of anticonciliationists: "I will suffer death before I will consent or will advise my friends to consent to any concession or compromise which looks like buying the privilege of taking possession of this government to which we have a constitutional right; because, whatever I might think of the merit of the various propositions before Congress, I should regard any concession in the face of menace the destruction of the government itself, and a consent on all hands that our system shall be brought down to a level with the existing disorganized state of affairs in Mexico."[67]

Meanwhile, alarmed at reports of the defection of "one of the most immovable of the Republican members," Republican stalwarts set out to defeat Kellogg. Their actions are a lesson in the pressure that party machinery could bring to bear and a reminder of the close ties and ease of communication among national and state party leaders. From Springfield, a group of radical state legislators fired off a telegram to Washington to determine whether the congressional delegation was really in favor of compromise. They received an immediate reply in the negative. The outraged legislators then accosted Kellogg, who acknowledged that he had "suggested the propriety of taking up with the border States' proposition" but insisted that he would never pressure Lincoln to abandon the Chicago platform (which meant little, of course, given the range of interpretations given to that phrase). From Washington, Senator Trumbull worked to subvert his colleague's mission with a telegram of his own, ordering Judd cryptically, "Do not proceed reaction has commenced tell Lincoln to await letters." Upon being handed Trumbull's message, Lincoln correctly interpreted it as alluding to Kellogg's inquiries and took the opportunity to delay a final response to the fretful congressman. He would, he told Kellogg, write Seward with his views as soon as he had received Trumbull's mysterious letters (which he no doubt realized did not exist). With that, Kellogg had no choice but to return to Washington. As he was leaving, a second telegram arrived from the national delegation, instructing legislative Republicans to "make no concessions and pass no resolutions" regarding compromise.[68]

Kellogg did not abandon his new course after completing his mission for Seward. In early February he proposed to the House a compromise consisting of four constitutional amendments, the chief one re-instituting the Missouri Compromise line for all current territories. A week later he elaborated on his plan in a lengthy address in which he blamed the crisis on partisanship and called on extremists from both sides to lay aside political considerations and save the Union.[69] Charles Francis Adams, who despised Kellogg both personally and politically, noted that the address "ended with loud congratulations from the democrats of the Northwest, and as loud jeers from his colleagues on our side of the House." That seems to have been accurate. John McClernand, who at one point during the speech joined hands with Kellogg and recited a line of poetry, wrote triumphantly to Lanphier, "His speech is a bombshell among the republicans, who are now divided and virtually dispersed." That is, he added grimly, "*if* we can save the Union."[70]

Even before Kellogg delivered the speech, a mass meeting in his district repudiated his compromise proposal, denouncing all compromise as "subversive of the dearest rights of the people of the free states, and eminently dangerous to our future prosperity as a nation." A letter to Trumbull enclosing that meeting's resolutions raved, "Kellogg has by his Resolutions committed himself boddy & Breeches to the South. . . . If the south wants to fight let them 'Pitch in' as soon as [they] please[.] We would rather fight (then) allow Slavery to go into one more Territory." The speech itself "created a furious storm," inducing a flood of shocked and indignant correspondence. "Democrats as well as Republicans are astonished at Mr. K's course especially after his manly & earnest protest against the measures proposed by Mr. Adams in the Com. of 33," one constituent sputtered. "The Republicans of this Congressional district, so far as I have heard an expression, would much prefer a separation from the Southern States than any longer to submit to the dictation of a Slave Oligarchy—We consider it an insult to the Republican party to demand of them to offer terms or compromise being conscious of no wrong or intention of it." Another reported, "Illinois is all right for . . . *coercion. Kellogg is politically dead* in all parts of the state but among democrats."[71]

Two weeks after his speech, a formal meeting of delegates from throughout Kellogg's district officially repudiated his course. The *Illinois State Journal*, denouncing his conversion to "the most obnoxious wing of the Democratic party," reported his universal condemnation among the party rank and file and his isolation from prominent party leaders. "He has sold himself to the slave power for a very small sum," it concluded. The *Chicago Tribune* completed the proceedings by reading him out of the party. Stunned at the rapid turn of events, a local Republican activist observed, "Little did I ever dream—that I would have to listen to the taunts of democracy over the fall of Mr. Kellogg. . . . He has no followers in this part of the country amongst the republicans—his sympathy is all from the treason excusing democracy."[72]

By February, the lines were clearly drawn. The price for crossing them was high.

✳ The experiences of Edward Everett, Amos Lawrence, John Munn, and William Kellogg illustrate the fate of conciliationists and, in a larger sense, conciliationism. Each came to the movement from a different angle, each operated at a different point in the political system, and each had different immediate goals, but their stories contain striking similarities. Most important, each believed that the best way to save the American Union was through diplomacy and compromise rather than brinkmanship, and each worked through traditional political channels—a petition, a party convention, congressional resolutions—to achieve his goals. In those ways, if not in their socioeconomic or political backgrounds, they were representative of most Northerners at that point in time. And like most Northerners, they were powerless to alter the course of the crisis. As the *New York Herald* editorialized, "Union meetings are good things, Union resolutions are good things, offers of compromise for the sake of the Union are good things; but practically they amount to nothing, emanating from parties which have no power to do anything."[73] The final decision regarding compromise lay in the hands of one party, and ultimately of just one man: Abraham Lincoln.

✳ For a moment in early January there had been near unity among Northerners. However, Buchanan's failure to take firm action and the redoubled efforts of procompromise leaders in Washington and the state capitals energized constituents and ensured that the moment was but brief. When it had passed, it appeared to leave the parties more unstable than ever. Although Democrats had rallied to the flag following South Carolina's aggression, the party was nevertheless divided over preventing secession through force. Most Republicans continued to toe the party line, but they still disagreed on just how threatening the situation really was, whether compromise was desirable, and just what their party's principles were and what would constitute their sacrifice. Many observers believed the partisan realignment that had been threatening since mid-December to be closer than ever. Yet the longer the crisis dragged on without its occurrence, the more frustrated and demoralized conciliationists became.

The failure of the anti-Republican compromise campaign is the story of Edward Everett, Amos Lawrence, and John Munn and their growing realization that no amount of effort on their parts would change the decisions that were being made in Washington. But even more it is the story of Stephen Douglas and John J. Crittenden, the dogged leaders of the movement and among the few who continued to fight all the way to the end, and beyond. In a similar fashion, the Republican coalition's unlikely success in hanging together is the story of William Kellogg and the mobilization of congressmen, state legislators, local editors, and constituents against his apostasy. But even more it is the story of Abraham Lincoln and William Seward, the two most powerful Republicans, and their long, subtle dance around compromise, coercion, and control of the party. Our story returns, then, to Washington.

Chapter 7 ✳ The Storm Is Weathered ✳ January– February, Revisited

By late January the crisis had stalled, the brief explosion of patriotic unity subsiding into more familiar partisan and factional wrangling; by mid-February, many proponents of compromise were giving in to frustration and hopelessness. Despite a sharp burst of initial excitement and anxiety, even the opening of yet another front for the crisis debates—a national peace conference in Washington— did little more than prolong the incessant and fruitless arguing for a few more weeks. By early March, in Congress and in the state legislatures, the Republican coalition had withstood the buffeting of internal division and external demands and prevented any significant action on compromise, due in large part to the behind-the-scenes maneuvering of Abraham Lincoln. To that point, his most powerful tool was silence: delaying announcements of both patronage and secession policies enabled him to retain the loyalty of both of his party's dueling factions. The day was approaching when he must take a stand on both issues, and his party's reaction was by no means foregone.

In the South, meanwhile, the seven cotton states went about the business of organizing a permanent government. That did not dismay conciliationists, however, for the eight border slave states decisively rejected disunion in February. The success of the Upper South unionists reinvigorated the movement in Congress to conciliate them, now made more desperate by the imminence of adjournment. As the inauguration of the new Republican president approached, the crisis appeared no nearer a resolution —either violent or peaceful—than before Anderson's controversial move into Fort Sumter.

✳ Despite the intense reactions from home that greeted many procompromise Republicans, Charles Francis Adams's and William Kellogg's conversions to conciliationism were, if more advanced than most, not unique: from mid-January to mid-February congressional Republicans displayed a surprising willingness—or at least a grudging desire to appear willing—to make some sort of concession for the sake of fostering Southern union ism. As Indiana representative (and cabinet hopeful) Schuyler Colfax observed, "The gasconade & bluster & threats of the Seceders, or rather the Traitors they should be called, we can all stand easy enough & defy. But the appeals of the Union men in the Border States to give them something to stand on & fight the battle for Union are harder to resist."[1]

On January 18, just two days after startling even themselves by successfully replacing the Crittenden plan with Daniel Clark's hard-line resolutions, Senate Republicans allowed reconsideration of the vote. Democrats reintroduced Crittenden's proposals, the substitution was reversed, and the Kentucky senator's popular compromise plan was back on the table. Republicans also refused to pass a force bill to give the president the power he insisted he needed to forcibly subdue rebellion. The only such bill introduced thus far had been buried in committee; by January 22 its author was grumbling that his proposal found "but little favor on either side of this House." Perhaps most shocking, in February, Congress organized three new territories, all of them north of 36°30′, without any mention of slavery—a de facto establishment of popular sovereignty.[2]

Much of the new feeling, of course, was due to the post-Sumter reaction and the resulting popular sympathy for peace. Nevertheless, it should not be surprising that congressional action, and inaction, was also being discreetly but effectively encouraged by Representative Adams's good friend Senator Seward.

Although Seward's January 12 speech had elicited high praise from conservative quarters—John Greenleaf Whittier even wrote a poem in praise of it—response to it left the crafty New Yorker more despondent than ever.[3] Hard-liners were quick to damn it as weak and destructive to the cause; even Seward's wife, who held strong abolitionist views, wrote from New York, "Eloquent as your speech was it fails to meet the entire approbation of those who love you best. . . . You are in danger of taking the path which led Daniel Webster to an unhonored grave."[4] In Washington, Seward conceded privately, "Two-thirds of the Republican Senators are as reckless in action as the South. . . . I could not compromise a principle, if I would, for there is nobody to go with me." The following week, he felt obliged to inform the Republican caucus that "what he had said was only for a speech—*he had no idea of bringing [his propositions] forward*—that they would split the Republ[ican] party."[5]

Yet if Seward's immediate goal had been to rally his party behind a goodwill gesture that would encourage border South unionists, the most important response was Lincoln's. With that in mind, Seward's decision to take his conciliation campaign from the shadows of the Capitol's back-rooms into the glare of the national spotlight, especially just two days after news of the *Star of the West* incident reached Washington and the North, had been dangerous. His acceptance of the State Department was just two weeks old; public repudiation from Lincoln would strip away the consider-able influence he had just gained as chief adviser in the incoming admin-istration. As usual, however, the president-elect's position was difficult to judge; Lincoln passed over the speech with a single complimentary but noncommittal sentence in a note concerning other matters.[6] Thus Sew-ard's dispirited caution in the caucus.

But the buoyant senator soon rallied. With characteristic optimism and boldness, he decided to interpret Lincoln's reserve as tacit approval. Giv-ing few hints of his precarious situation, Seward exuded his usual charm and good cheer while building up the confidence of border-state unionists. With obtaining a cabinet seat for one or more of them still a primary goal, he maintained his pursuit of John Gilmer. He also massaged his vast net-work of Southern contacts, assuring Virginia unionists of Lincoln's peace-ful intentions and urging them to push a call for a national convention through their state legislature.[7]

In a move that reflected both desperation and an appreciation for the growing popular sentiment for peace, Seward also spread rumors that a compromise was imminent. The details are hazy, but according to John Gilmer, in a private meeting on the evening of January 18 Seward pur-ported to come "to some definite arrangement on our present national dif-ficulties" with Douglas, Crittenden, and conservative Republican James Dixon of Connecticut. The four probably met again a week later, and may also have met with other senators as well.[8] What "arrangement" Seward offered is not certain, but the talk left Douglas and Crittenden genuinely optimistic, Douglas more so than at any time since his party's disastrous national conventions the previous summer. Beginning on the nineteenth, the two senators drafted several joint messages to the people of the border slave states expressing hope of an imminent settlement. Making use of his own extensive Southern connections, Douglas reported in a public letter to Virginia unionist James Barbour, "I can say with confidence that there is hope of adjustment, and the prospect has never before been better." He also hinted in the Senate at a "disposition" toward compromise, adding cryp-tically, "I have reasons satisfactory to myself upon which to predicate that firm hope that the Union will be preserved." The meeting inspired other influential figures to express confidence as well: Gilmer, who almost cer tainly had learned of it from Seward, wired to his district, "We will pass in substance Mr. Crittenden's plans. Give no ear to alarms."[9]

Rumors of an agreement soon reached the national press: Washington correspondents for the major New York papers reported with assurance that congressional Republicans were almost ready to accept a territorial compromise, possibly even Crittenden's. "The next few days will develop a complete change of policy on the part of the republican party," the *New York Herald*'s reporter affirmed positively. "Mr. Lovejoy, of Illinois, is open in his declaration that the party is sold out." The stories quickly grew to include Lincoln himself: "It is now certain, that all the influence of incoming Republican administration will be thrown in favor of a speedy settlement of our national difficulties," the *Herald*'s correspondent declared, implying that he had actually seen letters "from eminent chiefs of the Republican party, fresh from an interchange of opinion with the President elect, urgently counselling the republicans in Congress to adopt speedy measures of pacification," counsel that the congressional party leadership was in the midst of following. He even had it "on good authority" that Lincoln himself had written "one of his Cabinet Ministers" in support of the border-state plan. The rumors disturbed hard-liners enough that Wisconsin radical Carl Schurz warned Lincoln, "The moment seems to have arrived which will put manhood to a final test. Next week a desperate effort will be made to crowd the Crittenden—or the border state—resolutions through Congress, and many Republicans have already signified their willingness to yield."[10]

Reports such as these were critical to the three senators' efforts to buoy unionism in the Upper South, which explains why Douglas's and Crittenden's hopeful expressions had all been designed for public consumption. Indeed, projecting a hopeful air was more important now than ever: Virginia was scheduled to elect delegates to its secession convention on February 4, and Tennessee would hold a referendum five days later on whether to hold such a convention. Kentucky, Missouri, Arkansas, and North Carolina all stood poised to follow. The campaign to contain secession within the Deep South would be decided in the coming days, and success depended on how threatening the people of the border slave states believed the Republicans to be.

Seward did what he could to encourage optimism, at one point even allowing a reporter to record his assertion that "the question of slavery is not now to be taken into account. We must save the Union." But without Lincoln's explicit support for conciliation, he could neither negotiate nor even speak openly in the way that the other two could; quietly planting stories, dropping hints, and maneuvering Douglas and Crittenden into issuing declarations of confidence were his only available weapons. In fact, whatever false assurances Seward offered his fellow senators and the Virginia unionists dangerously exceeded his limited authority from Lincoln, an especially hazardous maneuver given the hard-line spirit among Republican senators and his reluctance to risk a party schism. He dared not go further without securing Lincoln's blessing.[11]

But that he was already angling for. By the time Seward met with Douglas and Crittenden on the eighteenth, William Kellogg was on a train to Springfield. Moreover, Joseph Medill's suspicions that Kellogg was part of a "d—d conspiracy" with Swett and Weed were well founded; Seward had not trusted the campaign wholly to one congressman. Swett left Washington for Springfield within a day or two of Kellogg, reportedly to convince Lincoln to come to Washington and help resolve the crisis, and Seward dashed up to Albany to persuade Weed to proceed there as well. As it turned out, Swett took sick and never made it past Pittsburgh before being confined to bed for three weeks, while Weed made it as far as Toledo before having second thoughts. He decided that it would be folly for him to "appear unbidden" in Springfield and turned back. Thus only Kellogg made it to Springfield, and we are already familiar with the results of his efforts.[12]

Kellogg's failure pushed the fretful Seward into more direct action: he would finally put his conciliatory views on record with the president-elect. On January 27, he penned a long letter to Lincoln describing the "very painful" appeals of Southern unionists, who warned that without "something of concession or compromise" their states would secede before Lincoln was inaugurated. "It is almost in vain," he wrote sorrowfully, "that I tell them to wait, let us have a truce on slavery, put our issue on Disunion and seek remedies for ultimate griefs in a constitutional question." Yet whether the Upper South seceded or not, Seward pointed out, Lincoln would face "a hostile armed confederacy." Echoing Douglas's January 3 speech (unconsciously, no doubt), he asserted that the only question was whether to subdue it through force or conciliation. "For my own part," Seward assured his chief, "I think that we must collect the revenues— regain the forts in the gulf and, if need be maintain ourselves here [in Washington]." However, he warned, although "much the largest portion of the Republican party are reckless now of the crisis before us," the North would not support a protracted civil war. Therefore, "every thought that we think ought to be conciliatory forbearing and patient, and so open the way for the rising of a Union Party in the seceding states which will bring them back into the Union."[13]

Here at last was his position, out in the open and committed to writing: Republicans must make sufficient concessions to keep alive the latent Southern unionism that he still insisted would rise to the fore. If Seward was disingenuous in insisting that the revenues be collected and the forts recaptured, the letter was still remarkable for its frank conciliationism. The question now was how Lincoln would respond. As after presenting his watered-down resolutions in the Committee of Thirteen and making his mild speech in the Senate, Seward could do nothing more but await a reply.

✳ Lincoln, like Seward, was playing a double game. Like all but the most radical hard-liners, he had been struggling throughout the crisis to strike his own balance between firmness and magnanimity, trying to uphold the principles on which he had been elected while still leaving room for the expected unionist reaction in the South. Despite his strong words to Kellogg, he had been careful not to criticize any particular plan; indeed, mindful of the damage that the appearance of absolute intransigence might do to Southern unionism, he had added that "this thing" was "in the hands of the people"—if they chose to call a convention to settle the crisis, he would not stand in the way.[14] Like Seward, Lincoln was particularly mindful of Southern unionism now, with Upper South convention elections looming. He was especially concerned with Virginia: not only was it the wealthiest and most populous slave state, but it was widely believed that if Virginia seceded, Maryland would follow, cutting Washington off from the loyal states. The situation was growing considerably more complex, and Lincoln's balancing act proportionately more difficult.

Lincoln responded to the opposing pressures by working to mollify both sides. On the one hand, he issued a prompt public denial to the *Herald*'s report that he had sent a letter advocating the border-state plan.[15] He also used the resources he had on hand—the local *Illinois State Journal* and young Henry Villard, the *New York Herald* correspondent assigned to Springfield—to deliver to concerned Republicans the firm message that Lincoln "stands immovably on the Chicago Platform, and he will neither acquiese in nor counsel his friends to acquise in any compromise that surrenders one iota of it." Villard went so far as to predict that "one of the first acts of his administration will be to renew the attempt to reinforce Fort

Sumter [and] demand the restoration of the federal property of the rebellious sovereignties."[16] Lincoln also must have assumed that some account of his statement to Kellogg about suffering death before bowing to secessionist threats would leak out (as of course it did).

On the other hand, Lincoln carefully balanced reports of his resolve with more moderate statements. For example, he personally oversaw the writing of a January 21 *Journal* editorial that distinguished between coercion and enforcement of the laws and declared that force would be used only to defend federal property against aggression. Villard summarized that editorial for national exposure in the *Herald*, and he continued to outline Lincoln's fair and balanced policy in subsequent dispatches.[17]

But Lincoln's chief means of encouraging Southern unionism lay in giving his future secretary of state free rein in Washington—to a point. He replied to Seward's letter on February 1, laying out precisely how far he would go in support of the senator's efforts to bolster the border slave states. He made sure to state up front, "I say now . . . as I have all the while said, that on the territorial question—that is, the question of extending slavery under the national auspices—I am inflexible." That opposition, he specified, applied to both present and future territories, for "I take it that to . . . put us again on the high-road to a slave empire is the object of all these proposed compromises. I am against it." However, Lincoln then conceded that "as to fugitive slaves, District of Columbia, slave trade among the slave states, and whatever springs of necessity from the fact that the institution is amongst us, I care but little, so that what is done be comely, and not altogether outrageous." Regarding the Corwin-Adams plan, he added, "Nor do I care much about New-Mexico, if further extension were hedged against." Lincoln presumably intended, or at least expected, that Seward would share the letter's substance with his extensive Southern unionist connections.[18]

The contradictory signals emanating from Springfield represented Lincoln's effort to assuage Southern unionism without encouraging secessionists or demoralizing his own party. Like most Northerners, his chief concern was to buy time—time for Southern unionists to defeat secession in the upcoming elections, time for Congress to adjourn without passing a compromise that would undermine his party's victory, and time for Lincoln himself to actually take office. Once those things had safely occurred, and especially once he held an official position in the government, then would be the time to announce his formal policy. With that in mind, Lincoln spent the last days of January composing his inaugural address. Could he have seen the speech in which the new administration's strategy would at last be made public, Seward would have been devastated. While Lincoln's restrained and temperate tone did not reflect the attitude of his most radical colleagues, neither did his views signal the movement toward conciliation that Seward perceived in the February 1 letter. As they had throughout the winter, Lincoln's ideas on secession harmonized with those of the hard-line moderates who made up his party's majority.

Following the same conservative strategy that had led the Chicago convention to reject Seward as too radical nine months earlier, in his address Lincoln emphasized his party's moderation: its unwillingness to threaten slavery in the states, its inability to do so even if it desired, and its commitment to upholding constitutional rights such as the return of fugitive slaves. This was a theme he returned to and elaborated on throughout the address. The points of disagreement between North and South, Lincoln explained, were not matters of constitutional violation or breaches of trust but honest disagreements over ambiguous constitutional provisions. Reiterating the plea for calm that he had made privately to a few Southern unionists back in December—and displaying the same ignorance of slavery's centrality in Southern culture that suffused moderate Republican ranks—he maintained that there was no real cause for hostility: "One section believes slavery is *right*, and ought to be extended, while the other believes it is *wrong*, and ought not be extended. That is the only substantial dispute."[19]

Lincoln maintained the same composed, reasonable tone while announcing his stalwart refusal to budge from his party's principles. Indeed, he opened his address with the frank statement that he had been elected on a party platform and could not, "upon the plainest grounds of good faith," alter his position. In fact, he wrote, his persistent refusal to submit to procompromise pressure was rooted in a duty to those who voted for him. That was not mere partisanship, however. To abdicate that responsibility, he asserted, would strike at the heart of American government and indeed the very idea of a republic: "If, when a Chief Magistrate is constitutionally elected, he cannot be inaugurated till he betrays those who elected him, by breaking his pledges, and surrendering to those who tried and failed to defeat him at the polls, this government and all popular government is at an end. Demands for such surrender, once recognized, are without limit. . . . They break the only bond of faith between public and public servant; and they distinctly set the minority over the majority." The same commitment to the rule of law and the electoral process informed Lincoln's unequivocal rejection of secession, his discussion of which continued to revolve around majority rule. He reasoned that "if the minority will not submit, the majority must," thereby establishing a pattern that would make future government untenable, for a disgruntled portion of the ruling minority would surely repeat the process. "Plainly," he concluded, "the central idea of secession, is the essence of anarchy."[20]

As to his secession policy, Lincoln declared unambiguously that he did not consider federal authority to have diminished in the seceded states, and that he considered it his "simply duty" as chief executive to ensure "that the laws of the Union be faithfully executed in all the States." With this in mind, he was determined to use "all the power at my disposal" to maintain federal authority in the South: to collect import duties, to deliver the mails, and most importantly, to defend the public property still under government control and recapture that which had been seized.[21] He insisted that such action would constitute not aggression but self-defense. He closed with that point: "In *your* hands, my fellow countrymen, and not in *mine*, is the momentous issue of civil war. . . . You can have no conflict, without being yourselves the aggressors. . . . With *you*, and not with *me*, is the solemn question of 'Shall it be peace, or a sword?' "[22]

The great majority of Republicans, could they have seen it, would have praised the address as striking perfectly that fine balance between generosity and resolve that moderates had been preaching since November. Lincoln's tone was mild and unthreatening, yet he deviated not an inch from the Chicago platform. Regarding the two primary issues of the day, he rejected compromise—explicitly spurning the notion of amending the Constitution, though he consented halfheartedly to follow the wishes of the public[23]—and vowed to enforce the laws and protect or recapture federal property—the latter an inherently aggressive, violent policy that was certain to spark widespread hostilities. His argument for both was grounded in the necessity for law and order that had come to serve as the foundation of the Republican position.

That was precisely the kind of reasoning that continually frustrated Seward's efforts to convince his party of the need for conciliation. The horror with which he would have reacted to Lincoln's intended policy can be estimated by the response of one of the only individuals to whom Lincoln showed the speech before leaving for Washington. Shortly before he left Springfield, Lincoln met with Carl Schurz, who had recently warned him of the danger of compromise in Congress. To assure his radical colleague that the newspaper reports about him were false, he locked the door and read his speech aloud. "Now you know better than any man in the country how I stand," he declared, "and you may be sure that I shall never betray my principles and my friends." Schurz declared himself thrilled with what he had heard.[24]

✳ Mercifully ignorant of the contents of Lincoln's inaugural, Seward was ecstatic over the president-elect's letter. His risky schemes appeared to have succeeded gloriously. On the day he received the letter, Virginians elected more than twice as many unionist delegates to their convention as secessionists. The next morning, Seward called Adams into the Senate chamber to celebrate "the complete defeat of the secession party." So excited that his friend could scarcely understand what he was saying, he whispered that Lincoln had approved his course "but was so badgered at Springfield that he felt compelled to keep uncommitted on it at present." Three days later he was still in raptures, reported Adams's son Henry: "The ancient Seward is in high spirits and chuckles himself hoarse with his stories. He says it's all right. We shall keep the border states, and in three months or thereabouts, if we hold off, the Unionists and Disunionists will have their hands on each other's throats in the cotton states. The storm is weathered."[25]

Seward's glee seemed both justified and well earned. Tennessee voters decided not even to call a convention. Two days later the Kentucky legislature adjourned without calling one, and a week after that Arkansas and Missouri voters elected unionist-dominated conventions. The wave of secession that had swept away the cotton states had broken against large unionist majorities in the Upper South. The Republicans' restraint regarding a force bill and the open support of Republican conciliationists like Adams and Kellogg were clearly important factors, as were the hopes engendered by a national peace conference that the Virginia legislature had recently summoned to meet in Washington. But Seward had the satisfaction of learning from a leader of the Virginia unionists that the decisive factor had been the "tolerable evidences" they had received that the Northern people were willing to grant the necessary assurances for the security of slavery—evidences Seward had been critical in producing. "The most potent campaign paper in this part of the state was the statement of Messrs. Douglas and Crittenden that an adjustment was to be expected," wrote James Barbour, to Seward's undoubted gratification; it had been he, after all, who had manufactured Douglas's and Crittenden's optimism.

But Seward's work was not complete; Barbour's letter contained a warning, too. "If these representations are disappointed," he continued, "our men . . . will become unconditional secessionists. . . . If you stand back and leave us unsupported in this great contest the secession of Va. is as inevitable as fate. I tell you this as no menace *but as a fact*."[26] Had he known the policy outlined in Lincoln's inaugural draft, Seward would not have been so optimistic.

✳ While Congress debated, maneuvered, and temporized, Buchanan had continued to deal with the more practical issues raised by secession— matters that other Northerners had the luxury of considering abstractly. The president's hands were continually tied by his determination to hold the door open to a peaceful settlement by avoiding a collision, but he had nevertheless determined that he was obligated to presume that South Carolina was still in the Union and to defend federal property wherever practicable. Thus he and Secretary of War Joseph Holt delivered a consistent message to secessionist visitors that the government would not abandon Fort Sumter and that it maintained the right to reinforce the fort whenever it might be deemed necessary. Holt also hastened to remove the secessionist sympathizer Major P. G. T. Beauregard from his command at West Point, an act that Buchanan supported despite vehement protests from Southern congressmen. Secretary of State Black issued a circular ordering the United States' diplomatic corps to take steps against foreign recognition of the seceding states. And newly appointed Secretary of the Treasury John A. Dix tried in vain to compel the Southern customs officers, most of whom had continued in their posts but now acted under their states' authority, to remand the revenues they collected. Dix also ordered all U.S. revenue cutters in Southern ports to New York to prevent their seizure. He became something of a hero when, upon receiving word that one captain refused to obey, he ordered that the officer should be treated as a mutineer, then added, "If any one attempts to haul down the American flag, shoot him on the spot." Those words were trumpeted in newspapers throughout the North and for a time Dix enjoyed a bit of the celebrity that Anderson had achieved with his move to Fort Sumter.[27]

Buchanan had given up the notion of putting reinforcements into either Sumter or Pickens, but his pledge to have them ready should they be called for was no bluff. On January 30, anticipating the departure of Isaac Hayne, Governor Pickens's representative, and the end of Anderson's truce, Buchanan met with Holt, Secretary of the Navy Isaac Toucey, and General Scott to discuss preparations for another expedition. Scott had heard through Montgomery Blair that Blair's brother-in-law, a former navy officer named Gustavus V. Fox, had developed a scheme for getting troops into Charleston harbor. He summoned Fox to Washington, and for several days in early February the two met with Holt and Lt. Norman Hall from Fort Sumter to discuss the plan. It was quite simple. Since light, unarmed ships like the *Star of the West* were powerless against the harbor's defenses, and heavy warships like the *Brooklyn* were prevented from entering by obstacles placed in the harbor channel by South Carolina forces, Fox proposed a solution that combined the strengths of each. Two light-draft tugboats would carry reinforcements and provisions to Charleston, accompanied by two heavier warships. Supported by the guns of Fort Sumter (the presence of Hall ensuring that Anderson would be alerted to the relief mission this time), the warships would drive off any enemy vessels that challenged them while the tugs ran into the harbor at night to deliver the troops and supplies.[28]

Scott assured Fox that his tactic would be used if reinforcements were sent, but they never were. Despite the ever-tightening defensive cordon surrounding his garrison, Anderson continued to mount his own campaign to preserve the peace. The last opinion on reinforcements the War Department had received from him was dated January 30; it read, "I do hope that no attempt will be made by our friends to throw supplies in; their doing so would do more harm than good." Given that assessment, Buchanan saw no need to undermine either the deliberations of the peace conference or the new administration's dealings with the envoys appointed by the new Confederate government in late February. Instead, Holt and Toucey arranged for a small squadron to remain in New York, ready to head for Sumter with reinforcements and supplies. They were still there when Buchanan's successor was inaugurated.[29]

✳ Given the importance of the Old Dominion's loyalty, Virginia's call for a national peace conference created an immediate stir in state capitals throughout the North. The governor of Ohio, unsure as to what stance his state should take and assuming that Governor Yates would know Lincoln's will, telegraphed Springfield for advice. Yates conferred with Lincoln. Although no firsthand record of their conversation exists, the story quickly spread through the Illinois Assembly that "Lincoln said that he would rather be hung by the neck till he was dead on the steps of the Capitol before he would buy or beg a peaceful inaugeration."[30]

This echo of Lincoln's pronouncement to Kellogg was issued even as rumors of his support for conciliation circulated through Washington and even as he was pondering his reply to Seward. Its adamant firmness reflected Lincoln's automatic response to any suggestion of compromise. A no-nonsense rejection of concessions signaled his resolve, offering reassurance to the Republican masses and establishing his credentials as a strict hard-liner. At the same time, it bought him time to weigh alternatives in private, and possibly to act more moderately behind the scenes. As every good parent, teacher, and manager knows, one can always change a no to a yes; to give something and then change one's mind and take it back is far more difficult. Lincoln would continue to use this strategy in the coming weeks, with important consequences.

Meanwhile, other party leaders wrote Lincoln directly. Indiana's Speaker of the House warned him of strong support for conciliation there; only "by parliamentary tactics" had the legislature beaten back resolutions in favor of the Missouri Compromise, he reported. Sending delegates to the convention might be a harmless way to appease such sentiment: "We feel satisfied that nothing will come from the convocation," he wrote, "but some of our folks think that time will be gained and that is all important." Indiana's governor, Oliver P. Morton, agreed that the convention would gain needed time—it might, he noted, "delay fatal action" until after Lincoln's inauguration—but he also emphasized the need for Republicans to "take hold of it and control it." Pennsylvania, especially, had been showing ominous signs of leaning toward the Crittenden plan, which could ruin the party in other states. It was up to the strong Northwest to send "good men and true" who could "operate as a powerful restraint upon any disposition on the part of other states to compromise the integrity and future of the Republican party."[31]

These ideas would ultimately comprise Northern legislatures' chief motivation for participating in the convention: to provide a sop for conciliationists while ensuring that nothing serious came out of the gathering. Yet many hard-line Republicans resisted any involvement whatever, and tough battles took place before they could be convinced of the plan's wisdom. In Illinois, for example, the legislative party caucus was still deliberating post–*Star of the West* antisecession resolutions like New York's when Virginia's invitation came; now it deadlocked on a response to that as well. Not until January 31 did Republican members finally come to a decision. The next day, each house's committee on federal relations finally reported the long-debated resolutions under which Illinois would agree to send delegates to an official constitutional convention should one be called with the qualification that Illinoisans did not actually want the Constitution amended and the additional provision that "the whole resources" of the state were at the service of the national government for the preservation of the Union. This was Illinois Republicans' version of balancing magnanimity with firmness, as well as their means of keeping their dividing party together. The committees also recommended sending five delegates, chosen by the governor, to the peace conference, but they observed explicitly that it was not an official constitutional convention but "simply an assemblage of private persons" with no legal authority. Moreover, the delegates were to be subject "at all times" to the control of the legislature.[32]

The reasoning behind the Illinois Republicans' decision for action was threefold: to disarm the treasonous Democrats, who were playing upon the people's Union sentiments by charging the Republicans with refusing even to talk with the loyal slave states; to give strength to the Southern unionists; and, perhaps most importantly, to prevent "some of our knock kneed bretheren" from uniting with the Democrats and passing more liberal resolutions. As long as stalwart Republicans were appointed, many felt, the convention could do no harm. It helped that Lincoln let it be known that he endorsed that course. The Democrats, of course, recognized the strategy and fought fiercely to amend the clauses asserting that no constitutional amendments were necessary, authorizing the governor to choose delegates, and placing the delegation under the control of the Assembly. Nevertheless, the Republicans had little trouble in pushing their measures through unaltered.[33]

In New York, meanwhile, the legislature had already demonstrated a growing spirit of conciliation: just a week after the passage of the stanch Littlejohn resolutions, the House Committee on Foreign Relations (chaired by conciliatory Republican Lucius Robinson) voted to recommend a bill urging Congress to organize the western territories into two large states. Now, in presenting the Virginia resolutions to the legislature, Governor Morgan, a strong ally of Weed and Seward, noted that "the great mass of the people of this State, and of the entire North," desired a peaceful resolution to the crisis and advised acceptance of Virginia's invitation. On January 31 a joint committee reported in favor of sending delegates, though with the same reservations as the Illinois Assembly: that the people of New York did not think a constitutional amendment necessary and that the commissioners were to remain under the control of the legislature. The House approved the report on February 2, and the Senate did so three days later, the day after the convention began.[34]

In the Massachusetts legislature, there was no appreciable conciliatory reaction and no divided Republican Party. There the controlling factor was Governor John Andrew. On January 28, as the state's committees on federal relations debated the Virginia resolutions, in Washington Senator John Hale recommended to Charles Francis Adams that Massachusetts's congressional delegation urge Andrew to support the convention. Adams, believing like Indiana's Governor Morton that "it will be well enough to show interest in order to master the nature of the scheme," circulated a short note among his Bay State colleagues. All signed but Senator Sumner, who protested to his friend Adams that he had already recommended to Andrew that he "keep Massachusetts out of such schemes." He insisted that the convention was "summoned to make conditions which contemplate nothing less than surrender of cherished principles." Adams, to whom "this did not seem . . . to be very reasonable," retorted that if that were the case then it "was so much the more proper for delegates to be present, who might expose its nature and character to the country." He sent the delegation's note, along with a longer, private letter to Andrew explaining his reasoning. Sumner dashed off his own missive, grumbling that his colleagues had "signed without much reflection, certainly without any general conference."[35]

Despite his well-deserved reputation as a radical, back in December Andrew had been open to Adams's arguments that the Upper South needed to be appeased long enough for a popular reaction to take hold and that such appeasement could be accomplished without any sacrifice of Republican principles. He sided with Adams again now, replying to Sumner that whatever risks sending a delegation would incur would be offset by appointing "good men" as delegates. Sumner attempted to go over the governor's head by writing directly to state legislators, but Andrew prevailed. On the thirty-first, the committees on federal relations recommended that Massachusetts send a delegation appointed by the governor. Like those of Illinois and New York, the resolutions denied the need for any constitutional amendment and provided for legislative control over the delegates. Despite opposition from Republican radicals, the Senate passed the resolutions on February 2 and the House, on February 5.[36]

Each Northern state had its own scuffle over the convention, and the range of responses revealed the degree to which the conciliatory reaction had taken hold in various areas. Not surprisingly, Pennsylvania, New Jersey, and Rhode Island were the most eager to participate, while the other New England states followed Massachusetts's example of reluctant acceptance. Ohio and Indiana passed resolutions similar to Illinois's and New York's, the Indiana governor taking the added precaution of requiring written assurance of delegates' opposition to concessions. The governor of Iowa merely instructed the state's congressional delegation to attend, "if you shall think it advisable to do so," while the more radical upper northwest states of Michigan, Wisconsin, and Minnesota refused to send delegates at all.[37]

After the uproar its announcement had aroused, the conference itself was anticlimactic. On the opening day, February 4, delegations from only one-third of the states were present, the other states either rejecting the invitation or still being mired in legislative battles. In the end, twenty-one of the thirty-three states would participate, the exceptions being the seceded cotton states (whose representatives began meeting that same day in Montgomery, Alabama, to create their new government), the ultra-Republican states of the upper northwest, and the far western Pacific states. Northern delegations, most of them dominated by hard-line Republicans whose presence was intended to ensure the convention's failure, outnumbered those from the South fourteen to seven. It was not a situation that promised to accomplish much in the way of sectional reconciliation.

In its call for a peace conference, the Virginia legislature had endorsed a version of the Crittenden proposal. As that was unacceptable to most of the Northern delegations, the first order of business, to the dismay of the Virginians, was to draft an alternative plan to serve as the basis for negotiations. Former treasury secretary James Guthrie of Kentucky, a moderate Southerner whom Lincoln had sounded out for a cabinet position in late November,[38] chaired the committee appointed to craft such a plan. The committee, composed of one member from each state, began deliberations on the sixth and was scheduled to make its report two days later. When the appointed day came, Guthrie requested additional time. On the eleventh he did so again, then once more on the thirteenth. Meanwhile, the delegates, like the country at large, were forced to wait. "It is well that the sessions of the Peace Congress are secret," grumbled Massachusetts radical George S. Boutwell after the third postponement, nine days after the conference had convened, "for nothing has yet been done that is of the smallest consequence." Despite his crossness, Boutwell and other hard-liners were content with developments thus far. As his fellow Massachusetts delegate John Z. Goodrich observed in a report to Governor Andrew, "Good nature and masterly inactivity is the policy till Lincoln is inaugurated. . . . Our true policy is to delay matters—finally do nothing, relying on

Providence and honest 'Old Abe' to work out the problem of American destiny."[39]

Conciliatory Republicans were also relieved to see the conference extended; their primary goal was also to stretch out debate as long as possible while unionist feeling grew in the Upper South. Seward was taking advantage of the border-state elections and the hopes raised by the peace conference to nurture optimism among unionists. With the confidence gained from Lincoln's written assurance that he would accept at least the Corwin-Adams proposal, he reassured his contacts in the Virginia secession convention that the new administration would be supportive of their cause.[40]

✳ Meanwhile, Lincoln finally left Springfield on February 11 for his long journey to Washington, made even longer by a circuitous route that involved receptions at several state capitals and numerous stops along the way. The route had been made public, and massive crowds gathered at each stop and shouted for him to speak. Apparently heartened by the Virginia and Tennessee elections, he took advantage of the opportunity to bolster Northern resolve. Lincoln had granted Seward as much leeway as he could, but now that Southern unionism had proved itself he began to rein his secretary of state–designate back in.

He wasted no time. On the evening of the journey's first day, speaking from the balcony of his hotel room in Indianapolis, Lincoln pronounced that it would not be coercion for the government to hold or retake its forts. To great laughter and loud cheers, he added in regard to anyone who might disagree, "It occurs to me that the means for the preservation of the Union they so greatly love, in their own estimation, is of a very thin and airy character. . . . In their view, the Union, as a family relation, would not be anything like a regular marriage at all, but only as a sort of free-love arrangement." Lincoln ridiculed secession, inquiring, "By what principle of original right is it that one-fiftieth or one-ninetieth of a great nation, by calling itself a State, have the right to break up and ruin that nation as a matter of original principle?" To the amusement of his audience, he concluded innocently that he was "deciding nothing, but simply giving you something to reflect upon."[41]

The Indianapolis speech was a thunderbolt to Seward. Over the next week and a half, as the president-elect wound his way eastward, his agony only intensified. To the ears of Southern unionists and Northern conciliationists, Lincoln's frequent wishes for peace and promises not to interfere with the rights of states were lost amid what they perceived to be most ominous assertions. What most concerned them was Lincoln's flippant attitude toward Southern concerns. At Columbus, Ohio, he asserted that "there is nothing going wrong . . . there is nothing that really hurts anybody." Refining the idea somewhat, he elaborated at Pittsburgh the next day, "Notwithstanding the trouble across the river, there is really no crisis, springing from anything in the government itself. In plain words, there is really no crisis except an *artificial one!* . . . There is no crisis, excepting such a one as may be gotten up at any time by designing politicians." And the following day at Cleveland: "Have they not all their rights now as they have ever had? . . . What then is the matter with them? Why all this excitement? Why all these complaints? As I said before, this crisis is all artificial. . . . Let it alone and it will go down of itself [Laughter]." At Poughkeepsie, New York, he jibed to Democrats in the audience, "I see that some, at least, of you are of those who believe that an election being decided against them is no reason why they should sink the ship."[42]

Thurlow Weed met Lincoln's train at Rochester and tried to persuade him to tone down his remarks, but to no avail. Shortly afterward, at Trenton, New Jersey, the president-elect introduced a powerful new theme, remarking pointedly, "I shall do all that may be in my power to promote a peaceful settlement of all our difficulties. The man does not live who is more devoted to peace than I am [Cheers]. . . . But it may be necessary to put the foot down firmly." "Here," according to the *Tribune* reporter who recorded the speech, "the audience broke out into cheers so loud and long that for some moments it was impossible to hear Mr. L.'s voice." The next day in Independence Hall, Philadelphia, he reiterated the Republican rationale for the use of force: "There will be no blood shed unless it be forced upon the Government. The Government will not use force unless force is used against it." Conciliationists cringed, wondering why he felt the need to bring up force at all.[43]

The truth behind Lincoln's remarks was merely common sense to most Republicans. To both the endless cheering crowds and a great many readers at home, the declarations of the president-elect were encouraging after two and a half months of Buchanan's wavering and congressional temporizing, as he intended them to be. But to Southerners they stank of coercion, and Seward and other conciliationists were astonished and dismayed that Lincoln felt compelled to make them. Charles Francis Adams mourned, "Nothing has so much depressed my spirits as the account of [Lincoln's remarks]. They betray a person unconscious of his own position as well as of the nature of the contest around him. Good natured, kindly, honest, but frivolous and uncertain." He concluded, "I am much afraid that in this lottery we have drawn a blank."[44]

To make matters worse, Lincoln's speeches seemed to have emboldened congressional stalwarts. On February 18, the House Committee on Military Affairs reported a new force bill, which was passionately debated for the next several days. Frantic Virginia unionists begged Seward to secure Lincoln's silence and to defeat the force bill, which "has done us more injury than an invading army." Seward, Adams observed, "seemed to be more discouraged than I had yet seen him." He told Adams that the Virginia convention appeared to be growing more radical. They agreed that "the danger of secession seemed to be imminent."[45]

✳ At the peace conference, meanwhile, a number of Northern delegates made the same discovery that many free-state congressmen had made in early December: it was much easier to be resolute against compromise from a distance than it was when faced with the pleas of Southern unionists in Washington. Despite Northern dominance of the convention and the stalwart spirit with which most Northern delegations were selected, the report that the Guthrie committee finally presented to the peace conference on February 15 closely resembled the border-state plan. Like that proposal, it extended the 36°30' Missouri Compromise line, prohibited slavery north of it, and eliminated Crittenden's guarantees for the security of slavery in territories south of the line, instead simply denying the authority of either Congress or territorial governments to interfere with the institution there. Yet the Guthrie proposal dealt with the Republicans' other major concern, that of territory "hereafter acquired," more strongly than the border-state plan, requiring the consent of four-fifths of the Senate for the acquisition of any new territory. Other provisions expressly denied the federal government authority to interfere with slavery in the District of Columbia or the Southern states, required the unanimous consent of all states to amend the constitutional provisions dealing with slavery, and provided for compensation for owners of fugitive slaves who were prevented by violence from claiming their property. The new proposal took the form of a single, multipart constitutional amendment.[46]

Needless to say, the report was unsatisfactory to either Northern or Southern hard-liners. The former presented a minority report simply calling on the states to request that Congress convene a national constitutional convention, rallying around the modest gesture proposed in Seward's January 12 speech; the latter demanded a radical overhaul of the national government that would give the South veto power over legislation and executive appointments and explicitly grant states the right of secession. For the next week and a half the entire conference gave itself over to passionate speech-making and sharp—at one point nearly violent—debate. Several amendments to the Guthrie report were approved, two of them significant: reestablishment of the Missouri Compromise line was revised to apply only to existing territory, and acquisition of new territory was to be permitted only with the concurrence of two-thirds of the Senate, including concurrent free-state and slave-state majorities.[47]

Not until February 26 did the convention finally vote on the propositions. Immediately the territorial piece was voted down, eleven to eight, rendering the rest of the plan superfluous. After voting to reconsider, the suddenly subdued convention adjourned. The next day found a new situation. The absence of a New York radical who was arguing a case before the Supreme Court left a tie in that state's delegation, canceling its vote. Missouri decided to abstain, and two of the five Illinois delegates reversed their votes, moving their state from the "no" to the "yes" column and producing a narrow nine to eight victory. Although the rest of the plan was then passed by wider margins, members did not feel confident enough to submit the whole to a vote. They quickly sent the proposal off to Congress. With that, the peace conference adjourned.[48]

The convention's agreement on a plan was met by an initial burst of excitement; President Buchanan announced at a reception that the country was saved, and General Scott ordered a 100-gun cannonade.[49] However, there was little chance of anything's coming of it. Congress was set to adjourn in just four days, and it was unreasonable to think that it would be able to accomplish in that time what it had been unable to accomplish in the previous three months. For Republicans, the conference had achieved its purpose, buying time until the inauguration. Accordingly, the House refused even to receive the document: Speaker Pennington did not present it until March 1, when, despite the support of conciliatory Republicans such as Adams and Kellogg, the plan failed to muster the two-thirds necessary to suspend the previously scheduled order of business and allow debate.[50]

The Senate agreed to consider it at least, despite the ironic suggestion of Vermont's Jacob Collamer "not only that it be made the order of the day for twelve o'clock tomorrow, but that it be adopted by three-fourths of the States the next day." Over the final days of the session, Crittenden and

Douglas fought futilely for the plan, Crittenden even substituting it for his own proposal. They did not have the cooperation of Seward. Recognizing that substantive concessions were a pipe dream at this point, he satisfied himself that the inauguration had been reached without the further spread of disunion and concerned himself now with boosting his influence with Lincoln. Rather than argue for any particular compromise plan, Seward partnered with stalwart leader Lyman Trumbull in calling for a national constitutional convention, an idea for which he probably had little real hope but which might offer Southern unionists some slight sign that the Republicans were not completely inflexible.

Over the long, hectic days before Congress adjourned, the peace conference proposals were debated, delayed, and ultimately rejected. So, too, was almost every compromise measure that had been brought before Congress. Only one proposal survived the ordeal: Seward's constitutional amendment guaranteeing the security of slavery in the states, a concession whose chief objection arose not from its substance—Republicans denied the federal government's right to interfere with slavery in the states as it was—but from its language: it introduced the word "slavery" into the Constitution. The amendment was approved by the House on February 28 and by the Senate in the early dawn of March 4, and sent off to the states for ratification.[51]

Although they voted solidly against even the one measure that was passed, the hard-liners, it seemed, had won. Lincoln's inauguration had arrived, the party was still intact, and no real concessions had been made.

✳ By the end of February, after months of rising and falling hopes and fears, of partisan struggle and governmental paralysis, Northerners were emotionally and intellectually drained. They had kept a close eye on events at the South, in Washington, in Springfield, and in their own state capitals. They had sustained long, impassioned campaigns for and against compromise. And at the end of it, careworn and spent, they still did not know the fate of the Union. In the Deep South, the seceded states had taken control of all federal property save for a few coastal forts; they had written a constitution and organized a government. Would their new confederacy endure? In the Upper South, unionists had somehow defeated secession despite receiving little of the encouragement they had demanded from congressional Republicans. Would they continue to do so after the new administration took control? And in the North, the long-anticipated reshuffling of parties had failed to materialize; the Republican coalition whose victory had sparked this fearsome crisis was on the verge of taking power.

Would its factions stand together behind whatever policy the new president revealed? Northerners could not know the answers to any of these questions, upon each of which hung the larger, more solemn matters of peace or war, the survival or destruction of the nation.

All would depend on Abraham Lincoln, and Northerners had watched carefully as he made his circuitous way to the capital, weighing his words and trying to take the measure of the man in whose hands their future rested. As February came to a grateful close, a tired, anxious people waited for their new leader to speak.

Chapter 8 ✳ A Calm Pervades the Political World ✳ March

By inauguration day, Lincoln had reason to be optimistic, if only cautiously. The capital was secure, and there seemed little chance that the inauguration would be interrupted by violence. Upper South unionists had beaten back secession and, despite continued warnings, seemed to have gotten safely past the worst danger. Congress had rejected substantive compromise before adjourning until December, so that issue would not agitate the country for another nine months. By the time it reconvened, the disunion furor would, with luck and a bit of encouragement, have died out in the border slave states and even begun to wither in the Deep South. Finally, all this had been accomplished without upsetting the fragile Republican coalition, the essential tool for ensuring that the republic of the Founders would not be corrupted by the further expansion of slavery.

It is not certain what Lincoln's precise plans for governance were. His initial concerns revolved around organizing the government, which meant distributing federal offices. That was not only for bureaucratic purposes. Through a successful patronage policy he could hope to unify his party; fortify the loyalty of the Upper South and even begin to establish viable Republican organizations there; and assist nature in ensuring that the new territories Congress had just organized would one day be free states. All of that would strengthen his hand in dealing with the very real problem casting a pall over all the gains of the past month: the seven states of the Lower South and their supposed Confederacy. Lincoln laid out his immediate plans for dealing with that matter in his inaugural address: he would refuse to recognize their departure from the Union, hold on to the few remaining federal possessions there, find a way to collect the customs duties, and for the time being refrain from delivering the mail or appointing federal officials. Aside from revenue collection, what he proposed was essentially passive. He would not sacrifice the Union in order to maintain peace, but neither did he intend to provoke a needless civil war.

Lincoln never got a chance to institute his policy. Immediately after he took office, the crisis shook off the brief, unsteady lull into which it had slipped and cast the government once more into convulsions. As usual, the focal point was the federal garrison at Fort Sumter, which was now revealed to be dangerously low on food. The question of what to do with Major Anderson and his small command would dominate the administration's first month, throwing the president and his cabinet into turmoil. Oddly, the storm had little visible impact outside of the White House, where a wait-and-see attitude much like November's prevailed. In the first weeks after the inauguration most Northerners accepted the evacuation of Fort Sumter, some from an earnest desire for conciliation, others from a grudging resignation to military necessity. The question was whether the president would submit to the seeming imperative of the new situation.

❋ For those seeking an indication of the day's meaning for the future, nature offered a hopeful one: after a blustery, chill morning, the sun came out shortly before the inauguration ceremony was scheduled to begin and the air grew warmer and more springlike. As omens went, the domeless Capitol building that rose up behind the scaffolding where the president-elect would swear the oath of office was more ambiguous. On the one hand, it could be read as an obvious metaphor for the half-finished nation itself. On the other, more optimistic hand, the Capitol was in the midst of being improved, not torn down, its wooden dome replaced by marble— as, perhaps, the new administration would render the Union itself more permanent.

A third, even more uncertain sign was also apparent. To the new administration's warmest supporters, the armed soldiers lining the streets along Lincoln's route, the occasional menacing clusters of cannon, the bustling officers on horseback, and even the unseen sharpshooters stationed on strategic rooftops were a comforting reminder that government authority was still in place—that the country had survived to reach this day when the people's constitutionally chosen leader would be duly instated. To others, however, the show of force was a disconcerting sight, jarringly out of place at one of the country's most important national rituals: the celebration of the successful operation of the political system, the peaceful transfer of power in response to the people's will. It could bode no good.

Abraham Lincoln, the central figure in the day's proceedings, shared a carriage with his predecessor from the hotel to the Capitol. Despite being accompanied by an armed escort that frustrated curious spectators' attempts to see inside, Lincoln seemed to take notice of neither the elaborate defenses nor the uneasy, expectant air they produced. Once upon the platform erected outside of the east portico, even the muted ripple of applause that greeted his introduction, so different from the rowdy exuberance of the western crowds he was used to addressing, elicited no discernible reaction. He simply began to speak, his high voice carrying his words almost to the back of the massive audience, making known at last the views Americans had been waiting to hear throughout that long, bleak winter. All of the apprehensions and hopes, the warnings and assurances, the accusations, indignation, and resentment of the last four months had come down to these words. The stakes, both he and his listeners well knew, were profound: with compromise defeated and Congress adjourned (although the Senate would stay on to confirm the new president's appointments), the response to secession now lay entirely in Lincoln's hands.

The speech he delivered differed significantly from the draft he had shown an elated Carl Schurz a month earlier. The calm, reasonable, inoffensive tone remained, as did the assurances that the administration had neither ill will toward Southerners nor malign intentions toward their peculiar institution. Still present as well were the condemnation of secession as the essence of anarchy and the vow to enforce the Constitution and protect federal property, which together formed the heart of his disunion policy. Gone, however, were any references to Lincoln's obligation to party principles or his refusal to compromise. The latter, in fact, had been replaced by an explicit endorsement of the constitutional amendment protecting slavery that the Senate had approved early that morning before finally adjourning. Absent also was the vow to retake federal property seized by secessionists. And no longer did the speech end abruptly with the implied threat, "With *you*, and not with *me*, is the solemn question of 'Shall it be peace, or a sword?'"—that line had been deleted entirely and the whole final paragraph reworked to emphasize the administration's desire to avoid conflict. The address now closed with an eloquent plea for forbearance and peace, rooted in a heartfelt appeal to Americans' shared history and mutual devotion to the Union: "We are not enemies, but friends. We must not be enemies. Though passion may have strained, it must not break our bonds of affection. The mystic chords of memory, stretching from every battle-field, and patriot grave, to every living heart and hearthstone, all over this broad land, will yet swell the chorus of the Union, when again touched, as surely they will be, by the better angels of our nature."[1]

Just over a week earlier, Southern unionists and their Northern allies had winced at Lincoln's blithe allusions to an artificial crisis and the need to put the foot down firmly, convinced that the new administration would drive the border states into the new Confederacy and render the Union's destruction permanent. Now, although he had not conceded all they could have asked for, his words offered hope that secession might be contained and the Union eventually restored. Clearly something had happened since Lincoln's arrival in Washington to alter his perception of the crisis.

It was only natural that William Seward had been intimately involved.

✳ As Lincoln had wound his way across the North, Seward's desperation had grown. He did score a minor victory when Lincoln took his advice and announced that in Washington he would stay at a hotel rather than in the private home arranged by Illinois hard-liners Elihu Washburne and Lyman Trumbull; Seward was anxious that the president be surrounded by the right people.[2] Seward also took advantage when General Scott informed him of a plot to assassinate Lincoln in Baltimore, sending his son Frederick to tell Lincoln of it personally. Lincoln had taken the advice of Seward and others and arrived in Washington unannounced, several hours ahead of the scheduled train that carried his family and entourage. The move had backfired somewhat when the opposition press ridiculed the president-elect for sneaking into the city under cover of night, but Lincoln showed no disposition to hold Seward responsible for that.[3] In any case, whatever small triumphs Seward might claim, Lincoln's public remarks continued to show that trying to surround him with right-thinking allies during the last days of the trip had failed to make any dent in his hard-line views. Seward would have his work cut out for him.

The senator took full advantage of finally having Lincoln personally at hand. On the first day—Saturday, February 23—he escorted the president-elect around town, making introductions at the White House, the Capitol Building, and the Supreme Court, taking him to see General Scott (who was not in but called at Lincoln's hotel later), and escorting Mary Lincoln and the rest of the family from the train depot in the afternoon. He took Lincoln to church the next morning and maintained a constant presence throughout the following week, missing no opportunity to surround Lincoln with conciliatory Northerners and, more importantly, Southern unionists. Between Monday and Wednesday, Lincoln met with numerous conciliationist leaders, including multiple times with Crittenden, Douglas, and John Bell of Tennessee, the Constitutional Union presidential candidate. Of course, Lincoln also spoke with a great many Republican stalwarts, but none were as omnipresent as Seward and his allies from the border slave states.[4]

From the beginning, Seward knew what he was up against; on his first day in Washington, Lincoln had given him a copy of the inaugural draft. Aside from some minor stylistic changes, it was unaltered from its original form. The appalled senator went through it line by line and on Monday morning presented Lincoln with six pages of suggested revisions, intended, he wrote, "to soothe the public mind." Accompanying them was an explanatory note that echoed much of what he had written in late January, including a claim that, having "devoted myself singly to the study of the case here, with advantages of access and free communication with all parties of all sections," he understood the situation better than the hard-liners, who "know nothing of the real peril of the crisis." Indeed, he claimed boldly, "only the soothing words which I have spoken have saved us and carried us along thus far."

Seward pulled no punches with his advice. Granting concessions, he wrote, would not disrupt the Republican Party—"they will be loyal, whatever is said"—but refusing them would utterly alienate its rivals. In particular, retaining the opening paragraphs pledging the administration's loyalty to the Chicago platform "will give such advantage to the Disunionists; that Virginia and Maryland will secede; and we shall within ninety, perhaps within sixty days, be obliged to fight the South for this capital, with a divided North for our reliance." Instead, he proposed, Lincoln should follow the example of Thomas Jefferson's 1800 inaugural, in which the new president had mollified his enemies by announcing his intention to govern for the good of all, not just his own party.[5]

Most of Seward's specific suggestions involved subtle changes in phrasing—for example, replacing "on our side, or on yours" with "on the side of the North, or of the South," or describing the secession movement as "revolutionary" rather than "treasonable." He advocated more substantive alterations as well, eliminating Lincoln's blunt rejection of compromise as well as his pledge to "reclaim" the Southern forts. Finally, Seward tried to take the sting out of Lincoln's closing words by framing a final paragraph that stressed the sections' shared heritage and the need for unity.[6]

Seward was taking a great chance with his bold letter and lengthy revisions, and he waited apprehensively for a response. None came. Lincoln kept the same busy schedule, meeting endlessly with delegations and individuals from all parties and factions and listening patiently to each. He shook hands, slapped backs, compared heights, told his jokes and stories, and gave little indication of what he was really thinking As inauguration day approached, Seward's fear became acute. Everything he had worked for all winter—the very survival of the nation itself, he believed—depended on Lincoln's reaction.

The speech, of course, represented only one part of the drama. The war for control of the party raged on unabated, and Seward was in the thick of that conflict also. Cabinet selection would not only indicate Lincoln's factional preference but greatly influence the distribution of all lesser offices. On this subject, Lincoln had deliberately kept silent for close to two months, a long period of uncertainty that had only intensified the resolve of both sides. With Seward and Edward Bates (as attorney general) already announced (although Seward's enemies kept up their efforts to oust him right to the end), the paramount question was whether Salmon Chase or Simon Cameron would win the chief patronage plum, the Treasury Department. Yet Seward was equally concerned that militant hardliner and outspoken Seward-hater Montgomery Blair would become Lincoln's Southern choice should John Gilmer refuse. He continued to pursue Gilmer even while mounting a fallback campaign for the Blair family's Maryland rival, Henry Winter Davis. There was also the question of the New England representative: Seward would have been thrilled with the selection of his close friend and ally Charles Francis Adams, whose name had been circulated quite a bit earlier in the winter, but if the press was to be believed, the contest had come down to Gideon Welles, a hard-liner and former Democrat from Connecticut, or former Massachusetts governor Nathaniel P. Banks, a moderate who seemed to favor conciliation.[7]

Lincoln's decision in January to delay further cabinet decisions and keep his own counsel in the meantime had probably been critical in keeping the party together through the bitter winter. As long as both sides thought they had a chance at favorable treatment when it came time to hand out offices, neither would risk estranging the president-elect by deviating too widely from the party line on compromise. On the other hand, had one side or the other actually gained supremacy in the cabinet, as both hoped to do, retaining the loyalty of the disappointed faction in the midst of the conflicting pressures of the crisis would have been difficult.[8] But Lincoln had to make a decision eventually, and a few days before the inaugural he made his choices public.[9]

As he had sworn to do since before the election, he followed the formula of "justice for all," a balance-of-power strategy that had been hugely successful for him in dealing with the vicious personal and political feuds among Illinois Republicans. Chase would head the Treasury and Cameron the War Department—the latter a startling indication of how lightly Lincoln took the potential for actual war. Welles was named to the Navy Department. Gilmer, in a move that would have enormous repercussions over the next month, had finally removed himself from consideration for any position. The Republicans' refusal to offer concessions had already alienated him, and reports that Chase had been selected to the cabinet confirmed the North Carolinian's conviction that Lincoln's administration would lean too far toward the radicals. Gilmer's withdrawal left Blair as postmaster general. The final spot, the Interior Department, went to Caleb B. Smith, a former Whig from Indiana who had been pressed by Seward's Illinois ally David Davis.[10]

Given the vulnerable state of the national party, Lincoln's "justice for all" was the only policy that had any chance of working, but a mere share of power and patronage satisfied neither faction. Given Lincoln's relative obscurity and rural bumpkin image, both sides believed they could dominate the administration and were determined to do so. Seward felt his hopes crushed by the prospective cabinet. Not only had he still not heard from Lincoln about the inaugural address, whose delivery was imminent, but the nominations of Chase, Blair, and Welles were a clear signal that his own views held no favor in the new administration. Not only did former Democrats (Chase, Welles, Blair, and Cameron) outnumber former Whigs (Seward, Bates, and Smith), but when it came to disunion policy, Seward was not sure he could count on his fellow old Whigs: Bates was a hard-liner and Smith an unknown with a colorless reputation. Seward would have only one reliable ally, Cameron. Even more desperate now than he had been in late January, he decided once more to wager everything.[11]

Seward's first move was to talk to Winfield Scott. The two men had a long history together, one in which the master politician dominated the politically naive but ambitious soldier. Throughout the secession winter, the senator and the general had been in close contact. Seward had advised Scott about defending the capital when danger had threatened in early January, and it had been Seward to whom Scott had entrusted his intelligence of an assassination plot. It made perfect sense for Seward to turn to Scott now; he might not be supported in the cabinet, but if Lincoln's top political and military advisers joined in counseling caution and diplomacy, how could the president-elect resist? Despite Scott's resolute lobbying of Buchanan to strengthen the Southern forts—most recently in summoning Gustavus Fox to Washington to discuss the reinforcement of Sumter—by the inauguration, the old Virginian had been converted to Seward's conciliatory view.[12]

On the day before the inauguration, Scott gave a letter to Seward, which the latter, by obvious prearrangement, passed on to Lincoln. It outlined four possible courses for the incoming administration. To the options of collecting the duties from Southern ports offshore and permitting peaceable secession—saying to the "*wayward sisters, depart in peace!*"—Scott offered no comment. He advised that the third, attempting to conquer the seceded states, would entail a two- to three-year war that would require a massive army, incur tremendous loss of life on both sides, and cost at least a quarter of a billion dollars. The result? "Fifteen devastated *provinces*—not to be brought into harmony with their conquerors; but to be held, for generations, by heavy garrisons—at an expense quadruple the net duties or taxes which it would be possible to extract from them—followed by a Protector or an Emperor."

On the other hand, the administration could reorganize the Republican Party, taking on a "Union" designation and endorsing either the Crittenden or peace conference proposals. Such a course would not only prevent further secession but bring back many and possibly all of the seceded states. Without this or "some equally benign measure," Scott warned, echoing Seward's recent admonition, "the remaining slave holding states will, probably, join the Montgomery confederacy in less than sixty days." If that happened, "this city—being included in a foreign country—would require a permanent Garrison of at least 35,000 troops to protect the Government within it"—a massive number given that the entire army presently consisted of only about 16,000. The letter offered no explicit recommendations, but it was obvious which alternative the general advocated.[13]

But Scott's letter was merely Seward's insurance plan, in case his primary strategy miscarried. On Saturday, March 2, he informed Lincoln that he would not accept an appointment to head the State Department. His note was brief and offered no explanation, but the implication was unequivocal: if Lincoln was going to maintain a hard-line stance toward the crisis and back it up by filling his cabinet with radicals, he would have to do without William Seward.[14]

Having thrown down the gauntlet, Seward waited. The game was in Lincoln's hands.

✳ Seward's note found the president-elect already privately softening his position; despite Lincoln's apparent intransigence, the New Yorker's earlier labors had unknowingly borne fruit. As Lincoln had proved typical of mainstream Republicanism in so many ways throughout the winter, so now did the resolve against conciliation that he had shown in the bosom of his home, far from the battleground of Washington, soften in the face of the capital's realities. The process had occurred first among moderate Republican congressmen in December, when only the intervention of outraged constituents and Lincoln himself had prevented a significant movement for compromise. It had been repeated in February at the peace conference, where a body dominated by Northerners, many of them chosen expressly for their hard-line views, had somehow cobbled together a compromise plan. In both instances the central factor had been the entreaties of Southern unionists, and in this case, too, it was their earnest pleas that led Lincoln to soften his stance.[15]

Not that he was as inflexible as he appeared. True, his numerous speeches along the road from Springfield made it clear to all that the president-elect was not prepared to compromise his position. The glibness with which he fended off appeals from peace conference delegates on his first night in the capital confirmed that view.[16] Yet Lincoln had already displayed a predilection for using strong anticompromise language as cover while he quietly considered mild movements toward conciliation, and it is likely that his speeches and his rebuff of the peace delegates were calculated both to raise morale among disheartened rank-and-file Republicans and to cement his hard-line reputation in official Washington, freeing him to make whatever minor concessions might prove necessary without alienating party stalwarts. The strategy was in perfect keeping with the balance of resolve and magnanimity that he had been trying to strike throughout the crisis.

That Lincoln had again adopted this approach is suggested by his reaction to a bit of advice from his old friend Orville H. Browning, a fellow Illinois lawyer. Browning, a rare anticompromise conservative, had looked over the draft of Lincoln's inaugural prior to the latter's departure from Springfield. Though admiring of its "clear, bold and forcible statement of principles," he advised Lincoln to remove the word "reclaim" from the section dealing with the Southern forts—not because he disagreed with the idea, but because there was no need to announce it. Give the rebels enough rope, he explained, and they would, by assuming the role of aggressor, hang themselves. That is, if the administration maintained an overtly defensive posture, the secessionists would inevitably hand it an opportunity to recapture the forts without ever having to take a belligerent stance. Not only was the point all the more powerful for coming from a firm stalwart like Browning, but it was in line with Lincoln's own efforts to avoid giving offense while still upholding the laws. Indeed, the logic of it struck Lincoln so forcefully that he was inspired to scrawl across the back of Browning's letter a line about the need for North and South to remain friends, which later found its way into the address's peroration.[17]

Although toning down his rhetoric on a key policy issue may have contradicted Lincoln's well-crafted public image of unwavering resolve, the reasoning behind it was consistent with his temperate hard-line views; like most moderates, he had never been as aggressively stalwart as the radicals. In contrast, a more substantive action such as, say, offering to evacuate Fort Sumter in exchange for a guarantee of Virginia's loyalty would seem a significant departure from his position. Yet Lincoln made just such an offer. A few days after his arrival in Washington, Lincoln met with a number of important border-state unionist leaders, including William C. Rives and George W. Summers of Virginia, John Bell of Tennessee, and Charles S. Morehead of Kentucky. Stephen Douglas was probably also in attendance; the most prominent Northern advocate of conciliation, Douglas, like Seward, was working closely with Southern unionists.[18]

According to Morehead's later account—the only one extant—Lincoln began the interview by emphasizing his and his party's lack of ill will toward the South.[19] He promised to uphold the constitutional rights of all the states and expressed bewilderment at the widespread antipathy Southerners held toward him. Nevertheless, he told them, he was not only personally committed to excluding slavery from the territories but obligated to respect the wishes of the voters who had elected him. Trying to get a feel for his visitors' views, he asked how he could fulfill his oath as chief executive to uphold the Constitution and the laws while avoiding what they considered coercion. Unsatisfied with their replies, Lincoln related a fable about a lion who loved a lady so much that he permitted her family, who professed to be concerned about her safety, to remove his claws and teeth. The operation safely concluded, they proceeded to beat the lion with clubs. The message was clear: if the federal government surrendered its right of self-defense in order to assuage Southern fears, it would be left helpless to prevent its own destruction.

Morehead responded by launching into the Southern unionists' oft-repeated warnings of a long and bloody civil war, but he was interrupted by Rives, a well-respected elder statesman of whom Northern conservatives had widely spoken for a position in Lincoln's cabinet. The Virginian offered a powerful and eloquent appeal for the Union but warned sadly that if Lincoln resorted to coercion, Virginia would leave the Union—and, he added, "As old as I am, and dearly as I have loved this Union, in that event I go, with all my heart and soul." Morehead claims that Lincoln was so moved that he sprang from his chair crying, "Mr. Rives! Mr. Rives! if Virginia will stay in, I will withdraw the troops from Fort Sumpter." Rives denied any authority to speak for his state, but he applauded Lincoln's wisdom and pledged to exert "whatever influence I possess" to restore the Union. The interview broke up shortly thereafter.

Lincoln's motivation in offering to evacuate Sumter is uncertain. Perhaps, as Morehead believed, he was overcome by the power of Rives's speech—or in a broader sense, the heartfelt appeals of the unionists Rives represented. It is likely, though, that he was also testing their sincerity. For months now, arguments for conciliation had revolved around the need to support Upper South unionists; Lincoln would naturally have wanted to find out how willing they were to meet Republican concessions. It is doubtful that he expected a positive response, at least not in the form of the guarantee he required. If they had accepted his overture, the sacrifice might prove worthwhile—after all, he remarked drolly to a foreign dignitary a few days later, "a State for a fort is no bad business"[20]—but that was unlikely to happen.

Whatever Lincoln's reasoning, the proposition marked a significant departure from the unyielding firmness he had maintained in Springfield; two months earlier his idea of encouraging Southern unionism had been to offer vague expressions of goodwill in private letters to unionist leaders; at around the same time, he had pronounced that Buchanan should be hanged if he abandoned the Charleston forts. His appreciation for the complexity of the situation was growing. On the other hand, Lincoln's change of heart should not be exaggerated. Offering to evacuate Sumter in return for Virginia's guaranteed loyalty was considerably different from capitulating to the mere threat of attack, as he had thought Buchanan had done. Moreover, whatever his calculations may have been in making the proposition, there is no evidence that he repeated it over the next few weeks. Just a few days later, in fact, Virginia representative Sherrard Clemens concluded after meeting with Lincoln that the president-elect was "an abolitionist of the Lovejoy and Sumner type" and predicted dourly that "his follies and puerilities" would drive Virginia and the other border slave states out of the Union.[21] Lincoln's first days in Washington had not completely altered his position.

Nor did Seward's last-minute refusal of the State Department have that effect. That is not to say that Lincoln simply recognized Seward's action as a bluff and called it, as historians have traditionally concluded.[22] Seward was far too powerful among the old Whig majority for Lincoln to risk an open rupture with him at the outset of the administration. As historian Patrick Sowle argues, Lincoln's response was more complex. To begin with, he would have recognized immediately that the move was prompted by two considerations: the cabinet battle and secession policy. Having resisted the attempts of both sides to dominate the cabinet throughout the winter, he was determined not to give in now—perhaps more than any other Republican, Lincoln believed that the survival of the party required unity between former Whigs and former Democrats. The Seward faction must not be permitted to dominate; Chase and the other radicals must stay.

The inaugural address was a different story. How many of Seward's revisions Lincoln had agreed to before receiving the senator's ultimatum is uncertain, but given his prior acceptance of Browning's idea and his recent Sumter-for-Virginia offer, there is every reason to believe that he had already integrated at least some of the proposed changes into his address, or planned to. It is impossible, then, to judge with any precision the influence of Seward's letter. What we do know is that Lincoln spent much of March 3 and part of the morning of March 4 revising the text, and that the final document incorporated most of Seward's modifications. We also know that it was not until after he had delivered the revised speech that he sent a note asking Seward to reconsider, which suggests that Seward probably did not know what Lincoln would say before he heard it along with the rest of the audience.[23]

The two men spoke for several hours that evening. The next morning, no doubt after analyzing the situation with Weed, who was in Washington as part of the cabinet lobbying campaign, Seward accepted the State Department. He was still unsatisfied with the cabinet, but ultimately his tactic *had* been a bluff—he knew that he could be far more useful inside the administration than outside. Despite his doubts about Lincoln's "compound Cabinet," he consoled himself, "I believe I can endure as much as any one; and may be that I can endure enough to make the experiment successful. At all events I did not dare to go home, or to England"—rumors had Lincoln appointing him minister to Great Britain—"and leave the country to chance."[24]

In the end, if Seward's March 2 letter was, as Sowle has characterized it, "his most successful maneuver of the secession winter," that success was qualified. The inclusion of Chase and, perhaps more significantly, Blair in the cabinet were frightening to Upper South unionists and signaled to Seward that Lincoln would not be easily influenced. Moreover, for all the mollifying alterations to the inaugural address, the end product was entirely consistent with Lincoln's brand of conciliation. The speech's tone was softened by the suggestions that he took from Seward, but ultimately it conceded nothing of substance. Even endorsing Congress's new thirteenth amendment was in keeping with Lincoln's policy of surrendering minor, irrelevant points; the amendment said nothing more than most Republicans already believed the Constitution to imply. Ultimately, Seward's changes were an enlargement on the basic idea that Lincoln had already received from Browning: that he should emphasize his peaceful intention while saying the minimum necessary to sustain federal authority.

In this regard, perhaps the most significant of Seward's proposals was one of the few that Lincoln rejected. With reference to the Southern forts and collection of the tariff, rather than adopt Seward's deliberately ambiguous line supporting "a peaceful solution of the national troubles and the restoration of fraternal sympathies and affections," Lincoln instead kept Browning's suggestion to simply eliminate the word "reclaim" while still pledging to "hold, occupy, and possess" government property and collect import duties.[25]

Lincoln's brief days in Washington had led him to make more concessions than he had during his long months in Springfield, and Seward's lobbying efforts (both direct and indirect) and his March 2 ultimatum had played an important role in Lincoln's delivering an inaugural address that Southern unionists could, if they chose, interpret as conciliatory. But it would be too much to claim that Lincoln had been won over to Seward's policy. He might have developed a greater comprehension of the subtleties of the crisis, but nothing he had done so far indicated a rejection of the moderated hard-line stance—the balance of firmness and forbearance—that he had embraced throughout the winter.

✳ A bit earlier that day, when James Buchanan rode from the White House to pick up Lincoln and drive him to the Capitol, he was inspired not by any desire to offer support or impart advice but by tradition. Indeed, the two men had little to say to each other, no more on this occasion than during the formal calls each had paid the other after the president-elect's arrival. Given the magnitude and complexity of the crisis facing the nation, it might seem reasonable for Lincoln to have questions or for Buchanan to communicate important information. But as the president's carriage rolled along the muddy streets, they merely exchanged bland pleasantries.

Once they arrived at their destination, they made a brief appearance together before the members of the two houses of Congress and the justices of the Supreme Court, all crowded into the Senate chamber. The entire body then proceeded out onto the Capitol's east portico, where seats had been arranged around the small, makeshift platform on which the ceremony took place. When it was over they returned to the White House, exchanged formal farewells, and went their separate ways. Buchanan's only recorded comment, which may well be apocryphal, was an expression of relief: "My dear sir," he is said to have told Lincoln, "if you are as happy in entering the White House as I shall feel on returning to Wheatland [his Pennsylvania estate], you are a happy man indeed."[26]

If those were the outgoing president's words, his well wishes were tinged with an unbecoming irony; he knew that any happiness his successor might be feeling would be short-lived. Convinced from the beginning that Lincoln and his party were responsible for the crisis, he no doubt thought it fitting that they would be left to deal with its latest and cruelest twist. At eleven o'clock that morning, shortly before Buchanan left the White House to carry out his final duty as chief executive, Secretary of War Joseph Holt had arrived, considerably late, to the administration's last cabinet meeting. After waiting for his colleagues to finish whatever they were doing, he stunned them by revealing the contents of the latest dispatch from Major Anderson: it would now take a force of twenty to thirty thousand men to overcome the elaborate Charleston defenses, Anderson reported, a force impossible to raise within the time his limited provisions would allow his garrison to remain at the fort. With the inauguration set to begin shortly, there was nothing that could be done beyond delegating Holt, at his own request, to convey the momentous intelligence to the new president. That settled, the outgoing president finished signing the last-minute bills Congress had sent him and left to find his carriage. At no point that day did he give Lincoln any hint of the new development.[27]

Lincoln's own recollection just a few months later was that Anderson's report was the first thing handed him when he entered his office after the inaugural, but that reflected the enormity of his shock more than the actual chronology of events. In fact, Holt discussed the matter at greater length with his colleagues that evening, then returned home to compose a lengthy cover letter to Lincoln, who meanwhile hosted his first White House dinner, attended the inaugural ball, and worked out his differences with Seward. By the time Holt handed his letter and its fateful enclosures to the unsuspecting president the next morning, Lincoln had submitted his list of cabinet appointments to the Senate and received several delegations of cheering well-wishers.[28] Nevertheless, his impression reminds us that he was given no time at all to settle into his new role. Lincoln's presidential term prior to being faced with the military crisis that would soon explode into a devastating internecine war could be measured in mere hours.

The first line of Holt's letter referred to the several "important and unexpected" dispatches from Fort Sumter that were enclosed, but Lincoln had to read quite a while before discovering their content. First, quoting extensively from his own letters and Anderson's reports, Holt detailed the administration's offer to send reinforcements at any time they were requested and the major's consistent expressions of satisfaction with the security of his position. Nevertheless, he wrote, an expedition had been held ready should Anderson indicate any change. However, that expedition was wholly inadequate to the "seemingly extravagant estimates" of 20,000 men that arrived the previous day from Fort Sumter, estimates that came as a complete surprise to the War Department.[29]

The main purpose of Holt's lengthy missive was plainly to absolve the outgoing administration of any suspicion that it had engaged in the kind of vacillating behavior it was so often charged with, or worse, that it had dropped this situation in Lincoln's lap intentionally. Lincoln's first act was to transmit the letter and dispatches to Winfield Scott, whose reply revealed that the general had other ideas. Taking advantage of this long-awaited opportunity to simultaneously denounce and distance himself from Buchanan's whole secession policy, Scott argued that the fort could have been reinforced easily in late December and that it had still been possible as recently as three or four weeks before, but that a series of truces with the secessionists had precluded any action. Now the opportunity had been lost. As the Sumter officers knew, it would take the government months to arrange an expedition even one-third the size they deemed necessary. "Evacuation seems almost inevitable," he concluded grimly, ". . . if indeed, the worn out garrison be not assaulted & carried in the present week."[30]

The administration's powerlessness to control or even adequately respond to constantly changing conditions, the president's inclination to remain aloof from important decisions and allow his assertive new cabinet to handle affairs, the squabbling over responsibility and blame—all of these patterns of the last few months were captured in miniature in the final hours of James Buchanan's presidency. The incident also foreshadowed the bitter struggle to control Buchanan's historical legacy—particularly his handling of the secession crisis—that would preoccupy most of the administration's key members over the next years and even decades. Already, before the drama had even reached its climax, the actors seemed as much concerned with criticism of their own performances as with the tragedy's denouement. All in all, the episode marked a fitting close to Buchanan's term.

✳ The news, Lincoln soon discovered, was even worse than it had first seemed. The next day, another dispatch arrived from Fort Sumter, this one containing a list of stores. In his earlier report Anderson had referred vaguely to the "limited supply of our provisions," and he now specified what that meant: the garrison had on hand just twenty-eight days' worth of flour and hard bread, the staple of the soldiers' diet.[31] Lincoln was understandably concerned about the loyalty of the Kentuckian officer, but Holt assured him that Anderson was no secessionist. That assuaged the president's doubts for the time being, but the thought would remain in the back of his mind.[32]

Over the next two days Scott, Holt, and several high-ranking military officers briefed Seward and Secretary of the Navy Welles, but when Lincoln first assembled the full cabinet on March 6, he made no mention of the crisis, preferring to keep the meeting brief and formal. No doubt he was having enough trouble getting his own mind around the new situation without risking civil war within his fragile "compound cabinet." It was not until Saturday, the ninth, that Lincoln held his first real cabinet session and broke the news to the rest of his advisers. Assuming, like Lincoln, that there would be plenty of time to examine and discuss the Sumter situation, all had occupied themselves with the endless chore of organizing their departments. Now, Bates recorded, they were "astonished to be informed that Fort Sumter *must* be evacuated."[33]

Indeed, that seemed to be the consensus. The military challenge appeared insuperable, and after hearing the opinions of Scott, Anderson, and army chief engineer General Joseph Totten, only Montgomery Blair among Lincoln's political advisers remained unconvinced. By Monday, just a week after Lincoln's long-awaited inauguration, newspapers across the North were reporting that the cabinet had decided that the evacuation of Sumter was an unavoidable military necessity. By Tuesday readers of the Charleston papers knew it, too. General Scott drew up the orders for

Anderson's withdrawal and submitted them to the War Department. For all Lincoln's resolve to maintain possession of the Southern forts, it appeared that his first major act as president would be to abandon the most prominent of them.[34]

✳ On Tuesday evening, three days after the cabinet meeting, Seward remarked over dinner at the Adams house that "the violent remonstrances from the north and east against the abandonment of Fort Sumter, had alarmed the President and delayed a decision."[35] Seward's assessment of Lincoln's thinking no doubt reflected the outrage Republican editors were expressing at reports of Sumter's imminent evacuation. It was probably also inspired by an incident at the White House the previous day. After listening to angry talk about Sumter among Republicans in the Senate and around Washington, Frank Blair Sr., former adviser to President Jackson and patriarch of the powerful and intensely hard-line Maryland clan that had produced Lincoln's postmaster general, stormed into the president's office in a rage. "The surrender of Fort Sumter, [is] virtually a surrender of the Union," he raved. "Compounding with treason [is] treason." What Seward apparently did not know was that, by the next day, once Blair had learned of General Scott's recommendations, he had regretted his rashness and written a letter asking his son Montgomery to "contrive some apology for me." Meekness in a Blair went only so far, though: he accompanied his regrets with an agitated appeal for the president to issue a proclamation, on the model of Jackson's 1832 nullification message, that would place blame on the previous administration and pledge to maintain the nation's remaining seaboard defenses.[36]

Although no other Republican was brazen enough to give Lincoln a tongue-lashing, Blair's reaction to news of the evacuation was typical. Gideon Welles later recalled that cabinet members' initial responses were that the fort must be reinforced, until the grim counsel of the military experts reconciled them to the unpleasant state of affairs. Public response among Republicans followed a similar pattern of knee-jerk resistance followed by grudging acceptance. Writing just a few days after the initial newspaper reports, Welles—no conciliationist, surely—observed, "An impression has gone abroad that Sumter is to be evacuated and the shock caused by that announcement has done its work. The public mind is becoming tranquilized under it and will become fully reconciled to it when the causes which have led to that necessity shall have been made public and are rightly understood. They are attributable to no act of those who now administer the government."[37] His judgment was confirmed both by the press, whose early reports that "the act is deprecated and denounced in every form of anathema" were accompanied by acknowledgments that leaving Sumter was unavoidable,[38] and by individual Republicans. Neal Dow, a Maine radical, virtually echoed Welles when he explained to Lincoln that Republicans in his state recognized that evacuation "is undoubtedly a Military *necessity*; and admits of no question as to its expediency. At first, the suggestion struck us unpleasantly, but when we learned the actual position of affairs, we saw that the measure is inevitable, and is a legacy of humiliation from the last administration, which cannot be declined." At a caucus of Republican senators, no less stanch a hard-liner than Charles Sumner suppressed a proposal to demand that Sumter be maintained, arguing that it was a military matter that the Senate should let alone.[39]

Thus the initial public outcry faded remarkably quickly, long before Lincoln's misgivings. It was not the last time Seward would misread the president over Fort Sumter. The popular indignation among Republicans no doubt confirmed Lincoln's reluctance to issue the order for Anderson's withdrawal, and it may even have been the explanation he offered to his secretary of state, but the next few weeks would reveal that his hesitation stemmed less from fear of public censure than from his own commitment to upholding the most visible symbol of federal authority in the seceded states, especially so soon after his public vow to "hold, occupy, and possess" it.

Already, in fact, Lincoln had acted to keep his options open. On the fifth, as soon as he learned of Sumter's situation, he had told Scott to take whatever steps were necessary to ensure the security of the three remaining Southern forts—Fort Pickens at Pensacola and two smaller outposts in the Florida Keys. His greatest concern was that the Fort Pickens reinforcements, who had been held onboard their ship since early February, be landed. Four days later, finding that Scott had not yet acted, he followed up his verbal instructions with a written order. (Whether Lincoln's initial instructions were simply vague or Scott delayed deliberately in order to avoid bringing on a conflict is not clear, but as we shall see the incident would linger in Lincoln's mind for some time.) The president also asked Scott to elaborate on his evaluation of the situation at Sumter: Exactly how long could the garrison hold out without reinforcements? Could the fort be resupplied or reinforced in that time, and if so, how long would it take? Seward might find comfort in the thought that public opinion was all that prevented Lincoln from issuing the critical order to evacuate Fort Sumter, but in fact the president was simply not yet ready to admit defeat.[40]

✳ When Lincoln and Seward conferred on the night of the inaugural, blissful in their ignorance of the recent turn of events, they had reason to hope that their respective policies for dealing with secession were not incompatible. Despite his insistence on bringing radicals and hard-liners into his cabinet, Lincoln had pledged in his inaugural to avoid any aggressive action and to refrain from aggravating secessionists by appointing unwanted officials or even trying to deliver the mail. In essence, the government would engage in the "masterly inactivity" that the Republican Party had called for back in November, avoiding any appearance of hostility while the secession fever ran its course. Thus, unless there was some unexpected and disastrous turn of events—a collision at one of the Southern forts being the greatest danger—the government would simply keep its hands off. It would refuse to recognize secession and be sure to maintain a symbolic authority, but would not push the issue. Whether Lincoln realized it or not, in practical terms the policy he had marked out was quite similar to Buchanan's. Given the distorted image of Buchanan's administration that prevailed throughout the North, he probably did not.

Of more immediate significance was that Lincoln's approach was also in line with Seward's policy of delay. Seward had built that strategy around two basic convictions. The first was that the cotton-state Confederacy could not survive unless the remaining slave states joined it. Once the Upper South had been secured to the Union, it would be only a matter of time until the seceded states came crawling back and the Union was reconstructed on Republican terms. The second was that unless provoked by a collision between the federal government and the secessionists, disunion sentiment in the Upper South would become progressively weaker, until eventually any danger would vanish altogether. The prospect of that depended upon how Southern unionists interpreted the intentions of the new administration, a consideration that had rendered Seward's inclusion in the administration vital.

Regarding the border slave states in particular, Seward had reason to be hopeful. Over the past few months, the question of Union or secession had become the central issue of Upper South politics, to the point that old political loyalties were falling away and a new bipartisan Union coalition was gathering strength. Seward believed that if he could nurture unionist faith until Virginia's May elections, the new party would emerge as the dominant political organization in the Upper South and the danger of disunion would pass. Moreover, as Seward's late-January letter to Lincoln had suggested (and Scott's March 3 letter had reminded the president), the new coalition offered the Republicans a golden opportunity to expand their organization into the South. That, Seward believed, was necessary if theirs was to be a viable, lasting party. In fact, Seward had made several comments over the past several weeks (though not to Lincoln) that suggest that he envisioned a new conservative national organization with himself at its head.[41]

Thus Lincoln's agreement to tone down the inaugural address was critical to Seward's plans. That the president continued to embrace the spirit of Seward's vision after the inauguration could be seen in the conciliatory tone of his speeches to various congratulatory delegations, and more substantively in the influence that Upper South unionists exerted over federal appointments, at Seward's suggestion.[42] Lincoln also assured Southern unionists that his inaugural signified a peaceful policy.[43] The two men, it seems, had come to an understanding; more, they had managed to form a working partnership.

It was, more than Seward recognized, an alliance to which both partners made critical contributions. Ironically, Lincoln's remarks on the road from Springfield had provided a vital boost to the conciliationist cause. Had the expectations of Southern unionists remained as high in late February as they had been when rumors of an impending settlement were circulating a month earlier, congressional Republicans' refusal to pass significant compromise legislation would likely have wrecked their hopes and made the inaugural address seem a war message. By the time the president-elect had arrived in Washington, however, Southern unionists expected the worst. Thus they took great comfort in things that they otherwise would have taken for granted, such as Lincoln's numerous meetings with unionist delegations, or viewed as sources of disappointment, such as Congress's failure to pass any compromise measures beyond the slavery amendment. Unionists also read conciliatory intentions into several instances of inaction: Republicans did not organize the new western territories on a free-soil basis, repeal New Mexico's slave code (something they had attempted in the previous session), or most importantly, pass a force bill. As there was no chance of congressional Republicans' going further than they did without Lincoln's express encouragement—which he was not about to give—Lincoln's strategy of creating a strict hard-line image while actually considering minor concessions probably proved more effective than Seward's encouragement of optimism and his open conciliationism. Perhaps the most reasonable conclusion is that both strategies were necessary and in fact complemented each other. Seward, of course, did not recognize this; as far as he was concerned, it was his intervention alone that had saved the Union thus far.[44]

The question was, how would this odd partnership hold up once Anderson's fateful dispatch fundamentally altered the situation? As it happened, news of the situation at Fort Sumter could not have come at a better time for Seward. In the days immediately following the inauguration he was frantically trying to contain a new, potentially explosive development. Martin J. Crawford, one of three commissioners appointed by the new Confederate government to negotiate the terms of separation, had arrived in Washington the day before the inauguration. The following day, Seward learned that Crawford intended to apply immediately to be formally received by the State Department, and that if his mission were rejected Confederate authorities did not believe they would be able to prevent an attack on the forts. Within a few days, Seward found himself discussing the matter with former California senator William Gwin, whom the Confederate commissioners (a second envoy, John Forsyth, arrived on March 5) had enlisted to sound out the administration for them. Seward assured Gwin that the administration desired peace.[45]

Desperate to buy time, Seward encouraged the commissioners to think that he might be able to help them. His assurances encouraged Crawford and Forsyth to press harder. Per their instructions, Gwin informed the secretary of state that as long as Sumter and Pickens were held by the United States, negotiations could not be postponed, and that the Confederates were "ready to accept war" if it came to that. In vain did Seward point out that the government was not even organized yet; finally he agreed that Gwin would deliver "the terms upon which [the commissioners] would consent to, and stipulate for, a brief respite" from their demands, in order to give the new government more time to compose itself. The commissioners were overjoyed, not at the prospect of the terms' being accepted but because Seward's receiving them would represent "a virtual recognition of us as the representatives of a power entitled to be treated with by this government."[46] Three months earlier, Buchanan had dealt with an identical situation by insisting that he could meet with South Carolinians only as private citizens, not official representatives. The new commissioners would accept no such splitting of hairs; they had been officially appointed by an organized national government and they were determined to secure formal recognition. Seward gained some time with a convenient illness—he was home in bed when Gwin arrived at the State Department, terms in hand, on the morning of March 8—but he was in a serious bind.[47]

Thus Anderson's report, so devastating to Lincoln, was a godsend to Seward. For months, the chief concern he had been hearing from the Upper South was that a collision must be avoided or all was lost. Now that Congress had adjourned and the thorny territorial issue no longer pressed, the unionists' fixation on maintaining peace was even more pronounced.[48] Throughout the crisis, the garrison at Charleston harbor had been the tinderbox that threatened to set the country alight. Withdrawing the troops would ease tensions and buy critical time with the commissioners, and Anderson's ultimatum would force Lincoln to make that decision. Moreover, it would cost Seward no political capital and would create a minimum of fallout, as all but the most diehard stalwarts would recognize that this was a necessity forced on Lincoln by the incompetence of the previous administration. The situation was far from ideal—nothing about the predicament was ideal—but to Seward this unexpected development must have seemed a blessing.

Two days later, as the news of evacuation was breaking across the country, Seward met with Virginia senator R. M. T. Hunter, who had replaced Gwin as intermediary.[49] Hunter reported afterward that Seward was "perceptibly embarrassed and uneasy," but it turned out that the rumors about Sumter had done their work. The commissioners were confused by the contradiction between, on the one hand, the administration's refusal to receive them and continued occupation of Sumter and Pickens and, on the other hand, its peaceful posture and the apparently credible rumors that the forts were to be evacuated. They decided to await further developments and instructed Hunter not to deliver their terms. However, Hunter did request that Seward meet informally with the commissioners. This was a significant improvement but did not solve Seward's problem: simply meeting with them would give an air of legitimacy to their mission. The harried secretary bought another day by pleading the necessity of conferring with the president, but he was running out of time.[50]

Whether Seward actually discussed the matter with Lincoln is uncertain, but the next day he informed Hunter that he was unable to receive the gentlemen in question. Prepared for that, they abandoned the backchannel approach and registered an official request with the State Department for a formal interview.[51] Seward continued to delay, but his back was now against the wall. He could not accept their request, of course, but as the situation stood, either rejecting it outright or doing nothing would result in their leaving Washington, which might well mean an attack on the forts. Lincoln's order to evacuate Sumter was just what Seward needed to keep the commissioners in the capital, but until it was issued all he could do was stall. As he had done so often in the last three months, Seward waited impatiently to see what Lincoln would do.

✳ Seward was not the only leader of the conciliation movement to find himself on the defensive, scrambling to adjust to the new conditions. Stephen Douglas, too, found himself in the now-familiar position of struggling to save his country and his party while forced to respond to his opponents' lead. The role of opposition leader did not suit Douglas's pugnacious style, especially when taking too strong a stand either for or against federal authority could alienate a significant portion of his own divided party. The Northern Democracy had been split on the question of using force against disunion from the beginning. Douglas had been careful to maintain a moderate position, insisting on the need to uphold federal authority but emphasizing the need for compromise and the dangers of Republican stubbornness. But passing compromise legislation was not an issue now that Congress had adjourned, and attacking the administration during a time of national crisis was difficult.

Keeping Northern Democrats together, challenging as it was, was only part of the Little Giant's strategy. He believed restoring peace and stability to the Union required bringing the Democracy back to its former glory, which entailed reunifying its estranged Northern and Southern wings. Having no illusions about the depth of the Gulf states' commitment to independence—or, for that matter, the animus Deep South Democrats held for him—Douglas, like Seward, was closely tracking and encouraging the growing alliance of unionist Democrats and Whigs in the Upper South. Like Seward's, his interest was actively encouraged by the leaders of the growing Union Party. Believing that Northern conservatives would follow their lead in dissolving old party ties in a time of crisis, the Southerners sought to attract both Northern leaders to "a national conservative party which will domineer over all other party organizations North and South for many years to come." From their point of view, "the course of the shrewd partisan and the wise patriot is now upon the same line."[52]

Despite their clandestine meetings back in January, neither Seward nor

Douglas was willing to cut old ties and join forces. While each was willing to use the other to further his own goals, they had opposed each other too long, worked too hard to get where they were, and had too many deeply held political differences. Rather, each looked to bring Southern unionists and Northern conservatives into his own respective organization. In some respects that was easier for Douglas, who was simply trying to restore what had always been a national party, than for Seward, whose efforts were crippled by his party's anti-South foundation as well as the hard-line views of most of his Republican colleagues. On the other hand, Douglas faced the same problem that had plagued him since the election: being powerless to shape policy, he had little to offer the new party, while Seward held forth the possibility of influencing Lincoln, who throughout the crisis had shown himself to be the only one wielding any real authority.

But the Southern unionists had a single overriding concern, and Douglas and Seward both knew that they would rally behind whomever they believed responsible for maintaining peace. Thus, during the long, hectic final days of the congressional session, Douglas had fought desperately for either Crittenden's or the weaker peace conference plan, while Seward, recognizing that his party would support no substantive concessions, had concerned himself with boosting his influence with Lincoln. The high profile he maintained while doing so was no accident; the newspapers were filled with stories of Seward's closeness with and influence on the president-elect.

Now Douglas was forced to follow Seward's lead; once congressional compromise had failed, influencing Lincoln was all he could do, either. At his meetings with Lincoln prior to the inauguration—which he, too, made sure were noticed in the press—Douglas emphasized the need to encourage Southern unionism through conciliation. He pledged not to take political advantage if Lincoln split with his party over what he carefully termed an "act of patriotism which would preserve the Union."[53] At the inaugural ceremony, he pushed to the front of the platform "in order to leave no doubts," his biographer writes, "that he would stand by the new administration in its effort to maintain the Union." Taking advantage of old social ties, that evening he escorted Mrs. Lincoln, whom he had once courted, to the inaugural ball, and he danced the quadrille with her at midnight.[54]

Ironically, it was the prospect that Lincoln's inaugural address might actually be moderate that presented Douglas with his greatest challenge. Even though it would afford him tremendous relief in terms of the danger to the country, if the Republican administration actually followed the conciliatory policy he had urged, it was likely to win over the very constituency he was trying to attract himself. As neither politics nor patriotism would permit him to change his position, however, Douglas decided that his best strategy lay in loyally supporting the administration while moving out ahead of it on the question of conciliation. His first move was to tout the inaugural as a peace manifesto, "for the purpose," he explained bluntly to John Forsyth, a former supporter who was now bedeviling Seward as a Confederate commissioner, "of fixing that construction on it and of toma-hawking [the administration] afterwards if it departed from it." To judge by his show of support before Lincoln even began speaking, he had de-termined to follow that course no matter what the address actually said. When he did finally hear the new president's policies, though, the mur-murs of approval he uttered throughout the address were, if a bit overdone, no doubt sincere. Afterward, when reporters pressed him for a reaction, he pronounced that Lincoln did not intend coercion. And to mollify the con-cerns of Virginia unionists at the Richmond convention, he and Crittenden issued another of their joint assurances: "Yes," they affirmed, "there is hope."[55]

Two days after the inauguration, on Wednesday, March 6, Douglas carried his plan a step further and defended Lincoln's address on the Senate floor. It should be considered "a peace offering rather than a war message," he declared. To reassure Northern Democrats that he had not sold them out, he made it clear that he had no "political sympathy" with Lincoln and expected to oppose the administration on traditional political questions. However, "on this one question, that of preserving the Union by a peaceful solution of our present difficulties . . . I am with him." What Lin-coln intended, he claimed, was that "if the enforcement of the laws in the seceding States would tend to facilitate a peaceful solution, he is pledged to their enforcement; if the omission to enforce these laws would best facili-tate peace, he is pledged to omit to enforce them." More specifically, "if maintaining possession of Fort Sumter would facilitate peace, he stands pledged to retain its possession; if, on the contrary, the abandonment of Fort Sumter and the withdrawal of troops would facilitate a peaceful solu-tion, he is pledged to abandon the fort and withdraw the troops."[56]

In this instance, Douglas's imaginative construction of Lincoln's inten-tions went beyond bluff; the Illinois senator had inside information and he was determined to exploit it. Fort Sumter's garrison, he announced to the Senate the next day, was dangerously low on food, and the country's top military experts estimated that it would take over ten thousand men to resupply it. Since Lincoln had neither ten thousand men nor the money to raise them before Congress reconvened, Douglas concluded, he must intend to evacuate.[57]

Although Douglas professed to have "stated casually what I supposed was well known to everybody,"[58] at that point—March 7—few people even inside the administration were aware of Anderson's plight. Of those few there can be little doubt which one revealed it to Douglas. If the leak was a replay of Seward's January scheme of covert bipartisanship, it succeeded: numerous Southern unionists reported to both men their tremendous relief at the news. Moreover, despite Douglas's insistence that his conclusion was based on logic rather than concrete knowledge of administration policy, his speech convinced many Upper South unionists that Douglas was in a position of great influence, even that he spoke for the president. From North Carolina, John Gilmer wrote urgently, "I fully believe you can quiet the border states. You can place in the hands of the Union men weapons of offence and attack" against secessionists.[59]

What Douglas probably did not know was that, reflecting the Southern unionists' dismissal of existing parties, Gilmer was writing to Seward at the same time, "You can do much to quiet Virginia. . . . I have full confidence that you in some ways wiser and better than I can devise or suggest can prevent" a collision.[60] Despite their efforts, neither Seward nor Douglas had gained any advantage over the other in the border states. They had managed, however, to place enormous pressure on Lincoln to order Anderson's garrison out of Fort Sumter.

✳ Such pressure was mounting; more and more it seemed that evacuation was inescapable. Responding to Lincoln's request for a more detailed analysis of the situation, General Scott estimated that the garrison's supplies could be stretched to forty days "without much suffering," but added that an assault would carry the fort easily any time the secessionists decided to make one. Worse, the government could not possibly supply or reinforce the fort before its supplies ran out: raising the necessary force, including getting authorization from Congress to expand the army beyond its current total of just 16,000 troops, would take at least six to eight months. Scott's brief conclusion was chilling: "It is, therefore, my opinion and advice that Major Anderson be instructed to evacuate the Fort . . . immediately on procuring suitable water transportation."[61]

Meanwhile, the almost daily cabinet discussions were getting nowhere. Desperate to hear a positive opinion, Lincoln agreed to meet with Montgomery Blair's brother-in-law, Gustavus Fox, to hear the plan for resupplying Sumter he had presented to Buchanan. He was impressed enough to invite Fox to join Scott and other military leaders in presenting their views at a cabinet meeting on Friday, March 15. After the military men had spoken, Lincoln took a formal poll of the cabinet, requesting written responses to the query, "Assuming it to be possible to now provision Fort Sumter, under all the circumstances, is it wise to attempt it?"[62] Predictably, Seward and Montgomery Blair represented the two extremes in the ongoing debate.

Seward spoke boldly for evacuation, spelling out his approach to the crisis more explicitly than ever before. He argued that since disunion was so clearly unjustified, in both the seceded states and the border slave states prosecession sentiment would die out, if left alone. But it was imperative that it be left alone. Seward acknowledged that the administration was obligated to use force if preserving the Union required it but insisted that its primary goal should be to avert both disunion *and* war. The way to do that was to give Southern unionists time to bring about the inevitable reaction in their states, which entailed avoidance of anything that might possibly be interpreted as military coercion. Even a successful provisioning of Fort Sumter—which General Scott and Major Anderson showed was impossible—would be too short-lived to represent anything of value. But whether it succeeded or failed, the attempt would inaugurate civil war and thereby make disunion permanent. The key point was to encourage the Upper South and unite the North by avoiding any appearance of belligerence. "I would defer military action on land until a case should arise when we would hold the defence," Seward concluded. "In that case, we should have the spirit of the country and the approval of mankind on our side."[63]

Blair's counterargument reflected the same reasoning strict hard-liners had followed throughout the crisis. Further delay would be disastrous, he insisted, for two reasons. First, "every hour of acquiescence in this condition of things and especially every new conquest made by the rebels strengthens their hands at home and their claim to recognition as an independent people abroad." The longer the federal government treated the seceded states as a separate country, the more people were growing accustomed to the idea. Second, what had emboldened the secessionists to attempt their scheme to begin with was their contempt for Northerners' will to resist. Evacuating Fort Sumter would merely encourage the rebels to seize additional property; already "Mr. Buchanans policy has . . . rendered collision almost inevitable & a continuance of that policy will not only bring it about but will go far to produce a permanent division of the Union." Reinforcing the fort, however—which he thought Fox proved could be accomplished "with little risk"—"would completely demoralize the rebellion" and inspire "a reactionary movement throughout the South which would speedily overwhelm the traitors."[64]

The replies of the rest of the cabinet showed Seward's ideas to have been the more persuasive. Only Chase agreed with Blair, and he was considerably less zealous. He declared that although he was persuaded that an attempt to provision the fort had a good chance of success, he would oppose it if he thought it was likely to inaugurate civil war. However, he did not think that was likely, as long as the expedition was accompanied by a proclamation "setting forth a liberal & generous yet firm policy towards the disaffected States." Though opposing evacuation, then, Chase agreed with Seward that the administration must not be perceived as acting belligerently.[65]

The rest echoed various arguments made by Seward and Scott. Bates concurred with the secretary of state in the importance of encouraging Southern unionism, while Smith reiterated that provisioning the fort would do no more than buy a small amount of time until the provisions ran out again. Bates, Welles, and Smith all agreed that the federal government must not appear to strike the first blow of the civil war that would surely result from a resupply attempt, making this the most widely agreed upon position in the cabinet. In Smith's words, "If such a conflict should become inevitable, it is much better that it should commence by the resistance of the authorities, or the people of South Carolina, to the legal action of the government, in enforcing the laws of the United States. The public sentiment of the North would then be united in the support of the government, and the whole power of the country would be brought to its aid." Finally, Cameron rested his opinion primarily on military considerations: he endorsed the judgment of Scott and the other officers that provisioning was impracticable but added that he would have supported Fox's plan anyway were he not convinced it would "initiate a bloody and protracted conflict."[66]

Judging by Lincoln's phrasing—"assuming it to be possible to now provision Fort Sumter"—the purpose of his question was to separate the political aspects of the situation from the military. It is odd, then, that he asked the question immediately after the military officers had presented their analyses. Predictably, several of the responses were plainly (sometimes explicitly) influenced by the military reality in Charleston; in other words, they did not assume provisioning the fort to be possible. On the other side of the question, Scott had already shown, and would show again, his proclivity to allow political factors to influence his military analysis. By month's end, Lincoln's intense frustration at being unable to get straight answers from his military and political advisers would play a key role in his final decision.

But that lay in the future. For now, a week and a half had passed since Lincoln's inauguration and his discovery of the new crisis. Over that time, the conviction had grown that Fort Sumter had to be abandoned. All of Lincoln's top military advisers concurred in the impossibility of sending provisions, and most of his top political advisers agreed that, for various reasons, to attempt it would be unwise. Most of the cabinet left the March 15 meeting convinced—again—that a decision had been reached.[67]

✳ That Seward assumed that Sumter's evacuation was imminent is demonstrated by the alacrity with which he made use of the intelligence. Among his first actions after the cabinet meeting was to pass the news to George W. Summers, leader of the Union delegates at the Virginia secession convention, still meeting in Richmond. The message had its desired effect. A grateful Summers replied a few days later, "The removal from Sumter acted like a charm—it gave us great strength. A reaction is now going on in the State. The outside pressure here has nearly subsided. We are masters of our position here, and can maintain it if left alone."[68]

Seward also took advantage of an unexpected opportunity to inform the Confederate commissioners of the cabinet's decision. Shortly after the meeting, Supreme Court justices Samuel Nelson of New York and John A. Campbell of Alabama called on Seward at the State Department to impress upon him the wisdom of receiving the commissioners. Seward put them off. The administration, he said, would never consent—and besides, he added, "the surrender of Sumter is enough to deal with." The offhand remark did the trick: a startled Campbell agreed that of course "only one matter should be dealt with, at a time," and offered not only to speak with the commissioners but also to write of the matter to Jefferson Davis, recently a Mississippi senator and now newly elected president of the Deep South's Confederacy. But what exactly, Campbell inquired delicately, should he tell Davis? Here was Seward's opportunity for a dramatic pronouncement that would, by impressing the secessionists with the administration's goodwill, gain some of the time he so desperately needed: "You may say to him, that before that letter reaches him: (How far is it to

Montgomery?) three days. You may say to him that before that letter reaches him, the telegraph will have informed him that Sumter shall have been evacuated."[69]

With an additional, intentionally vague assurance that no action was contemplated regarding Fort Pickens (in fact, Lincoln's orders to land the reinforcements had been sent three days earlier), the prestigious messengers were on their way. Crawford took some convincing, but Campbell swore to him that he had "perfect confidence" that Anderson and his men would leave Sumter within—he extended the time to be on the safe side—five days. To act precipitously in the face of such knowledge, he reasoned, would only hurt the Confederate cause.

The commissioners decided they could afford to wait. They knew very well that Seward was playing for time, waiting for a unionist reaction in the South. Confident that such a reaction would never occur, they calculated that delay would benefit their own cause by allowing their new government time to get organized. As Forsyth explained later, their instructions were "to play with Seward, to delay and gain time until the South was ready." In the meantime, it seemed to them that Lincoln's cabinet was headed for rupture and a peace movement appeared to be growing in the North. If Seward was aware of their calculations, he did not mind. For him as for them, "a policy of 'masterly inactivity'" seemed to be "wise in every particular."[70]

✳ As if the situation were not complicated enough, a new problem now arose, one that threatened to make all previous calculations concerning the fragile national situation obsolete. On March 1, the first Confederate tariff, or import tax, went into effect, lowering import duties to the level of the United States' 1857 tariff. On April 1, the new Morrill tariff, which the Republicans had passed after the departure of the Deep South delegates had left them in control of Congress, was scheduled to raise U.S. rates to almost twice that level. Northeastern merchants, especially in New York, began to panic as they realized that "when the tariffs get into working order in opposition to each other, not only will the people of the Gulf States do all their own importing, but they will drive Northern importers out of the Western market also."[71] The worry was that the smuggling of cheap European imports from New Orleans into the western states and territories would disconnect the East from the West economically; moreover, the Confederacy's lower tariff might lure the border states out of the Union altogether.[72]

Here was evidence that a hands-off policy might not be viable, even in the short term. Lincoln had been sure to point out in his inaugural that the government retained the authority "to collect the duties and imposts"—that is, the federal tariff—in the Southern ports, even though the Treasury Department had no way to enforce it. He now began to give serious consideration to collecting the revenue via warships anchored offshore. It was an idea that had been batted around since the crisis began—Winfield Scott had suggested it in his "Views" back in late October—but the House had never passed a proposed bill to authorize such collections.[73] On March 18, Lincoln requested opinions from relevant cabinet officials as to whether offshore vessels could be used effectively to collect import duties, how large a force could be made available for revenue collection and how long it would take to assemble, and whether collecting duties offshore was constitutional if no other method were possible.[74]

Both secessionists and most Upper South unionists warned that stationing warships off of Southern ports would provoke hostilities.[75] With the new tariff due to go into effect in two weeks, though, Lincoln could see few alternatives: the economic competition would inflict further damage on an already deeply wounded economy, and to forego the collection of taxes would be to sacrifice one of the most basic tasks of government. As with Sumter, he could not postpone a decision for long.

✳ In the same letter in which he expressed his gratitude for news of Sumter's imminent evacuation, George Summers added an anxious postscript: "What delays the removal of Major Anderson? Is there any truth in the suggestion that the thing is not to be done after all? This would ruin us." The query from Richmond echoed Seward's own thoughts; as the deadline he had given the commissioners expired, it was becoming obvious that the flaw in Seward's calculations lay, once again, with Lincoln: the president still had not issued the long-expected order. When the five days Justice Campbell had conveyed to the commissioners had elapsed, he returned to the State Department for an explanation. Seward assured him that there had been no change in policy. The delay, he said, was due merely to the president's disorganization and inability to set priorities—a rationale that he may actually have believed, for he frequently grumbled about Lincoln's lack of system and his preoccupation with distributing the patronage. If Seward was beginning to suspect that Lincoln was still ambivalent, though, he was playing a dangerous game, gambling heavily that the president would ultimately come down on the side of evacuation: he renewed his pledges to Campbell, who accepted them and gave his own to the commissioners. Seward also arranged through the Russian minister to meet the commissioners informally, then backed out for fear that word of the meeting would leak to the press.[76]

What Lincoln was actually thinking is not certain, but he seemed less determined than ever to abandon Sumter. Instead, he was trying to gather more information about the situation in Charleston harbor. On March 19, the same day Summers wrote to ask when Sumter was to be abandoned, Lincoln asked Cameron to send Gustavus Fox to Charleston to review the situation at the fort firsthand. Fox left for South Carolina that same evening.[77] Two days later, Lincoln sent two more emissaries to investigate conditions in Charleston. His motivation this time was to gauge unionist sympathy there in order to verify Seward's conviction that holding the Upper South in the Union would bring the Deep South back. The agents he chose for this mission were not only Illinoisans but native Southerners. Stephen Hurlbut, an influential state assemblyman whom William Jayne had praised as "the man of this legislature," was a native South Carolinian who still maintained contact with family and friends in Charleston. Ward Hill Lamon, a young lawyer whom Lincoln knew from their days riding the circuit, had weaker ties to his native region, having moved from Virginia at the age of nine. His personal loyalty to Lincoln, however, was undisputable. Lamon would present himself to the governor in an official capacity, under the pretense of settling postal accounts, while Hurlbut, saying nothing of his connection with the administration, would quietly sound out his personal contacts.[78]

Plainly Lincoln was torn. On the one hand, even if the fort could be provisioned without starting a war, which did not seem possible, it could not be held indefinitely. It had no real military value, and could not even be used for collecting the revenue offshore. Evacuation would remove the primary irritant to Southerners and, by signaling the administration's pacific intent, strengthen Southern unionism by cutting the ground from under those who charged coercion. It would also remove the danger that a successful attack would invigorate disunionism. On the other hand, evacuation might embolden secessionists and could have a demoralizing effect on the already strained Republican Party.[79] The results of evacuating Sumter were simply impossible to predict. Would it encourage border-state loyalty and lead to the peaceful restoration of the Union, as Seward and his Southern friends believed? Or would it encourage disunionism and cement the existing division, as Blair and the stalwart Republicans insisted? Lincoln wanted as much information as possible before making his final determination.

✳ William Howard Russell, the celebrated war correspondent of the *London Times*, arrived in New York on March 16, ready to analyze the growing risk of schism among the United States and get a feel for Americans in general. The Americans he found on the crossing were all Southerners, so it was not until he reached the Empire City that he came into contact with residents of the free states.[80] With the careful eye of a journalist he observed the customhouse, the Irish dockworkers, the attitudes of servants, the appearance and behavior of the wealthy, the stores and restaurants and hotels, and of course the local press.[81] But his real interest lay in ferreting out Americans' views on the looming conflict. Among his first notations was that the focus of public attention at that moment was two federal forts, Sumter and Pickens. The president, he was told, was vacillating and temporizing as a result of his reluctance to acquiesce to the impossible military situation, and "every one," he found, "is asking what the Government is going to do." Strangely, however, it seemed that although everyone he spoke with had something to say about "the troubled condition of the country," they evinced little real concern—their comments, he wrote, were "principally of a self-complacent nature."[82]

Russell had little interest in the views of the city's poor and middle-class citizens, so it was fortunate that his reputation and the stature of his employer gained him access to the leaders of New York politics and business. The first notable he spoke with was George Bancroft, the Democratic former minister to England most known for his celebratory history of the United States. Bancroft talked at length about the crisis but seemed unable to come to any conclusions: while believing that "the republic, though in danger, was the most stable and beneficial form of government in the world," he was insistent that "as a Government it had no power to coerce the people of the South or to save itself from danger." This was among the first examples of an "astonishing" tendency that Russell would observe of New Yorkers' preoccupation with the philosophical abstractions of constitutional power, particularly the government's lack of authority to prevent secession.[83]

Russell continued to record the views of New York residents for the next week. He found that talk in his hotel bar centered on the disgust of "respectable people" at Lincoln's election; one gentleman pronounced that "if it came to a split," he would support the South. Among the occupants at his hotel he found "not the smallest evidence of uneasiness." At a dinner that included the cream of respectable Democratic politics (those who looked down upon the infamous ward bosses and their minions), he found that such luminaries as Horatio Seymour, Samuel Tilden, and Bancroft embraced the Southern interpretation of the nature of the Union: that is, that the federal government was not sovereign but merely the "machine" created by the states to facilitate union. No one present admitted the government's right to force a state to remain in the Union, and all seemed to enjoy watching the Republicans squirm under the pressure of the national crisis they had brought on. Russell also attended a breakfast at which the editors of the city's leading papers bickered cheerfully over topics from the Southern forts to local politicians to New York life. Much of the conversation revolved around a recent boxing match between English and American favorites.[84]

In his unfamiliarity with the nuances of Northern political views, Russell somewhat exaggerated the radical spirit in New York. Even among the Hardshell-dominated anti-Republican press, historian David Osborn has found, only one newspaper actually welcomed disunion—most advocated peaceable secession only as an unhappy necessity, preferable to coercion. Like George Bancroft, in fact, most anti-Republicans were "unable to arrive at any settled conclusion." They loved and admired the Union and had no wish to see it broken up, but they also firmly believed that a military solution would destroy it more effectively, more permanently, than peaceable secession ever could. Avoiding war was necessary in order to maintain the possibility of a compromise, either before or, if necessary, after disunion.[85]

Even given these caveats, it must be noted that at no point during the crisis (or before) had New York ever been typical of even anti-Republican popular sentiment. As it was the nation's largest city and most important port, public opinion in New York was of intrinsic importance to the crisis, but it is unfortunate for the historian that after his time there Russell decided to head south to Washington rather than explore a few more Northern towns and cities. If he had, he may have discovered that the sentiments of Northern anti-Republicans elsewhere reflected a significantly more complex perception of the situation.[86]

An Illinois writer captured the basic dilemma moderate anti-Republicans faced, a dilemma very similar to that which drove Seward and other conciliatory Republicans. "Our great object is to avert fratricidal war, both on account of its horrors & direct consequences, and to preserve the border slave states, and leave a hope of a reunion yet of our whole country," he wrote. "It is also an object of primary importance for the stability & efficiency of our government, & a constitutional necessity, that we do not acknowledge the right of secession." Or as a Philadelphian phrased it, "The dignity of the government must be maintained, the authority of the Law must be vindicated, the integrity of the Union be preserved; yet all may be done in that spirit of mildness and forbearance, which shall subdue rather than alarm or exasperate our deluded fellow citizens of the South."[87]

Few anti-Republicans acknowledged (at least outwardly) the potential conflict between avoiding war and rejecting secession. Most simply called for an evacuation of the forts and continued to emphasize the need for a sectional adjustment without speculating about what would happen if compromise failed. In that regard, Douglas's endorsement of the inaugural address pleased many of them: it not only showed that Douglas was willing to put the Union before party considerations but also held forth hope that the administration might be swayed in a conciliatory direction.[88] However, as the weeks passed the contradiction in goals was beginning to show. For some, the controlling issue was the need to uphold government authority, and there was some grumbling that Douglas had gone over to the side of the South.[89] In others, the growing tension over Fort Sumter had created a sense of resignation. Peaceable secession, they decided, was preferable to forcing the seceded states to remain in the Union. In Utica, John Munn wrote sadly, "I have lost hopes of any Union, but pray for some amicable settlement of our difficulties—each section left to its own policy."[90]

Nevertheless, Russell's observations illustrate some important points that pertain to the North more broadly. For one, as we have seen, Americans in general (that is, North and South) exhibited great concern for bringing their political views into line with the Constitution, or vice versa. That habit tended to polarize debate by denying the legitimacy of their opponents' views, much like different Christian sects' use of the Bible to discredit each other's beliefs.[91] For another, while secession and its attendant issues did tend to dominate public conversation, it did not consume people's lives during every moment between Lincoln's election and the outbreak of war. The impending crisis over Fort Sumter had generated tremendous anxiety, but Northerners had been living with the question of disunion for four and a half months and were learning to cope with the constant uncertainty and the rise and fall of emotion.

✳ In Washington, the sense of Northern opinion that Lyman Trumbull was getting was very different from that of William Howard Russell. In contrast to the anticoercion principles of the New York elites to whom the London journalist spoke, those of Trumbull's constituents who wrote about national affairs all echoed the sentiments of the Illinois writer who reported, "The people here are all for the Union & generally for the enforcement of the laws and all hope much from the new administration." Some went further. One older citizen related the travails of his father's service under Washington in the Revolution, and demanded, "Shall all this be thrown away to please a few villains and Traitors[?] *I say nay, verryly*; why it makes my very blood boil, to think of the coolness of these unwashed Scoundrels." William Butler, an influential party manager and close ally of Trumbull's, sputtered, "Is it possible that Mr Lincoln is getting scared[?] I know the responsibility is grate; But for god sake tell Mr L to live by it; Or have the credit (If credit it may be termed) Of Sinking in a richous cause and an honest Administration of this Government. I don't want to bequeath this damnable question to any posterity. Let us stand firm."[92]

A closer look at Trumbull's correspondence in mid-March reveals some curious features. First, the volume of mail touching on the crisis that he received in the fortnight following the inaugural was dramatically lower than it had been at any point since the anxious waiting period back in November. Second, only a few letters mentioned the Sumter question explicitly. Some protested news stories of the administration's treating with the Southern commissioners,[93] while others complained about the need to collect the revenue at Southern ports.[94] The Charleston fort was not the only thing on Republicans' minds. Third, in almost every instance those who did discuss the fort did so in the context of its effect on the Republican Party. "How is it," inquired Butler acidly, "do we surrender Sumpter on the grounds of expediency or from necessity[?] If it is done for Expediency, I tell you our party will go under, Such expediency wont do for western feeling." Those without Butler's insider perspective agreed; already the Democrats "are exulting over the rumor that fort Sumpter is to be abandoned," grumbled a Minnesota writer.[95]

Despite their indignation (and correspondents of Illinois's Democratic senator testified that it was great),[96] by not bothering to express their feelings to their national representative, most Illinois Republicans indicated tacit submission to an unpleasant reality. It would seem that Trumbull's correspondents, who throughout the crisis had been among the most stalwart of Republicans, had grudgingly accepted the inevitability of withdrawal. They did not like it; they feared its effects on Republican unity; but like most of Lincoln's cabinet they saw no viable alternative. In spite of the continued focus on enforcing the laws, it can be argued that the most characteristic sentiment came from an office-seeker from Atlanta, Illinois: "Our people are alarmed at the proposed abandonment of Sumter," he reported, but "if it is deemed a military necessity I suppose they will become reconciled."[97]

Trumbull kept his own feelings on Sumter to himself. It was not that he had no opportunity to make it known whether he supported or opposed the administration's policy: the Senate was still in special session, and he could always stroll over to the White House and share his thoughts with the president directly. But Republicans in the Senate had decided to remain silent and wait for the administration's appointments to conclude so that they could adjourn without any further trouble. As long as they controlled the votes, they had no need to engage in the running battles that dominated the floor between Douglas and the few remaining Southern radicals.[98] As for the second option, Trumbull had given up trying to talk to Lincoln.

Back in December the junior senator from Illinois had been one of the president-elect's most trusted advisers: Lincoln had chosen him to deliver his remarks at the Jubilee, and had even awaited his approval before finalizing major decisions such as asking Seward into the cabinet or formally rejecting Buchanan's compromise overture. Trumbull had reciprocated by writing to Springfield regularly to keep Lincoln informed of developments in Washington. In early January, however, their relationship had become strained, a casualty of the war of the factions that had dominated so much of the party's energies over the winter. Like other Republican leaders, Trumbull had been anxious for Lincoln to be surrounded by right-thinking friends, and as a former Democrat and a strict hard-liner he tended to side with the radical wing. Not that he was really a radical—he was realist enough to know that Seward's place on the cabinet was a foregone conclusion, and he never lobbied for Chase the way most of them did. But he had actively engaged in the fights to prevent the inclusion of Cameron and secure that of Illinois radical Norman B. Judd, a friend and ally.

News of Lincoln's (later aborted) offer to Cameron disappointed him, but it was Judd's exclusion that had really hurt. Trumbull had good reason to trust his influence with the president-elect, so when he told Lincoln that it was Judd "in whom I personally feel more interest than in any other person named," and even presented a petition for Judd signed by every Republican senator from the Northwest, he thought his arguments would carry some weight.[99] However, a visit to Springfield from Judd's chief rival, David Davis, and a letter from Jesse W. Fell, a relative neutral in the state battles, convinced Lincoln that to favor either Illinois faction with a cabinet position would split the state party and incur the resentment of Republicans in other states. In the end Judd got a foreign mission and the unexceptional Caleb Smith, a former Whig, was named the Northwest's representative in the cabinet.[100]

The whole affair left a bad taste in the mouths of Illinois's former Democrats, who concluded that Lincoln had gone over to the old Whigs and grew disenchanted with the president-elect.[101] Still, Trumbull's actual break with Lincoln did not come until the latter arrived in Washington. Lincoln's decision not to stay in the private home he and Washburne had arranged, a perception that Lincoln did not make any effort to see his old friends, and a feeling of being ignored on patronage decisions all contributed to his frustration. It was not mere oversensitivity: shortly after Lincoln's arrival, the *Herald*'s Washington correspondent noted, "Judge Davis, of Illinois, is already recognized as a power behind the throne, and is almost as much sought after as Mr. Lincoln himself. . . . The Judd faction look decidedly blue at the prevalence of their rivals."[102]

By the time Lincoln dispatched his agents to Charleston, Trumbull had decided that he had had enough. "No other delegation from any other state would stand this without a blow up, nor do I know how long we shall," he complained to a friend, adding, "I see very little of Mr. L. His surroundings at the White House are such as to make it extremely distasteful for me to go there. He is constantly beset by a crowd, & it is difficult to get to see him at all, & when you do, it is only for a hurried interview." His brother-in-law, William Jayne, reported that in person Trumbull revealed stronger emotion: "Mr L has not treated Mr Trumbull as he should," he revealed, "& Mr T said this morning that he should not step inside the White House again during Mr Lincoln's four years, unless he changed his course."[103]

In itself, Lincoln's falling out with Trumbull was relatively inconsequential. The two had never been close friends; on a personal level a rupture would have left neither terribly distraught. Yet the incident is significant in two respects. First, it is an important reminder that even at a critical moment of decision at the highest level of government, Northern leaders found their attention occupied by concerns other than statesmanship. The patronage had been a consuming issue among Republicans since Lincoln's election, and it continued to be as the crisis approached its climax. Second, the strain had important political implications. Trumbull was not alone in his estrangement from Lincoln. Having been the most influential Illinoisan in Washington earlier in the crisis, he felt the perceived fall from grace most keenly, but much of the state's delegation felt similarly.[104] The result was to alienate Lincoln from the people he knew best in Washington at the very time he was most in need of advice he could trust.

✳ "A calm pervades the political world," John Munn observed at the end of Lincoln's third week in office.[105] His own relative silence on national affairs through much of March underscores the remark. The stillness he perceived, though, was not a relaxation of tension but the oppressive hush of the hurricane's eye. Outside of the White House there was an air of restless anticipation, as Northerners waited anxiously to see what the administration would do. Would Lincoln yield to the traitors and submit to a cowardly surrender of his party and his country? wondered Republicans. They had expected his inauguration to bring an end to vacillation and drift, but his wavering over Fort Sumter boded ill. Would he submit to the warmongering of his party and lead the country to destruction and ruin? wondered Democrats and conservatives. They had been gratified at the conciliatory tone of his inaugural address and relieved at reports of Sumter's imminent evacuation, but the long weeks of inaction worried them.

The lack of action inside the White House, meanwhile, was even more nerve-racking. Amid all the debating and calculating and maneuvering, pressure was rising. General Scott and every other high-ranking military officer had pronounced Sumter's evacuation necessary. Five of Lincoln's seven cabinet officers had declared it unavoidable, even wise. All seemed to think the issue had been decided, and Seward had used that knowledge to forestall Confederate action against the fort and encourage unionism in Virginia. Yet Lincoln would not act. The days passed into weeks and he simply would not act. By late March nerves were taut and tempers thin as the administration worked frantically to juggle never-ending patronage issues and the pressing question of peace or war.

Chapter 9 ✳ Any Decision Would Be Preferable to This Uncertainty ✳ March–April

Whatever optimism Lincoln may have felt in early March had evaporated within twenty-four hours of his inauguration; with each passing day the noose drew tighter around his administration. The decision facing the new president was grave, graver than any faced by his predecessors. From a military standpoint there was no question what should be done with Major Anderson's small garrison at Fort Sumter. Its position was untenable and the fort had almost no strategic value. But Sumter had tremendous symbolic importance due to its location in the principal city of the most radical secessionist state, and had assumed even greater significance with Anderson's dramatic move from Fort Moultrie, the seizure of almost every other federal possession in the Deep South, and the firing on the *Star of the West*. To many Americans North and South the fort's evacuation would signal the surrender of federal authority in the seceded states and a de facto acknowledgment of disunion.

Now the garrison was running out of food, and any attempt to reinforce or even reprovision it would almost certainly provoke a collision of arms, which would mean civil war. Lincoln wished desperately to avoid open hostilities, but he could not bring himself to abandon the fort. For three weeks he delayed making a decision, in the meantime pondering his choices, trying to gather all possible information, and busying himself (far too much, his critics said) with the complexities of organizing his administration.

Although the correlation of the North's hard-line/conciliationist division to the major parties was not perfect—Lincoln's own secretary of state was foremost among a conciliatory Republican minority—it was close enough that Sumter's fate became not only a national concern but also a partisan one. Most Republicans opposed evacuation because they thought nothing was more certain to destroy the country than capitulation to rebellion, while most Democrats urged evacuation because they thought nothing was more certain to destroy the country than civil war. By early

April, the political overtones were increasing in importance, for Republicans especially. While many party hard-liners were still willing to accept evacuation as a military necessity, a growing number grew restive at Lincoln's inaction. Once more there were rumblings that weakness among party leaders would split the organization. If that happened, most Republicans believed, the country would be lost to the slave interest.

From a variety of fronts, then, pressure was mounting for Lincoln to make a decision. And it was his decision to make—no matter how vehemently Northerners argued or how mightily political leaders struggled to exert influence, the government was structured such that the choice would be Lincoln's alone.

✳ On Thursday, March 28, matters in Washington finally came to a head. Intelligence arriving from Charleston played an important role. Gustavus Fox had returned from Fort Sumter on Sunday and reported that the garrison could hold out until April 15 on half-rations. He also announced that after surveying the harbor, he believed his plan to run in supplies at night on tugboats to be feasible. However, a dispatch from Sumter's commander arrived the next day strongly suggesting that Fox's plan would not work. Anderson warned that even at the best landing point, the one Fox favored, the tugboats would be able to approach no closer than forty feet from shore. That meant that the supplies would have to be taken in the rest of the way by rowboat, probably under fire from Confederate-occupied Fort Moultrie.[1] Except that he now had a fixed deadline, the fifteenth, Lincoln was no further ahead.

On Wednesday, Stephen Hurlbut and Ward Hill Lamon had come back with more information. "I have no hesitation in reporting as unquestionable that Separate Nationality is a fixed fact," Hurlbut affirmed, "that there is an unanimity of sentiment which is to my mind astonishing—that there is no attachment to the Union." Lamon concurred, adding that Governor Pickens had made it clear that should Lincoln not acquiesce in secession, South Carolina intended to fight. Hurlbut agreed that the secessionists would permit no attempt to provision Sumter. He recommended evacuating the fort—quickly. "At present the garrison can be withdrawn without insult to them or their flag," he said. "In a week this may be impossible and probably will." He suggested that the government maintain its authority in the South by strengthening Fort Pickens. Hurlbut later recalled that after he presented his verbal report to Lincoln, the president asked him to repeat it to Seward, who was continuing to insist "that there was a strong Union party in the South which would stop the movement." Lincoln then had Hurlbut make up a written report for the entire cabinet.[2]

By the twenty-seventh, then, Lincoln had reliable firsthand testimony that there was no latent unionist movement in South Carolina (or any of the Gulf states, Hurlbut reported), something Republicans had long suspected but which jarred the president no less deeply for that. If no groundswell of latent loyalty was waiting to sweep the Deep South back into the Union, what was the point of the government's policy of delay? What could masterly inactivity accomplish but a strengthening of the rebellion's defenses? As for Sumter itself, between Fox's confirmed belief that provisions could be gotten into Fort Sumter and Anderson's continued insistence that they could not, Lincoln could no better predict the military outcome of a supply expedition than he could two weeks earlier.

The next day, the special session of the Senate adjourned. That meant that the frenzy to fill federal offices would finally subside and Lincoln could devote more attention to the problem of the Southern forts.[3] The departure of the senators came none too soon; he was receiving unmistakable signs that Republican disapproval of his hands-off policy was growing. A week earlier, a caucus of indignant Senate Republicans had "violently and bitterly opposed" the evacuation of Sumter; now, on the last day of the extra session, their anger manifested in more public fashion. Early in the afternoon of that fateful Thursday, Lincoln's erstwhile adviser, Lyman Trumbull, introduced a resolution that read, "Resolved, That in the opinion of the Senate, the true way to preserve the Union is to enforce the laws of the Union; that resistance to their enforcement, whether under the name of anti-coercion or any other name, is encouragement to disunion; and that it is the duty of the President to use all the means in his power to hold and protect the public property of the United States, and enforce the laws thereof, as well in the States of South Carolina, Georgia, Florida, Mississippi, Alabama, Louisiana, and Texas, as within the other States of the Union."[4]

Already the president was visibly sagging under the oppressive weight of his first twenty-five days in office. The strain of the crisis at Sumter was onerous enough, but the added challenge of organizing the government, and especially dealing with the relentless crush of office-seekers, had worn his nerves thin. One Republican senator observed, "Our poor President is having a hard time of it. He came here tall, strong, and vigorous, but has worked himself almost to death."[5] Now Trumbull's resolution represented a direct challenge from the hard-liners and carried with it the renewed prospect of that chronic menace, a split in the party. Coming on the heels of Hurlbut's report from Charleston, it goaded Lincoln into taking at least preliminary action regarding Fort Sumter.[6] With Anderson's supplies dwindling and passions in Charleston running high, the president ordered Fox to make a list of whatever ships and stores he would need. If Lincoln was going to keep his options open any longer, he must have a supply expedition ready if called for, and he would put off its preparation no more.[7]

In addition, Lincoln was still considering the thorny problem of collecting import duties in the seceded states. Chase had offered his opinion that collecting federal revenues from ships stationed outside the Southern ports would be feasible, though not foolproof, and Welles had submitted a list of the naval support available for such a mission. Knowing that his advisers considered offshore collection to be a realistic possibility no doubt offered some relief, but Lincoln's decision had to take into account the larger question of whether executing such a policy would trigger the collision he was trying so hard to avoid. With the Morrill tariff due to go into effect in just four days, this was another critical decision that he must make soon, another weight pressing upon him.[8]

Given all that was going on, hosting his first state dinner that evening was likely the last thing the harried president wanted to do. Still, authorizing Fox to begin making plans bought a little time, and must have afforded Lincoln some small measure of relief. When he sent a last-minute note asking General Scott to come to the White House before dinner, he no doubt intended to inform him of the order to Fox. The general, however, assumed that Lincoln wanted to talk about a momentous—and, as it would turn out, preposterous—piece of intelligence that Hill Lamon had just brought back from Charleston: that Governor Pickens wanted South Carolina to reenter the Union. Moreover, Scott and Lamon had had a long conversation about the necessity of evacuating not only Fort Sumter but also Fort Pickens. Understanding from Lamon that Lincoln would approve such an idea, Scott drew up a memorandum recommending the evacuation of both forts, which he presented to Lincoln that evening before dinner.[9]

Sumter would be evacuated as a matter of course, Scott began. Even if an expedition like that proposed by Fox were to succeed, it would have to be repeated every few weeks, and yellow fever season was coming on in Charleston. "The sooner the more graceful on the part of the Government," he suggested (echoing a remark Seward had made privately some two weeks earlier). However, Scott continued, it was unlikely that the evacuation of Sumter would have "a decisive effect" on the "wavering" border states because it would be interpreted as bowing to necessity rather than a gesture of goodwill. As a result, information from the Upper South now indicated that Fort Pickens must be evacuated, too. Referring to Governor Pickens's alleged change of heart, about which Lincoln was entirely ignorant, Scott concluded, "The giving up of Forts Sumter and Pickens may be best justified by the hope that we should thereby recover the State to which they geographically belong by the liberality of the act, besides retaining the eight doubtful States."[10]

Upon hearing this recommendation, Lincoln felt what he later described as "a cold shock."[11] None of his advisers had ever mentioned a need to abandon Fort Pickens before. On the contrary, it had been assumed that an evacuation of Sumter must be accompanied by the reinforcement of Pickens in order to fortify the government's authority in the South and the administration's credibility in the North. What shook Lincoln, though, was not just the advice but the reasoning behind it: Scott made no pretense of recommending Fort Pickens's evacuation on military grounds but cited purely political arguments. Lincoln's and the cabinet's reluctance to reinforce Sumter rested chiefly on Scott's resolute opposition—had that been politically motivated as well? What of Lincoln's need to put his order to reinforce Pickens in writing earlier in the month—had Scott been deliberately undermining attempts to strengthen the forts all along? And did this mean that Lincoln could not count on any of the advice given him on Sumter by Southern-born officers—could he trust Anderson's opinion on the impracticality of Fox's plan?

With the staggering load of the past weeks bearing down upon him and the very foundation of his Sumter policy abruptly and profoundly shaken, Lincoln lashed out at the astounded general. A humbled and deeply wounded Scott told his military secretary the next morning that the president charged that "*Anderson had played us false*" and criticized Scott's "want of consistency" regarding Pickens. With Trumbull's resolutions of earlier that day in mind, Lincoln exclaimed in bitter frustration "that his administration would be broken up unless a more decided policy was adopted." Finally, he declared pointedly that if Scott would not follow his orders, he would find someone who would.[12]

By the time he was through upbraiding the general, the other dinner guests were waiting. Scott asked that Lincoln convey his apologies and left. Lincoln composed himself, then went inside, reported that General Scott was not feeling well, and somehow managed to act the charming and gracious host. William Howard Russell, who had traveled down from New York two days earlier and been invited to the dinner by Mary Lincoln, even remarked on the president's ability to keep the mood light with his jokes and stories. Despite the intense strain of the last weeks, and especially the past several hours, the evening was a success. Nobody seems to have suspected the drama that had just been played down the hall.[13]

Lincoln asked his cabinet advisers to stay behind when the other guests left. Once they were alone, he informed them of Scott's recommendation. A long silence followed, broken finally by the administration's most fervent hard-liner, Montgomery Blair, who pointed out angrily what had already struck Lincoln—that Scott was playing at politician rather than general. Livid at this apparent betrayal, Blair raved for some time. When he had finished, nobody had anything more to say. Lincoln asked them all to return the next day, and the somber cabinet filed out.[14] No sleep came to the beleaguered president that night. He spent the long hours until daylight alone with his thoughts.[15]

As Blair recalled it later, his response to Scott's recommendation had a decisive effect upon Lincoln, who immediately began ordering the arrangements for a supply expedition. In reality, Lincoln had ordered those arrangements earlier in the day and had already arrived at Blair's conclusion on his own. Moreover, Blair's remarks did not have the electrifying influence he envisioned upon the cabinet, either. Attorney General Bates recorded in his diary that after a "desultory" and unproductive discussion the next day, he suggested that the members submit written memoranda of their views, as they had done two weeks earlier. Lincoln approved, and each cabinet secretary wrote and read his opinion.[16] Whether because of a reaction against General Scott's advice of the night before, because the deadline by which a decision must be made now loomed, or because a feeling of unrest and discontent that was spreading through the party had infected the cabinet as well—probably all of these—the results differed significantly from those of the fifteenth.

Bates, who spoke first, argued for the reinforcement of Pickens and the strengthening of the navy's presence outside of the Southern ports and concluded that the time had come to make a decision one way or the other on Sumter.[17] Four more members—Chase, Welles, Smith, and Seward—agreed that Pickens must be reinforced; no one dissented. Welles and Smith also concurred with Bates in the necessity of increasing the naval force along the Southern coast; again, no one disagreed. On Sumter, on the other hand, there was no consensus. Blair, of course, spoke vigorously in favor of reinforcing the fort. His passion overcoming his grammar, he avowed, "S[outh] C[arolina] is the head & foot of the rebellion & when that State is safely delivered from the authority of the US it will strike a blow ag[ain]st our authority from which it will take us years of bloody strife to recover from." Seward continued to lead the opposition, arguing— prophetically, as it would turn out—that any attempt to provision the fort would trigger an attack and start a war, probably before the expedition even got there. Sumter was an untenable position and should be abandoned, he declared. Unlike two weeks earlier, however, this time only Smith agreed; Chase and Welles both advocated sending in supplies. On the critical issue of Fort Sumter, the cabinet now stood three to two in favor of maintaining the garrison.[18]

Historians have naturally emphasized the shift between this vote and that of March 15. However, the memoranda of March 29 reveal more than just a change in opinion. They also demonstrate that the cabinet continued to be split along factional lines: all three former Democrats favored a hard-line approach, while the former Whigs either advocated evacuation or expressed no opinion. (Cameron, who was conveniently absent, had favored conciliation throughout the crisis and if pressed would undoubtedly have sided with Seward now. However, he had been a Democrat only out of opportunism and had never demonstrated the radicalism associated with that faction of the party.)

Moreover, a close examination of the replies discloses a less dramatic change than is generally presented. Only Welles actually changed his mind, for one thing. More important, his and Chase's remarks revealed a much more complex understanding of the situation than Blair's. Welles supported the idea, first raised two weeks earlier, of sending provisions to the fort not secretly but openly—that is, announcing the government's intention to deliver them. After the delivery was opposed—as of course it would be—both provisions and reinforcements would be forced in. He explained, "Armed resistance to a peaceable attempt to send provisions to one of our own forts will justify the government in using all the power at its command, to reinforce the garrison and furnish the necessary supplies." In other words, the government should reinforce Sumter in such a way as to remain on the defensive, thereby placing the burden of opening hostilities where it properly belonged—on the Confederates.[19]

Chase agreed. War, he said, would result from an attempt to resupply either Sumter or Pickens. Since Pickens could not be surrendered, a conflict was inevitable. Therefore, "I perceive no reason why it may not be best begun in consequence of military resistance to the efforts of the administration to sustain troops of the Union stationed, under the authority of the Government in a Fort of the Union, in the ordinary course of service."[20] These analyses expressed a far more subtle strategy than Blair's intention of teaching the impudent secessionists respect for federal authority, and one much more conducive to the president's own thinking. In fact, Welles and Chase's suggestion reflected the same concern that had motivated Lincoln to take O. H. Browning's advice on the inaugural address weeks earlier: if fighting should occur, if it could not be avoided, the administration must not be perceived as the aggressor.

Even after the cabinet meeting, however, it was still not clear whether Lincoln had made up his mind on any course. He did put the wheels in motion to prepare an expedition, however. On the bottom of the list of necessaries Fox had submitted, Lincoln wrote to Cameron, "I desire that an expedition, to move by sea, be got ready to sail as early as the 6th of April next." Fox set out for New York to make the arrangements.[21]

✳ Certain that they knew what really needed to be done to save the Union from destruction, William Seward, Stephen Douglas, and countless other Northerners would have given much to have Lincoln's authority in those frantic final days of March. That was an easy attitude to maintain while looking in from outside the seat of power, but the president himself showed signs of cracking under the strain of his profound responsibility. The weeks of steadily growing pressure were taking a harsh toll. Exploding at Scott on the evening of the twenty-eighth was out of character, if understandable. The day after the cabinet meeting, he again lost his temper, this time with a group of California politicians with whom he was discussing patronage. Frustrated at their leader's arrogance, Lincoln barked at him heatedly, then grabbed his speech, crumpled it, and threw it into the fire before angrily inviting the entire deputation to leave. Later that day the president collapsed, felled by a "sick headache," his first in years.[22]

Lincoln's short temper and especially his collapse are important reminders that the momentous decisions of those hectic days cannot be understood solely from the perspective of logic. The stress of the situation was enormous and had to have been increased by Lincoln's unfamiliarity with Washington, which not only made it difficult for him to utilize available resources but also left him isolated. That sense of solitude had been heightened by the alienation of his resentful Illinois friends and now by Scott's apparent betrayal. There was no one around him he felt he could trust. On top of all that, he was "haunted continually," his private secretary reported, "by some one who 'wants to see the President *for only five minutes*'"—office-seekers, party leaders requesting or complaining about patronage, and hundreds of visitors who wanted to present a problem, ask his views, or simply get a close look at the president.[23] Any evaluation of Lincoln's motives at this time must take into account that by late March he was physically and emotionally exhausted. Thursday's "cold shock" and sleepless night and the overwhelming weight of the issues facing him were pushing him to the edge of his endurance.

✳ Chances are that it was Seward as much as Lamon who had convinced Scott of the wisdom of evacuating both forts: not only had unionists in the Virginia convention and elsewhere been warning him adamantly about the need to remove all troops from the seceded states, but he and Scott had been "working like hand in glove" for months in pursuit of Seward's goals.[24] When the general's advice backfired and it became clear that Lincoln was preparing reinforcements, Seward backpedaled furiously, taking immediate steps to make Pickens rather than Sumter the focus of the administration's attention. It was still unknown whether Scott's earlier orders to land the reinforcements at Fort Pickens had been carried out yet, but Seward determined that the fort must be strengthened either way. If the government's presence at Pensacola were secured, perhaps Lincoln could be persuaded even now to cast off the albatross in Charleston harbor. Chase might be right that reinforcing either fort would lead to hostilities, but that prediction was less certain in Florida than South Carolina, and Seward was so far out on his wobbly limb that playing the odds was all he had left.

Never short of ideas, Seward put two plans into effect now. First, shortly after Friday's momentous cabinet meeting ended, he summoned to the White House Capt. Montgomery Meigs, a young army officer who had not only won popularity among Republicans by criticizing the previous administration but had recently been stationed in Florida. In response to queries from Seward and Lincoln, Meigs asserted firmly that Fort Pickens could be held. Seward assured Lincoln that this was their man and instructed the captain to begin drafting a specific plan for putting in additional troops.[25]

On March 31, Easter Sunday, General Scott sent his military secretary, Lt. Col. E. D. Keyes, to brief Seward on the difficulties of further reinforcing Fort Pickens. Seward no longer had the luxury of caring about difficulties—he sent Keyes to find Meigs and finalize a strategy that day to get troops into the fort. The two officers hammered out their ideas and joined Seward at the White House by midafternoon. When they had finished explaining their plan, Lincoln sent them to tell General Scott "that he wished this thing done and not to let it fail unless he can show why the refusing him something he asked is necessary." Scott, who had spent the previous day composing a lengthy (and not altogether straightforward) defense of his actions over the previous five months, could not have missed the president's pointed stab. He reluctantly approved the plan, Lincoln signed whatever orders were placed in front of him, and within a few days Meigs, Keyes, and two other of Seward's handpicked army and naval officers had followed Fox to New York with $10,000 that Seward had procured from the secret service budget. The expedition would depart for Pensacola on April 6.[26]

In meddling with Fort Pickens's defense, the embattled secretary of state had passed far beyond the jurisdiction of his department, and he was acting so much in isolation that no one in the administration even knew of the expedition but Lincoln—a circumstance that led him, probably intentionally, to order to Pensacola the same warship Welles was planning to lead Fox's Sumter fleet. (When a bewildered Welles notified the president that there had been some kind of mix-up, Lincoln immediately ordered that the ship be used for the Sumter expedition. It was too late; the Pickens expedition had gone.)[27] The fact is that Seward was under pressure almost as great as that of the president and, after weeks of watching Lincoln's vacillation over Sumter with growing dread, was now close to full-scale panic. He had assured Southerners from both the Gulf states and the border states that Sumter's evacuation was assured, and he was convinced that only his pledges had kept the unionists in control of Virginia's secession convention and the Confederate commissioners from leaving Washington and instigating a war.

That rejection of the commissioners would have meant war was doubtful—the leaders of the Confederacy were no hawks, and they knew that Anderson would soon be forced to withdraw without any effort on their part—but Seward did exert a powerful influence in the Upper South. The changes he had suggested to Lincoln's inaugural and his subsequent assurances that Sumter was to be evacuated had a decided impact in the border states. Bolstered by the belief that the administration meant to avoid a collision, unionist strength in Virginia, Tennessee, and North Carolina peaked between mid-March and early April. Old partisan allegiances continued to fade as the new Union Party rose to the fore. In the Richmond convention, Unionists expected to adjourn the convention in triumph within two weeks, secession vanquished; meanwhile, they put finishing touches on a plan of adjustment, based on the peace conference proposal, that they intended to present to a conference of the border states in June. Their victory in Virginia's upcoming May elections seemed assured. In Tennessee and North Carolina, Unionist predominance was equally apparent; elections there were to be held in August.[28]

With a key vote looming in the Virginia convention and an expedition to reinforce Sumter being prepared, Seward was not content simply to send additional troops to Pickens and hope Lincoln would see the light. On April 1 he put into execution the second part of his plan, his boldest and in many ways most bizarre gamble yet. He addressed to Lincoln a memorandum blandly titled "Some thoughts for the President's consideration." The first thought he presented was that the administration had neither a domestic nor a foreign policy. In a not-so-subtle dig at Lincoln's lack of method and inability to set priorities, he granted that this was understandable, as "the presence of the Senate, with the need to meet applications for patronage have prevented attention to other and more grave matters." But the danger to the country was now too great, and the distribution of offices must be delegated to lesser officials.[29]

Noting that perhaps he had not adequately explained the domestic policy he advocated, Seward elaborated. "My system," he wrote, "is built on this *idea* as a ruling one, namely that we must *Change the question before the Public from one upon Slavery* . . . for a question upon *Union or Disunion*. In other words, from what would be regarded as a Party question to one of *Patriotism* or *Union*." That was, in essence, the idea Thurlow Weed had elucidated to Lincoln in Springfield back in December. Now Seward applied it to the forts: since the controversy over Sumter had clearly become a partisan matter, he argued, the administration should dispense with it while simultaneously strengthening the Gulf forts. He concluded vaguely, "This will raise distinctly the question of *Union* or *Disunion*." The rationale behind Seward's foreign policy ideas was equally indistinct: he recommended (not in so many words, but almost) instigating a war with Spain or France while "send[ing] agents into *Canada, Mexico* and *Central America*, to rouse a vigorous continental *spirit of independence* on this continent against European intervention."[30]

The assertion that Lincoln had no policy was a direct slap, the explanation of Seward's ideas patronizing, and the foreign-war notion reckless, to say the least. The true audacity of Seward's memorandum, however, came in the final lines: "Whatever policy we adopt," he wrote, "there must be an energetic prosecution of it. For this purpose, it must be somebody's business to pursue and direct it incessantly. Either the President must do it himself and be all the while active in it, or Devolve it on some member of his Cabinet. Once adopted, debates on it must end, and all agree and abide." He concluded modestly, "It is not in my especial province But I neither seek to evade nor assume responsibility." Here, then, was the crux of Seward's new strategy: if Lincoln, obviously exhausted and well beyond his depth, could not be trusted to follow the right path, Seward would take power himself.

It was a brazen maneuver born of desperation and acute frustration at Lincoln's haphazard, slapdash approach to governance.[31] It would seem in hindsight that Seward had to have expected dismissal; surely he could not have thought Lincoln would simply hand over responsibility for the administration's secession policy. Yet he seems to have believed just that, and perhaps not so irrationally. In light of Lincoln's administrative inexperience, prolonged indecision, preoccupation with details of the patronage, and obvious fatigue—Seward certainly knew of his collapse two days earlier—the secretary's presumption is not so difficult to understand.

Moreover, Patrick Sowle has argued persuasively that Seward was able to convince at least two other important Republican leaders to support him. It seems that on April 1 a last-minute summons from Seward brought *New York Times* editor Henry J. Raymond, a longtime ally, on a last-minute trip to Washington. For several hours Raymond kept open both the telegraph line and the front page of the *Times* in expectation of an announcement that Seward would take control of the administration. Over the following days, editorials in the *Times* and Thurlow Weed's *Albany Evening Journal* echoed Seward's criticism of Lincoln's lack of policy and preoccupation with the patronage, his need to decide between enforcing the laws and encouraging Southern unionism, and even his foreign policy notions.[32] If the secretary of state was suffering delusions, he was not alone.

Whatever his expectations, Seward was now left, once more, to await Lincoln's response. Though the stakes climbed ever higher, the situation had become all too familiar.

✳ The tension was taking its toll on everyone. By the end of March, Stephen Douglas, like Seward, had grown desperate. Despite the initial enthusiasm his actions in the Senate had generated among Southern unionists, his efforts went for naught. Senate Republicans ignored his overtures; the White House was impassive. Still he continued to insist on the essential peacefulness of the administration—he was, in fact, its only defender in the Senate, since the Republicans were still holding their silence. When Douglas tried to force the issue by proposing a resolution demanding information on the Southern forts (information that Lincoln himself had just requested from General Scott), the Republicans simply refused to adopt it.[33] Eventually the strain began to show and Douglas fell to attacking those whose confidence he was trying to win. At one point he and Senator William Fessenden of Maine came close to declaring a duel. Another time his frustration exploded in a fit of temper on the Senate floor. "The country is going to pieces, just because I was unable to defeat you," he shouted wildly. ". . . You can boast that you have defeated me, but you have defeated your country with me."[34]

More ominously, Douglas began to fall back on an old idea he had for an American customs union, a free-trade zone from Canada to Central America modeled on the German zollverein. Initially he raised the idea as a means of pressuring the seceded states back into the Union. By late March, however, a customs union began to hold a different appeal. Even if conflict over the Southern forts was avoided, with the Morrill tariff set to take effect, the prospect loomed that Douglas's beloved West would be torn apart by a trade war, which could easily become a shooting war. The customs union morphed into a commercial alliance between North and South, a plan to ensure peace should disunion prove unavoidable. As long as war could be averted, there would be a possibility of future reunification. Stephen Douglas, the champion of the Union who had campaigned against secession in the Deep South, who had declared even before the election that rebels ought to be hanged, who had argued that coercion was the essence of government, seems to have resigned himself, for a time at least, to a peaceable separation.[35]

Seward's April 1 memorandum and Douglas's customs union were final, frightened attempts to save a Union that they feared would perish with the onset of civil war, and at the same time to salvage the dreams each cherished of presiding over a new national party and eventually rebuilding a revitalized national party system. In their minds those goals were intimately linked; looking beyond the immediate need to prevent civil war, they believed partisan ties to be an essential bond between the estranged sections.[36]

Seward's and Douglas's chronic disappointment also illustrates the nature of the influence that parties exerted over the functioning of the government. As March passed into April and the administration lurched toward war, their frustrated helplessness was a product of the same factor that had impeded their efforts throughout the crisis: neither was able to maneuver himself into a position of genuine power. A year earlier, they had been the two most prominent and powerful political figures in the United States. Even after Lincoln had upset their presidential bids, Douglas and Seward had retained much of their enormous prestige and influence; moderate and conservative Republicans and Northern Democrats, respectively, continued to look to them for guidance. Yet their efforts to promote compromise and foster conciliation were thwarted at every turn—not by their rivalry for the same conservative constituency, which had led them to adopt similar strategies and even join forces on at least two occasions, but by Lincoln.

Their struggles for compromise and their appeals to Northern and Southern conservatives were rooted in the belief that political negotiation provided a better foundation for Union than did war. Lincoln's opposition to compromise and efforts to keep the current Republican coalition intact stemmed from his conviction that making concessions in the face of treason would corrupt and possibly destroy the Union. What enabled him to succeed in pursuing his vision where they failed was his command of Republican Party machinery. As Douglas had discovered back in December, congressional Republicans controlled the possibility of compromise. As Seward had discovered at about the same time, potentially conciliatory Republican congressmen were deeply vulnerable to pressure from their constituents and from the head of their party. The moderate Republicans' motivations for responding to that pressure varied, but if nothing else, knowledge that Lincoln would distribute the patronage had kept them in line during the winter. And after the inauguration, Lincoln had continued (so far, at least) to exert control, through the patronage and now also through management of the executive branch.

The whole dynamic illustrates the extent not only to which antebellum parties shaped the running of government but also, in time of crisis at least, to which national leadership controlled the parties and to which that leadership was concentrated. As long as Lincoln kept a tight grip on the reins, Douglas, the leader of the opposition party, and Seward, the leader of an opposition faction, were left on the defensive—no matter how popular they or their ideas might be.

✳ Lincoln would keep the reins; Seward had made his bid, but the president had no intention of relinquishing power. Yet he would not ask for Seward's resignation. He could not, really; not only would Seward's departure strike severe blows to his administration's credibility and his party's always-fragile unity, but the New Yorker's presence was vital if Lincoln was to have any chance of retaining the border slave states. In a brief response written the same day he received Seward's memorandum, he pointed out that the administration's policy of inactivity had been adopted in accord with Seward's own counsel. He also expressed puzzlement as to why the relief of Fort Sumter was a party question and the relief of Fort Pickens a patriotic one. Finally, after passing quickly over the proposal to stir up a foreign war, he politely but firmly declined to hand control of the government to any member of his cabinet.[37]

It is possible that the memorandum did serve as something of a wakeup call, however. Lincoln seems to have realized that he had been trying to handle too much at once. Already, after his collapse two days earlier, he had cut back slightly on his office hours; now he restricted them further. No longer would visitors wander constantly in and out.[38] He even took advantage of his new free time by going out riding, an activity he had not had the chance to do in weeks.[39] He continued to suffer enormous stress and anxiety over the next several days, but limiting his calling hours, in conjunction with the adjournment of the Senate, could not help but have improved his ability to analyze the increasingly complex situation, weigh his options, and, at long last, make decisions on the vital questions that faced him.

The most important of those, of course, was whether to send Fox's expedition to Sumter. The argument that relieving one fort would be seen as a partisan question while relieving another a patriotic one made little sense to Lincoln, but Seward's earlier point that Sumter was untenable even if reinforcements could be gotten through was an important consideration. Numerous people had suggested that evacuating Sumter and fortifying Pickens was the wisest move. Would reinforcing the Pensacola fort merely shift the trouble spot from South Carolina to Florida, gaining nothing? Or would it enable the administration to withdraw from Charleston without surrendering federal authority, losing credibility, or causing a serious rift among Republicans? The last continued to be a critical factor; among other considerations, Lincoln must have contemplated the impotence of John Tyler's Whig administration a generation earlier once his party had withdrawn its support.

The issue threatened to become moot when, also on April 1, word arrived from Pensacola harbor that as of a few days earlier the reinforcements waiting onboard ship had not yet received General Scott's March 12 order to land. It was doubtful that Meigs's expedition, which was still making preparations in New York, could reach Pensacola before Anderson's supplies ran out, and Lincoln would not even consider evacuating Sumter without knowing that Pickens was already secure. The president's options were dwindling.[40]

Looming over all was the Virginia secession convention; now that Lincoln knew that unionism was dead in South Carolina, the only reason left for delay was to appease the border slave states. Although the Unionists appeared to be in firm control in Richmond, reports from throughout the Upper South were unanimous that any indication of federal coercion would lead to secession and war. As Scott had reported, calls were widespread for the evacuation of all federal troops in the South. On that same hectic Monday, April 1, Lincoln authorized Seward to summon from Richmond George Summers, leader of the nascent Union Party. Summers balked; there was a critical vote on secession scheduled in a few days, and he seems to have suspected that the invitation was actually a secessionist ruse to get him out of town.[41] It is not clear whether Lincoln had received the latest report from Pensacola when Seward first wrote to Summers, but we do know that by April 3, when the White House dispatched a messenger to retrieve Summers personally, the president had had two days to digest the news about Pickens. That fact bears heavily on the controversial meeting that occurred when Summers's emissary, John B. Baldwin, arrived late on the morning of April 4.

It certainly explains Lincoln's peculiar opening remark. Baldwin later told the story thus: "As I was about sitting down, said he, 'Mr. Baldwin, I am afraid you have come too late.' 'Too late for what?' said I. Said he, 'I am afraid you have come too late; I wish you could have been here three or four days ago.'" That baffling comment—Baldwin had just received the summons the previous day and had come as quickly as he could—set the tone for an unsatisfying meeting on both sides. Lincoln asked why the unionists had not adjourned the convention yet, which bewildered Baldwin even more. " 'Adjourn it!' " he stammered back. " 'How? Do you mean sine die [that is, permanently]?' 'Yes,' said [Lincoln], 'sine die. Why do you not adjourn it? It is a standing menace to me, which embarrasses me very much.' " Baldwin could have no idea of the pressures on Lincoln at that moment, but we can see that Virginia's reaction to a possible Sumter expedition weighed on him heavily.[42]

Baldwin proceeded to lecture the agitated president on the delicate position of the Virginia unionists and the important role the convention played in maintaining their credibility and their ability to suppress disunionism. He concluded, "Sir, it seems to me that our true policy is to hold the position that we have, and for you to uphold our hands by a conservative, conciliatory, national course." Just what the Southern unionists had in mind when they demanded a conciliatory course was a question that had bothered Lincoln for quite some time, since December at least. He pressed his visitor to explain precisely what he meant. As he answered the president's queries, John Baldwin inadvertently stripped away every piece of ground on which Lincoln may have been willing to stand. As Hurlbut and Lamon had done a week earlier, Baldwin confirmed Lincoln's suspicion that the kind of conciliatory policy that would satisfy Seward's allies was incompatible with his own definition of preserving federal authority.

First of all, Baldwin said, the administration should issue a proclamation that signaled its pacific policy without surrendering national authority, a policy which would include, among other things, withdrawing from Forts Sumter and Pickens. To most Republicans, of course, vacating the forts was irreconcilable with maintaining federal authority. When Lincoln replied that his friends would not like such a policy, Baldwin responded that he would gain ten supporters for every one he lost—an argument that may have resonated with Seward but Lincoln had dismissed out of hand months earlier. Unless the current Republican coalition survived intact, he believed, the battle to depose the Slave Power could not be won.

Lincoln then raised the possibility of evacuating Sumter on the grounds of military necessity, not revealing that those were the only grounds on which he would even consider doing so. Baldwin was adamant that that would never do. Like Winfield Scott, he insisted that Lincoln must claim the "higher ground" by presenting withdrawal as a gesture of peace. To most Republicans, including Lincoln, this smacked of bowing to secessionists' threats, the kind of rank submission that would make future electoral government impossible.

Finally, the president inquired about an idea that had gained much ground within the administration over the last few days, and that was probably his own tentative plan at that point: what if only provisions were sent into the fort? In other words, what if relief was attempted in a way that could not reasonably be interpreted as aggressive? Absolutely not, Baldwin replied. Confederate forces would never allow it, and any conflict at all would chase the Upper South from the Union: "If there is a gun fired at Sumter—I do not care on which side it is fired—the opportunity for settlement is lost." "Impossible," Lincoln replied, stunned at the idea that the latent unionism on which his party's entire secession policy had rested could be that frail. Baldwin insisted that it was true. Lincoln continued to reject the notion, but Baldwin was adamant: in the event of a collision, he pronounced, "Virginia herself, strong as the Union majority in the convention is now, will be out in forty-eight hours."[43]

Over the next couple of weeks, Lincoln told other Virginia unionists that in speaking with Baldwin he had offered to withdraw the troops from Sumter if the Virginia convention would adjourn but that Baldwin had rejected his proposal outright.[44] Some witnesses later claimed that Baldwin also spoke of such an offer afterward, while others testified that he did not.[45] Baldwin himself denied Lincoln had said any such thing.[46] It is impossible to know what actually happened. Perhaps when Lincoln first agreed to speak with Summers on Monday, April 1, he had the idea of renewing the offer he had made to William C. Rives before the inauguration. Yet it is doubtful that he would still have proposed such a trade after discovering the unlikelihood of securing Fort Pickens before Anderson's supplies ran out. It could be that Lincoln's own ambivalence simply prevented him from making it clear to Baldwin what he was proposing. Equally plausible is the possibility raised by historian Daniel W. Crofts that although Lincoln did not make the offer to Baldwin, he did tell other Southern unionists that he had. He certainly had reason to present as conciliatory an image as possible. He knew that the rest of the Upper South would likely follow Virginia's lead in responding to whatever happened in the next week or so, and he knew also that what would happen was more and more likely to be an attempt to relieve Fort Sumter.[47]

In any event, the real significance of the Baldwin interview lay in Lincoln's discovery that there was little chance of maintaining a federal presence in the seceded states and also retaining the loyalty of the border slave states. It was a mighty blow to his continuing effort to balance firmness with magnanimity, to uphold national authority and still foster the Southern unionism that he had hoped held the key to resolving the crisis peacefully.

✳ The situation was developing rapidly; further events on April 4 confirmed that Lincoln's time had just about run out. His meeting with several Northern governors brought the imperative issue of party discontent to the fore.[48] As the long impasse wore on, Republicans across the North were growing restless, and resistance to abandonment of the forts increased. There were still many who judged that the party could tolerate Sumter's evacuation and even a few conciliationists who favored it,[49] but voices heralding the party's downfall were rising. "Unless our Republican Administration protects preserves & *holds* at the point of the bayonet if need be the *whole country* & *enforces the laws* at every port at least, we are ruined," insisted a leader of the Young Men's Republican Union in New York. An irritated Ohio man wrote to Chase that if Lincoln vacillated much longer, "the South will proclaim him a Damned fool, and the North a damned Rascal." From Springfield, William Jayne lamented to Trumbull, "I wish that the President and the Cabinet knew the feeling in the North West in regard to the do nothing policy of the Administration. . . . I think that unless our friends show more determination & resolution in enforcing the laws that the administration will be abandoned by the people." An irate Kansan grumbled to his cousin that he could not abide Sumter's abandonment from Lincoln any more than he could from Buchanan and added, "When it comes to getting down and licking spittle for the d—d hounds I am greatly opposed to it. My way would be to 'coerce' them, and hang every d—d traitor if I had to clean out the whole country." If relatively few went that far, a growing number would have agreed with the Illinoisan who wrote, "It is no use (however true it may be) to tell us, we can not keep or retake the public property of the South ('hold, occupy, and possess,') [—]we can try. We can shed our treasure and blood in the defence and support of our principles and lawful rights as our Fathers did. . . . War is bad civil war is worse, but if liberty and the right of the people to govern themselves was worth fighting for in the days of the Revolution, it is worth fighting for now."[50]

Local and state elections in late March and April gave more ammunition to Republicans who warned of the threat to the party. Around the North anti-Republicans either won or gained considerable support, and as they had after the Massachusetts municipal contests in early December, they trumpeted their success as a sign "that a formidable reaction has commenced in the North" against Republican belligerence. The *Stark County Democrat* of Canton, Ohio, in a typical reaction, crowed that the triumph there was "a glorious victory for the friends of our undivided American Union. . . . Whenever the country is in danger, safety is sought and found in the conservative and safe counsels of the Democratic party."[51] Republicans took the opposite stance, attributing their losses to dissatisfaction with Lincoln's apparent weakness. "The supposed evacuation & surrender of the Forts, has defeated your friends and your supporters," a Cincinnati Republican raged to Lincoln. "In our city we are about to be annihilated. Our municipal government all passes into the hands of the Democratic, Union party—and we are compelled to lay the fault at your door."[52]

Weeks of uncertainty had been followed by sudden expectation of action, and the strain was felt by all. Carl Schurz, who had just returned to Wisconsin from a trip across the North, reported to Lincoln, "There is a general discontent pervading all classes of society. Everybody asks: What is the policy of the Administration? And everybody replies: Any distinct line of policy, be it war or a recognition of the Southern confederacy, would be better than this uncertain state of things." Although most Northerners meant it no more literally than the ever-stalwart Schurz, that kind of impatience was indeed creeping into Northern minds. A New York woman who had nearly resigned herself to the necessity of peaceable secession wrote to Tennessee senator Andrew Johnson, "We are here awaiting with the greatest anxiety some exposition of the policy of the administration feeling that any decision would be preferable to this uncertainty." The Douglas organ in Detroit claimed to welcome even war, so long as something was done—"Some sort of certainty, be it ever so dismal, may be better than uncertainty," wrote the edgy editor. "Better almost anything than additional suspense," a Bell paper in New York echoed. The *New York Times*, until now a staunch supporter of conciliation, reflected both Seward's April 1 bid for power and the increasing popular restlessness when, in an editorial titled "Wanted—A Policy," it demanded, "We trust this period of indecision, of inaction, of fatal indifference, will have a speedy end. Unless it does, we may bid farewell to all hope of saving the Union from destruction and the country from anarchy." It cannot be known the precise effect of the April 4 governors' council, and the growing impatience within the party and around the North in general, but it could not but have added to the president's sense of urgency.[53]

✳ Contributing to that sense more immediately was another startling dispatch received that same day from Anderson. Dated April 1, the report indicated that his supplies would last only one week longer. When, he inquired, was the expected order for withdrawal to come?[54] Anderson's readers were not only taken aback at the shortened timeline—Fox had told them that the garrison's supplies would last until the middle of the month —but perplexed at the message as a whole. It soon became evident that Lincoln's unofficial envoys to Charleston had left in their wake a tangle of confusion and misinformation. Already Lincoln had seen Fox and Anderson's contrary view of Fox's plan; it turned out that that was not all on which they disagreed. Fox had left Sumter believing that Anderson would put his men on half-rations, which would carry them until April 15. Anderson now reported that he had told Fox the garrison could last on half-rations until "after the 10th," but having received no instructions to put them on half-rations, he had never done so. That he saw no reason to was understandable, for a few days after Fox left, Lamon had arrived, claiming to be a direct agent of the president and informing him that the fort was to be evacuated shortly.[55] For over a week now the garrison had been waiting for final confirmation to arrive.[56] With this latest twist, coming as it did on the heels of Scott's misguided foray into political counsel and Seward's frantic deceptions and hijacking of the Sumter relief fleet's flagship, the Lincoln administration's first major decision was threatening to become a comedy of errors.

The result of the miscommunications was to tie Lincoln's hands even more tightly. Unless he suddenly received unexpected news that Scott's March 12 order had finally reached Pensacola, there was no way he could command Sumter's evacuation with any guarantee of Pickens's safety— without which he would not command it at all. Accordingly, it was on April 4, after speaking with John Baldwin, receiving the latest bombshells from Forts Pickens and Sumter, and meeting with the governors, that Lincoln finally set the Sumter relief plan into motion. He had Cameron inform Anderson that an expedition was on its way and instruct him to try to hold out until the eleventh or twelfth. The secretary of war also notified Fox that an expedition had been decided upon and that he was to command it. Until the ships departed from New York harbor there would still be time to recall the mission, but for all practical purposes Lincoln had made up his mind that a masterly inactivity was no longer feasible. Sumter was to be relieved.[57]

Later on, once the dust settled, Lincoln told Congress that if Fort Pickens had been rendered secure in time, he would have evacuated Sumter on the grounds of military necessity.[58] The president had never shown any real enthusiasm for the idea, however; the record suggests that he was willing to keep the option available, but no more than that. He was simply not convinced the trade-off would gain anything.[59] But once it became apparent that Pickens would not be fortified before Anderson's supplies ran out, the question settled itself. At that point, Lincoln believed that his alternatives had narrowed to two: relieve Sumter or recognize disunion.

As it turned out, he was right about Pickens: on April 6, the same day Captain Meigs's relief fleet started for Florida, confirmation arrived from Pensacola that the fort had not been reinforced in time.[60] With that news, Lincoln could wait no more; he had delayed as long as he possibly could, but the final step must be taken. He dispatched messengers to notify the governor of South Carolina that Fort Sumter was to be relieved "with provisions only; and that, if such attempt be not resisted, no effort to throw in men, arms, or ammunition, will be made, without further notice, or in case of attack upon the fort."[61]

It is clear why Lincoln finally had to make a decision, and why his decision was not to evacuate Fort Sumter but to attempt its relief. But why did that attempt take the form it did? Why try first to deliver provisions only, but then, if the Confederates refused permission, use force to throw in reinforcements as well? And why formally announce to the governor that the ships were coming?

This method of Fort Sumter's relief differed fundamentally in its purpose from Fox's initial proposal to drive off any enemy ships by force before running in troops and supplies at night. The new plan represented an entirely different strategy, the one Welles and Chase had advocated at the March 29 cabinet meeting. There is evidence that Seward was involved in the adoption of this new plan,[62] but although the secretary of state was the champion of conciliation within the administration, a great many Republicans were concerned, and had been for some months, that the government not appear the belligerent in any collision. Welles's and Chase's recent support for that notion demonstrated that even many hard-liners shied away from the aggressiveness of extremists like Blair, just as Browning's inaugural advice and the March 15 recommendations of most of the cabinet —to include Seward—showed a widespread sensitivity to the danger of appearing aggressive.

These concerns had risen rapidly in prominence in the past week. Earlier, Lincoln's primary concern was to maintain the status quo. The priority had been to retain Fort Sumter as a symbol of continuing federal authority in the seceded states. Thus, if an attempt to relieve the fort were to be made, it made sense to gamble on Fox's plan for doing it quickly, forcefully, and without warning. However, Hurlbut's report had brought the purpose of maintaining the status quo into serious question, while the latest dispatches from Sumter and Pickens had rendered it impracticable anyway. Therefore, it was now the *attempt* to reprovision the fort that would signal the maintenance of federal authority—yet the attempt must be made in such a way that observers would see that the government was acting defensively.

With the new plan, Lincoln upheld the twin facets of his inaugural address, both his resolute vow to "hold, occupy, and possess" federal property and his more conciliatory pledge to forebear from aggression. In that sense the president's final Sumter strategy rested on his ongoing quest for that elusive balance of firmness and magnanimity that he and other moderate Republicans had been seeking throughout the crisis. That is not to say that he believed his plan might actually succeed in securing Sumter without a fight. There can be no question that Lincoln deliberately discarded Fox's plan for one that was destined to fail. If anyone still had any real hope that the supplies could be delivered peaceably, on April 6 the War Department learned that the Charleston batteries had opened fire on an unarmed merchant ship that had wandered into the harbor accidentally.[63] There could be little doubt of the response when an actual relief expedition appeared, especially if the Confederate defenses had advance warning that it was coming. Rather, Lincoln's decision on Sumter was consistent with his stance throughout the crisis in that he leaned as far toward conciliation as he could without sacrificing federal authority. That is to say, as circumstances at Charleston grew dire, the need for firmness became paramount; it was now the appearance of magnanimity that counted.

The relief fleet, then, would inevitably be met with force, and Lincoln would have no choice but to call up the militia and forcibly subdue the rebels. They would resist, and the result would be civil war, hopefully in the form of a single pitched battle but possibly a longer campaign. There the situation became particularly thorny. Lincoln was supremely conscious of the importance of public opinion in a republic, and he knew that his ability to fight and win that battle or campaign would rest on two things: unified Northern support and the continued loyalty of the border slave states. The former did not seem likely given the polarization of recent months, but Lincoln had witnessed the brief moment of patriotic unity that followed South Carolina's seizure of federal property and attack on the *Star of the West*. A Southern attack on Sumter now might trigger such solidarity again. As for the latter, he was mindful of the threat to the capital should Virginia and Maryland secede and Washington be cut off, and knew as well that the addition of the more populous and economically diverse states of the Upper South would strengthen the new Confederacy immeasurably. Baldwin's warning notwithstanding, the one chance Lincoln had of retaining the Upper South lay in not appearing the aggressor.[64]

Thus, since a perception of federal belligerence would alienate both border-state unionists and a large segment of Northerners, preserving the Union required that the government appear to act defensively. From Lincoln's perspective, this was not manipulation but fidelity to the truth. To him, the image he later presented to Congress and the nation was essentially accurate: he knew that the immediate situation involved more than merely an innocent "giving of bread to the few brave and hungry men of the garrison," but he firmly believed that in the larger view his administration had done all it could to avoid a conflict, short of surrendering the government. It had been the secessionists who had created this crisis, who had pushed and prodded and backed him into this corner; why should it be the government that now appeared the aggressor? As he explained to Congress a few months later, Lincoln planned the Sumter mission in such a way as "to keep the case so free from the power of ingenious sophistry, as that the world should not be able to misunderstand it."[65]

✳ Fox's fleet sailed out of New York four days later, on April 10, but its real work had already been accomplished by the time its storm-blown remnants reassembled outside of Charleston harbor on the morning of the twelfth. Judging that they had to act before the relief mission arrived, Confederate authorities had demanded Anderson's immediate surrender the previous afternoon. With his supplies virtually exhausted, Anderson was willing to schedule a voluntary departure on the fifteenth, but knowing Fox's expedition might arrive in the meantime, he refused to assent to an unconditional cease-fire in the interim. That was unacceptable to the Confederates, of course, since it was the imminent arrival of the relief ships that had prompted them to demand his surrender to begin with. In the early morning of Friday, April 12, even as the relief mission was beginning to gather outside the harbor, the long-anticipated attack on Fort Sumter commenced.

Heavy seas, the loss of his tugboats in the storm, and the absence of his main warship prevented Fox from trying to run in supplies during the long bombardment, but it did not matter; Sumter was less secure than it was thought to be, and on Sunday morning raging fires forced Anderson to discard most of his remaining gunpowder. A few hours later a truce was called and he agreed to evacuate the fort. On April 14, for the first time since it had stolen in under cover of night three and a half months earlier, the federal garrison left Fort Sumter. Astonishingly, no one on either side of the barrage had been killed.[66]

✳ Lincoln could not have been pleased with the outcome, but he was prepared for it. On April 13, while the cannon still thundered at Charleston harbor, he addressed a small delegation of Virginians who had been sent from the convention to express the unionists' grave concerns over rumors of a change in the president's policy. They were the first to hear the administration's position on what was happening. Lincoln claimed "deep regret, and some mortification" that they felt any "uncertainty" as to his policy, for it represented the pledge he had made in his inaugural address to "hold, occupy, and possess" the public property. Emphasizing the administration's defensive posture, he added that "if, as now appears to be true, in pursuit of a purpose to drive the United States authority from these places, an unprovoked assault, has been made upon Fort-Sumpter," he also felt at liberty to repossess those places seized before he took office. The attack, he emphasized, had marked "the commencement of actual war against the Government."[67] The administration would hold firmly to that interpretation of events throughout the ensuing war.

Two days later, with the fall of Sumter confirmed, Lincoln announced his policy to the country, in the form of the proclamation that advisers from Frank Blair to John Baldwin had long urged—though it cannot be doubted that Blair was significantly more pleased than Baldwin with the president's final effort. In it, he called up a militia force of 75,000 to "suppress" the "combinations" that had been opposing the execution of the law in seven states. He also convened a special session of Congress to meet on July 4. In identifying the threat facing the country, Lincoln was careful not to mention secession or even the involvement of the state governments—as far as he was concerned, secession was not constitutionally possible and so had not occurred. That, too, was a position he would maintain throughout his presidency.

The proclamation also called on the American people to assist the president in his twofold mission: first, "to maintain the honor, the integrity, and the existence of the National Union, and the perpetuity of popular government," and second, "to redress wrongs already long endured."[68] The first part captured as neatly as anything said or written during the preceding months the determination to defend the Union, and thus the very idea of self-government, to which virtually all Northerners subscribed; in effect, Lincoln had identified the lowest common denominator of Northern political thought, much as Samuel Tilden had sought to do among anti-Republicans almost six months earlier. The second part reinforced the government's blamelessness and tried to tap into the sense of outrage that he hoped would well up throughout the loyal states following the attack on Fort Sumter.

As far as the Upper South went, Lincoln's pains to avoid the role of aggressor had mixed results. As recently as April 4, unionist strength in the Virginia convention was such that an ordinance of immediate secession was rejected by a margin of eighty-nine to forty-five. (It would have been a clean two-thirds had John Baldwin not been absent in Washington.) Thirteen days later, delegates voted overwhelmingly to secede; it took a bit longer than Baldwin's prediction of forty-eight hours, but not much. In the May elections that were to have provided a mandate for the new Union Party, a stunning 85 percent of voters ratified disunion. On May 4, Tennessee also withdrew from the Union, followed two days later by Arkansas and two weeks after that by North Carolina. All four quickly joined the Southern Confederacy. Those states might have survived the Sumter battle had it been followed by a patently conciliatory response from the administration, but to most Southern unionists Lincoln's proclamation signaled naked coercion and could not be tolerated.[69] Of the four remaining slave states, Delaware was too conservative to foster a serious secession movement, while a wide range of sometimes desperate maneuvers from the administration somehow kept Kentucky, Maryland, and Missouri in the Union throughout the long ordeal that followed, despite the divided sympathies of their citizens.

Thus, as of April 15, the country was engaged in civil war, with at least eleven states allied (or soon to be) against the government and three others of dubious loyalty. The question facing Lincoln then was whether his own deeply polarized section would rally to his call.

✳ Lincoln had delayed for a month before finally committing to the relief of Sumter. In the end, he made a decision only when he was forced to, when incoming intelligence and the course of events had stripped all other options away and left him a stark choice between sending supplies and vacating the fort. Fox's March trip helped him not at all in determining whether relief was possible, but the reports of Hurlbut and Lamon came close to rendering that question moot: if the rebel defenses were determined to attack any relief effort, then even a successful mission would provoke the fight Lincoln wanted desperately to avoid. Moreover, if there was no latent unionism in South Carolina, there was no point anyway in delaying a conflict long enough for a unionist reaction to take hold. Meanwhile, the Trumbull resolutions, the Northern governors, and his own never-ending correspondence kept Lincoln aware of a growing impatience within his party; that and the threat of a trade war once the Morrill tariff went into effect added significantly to the president's strain. Between the political pressure, the quandary of Anderson's dwindling supplies, and General Scott's disastrous self-inflicted wound to his own credibility, Lincoln scarcely knew where to turn or what to believe—and that was before John Baldwin informed him that Virginia would secede unless Sumter were evacuated.

Withdrawing from Sumter and retaining Pickens seemed an unsatisfactory solution, especially in light of Republican unrest, but then even that option evaporated. By April 6, Lincoln could either pull out of Charleston and hope Fort Pickens could still be reinforced and a symbolic presence maintained in the South a while longer, or he could uphold federal authority by sending an expedition to Sumter that was predestined to fail and ignite hostilities. At that point the only real question was how to organize the Sumter mission in such a way as to minimize the fallout and maximize the government's chances of winning the war. As he had discovered in the wake of the March 9 and 15 cabinet meetings, he simply could not bring himself to abandon Fort Sumter. To do so, he would later explain to Congress, "would be our national destruction consummated."[70]

It is fitting in a way that Lincoln agonized over the crisis's critical decision until the last possible moment: that was what Northerners collectively had done all winter. Recognizing the tremendous risk involved in any choice he selected, Lincoln delayed and postponed and hoped for the impossible to happen, debating with himself and his cabinet in much the same way that Northerners argued among themselves and with their elected representatives. The difference, of course, was that they—everyone from ordinary citizens to William Seward and Stephen Douglas—could only try to influence those with more power than they had, and so had the luxury of choosing a side and condemning all who disagreed. Lincoln, like Buchanan before him, held in his hands final responsibility, and so was forced to grapple with the complexities and nuances that others could afford to be ignorant of or ignore.

As expected, the Sumter mission and Lincoln's subsequent call to arms drove several more slave states into the new Confederacy, which would make the task of salvaging the Union considerably more difficult. As for whether he would be able to undertake that task, it was now the president's turn to play the role to which Seward, Douglas, and the rest of the North had unwillingly become accustomed throughout the crisis—he must wait to see how those with more power than he responded. Lincoln had done all he could to ensure that the public recognized who was truly at fault. What happened next would depend upon the people of the North.

Chapter 10 ✳ **Everybody Now Is for the Union** ✳ April–May

In early January Northerners of all political persuasions had responded with anger and resentment to South Carolina's seizure of Fort Moultrie and the other federal defenses at Charleston, and with fury to the attack on the *Star of the West*. Passionate differences over slavery's extension and fugitive slaves, compromise, and coercion had disintegrated in a burst of patriotism, a reaction grounded in the near-universal perception of unreasonable, unprovoked aggression on the part of the Palmetto State. But President Buchanan had retreated from his bold stance, conciliatory leaders in Congress had led a resurgent procompromise campaign, time had passed with no further excitement, and the groundswell of nationalist unity faded as quickly as it rose.

Buchanan's successor seems to have drawn two important lessons from that critical episode: one, that the perception of belligerence was all-important in determining how the public responded to hostilities, and two, that patriotic fervor could be a powerful force only if properly encouraged and channeled. In executing his Sumter strategy, Lincoln demonstrated a remarkable aptitude for shaping public opinion: first by alerting South Carolina to the coming of the relief ships, thereby provoking the preemptive attack he knew would result, and then by issuing an immediate, carefully phrased call for military support to put down a violent rebellion. Greatly aiding his cause was that his message had no real competition, with Congress out of session and the most visible champion of conciliation, Stephen Douglas, offering immediate and substantial cooperation. Across the North a tremendous wave of popular indignation translated into an outpouring of support for the administration and, of even more immediate importance, a superabundance of enlistments. Lincoln's gamble had succeeded; he would not have to try to fight a war in opposition to his constituents' wishes.

In the immediate wake of Sumter, it seemed to many that the old political lines were suddenly erased and the entire region brought together into a single, glorious unit. Yet even in those first passionate moments of the war the exaggeration of that view could be seen. Even as they rallied behind the president, Democrats began feeling their way into the delicate role of opposition wartime party, supporting the war effort while insisting on their freedom to criticize the administration's policies. With the benefit of hindsight one can recognize even in those first, rosy weeks after Sumter the outline of wartime politics: Democrats' insistence that they were supporting a war only to restore the Union, not to end slavery, and Republicans' agreement; Republicans' inclination to view dissent as treason and attempt to quash it, and Democrats' protests—quiet grumblings, really, at this early day—about violations of civil liberties; and even the emergence from the Democratic mainstream of a few pockets of antiwar radicalism, precursors to the wartime Copperhead movement.

But these patterns are more easily seen in hindsight; at the time, Northerners were right to wonder at the near unanimity that so quickly followed the long months of bitterness and discord. It would not last throughout the protracted war to come—nor even through the year—but in that moment of unity was laid bare the common Northern nationalism usually hidden by the fierce battles more typical of the political arena.

✳ In Oswego, New York, the brilliant autumn sunshine of early November lay forgotten under long months of snow and piercing cold, and now the dark clouds of yet another storm gave warning that this seemingly never-ending winter had not yet released its icy grip. Despite the looming tempest, young Gus Frey, bent over a new letter to his brother Lud, once more bubbled with an enthusiasm that was almost palpable. After a brief nod in the direction of personal news, he got straight to the main point. "Perhaps you feel like going to the wars," he suggested gleefully. "*I do and no mistake*—when I heard of the surrender of Fort Sumter my dander 'riz.' I felt like 'knawing a file and fleeing into the mountains of Hepsidam, where the lion roareth and the Whangdoodle mourneth for his first born.'" The whole town was excited about the recent news from Charleston, he reported, "and all party lines are for the time being obliterated. Every one is . . . for sustaining the Administration in maintaining the honor of the Stars and Stripes in upholding the Constitution and enforcing the laws. These miserable Rebels and Traitors must be made to feel the *full* power of the Federal Government. They must be taught a lesson that will ever after remain impressed on their minds, or on any others who may hereafter undertake similar matters."

According to the telegraph reports of the local paper, he noted, "the rebels are anxious for another battle." Well, this time they would not get off without casualties—someone was going to get hurt. "Now that Old Abe is thoroughly aroused, there will be no more tampering with the miscreants, but they must prepare for a blood-letting that they at present have no idea of." At a meeting the night before, the local militia had resolved to offer its services to the president, he added, closing cheerfully, "Do not be surprised if you hear some fine morning that, I have gone off to fight for my country."[1]

Gus Frey reported the town's fervor accurately. Despite the snowstorm, a mass meeting held that night, April 16, was packed with enthusiastic citizens eager to condemn disunion, declare their support for the national administration and for the legislature's recent strengthening of the militia, and rejoice in the submersion of partisan differences in this time of crisis.[2] For it did seem that party lines had been obliterated, and both parties were well represented. In a letter of his own the next day Gus's father marveled, "The *worst kind* of Democrats came *right in*!"[3]

Yet there were those in Oswego who seemed unaffected by the excitement, at least initially. For a few days after Sumter, Sarah Johnson took no notice of the uproar but continued to fill her diary with notations of daily affairs. Then the significance of what had happened began to sink in and she abruptly ceased writing. On the twenty-second of April she picked up her journal once more and pronounced in wonder, "The events of the past week are so startling that all personal things sink into littleness." For the first time all winter, she began to write extensively of national events: the fall of Fort Sumter, an attack on Massachusetts troops trying to pass through Baltimore, the remarkable outburst of patriotic zeal in New York City, the continuing threat to the nation's capital, the rumored lynching of a prominent Virginia unionist. She recorded personal effects of the recent occurrences as well, noting the enlistment of two young family friends.[4]

Still, despite the outpouring of popular support for Lincoln—even among "the *worst kind* of Democrats"—Sarah Johnson's analysis of the political situation had not changed since the election. "And all this might have been prevented," she concluded bitterly, "if the Rep party had only believed the south was in earnest, and by negotiation might have settled everything."[5]

✳ Whereas the decisive factor in the Upper South was Lincoln's proclamation, Northerners responded immediately to the attack on Fort Sumter itself. The eruption of popular anger and the widespread declarations of support for the administration that greeted news of the Confederate assault and Sumter's fall far exceeded anything the administration could have hoped for and anything most observers had believed possible. As Gus Frey observed in his small part of the country, the entire North had indeed come together. After five long months of bitter polarization, the free states were instantly united. Flags flew everywhere, Republicans and Democrats joined in condemning disunion and supporting its forcible suppression, and hundreds of thousands of men flocked to volunteer for the military. "And why this transformation?" inquired a Maine Democrat. His answer was remarkably astute: "Because the very foundations of our Republican government are assailed—all that the blood and treasure of the Revolution achieved—all that three quarters of a century of peaceful industry and national growth has done for us at home, and secured for us among the nations of the earth—is in peril by a formidable rebellion; because the glory of the past, the security of the present, and the hopes and just inheritance of posterity are threatened with annihilation—because the world's best promise in the success of popular government is in jeopardy!"[6] No historian could list the factors underlying Northern nationalism more comprehensively.

Nowhere was the phenomenon so pronounced—and so startling to many around the North—than in that most Southern of Northern cities, New York. For the first time since the crisis began, events and attitudes in the Empire City were typical of those throughout the region; to a remarkable extent the city displayed in microcosm the pattern by which Americans across the free states reacted to the attack on Sumter. An analysis of the Northern response to Fort Sumter can find rich ground in New York City.

Since both the Sumter and Pickens expeditions were organized in the Brooklyn Navy Yard, where the daily newspapers had reporters assigned, New York was abuzz over the prospect of action before either mission was even launched. Citizens speculated, and in some cases wagered, over where the ships were going, and visitors showed up to observe the proceedings themselves.[7] Fueled by weeks of expectation of Sumter's evacuation and months of apprehension over the fate of the country, curiosity was intense by the time the ships steamed off, first on the sixth and then again on the tenth. By the afternoon of Friday, April 12, when swarms of heavy-laden newsboys began crying, "Extry—a *Herald*! Got the bombardment of *Fort Sumter*!" anticipation had reached such a pitch that the streets thronged with buyers. Unable to wait until they got home to read, they broke into hundreds of small groups, each huddled around a paper. The hoarse newsboys and their eager customers remained until after midnight, exchanging coins for the new editions that appeared every few hours. The next morning they returned, braving a drenching rain to get the latest telegraphic reports.[8]

The rush for news was only the first manifestation of an explosion of support for Lincoln's course. Early hopes of victory dissolved into disappointment and confusion at the fort's surrender, followed quickly by anger, and finally resolve. "The war news" was the only topic of conversation for days, and for the first time during the crisis the debate was all on one side: "The Northern backbone is much stiffened already," G. T. Strong noted with satisfaction that first Saturday, even as the battle still raged in Charleston. Indeed it was, and the tide of demonstrative patriotism only rose higher after that. An observer might have been pardoned for thinking it had crested with the massive crowds who turned out on Thursday, the eighteenth, to cheer first a Massachusetts regiment passing through on its way to defend the capital and then a stunned Major Anderson when he and his command steamed into the harbor from Charleston. But the multitudes returned the next day to greet more Bay State soldiers, then reached a truly prodigious scale at an enormous rally that was held at Union Square on Saturday.[9]

By that time citizens' passions had been whipped into a frenzy—first by Lincoln's call for troops, which at last offered an outlet for the pent-up anxieties and frustrations of the past five months, then by reports that the Massachusetts troops they had cheered along their way on Thursday had been attacked by a secessionist mob in Baltimore on Friday, with four men killed and dozens more wounded. More than a few Northerners found it notable that it was on April 19, the anniversary of the battle of Lexington, that the first blood had been spilled in this war, and that it had once more been Massachusetts blood at that. "This is a continuation of the war that Lexington opened," Strong wrote grimly, "a war of democracy against oligarchy. God defend the right and confound all traitors." Around the city, another diarist observed, "the public mind is wrought up into a state of frenzy to day with the war question."[10]

It was no surprise, then, that New Yorkers jammed the streets, windows, and rooftops around Union Square the next day. They roared their approval of Anderson and the other speakers who manned the various stages erected around the area, gathered in "small mobs" to stare at the sentries in their dashing new uniforms posted outside the headquarters of passing regiments, and sang and cheered their way through the national anthem. The scene was breathtaking, and New Yorkers were stirred by the spectacle and speeches. "Few assemblages have equalled it in numbers and unanimity," Strong recorded in wonder. "Every other man, woman, and child bearing a flag or decorated with a cockade. Flags from almost every building. The city seems to have gone suddenly wild and crazy." A young medical student wrote home, "Is this not a glorious war?" A woman who was on a balcony overlooking the square but was too far away to hear the speakers nevertheless found assurance merely in the sight: "Now we don't feel that the social fabric is falling to pieces at all, but that it is getting gloriously mended."[11]

Hundreds of prominent men of all political leanings had signed the call for the meeting, which was presided over by Hardshell Democrat John A. Dix, the erstwhile secretary of the treasury who had achieved brief celebrity in late January by calling for a disloyal revenue cutter captain to be shot. Almost every political leader in the city was represented on the Union Defense Committee created that day. A few days later Mayor Wood, who three months earlier had issued an ill-advised call for New York to secede from the Union and declare itself a free city, joined the Board of Alderman in authorizing the expenditure of a million dollars, to be controlled by the new committee, to train and equip volunteers.[12]

The flags that Strong noted were ubiquitous throughout those heady days; overnight the national colors had become the most visible rallying point of the "rampant and demonstrative" patriotism that gripped the city. "The national flag flying everywhere," Strong had observed a few days earlier; "every horse cart decorated." He had to hunt through the city, in fact, to find one to raise over Trinity Church, and when he finally succeeded, the enthusiasm with which an impromptu crowd cheered the symbolic fusing of church and nation was startling. The reason he had difficulty was not hard to fathom—a city woman who had gone to see the Bay State regiment march through that same day wrote, "U.S. Flags displayed by thousands, & every person decorated by flag or rosette." The same was true even without a major public event to draw crowds: a few days later she observed again, "The city decorated with U.S. Flags from every House & Store & public building. Every one with rosettes on their breast or small flags in their hands." She bought three herself.[13]

The power of the flag lay in its convenient and compelling symbolism of that potent constellation of nationalistic values associated with the Union, the Constitution, and enforcement of the laws. Although the hard-line Republicans had been more aggressive in linking their message explicitly with those values, the burst of patriotic unity that had briefly united the

North in late December and early January showed that they had undergirded the outlooks of both hard-liners and conciliationists throughout the crisis. The differences between the two lay in their views regarding the nature of the Union, the proper interpretation of the Constitution, and the practicability of enforcing the laws given the explosive situation. Once the flag had been fired upon at Fort Sumter, such distinctions became obsolete; virtually all agreed that divergent understandings of national ideals meant little when the nation itself was under attack. Moreover, the assault on Sumter also brought to the fore another powerful symbolic meaning of the flag: the blood sacrifice the Revolutionaries had made to create the republic. The Confederate insult at Charleston reminded Northerners that secession was an attack not only on their freedom and security but on the Founders' noble experiment in self-government. Finally, as that frequently used word "insult" suggests, it cannot be forgotten that Northerners felt deeply the injury to the national honor posed by the assault on Sumter and by secession itself.

To New Yorkers, the ever-growing military presence in the city added a physical embodiment to the values associated with the flag—hence the massive crowds lining the streets to cheer the regiments on their way. Suddenly the city could not get enough of all things military. Prints of celebrated battles and books on military tactics, training, and history were instantly popular; war dramas and martial music dominated the theaters.[14] For thousands of families the proud image of smartly marching soldiers took on a bittersweet immediacy with the enlistment of waves of young men into the scores of volunteer regiments being formed around the city. They were inspired by any number of factors: the patriotic fervor, the insult to the flag, and the threat to the Union and the free institutions it represented, certainly, but also the debonair picture of the soldiers, the promise of adventure, enormous social pressure, and for those who had received the brunt of the months-long economic recession, a steady paycheck.[15]

With the exception of the last, such motives affected all social groups equally, and the Irish and German immigrants who formed the backbone of the city's Democratic Party enlisted in similar proportion to native-born Americans. Within days of Sumter's fall, a steady stream of passing troops and a rapidly growing body of volunteers from within and around the city had converted New York into an armed camp. By the end of the month, over 7,000 soldiers had departed for Washington. Eager to join in the excitement, older men unfit for volunteering formed home guard units and began to practice the rudiments of drill. Women, too, responded in unexpected numbers to a call from the *Times* to meet and prepare bandages and other medical necessities; some of the city's poor women, including prostitutes, former prisoners, and almshouse inmates, received training as nurses.[16]

In all of this, Lincoln's decision to leave the initiative in Confederate hands—his maneuvering them into the position of, as he said, attacking ships that were merely "giving . . . bread to the few brave and hungry men of the garrison"[17]—proved critical, for it ensured that the overwhelming majority of conciliationists, regardless of party, interpreted the assault as unprovoked Southern aggression. A city woman whose few observations on politics throughout the crisis had been submerged in the details of everyday life now expressed the connection most directly: "News arrived to day of the attack on Fort Sumpter, by the *Traitors* in Charleston, & that 5 or 6 Thousand men well fed, had out fired 70 or 80 half starved ones! Great excitement in New York, Men turning from indifference to good Union & government men." George T. Strong observed a similar phenomenon, noting that "many who stood up for 'Southern rights' and complained of wrongs done the South now say that, since the South fired the first gun, they are ready to go to all lengths in supporting the government."[18]

And Strong was not surprised that such should be the result, for he had been considering for some time the importance of which side fired first. As early as April 10, when the *Tribune* first reported that the relief expedition contained only a small fraction of the force Anderson and Scott thought was necessary, Strong had wondered whether "the Administration counts on a repulse as a tonic and stimulant to the North." The next day he judged Jefferson Davis's rumored order not to attack the ships "a politic move, for everything depends on being strictly right on the particular issue in which first blood is drawn."[19]

Strong was not the only one to appreciate the logic of Lincoln's strategy —it was openly debated in the press. Republicans praised the president's wisdom. The *Times*, which two weeks earlier had criticized Lincoln's lack of a policy and tried to help Seward seize the reins of power, now asserted admiringly that "the surrender of Fort Sumpter, instead of being a defeat, is, when we come to look at its effects, a most brilliant success. It has thrown upon the Confederated States the entire responsibility of commencing the war." That was no accident, the editor continued: "It was not the plan of the Administration that [the fleet] should go to [Anderson's] rescue at too great a peril. It was from the start destined to an entirely different field and mode of action. Neither the retention or surrender of Fort Sumpter could have any bearing on the policy the Government had marked out for it-self. . . . [The] Government could not allow its flag to be disgraced by retreat. *It is strengthened in every part by the surrender of the Fort.*"[20]

The city's Democratic newspapers, all Hardshell, did not speak so kindly of the plan. "We have no doubt," the *Evening Day-Book* seethed, "and all circumstances prove, that it was a cunningly devised scheme, contrived with all due attention to scenic display and intended to arouse and, if possible, exasperate the Northern people against the South. . . . And some Democrats have been just such dunderheads as to fall into this pit dug for their reception."[21] Both sides gave Lincoln too much credit for his far-sightedness, aware of neither the confusion and uncertainty that reigned in the capital in late March and early April nor the desperation that shaped the final decision, but they recognized his purpose with a fair degree of accuracy.

The Hardshell press did not express such outspoken criticism of the administration or the war for long. The spontaneous outburst of patriotism soon revealed a darker side when, on April 15, a mob appeared at the office of the *Herald* and compelled editor James Gordon Bennett to hang an American flag from his window;[22] two days later another crowd made the rounds of the rest of the city's pro-Southern papers and forced them to display flags as well. The action resulted in the conversion of all but one—the *Daily News*, edited by the brother of Mayor Wood—to grudging (and temporary) support for the war. After recounting the incident in his diary, a Democratic businessman observed, with no apparent disapproval, "Everybody now is for the Union, & even the Herald has come over."[23]

Some anti-Republicans objected strenuously, however, both to the news-paper mobs and to more subtle examples of political repression. "The despotism here is supreme," fumed Sidney Webster, a protégé of Caleb Cushing. "Men who have houses of business do not *dare* to denounce the war, or even criticize the acts of Lincoln. . . . Slavery of the worst and meanest kind is upon us." With patriotism and Republicanism linked in the public mind, he added, "democrats are compelled to adjourn discussion of party issues." David M. Turnure, one of many Northerners whose diary-keeping began with the attack on Fort Sumter, expressed similar resent-ment. The "war excitement," he wrote, was so intense that "those differing in sentiment with republicans or in any way opposed to the acts of the Administration scarcely dare express these sentiments for fear of bodily injury. The prevailing opinion is to day that the Govt must be sustained and rebellion suppressed and no matter what differences of opinion may exist as to the mode of meeting the rebellion they must be suppressed or treason is at once imputed to a person."[24]

Such criticism was uncommon, though, and not merely because not many dared express it. In the giddy days after Sumter, few anti-Republicans needed to be coerced into expressing their support for the war. A young Democratic businessman captured the common spirit when, after the first reports of the Sumter attack, he wrote resignedly, "My sympathy has been with the South, who would have been satisfied with the recognition of their just rights in the territories, but now that Mr Lincoln is our President, & lawfully elected, all good citizens must stand by him to see that the laws are enforced & that the U.S. property is everywhere protected." A few days later, upon reading Lincoln's proclamation, he declared succinctly, "Every good citizen now knows but one party *that of the Union*, & the laws must be enforced, else we are a ruined people." Tammany Hall itself echoed that sentiment, pledging that every Democrat in the city was "heartily united to uphold the constitution, enforce the laws, maintain the Union, defend the flag, and protect the Capital."[25]

That did not mean, of course, that New York Democrats determined en masse to dissolve their organization. Many party leaders expressed their support for the war in carefully qualified phrases. Brooklyn state senator Francis B. Spinola, who in early January had led the charge for a military response to the attack on the *Star of the West*, summarized the feelings of most anti-Republicans by declaring, "You of the majority have precipitated this war upon us, but we shall fight it to the end. We shall fight it side by side with every loyal citizen, so long as fighting may be necessary, but ever praying that, by equitable compromise, peace may be restored to our unhappy country." Nevertheless, almost all recognized that the stakes had risen beyond the level where traditional partisan differences could be indulged. Thus the wife of a Democratic officeholder could in the same diary entry chide Massachusetts abolitionists for causing the war and also observe, "The attack upon Fort Sumter has united all the North as one man against the South. Party is forgotten. All feel that our very nationality is at stake, and to save the country from anarchy (learning what South America and Mexico are) that every man must do his best to sustain the government, whoever or whatever the President may be." She concluded, "It is a sublime spectacle."[26]

✳ The spectacle was repeated throughout the free states. As in New York, the entire North was seized by a rage militaire that instantly rallied men and women of all parties behind the war. Everywhere men answered the president's call by enlisting in volunteer militia regiments. Massachusetts was the first to respond. From Boston, where, like New York, Republican strength was at its weakest in the state, Amos A. Lawrence informed Crittenden, "You have but a faint idea of the indignation which has seized the public mind since the defeat of Anderson. Everyman wishes to be a volunteer." The *Boston Evening Transcript*, one of that tiny minority of newspapers not affiliated with a political party, rejoiced, "The seven thousand conspirators who assaulted Fort Sumter have sown the dragon's teeth, which have instantly sprung up armed men. They have made the Free States a unit, and such a unit!"[27] Even hard-nosed radical Democrat Caleb Cushing announced his support for the administration and offered his services to Governor Andrew, hoping for a military commission. His followers applauded his course, one lifelong Jacksonian expressing resentment of Republican insults but declaring, "When the question is whether we shall have a Government or Anarchy, whether the Stars & Stripes must be lowered . . . I have no hesitancy in declaring my choice."[28]

The governor rejected Cushing's proposal out of hand, writing, "Were I to accept your offer I should dishearten numerous good and loyal men, and tend to demoralize our military service." Plainly the old political lines had not been obliterated completely. As if Andrew's pointed language were not insult enough, the justification he cited was bosh; not only had Andrew already accepted a similar offer from Cushing's Democratic colleague Benjamin Butler, but, like other Northern governors, he had his hands so full with volunteers that he had to turn many away. Fortunately, Massachusetts had reformed its militia some years earlier, and when the radical Andrew had taken office in January he was able to spend the next few months preparing the state's defense organization for this moment. When the request for men arrived from Washington on the fifteenth, he relayed the order immediately, and the first units began to arrive in Boston the next day. Thus it was that within two days of Lincoln's proclamation—on Wednesday, the seventeenth—the Sixth Massachusetts Volunteer Regiment left for the capital. It was the same unit that would stir hearts in New York on Thursday and suffer the first casualties of the war in Baltimore on Friday.[29]

By that time Boston, like New York and every other Northern city of any size, had been converted into a military encampment. Existing militia units poured into the city at the same time that applications for over 150 new companies were made; the militia soon numbered 10,000 men. Here, too, older men formed drill companies and women made bandages and trained as nurses; public funds were appropriated to train and equip soldiers and private money raised to support their families; the American flag was omnipresent, waving from homes, businesses, and government buildings, decorating horse carts and express wagons, and adorning the persons of men, women, and children. (Like George T. Strong, Edward Everett had to scour the city for a flag to display over the Boston Public Library—unlike Strong, he was unable to locate one.) And here, too, the symbolic power of the flag stirred all parts of society: on the twenty-seventh, a mob numbering several hundred, mostly Irish, forced a Georgia ship to replace the Confederate colors with American, then tore the secession flag into small pieces. The local Irish newspaper came out in support of the war (with the usual aside noting the culpability of Republican fanaticism in starting it), and a meeting of Irish Democrats pledged to defend the Union against treason.[30]

In Albany, where the state legislature was still in session, the government acted with a like alacrity. There a bill authorizing half a million dollars to equip the militia had languished in the House since early February, blocked by Democrats and conciliatory Republicans. Since then the crisis had settled into the background as the Assembly focused on the more ordinary business that had been shunted aside throughout January. But rumors of an impending conflict raised the militia issue again in early April, and news of Sumter now virtually erased opposition. The bill, slightly amended, passed easily. In the meantime, Governor Morgan met with state officials and relevant committees from the legislature to draw up a more sweeping bill, which provided for 30,000 two-year volunteers, a three-million-dollar appropriation, and a new state military board to oversee the militia. He transmitted it to the Assembly the next day along with Lincoln's request for troops. Democrats were so reluctant to appear partisan that party leaders found it impossible even to gather a caucus, and the bill was passed with only a handful of negative votes in either house.[31]

In Springfield, Governor Richard Yates had the luxury of neither a reformed militia—as in New York, Democrats and conciliatory Republicans had held it up earlier in the year—nor an in-session legislature. He acted immediately to rectify both situations, summoning the Assembly and pushing for a militia bill as soon as it met. By early May the militia had been reorganized and funds authorized for proper equipment.[32] In the meantime, Yates had begun recruiting new militia units; within two days the newspapers were reporting that between forty and fifty companies had been offered. The state's quota filled so quickly that by the time the legislature even met, Stephen Hurlbut was complaining to Lincoln that his volunteer company was among seventy that the governor had been forced to send home.[33]

✳ Despite the massive outpouring of support, rumblings of dissent could still be heard. A number of editors openly denounced the administration for eschewing compromise and bringing on the war. Several followed New York City's Hardshell press in condemning Lincoln's Sumter strategy as manipulative, and some even clung to the conviction, oft-expressed throughout the crisis, that a republic could not be preserved through force of arms.[34] In a few areas this sentiment transcended the editorial page and blossomed into outright protest. In Connecticut, for example, a few antiwar protesters began to raise "peace flags," white flags emblazoned with peace slogans.[35]

Probably the most widespread and outspoken antiwar feeling existed in the southern regions of the northwestern border states of Ohio, Indiana, and Illinois, long a core of Democratic strength in the North. These areas tended toward ideological extremism, dominated as they were by first- and second-generation Southern immigrants, many of whom found themselves genuinely torn in their loyalties. Party leaders from southern Illinois, or Egypt, as it was known, were the radicals who had championed resistance to federal coercion at the January state party convention. Now there were signs that Egypt might explode in rebellion. Public meetings in Pope and Williamson counties actually endorsed secession and protested Lincoln's call for troops. In Johnson County, the local paper reported that after news of Sumter's fall, fifteen cannons were fired in honor of a united South. The *Galconda Weekly Herald* advised citizens to arm themselves against black Republican armies. Republican leader John M. Palmer later recalled that in traveling through Egypt to observe public feeling in the week after Sumter, he found considerable support for making Cairo, at the confluence of the Mississippi and Ohio rivers, an independent city.[36]

Throughout the North, response to dissent varied, and occasionally included force. In Connecticut, someone took a shot at the man who raised the first peace flag.[37] Philadelphia mobs, like their counterparts in New York, forced pro-Southern editors to display the stars and stripes outside their offices; what was more, they actually attacked a number of suspected disunionists. The personal intervention of the mayor failed to quell the violence; it only stopped when he threatened that the police would shoot to kill.[38] In Egypt, forcible suppression of disunionism took a more institutional form: Governor Yates took no chances with stories of Egyptian secessionism but sent troops to secure Cairo. By May 6, about four thousand soldiers were stationed there.[39]

There is a temptation to generalize from such incidents, but we must be careful to exaggerate neither the extent nor the degree to which dissent was physically suppressed in the free states at this early stage of the war. Very few dissenters were hurt, if any at all, in the various incidents of urban mob intimidation; in fact, the occurrence of mobs was actually quite rare. Instead, early critics of Lincoln's policy were subject to more subtle pressure, the kind under which Sidney Webster and David Turnure chafed in New York. In Oswego, for example, Sarah Johnson wrote of a suspected secession sympathizer who "was advised to leave quietly before anything happened to his family." In Springfield, state assemblyman William Green complained that the presence of troops in the city was intimidating members—"Democrats . . . tell me no man can safely express himself in opposition to the policy of the President," he reported—but if any real threat existed outside of the imaginations of anxious radicals there, no evidence of it survives.[40]

For the most part, pressure was unnecessary: amid the post-Sumter surge of patriotism, most anti-Republicans in the North threw themselves into the war wholeheartedly. In Connecticut, peace flags were few and far between prior to the Battle of Bull Run in late July. In southern Illinois, commitment to the Union and the Constitution had trumped prosecession sympathy even before the militia arrived. The Williamson County resolutions against Lincoln's proclamation were denounced by a subsequent meeting in neighboring Jackson County, and a number of Egyptian editors decried secession and supported the administration. By late April there were even reports that the Northern war frenzy had gained sway and that secessionists were being threatened with hanging.[41] Democratic leaders such as Stephen Douglas and John A. Logan served as focal points for Unionist sympathies, the former by driving himself into an early grave speaking out in support of the war, the latter, a popular young Egyptian congressman, by raising a regiment and joining the army. While the relative influence that the public and political leaders exerted on each other is uncertain, it is safe to conclude that their leadership helped to ensure that Yates's military occupation succeeded in securing Cairo rather than inflaming resentment and rebellion. In any case, any real danger had passed by early summer; even as secessionist recruiters headed south having attracted a scant thirty-five men, Egypt contributed its first full regiment of Illinois militia.[42]

Despite a few overblown incidents, then, neither dissent nor its suppression generally took violent form; for the most part, anti-Republican opposition did not yet transcend those few rumblings. Criticism of the administration was left to Democratic Party leaders, who at this early stage in the war were concerned with two things: that their party survive the burst of political unity that so many Northerners thought was heralding the end of partisan conflict, and that the Republicans not convert this war into an antislavery crusade. Given their critical place in the machinery of party, Democratic editors were more conscious than most of their readers of the need to maintain a healthy distance from the Republicans. Thus even as Charles Lanphier's *Illinois State Register* asserted stoutly that patriotism demanded that all set aside the question of who was responsible for the war and rally to the flag, it also stated categorically, "We have not, nor do we now, indorse the principles of the administration. We condemn them." Democrats must sustain their constitutionally chosen government, the *Register* insisted, "not in its party principles, but in its resistance to rebellion." Lanphier's reasoning combined patriotic and partisan considerations: not only would submission to secessionist violence "bid havoc, anarchy and endless civil war," but opposition to the government in wartime would weaken the Democracy just as it had the Federalists in 1812 and the Whigs in 1846.[43] Other party organs echoed these sentiments, many warning explicitly that they would not condone Republicans' using the war as an opportunity to destroy slavery.[44]

Stephen Douglas himself epitomized the Democrats' tentative first steps toward loyal wartime opposition. On the night of April 25, after privately hashing out an agreement with Illinois Republicans on the pending militia bill, he addressed the state legislature in what became one of the most widely printed and talked-about speeches of the time. He had worked as hard as any man to save the Union through compromise, he said—had even leaned "too far to the Southern section of the Union against my own"—and he continued to hope for a peaceful outcome. But the fastest way to peace, he held now, was a vigorous prosecution of the war. Douglas was careful to urge Republicans not to use the war for partisan advantage and swore that "so far as any of the partisan questions are concerned, I stand in equal, irreconcilable, and undying opposition both to the Republicans and Secessionists." Still, he avowed, the time for indulging party differences would be after the danger had passed. For now, he continued, "I believe in my conscience that it is a duty we owe ourselves, and our children, and our God, to protect this government and that flag from every assailant, be he who he may." Shortly afterward, in a public letter intended to win over recalcitrant Democrats, he added that he was neither a supporter of Lincoln nor an apologist for his errors but, like all loyal Americans, was simply standing by "the Flag, the Constitution, and the Union."[45]

Writing the letter would be the last public act of Douglas's life. Overworked and suffering from almost a year of unremitting strain, he had already suffered a severe attack of rheumatism and had to dictate his words to a secretary. His condition declined rapidly and he died within weeks, on June 3. His last words were said to be advice to his sons: "Tell them to obey the laws and support the Constitution of the United States." Before departing, Douglas had offered his party a blueprint for balancing support for the war with legitimate political opposition, one most Democrats would adhere to closely in the years to come.[46]

✳ Aside from the rush of enlistments, perhaps the most telling sign of genuine bipartisan support for the war was the hundreds of Union rallies held throughout the free states in the weeks after Sumter. These mass meetings presented an astonishing contrast to those of January and February, in which hard-liners and conciliationists had vied for the label "unionist" and resolutions had revealed a sharply divided citizenry. Post-Sumter rallies were remarkable for their harmony and uniformity: in rallies held in big cities like Boston, Chicago, Cincinnati, and Philadelphia, as well as small towns like Oswego, New York; Norwich, Connecticut; and Springfield, Ohio—almost all of them aimed at inspiring enlistment—speakers preached a consistent message of the need to abandon parties, defend the Union, and uphold the Constitution and the laws.[47]

As well as demonstrating an apparent erasure of party lines, the Union meetings also reflected the symbiotic relationship between the parties' leaders and the rank and file during the tumultuous post-Sumter period. On the one hand, all were called by prominent citizens and announced a day or two ahead in the local press. Officers and members of the resolutions committees were recognized political leaders. On the other hand, the sheer enthusiasm of the attendees frequently influenced not only the call but also the actual form the meetings took. An example is New York's Union Square rally: although the city's elite carefully engineered the assembly's speakers and layout to produce maximum turnout, the crowd's enthusiasm differed little from the spontaneous gatherings of previous days.

An April 18 meeting in the small town of Hudson, New York, was more typical. Though it was originally called for the purpose of forming a volunteer company, the unexpected volume of participants forced its callers to alter their agenda: the first item, as the courthouse filled to overflowing, became figuring out how to hold the meeting at all. The people took the lead: at the suggestion of "hundreds in the back part of the house," everyone moved to the more spacious city hall. There the officers regained control and appointed a committee to frame resolutions, but as its members filed out to deliberate, the crowd asserted itself again, demanding to hear from particular speakers. The first was John Van Ness Philip, a local retired naval officer and a Democrat. "It was the most overpowering manifestation of enthusiasm that I ever saw," an awed Philip would write his brother afterward. "When I walked up on the stage I thought the house would come down."[48]

The speech Philip delivered reflected the same message as those of thousands of anti-Republicans in hundreds of such meetings, and of most of the party press. "I take the broad platform of the Constitution and the Union!" he proclaimed. "The booming of cannon in Charleston harbor has buried all parties in oblivion. . . . There are now only two sides—for the Union or against it." Philip was a committed Democrat and had worked to defeat Lincoln, but he asserted, "The question now is: Shall this Government be overthrown by traitors, or shall it be sustained?" Cries of "Sustained" came back from the audience. "Shall not they who have trampled under foot this sacred flag, which has so long floated over our country, be put down?" "Yes!" his listeners shouted. Philip broadened his appeal to include the Founders, echoing the Declaration of Independence in pledging his life, fortune, and sacred honor to the cause and reminding his audience that the government was a trust bequeathed by "our fathers," under whose watch no "heretical doctrine" of secession had been permitted.

He then gestured dramatically to the flag behind him on the stage and invoked it as a symbol of the nation's strength, ideals, and blood sacrifice: "For twenty years I have sailed under it, to all parts of the Globe, and everywhere seen it unfurled as the emblem of Liberty and the safeguard of American rights. Some of my best friends too have fallen at my side in its defence. And now to see it menaced and insulted by traitors! But are there not strong hearts and hands enough to avenge it?" "Yes!" the crowd roared.

It was a perfect ending note, but Philip was not quite finished. He wished he could stay and help his fellow citizens through the coming trial, he said, but he must go and serve his country in the navy. His heart would be with them, and he hoped they would remain true. He rejoiced in the display of patriotism among all parties and closed "in the words of the old hero of New Orleans"—here he was interrupted by great cheering for Andrew Jackson—" 'The Union—it Must and Shall be Preserved.' " As he left the stage, he recounted later, "the audience actually jumped up & down, and cheered most vociferously."[49]

By the time Philip finished speaking, the resolutions committee had just about completed its task; after some more calling for speakers from the crowd, the results were submitted. Like the resolutions of similar meetings across the North, they condemned the assault on the flag and the rebellion it represented; called on men of all parties to forget their past differences and unite in support of the government; expressed pride in the patriotic uprising so evident throughout the North; pledged to stand behind the actions of the governor and legislature; and in a popular and deliberately vague concession to the sentiments of conciliationists, looked forward to making a just peace with their Southern brethren, making "all such concessions as men of principle may make," once "the sober second thought shall recall them to a sense of their duty and obligations to their sister States." Such was the platform—the new lowest common denominator— upon which almost all Northerners were comfortable in standing. The Hudson meeting passed it immediately.[50]

Another Democratic speaker made a brief address echoing these sentiments, and then the meeting's leaders prepared to sign enlistees. The people intervened in the proceedings one last time, however, demanding to hear from a popular local politician, who obliged with a lengthy and fiery speech extolling the virtues of the Union. "All listened with emotion," the local paper reported, "and when he concluded with the declaration that the glorious old Flag of our Country should long wave over 'the land of the free and the home of the brave,' the enthusiasm of the meeting broke forth in loud and long applause." When the organizers again called for volunteers, this time "a large number immediately went upon the stand."[51]

So, in general form and result, went countless local Union meetings in the exhilarating days after the fall of Fort Sumter. The crisis had at last reached the point at which the deeper cords that bound the region's political culture together—commitment to the integrity of the Union, determination to enforce the authority of the Constitution, and devotion to the legacy of the Founders—overshadowed the partisan antagonism that had long dominated politics.

Yet the Hudson meeting also underscores the muted strength that partisan perspectives still held; just because Democrats pledged their support to the defense of the flag did not mean that past resentments and disagreements were forgotten. In the same letter in which John Van Ness Philip wrote his brother of his glorious political debut, he also complained that the government should have done more to conciliate the border states and wondered whether Lincoln was up to the task before him. "If we only had sent a man as John A. Dix," he mused regretfully, "Maryland may as well give up any idea of secession."[52] If Philip, like most Democrats, carried his anti-Republican grudge no further than that, his wistful pondering of what might have been still reflected elements of the same strong remnants of partisanship that led his more radical compatriots to murmur against the intense pressure they felt to fall into line behind the administration.

In numerous ways, then, did the Hudson meeting and hundreds like it represent in microcosm the Northern response to Sumter: in the passion with which Northerners charged vigorously into war, and in the motivation behind their zeal; in the melding of long-opposed parties into a remarkably united front, and in the hints of partisan opposition that continued to linger; and, with a bit of reading between the lines, in the informal negotiations that defined the relationship between people and political leaders—negotiations that, for a while in the immediate wake of Sumter, became more balanced than was usually the case.

With regard to that last point, it is worth recalling that three generations earlier, most of these Americans' Revolutionary-era forebears had refrained from formal participation in government but reserved the right to take to the streets as "the people out of doors"—mobs—when their "betters" failed to protect their interests. Though ordinary Americans now rejected the notion of deference to one's superiors and engaged formally in politics at an astonishing rate through the vote, the popular response to secession reminds us that in times of crisis the people continued both to look to political leaders for guidance and to find unofficial means of making their own voices heard, whether through sending letters, petitions, and resolutions to Congress or through compelling local politicians to respond to their demands at mass meetings.

Their influence was limited, as we have seen. In Hudson it was local political and social elites who called the meeting, staffed the resolutions committee, and comprised the speakers, as in Washington it was congressmen who acted for or against compromise and the president who not only made the ultimate decision on the use of force but executed his decision in such a way as to maximize his chances at winning the people's support—or as some argued, arranged events so as to manipulate public opinion in his favor. However one interprets Lincoln's actions, though, his Sumter strategy serves as a powerful reminder that no politician, be it a local activist organizing a rally, a congressman serving on a key committee, or the president deciding whether to take steps that would lead to war, could afford to ignore the will of the public altogether. How the government responded to disunion lay ultimately with the president; whether the government succeeded in carrying out its policy toward disunion lay ultimately with the people. If the people's role in government decisions should not be overstated, neither can it be overlooked.

✳ With the attack on Fort Sumter, the secession crisis ended and the Civil War began. Northerners of all parties united to support the Lincoln administration in upholding the Constitution and preserving the Union. As did so much of the Northern response to secession, the outpouring of patriotism exemplified both the importance of public opinion and the influence of political leaders; the former was genuine and spontaneous and provided the energy needed for the government to go to war, but strong leadership was necessary to give it shape and substance beyond the wispy phantasm that had so quickly melted away in January. When he offered his official account of the Sumter crisis to Congress in July, Lincoln would expand on the interpretation of events he had begun to establish in the war's first hours, casting the conflict in terms to which he knew Northerners would respond: "This issue embraces more than the fate of these United States. It presents to the whole family of man, the question, whether a constitutional republic, or a democracy—a government of the people, by the same people —can, or cannot, maintain its territorial integrity, against its own domestic foes. It presents the question, whether discontented individuals, too few in numbers to control administration, according to organic law, in any case, can . . . break up their Government, and thus practically put an end to free government upon the earth."[53]

It was an interpretation of events that resonated powerfully with the Northern people, and one that Lincoln felt deeply. For both of those reasons, he would continue to play on this theme throughout the long war to come, most famously in dedicating a cemetery for fallen soldiers on the site of one of the many horrific battles that lay for now in an unknown future. "We here highly resolve," he would pronounce in November 1863, "that these dead shall not have died in vain—that this nation, under God, shall have a new birth of freedom—and that government of the people, by the people, for the people, shall not perish from the earth."[54]

With so much at stake, the partisan differences that drove ideas and events during the winter now seemed petty and inappropriate. Certainly, Democratic leaders began feeling their way toward asserting their political independence and preserving their organization, and already some objected to early instances of patriotic repression. If the powerful gift of hindsight reveals to us in even these minor qualifications of support and small mutterings of discontent an outline of the mighty struggle to control the war that Republicans and Democrats would wage over the next four years, still, for now, amid the passion and the pageantry and the boundless optimism of the post-Sumter North, what mattered for most was suppression of the rebellion and defense of the Union.

Conclusion ✳ Shall It Be Peace, or a Sword?

In late January, Lincoln had thought to challenge secessionists to follow a course that would avert war. "In your hands, my dissatisfied fellow countrymen, and not in mine, is the momentous issue of civil war," he wrote in his original inaugural draft. "With you, and not with me, is the solemn question of 'Shall it be peace, or a sword?'"[1] Although he eliminated that particular line from the final draft of his address, the idea formed the basis of his entire secession policy. Throughout the crisis he sought to encourage Southerners to back away from secession and embrace the Union—to decide on peace—but always with the warning that if they did not, he had no choice but to uphold federal authority. In the end he was so convinced that responsibility lay with the disunionists that he even arranged the relief of Fort Sumter so that others would not misperceive the conflict as arising from Northern aggression.

It was characteristic of Lincoln that he arrived at this conclusion through use of the most basic tool of Euclidean geometry, the syllogism.[2] Seeing four possible outcomes of the crisis—compromise, peaceable secession, the use of force, or a Southern retreat from disunion—he reasoned something like this: A) Northerners could not submit to a compromise, because "buying" the right to take power after a constitutional election would not only encourage the rapacious appetites of the Slave Power but undermine the whole electoral system and destroy republican government. B) Northerners could not acquiesce in peaceable disunion, because secession was "the essence of anarchy" and would destroy republican government. Therefore, C) either secessionists must cease their efforts to break up the Union, or Northerners would have no alternative but to preserve the republic by force.

It is the nature of the syllogism that the conclusion follows only if the premises are true. During the secession winter a great many of Lincoln's fellow Northerners disputed his, particularly with regard to compromise and the probable results of force. It is also the nature of politics that reality is rarely, if ever, so black and white that it can be reduced to a syllogism; through much of the crisis Northerners saw not three clear and distinct options on their part—compromise, peaceable secession, or force—but a range of possible courses, including a variety of combinations and degrees of those three.[3] Although Lincoln and most Republicans believed that the crisis's outcome lay entirely with the secessionists, the protracted debates over compromise and coercion were actually arguments over what the *North* was willing to do and how far it was willing to go to prevent Southern secession. Ultimately, it was Northerners who were asking themselves, "Shall it be peace, or a sword?" Yet in the end, Lincoln's vision triumphed after all: in April, free-state residents supported his decision to draw the sword when he persuaded them that he did so only in self-defense.

The Northern decision for war cannot be understood without close study of how the region's complex and contradictory political culture framed questions, influenced decisions, and ultimately shaped a united response to the republic's impending dissolution. The common goal of virtually all Northerners was to preserve the Constitution and the Union. However, through most of the crisis Republicans and anti-Republicans disagreed fundamentally over just how to do that—which is to say that intense political and ideological differences molded individuals' and parties' responses to the dramatic events of that terrible winter. At the simplest level, Northerners agreed that the republic was in danger, but while Republicans blamed the Southern Slave Power and its Northern Democratic pawns, their opponents saw the Republicans, with their moral imperialism and their fanatical sectional agitation, as the instigators.

Still, as antagonistic and entrenched as partisan battles were, the sides did share that mutual aim of preserving the Constitution and the Union. And as that commonality indicates, Northern political conflict operated within certain defined boundaries dictated by a unified political culture. That culture rested upon a set of values and traditions that centered on a few basic elements: a devout reverence for and obligation to the Founders of the republic; a sense of duty to humanity to ensure the success of the United States' unique experiment in self-government; a strong faith in America's future glory and power; a deep emotional commitment to the Union and the Constitution that regulated it, which they believed were the bases of Americans' freedom and prosperity; and a passionate commitment to law and order.

Those shared principles ensured that all sides abided by the results of the political system's operation. That agreement on a fundamental set of rules for political discourse kept the country from immediate disintegration when seven of the thirty-three states seceded. For instance, no matter how infuriated and resentful conciliationists were when congressional Republicans rejected genuine compromise, only a handful of extremists even spoke of responding in an extralegal manner—advocating the secession of New York City or southern Illinois, for example. Even in the aftermath of Sumter, when the administration finally decided to suppress disunion forcibly, few Northerners advocated violent resistance.

Of course, it is impossible to say how extensive resistance would have been had there been widespread opposition to the war. That there was not, despite the long and bitter arguments over compromise and coercion, can be attributed in large part to Northerners' commitment to law and order and their devotion to preserving the legacy of the Founders. Those values underlay the widespread conviction that since the Southern forts were government property, the government had a right to defend them. Even among the large percentage of Northerners who advocated the forts' evacuation in mid- to late March—even among the growing number who had resigned themselves to disunion—the great majority believed that the government had the *right* to keep troops in the forts. Thus they perceived the Confederate attack on Fort Sumter, as Lincoln did, to be an unjustified assault on a defensive position. Such an act represented a gross violation of the law to those who denied the reality of secession, and of ordered, civilized standards of behavior to those few who acknowledged it. At a deeper level, it represented to both a deliberate attempt to destroy the Union, in all its symbolic and material meanings. Partisan differences dissolved instantly in a shared commitment to sustain the government. After April 12, opponents of the Republicans finally agreed that the secessionists' Confederacy was the real threat to the nation, and the North responded with war.

If an understanding of the complex of values and ideals that underlay Northern politics offers insight into why Northerners responded to secession as they did, so too does a close examination of the crisis help to illuminate antebellum political culture. At the very least, it points to the need for historians interested in political culture to focus on the actual workings of the political system, and it confirms that parties lay at the center of that system. More than that, the Northern response to secession offers some suggestive illustrations of the role parties and partisans played in politics and government. Most centrally, it illustrates the limited effect of popular pressure on governmental decision making: up to Lincoln's April 15 call for troops, the only popular influence of consequence was exerted by Republicans, and even that was indirect. In the end, it was Lincoln's choice to make.

As the crisis evolved, the principal political disputes facing the country shifted from the expansion of slavery to compromise, and from there to the use of force to preserve the Union. But despite the disordered state of the party system even before the crisis began, the major realignment of partisan allegiances that threatened at several points during the winter—that some major political figures actually worked to bring about—never happened. The party configuration that existed when Fort Sumter was attacked was essentially the same as the one that had produced Lincoln's election five tumultuous months earlier. That stability, frail as it so often was, demonstrates two things: the centrality of partisanship, and the importance of party leaders and party machinery to the workings of the political system.

With regard to the former, the paramount factor was the ideological importance of party to both the rank and file and party managers. That is, because both Democrats and Republicans believed their party to represent a vision of what the United States should be, and because they generally associated the opposing party with a vision of what they thought the United States should not be, it was exceedingly difficult for individuals to alter their party allegiance. For most Northern voters, then, ideology was inextricably tied to party loyalty and party identification. Thus, when political conditions shifted and a new issue rose to the fore, partisans tended to adapt to it as units, adopting a particular stance because it fit with their idea of what course the country should follow, because it was politically expedient, because their rivals took the opposite stance, and for many, simply because that is what their party was doing.

But with partisanship and ideology so closely intertwined, there was a danger that the party leadership would alienate the faithful by violating party principle. Such had been the case for Conscience Whigs in the early to mid-1850s, anti-Nebraska Democrats in 1854, and Douglas Democrats between 1857 and 1860. With that in mind, it can be argued that the principal reason that the Republican coalition held together through the secession crisis was Abraham Lincoln.

First, because Lincoln's views were representative of most moderate Republicans', through most of the crisis he naturally followed the course that a majority of his party supported. This is not say that he followed only his own ideas; his deep appreciation for the importance of keeping party policy in line with rank-and-file opinion may have kept him from moving too far in the direction of conciliation in March, for example. In any case, had he not kept the party leadership so consistently within the bounds of popularly accepted party ideals, the Republican organization could easily have collapsed around him—possibly to be replaced by the more conservative coalition that Seward envisioned, but, to judge from the similar strategies employed some years earlier by John Tyler and a few years later by Andrew Johnson, probably not.

Second, by communicating with key party leaders in December, Lincoln was able to exert a subtle but undeniable influence on Congress at a critical time. In that way he played a crucial role in preventing a sectional compromise that would have threatened his party's always-delicate unity.

Third, despite the Cameron fiasco in early January and alienating much of his own state's party leadership by mid-March, Lincoln proved adept at manipulating the distribution of the patronage in such a way as to at least satisfy the two major Republican factions. In fact, it would not be going too far to say that Lincoln's greatest success during the crisis came not from his statesmanship, which was limited, but from his expertise as a party manager—that is, from the same ability to rise above faction and to soothe egos and ambitions that had made him the unchallenged leader of the Illinois party, the position that had permitted his nomination and subsequent election.

Finally, by not ordering the evacuation of Fort Sumter, Lincoln ensured that the hard-line majority who were growing impatient with his inaction did not begin to fall away. And of course, the way in which he arranged the relief mission and described ("spun," we would say today) the battle that followed not only united Northerners of all parties for the moment, but brought his own party together behind the war that would complete their unique journey from fringe third party challenger in 1854 and 1855 to one of the core institutions of American government for the next century and a half.

✳ In the spring and early summer of 1861, the popular rage militaire that greeted the Confederate assault on Fort Sumter was so powerful that even the two centers of radical Democracy—eastern cities, especially New York, and those areas of the Northwest, like Egypt, where transplanted Southerners predominated—had been caught up in, or at least bowed to, its tremendous force. Democrats and old-line Whigs across the North joined Republicans in offering enthusiastic support for the suppression of the rebellion against the government.

The shared nationalism that led those bitter political enemies to join forces against disunion would carry the free states through a long, terrible civil war that nobody, not even the anti Republican Cassandras who had warned of such a thing all winter, could foresee. Yet the initial zeal would wear off before many months passed, and the differences that had fueled antebellum political conflict and produced opposing views during the crisis would once more rise to the fore. Few Northerners would actively oppose the war, especially after mounting casualty lists added the element of personal antipathy toward the South to their motivations, but growing numbers would object to the way it was carried out.

For the most part, the battle raged along the old party lines. As it had been before the crisis, when Republicans and Northern Democrats had vied over whether Northerners could or should dictate domestic policies outside of their own states, the fundamental question underlying most issues would be the power of the central government. In the name of waging war, Republicans would support a massive expansion of government power, instituting new policies ranging from a national banking system and income taxes to conscription and emancipation. That most of them equated opposition to the administration with disunion sympathy and even treason would polarize political conflict all the more, adding frustration and resentment to their rivals' motives for resistance.

On the other side, the conditional support that many anti-Republicans offered the administration even in the glorious early days would translate into increasing opposition to Republican policies and occasionally even calls for a negotiated peace. New York City and the southern regions of the Northwest, where many citizens distrusted Lincoln's intentions even in the aftermath of Sumter, would become centers of anti-administration and antiwar sentiment. Despite a few sensationalized, often grossly exaggerated exceptions, however, the nature of wartime politics would reflect the politics of the crisis that produced the war. Debate would almost always occur within well-respected boundaries, and while partisans would argue fervidly over means, few would dispute the value of the ends. From the opening of the secession crisis until the surrender at Appomattox, the question for Northerners was never whether the Union was worth saving, but what the best method was to save it.

Notes

Abbreviations

Adams Diary   Charles Francis Adams Diary, Adams Family Papers, Massachusetts Historical Society, Boston, Mass.

AL   Abraham Lincoln Papers, Library of Congress, Washington, D.C.

ALPL   Abraham Lincoln Presidential Library, Springfield, Ill.

CG   *Congressional Globe*, 36th Cong., 2nd sess. (Washington, 1861)

CHS   Chicago Historical Society, Chicago, Ill.

CWL   Roy P. Basler, ed., *The Collected Works of Abraham Lincoln*, 8 vols. (New Brunswick, N.J.: Rutgers University Press, 1953–55)

Everett Diary   Edward Everett Diary, Edward Everett Papers, Massachusetts Historical Society, Boston, Mass.

GLC   Gilder-Lehrman Collection, New-York Historical Society, New York, N.Y.

GTS   Allan Nevins and M. H. Thomas, eds., *The Diary of George Templeton Strong*, 4 vols. (New York: Macmillan, 1952)

JANY   *Journal of the Assembly, State of New York, Eighty-Fourth Session* (Albany, N.Y., 1861)

JHI   *Journal of the House of Representatives of the 22nd Assembly of the State of Illinois* (Springfield, Ill., 1861)

Journal of 13   *Journal of the Proceedings of the Special Committee under the Resolution of the Senate of the 18th of December, 1860*, 36th Cong., 2nd sess., Rep. Com. No. 288 (Washington, 1861)

Journal of 33   *Journal of the Proceedings of the Special Committee of Thirty-three under the Resolution of the House of Representative of the United States of the 4th of December, 1860*, 36th Cong., 2nd sess., House Report No. 31 (Washington, 1861)

JSI   *Journal of the Senate of the 22nd Assembly of the State of Illinois* (Springfield, Ill., 1861)

JSNY   *Journal of the Senate, State of New York, Eighty-Fourth Session* (Albany, N.Y., 1861)

Lawrence Diary   Amos A. Lawrence Diary, Amos A. Lawrence Papers, Massachusetts Historical Society, Boston, Mass.

LC   Library of Congress, Washington, D.C.

LT   Lyman Trumbull Papers, Library of Congress, Washington, D.C.

MHS   Massachusetts Historical Society, Boston, Mass.

Munn Diary	John Munn Diary, Chicago Historical Society, Chicago, Ill.
NES	Howard Cecil Perkins, *Northern Editorials on Secession*, 2 vols. (Gloucester, Mass.: Peter Smith, 1964)
NYHS	New-York Historical Society, New York, N.Y.
NYPL	New York Public Library, New York, N.Y.
NYSL	New York State Library, Albany, N.Y.
OR	United States, War Department, *The War of the Rebellion: A Compilation of the Official Records of the Union and Confederate Armies* (Washington, 1880) (unless otherwise specified, refers to series 1, volume 1)
SD	Stephen A. Douglas Papers, University of Chicago, Chicago, Ill.
UR	University of Rochester, Rochester, N.Y.

Note: When dating my sources, I have dropped the year in most instances. Unless otherwise specified, all dates between September and December refer to 1860, while all those between January and June refer to 1861.

Introduction

1. I take this phrase from Henry Adams, "Great Secession Winter."

2. See, for example, Channing, *Crisis of Fear*; Barney, *Secessionist Impulse*; Michael Johnson, *Toward a Patriarchal Republic*; Buenger, *Secession and the Union in Texas*; Woods, *Rebellion and Realignment*; Crofts, *Reluctant Confederates*; Olsen, *Political Culture and Secession*; Detzer, *Allegiance*; Link, *Roots of Secession*; and Freehling, *Secessionists Triumphant*. Charles Lee, *Confederate Constitutions*, and William C. Davis, *Government of Our Own*, have examined the formation of the Confederate government in Montgomery, Alabama, and analyzed its role in precipitating war, while Dew, *Apostles of Disunion*, explores the secession commissioners who traveled among the slave states.

This tendency to look southward for the subjects of state and regional studies of the period is far from new; see, for example, Dumond, *Secession Movement*; Denman, *Secession Movement in Alabama*; Shanks, *Secession Movement in Virginia*; Rainwater, *Mississippi*; Sitterson, *Secession Movement in North Carolina*; Phillips, *Course of the South*; Mary Campbell, *Attitude of Tennesseans*; and Wooster, *Secession Conventions*.

3. Eric Foner, *Free Soil*, 316.

4. *CWL*, 4:261. The "peace, or a sword" line was left out of the final draft of Lincoln's inaugural address on the advice of more moderate voices, but it clearly captures the attitude of not only Lincoln but also most rank-and-file Republicans at that point in the crisis. See below, especially Chapter 9 and conclusion.

5. Stampp, *And the War Came*.

6. Perkins, "Defense of Slavery"; Nichols, *Disruption*; Alton Lee, "Corwin Amendment"; Hesseltine and Gara, "New Governors"; Johannsen, "Douglas

Democracy"; Goldschmidt, "Northeastern Businessmen"; Hubbell, "Politics as Usual" and "Jeremiah Sullivan Black"; Cardinal, "Ohio Democracy"; Hess, "Mississippi River"; Anbinder, "Fernando Wood"; Osborn, "Queens County" and "Union or Slavery."

7. Meredith, *Storm over Sumter*; Swanberg, *First Blood*. Two exceptions should be noted. Catton, *Coming Fury*, offers that author's usual keen insight, but it looks only at high politics and makes little effort to probe deeper, more sophisticated elements of causation or motivation. Maury Klein, *Days of Defiance*, offers an effective blend of popular and academic history and is easily the best comprehensive account of the crisis. His approach differs from mine in two key ways. First, like Catton, he restricts his study to the handful of players at the top of the political process, whereas I try to place the crisis into the context of the political system as a whole and emphasize the interrelations among participants at the various levels of politics. Second, his Northern perspective is limited almost entirely to events at Washington, while I incorporate developments throughout the free states. That said, I have drawn much of value from Klein's work regarding the areas where we overlap.

8. Ramsdell, "Lincoln and Fort Sumter"; Randall, "When War Came"; Potter, *Lincoln and His Party* and "Why the Republicans Rejected"; Stampp, "Lincoln and the Strategy of Defense," *And the War Came*, "Comment," and "Lincoln and the Secession Crisis." See also Tilley, *Lincoln Takes Command*; Baringer, *House Dividing*; Dufwa, "Lincoln and Secession"; Current, *Lincoln Nobody Knows*, 76–130, and *Lincoln and the First Shot*; Woodward, "Lincoln and the Crittenden Compromise"; and Westwood, "President Lincoln's Overture."

9. On congressional actions, see Bancroft, "Final Efforts"; Glover, *Immediate Pre-Civil War Compromise Efforts*; Alton Lee, "Corwin Amendment"; Sowle, "Conciliatory Republicans"; and Tusa, "Congressional Politics." On the Southern forts, in addition to note 7, above, see Hoogenboom, "Gustavus Fox"; Dibble, "War Averters"; and Bearss, "Fort Pickens." On the Washington Peace Conference, see Keene, *Peace Conference*, and Gunderson, *Old Gentlemen's Convention*.

10. Stampp, *Peculiar Institution* and *Era of Reconstruction*.

11. Silbey, *Partisan Imperative*, 75. On the ethnocultural aspect of antebellum partisanship, other key works include Benson, *Concept of Jacksonian Democracy*; Holt, *Forging a Majority*; Kleppner, *Cross of Culture* and *Third Electoral System*; Formisano, *Birth of Mass Political Parties*; and Hansen, *Making of the Third Party System*.

12. Three historians of the antebellum United States who use very different approaches to political culture, all to great effect, are Howe, *Political Culture*; Formisano, *Transformation*; and Jean Baker, *Affairs of Party*. See my discussion of these works and the concept of political culture more broadly in McClintock, "Shall It Be Peace, or a Sword?" 7–11. A useful historiographical essay is Gendzel, "Political Culture."

13. A few exceptional authors have been able to do it, but it can make for an awkward and sometimes tedious tale. The late William Gienapp's magisterial *Origins* perhaps best reveals the tremendous analytical benefits as well as the narrative pitfalls of combining the new methods with traditional narrative. See also Holt, *Rise and Fall.*

14. Michael F. Holt makes a similar point, if more strongly stated, in *The Fate of Their Country.* Sean Wilentz also argues for a limited view of popular influence in his recent magnum opus, *Rise of American Democracy.* It would seem that the pendulum has begun to swing away from an overstated view of the ability of ordinary antebellum citizens to pressure government leaders and force negotiation over important issues, toward a more balanced picture that acknowledges the complex interactions among individuals and groups at various levels of government, even as it recognizes the significant restrictions on the influence of public opinion on government policy.

15. Compare this view to that of Susan-Mary Grant, who in *North over South* argues for a Northern nationalism defined chiefly by anti-Southern sentiment; in this she presents a wonderful explication of Republicanism, but her interpretation excludes the North's significant anti-Republican minority.

16. Sowle, "Conciliatory Republicans"; Crofts, *Reluctant Confederates.*

17. Lincoln's account is in Lincoln, "Message to Congress," July 4, 1861, in *CWL*, 4:424–25. The harsher criticism can be found in Jefferson Davis, *Rise and Fall*, 290–95; Tilley, *Lincoln Takes Command*; Ramsdell, "Lincoln and Fort Sumter," 278–88; and Barbee, "Line of Blood." More moderate accounts are Stampp, "Lincoln and the Strategy of Defense," 311–15; and Current, *Lincoln Nobody Knows*, 121–30, and *Lincoln and the First Shot*, 182–208. Lincoln's defenders are represented by Randall, *Lincoln the Liberal Statesman*, 94–117, and Potter, *Lincoln and His Party*, 358–75, xxxix–lii. The most balanced account is Stampp, "Lincoln and the Secession Crisis," 177–88. See also Chapter 9.

18. This study does not address the Pacific Coast states. First, that region presents a very different story from that of the contiguous free states, one that it would be impractical and needlessly confusing to include here, and second, the great distance and poor communication and travel conditions rendered West Coast Americans largely irrelevant to the decision-making process in the winter of 1860–61.

19. On women, see Pierson, *Free Hearts and Free Homes*; Gustafson, *Women and the Republican Party*; Freeman, *A Room at a Time*; Edwards, *Angels in the Machinery*; Ryan, *Women in Public*; and Endres, "Women's Press in the Civil War." On African Americans, see Rael, *Black Identity and Black Protest*; Horton and Horton, *In Hope of Liberty*; Blight, *Frederick Douglass' Civil War*; and Dick, *Black Protest.*

Chapter One

1. Quotation from Jordan, *White over Black*, 44.

2. My account of this incident is drawn from H. K. Craig to J. B. Floyd, Octo-

ber 31, J. L. Gardner to H. K. Craig, November 5, F. C. Humphreys to H. K. Craig, November 10, and F. J. Porter to S. Cooper, November 11, all in *OR*, 67–72; Detzer, *Allegiance*, 50–54; and Samuel Crawford, *Genesis*, 57–60.

3. *Charleston Mercury*, November 8. On this and the material in the following paragraph, see Channing, *Crisis of Fear*, 249–51; Samuel Crawford, *Genesis*, 9–19; Catton, *Coming Fury*, 111; Potter, *Impending Crisis*, 490–92; and Freehling, *Secessionists Triumphant*, 395–401.

4. Hunt, ed., "Narrative and Letter," 533. The order for Gardner to withdraw arms is H. K. Craig to J. B. Floyd, October 31, in *OR*, 67–68.

5. John G. Nicolay memorandum, December 22, in Burlingame, ed., *With Lincoln in the White House*, 21; Lincoln to David Hunter, December 22, Lincoln to P. H. Silvester, December 22, Lincoln to Trumbull, December 24, and Lincoln to J. W. Webb, December 29, in *CWL*, 4:159, 160, 163, 164.

6. Augustus B. Frey to Samuel L. Frey, November 3, Frey Family Papers, NYHS.

7. Mrs. Charles F. Johnson Diary, November 4 and 6, NYHS.

8. *GTS*, September 13 and October 23 entries, 3:41, 52–53. See also Luthin, *First Lincoln Campaign*, 173–75; Baringer, "Campaign Techniques"; Gulley, "Springfield Lincoln Rally"; and Fischer, "Republican Campaigns."

9. Gienapp, " 'Politics,' " 17–20; *GTS*, November 6 entry, 3:59; Alfred H. Satterlee Diary, November 6, NYHS.

10. Douglas himself conceded to his secretary, "Mr. Lincoln is the next President" (Johannsen, *Douglas*, 797–98). See also Abraham Lincoln to William H. Seward, October 12, in *CWL*, 4:126; *GTS*, October 9–10, 19 entries, 3:44–45, 52; and Hubbell, "Douglas Democrats," 125–26.

11. E. Wilcox to John A. McClernand, October 25, John A. McClernand Papers, ALPL. See also Munn Diary, November 4.

12. Edward N. Tailer Jr. Diary, November 6, NYHS. See also Munn Diary, November 5; Alfred Satterlee Diary, November 6, NYPL; *GTS*, November 6 entry, 3:58–59; and Lowell, "Election in November," 494.

13. Henry Moore to Thomas Ewing, November 9, Ewing Family Papers, LC. See also *Providence Post*, November 8, in *NES*, 1:85; James Buchanan, December 3, "Fourth Annual Message to Congress," in Richardson, ed., *Messages and Papers*, 5:637; and John Pearson to Stephen Douglas, December 7, SD.

14. Printed remarks of John A. Stevens, [September 19?], Stevens Papers, NYHS; *GTS*, October 24 entry, 3:53. My account of the panic of 1860 draws heavily on Philip Foner, *Business and Slavery*, and Goldschmidt, "Northeastern Businessmen."

15. Gienapp, "Who Voted for Lincoln?"

16. Potter, *Impending Crisis*, 41–43. An excellent discussion of the Southern view can be found in Genovese, *Slaveholders' Dilemma*. On the Northern view, see Paludan, *People's Contest*, xxv–xxx; Floan, *South in Northern Eyes*; Eric Foner,

Free Soil, 40–72; Grant, *North over South*. On free-soil ideology, see Eric Foner, *Free Soil*, ix–xxxix, 11–39.

17. On the political realignment of the 1850s, see Holt, *Political Crisis*, esp. 101–81, and *Rise and Fall*, 635–985; Silbey, *Transformation of American Politics*, 3–28, and *Respectable Minority*, 127–65; Kleppner, *Third Electoral System*, 48–96; Hansen, *Making of the Third Party System*, 1–20; Baum and Knobel, "Anatomy of a Realignment"; and Gienapp, *Origins*, esp. 13–67, 443–48. On the widening appeal of free-labor values, see Welter, *Mind of America*, 129–62; Collins, "Ideology of the Ante-Bellum Democrats," 104–5; and Gienapp, *Origins*, 380. On the rise of evangelical politics, see Howe, "Evangelical Movement," and Carwardine, *Evangelicals and Politics*.

18. A brilliant discussion of the ironies of the nationalist manifest-destiny movement is Potter, *Impending Crisis*, 7–17, 196–98.

19. On the role of the West in Jeffersonian thought, see McCoy, *Elusive Republic*. On antebellum Northern interpretations of this, see Welter, *Mind of America*, 298–328; Morrison, *Slavery and the American West*, 109–14; and Eric Foner, *Free Soil*, 27–29, 57–58. On racism and the West, see Bilotta, *Race and the Rise of the Republican Party*; Berwanger, *Frontier against Slavery*; Voegeli, *Free but Not Equal*; and Litwack, *North of Slavery*, 268–74.

20. *New York Evening Post*, May 23, 1856, quoted in Gienapp, *Origins*, 359. See also Donald, *Charles Sumner*, 278–311, and Gienapp, "Crime against Sumner."

21. Gienapp, "Crime against Sumner."

22. Potter, *Impending Crisis*, 356–80; Oates, *To Purge This Land with Blood*, 353. Historians' unfortunate tendency to focus on the responses of radical Northerners and ignore mainstream reaction is exemplified in Finkelman, ed., *His Soul Goes Marching On*. See also Betty Mitchell, "Massachusetts Reaction."

23. Potter, *Impending Crisis*, 44–50. The best introduction to abolitionism is Stewart, *Holy Warriors*.

24. Gienapp, "Who Voted for Lincoln?"

Chapter Two

1. Nichols, *Disruption*, 341; Gienapp, "Who Voted for Lincoln?" 62.

2. On the New York fusion movement, see Sears, "New York and the Fusion Movement"; Flick, *Tilden*, 119–21, 124–25; Nichols, *Disruption*, 343–44, 348–49; Katz, *August Belmont*, 77–83; Mushkat, *Fernando Wood*, 106–10; and Osborn, "Union or Slavery," 91–104.

3. This discussion is drawn primarily from Ginsberg, "Barnburners, Free Soilers"; Osborn, "Union or Slavery," 9–15; Gunn, "Antebellum Society and Politics," 383–415; Flick, *Tilden*, 81–87; and Mushkat, *Fernando Wood*, 21–22, 26–30.

4. *New York Evening Post*, October 9. Tilden's biographer denies that Tilden was prevented from speaking (Flick, *Tilden*, 121), and the local Democratic papers make no mention of the episode, but given that Tilden clearly did not deliver his

full remarks that night and that in his subsequent correspondence with the *Post* he never denied the incident, it seems that the *Post*'s account, although no doubt exaggerated in the details, is fundamentally accurate. See also *New York World*, October 9.

5. *New York Evening Post*, October 9; Samuel J. Tilden to the Editors, October 9, *New York Evening Post*, October 10 (both also printed in Bigelow, ed., *Letters of Tilden*, 132).

6. John Bigelow to Samuel J. Tilden, October 10 and 11, and Samuel J. Tilden to John Bigelow, October 11 and 27, printed in Bigelow, ed., *Letters of Tilden*, 137–39; *New York Evening Post*, October 30; Tilden, *Union!*

7. Tilden, *Union!* 1–3.

8. Ibid., 2–8.

9. Ibid., 8–10.

10. Ibid., 10–11.

11. Ibid., 12–13.

12. Ibid., 16.

13. *New York Journal of Commerce*, November 26. For Hardshell examples, see J. C. Spencer to Caleb Cushing, November 28, Cushing Papers, LC; Washington, D.C., *Constitution*, September 6, in *NES*, 1:32. On this aspect of Democratic culture, see Silbey, *Respectable Minority*, 14–23, and *Partisan Imperative*, 87–115; Kleppner, *Third Electoral System*, 50–59; Hansen, *Making of the Third Party System*, 38–39; Power, *Planting Corn Belt Culture*; and Etcheson, *Emerging Midwest*.

14. *Cincinnati Times*, September 22, 1860, in *NES*, 1:38.

15. Quotation in Hansen, *Making of the Third Party System*, 112; see also Jean Baker, *Affairs of Party*, 177–258.

16. Douglas's opening speech at Ottawa, August 21, 1858, in Angle, ed., *Complete Lincoln-Douglas Debates*, 111. See also Jean Baker, *Affairs of Party*, 177–96. On Republican racial attitudes, see Eric Foner, *Free Soil*, 261–300, and Bilotta, *Race and the Rise of the Republican Party*.

17. Douglas's rejoinder at Alton, October 15, 1858, in Angle, ed., *Complete Lincoln-Douglas Debates*, 400.

18. See, for example, *Illinois State Register*, September 28; *Chicago Times and Herald*, November 21, in *NES*, 1:95; and Osborn, "Union or Slavery," 7–8, 95–96. Breckinridge Democrats were, if anything, more dedicated to these ideas. See *New York Herald*, September 19; *Cleveland National Democrat*, November 19, in *NES*, 1:92; Haldeman, *Territorial Distractions*; P. M. Leland, December 1, W. Raymond Lee, November 30, and James D. Baker, December 1, to Caleb Cushing, Cushing Papers, LC; and Clark, *State of the Country*. For a fuller exposition of James Gordon Bennett's racial ideas, see Perkins, "Defense of Slavery," 506–9. Two excellent discussions of racism and Democratic political culture can be found in Jean Baker, *Affairs of Party*, 212–58, and Maizlish, "Race and Politics."

19. Goldschmidt, "Northeastern Businessmen," 150–52.

20. Joseph Ellis (*Founding Brothers*) makes an excellent case that this commitment to placing the political system ahead of one's personal interest or ideology was indeed the central theme of United States political culture from the first generation. See also Knupfer, *The Union as It Is*.

21. Nichols, *Disruption*, 335; Hubbell, "Douglas Democrats," 129–30; Dickinson, ed., *Speeches of Dickinson*, 1:691–93. See also Sanders, *George N. Sanders*, 4.

22. Nichols, *Disruption*, 336; Johannsen, "Douglas Democracy," 232–33; Johannsen, *Douglas*, 775–88, 803, 809; Hansen, *Making of the Third Party System*, 116–28. Breckinridge supporters were well aware of this aspect of Douglas's strategy. See, for example, Daniel S. Dickinson, "Speech Delivered on the Occasion of a Serenade, at the Kirkwood House, Washington City, August 1, 1860," in Dickinson, ed., *Speeches of Dickinson*, 1:692–93.

23. Douglas to William A. Richardson, June 20, 1860, in Johannsen, ed., *Letters*, 492, 498; *Peoria Democratic Union*, October 5, in *NES*, 1:47; D. H. Solomon, November 6, and A. Sherman, November 24, to Douglas, SD.

24. See William G. Maitland to [Joseph] Maitland, December 19, 1859, GLC.

25. Johannsen, *Douglas*, 788–93; Luthin, *First Lincoln Campaign*, 216; Milton, *Eve of Conflict*, 494.

26. P. M. Leland to Caleb Cushing, December 1, Cushing Papers, LC. Cushing's speech was printed in the *Boston Courier*, November 27 and 28 (quotation from November 28). See also Judge George W. Woodward to Jeremiah S. Black, November 18, Black Papers, LC, printed in Auchampaugh, *Buchanan and His Cabinet*, 102–6; *Boston Post*, September 26, *Brooklyn Eagle*, November 13, and *Concord (N.H.) Democratic Standard*, November 24, all in *NES*, 1:39, 167, 99; and Fermer, *James Gordon Bennett*, 158–59.

27. Johannsen, *Frontier, the Union*, 202–3; Bowden, *Voice for the Union*, 11; Indianapolis *Indiana Daily State Sentinel*, November 3, and *Providence Daily Post*, November 8, in *NES*, 1:72, 85.

28. Douglas to Ninety-Six New Orleans Citizens, November 13, in Johannsen, ed., *Letters*, 499–503.

29. My reading of Buchanan's November cabinet discussions relies heavily on Hunt, ed., "Narrative and Letter," 532–38; Nichols, *Disruption*, 378–91; and Auchampaugh, *Buchanan and His Cabinet*, 65–139.

30. Nichols, *Disruption*, 382–84 (quotation 383). See also Hunt, ed., "Narrative and Letter," 534–35.

31. *New York Tribune*, November 7–8, 12; quotation in November 7 dispatch in *New York Herald*, November 11.

32. Quotation in November 7 dispatch in *New York Herald*, November 11; November 7 dispatch in *New York Tribune*, November 12; Baringer, *House Dividing*, 5–6.

33. Beale and Brownsword, eds., *Diary of Gideon Welles*, 1:81–82. Lincoln had been considering the cabinet for some time, of course, and in fact had probably

discussed the matter with a number of Ohio and Illinois party leaders just two days earlier over tea. See Lincoln to John G. Nicolay, November 3, in *CWL*, 4:136. But this early-morning session seems to have been his first significant attempt to work out an actual list.

34. Beale and Brownsword, eds., *Diary of Gideon Welles*, 1:82.

35. The list Lincoln composed is probably the undated card enclosed in Kinsley S. Bingham, Solomon Foot, and Zachariah Chandler to Abraham Lincoln, January 21, AL. See also Donald, *Lincoln*, 261–62.

36. Salmon P. Chase to Lyman Trumbull, November 12, LT.

37. Eric Foner, *Free Soil*, 186–205.

38. Ibid., 103–48.

39. Compare this to Potter, *Lincoln and His Party*, 22.

40. Eric Foner, *Free Soil*, 205–16, 219. Compare this to Potter, *Lincoln and His Party*, 20–24.

41. Fehrenbacher, *Prelude to Greatness*, 143–61; Stampp, "Republican National Convention"; Potter, *Impending Crisis*, 418–30; Nevins, *Emergence of Lincoln*, 2:229–60; Gienapp, "Who Voted for Lincoln?" 52–57.

42. Gienapp, "Who Voted for Lincoln?" 63–77.

43. The best sources on this feud are Fehrenbacher, *Chicago Giant*; Willard King, *Lincoln's Manager*, 125–34; and Hansen, *Making of the Third Party System*, 95–98.

44. John D. Defrees to Jesse K. Dubois, November 12, and George W. Gans to Lincoln, November 30, AL. See also J. R. Doolittle, November 10, and B. F. Wade, November 14, to Lyman Trumbull, LT.

45. See, for example, Joseph Medill to Lincoln, July 5, 1860, AL; *Pittsburgh Post*, October 10, in *NES*, 1:51; *Albany Atlas and Argus*, November 10; *Illinois State Register*, November 22; and R. W. Massey to Stephen Douglas, November 28, SD.

46. Hamlin, *Life and Times*, 367–70.

47. Carman and Luthin, *Lincoln and the Patronage*, 20 50; Baringer, *House Dividing*.

48. Lowell, "Election in November," 501; *New York Tribune*, July 28, 1860; Baker, ed., *Works of Seward*, 4:344. See also *New York World*, November 1 and 6; as well as *Lowell Daily Journal and Courier*, September 5; *Hartford Evening Press*, October 25–26; and *Daily Pittsburgh Gazette*, November 2, in *NES*, 1:29, 60, 69.

49. *Chicago Tribune*, November 10; Bryant quoted in Stampp, *And the War Came*, 14. See also George G. Fogg to Lincoln, October 26, and Pleasant A. Hackleman to David Davis, November 27, AL; S. C. Hewitt to Nathaniel P. Banks, November 30, Banks Papers, LC; and John Bigelow to Hargreaves, November 10, Bigelow Papers, NYPL.

50. Mason Brayman to William H. Bailhache, November 10, Bailhache-Brayman Papers, ALPL. See also S. S. Harding to George W. Julian, October 18,

Giddings-Julian Papers, LC; Henry C. Stimson to Henry A. Stimson, October 26, Stimson Papers, NYHS; and Alfred W. Upham to Lincoln, November 26, AL. According to the later recollection of Ohio Republican leader Donn Piatt, Lincoln expressed the same opinion. See Piatt, *Memories*, 30–34.

51. *Boston Atlas and Bee*, November 12, in *NES*, 1:88. See also *New York World*, November 7, and *New York Times*, November 13.

52. Potter, *Lincoln and His Party*, 2–3; Eric Foner, *Free Soil*, 88–89; and Charles Sumner, October 11, "Threat of Disunion by the Slave States, and its Absurdity," in Sumner, *Works*, 5:295–96. See also *Daily Pittsburgh Gazette*, November 14, in *NES*, 1:91; James Watson Webb to Lincoln, November 5, AL; and *Boston Traveller*, November 19.

53. Boutwell, "Slavery the Enemy of the Free Laborer . . .," in Boutwell, *Speeches and Papers*, 32; William Cullen Bryant to John Bigelow, February 20, in Bigelow, *Retrospections*, 1:253; *Douglass' Monthly*, December issue, in Philip Foner, ed., *Life and Writings of Douglass*, 2:528.

54. S. S. Harding to George W. Julian, November 18, Giddings-Julian Papers, LC; F. D. Parish to John Sherman, November 23, Sherman Papers, LC. See also *Chicago Daily Democrat*, in November 5, *NES*, 1:76; B. F. Wade to Lyman Trumbull, November 14, LT; and Leonard Swett to Lincoln, November 30, AL.

55. Pleasant A. Hackleman to David Davis, November 27, AL; *New York Tribune*, November 28; John D. Defrees to Lincoln, November 25, AL; Henry Frey to [John Frey], November 28, Frey Family Papers, NYHS. See also E. Littell to N. P. Banks, November 9, Banks Papers, LC; George Ashmun to Lincoln, November 13, AL; Anson S. Miller to Lyman Trumbull, November 16, LT; *Springfield (Mass.) Republican*, October 27 and 31, and November 10, 12, 15; *New York World*, November 8, 10, 12–14; *New York Times*, November 9, 12–16; *Albany Evening Journal*, November 10; and *Pittsburgh Daily Gazette*, November 14, in *NES*, 1:91.

56. Thomas Corwin, October 28 and November 4, and Henry J. Raymond, November 14, to Lincoln, AL. See also W. T. Early, October 30, George T. M. Davis, October 31, Truman Smith, November 7, Alexander Jenkins, November 7, William H. Trescott, November 9, and Rodney L. Adams, November 10, to Lincoln, AL; George T. Curtis to Thomas Ewing, November 7, Ewing Family Papers, LC; and William L. Hodge to Lyman Trumbull, November 23, LT. Editorials beseeching Lincoln to issue a statement appeared in most Democratic and Constitutional Union journals in these weeks, but the most persistent (and widely read) anti-Republican periodical was the *New York Herald*. See November 8–14, 16, 19–20. See also Fermer, *James Gordon Bennett*, 160.

57. J. H. Wigand to Lincoln, November 9, AL; E. D. Morgan to Lincoln, November 20, Morgan Papers, NYSL. See also Fred Stephenson, November 12, J. B. McKeehan, November 13, and Henry S. Sanford, November 15, to Lincoln, AL; and Mason Brayman to William H. Bailhache, November 10, Bailhache-Brayman Papers, ALPL. For party managers, see William Cullen Bryant, Novem-

ber 1, James Watson Webb, November 5, Thurlow Weed, November 7, George G. Fogg, November 7, Benjamin Welch Jr., November 8, and James E. Harvey, November 8, to Lincoln, and Weed to David Davis, November 17, AL; Joseph Medill to O. M. Hatch, November 16, Hatch Papers, ALPL; and Henry Hardy to Richard Yates, November 19, AL.

58. John G. Nicolay to unknown, n.d. [1860], AL.

59. Lincoln to George T. M. Davis, October 27, and Lincoln to Nathaniel P. Pascall, November 16, in *CWL*, 4:134–35, 139–40. See also Lincoln to George D. Prentice, October 29, and Lincoln to Truman Smith, November 10, in ibid., 132–33, 138–39. See also *New York Times*, November 8; *New York Tribune*, November 9, 10; *Illinois State Journal*, November 16; November 16 and 18 dispatches in *New York Herald*, November 22; and *Chicago Tribune*, November 17, clipped in *New York Herald*, November 20.

60. These sentiments may be found in most of Lincoln's speeches from 1854 to 1860, but good examples are his addresses at Springfield, June 16, 1858; at Quincy, Illinois, October 13, 1858; at the Cooper Union Institute in New York, February 27, 1860; and at New Haven, March 6, 1860, in *CWL*, 2:461–69, 3:245–57, 522–50, and 4:13–30. Quotation from ibid., 4:16.

61. Truman Smith to Lincoln, November 7, AL.

62. L. F. Holbrook to Lincoln, November 12, AL; John Olney to Lyman Trumbull, November 16, LT.

63. See Baringer, *House Dividing*, 32–33.

64. *Illinois State Journal*, November 21; *Illinois State Register*, November 21; *New York Herald*, November 20; *New York Times*, November 21; *Boston Courier*, November 22.

65. Trumbull's speech is printed in *Illinois State Journal*, November 21.

66. For Lincoln's contribution to Trumbull's speech, see *CWL*, 4:141–42.

67. David Donald (*Lincoln*, 261) charges Trumbull with "undermining" Lincoln's conciliatory message with his "woe to the traitors" passage. In that Trumbull provided ammunition for hostile analysts eager to denounce the Republicans, Donald is correct. However, as I indicate below, this was a mild expression of Republican-style pro-Union sentiment, and, as it also jibed with Lincoln's own antisecession attitude, it is difficult to believe that Lincoln did not condone Trumbull's firmness.

68. Lincoln to Henry J. Raymond, November 28, in *CWL*, 4:146.

69. Yates's speech is printed in *Illinois State Journal*, November 22.

70. Wilson in *Boston Advertiser*, November 10, and *Boston Courier*, November 10; *Chicago Democrat*, November 8, quoted in Baringer, *House Dividing*, 60; Z. Chandler to Lyman Trumbull, November 13, Lyman Trumbull Correspondence, ALPL.

71. D. R. Martin to E. D. Morgan, October 26, Morgan Papers, NYSL; J. H. Whitney to Lyman Trumbull, November 19, LT; Indianapolis *Indiana American*,

November 21, in *NES*, 1:97. See also Andrew, "Speeches"; Sumner, "Threat of Disunion," in Sumner, *Works*, 5:294–95; and *GTS*, October 27–29 and 31, November 2 entries, 3:54–57.

72. *New York Tribune*, November 9.

73. B. F. Wade to Lyman Trumbull, November 14, LT; *New York Times*, November 13, 15; Henry C. Stimson to Henry A. Stimson, October 26, Stimson Papers, NYHS; George N. Eckert to Lincoln, November 14, AL; *GTS*, November 15 entry, 3:63. On Greeley and peaceable secession, see Potter, "Horace Greeley"; Bonner, "Horace Greeley"; and Weisberger, "Horace Greeley." The idea was not new: through the 1850s, Garrisonian abolitionists had even advocated Northern secession from the slave states and held their own secession convention in Worcester, Massachusetts, in 1857. See *The Liberator*, January 23, 1857.

74. E. Littell to N. P. Banks, November 9, Banks Papers, ALPL. Baringer, *House Dividing*, 64. See also *GTS*, October 19, 23, and 24 entries, 3:52, 53, 54.

75. *New York Times*, November 14. See also *New York Times*, November 16, 17, 22, 27; Potter, *Lincoln and His Party*, 63–65; and Krummel, "Henry J. Raymond," 388–89.

76. For anti-Republican support, see Charles A. Davis to Edwin D. Morgan, November 27, Morgan Papers, NYSL; *Sioux City Register*, December 1, and *Dubuque Herald*, November 11, in *NES*, 1:109, 158; and Fermer, *James Gordon Bennett*, 163. For Republican support, see William D. Hart, November 13, and George D. Morgan, November 27 and 28, to Edwin D. Morgan, Morgan Papers, NYSL; Henry Hardy to Richard Yates, November 19, and John Benton, November 23, to Lincoln, AL; and *New York World*, November 15. See also Morris, *Free Men All*, 203–18.

77. *Albany Evening Journal*, November 22, 27, 30.

78. Ebenezer Griffin to Lyman Trumbull, December 3, LT; Preston King to Thurlow Weed, December 7, in Weed, ed., *Autobiography*, 309; *GTS*, November 20 entry, 3:64. See also John Benton to Lincoln, November 23, AL; and W. Kitchell, November 28, and J. Grumhan, [November], to Trumbull, LT.

79. See late November and early December, passim, Weed Papers, UR.

Chapter Three

1. Buchanan's inquiry and Black's response are both printed in Curtis, *Life of James Buchanan*, 2:319–24 (quotations 323). See also Nichols, *Disruption*, 382–91; Philip Klein, *Buchanan*, 357–61; and Hunt, ed., "Narrative and Letter," 534–35. Thompson's account of his argument against the right of coercion is printed in Auchampaugh, *Buchanan and His Cabinet*, 137–39.

2. Nichols, *Disruption*, 385–86; Job 9:33. Buchanan's allusion here is telling. Throughout this chapter, Job discusses the powerlessness of man before God's will; the president doubtless felt much the same.

3. November 22 dispatch in *New York Herald*, November 23.

4. S. Cooper to Robert Anderson, November 12, and L. Thomas, November 15, in *OR*, 72–73.

5. Hunt, ed., "Narrative and Letter"; Samuel Crawford, *Genesis*, 30–31; Robert Anderson to S. Cooper, November 23, in *OR*, 74–76.

6. Scott's "Views" are printed in [Buchanan], *Mr. Buchanan's Administration*, 287–90.

7. Hunt, ed., "Narrative and Letter"; [Buchanan], *Mr. Buchanan's Administration*; Nichols, *Disruption*, 387; Elliott, *Winfield Scott*, 678–79.

8. Richardson, ed., *Messages and Papers*, 5:626–39.

9. Ibid., 626–27. I have transposed two phrases in this quotation.

10. Ibid., 627–34.

11. Ibid., 634–36. For a provocative modern argument for this point, see Hummel, *Emancipating Slaves*, 351–53, 360.

12. Richardson, ed., *Messages and Papers*, 5:636–39.

13. *New York Herald*, December 5; Curtis, *Life of James Buchanan*, 2:353–55.

14. *Boston Advertiser*, December 7; *New Haven Morning Journal and Courier*, December 6; and *Quincy (Ill.) Whig and Republican*, December 10, all in *NES*, 1:146, 137, 152.

15. *Buffalo Courier*, December 6, in *NES*, 1:139. See also *Cincinnati Enquirer*, December 6, in ibid., 1:141.

16. Stampp, *And the War Came*, 47.

17. J. J. Harney to Stephen Douglas, December 4, SD. See also John T. Cooley, n.d., and John Pearson, December 7, to Douglas, ibid.; Silas Reed to Lyman Trumbull, December 6, LT; and Dwight Jarvis, December 5, and Benjamin Benson, December 27, to John Sherman, Sherman Papers, LC.

18. William Seward to Frances Seward, December 5, in Seward, *Seward at Washington*, 2:480. On the frequent repetition of this analysis, see *GTS*, December 7 entry, 3:71.

19. Tusa, "Congressional Politics," 29–33, 40–59, 64.

20. John T. Cooley, n.d., and Albert M. Billings, December 25, to Stephen Douglas, SD. See also Charles D. O'Kelly, December 7, I. F. Johnston, December 16, John Stevens, December 21, and Stephen Thomas, December 25, to Douglas, ibid.; and August Belmont to William Sprague, December 19, in Belmont, *Letters*. On the Boston elections, see *Boston Courier*, December 13; and Richard Vaux to Douglas, December 12, SD.

21. For expressions of Douglas as savior, see H. D. Horton, n.d., R. Hamilton, December 4, John Pearson, December 7, Charles W. Baker, December 13, and W. M. Flanders, December 15, to Douglas, SD. For faith in nonintervention, see J. J. Harney, December 4, David A. Neal, December 4, and George Berry, December 10, to Douglas, ibid. For predictions about 1864, see George W. Besore, December 5, and "Amicus" to Douglas, December 17, ibid.

22. Stephen Douglas to William S. Prentice, December 5, in Johannsen, ed., *Letters*, 503.

23. Johannsen, *Douglas*, 812–13.

24. *CG*, December 10, pp. 38–39; Nichols, *Disruption*, 392–404; Johannsen, *Douglas*, 809–14.

25. *New York Times*, December 4; *New York Herald*, December 4.

26. Lyman Trumbull to Julia Trumbull, December 4, Lyman Trumbull Correspondence, ALPL. See also Preston King to John Bigelow, December 3, in Bigelow, *Retrospections*, 1:316–17; and Lyman Trumbull, December 4, James E. Harvey, December 5, and W. G. Snethen, December 8, to Lincoln, AL.

27. Paludan, *Presidency of Lincoln*, 38. See Van Deusen, *William Henry Seward*, 206–10, and Major Wilson, *Time, Space, and Freedom*, 211–34.

28. On Seward's ties to Weed's proposals, see Bancroft, *Seward*, 2:26–29; Crofts, "Secession Winter," 238. On his way to Washington, Seward met again with Weed, after which Weed wrote a lengthy editorial explaining his ideas in greater detail but pointing out explicitly—twice, even—that "we speak only for ourself." See *Albany Evening Journal*, November 30. Compare this interpretation to Potter, *Lincoln and His Party*, 83–84, and Van Deusen, *William Henry Seward*, 238–39.

29. Seward to Weed, December 3, in Barnes, *Memoir*, 308; December 4 dispatch in *New York Herald*, December 5.

30. Seward to Weed, December 2 and 3, in Barnes, *Memoir*, 307–8.

31. David Clopton to Clement C. Clay, December 13, Clement C. Clay Papers, Duke University, quoted in Johannsen, *Douglas*, 811. On Seward's influence, see Preston King to John Bigelow, December 3, in Bigelow, *Retrospections*, 316–17; J. E. Harvey, December 5, Lyman Trumbull, December 4, W. G. Snethen, December 8, and E. B. Washburne, December 9, to Lincoln, AL; and E. B. Lee to S. P. Lee, December 5, in Laas, ed., *Wartime Washington*, 13.

32. *CG*, December 5, pp. 9–12; E. B. Washburne to Lincoln, December 9, AL.

33. Although Republicans cast all thirty-eight nay votes, sixty-two of them supported the committee. Twelve did not vote.

34. E. B. Washburne, December 9, J. A. Gurley, December 3, James E. Harvey, December 5, William Kellogg, December 6, Thomas Corwin, December 10, George G. Fogg, December 13, 17, and 19, John D. Defrees, December 15, and E. B. Washburne, December 18, to Lincoln, AL; Henry Adams to C. F. Adams Jr., December 9, 13, and 18, in Ford, ed. *Letters of Henry Adams*, 62–67; George G. Fogg to William Butler, December 19, Butler Papers, CHS; John Cochrane to Samuel J. Tilden, December 20, Tilden Papers, NYPL. See also Sowle, "Conciliatory Republicans," 46–53, and Crofts, *Reluctant Confederates*.

35. See Trumbull, December 4, and James E. Harvey, December 5, to Lincoln, AL; Adams Diary, December 4; Curtis Journal, December 6, ALPL; and Sowle, "Conciliatory Republicans," 40–44.

36. *CG*, December 12, pp. 76–78; Sherman to William Read et al., December 22, in Thorndike, ed., *Sherman Letters*, 92–104.

37. *CG*, December 12, pp. 76–78; Sowle, "Conciliatory Republicans," 107–30; Potter, *Lincoln and His Party*, 95–98.

38. On the Boston riot, see *Boston Traveller*, December 3–4, 17; *Boston Post*, December 4, clipped in *New York Herald*, December 5; and O'Connor, *Civil War Boston*, 42–43. On the Philadelphia meeting, see Goldschmidt, "Northeastern Businessmen," 241, and Dusinberre, *Civil War Issues*, 103–4.

39. The address is printed in Dix, ed., *Memoirs*, 1:350–60; quotations from 351–52. See also Philip Foner, *Business and Slavery*, 227–32, and Dickinson, ed., *Speeches of Dickinson*, 1:696–702.

40. Dix, ed., *Memoirs*, 1:352–57.

41. Ibid., 358–60.

42. Philip Foner, *Business and Slavery*, 208–23; Goldschmidt, "Northeastern Businessmen," 166–85; Osborn, "Union or Slavery," 138–39; O'Connor, *Lords of the Loom*, 144–45; Ware, *Political Opinion in Massachusetts*, 47–49.

43. Goldschmidt, "Northeastern Businessmen," 215–28; O'Connor, *Lords of the Loom*, 144.

44. *New York Courier and Enquirer*, December 2; *New York Times*, November 26, December 7; *Indianapolis Journal*, November 29, December 4 and 21, quoted in Stampp, *Indiana Politics*, 52; *Detroit Journal*, *Cincinnati Commercial*, *Cincinnati Press*, and *Pittsburgh Gazette* cited in Sowle, "Conciliatory Republicans," 85–86; *Springfield (Mass.) Republican*, December 11.

45. December, passim, Crittenden Papers, LC; Potter, *Lincoln and His Party*, 189–92.

46. George Opdyke to Lyman Trumbull, December 17, LT.

47. In what has long been the standard analysis of the business world's response to secession, Philip Foner (*Business and Slavery*, 232–38) emphasizes the pro-compromise sentiment of Republican businessmen, but Eli Goldschmidt ("Northeastern Businessmen," 220–54) offers a valuable corrective, noting the general loyalty of Republican businessmen to party principles. For Republican reaction to the Pine Street meeting, see Opdyke to Trumbull, December 17, LT; *GTS*, December 17 entry, 3:76; Thomas W. Ludlow to Hamilton Fish, December 24, Fish Papers, LC; and Goldschmidt, "Northeastern Businessmen," 239–40.

48. G. D. Morgan to E. D. Morgan, October 20 and 22, November 27 and 28, December 4 and 15, January 8, Morgan Papers, NYSL; G. D. Morgan to Thurlow Weed, December 18, Weed Papers, UR.

49. Sowle, "Conciliatory Republicans," 83; Philip Foner, *Business and Slavery*; December, passim, Weed Papers, UR; J. T. Sherman to Weed, December 8, Weed Papers, LC.

50. The Boston memorial can be found in *Boston Courier*, December 18. See also Everett Diary, December 3, 10, and 17, and Lawrence Diary, December 10.

51. August Belmont to William Sprague, December 19, and Belmont to Stephen Douglas, December 31, in Belmont, *Letters*, 16, 28–29; Daniel Lord to Hamilton Fish, December 31, Fish Papers, LC; Sidney Webster to Caleb Cushing, December 31, Cushing Papers, LC; Philip Foner, *Business and Slavery*, 237–38; Sowle, "Conciliatory Republicans," 92.

52. E. G. Spaulding to Thurlow Weed, Weed Papers, UR, quoted in Sowle, "Conciliatory Republicans," 51. See also Adams Diary, December 15.

53. Lincoln to Trumbull, December 10 and 17, E. B. Washburne, December 13, William Kellogg, December 11, Thurlow Weed, December 17, and John D. Defrees, December 18, all in *CWL*, 4:149–55; December 10 dispatch in *New York Herald*, December 15. Eli Thayer, a Massachusetts Republican, had introduced a compromise proposal involving popular sovereignty to the House on December 12.

54. W. S. Gillman, December 11, and Isaac Lee, December 26, to Trumbull, LT; James T. Sherman to Thurlow Weed, December 8, Weed Papers, LC. See also G. F. Brown, December 18, Henry Asbury, December 23, and Pliny Thayer, December 27, to Trumbull, LT; D. S. Gregory to E. D. Morgan, December 17, Morgan Papers, NYSL; and John Wilson to Richard Yates, January 1, Yates Family Papers, ALPL.

55. Lincoln to Kellogg, December 11, in *CWL*, 4:150. See also Lincoln to Trumbull, December 17, in ibid., 153.

56. Gideon Welles to James Dixon, December 5, AL; S. P. Chase to Henry Wilson, December 13, in Chase, "Diary and Correspondence," 294–95.

57. P. V. Wise to Lincoln, December 13, AL. See also Carl Schurz, December 18, and George G. Fogg to Lincoln, December 13, 17, and 19, ibid.

58. E. Stafford, December 20, J. R. Woods, December 20, and G. T. Allen, December 27, to Trumbull, LT; William Bacon to John Sherman, December 5, Sherman Papers, LC.

59. George G. Fogg to Horace Greeley, December 1, Greeley Papers, LC; G. O. Foss to Trumbull, December 23, LT. See also G. P. Edgar, December 14, Thomas Richmond, December 14, and Wait Talcott, December 16, to Trumbull, ibid.; Carl Schurz to Lincoln, December 18, AL; and J. Y. Scammon to Richard Yates, December 27, Yates Family Papers, ALPL.

60. F. K. Phoenix, December 23, John Olney, December 21, David J. Baker, December 22, Henry Asbury, December 23, and S. York, December 28, to Trumbull, LT; George G. Fogg to William Butler, December 13, Butler Papers, CHS.

61. A. W. Metcalf, December 18, and John Olney, December 21, to Trumbull, LT. Among the most explicit expressions of this view are W. H. Hanna, December 19, W. H. Herndon, December 21, S. York, December 28, Thomas Gregg, December 29, and Hurlbut Swan, December 29, to Trumbull, LT.

62. D. Kidling to John Sherman, December 29, Sherman Papers, LC. For examples of other such sentiments, see December, passim, Trumbull Papers, Sherman Papers, and E. B. Washburne Papers, LC; and Adams Papers, MHS.

63. Lincoln to William Kellogg, December 11, and Trumbull, December 10, in *CWL*, 4:150, 149; G. O. Foss to Trumbull, December 23, LT. See also D. J. Linegan, December 10, W. H. Herndon, December 21, F. K. Phoenix, December 23, Thomas Gregg, December 29, and F. S. Rutherford, January 1, to Trumbull, LT; F. M. Keith to John Sherman, December 29, Sherman Papers, LC; W. P. Fessenden to Hamilton Fish, December 15, Fish Papers, LC; and J. P. Sanderson to Leonard Swett, December 7, AL.

64. Trumbull to Richard Yates, December 19, Yates Family Papers, ALPL; J. B. Haskins to E. D. Morgan, December 20, Morgan Papers, NYSL; Sowle, "Conciliatory Republicans," 152–60.

65. E. B. Washburne to Lincoln, December 18, AL; Adams Diary, December 21 and 22; John M. McClernand to Charles H. Lanphier, December 25, Lanphier Papers, ALPL. See also Curtis Journal, December 28, ALPL; and Henry Adams to C. F. Adams Jr., December 22, in Ford, ed., *Letters of Henry Adams*, 70.

66. *CG*, December 17, pp. 99–104.

67. E. B. Washburne, December 17 and 18, Francis P. Blair Sr., December 18, Joseph Medill, December 18, and George G. Fogg, December 19, to Lincoln, AL.

Chapter Four

1. Trumbull to Lincoln, December 24, AL.

2. Buchanan memorandum, [December 10], in John Moore, ed., *Works of James Buchanan*, 11:56–57; Samuel Crawford, *Genesis*, 38–39; Philip Klein, *Buchanan*, 368.

3. [Buchanan], *Mr. Buchanan's Administration*, 167–69; Philip Klein, *Buchanan*, 371–72.

4. Buchanan memorandum, [December 11], Lewis Cass to Buchanan, December 12, Buchanan memorandum, [December 15], and Buchanan to Lewis Cass, December 15, all in John Moore, ed., *Works of James Buchanan*, 11:57–61.

5. Samuel Crawford, *Genesis*, 28.

6. Winfield Scott to John J. Crittenden, November 12, in Mrs. Chapman Coleman, *Life of Crittenden*, 2:219; Elliott, *Winfield Scott*, 678; Keyes, *Fifty Years' Observation*, 370.

7. Scott describes the interview and quotes his note of December 15 in Winfield Scott to Lincoln, March 30, AL. Buchanan's perspective is presented in [Buchanan], *Mr. Buchanan's Administration*, 168–70.

8. *GTS*, December 13 and 15 entries, 3:74–75; J. C. Oliver to Douglas, December 21, SD. See also John Bigelow to Hargreaves, December 12, Bigelow Papers, NYPL; Jonas Nolestine to Trumbull, December 12, LT; George G. Fogg, December 13, A. Williams, December 19, and Trumbull, December 24, to Lincoln, AL; O. W. Wright, n.d., and J. B. Haskins, December 20, to E. D. Morgan, Morgan Papers, NYSL; A. W. Spies to Douglas, December 17, SD; and C. B. Phillips to J. M. McClernand, December 17, McClernand Papers, ALPL.

9. Villard and Villard, eds., *Lincoln on the Eve of '61*, 38.

10. E. B. Washburne, December 17, Trumbull, December 14 and 17, and Francis P. Blair Sr., December 18, to Lincoln, AL.

11. Lincoln to Elihu Washburne, December 21, and F. P. Blair Sr., December 21, in *CWL*, 4:159, 157.

12. John G. Nicolay memorandum, December 22, in Burlingame, ed., *With Lincoln in the White House*, 21; Lincoln to David Hunter, December 22, P. H. Silvester, December 22, Trumbull, December 24, and J. W. Webb, December 29, in *CWL*, 4:159, 160, 163, 164.

13. W. C. Bryant to Lincoln, November 10, AL; Niven, *Salmon P. Chase*, 228; Joshua Giddings to Laura Giddings, December 2, Giddings-Julian Papers, LC; Giddings to John Allison, December 25, AL; George G. Fogg to Lincoln, December 13, AL.

14. Weed, ed., *Autobiography*, 605–7.

15. Hamlin, *Life and Times*, 367–70; Hamlin to Lincoln, December 4, AL; John Bigelow Diary, May 8, 1861, quoted in Clapp, *Forgotten First Citizen*, 143–44.

16. Lincoln to Trumbull, December 8, Seward, December 8, and Hamlin, December 8, in *CWL*, 4:147–49; Seward to Lincoln, December 13, AL.

17. George G. Fogg, December 13, and Hannibal Hamlin, December 4 and 10, to Lincoln, AL; Hamlin, *Life and Times*, 370.

18. Lincoln to John A. Gilmer, December 15, and Alexander H. Stephens, December 22, in *CWL*, 4:160.

19. *Illinois State Journal*, December 12, in *CWL*, 4:150.

20. November through January, passim, AL; Hamlin, *Life and Times*, 367–70; Baringer, *House Dividing*; Carman and Luthin, *Lincoln and the Patronage*, 18–20. David Potter writes that Lincoln actually offered Guthrie a position, but Joshua Speed, Lincoln's agent in the matter, claimed otherwise. See Potter, *Lincoln and His Party*, 150–51; W. H. Herndon interview with Joshua Speed, n.d. [1865–66], in Wilson and Davis, eds., *Herndon's Informants*, 475; and Joshua Speed to Ward H. Lamon, June 24, 1872, in Lamon, *Recollections of Lincoln*, 286. See also Herndon and Weik, *Herndon's Life of Lincoln*, 386, and Baringer, *House Dividing*, 89. If Guthrie had been offered and rejected a position, Hamlin knew nothing about it: in early December he wrote to Lincoln as if the matter was still under consideration. See Hannibal Hamlin to Lincoln, December 4, AL.

21. Beale, ed., *Diary of Edward Bates*, 164–65, 166n.

22. Seward to Lincoln, December 13, AL.

23. Leonard Swett and David Davis to Thurlow Weed, December 10, in Barnes, *Memoir*, 301–2; Seward to Lincoln, December 16, AL; *Albany Evening Journal*, December 17.

24. Weed, ed., *Autobiography*, 604–14. For Weed's theory on the crisis, see especially *Albany Evening Journal*, November 24 and 30 and December 17; Thur-

low Weed to Preston King, December 10, in Barnes, *Memoir*, 309; and Thurlow Weed to Lincoln, December 11, AL.

25. Weed, ed., *Autobiography*, 604.–14. Shortly afterward, Lincoln told Lyman Trumbull that he intended to offer Blair a seat but could not yet commit. See Lincoln to Trumbull, December 24, in *CWL*, 4:162.

26. Lincoln, "Resolutions," [December 20], and Lincoln to Trumbull, December 21, in *CWL*, 4:156–58.

27. Potter, *Lincoln and His Party*, 169–70.

28. Crofts, *Reluctant Confederates*, 104–6, 122–26.

29. Lincoln to John Gilmer, December 15, and Alexander Stephens, December 22, in *CWL*, 4:152, 160; Henry Villard, December 19 dispatch, in Villard and Villard, eds., *Lincoln on the Eve of '61*, 42. Stephens's December 30 reply to Lincoln is excerpted in Catton, *Coming Fury*, 113–14. Lincoln's vaunted Southern roots were actually quite shallow. No generation of Lincolns had spent an entire lifetime in the slave states, his grandfather moving from Pennsylvania to Virginia and then Kentucky, and his father from there back North to Indiana. See Winkle, *Young Eagle*, 1–9.

30. Lincoln to Nathan Sargent, June 23, 1859, in *CWL*, 3:387–88. On Republican attitudes toward the territories, see J. R. Woods, December 20, and George Banell, December 21, to Trumbull, LT; George G. Fogg, December 19, and T. C. Jones, December 24, to Lincoln, AL; and Eric Foner, *Free Soil*, 54–65. On Southern unionism, see Crofts, *Reluctant Confederates*, 122–25.

31. Lincoln to Trumbull, December 21, in *CWL*, 4:158.

32. Lanphier to McClernand, December 19, McClernand Papers, ALPL; McClernand to Lanphier, December 21, Lanphier Papers, ALPL; Johannsen, *Douglas*, 815–17.

33. W. L. Helfenstein, December 15, A. W. Spies, December 17, J. T. Cooley, n.d. [c. December 4], R. Hamilton, December 4, John Dovan, December 13, and "Amicus," December 17, to Douglas, SD.

34. J. W. Sheahan, December 17, L. Larmon, December 19, W. B. Scotes, December 17, A. F. Johnston, December 16, and A. Bainbridge, December 13, to Douglas, SD. A more extreme version of this sentiment can be found in G. C. Sampson to Douglas, December 24, ibid.

35. See December, passim, ibid.

36. Douglas to Lanphier, December 25, in Johannsen, ed., *Letters*, 504; *Journal of 13*, 8–13. See also Douglas to August Belmont, December 25, in Johannsen, ed., *Letters*, 505.

37. *CG*, December 18, pp. 112–14; Crittenden, "Drafts & Notes of Speeches & of Letters," 143–55, 267, Crittenden Papers, Duke University, cited in Sowle, "Conciliatory Republicans," 166–67.

38. *Journal of 13*, 2–5. The plan would have been defeated even if the senators

from Georgia and Mississippi had not added their negative votes to the Republicans', as the committee had adopted a rule that no proposal would be accepted that did not win the approval of dual majorities of both the Republicans and non-Republicans. See ibid., 2.

39. Ibid., 8–10.

40. Adams Diary, December 22.

41. Ibid., December 22, 20; Henry Adams to C. F. Adams Jr., December 26, in Ford, ed., *Letters of Henry Adams*, 72.

42. Quotations from Adams Diary, November 12 and December 15, and C. F. Adams to E. Farnsworth, December 9, Adams Papers, MHS. See also Henry Adams to C. F. Adams Jr., December 9, in Ford, ed., *Letters of Henry Adams*, 62.

43. *Journal of 33*, 10–12; Adams Diary, December 17 and 18.

44. *Journal of 33*, 13.

45. Ibid., 13–14; Adams Diary, December 20; Henry Adams to C. F. Adams Jr., December 22, in Ford, ed., *Letters of Henry Adams*, 69–70.

46. Adams Diary, December 21.

47. Ibid.; Curtis Journal, December 28, ALPL; Henry Adams to C. F. Adams Jr., December 22, in Ford, ed., *Letters of Henry Adams*, 69.

48. Adams Diary, December 22–26; Henry Adams to C. F. Adams Jr., December 26, in Ford, ed., *Letters of Henry Adams*, 72; Henry Adams, "Great Secession Winter," 13–14, 18–20; [Henry Adams], December 28, in *Boston Advertiser*, January 1.

49. Adams Diary, December 27–29; *Journal of 33*, 15–21; Sowle, "Conciliatory Republicans," 207–17; Crofts, *Reluctant Confederates*, 234–35.

50. Seward to Lincoln, December 26, AL; *Journal of 13*, 5–13. On Seward's possible support for the Crittenden plan, see Potter, *Lincoln and His Party*, 182–84.

51. *Journal of 13*, 14–19; Sowle, "Conciliatory Republicans," 190–93, 213; Seward to Lincoln, December 28, AL.

52. Weed to Preston King, December 10, in Barnes, *Memoir*, 309.

Chapter Five

1. *GTS*, December 21 entry, 3:79. See also Henry Veeder to Stephen Douglas, December 21, SD; and Andrew Lester Diary, December 22, NYHS.

2. Robert Anderson to S. Cooper, November 28, December 1, 6, and 9, in *OR*, 79, 81–82, 87, 89. See also engineer J. G. Foster's reports of December 4 and 13, in *OR*, 85, 91–92.

3. Major Don Carlos Buell, "Memorandum of verbal instructions . . . ," December 11, and John Floyd to Robert Anderson, December 21, in *OR*, 89–90, 103; Samuel Crawford, *Genesis*, 71–73.

4. John Moore, ed., *Works of James Buchanan*, 11:295; [Buchanan], *Mr. Buchanan's Administration*, 168.

5. Robert Anderson to S. Cooper, December 22, in *OR*, 105.

6. J. G. Foster to R. E. DeRussy, December 27, Robert Anderson to S. Cooper, December 27, Robert Anderson to J. B. Floyd, December 27, and Robert Anderson to S. Cooper, December 27, in ibid., 108–9, 2–4; Samuel Crawford, *Genesis*, 100–108.

7. F. C. Humphreys to W. Maynadier, December 28–31 and January 3, John Cunningham to F. C. Humphreys, December 30, F. W. Pickens to John Cunningham, December 29, and F. C. Humphreys to John Cunningham, December 30, in *OR*, 5–8; Robert Anderson to S. Cooper, December 28, in ibid., 112–13.

8. Duff Green to Buchanan, December 28, printed in Curtis, *Life of James Buchanan*, 2:426; Philip Klein, *Buchanan*, 385.

9. Horatio King, *Turning on the Light*, 26–38, 109–19; Buchanan to W. M. Brown, December 25, in John Moore, ed., *Works of James Buchanan*, 11:75; Philip Klein, *Buchanan*, 373–74.

10. Philip Klein, *Buchanan*, 377–78; Nichols, *Disruption*, 423–27.

11. John A. Turley to John Sherman, December 28, Sherman Papers, LC.

12. *Boston Courier*, December 28.

13. *Springfield (Mass.) Republican*, December 28; Trumbull to Lincoln, December 27, AL; Sidney Webster to Caleb Cushing, December 31 and January 5, Cushing Papers, LC. See also Sardis Allen to John Frey, December 31 and January 3, Frey Family Papers, NYHS; Trumbull to Richard Yates, January 2, Reavis Collection, CHS; and John M. McClernand to Charles H. Lanphier, December 27, Lanphier Papers, ALPL. On Northern praise for Anderson, see January, passim, Anderson Papers, LC; Detzer, *Allegiance*, 151; Maury Klein, *Days of Defiance*, 168–69; and Stampp, *And the War Came*, 71 72.

14. Edward Everett to Rev. Dr. Farley, January 11, Everett Papers, MHS. See also Sidney Webster to Caleb Cushing, December 28, Cushing Papers, LC; Sam Hoard to Lyman Trumbull, December 31, LT; and Leonard Swett to Lincoln, December 31, AL.

15. Henry Adams to C. F. Adams Jr., December 29, in Ford, ed., *Letters of Henry Adams*, 74–75; January 2 dispatch in *Chicago Tribune*, January 7; Seward, December 28, and Leonard Swett, December 31, to Lincoln, AL; E. D. Morgan to Seward, January 5, Seward Papers, UR; Adams Diary, January 3; C. F. Adams to John Andrew, January 4, Andrew Papers, MHS; Henry Adams, "Great Secession Winter," 7.

16. *Chicago Tribune*, January 7; *Albany Evening Journal*, January 9; P. W. Curtenius, December 31, B. G. Noble et al., n.d. [January], Kansas Army of Freedom, January 1, James H. Lane, January 2, Peter Page, January 3, and S. S. Goode, January 4, to Lincoln, AL; Thomas Earl to John Sherman, December 28, Sherman Papers, LC; J. M. McClernand to C. H. Lanphier, December 25, Lanphier Papers, ALPL; Resolutions of the New York Central Club, January 10, in Treadwell, *Secession an Absurdity*. On Everett, see Everett to Mrs. Charles Eames,

December 31 (typescript), and Everett to General R. K. Call, December 31, Everett Papers, MHS.

17. Eber B. Ward to Lincoln, January 4, AL; J. Depeyster Ogden to John J. Crittenden and *New York Herald*, January 4, both quoted in Philip Foner, *Business and Slavery*, 239–40; S. Webster to C. Cushing, December 31, and E. S. Williams to C. Cushing, January 9, Cushing Papers, LC; E. B. Washburne, December 31, and Isaac N. Morris, December 29, to Lincoln, AL.

18. Thurlow Weed to Lincoln, January 4, AL.

19. Brigance, *Jeremiah Sullivan Black*, 97–101; Nichols, *Disruption*, 430–32. Contemporaries speculated that Floyd's radical course over that final, scandal-ridden week—especially in regard to Pittsburgh arms—was motivated by his need for a pretext on which to resign honorably. That is as likely an explanation as any. See Philip Klein, *Buchanan*, 380.

20. Duff Green to Buchanan, December 28, in Curtis, *Life of James Buchanan*, 2:426; Lincoln to Green, December 29, and Trumbull, December 29, in *CWL*, 4:162–63; Green to Lincoln, January 7, AL; January 6 dispatch in *New York Herald*, January 8. Considering who was behind Green's mission, Lincoln could hardly dismiss the plea outright; instead he promised to produce a letter for Green by the next morning. Although the report Green wrote to Buchanan that evening is unlikely to have reached Washington in time to influence the reply to the commissioners, in it Green stated his intention to wire the president Lincoln's reply of the next morning. The contents of Lincoln's letter indicate that that verbal reply could have given Green no cause for hope. Thus, although no telegram from Green survives, Buchanan's biographer points out that if it was sent it would have informed the president of his failure, and if it was not, Green's silence would have conveyed the result equally well. See Philip Klein, *Buchanan*, 385–86.

21. Buchanan to South Carolina commissioners, December 31, in John Moore, ed., *Works of James Buchanan*, 11:79–84, and in *OR*, 115–18; Hunt, ed., "Narrative and Letter," 543–46; Samuel Crawford, *Genesis*, 145–58; Nichols, *Disruption*, 427–33; Philip Klein, *Buchanan*, 378–81.

22. Winfield Scott to Buchanan, December 28, 30, and 31, and to Col. Dimick, December 31, in *OR*, 112, 114, 119, 128; L. Thomas, Memorandum of arrangements, January 2, L. Thomas to Winfield Scott, January 4, C. R. Woods, January 5, and Robert Anderson, January 5, in ibid., 130–33; Winfield Scott to Commanding Officer, Detachment U.S. Army, January 7, and Joseph Holt to Robert Anderson, January 10, in ibid., 134, 136–37; [Buchanan], *Mr. Buchanan's Administration*, 188–90; Samuel Crawford, *Genesis*, 151–70; Detzer, *Allegiance*, 141–44.

23. Nichols, *Disruption*, 435–36; Hermann Hirsch to W. H. C. Whiting, January 3, and W. H. C. Whiting to J. G. Totten, in *OR*, 318–19; J. L. Reno to W. Maynadier, January 4, S. Patterson to S. Cooper, January 5, and A. B. Moore to Buchanan, January 4[?], in *OR*, 327–28; E. Powell to W. Maynadier, January 6 (three letters), and Henry Douglas to H. K. Craig, January 7, in *OR*, 332–33.

24. On reports of Seward's support, see Johannsen, *Douglas*, 819; Kirwan, *John J. Crittenden*, 390–93; and Potter, *Lincoln and His Party*, 182–84.

25. The joint letter is in Johannsen, ed., *Letters*, 506. For popular support for the Crittenden plan, see December–January, passim, SD and Crittenden Papers, LC; and Potter, *Lincoln and His Party*, 189–92. Crittenden's January 3 proposition is in *CG*, 237.

26. Douglas's speech is in *CG*, appendix, 35–42. See also Johannsen, *Douglas*, 819–21.

27. See January, passim, SD and Crittenden Papers, LC; and Johannsen, *Douglas*, 821–22.

28. James T. Hale to Lincoln, January 6, AL; *New York Tribune*, January 7; *New York Times*, January 7–8. The best secondary account of the border-state plan is Sowle, "Conciliatory Republicans," 221–27. See also Crofts, *Reluctant Confederates*, 201–4, 232.

29. Adams Diary, January 5.

30. *Journal of 33*, 23–25; Adams Diary, January 2; Henry Adams to C. F. Adams Jr., January 2, in Ford, ed., *Letters of Henry Adams*, 75.

31. January, passim, Adams Papers, MHS. During the January 5 caucus, radicals such as Owen Lovejoy and Thaddeus Stevens attacked both Hale's border-state plan and Adams's New Mexico statehood proposal, accusing their colleagues of offering protection to slaveholders and leaving the door open to the acquisition of additional slave territories. The rank and file of the party would never permit such a sacrifice of principle, they asserted, and displayed numerous letters to prove it. That evidence would have been unnecessary, as we have seen, but the reminder no doubt hit home with conciliatory moderates. See Sowle, "Conciliatory Republicans," 224–26.

32. Adams Diary, January 5.

33. *Journal of 33*, 32–40; Adams Diary, January 6–14; Sowle, "Conciliatory Republicans," 235–43, 246.

34. Etheridge's plan watered down Crittenden's propositions even more than the border state representatives had, making it impossible for future territory to be added without Republican approval. See *CG*, January 7, p. 279, and Crofts, *Reluctant Confederates*, 233. The final vote was eighty-three to seventy-eight in favor. Northern Democrats supported suspension of the rules twenty-six to four, while Republicans opposed it seventy-one to fourteen. The mid-Atlantic states, with their large cities and extensive Southern trade, were virtually the only source of Republican dissension: of the fourteen Republican supporters, twelve were from Pennsylvania, New York, and New Jersey. Pennsylvania was the most torn: its Republican representatives actually supported the measure eight to six. Significantly, seven New Yorkers and five Pennsylvanians did not vote at all. Although it is impossible to know how many were simply absent for the vote, such high numbers suggest intentionality.

35. *CG*, January 7, pp. 280–82. Burch of California also opposed both the suspension of the rules and the Anderson resolution.

36. Clement Vallandigham of Ohio, one of the tiny group of Northern Democrats who opposed the Anderson resolution, remarked on a distinction that few others perceived: "I voted for peace and adjustment [that is, for Etheridge's motion] a moment ago; you refused it. I vote now against force." New York Hardshell Dan Sickles was closer to the prevailing spirit of his party when he declared, "Believing that my constituents are inflexibly opposed to coercion employed against a sovereign State; nevertheless, convinced as I am, that they regard the act of Major Anderson as one done . . . from patriotic motives; and that it is the sworn duty of the President, according to his oath, to preserve the Union by the employment of all constitutional means, I believe I only give expression to the sentiment of the city of New York, when I vote 'ay'" (*CG*, January 7, pp. 280–81).

37. Robert Anderson to S. Cooper, December 31, in *OR*, 120. See also January 6, ibid., 133. Reports detailing the expedition's preparations are in *OR*, 128–32. On General Scott's role, compare Winfield Scott to Lincoln, March 30, AL, with [Buchanan], *Mr. Buchanan's Administration*, 190.

38. Robert Anderson to S. Cooper, December 31, and Winfield Scott to Robert Anderson, January 5, in *OR*, 120, 132. Ironically, Anderson and his officers had seen a newspaper report of the expedition but they did not believe that the government would order such a mission without informing them. See Doubleday, *Reminiscences*, 101–4.

39. C. R. Woods to L. Thomas, January 13, in *OR*, 9–10, and Samuel Crawford, *Genesis*, 178–82. On South Carolina's intelligence, see Detzer, *Allegiance*, 140, 153–55.

40. The effect was heightened when Crittenden's speech was followed by the belligerent assertion of Robert Toombs of Georgia that "the Union, sir, is dissolved. That is an accomplished fact." Republicans appreciated such claims no more from Toombs than they had from Douglas. See *CG*, January 7, pp. 265, 267.

41. *CG*, January 9, p. 283.

42. Seward, January 12, in *CG*, 341–43 (quotations on 343, 341).

43. Ibid., 343–44 (quotation on 344).

44. Ibid., 283, 289.

45. Ibid., 344.

46. Quotation from December 30 dispatch in *New York Herald*, January 7.

47. See, for example, Joseph Casey to David Davis, November 19; and Andrew H. Reeder, November 21, John W. Forney, November 22, Pennsylvania Republicans in Congress, December 12, and David Wilmot, December 12, to Lincoln, AL; and Lincoln to Hannibal Hamlin, November 27, in *CWL*, 4:145. See also Bradley, *Simon Cameron*, 163–66, and Carman and Luthin, *Lincoln and the Patronage*, 25. Compare to Baringer, *House Dividing*, 126–28.

48. Lincoln compiled a memorandum on Cameron's liabilities and assets; see

CWL, 4:165–67. That no similar list exists for any other candidate indicates the degree of Lincoln's uncertainty.

49. Lincoln to Cameron, December 31, in ibid., 4:168.

50. Trumbull to Lincoln, December 31, AL. See also ibid., January 3.

51. On the substance of McClure's meeting with Lincoln, see A. K. McClure to Lincoln, December 29, AL (quoted); and McClure, *Abraham Lincoln*, 41–49, 140–41. Lincoln knew McClure through the latter's frequent letters during the campaign on the situation in Pennsylvania; see A. K. McClure to Lincoln, June 16, July 2, 7, and 18, August 11, 21, and 27, September 12, 14, and 24, and October 10, 15, and 19, 1860, AL. Lincoln's January 3 letter to Cameron is in *CWL*, 4:169–70.

52. Quotation from E. B. Washburne to Lincoln, January 10, AL. See also G. Rush Smith, January 2, Russell Errett, January 2, B. Rush Petrikin, January 2, Trumbull, January 9, and A. K. McClure, January 11, to Lincoln, ibid.; Trumbull to William Butler, January 9, Butler Papers, CHS; January 3 dispatch in *New York Herald*, January 4; January 2 dispatch in *New York Tribune*, January 3; William S. Thayer to John C. B. Davis, January 6, in Bradley, *Simon Cameron*, 167–68; Carman and Luthin, *Lincoln and the Patronage*, 26; and Martin Crawford, ed., "Politicians in Crisis," 237.

53. See Baringer, *House Dividing*, 152–89 (quotation on 152). Even the most cursory look through the Lincoln Papers for this period shows the grossly unbalanced volume of correspondence related to cabinet advice compared to that related to disunion. See January, passim, AL. The two were far from unrelated, of course, as I will discuss below.

54. See Chapter 4.

55. Quotations from Lincoln to Trumbull, in January 7, *CWL*, 4:171. See also Koerner, *Memoirs*, 2:114.

56. See Crofts, "Reluctant Unionist."

57. Lincoln to Seward, January 12, in *CWL*, 4:173; January 22 dispatch in *New York Herald*, January 24.

58. Angle, *"Here I Have Lived,"* 83–85, 160–203; Cole, *Era of the Civil War*, 4–8; James L. Anderson to John C. Bagby, January 12, Bagby Papers, ALPL; W. H. L. Wallace to Ann Wallace, January 6 and 11, Wallace-Dickey Papers, ALPL.

59. Republicans were particularly vocal in their concerns. See St. G. McPike, December 5, George F. Brown, December 10, William H. Bailhache, December 12, John Trible, December 18, N. B. Judd, December 21, Richard Yates, December 21, David J. Baker, December 22, Russell Hinckley, January 1, Henry Logan, January 2, and D. T. Linegan, January 9, to Trumbull, LT; J. D. Glover to William Butler, December 10, Butler Papers, CHS; and *Illinois State Journal*, December 19. On the Judd-Wentworth feud, see Chapter 2.

60. *JHI*, January 7, pp. 4–6; Virgil Hickox to Stephen Douglas, January 8, SD. Edward L. Baker, editor of the local Republican journal, speculated that they

intended to stay away until the Republicans agreed to elect someone other than Trumbull senator. See *Illinois State Journal*, January 8. The party affiliation of members is in *Illinois State Journal*, December 11.

61. The resolutions and parliamentary process can be found in *JHI*, January 8, pp. 13–15. The debates are printed in *Illinois State Journal*, January 9. The following paragraphs are drawn from these sources, except as otherwise indicated.

62. References to Jackson dominate public and private writings during the crisis. For a small sampling, see Silas Reed to Trumbull, December 6, LT; Charles W. Baker to Stephen Douglas, December 13, SD; Hawkins Layton to Lincoln, December 21, AL; John B. Haskins to E. D. Morgan, December 20, Morgan Papers, NYSL; George G. Fogg to William Butler, December 28, Butler Paper, CHS; Cyrus Bryant to Cullen Bryant, December 31, Bryant Family Papers, NYPL; General John E. Wool to N. P. Banks, January 6, Banks Papers, LC; and James F. Austin to O. M. Hatch, January 7, Hatch Papers, ALPL.

63. Lists of Jackson Day memorials are in *New York Times*, January 9; *Albany Atlas and Argus*, January 8; *Boston Traveller*, January 8; and *Illinois State Register*, January 9.

64. On Scammon's hard-line views, see J. Y. Scammon to Richard Yates, December 27, Yates Family Papers, ALPL.

65. Such accusations dotted both legislative and editorial debates across the North; a local, contemporary example is the editorial war in *Illinois State Journal*, December 29 and January 1 and 16, and *Illinois State Register*, December 31 and January 3 and 15.

66. As one Springfield observer reported perceptively, "Neither Republicans or Democrats agree among themselves," but "in general, the Republicans believe that coersion ou[gh]t to be used to compel the sesceding States while the Democrats generally express the belief that the Union can be more lik[e]ly preserved without it." The same was true across the free states. See James L. Anderson to John C. Bagby, January 12, Bagby Papers, ALPL.

67. *JANY*, January 2, pp. 39–40, and *JSNY*, January 2, p. 34; *Albany Atlas and Argus*, January 4.

68. *JANY*, January 7, p. 52.

69. On the Democratic caucus, see *New York Tribune*, January 4, and *New York Herald*, January 4. For the resolutions, see *JANY*, 35, 48–52.

70. *Albany Atlas and Argus*, January 11. This debate is explored in greater detail in McClintock, "Shall It Be Peace, or a Sword?" 316–24.

71. The two dissenters requested and were denied permission to abstain. Both argued that protection of federal property was up to Congress, not the states, while one explained in addition that he could not support any resolutions that placed New York in favor of coercion without having exhausted all peaceful alternatives. See *JANY*, January 11, pp. 76–77; and *Albany Atlas and Argus*, January 12.

72. *JSNY*, January 11, pp. 57–59; *Albany Atlas and Argus*, January 12. The

senator who cast the dissenting vote was quick to explain that he did not disapprove of the resolution but could not agree to a minor amendment that the Senate adopted (on Spinola's motion) to clear up a disagreement over whether a state could technically declare war or could only commit treason.

73. *Joint Resolutions of the General Assembly of the State of Ohio*, January 12; *Resolves Tendering the Aid of the Commonwealth to the President of the United States, in Enforcing the Laws and Preserving the Union*, January 21 (Massachusetts); *Joint Resolutions Co-operating with Friends of the Union throughout the United States*, January 21 (Wisconsin); *Joint Resolutions of the Legislature of the State of Minnesota, on the State of the Union*, January 22; *Resolutions Adopted by the Legislature of Pennsylvania*, January 24; *Joint Resolutions in Relation to the Union of the States*, January 29 (New Jersey).

Chapter Six

1. Robert Anderson to Francis Pickens, January 9, Francis Pickens to Robert Anderson, January 9, and Captain J. G. Foster to General Joseph Totten, January 9 and 12, in *OR*, 134–37. See also Samuel Crawford, *Genesis*, 187–97.

2. [Buchanan], *Mr. Buchanan's Administration*, 193, 95–96; J. S. Black to Winfield Scott, January 16, in *OR*, 140–42.

3. Joseph Holt to B. Fitzpatrick, S. R. Mallory, and J. Slidell, January 22, and Joseph Holt to I. W. Hayne, February 6, in *OR*, 149–50, 66–68; Buchanan memorandum, [January 16], in John Moore, ed., *Works of James Buchanan*, 11:109–11, and in [Buchanan], *Mr. Buchanan's Administration*, 196–200; Samuel Crawford, *Genesis*, 218–34. It is unlikely that Buchanan would have ordered reinforcements anyway. As Secretary of War Joseph Holt informed Anderson, "Your late dispatches . . . have relieved the Government of the apprehensions previously entertained for your safety. In consequence, it is not its purpose at present to re-enforce you." See Joseph Holt to Robert Anderson, January 16, (quoted); J. S. Black to Winfield Scott, January 16; Joseph Holt to B. Fitzpatrick, S. R. Mallory, and J. Slidell, January 21; and Robert Anderson to S. Cooper, January 30, in *OR*, 140–42, 144, 159. Buchanan's own recollection emphasizing Anderson's truce is in [Buchanan], *Mr. Buchanan's Administration*, 194–96.

4. Bearss, "Fort Pickens," 6–19; [Buchanan], *Mr. Buchanan's Administration*, 214–17; John Moore, ed., *Works of James Buchanan*, 11:285; A. J. Slemmer to L. Thomas, February 5, in *OR*, 334–41; L. Thomas to Justin Dumick, January 21, L. Thomas to Israel Vogdes, January 21, J. S. Saunders to J. Holt, January 23, S. R. Mallory to John Slidell, January 28, J. Holt to Adam J. Slemmer, January 29, J. Holt and Isaac Toucey to James Glynn, January 29, and I. Vogdes to L. Thomas, January 31, all in *OR*, 351–59.

5. Robert Anderson to S. Cooper, February 6 and February 7, in *OR*, 169.

6. *JANY*, January 7, 8, and 12, pp. 59, 75–76, 82; *Albany Atlas and Argus*, January 9 and 12.

7. *Albany Atlas and Argus*, January 14. A detailed discussion of this debate is in McClintock, "Shall It Be Peace, or a Sword?" 319–24.

8. *Albany Atlas and Argus*, January 14.

9. See the farewell address of Governor John Wood and the inaugural address of Governor Richard Yates in *JHI*, 26, 94. See also *Illinois State Register*, January 21. Edward L. Baker, editor of the *Illinois State Journal*, claimed to be "rather astonished" that Democrats would oppose the proposed reform. "There is certainly nothing in the bill which anybody need be alarmed about," he said. "It provides only for what was before the Legislature two years ago, and it smells no more of war and carnage now than it did then" (*Illinois State Journal*, January 12).

10. See *Illinois State Journal*, January 11; J. Y. Scammon to Richard Yates, December 27, Yates Family Papers, ALPL; December 29 dispatch in *New York Herald*, January 3; Trumbull to Richard Yates, January 2, Reavis Collection, CHS; and Horace White to Trumbull, December 30, LT.

11. *Illinois State Register*, January 15, 16, and 21.

12. Ibid., January 14. See also *Joliet Signal*, January 15, quoted in Barns, "Attitude of Illinois," 48; and D. H. Brush to Trumbull, January 21, LT.

13. For the various forms taken by the proposed Militia Bill, see *Massachusetts House Documents*, Nos. 6, 7, 18, 27, 37, and 41. For an excellent review of Massachusetts's militia reforms in the 1840s and 1850s, see McGraw, "Minutemen of '61."

14. See, for example, "Non-Secessionist," "Letter to Mr. Green," January 12, in *Illinois State Journal*, January 14; ibid., December 29; and *Illinois State Register*, January 17.

15. *Illinois State Register*, January 17; William Jayne to Trumbull, January 17, LT.

16. *Illinois State Register*, January 17.

17. *Illinois State Journal*, January 17; C. H. Ray to Trumbull, January 16, LT. See also Gustave Koerner, January 21, D. H. Brush, January 21, and Jesse K. Dubois, January 22, to Trumbull, ibid.

18. N. B. Judd to Trumbull, January 17, LT. On the popularity of the border state plan, see William Jayne, January 21, and O. M. Hatch, January 25, to Trumbull, ibid. (quotation from Hatch). See also William Jayne to Trumbull, January 18, ibid. For a good example of the shifting views of a formerly stalwart Republican, compare Gustave Koerner's December 10 and January 21 letters to Trumbull, ibid.

19. William Jayne to Trumbull, January 18 and 21, LT (quotation from January 21). For a discussion of the various state resolutions on the crisis, see Chapter 5. For the Blades resolutions, see *JHI*, January 14, pp. 82–83.

20. William Jayne to Trumbull, January 18, LT.

21. For the most part, public figures tended to attract correspondence from like-minded constituents. A number of sizable collections of rank-and-file letters sur-

vive. For representative views of hard-line Republicans, see the Trumbull, Washburne, and Chase Papers, LC, and the Adams and Andrew Papers, MHS. For a mix of conciliatory and stalwart Republicans, see Seward Papers, UR, and Sherman Papers, LC. For procompromise sentiment, see Douglas Papers, University of Chicago, and Crittenden Papers, LC (the latter of which includes numerous letters from both Republicans and anti-Republicans).

22. Presentations of petitions and memorials can be found throughout *CG* for these weeks. The easiest way to get an idea of the sheer numbers, as well as their subjects and points of origin, is to consult the indexes to the House and Senate *Journals*.

23. *St. Paul Minnesotian*, January 19, in *NES*, 1:251. Another succinct example of this sentiment is Salmon P. Chase to N. B. Judd, January 20, AL.

24. E. Danforth Jr. to Lincoln, January 30, AL; C. D. Hay, January 13, Charles G. Ames, January 12, and Coleman Gaines, January 20, to Trumbull, LT.

25. Benjamin Franklin Thomas, *A Few Suggestions*, 18–19; Ebenezer Peck to Lyman Trumbull, January 1, LT. On Northerners' devotion to law and order, see Paludan, "American Civil War Considered." On the importance of the Constitution to the formation of American nationalism, see Murrin, "Roof without Walls"; Parish, "American Nationalism"; and Knupfer, *The Union as It Is*. Devotion to both the Constitution and the Union was carefully cultivated in the nineteenth century; see Curti, *Roots of American Loyalty*, 124–41; Horn, "Edward Everett"; and Simpson, "Daniel Webster." Numerous studies place the idea of freedom at the center of American nationalism; see especially Arieli, *Individualism and Nationalism*; Kohn, *American Nationalism*; Somkin, *Unquiet Eagle*; and Major Wilson, *Time, Space, and Freedom*. More recently, Rogan Kersh has examined the importance of the concept of union itself. See Kersh, *Dreams of a More Perfect Union*.

26. John Wilson to Richard Yates, January 1, Yates Family Papers, ALPL; John McClernand, January 14, in *CG*, 369; Boutwell, *An Address upon Secession* (January 8), 19–20; *Illinois State Journal*, February 8.

27. *Chicago Post*, December 29, and *New Haven Palladium*, January 11, both in *NES*, 1:202, 211. Compare these paragraphs to Siddali, " 'Sport of Folly,' " which emphasizes an economic basis for Northern outrage at Southerners' seizures of federal property.

28. Horatio King to Nahum Capen, January 21, in Horatio King, *Turning on the Light*, 42; January 14 entry in Wainwright, ed., *Philadelphia Perspective*, 377; Moses Grinnell to William Seward, January 28, printed in Bancroft, *Seward*, 2:532–33; *GTS*, January 31 entry, 3:95–96. See also Thomas Ewing Sr. to Thomas Ewing Jr., January 15, Ewing Family Papers, LC.

29. William Jayne to Trumbull, January 21, LT.

30. For a persuasive elaboration of this argument, see Potter, *Lincoln and His Party*, 195–200. Even Kenneth Stampp, who argues that the North was united

behind war from mid-January on, acknowledges that "the evidence was strong that the majority of Northerners favored some kind of an adjustment" (Stampp, *And the War Came*, 131–32, 141).

31. George Trumbull to Lyman Trumbull, January 27, LT; *Illinois State Journal*, February 5. On the *Journal* as Lincoln's organ, see below. Two excellent examples of this sentiment are *Chicago Tribune*, January 23 and 25.

32. Cullen Bryant to [Cyrus Bryant], January 10, and Mark Bryant to [Cullen Bryant], January 12, Bryant Family Papers, NYPL; see also F. K. Bailey, January 16, William T. Barron, February 2, and G. O. Pond, February 18, to Trumbull, LT.

33. John Wilson to Richard Yates, January 1, Yates Family Papers, ALPL; Benjamin Franklin Thomas, *A Few Suggestions*, [January 1], 19; Isaac N. Morris, January 16, in *CG*, appendix, 54; John McClernand, January 14, in *CG*, 371; D. H. Brush to Trumbull, January 21, LT. Virtually all conciliatory Republicans embraced the need for coercion as a last resort; see, for example, Thomas Ewing Jr. to Hugh Ewing, January 17, Ewing Family Papers, LC.

34. George Pendleton, January 18, *CG*, appendix, 72.

35. A. E. Harmon to Douglas, January 23, SD; Douglas to C. H. Lanphier, December 25, Lanphier Papers, ALPL. See also James M. Lucas, January 5, and A. Bainbridge, January 18, to Douglas, SD; and John Logan to Isaac N. Haynie, January 1, typescript in Logan Papers, LC.

36. J. M. Sturtevant to Trumbull, January 30, LT; Abraham Lincoln, "Speech at Peoria, Illinois," October 16, 1854, in *CWL*, 2:277; Richard Oglesby, February 1, in *Illinois State Journal*, February 4. A few radicals, including Charles Sumner, were explicit about favoring disunion over war: "If possible, we must avoid civil war; indeed, to avert this dread calamity, I will give up, if necessary, territory and state; but I will not give up our principles" (Sumner to John Andrew, January 18, in Palmer, ed., *Letters of Sumner*, 2:41).

37. On the Shaw memorial, see Chapter 3. On the anti–personal liberty law petitions, see Lawrence Diary, December 11 to January 1. On the Boston petition, see *CG*, January 28, p. 597; and Edward Everett to A. H. Rice, January 25, Everett Papers, MHS.

38. Robert C. Winthrop to Edward Everett, January 21, Everett Papers, MHS.

39. This attitude is revealed throughout Everett's correspondence of November and December. See, for example, Edward Everett to Joshua Bates, November 13, and John R. Thompson, December 17, Everett Papers, MHS. Quotation is from the latter.

40. Edward Everett to Nahum Capen, November 27, and John B. Robinson, December 11, and Everett Diary, December 17, Everett Papers, MHS. See also Everett to John R. Thompson, December 17, ibid.

41. Everett Diary, January 21.

42. Lawrence Diary, December 6–21, January 8 and 21–22.

43. See Chapter 5.

44. Edward Everett to J. L. Petigru, January 19, and Sir Henry Holland, January 21, Everett Papers, MHS; Lawrence Diary, December 24–January 12 (quotation from January 10).

45. Edward Everett to Alexander H. Rice, January 25, Everett Papers, MHS; Everett Diary, January 25–26.

46. *New York Times*, January 25, clipped and pasted into Lawrence Diary, January 25. Lawrence confirmed the accuracy of the exchange by noting that the exchange "must have been overheard by some reporter who stood near, or by some one who repeated it to a reporter."

47. Adams Diary, January 28. Incidentally, Adams was Everett's brother-in-law; his and Everett's wives were sisters. See also January 24 dispatch in *New York Herald*, January 25.

48. Lawrence Diary, January 25–28; Everett Diary, January 25–28.

49. Lawrence Diary, January 28; Everett Diary, January 28; *CG*, January 28, p. 597.

50. Lawrence Diary, January 28–30, February 6, 7–25.

51. Munn Diary, January 27.

52. Ibid., January 30, 27.

53. For all Everett's and Lawrence's contacts among influential Southerners, Munn's Southern connections were more direct than theirs. Connecticut-born, he had migrated South in his early twenties and stayed, as a store owner, bank manager, and land speculator based primarily in Mississippi, for over twenty years. In 1849, just as sectional relations were souring, he had moved with his family to Utica, New York, where he was able to live comfortably on earnings from his real estate and railroad investments. Since then he had become a well-respected citizen in Utica, as evidenced by the repeated invitations to run for mayor. See "Biographical sketch of John Munn," Munn Diary.

54. Munn Diary, February 1.

55. *Albany Atlas and Argus*, February 1; *New York Herald*, February 1–2.

56. Munn Diary, February 1. Munn identified those of Horatio Seymour, Lyman Tremain, James S. Thayer, and Chancellor Walworth. Seymour's, Tremain's, and Thayer's speeches are printed in full in *Albany Atlas and Argus*, February 6, 16, and 18, respectively; Walworth's (and Tilden's) are printed in briefer form in *Albany Atlas and Argus*, February 2, which also relates the enthusiasm that greeted Tremain's mention of Robinson and Weed.

57. *Albany Atlas and Argus*, February 18 and 2.

58. Ibid., February 2.

59. Munn Diary, February 1 and 3, 4–12.

60. *CG*, January 14, pp. 367–72.

61. *CG*, January 30, pp. 649–52; Roscoe Conkling to G. Burke, February 5, GLC.

62. Adams Diary, December 26, and C. F. Adams to E. Hopkins, January 19, Adams Papers, MHS. The speech is in *CG*, appendix, January 31, pp. 124–27.

63. William Kellogg to Lincoln, December 6, AL; Lincoln to William Kellogg, December 11, in *CWL*, 4:150; *New York Herald*, December 15.

64. *Journal of 33*, December 28 and 29, pp. 19–21; Adams Diary, December 26.

65. Joseph Medill to N. B. Judd, January 20, Butler Papers, CHS. I have inverted a phrase in this quotation. On the suspected "conspiracy," see Chapter 7.

66. Lincoln to Seward, February 1, in *CWL*, 4:183.

67. January 27 dispatch in *New York Herald*, January 28, printed in ibid., 4:175–76. For reports of similar statements by Lincoln at around the same time, see William Jayne to Lyman Trumbull, January 28, LT; and William Herndon to Samuel E. Sewall, February 1, cited in Donald, *Lincoln's Herndon*, 145.

68. January 19, 21, and 22 dispatches in *New York Herald*, January 21, 26, and 28; January 21 dispatch in *Chicago Tribune*, January 24. With regard to the alleged letters from Trumbull, one wonders how Lincoln viewed this lack of confidence in his ability to resist Kellogg without subterfuge from Washington. See Lincoln to Seward, February 1, in *CWL*, 4:183.

69. *CG*, February 1, p. 690; *CG*, appendix, February 8, pp. 192–96.

70. Adams Diary, February 8; John McClernand to Charles Lanphier, February 8, Lanphier Papers, ALPL.

71. J. H. Smith, February [misdated January] 7, John D. Amolet, February 11, and A. P. Bartlett, February 9, to Trumbull, LT.

72. *Illinois State Journal*, February 7 and 14 (quotation from February 14); *Chicago Tribune*, February 4, 13, and 23; G. O. Pond to Trumbull, February 18, LT.

73. *New York Herald*, January 29.

Chapter Seven

1. Schuyler Colfax to O. H. Browning, January 19, Browning Papers, ALPL.

2. Reconsideration of the Clark resolutions can be found in *CG*, 402–10, 443. Although it was Simon Cameron who first moved a reconsideration of the Clark substitution on January 16, I use the term "allowed" because no Republican actually voted for the measure when it came up again on the eighteenth; rather, enough of them abstained to permit it to pass by a vote of twenty-seven to twenty-four. On John A. Bingham's Force Bill, see ibid., 219, 246, 282; and *CG*, appendix, 80–84 (quotation on 81). On territorial organization, see *CG*, 729, 765, 1005, 1207–8, 1334–35.

3. See, for example, Robert C. Winthrop to H. B. Grigsby, [misdated January 11], in "Extracts from correspondence and diaries of R. C. Winthrop, Sr.," Winthrop Family Papers, MHS; *GTS*, January 14 entry, 3:89; and *New York Times*, January 14 and 16.

4. Frances Seward to William Seward, January 19, Seward Papers, UR.

5. Seward to Home, January 13, in Seward, *Seward at Washington*, 2:496;

Charles Sumner to John Andrew, January 18, in Palmer, ed., *Letters of Sumner*, 2:41. Others also commented on the speech's potential to disrupt the party: see E. B. Washburne to Lincoln, January 13, AL; Henry Adams to C. F. Adams Jr., January 17, in Ford, ed., *Letters of Henry Adams*, 81; and Charles Sumner to John Andrew, January 17, in Sumner, *Works*, 5:455.

6. Lincoln to Seward, January 19, in *CWL*, 4:176.

7. Crofts, *Reluctant Confederates*, 267, 270; Potter, *Lincoln and His Party*, 282–85.

8. On the January 18 meeting, see Thomas Fitnam to James Buchanan, January 25, cited in Milton, *Eve of Conflict*, 534. Fitnam's account and Gilmer's reliability (or at least his sincerity) are supported by the latter's contemporaneous telegram, cited in note 9, below. Regarding other possible meetings, the most explicit evidence comes from the *Cincinnati Commercial*'s Washington correspondent, who reported on January 26 that "Mssrs. Douglas, Seward, Crittenden and Dixon held an important meeting last night on compromise. Crittenden says he has great hopes of its results. It is believed a modification of the Crittenden resolutions will be agreed on" (January 26 dispatch in *Chicago Tribune*, January 29). Historian Robert Johannsen asserts that "the four Senators apparently continued to meet for several days" after the eighteenth, but he provides no source and may be referring to the *Commercial* correspondent's report. Prominent New York Republican John A. Stevens told George T. Strong on the twenty-ninth that he had "authentic, private, confidential information that Seward, Crittenden, Hunter of Virginia, and Douglas agreed last night on certain 'conciliatory' measures, and the whole slavery question is settled." Whether Stevens had genuine intelligence of another conference or whether he had heard a garbled rumor of the meeting on the twenty fifth is not clear. See Johannsen, *Douglas*, 827; and *GTS*, January 29 entry, 3:94.

9. On the joint messages, see Crittenden and Douglas, January 19, in *Raleigh (North Carolina) Register*, cited in Milton, *Eve of Conflict*, 532; and January 26 dispatch in *New York Herald*, January 27 and February 9. Douglas alluded to them in the Senate on January 28 (*CG*, 668). See also Douglas to James Barbour, January 27, in *Illinois State Register*, February 2. For Gilmer's telegram, see John Gilmer to Jesse J. Yeates, January 22, in *OR*, series 1, volume 51, part 2, p. 7.

10. January 25 dispatches in *New York Tribune*, January 26; January 28 AP dispatch in *New York Herald*, January 29, and *New York Times*, January 29; January 29 and 31 dispatches in *Chicago Tribune*, January 31 and February 2 and 4; Carl Schurz to Lincoln, January 31, AL. On the possible existence of at least one such letter, see (St. Louis) *Missouri Democrat*, January 18; and Samuel Treat to Stephen Douglas, January 18, SD. On a possible letter from Lincoln, see below, note 15.

11. Quotation from January 28 AP dispatch in *New York Herald*, January 29. Despite his cheerful facade, Seward did reveal his anxiety on occasion. It was at this time that Seward spoke to Everett, Lawrence, etc., about the apparently hopeless

state of the compromise movement, including his inability to win the support of Lincoln. See Chapter 6.

12. On Swett and Weed, see January 20 and 24 dispatches in *New York Herald*, January 21 and 25; Leonard Swett to Lincoln, January 24, AL; and Thurlow Weed to William Seward, January 18 and 19, Seward Papers, UR. See also Weed to Swett, January 20, AL.

13. Seward to Lincoln, January 27, AL.

14. January 27 dispatch in *New York Herald*, January 28, printed in *CWL*, 4:175–76. Kellogg indicated that Lincoln had even agreed to submit to the border state plan "if the Republican party desire it," but that would have gone far beyond any other statement he was reported to have made during that period. If he did make such a statement, it could only have been out of confidence that the party did not desire it; most likely the border state claim was Kellogg's invention, or at least a product of his own wishful thinking. See Baringer, *House Dividing*, 228, and note 15, below.

15. Denials in January 29 and 31 dispatches, in *New York Herald*, January 30 and February 1; *Illinois State Journal*, January 29; and *New York Tribune*, January 29. It is difficult to account for the *Herald* correspondent's report of a Lincoln letter. William Baringer, one of the closest and ablest scholars of Lincoln during these months, argues that Seward actually showed the reporter Lincoln's February 1 letter to him, which Lincoln must have written on January 25 or 26 and intentionally postdated (as he had done with a letter to Cameron a few weeks earlier). Lincoln's motive for doing so, Baringer posits, was to maintain deniability for engineering the compromise that he presumably thought would pass Congress in the last week of January. See Baringer, *House Dividing*, 229–32. That makes some sense given the extensive movement for compromise—numerous letters and discussions among high party leaders in and out of Congress—that the *Herald* reporter describes in the same dispatch. However, I have found (and Baringer offers) little evidence to confirm such activity, and I have argued above that it was largely smoke generated by the statements of Douglas and Crittenden and rumors of their deal with Seward. It certainly does not seem that Lincoln had any reason to think Congress would pass any compromise measures that week, so dating the letter February 1 would have gained him nothing.

There is a simpler explanation. Since Lincoln had told Kellogg that he would write to Seward, and Kellogg claimed that Lincoln had agreed to abide by the border state compromise, it is probable that Kellogg merely predicted to the correspondent what the letter to Seward would say. That would not have been out of character: Kellogg had already displayed a tendency to presume that he knew Lincoln's views on compromise (in December, on the Committee of Thirty-three). Moreover, he had just spoken the previous day with that particular reporter on the subject of Lincoln's supposed endorsement of the border-state plan.

16. *Illinois State Journal*, January 29; January 27 dispatch in *New York Herald*,

February 1. On this and the following paragraphs, see also Baringer, *House Dividing*, 224–31.

17. *Illinois State Journal*, January 21. Villard described the editorial as "being carefully prepared under the eyes of the President elect" (January 22 dispatch in *New York Herald*, January 28). The *Journal* continued to explore the subject in editorials of February 5 and 20. See also Villard's January 20 dispatch in *New York Herald*, January 25. On the perception of the *Journal*'s being Lincoln's organ, see January 27 Washington dispatch in *New York Herald*, January 28.

18. Lincoln to Seward, February 1, in *CWL*, 4:183.

19. *CWL*, 4:250–52, 255–58 (quotation on 258).

20. Ibid., 4:250, 252–53, 256–57, 259 (quotations on 250, 259, 256).

21. Ibid., 4:253–55 (quotations on 253, 254).

22. Ibid., 4:254, 261 (quotation on 261).

23. Ibid., 4:260.

24. Carl Schurz to Margarethe M. Schurz, February 10, in Bancroft, ed., *Speeches of Carl Schurz*, 1:179.

25. Adams Diary, February 5; Henry Adams to C. F. Adams Jr., February 8, in Ford, ed., *Letters of Henry Adams*, 87.

26. James Barbour to William Seward, February 8, in Bancroft, *Seward*, 2:535.

27. Dix, ed., *Memoirs*, 1:366–67, 370–72; Stampp, *And the War Came*, 103–9.

28. Buchanan to Holt, January 30, in Curtis, *Life of James Buchanan*, 2:474; Montgomery Blair to G. V. Fox, January 30, Winfield Scott to G. V. Fox, January 30, G. V. Fox to Virginia Fox, February 6 and 7, and G. V. Fox to Winfield Scott, February 8, all in Thompson and Wainwright, eds., *Confidential Correspondence of Fox*, 1:3, 6 9; G. V. Fox memorandum, February 6, in *OR*, 203–4.

29. G. V. Fox to Virginia Fox, February 7, in Thompson and Wainwright, eds., *Confidential Correspondence of Fox*, 1:6; Robert Anderson to S. Cooper, January 30, Joseph Holt to Robert Anderson, February 23, and S. Cooper to Robert Anderson, February 28, in *OR*, 159, 182–83, 187; Horatio King Diary, February 19, in [Buchanan], *Mr. Buchanan's Administration*, 209–10; Samuel Crawford, *Genesis*; Horatio King, *Turning on the Light*, 45.

30. William Dennison to Richard Yates, January 26, AL; William Jayne to Lyman Trumbull, January 28, LT. On the assumption that Yates spoke for Lincoln, see January 28 dispatch in *Chicago Tribune*, January 29.

31. Cyrus Allen, January 25, and Oliver P. Morton, January 29, to Lincoln, AL.

32. The House passed the antisecession resolutions the next day, while the Senate let them lie until February 12 before passing them. The peace conference resolutions were passed by both houses on February 1. See *JHI*, 297–311, 534; and *JSI*, 224–29, 358–64.

33. William Jayne, January 31 and February 1, and Ebenezer Peck, February 2, to Lyman Trumbull, LT. Debates are printed in *Illinois State Journal*, February 4, 12, 14, and 19, and *Illinois State Register*, February 2 and 5. On Lincoln's role, Judd

reported some years later that the president-elect actually drafted the resolutions and directed Republicans in the Assembly to pass them. That may or may not be true, but his involvement on some level is supported both by rumors to that effect in the legislature and by the similarity of the resolutions to the anticompromise statement Lincoln was reported to have given Kellogg (see Chapter 6). See John G. Nicolay interview with Norman B. Judd, February 28, 1876, in Burlingame, ed., *Oral History*, 47–48; and William Jayne to Trumbull, January 21 and 28, LT.

34. *Documents of the New York Assembly*, no. 18, pp. 38–39; *JANY*, 115–16, 157–60, 166–79, 205, 225–27, 256–61; *JSNY*, 94–95, 104, 127, 133–34, 139–43. On the Littlejohn resolutions, see Chapter 5.

35. Adams recorded that they had a "rather warm" discussion in the House, which lasted until "the sweepers drove us from the Hall." The next day it resumed but in more formal, strained tones. Two days later Sumner failed to show up for Adams's speech, and the following Sunday Sumner was absent from dinner at the Adams house for the first time that session. The ultimate result of the incident was a permanent rupture in their friendship. See Adams Diary, January 28–29 and February 3; Charles Sumner to John Andrew, January 26 and 28, Andrew Papers, MHS, in Sumner, *Works*, 5:459–62; and Henry Adams to C. F. Adams Jr., February 5, in Ford, ed., *Letters of Henry Adams*, 85–86. See also Henry Wilson to John Andrew, January 29, Andrew Papers, MHS.

36. John Andrew to Charles Sumner, January 30 and February 6, cited in Pierce, ed., *Letters of Sumner*, 2:48 n. 3, 51 n. 2; Charles Sumner to William H. Claflin, February 4, in ibid., 51–52; *Documents Printed by Order of the Senate of the Commonwealth of Massachusetts*, no. 32; Schouler, *History of Massachusetts*, 26–28.

37. Gunderson, *Old Gentlemen's Convention*, 35–41; Stampp, *And the War Came*, 394–97.

38. See Chapter 2.

39. Gunderson, *Old Gentlemen's Convention*, 49–50; George S. Boutwell to N. P. Banks, February 13, Banks Papers, LC; John Z. Goodrich to John Andrew, February 7 and February 9, Andrew Papers, MHS.

40. James Barbour to William Seward, February 8, in Bancroft, *Seward*, 2:534–36; Crofts, "Secession Winter," 245.

41. *CWL*, 4:194–96.

42. Ibid., 4:204, 211, 215–16, 228.

43. Ibid., 4:237, 241. Thurlow Weed to William Seward, February 21, Seward Papers, UR, quoted in Gunderson, *Old Gentlemen's Convention*, 83.

44. Adams Diary, February 16, 18, and 20.

45. *CG*, 1031–33, 1066, 1097–98; *CG*, appendix, 231–34; Sherrard Clemens, February 18, Thomas Fitnam, February 19, Alfred Barbour, February 21, Joseph Segar, February 21, and F. W. Lander, February 22, to Seward, Seward Papers, UR, printed in Bancroft, *Seward*, 2:536–41; Adams Diary, February 19. See also

C. F. Adams Jr. Diary, February 19, quoted in Adams Jr., *Charles Francis Adams*, 77; and C. F. Adams Jr. to John Andrew, February 22, Andrew Papers, MHS.

46. Gunderson, *Old Gentlemen's Convention*, 62.

47. An excellent analysis of the speeches and debates is found in ibid., 62–71. For amendments to the Guthrie report, see ibid., 86.

48. Ibid., 87–90. On the Illinoisans' switch, see Thomas Turner to Lincoln, February 28, AL.

49. "The Washington Diary of Horatio Nelson Taft," February 27 and 28 entries, LC.

50. *CG*, 1331–33.

51. Ibid., 1254–55, 1260–62, 1269–74, 1283–85, 1306–18, 1338–40, 1349–1405. Quotation on 1255.

Chapter Eight

1. The final draft of Lincoln's inaugural address is in *CWL*, 4:262–71 (quotation from 271).

2. Lincoln to E. B. Washburne, February 15, in ibid., 4:217; E. B. Washburne to Lincoln, February 19, AL; Thurlow Weed to Willard's Hotel, n.d. [February 18], in Lamon, *Recollections of Lincoln*, 34.

3. See Seward, *Seward at Washington*, 2:510; and Seward to Home, February 23, in ibid., 511. Seward probably knew that Lincoln had already heard of a plot in Baltimore and was being urged by N. B. Judd and Allan Pinkerton to alter his schedule. See Pinkerton Agency report, n.d., 1861, and Allan Pinkerton to William H. Herndon, August 23, 1866, both in Wilson and Davis, eds., *Herndon's Informants*, 267–314, 317–25; Cuthbert, *Lincoln and the Baltimore Plot*; and Baringer, *House Dividing*, 292–96.

4. The best account of Lincoln's first days in Washington is Baringer, *House Dividing*, 304–30. See also Sowle, "Conciliatory Republicans," 406–15, 421–29.

5. Seward to Lincoln, February 24, in Seward, *Seward at Washington*, 2:512.

6. Seward to Lincoln, [February 24] (filed under [February]), AL; *CWL*, 4:249–61.

7. Baringer, *House Dividing*, 311–13, 318–19, 321–29; Carman and Luthin, *Lincoln and the Patronage*, 44–51; Sowle, "Conciliatory Republicans," 422–29; Crofts, *Reluctant Confederates*, 245–47.

8. Patrick Sowle ("Conciliatory Republicans," 427–28) credits this policy with demoralizing both factions, but the evidence he cites seems more to indicate last-minute anxiety.

9. *New York Herald*, March 1.

10. On Gilmer, see Crofts, *Reluctant Confederates*, 246–47.

11. See Sowle, "Conciliatory Republicans," 448–49.

12. See Beale and Brownsword, eds., *Diary of Gideon Welles*, 1:12; Bancroft, *Seward*, 2:95–101; and Elliott, *Winfield Scott*, 696–700.

13. Winfield Scott to Seward, March 3, AL (also printed in John Moore, ed., *Works of James Buchanan*, 11:300–301); Seward to Lincoln, March 4, AL. In addition to passing the letter along to its intended recipient, Lincoln, Seward also distributed copies of it freely.

14. Seward to Lincoln, March 2, AL. Seward's resignation has traditionally been interpreted as a naked bid for power, an effort to force Lincoln to exclude Chase from the cabinet. See Nicolay and Hay, *Abraham Lincoln*, 3:370; Baringer, *House Dividing*, 326–29; Nevins, *Emergence of Lincoln*, 2:454–55; Oates, *With Malice toward None*, 215; Van Deusen, *William Henry Seward*, 253; and Niven, *Salmon P. Chase*, 237. I have followed Patrick Sowle's persuasive argument that Seward's main concern was with preventing the secession of the Upper South. See Sowle, "Conciliatory Republicans," 448–49. See also Crofts, *Reluctant Confederates*, 254.

15. Patrick Sowle ("Conciliatory Republicans," 421, 454) and Maury Klein (*Days of Defiance*, 310) both remark on the influence of Washington on Lincoln's outlook.

16. What was said during Lincoln's meeting with the peace conference delegates is not known with any precision. Many historians accept the account of conference secretary Lucius Chittenden, who describes a lengthy conversation that he claims was recreated from contemporary notes. However, Don E. Fehrenbacher points out inconsistencies in Chittenden's account, including his claim to have introduced the members to Lincoln himself (a *New York Herald* correspondent credits Chase with that duty) and, more significantly, the unlikelihood that both the introductions and the extended dialogue Chittenden describes could have occurred in the half hour or so that the interview occupied. See Chittenden, *Recollections of President Lincoln*, 68–78; Fehrenbacher and Fehrenbacher, eds., *Recollected Words*, 99–101; and February 23 AP report in both *New York Herald*, February 24, and *New York Tribune*, February 24. On Chittenden's general unreliability, see Fehrenbacher and Fehrenbacher, eds., *Recollected Words*, 98–99, 521 nn. 98–99.

However, there is no reason to believe that Chittenden invented his conversation out of whole cloth. On the contrary, his description of the exchange between Lincoln and William Cabell Rives of Virginia, for example, fits roughly with Rives's brief contemporary description. The basic thrust of Chittenden's account of Lincoln's remarks—generally noncommittal but clearly nonconciliatory—is probably fairly accurate. See William C. Rives to William C. Rives Jr., February 24, Rives Papers, LC. I am grateful to Drew McCoy for providing me with this letter.

17. O. H. Browning to Lincoln, February 17, with endorsement in Lincoln's hand, AL. See also Pease and Randall, eds., *Diary of Browning*, February 11 entry, 455–56; and John G. Nicolay interview with O. H. Browning, June 17, 1875, in Burlingame, ed., *Oral History*, 5–6.

18. There is some minor confusion regarding some of the details of the meeting,

but I agree with Don and Virginia Fehrenbacher in linking it with the one an AP reporter describes in a February 27 dispatch that appeared the next day in the *New York Tribune* and *New York Times*, which places the meeting on February 26. See Fehrenbacher and Fehrenbacher, eds., *Recollected Words*, 538 n. 340. Compare to Baringer, *House Dividing*, 315–18.

19. The following description of this interview is drawn from Charles S. Morehead's speech to the Southern Club at Liverpool, England, October 9, 1862, partially reprinted in Barbee and Bonham, "Fort Sumter Again." See also Morehead to John J. Crittenden, February 23, 1862, partially printed in Mrs. Chapman Coleman, *Life of Crittenden*, 2:333–36.

Morehead's account must be viewed cautiously, not only because of the magnitude of the events that occurred during the year and a half between the interview and the time he revealed his story publicly, but also because the Lincoln administration had him imprisoned for four months in the fall of 1861. It was fear of another arrest that had driven him to England, where he delivered the speech describing this meeting. Yet his account jibes well not only with Lincoln's private statements throughout the crisis but also with the draft of his inaugural as it was then written, including points that were expunged before its delivery. That would seem to support Morehead's assertion that he was working from notes written "shortly afterward." See Barbee and Bonham, "Fort Sumter Again," 67. Of more significance is that two contemporary accounts have Lincoln himself corroborating the most controversial claim in Morehead's account: a report by the minister from Bremen dated a few days later and a diary entry by one of Lincoln's private secretaries later that year. See Lutz, "Rudolf Schleiden," 210–11; and Burlingame and Ettlinger, eds., *Inside Lincoln's White House*, October 22, 1861, entry, 28.

20. Lutz, "Rudolf Schleiden," 211.

21. Sherrard Clemens to unknown, March 1, W. P. Palmer Manuscripts, Western Reserve Historical Society, quoted in Baringer, *House Dividing*, 313. See also Crofts, *Reluctant Confederates*, 252.

22. See the references at note 14, above.

23. *Washington Star*, March 4, cited in Miers, ed., *Lincoln Day by Day*, 3:22; Sowle, "Conciliatory Republicans," 451; Crofts, *Reluctant Confederates*, 254; Lincoln to Seward, March 4, in *CWL*, 4:273.

24. Seward to Lincoln, March 5, AL; Seward to Frances Seward, March 8, in Seward, *Seward at Washington*, 2:518 (quoted). See also Sowle, "Conciliatory Republicans," 454–56. This is one of the numerous points at which the historian of the secession crisis finds himself grappling with the puzzling "Diary of a Public Man," an anonymous work published in 1879 that purported to be an excerpt from a diary written by an individual who was on intimate terms with virtually every person of importance in Washington. This "diary" raises so many questions that I made the decision early in my research simply to ignore it, following the advice of the closest researcher into its authorship and nature, Frank Maloy Anderson, who

debunked it in the 1940s (Anderson, *Mystery of "A Public Man"*). As my own study was reaching the final stages of publication, however, I was fortunate enough to be privy to a draft manuscript of a new study of the "Diary" by Daniel W. Crofts, who confirms Anderson's conclusion that it was not a genuine diary but argues persuasively that it has significant historical value nonetheless. Crofts identifies several points in the "Diary" that can be corroborated by contemporary sources that were not available to an 1879 writer (Crofts, "Public Man Revealed," esp. chs. 8–9). This could be one of those: Seward's private reference to the possibility of an appointment to England may bear out a story the diarist tells of Lincoln's outmaneuvering a group of pro-Seward lobbyists who were urging the president-elect not to appoint Chase to a cabinet position on the grounds that Seward could never work with the radical Ohioan. The diarist relates how Lincoln stunned them into silence by telling them that if that was the case he would have to send Seward to the Court of St. James. See "Diary of a Public Man," March 2 entry, 220–22; and Crofts, "Public Man Revealed," 113–15.

25. *CWL*, 4:254. Lincoln did use Seward's passage, moving it into the next paragraph. See ibid., 266.

26. Philip Klein, *Buchanan*, 402.

27. Buchanan memorandum, March 9, in John Moore, ed., *Works of James Buchanan*, 11:156. Anderson calculated his estimate of 20,000 troops after polling his fellow officers. All nine reports are in AL. See Anderson to S. Cooper, February 28; and Theodore Talbot, February 28, Abner Doubleday, February 28, Richard K. Meade, February 28, Truman Seymour, February 28, George W. Snyder, February 28, John G. Foster, February 28, Norman J. Hall, February 28, and Jefferson C. Davis (no relation), February 28, to Robert Anderson, AL.

28. Buchanan memorandum, March 9, in John Moore, ed., *Works of James Buchanan*, 11:156; Joseph Holt and Winfield Scott to Lincoln, March 5, AL; Miers, ed., *Lincoln Day by Day*, 3:25–26.

29. Joseph Holt and Winfield Scott to Lincoln, March 5, AL.

30. Ibid.; Lincoln to Winfield Scott, March 9, in *CWL*, 4:279.

31. Robert Anderson to S. Cooper, March 2, enclosing Norman J. Hall memorandum, March 1, AL.

32. John G. Nicolay interview with Joseph Holt, April 2, 1874, in Burlingame, ed., *Oral History*, 72.

33. Beale and Brownsword, eds., *Diary of Gideon Welles*, 1:4–6; Beale, ed., *Diary of Edward Bates*, March 6 and 9 entries, 177.

34. *New York Tribune*, March 11–14; *New York Times*, March 11–13; *New York Herald*, March 12–15; *Chicago Tribune*, March 12–13. Southern newspapers are cited in Nevins, *War for the Union*, 1:43. For Scott's order, see Winfield Scott to Robert Anderson, March 11, AL.

35. Adams Diary, March 12.

36. Frank Blair Sr. to Montgomery Blair, March 12, and Montgomery Blair to Lincoln, March 12, both in AL.

37. Beale and Brownsword, eds., *Diary of Gideon Welles*, 1:4–5; Gideon Welles to Lincoln, March 15, AL. See also Caleb Smith to Lincoln, March 16, AL.

38. Quotation from March 11 dispatch in *New York Tribune*, March 12. See also *New York Times*, March 12; *Springfield (Mass.) Republican*, March 12; *Chicago Tribune*, March 12–14; Lincoln's interview with John Covode in March 14 dispatch in *New York Herald*, March 15; and Stampp, *And the War Came*, 267.

39. Neal Dow to Lincoln, March 13, AL; Rudolph Schleiden to Bremen government, March 12, cited in Donald, *Charles Sumner*, 386–87. Even many of those who disapproved of the decision and urged Lincoln to reconsider grudgingly pledged to support the administration if evacuation was in fact unavoidable. See, for example, James Watson Webb, March 12, and James L. Hill, March 14, to Lincoln, AL.

40. Lincoln to Scott, March 9 (two letters), in *CWL*, 4:280, 279. Scott issued the order on the twelfth, a full week after Lincoln directed it. See Winfield Scott to Israel Vogdes, March 12, in *OR*, 360. On Lincoln's understanding of his order, see Meigs, "General M. C. Meigs," 300, and Keyes, *Fifty Years' Observation*, 379.

41. See, for example, Lawrence Diary, January 25; Lord Lyons to Lord John Russell, February 4, quoted in Nevins, *Emergence of Lincoln*, 2:401; and M. J. Crawford and J. Forsyth to Robert Toombs, March 8, Toombs Papers, University of South Carolina, in Nicolay and Hay, *Abraham Lincoln*, 3:399, and in Samuel Crawford, *Genesis*, 322–23. See also Sowle, "Conciliatory Republicans," 408, and Crofts, *Reluctant Confederates*, 270–73. For an intriguing evaluation of the feasibility of Seward's ideas, see Crofts, *Reluctant Confederates*, 356–59.

42. Lincoln's replies to delegations from New York, Pennsylvania, Massachusetts, and Illinois, March 4 and 5, in *CWL*, 4:272, 273–75. On Southern patronage, see Crofts, *Reluctant Confederates*, 272–73; Adams Diary, March 12; and Edwin Stanton to Lincoln, March 6, AL.

43. Crofts, *Reluctant Confederates*, 262.

44. See Seward to Frances Seward, March 8, in Seward, *Seward at Washington*, 2:518–19. On Southern unionist response to these congressional measures, see Crofts, *Reluctant Confederates*, 255–56.

45. Samuel Ward memorandum, March 4, in Bancroft, *Seward*, 2:544; M. J. Crawford to Robert Toombs, March 6, Toombs Papers, University of South Carolina, in ibid., 2:108 n.

46. M. J. Crawford and John Forsyth to Robert Toombs, March 8, in ibid., 2:109–11.

47. Ibid., 111 n.

48. Crofts, *Reluctant Confederates*, 256–57.

49. Gwin later recalled that after Seward declined to meet with him he removed

himself from the negotiations in disgust at such a puerile tactic, but Seward was, in fact, quite sick. See Evan Coleman, ed., "Gwin and Seward," 469; Seward to Frances Seward, March 8, in Seward, *Seward at Washington*, 2:519; and Seward to Douglas, March 9, SD.

50. M. J. Crawford and John Forsyth to Robert Toombs, March 12, Toombs Papers, University of South Carolina, in Nicolay and Hay, *Abraham Lincoln*, 3:402–3; Bancroft, *Seward*, 2:111–12; Nevins, *War for the Union*, 1:40–41.

51. M. J. Crawford and John Forsyth to Robert Toombs, March 12, Toombs Papers, University of South Carolina, in Nicolay and Hay, *Abraham Lincoln*, 3:402; Seward to R. M. T. Hunter, March 12, in Nicolay and Hay, *Abraham Lincoln*, 3:402.

52. James Barbour to William Seward, February 8, in Bancroft, *Seward*, 2:535; James Barbour to Douglas, February 6, SD. On Seward, Douglas, and the Union Party in the Upper South, see Crofts, *Reluctant Confederates*, 262–73; Johannsen, *Douglas*, 848, 851–52, 857–58; and Nichols, *Disruption*, 492–93.

53. Lincoln thanked him politely. See February 27 dispatch in *New York Herald*, February 28; and *Illinois State Register*, March 4.

54. Miers, ed., *Lincoln Day by Day*, 3:26; Johannsen, *Douglas*, 843–45. There is also the story that when Lincoln fumbled awkwardly for a place to put his hat while he spoke, Douglas took it and held it throughout the address. On that controversial incident, see *Cincinnati Commercial*, March 11, and "Diary of a Public Man," March 4 entry, 231. Frank Maloy Anderson (*Mystery of "A Public Man,"* 97–112) makes a strong case that the story of the hat is likely false, while Allan Nevins ("He Did Hold Lincoln's Hat") and Daniel W. Crofts ("Public Man Revealed," 116–17) argue for its veracity. Whatever the truth of this occurrence, it would have been in keeping with Douglas's demeanor at the inaugural.

55. John Forsyth to Robert Toombs, March 8, Toombs Papers, University of South Carolina, quoted in Nicolay and Hay, *Abraham Lincoln*, 3:399; Johannsen, *Douglas*, 844–46 (quotation on 846).

56. *CG*, March 6, pp. 1436–39. Quotations on 1436, 1438, 1437.

57. Ibid., March 7, pp. 1442, 1445.

58. Ibid., 1445.

59. John Gilmer to Douglas, March 8 and 10, quoted in Johannsen, *Douglas*, 848.

60. John Gilmer to Seward, March 8, in Bancroft, *Seward*, 2:546. I have inverted two sentences in this quotation. See also Gilmer to Seward, March 7 and 12, in ibid., 545–48, and Gilmer to Seward, March 9, AL.

61. Lincoln to Winfield Scott, March 9, in *CWL*, 4:279; Winfield Scott to Lincoln, March 11 and 12, AL.

62. Lincoln to Seward, March 15, in *CWL*, 4:284. Fox's plan is described in Chapter 7.

63. Seward to Lincoln, March 15, AL.

64. Montgomery Blair to Lincoln, March 15, AL.

65. Salmon Chase to Lincoln, March 16, AL.

66. Gideon Welles, March 15, Edward Bates, March 16, Caleb B. Smith, March 16, and Simon Cameron, March 16, to Lincoln, AL.

67. Sowle, "Conciliatory Republicans," 469–70. Cameron recalled later, "The Sumter question was not absolutely decided in Cabinet—nothing was ever decided —there was general talk. Everybody understood Sumter was to be given up" (John G. Nicolay interview with Simon Cameron, February 20, 1875, in Burlingame, ed., *Oral History*, 42).

68. How much Lincoln knew of Seward's activities has long troubled historians. Most have been willing to charge Seward with acting entirely on his own and attribute his presumptuousness to either his desire to control the administration or his belief that he did. Daniel W. Crofts, who (as I do) follows David M. Potter's and Patrick Sowle's more complex and sympathetic interpretations of Seward's motives, contends that Lincoln was aware that Seward informed George Summers of the evacuation. His argument goes something like this: 1) On March 19, Summers wrote to thank J. C. Welling for informing him of the evacuation. The letter to which Summers was responding is not extant, but Welling later claimed that he had written Summers at Seward's direct request. 2) On the same day, March 19, Seward wrote Lincoln as follows: "I think I told you of John Cochrane late Democratic member from New York and his visit to Richmond. He has this morning a noble letter from Summers, which was written upon explanations made to him by Mr Cochrane from me. I have advised him to show it to you. You can converse freely with Mr Cochrane." We do not have that "noble letter" from Summers to Cochrane, unfortunately, but since Seward had clearly sent Cochrane to Richmond to speak with Summers, it makes sense that the message was the same one he had sent through Welling: that Sumter was to be vacated. 3) It is logical to conclude that the Summers letter Cochrane showed Lincoln said essentially the same thing as the one Summers wrote the same day to Welling, thanking him for the news about Sumter's evacuation. 4) We can conclude, then, not only that as of March 19 Lincoln knew of Seward's assurances to the Virginia unionists but also, since Seward had no apparent qualms about telling him, that he assumed Lincoln would approve. See George W. Summers to J. C. Welling, March 19, in *The Nation* 29 (December 4, 1879), 384; J. C. Welling to the Editor, November 21, 1879, ibid., 383–84; Seward to Lincoln, March 19, AL; and Crofts, *Reluctant Confederates*, 275–76.

It is a compelling argument, but as Crofts admits, even if it is sound, there are reasons why Seward would send Cochrane to speak with Lincoln other than that Lincoln already knew of Seward's actions: for example, Crofts writes, Seward may have told Summers of the evacuation on his own authority and then sent Cochrane to Lincoln to convince the president to honor his assurances. There are at least two more possibilities as well. First, if Crofts's reasoning is correct and Lincoln did know of Seward's assurances on or before the nineteenth, he may have been deliberately allowing Seward to mislead the Virginia unionists, as Crofts suggests he himself did in early April after the John B. Baldwin interview (see Crofts, *Reluctant Confederates*, 304, and Chapter 9, below). Second, one or both of Crofts's premises could be wrong: that is, Welling's claim to be acting on Seward's behalf was inaccurate (without the original letter to Summers we cannot be sure), or the message Seward sent through Cochrane was not the same as the one he sent through Welling.

With regard to the latter possibility, the language Cochrane uses in a March 16 letter describing his trip to a political ally is suggestive: "The Administration I think is inclining to peaceful measures[.] If it adopt them I have hopes that we shall ultimately quell our present diffrenses." It is possible that Seward simply swore him to secrecy, but considering the certainty with which newspapers at the time were reporting the cabinet's decision to evacuate Sumter, Cochrane's vagueness may indicate that Seward had not given him the same message Welling claimed to have conveyed. Also casting doubt is that Cochrane arrived in Richmond on March 13 and was back in Washington by March 15, the day of the critical cabinet meeting. See John Cochrane to Fernando Wood, March 16, Wood Papers, NYPL; *New York Herald*, March 14.–16; and *New York Times*, March 14.–15.

In fact, all of the possible explanations raise both sticky problems and fascinating possibilities. There is simply not enough evidence to conclude which is true, if any, or whether Lincoln was aware of Seward's actions at all. The significance of the question, of course, is that if Seward were acting with Lincoln's prior knowledge, it might indicate that Lincoln had in fact determined to withdraw the Sumter garrison around the fifteenth, before changing his mind later, which is what Crofts believes. Again, the evidence is not conclusive either way, but as I argue in this and the following chapter, I am convinced that Lincoln never did resign himself to evacuation, even briefly, but instead searched continually for an alternative course.

69. For this and the following paragraph, I have followed Campbell's retrospective account, written in 1873, which is corroborated in numerous details by contemporary sources. See John Campbell, "Papers," 30–33. See also J. A. Campbell to Seward, March 15 and 16, in Bancroft, *Seward*, 2:115 n. 116; and "Copy 'A.' Notes of Justice J. A. Campbell. No. 1," March 15, in Samuel Crawford, *Genesis*, 330. Campbell's letter to Davis is not extant, but see J. A. Campbell to Jefferson Davis, April 3, in Crist and Dix, eds., *Papers of Jefferson Davis*, 7:88.

70. Samuel W. Crawford interview with John Forsyth, 1870, in Samuel Crawford, *Genesis*, 333 n; M. J. Crawford to Robert Toombs, April 1, Toombs Papers, University of South Carolina, in Bancroft, *Seward*, 2:119; M. J. Crawford et al. to Robert Toombs, March 8, Toombs Papers, University of South Carolina, cited in Nicolay and Hay, *Abraham Lincoln*, 3:399; John Forsyth to Robert Toombs, March 14, Toombs Papers, University of South Carolina, in Nicolay and Hay, *Abra-*

ham Lincoln 3:404; M. J. Crawford et al. to Robert Toombs, March 26, Toombs Papers, University of South Carolina, in Nevins, *War for the Union*, 1:49–51.

71. *New York Herald*, March 1, quoted in Philip Foner, *Business and Slavery*, 280. See also *New York Post*, March 13, and *New York Times*, March 22, 29, and 30, all quoted in ibid., 281.

72. Philip Foner, *Business and Slavery*, 275–83; Stampp, *And the War Came*, 231–35.

73. Winfield Scott, "Views," October 31, printed in [Buchanan], *Mr. Buchanan's Administration*, 287–90; *CG*, March 2, pp. 1422–23. Buchanan judged that once the Charleston customs officer resigned and the Senate neglected to confirm his replacement, he was powerless to collect the duties in Charleston. See [Buchanan], *Mr. Buchanan's Administration*, 159. On John A. Dix's frustration at not being able to control the Southern customs officers, see Chapter 6.

74. Inaugural address, March 4, Lincoln to Salmon P. Chase, March 18, Lincoln to Gideon Welles, March 18, and Lincoln to Edward Bates, March 18, in *CWL*, 4:266, 292, 293, 290.

75. On Seward's support for the offshore tariff collection, see Seward to Lincoln, March 15, Gilmer to Seward, March 9, and Seward to Lincoln, January 27, AL.

76. The Summers quotation is in George W. Summers to J. C. Welling, March 19, in *The Nation* 29 (December 4, 1879), 384. On Seward and Campbell, see John Campbell, "Papers," 33–34; Campbell, "Copy 'B.' Notes of Justice J. A. Campbell. No. 2," March 21, and Campbell, "Copy 'C.' Notes of Justice J. A. Campbell. No. 3," March 22, both in Samuel Crawford, *Genesis*, 331; and A. B. Roman to Robert Toombs, March 24, and M. J. Crawford et al. to Robert Toombs, March 26, Toombs Papers, University of South Carolina, cited in Bancroft, *Seward*, 2:117. On Lincoln's sloppy work habits, see Seward to home, March 16, in Seward, *Seward at Washington*, 2:530; and Adams Diary, March 10, 12, 28, 31. Seward's complaints about Lincoln's lack of system were legitimate. One of the president's personal secretaries later recalled that Lincoln "was extremely unmethodical; it was a four-years struggle on Nicolays part and mine to get him to adopt some systematic rules. He would break through every Regulation as fast as it was made. Anything that kept the people themselves away from him he disapproved—although they nearly annoyed the life out of him by unreasonable complaints & requests" (John Hay to William H. Herndon, September 5, 1866, in Wilson and Davis, eds., *Herndon's Informants*, 331). On the abortive meeting, see Baron Edouard de Stoeckl to the Russian Foreign Office, April 9, in Woldman, *Lincoln and the Russians*, 50. See also Sowle, "Conciliatory Republicans," 468–76.

77. According to the written orders, Lincoln delegated selection of the envoy to Cameron, who delegated it to Scott. However, the disparity between Scott's and Fox's positions on Sumter made it unlikely that Fox would have been the general's choice, suggesting that Lincoln probably specified verbally whom he wished to

undertake the assignment. This interpretation is corroborated by Fox's proud remark to his wife that "our Uncle Abe Lincoln has taken a high esteem for me." See Simon Cameron to Winfield Scott, March 19, in *OR*, 208–9; and Winfield Scott to G. V. Fox, March 19, and G. V. Fox to Virginia Fox, March 19, in Thompson and Wainwright, eds., *Confidential Correspondence of Fox*, 10.

Of more potential significance is Fox's description of his mission in the same letter. Lincoln, he wrote, "wishes me to take dispatches to Major Anderson at Fort Sumpter with regard to its final evacuation and to obtain a clear statement of his condition which his letters, probably guarded, do not fully exhibit" (G. V. Fox to Virginia Fox, March 19, in Thompson and Wainwright, eds., *Confidential Correspondence of Fox*, 10). As neither Cameron's written order nor Scott's letter to Fox mention any dispatches about the fort's evacuation, it is impossible to say what Fox may have been referring to. Samuel W. Crawford (*Genesis*, 370) writes that Fox carried three letters to Anderson, which Fox showed Crawford "in confidence." He details the letters: a laudatory one from Scott, promising a recommendation for promotion; the brief order from Cameron to Scott generating the mission; and a third from Governor Pickens permitting Fox to enter the fort. The most likely explanation for Fox's comment is that, being aware of the widespread reports of the fort's imminent evacuation, his initial assumption was that the letters he carried to Anderson concerned that weighty topic. There is no evidence to suggest that in ordering the mission Lincoln was motivated by anything other than a desire to gain more direct information about conditions at Sumter. Compare this interpretation to Detzer, *Allegiance*, 339 n. 322.

78. The precise origin of Hurlbut's mission is not certain, as none of the contemporary accounts address it. Hurlbut recalled later, "Mr. Lincoln told me one day that Mr. Seward insisted that there was a strong Union party in the South—even in South Carolina. I told him that my advices . . . were, that the secession element had absolute controll—that there were no Union people there. He said he would like very much to know. I told him he could know—that I would go down there and find out for him." As Lamon told it, however, Hurlbut attached himself informally to Lamon's mission in order to visit with family and friends, and Lincoln knew nothing about his going along until afterward when Lamon told him. See John G. Nicolay interview with Stephen A. Hurlbut, May 4, 1876, in Burlingame, ed., *Oral History*, 62–64; and Lamon, *Recollections*, 70, 79. Lamon's story can be dismissed not only because of the self-serving inaccuracies that litter his entire account of the episode and his general untrustworthiness (see Chapter 9), but also because Hurlbut's contemporary written report to Lincoln describes his journey as having begun "in compliance with the suggestion made on Thursday last" (i.e., March 21). Whether Hurlbut's story is correct cannot be verified, but it does fit with what is known of both Seward's and Lincoln's mind-sets at the time.

79. Memorandum, March 18[?], in *CWL*, 4:288–90.

80. Russell, *My Diary North and South*, 2–4, 9. An excellent review of Russell's visit to New York is in Maury Klein, *Days of Defiance*, 3–14.

81. Russell, *My Diary North and South*, 7–28.

82. Ibid., 10, 13.

83. Ibid., 13–14. For similar comments, see p. 20.

84. Ibid., 14, 19–22.

85. Osborn, "Union or Slavery," 239–51, 255; Russell, *My Diary North and South*, 13.

86. As it did throughout the crisis, the correspondence of Stephen Douglas represented a good cross-section of the geographical and political views of Northern Democrats, and the following discussion relies heavily on March 5–22, passim, SD. To underscore the geographic diversity of the writers, I have included their places of origin in the citations below.

87. A. G. Dickerhoff, Quincy, Ill., March 15, and Joshua T. Owen, Philadelphia, March 8, to Douglas, SD.

88. See, for example, J. C. Greene, Brooklyn, March 7; Benjamin Rush, Mt. Airy, Ill., March 7; Richard Vaux, Philadelphia, March 8; S. J. Anderson, New York, March 8; William Shomo, Hollidaysburg, Pa., March 8; Joseph Knox, Chicago, March 10; Nahum Capen, Boston, March 13; and S. Churchill, New York, March 16, to Douglas, SD.

89. S. J. Anderson, New York, March 8; Daniel Gardner, New York, March 9; George Whitaker, Lewistown, Ill., March 9; "A Friend," Boston, March 11; John A. Snyder, Philadelphia, March 15; and B. Watson, Lawrence, Mass., March 19, to Douglas, SD.

90. Munn Diary, March 24. See also A. G. Dickerhoff, Quincy, Ill., March 15; [F. F. H.?] Miller, Columbus, Ohio, March 14; and Joseph Weinmann, Carver, Minnesota, March 18, to Douglas, SD.

91. Howe, *Political Culture*, 23–24.

92. C. F. Noetling, March 12, John Estabrook, March 6, and William Butler, March 14, to Trumbull, LT. See also William Thomas, March 12, William Butler, March 20, and Daniel Baldwin, March 15, to Trumbull, LT.

93. C. F. Noetling, March 12, and William Butler, March 20, to Trumbull, LT.

94. Grant Goodrich to Trumbull, March 18, LT.

95. William Butler, March 12, and Daniel Baldwin, March 15, to Trumbull, LT. See also John Estabrook to Trumbull, March 6, LT.

96. Charles H. Fox, March 13, and William Fahnestock, March 26, to Douglas, SD.

97. Jerome B. Lenney to Trumbull, March 15, LT. The Lincoln Papers, Chase Papers, and Washburne Papers, all at LC, follow a similar pattern for this period. The Seward Papers, UR, contain more expressions of explicit acceptance of the evacuation but otherwise demonstrate the same tendency.

98. Johannsen, *Douglas*, 848–51; Nichols, *Disruption*, 499–500.

99. Trumbull, December 27, January 3 and 7, and Republican Senators, January 7, to Lincoln, AL. See also Trumbull to William Butler, January 12, Butler Papers, CHS; N. B. Judd to Lincoln, January 11, AL; Krug, *Lyman Trumbull*, 166–68; and Willard King, *Lincoln's Manager*, 170–72.

100. Jesse W. Fell to Lincoln, January 2, AL; Willard King, *Lincoln's Manager*, 172; Krug, *Lyman Trumbull*, 168–69; Baringer, *House Dividing*, 175–86; Carman and Luthin, *Lincoln and the Patronage*, 29–32.

101. See, for example, Joseph Medill to N. B. Judd, January 20, Butler Papers, CHS.

102. February 27 dispatch in *New York Herald*, February 28. For Lincoln's concern with giving too much to his home state in general, see Lincoln to W. W. Dananhower, March 25, GLC. The demands made by his state were indeed substantial; on that same day, an Illinoisan wrote to a friend, "I dont go to the White House, Too many hungry Illinoisans there" (D. L. Phillips to O. M. Hatch, March 25, Hatch Papers, ALPL).

103. Trumbull to Jesse K. Dubois, March 21, Dubois Papers, ALPL; William Jayne to William Butler, March 21, Butler Papers, CHS. See also William Jayne to Pascal T. Enos, March 2, Jayne Papers, ALPL; William Butler to Trumbull, March 15, Trumbull Correspondence, ALPL; Trumbull to O. M. Hatch, March 24, Hatch Papers, ALPL; and Krug, *Lyman Trumbull*, 169–70.

104. That Trumbull's brother and brother-in-law both received prestigious offices underscores that his pique arose from the party's factional war rather than any personal patronage resentments. For Lincoln's attitude, see Memorandum: Appointment of William Henshaw, [April 3], in *CWL*, 4:321.

105. Munn Diary, March 24.

Chapter Nine

1. G. V. Fox, "Official Report," February 24, 1865, in *Chicago Tribune*, September 14, 1865, in Nicolay and Hay, *Abraham Lincoln*, 3:389; Simon Cameron to Robert Anderson, April 4, and Robert Anderson to L. Thomas, March 22, in *OR*, 235, 211; Samuel Crawford, *Genesis*, 369–72; Detzer, *Allegiance*, 228.

2. Stephen A. Hurlbut to Lincoln, March 27, AL; John G. Nicolay interview with Stephen A. Hurlbut, May 4, 1876, in Burlingame, ed., *Oral History*, 62–64; Lamon, *Recollections*, 74–79.

3. Three days earlier, Lincoln had written, "The Senate is about adjourning, and hence my time is next to a matter of life and death with me" (Lincoln to W. W. Dananhower, March 25, GLC).

4. M. J. Crawford et al. to Robert Toombs, March 22, Toombs Papers, University of South Carolina, cited in Nevins, *War for the Union*, 1:55 n; *CG*, March 28, p. 1519.

5. William P. Fessenden to Home, March 17, in Fessenden, *Life and Public Services*, 127.

6. Gideon Welles later asserted that the deciding factor for Lincoln was an angry interview with Frank Blair Sr. on the night of the twenty-ninth, in which Blair "denounced" Lincoln's policy of inaction as "the offspring of intrigue." Welles writes, "His earnestness and indignation aroused and electrified the President; and when, in his zeal, Blair warned the President that the abandonment of Sumter would be justly considered by the people, by the world, by history, as treason to the country, he touched a chord that responded to his invocation" (Beale and Brownsword, eds., *Diary of Gideon Welles*, 1:13–14). Welles later backed away from that claim and attributed Lincoln's decision to Blair's son, Montgomery. In both interpretations, he seems to have been influenced by Montgomery Blair, his source for this meeting, who, Welles noted in 1865, "in talking over the events of that period, gives me always some new facts, or revises old ones." It is interesting, though, that Blair himself does not seem to have credited his father's words with determining Lincoln's course; why Welles decided that they had is uncertain. See the February 22, 1865, entry in ibid., 2:248.

In addition to telling the story to Welles, Blair also wrote of it some thirty years after the fact to Samuel W. Crawford, adding the significant detail that his father had told Lincoln "that such a course would not be endorsed by the people, that it would destroy the formation of the Republican party, and that impeachment would surely follow" (Samuel Crawford, *Genesis*, 364). See also W. E. Smith, *Francis Preston Blair Family*, 2:7–10. If the elder Blair did make such an argument on the night of March 29, not only would his warnings have fit perfectly with the message Lincoln had already drawn from Trumbull's Senate resolution, but in making them Blair was probably also influenced by the resolution's presentation to the Senate the previous day.

7. G. V. Fox to Lincoln, March 28, cited in Nicolay and Hay, *Abraham Lincoln*, 3:433. For Fox's requisition, see the two enclosures in Lincoln to Simon Cameron, March 29, in both *OR*, 227, and *CWL*, 4:301. That Lincoln authorized these requisitions *before* the cabinet meeting that evening is demonstrated in Hoogenboom, "Gustavus Fox," 387.

8. Salmon P. Chase to Lincoln, n.d., and Gideon Welles to Lincoln, March 20, AL. Bates's response regarding the constitutionality of the endeavor is not in the Lincoln Papers. Lincoln's decision on offshore collection may have been held up by a delay in the attorney general's response, or perhaps by an unfavorable opinion, but that is purely speculative.

9. E. D. Keyes Diary, March 29, in Keyes, *Fifty Years' Observation*, 377–78. The dating of Scott's memorandum is problematic, which is unfortunate given its apparent importance. In *OR* (pp. 200–201) it is included among the documents supporting Simon Cameron's March 15 opinion on Sumter. Some historians have

accepted that date. See Samuel Crawford, *Genesis*, 365–66; Kenneth Williams, *Lincoln Finds a General*, 1:387–88; Hoogenboom, "Gustavus Fox," 387; and Potter, *Impending Crisis*, 574. Most, however, have followed Nicolay and Hay in dating it March 28 and in placing great significance on it as a determinant in Lincoln's decision. In addition to Nicolay and Hay, *Abraham Lincoln*, 3:394, see also Potter, *Lincoln and His Party*, 360–61; Stampp, *And the War Came*, 277; Sowle, "Conciliatory Republicans," 484–85; Crofts, *Reluctant Confederates*, 296–97; Maury Klein, *Days of Defiance*, 354; and Detzer, *Allegiance*, 224. Finally, Allan Nevins (*The War for the Union*, 1:55 n) splits the difference, concluding a bit oddly that Lincoln had received Scott's memorandum on the fifteenth but informed a shocked cabinet of it on the twenty-eighth.

There is good reason for following Nicolay and Hay in assigning the later date. Not only did two of Lincoln's cabinet members, Montgomery Blair and Gideon Welles, later discuss Scott's advice regarding Pickens in that context, but two contemporary accounts independently confirm both the March 28 date and Lincoln's response. See Welles, *Lincoln and Seward*, 57–60; Montgomery Blair to Gideon Welles, May 17, 1873, in Welles, *Lincoln and Seward*, 64–65; Montgomery Blair to Samuel W. Crawford, May 6, 1882, in Samuel Crawford, *Genesis*, 365; E. D. Keyes Diary, March 29, in Keyes, *Fifty Years' Observation*, 377–78; and M. C. Meigs Diary, March 31, in Meigs, "General M. C. Meigs," 300.

10. Winfield Scott memorandum, n.d., in *OR*, 200–201. On Seward's private remark, see Adams Diary, March 12.

11. M. C. Meigs Diary, March 31, in Meigs, "General M. C. Meigs," 300.

12. E. D. Keyes Diary, March 29, in Keyes, *Fifty Years' Observation*, 377–78.

13. Russell, *My Diary North and South*, 42–44.

14. There are no contemporary accounts of that meeting. The two witnesses who provided later descriptions, Gideon Welles and Montgomery Blair, do agree on the details, but that may be because Blair, who is the hero of his own story, influenced the recollection of Welles (see note 6, above). Note the change between the opening essay in Welles's diary and his 1874 account, which corresponds closely with the contemporary letter of Blair's that he includes in full (all cited below). However, that Blair was anxious to be recognized later as the only member of Lincoln's cabinet who consistently supported holding Sumter does not mean that what he said was not true. His role in his version of events does fit with the views he was known to hold at the time, and his 1882 description of that cabinet meeting is remarkably similar to the account he wrote for Welles nine years earlier. Of course, that may just reflect the frequency with which he told the story, the zeal with which he believed it, or both. See Beale and Brownsword, eds., *Diary of Gideon Welles*, 1:13–14; Welles, *Lincoln and Seward*, 57–60; Montgomery Blair to Gideon Welles, May 17, 1873, in Welles, *Lincoln and Seward*, 64–65; and Montgomery Blair to Samuel W. Crawford, May 6, 1882, in Samuel Crawford, *Genesis*, 365–66. On Blair's views at the time, in addition to his March 15 and March 29

cabinet opinions, see Blair to G. V. Fox, January 31, in Thompson and Wainwright, eds., *Confidential Correspondence of Fox*, 4–5.

15. M. C. Meigs Diary, March 31, in Meigs, "General M. C. Meigs," 300.

16. Montgomery Blair to Samuel W. Crawford, May 6, 1882, in Samuel Crawford, *Genesis*, 365–66; Beale, ed., *Diary of Eward Bates*, March 29 entry, 180.

17. Historians have generally emphasized Bates's vacillation on Sumter, but his opinion was not as useless as it has been made out to be. His insistence that a determination on Sumter could no longer be deferred must be read in the context of the administration's long indecisiveness on that issue. His stance makes it difficult for the historian to tabulate the cabinet vote neatly, but it is a stronger position than Lincoln had yet taken.

18. The opinions of Bates, Seward, Chase, Welles, and Smith, most of which are undated but all of which are noted in Lincoln's hand as having been written "in cabinet," are filed under [March 29] in AL. Blair's opinion, which is not so endorsed, is filed under [March]. Cameron was not present.

19. Gideon Welles memorandum, [March 29], AL. On the discussion of these ideas at the March 15 meeting, see Chapter 8.

20. Salmon P. Chase memorandum, [March 29], AL.

21. Lincoln to Simon Cameron, March 29, in *OR*, 226–27.

22. March 30 dispatch in *New York Herald*, March 31; Samuel Ward to S. L. M. Barlow, March 31, Barlow Papers, Huntington Library, cited in Nevins, *War for the Union*, 1:58.

23. J. G. Nicolay to Therena Bates, March 24, in Burlingame, ed., *With Lincoln in the White House*, 31.

24. Bancroft, *Seward*, 2:124 (quoted); Samuel Crawford, *Genesis*, 362; Crofts, *Reluctant Confederates*, 271, 274, 297.

25. M. C. Meigs Diary, March 29, in Meigs, "General M. C. Meigs," 299–300; Seward to Lincoln, March 15, AL. For Meigs's clash with John B. Floyd, Buchanan's secretary of war, see Nichols, *Disruption*, 329–30.

26. M. C. Meigs Diary, March 31–April 4, in Meigs, "General M. C. Meigs," 300–301; Keyes, *Fifty Years' Observation*, 380–91. See Lincoln's orders to Andrew H. Foote, Samuel Mercer, David D. Porter, and E. D. Keyes in *CWL*, 4:313–15, 320. His April 2 requisition of the secret service funds is in *CWL*, 4:320. According to Welles, Lincoln admitted signing these orders for Seward without reading them. See Beale and Brownsword, eds., *Diary of Gideon Welles*, 1:17–18.

27. Beale and Brownsword, eds., *Diary of Gideon Welles*, 1:23–25; Samuel Crawford, *Genesis*, 407–16.

28. Crofts, *Reluctant Confederates*, 262–69, 276–83.

29. William H. Seward memorandum, April 1, AL.

30. Ibid. Seward's failure to develop his ideas more explicitly is odd; perhaps he intended to (or, most likely, did) elaborate on them in person. With regard to the forts, Seward meant that because of the attention being given to Sumter by all

parties in all parts of the Union, it had taken on a symbolic importance completely out of proportion to its military value. Pickens, having received far less attention, was correspondingly less politicized. As for provoking a foreign war, Allan Nevins (*War for the Union*, 1:62–63) has pointed out that the idea was neither as simplistic nor as ham-fisted as it first seems. What Seward had in mind was not merely relying on the seceders' latent patriotism to bring them back but picking a fight with Spain in particular in order to win Cuba. Southern expansionists had long hungered after that island's sugar wealth and slaves, and Seward believed that the specter of a free Cuba would bring the Confederacy back. If that was his thinking, it is difficult to see how he could have expected luring the South back with the prospect of Cuba to appeal to the president; in his February 1 letter, Lincoln had specifically noted that his opposition to permitting the spread of slavery was grounded in part in a determination to prevent the establishment of a Caribbean slave empire. See Lincoln to Seward, February 1, in *CWL*, 4:183, and above, Chapter 7. See also Lincoln to Elihu B. Washburne, December 13, Thurlow Weed, December 17, and John D. Defrees, December 18, in *CWL*, 4:151, 154, 155.

31. For evidence of Seward's continued irritation with Lincoln's leadership style, see Adams Diary, March 28 and 31.

32. Sowle, "Reappraisal," 234–39.

33. *CG*, March 14 and March 28, pp. 1452, 1519–20; Johannsen, *Douglas*, 848–51.

34. *CG*, March 25, p. 1503; Johannsen, *Douglas*, 850.

35. Milton, *Eve of Conflict*, 539–41; Johannsen, *Douglas*, 852–53.

36. Some modern historians, at least, agree with that assessment; see Holt, *Political Crisis*. See also Chapter 1.

37. Apparently Lincoln handled the matter in person, however, as it appears that this reply was never sent. See Lincoln to Seward, April 1, in *CWL*, 4:316–17.

38. J. G. Nicolay to Therena Bates, March 31, April 2, and April 7, in Burlingame, ed., *With Lincoln in the White House*, 32–33.

39. Washington correspondent to the *Cincinnati Gazette*, April 8, in *Illinois State Journal*, April 11.

40. Winfield Scott to Lincoln, April 1, and M. C. Meigs to Seward, April 1, AL.

41. Crofts, *Reluctant Confederates*, 301.

42. John B. Baldwin testimony, February 10, 1866, in *Report of the Joint Committee on Reconstruction*, pt. 2, pp. 102–3. (This testimony has been reprinted in Baldwin, *Interview*.) See also Magruder, "Piece of Secret History," 438–40.

43. Baldwin testimony, February 10, 1866, in *Report of the Joint Committee on Reconstruction*, 103–4.

44. John Minor Botts testimony, February 15, 1866, in *Report of the Joint Committee on Reconstruction*, 114–23; John F. Lewis testimony, February 7, 1866, ibid., reprinted in Botts, *Great Rebellion*, 197 n; George Plumer Smith to John Hay,

January 9, 1863, AL; John G. Nicolay interview with George Plumer Smith, March 5, 1878, J. G. Nicolay Papers, LC, quoted in Fehrenbacher and Fehrenbacher, eds., *Recollected Words*, 410; Garret Davis to the Senate, February 17, 1868, in *CG*, 40th Cong., 2nd sess., 1207. None of these accounts is contemporary, but Lincoln's own later confirmation that he made such an offer suggests that they are reliable. See October 22, 1861, entry in Burlingame and Ettlinger, eds., *Inside Lincoln's White House*, 28; and John Hay to George Plumer Smith, January 10, 1863, AL.

45. See Botts, *Great Rebellion*, 195–202, and Baldwin, *Interview*, 24–27.

46. Baldwin testimony, February 10, 1866, in *Report of the Joint Committee on Reconstruction*, 105–6.

47. Crofts, *Reluctant Confederates*, 304–6.

48. Ramsdell, "Lincoln and Fort Sumter," 275–76; Lincoln to Andrew Curtin, April 8, in *CWL*, 4:324; Miers, ed., *Lincoln Day by Day*, 3:33.

49. For examples of a "military necessity" view, see J. Blanchard, March 28, William H. Aspinwall, March 31, O. B. Pierce, March 31, H. B. Small, April 2, and J. H. Jordan, April 5, to Lincoln, AL. See also Sowle, "Conciliatory Republicans," 478–80. For examples of a conciliatory view, see John H. Strider to Joseph Gillespie, March 16, Gillespie Papers, CHS; Rufus King to Lincoln, March 19, AL; David Davis to W. H. Lamon, March 30, photostat in Davis Papers, CHS; and William L. Hodge to J. A. Stevens, April 5, Stevens Papers, NYHS.

50. Dexter A. Hawkins [vice president, Young Men's Republican Union, New York] to John Sherman, March 23, Sherman Papers, LC; H. Abram to S. P. Chase, March 25, Chase Papers, LC, quoted in Potter, *Lincoln and His Party*, 359–60; William Jaync to Trumbull, April 4, LT; Peter Bryant to [Cullen Bryant], April 7, Bryant Family Papers, NYPL; W. B. Plato to Trumbull, March 29, LT. See also J. J. Walpole, March 25, and M. D. Wellman, April 10, to John Sherman, Sherman Papers, LC; A. C. Woolfoek to O. M. Hatch, March 28, Hatch Papers, ALPL; Timothy C. Day to John Bigelow, April 1, Bigelow Papers, NYPL; Stampp, *And the War Came*, 266–72; and Sowle, "Conciliatory Republicans," 476–78.

51. *Cincinnati Enquirer*, April 2, quoted in Hubbell, "Politics as Usual," 29; *Stark County Democrat*, April 3, quoted in Cardinal, "Ohio Democracy," 33. See also Sowle, "Conciliatory Republicans," 481–82, and Osborn, "Union or Slavery," 236–39.

52. John W. B. Autram to Lincoln, April 2, AL. See also J. H. Jordan, April 4, and Carl Schurz, April 5, to Lincoln, AL; R. B. Hayes to S. Birchard, March 17, in Charles Richard Williams, ed., *Diary and Letters of Hayes*, 6; Stampp, *And the War Came*, 270; and Sowle, "Conciliatory Republicans," 482–83.

53. Carl Schurz to Lincoln, April 5, AL; Eleanor F. Strong to Andrew Johnson, March 26, in Graf and Haskins, eds., *Papers of Andrew Johnson*, 4:434; *Detroit Free Press*, March 20, and *New York Morning Express*, April 5, both quoted in

Stampp, *And the War Came*, 268; *New York Times*, April 3. See also Stampp, *And the War Came*, 266–70; Osborn, "Union or Slavery," 232–33; and Sowle, "Conciliatory Republicans," 476–77.

54. Robert Anderson to L. Thomas, April 1, in *OR*, 230.

55. Ibid.; Simon Cameron to Robert Anderson, April 4, in *OR*, 235. Lamon also told Governor Pickens that Sumter was to be evacuated. See Francis Pickens to P. G. T. Beauregard, March 25, P. G. T. Beauregard to L. P. Walker, March 26, and P. G. T. Beauregard to Robert Anderson, March 26, in ibid., 281, 282, 222. See also John Campbell, "Papers," 34. Why Lamon spread such news around Charleston is unclear. It is possible that he got that impression from Lincoln, but more likely is that, like most other people in Washington, Lamon simply assumed it was true. Either way, his imparting the information was plainly a function of his self-importance and his tendency to embellish the truth; even if Lincoln had left the impression that Sumter was to be abandoned, he certainly did not direct Lamon to tell Major Anderson, Governor Pickens, or anyone else.

The real question is why, given Lamon's unstable personality, Lincoln sent him to begin with. Perhaps this was another consequence of Lincoln's relative isolation in Washington; there were few people available whom he trusted. There is always the possibility, of course, that Lamon was acting under Seward's instructions, or at least influence—suggestive in this regard is that one of his only contemporary writings regarding his mission is a letter he wrote to the secretary of state from Charleston. See Ward H. Lamon to Seward, March 25, in Bancroft, *Seward*, 2:107 n. One begins to wonder, though, whether Seward could possibly have been behind half of what he seems to have been, or whether it simply becomes an involuntary reflex on the part of the historian to attribute to his influence anything that fit with his plans.

56. It was around that time that Lincoln received confirmation of the demoralizing effect of that long wait by reading letters sent from the fort by Captain Abner Doubleday to his wife. See Mary Doubleday to Lincoln, n.d., and Abner Doubleday to Mary Doubleday, March 27, 29, and April 2, AL. On conditions in the fort in the wake of Lamon's visit, see Detzer, *Allegiance*, 223–24, 232–39, 242–44.

57. Simon Cameron to Robert Anderson, April 4, Simon Cameron to G. V. Fox, April 4, and Gideon Welles to Samuel Mercer, April 5, in *OR*, 235–36, 240; G. V. Fox to Daniel Jackson, April 12, and G. V. Fox to Francis Pickens, April 12, in Thompson and Wainwright, eds., *Confidential Correspondence of Fox*, 18.

58. Lincoln, "Message to Congress," July 4, 1861, in *CWL*, 4:424–25.

59. Lincoln to Seward, April 1, in *CWL*, 4:316.

60. Capt. Israel Vogdes, who commanded the reinforcements, finally received Scott's March 12 orders on the night of Sunday, the thirty-first—an Easter miracle, he must have thought. However, the next day when he brought them to Capt. Henry A. Adams, who commanded the fleet, Adams decided that General Scott's orders did not supersede those of Secretary of the Navy Isaac Toucey, who had

given him strict instructions in February to avoid provoking a collision. He refused to allow Vogdes to reinforce the fort. Vogdes immediately sent a messenger to Washington. The messenger arrived on the sixth, at which point Welles at once dispatched a second messenger with new orders for Adams, but by that time the last chance that Pickens might be held in lieu of Sumter had passed. See Winfield Scott to Lincoln, April 6, I. Vogdes to H. A. Adams, April 1, and H. A. Adams to I. Vogdes, April 1, AL; Beale and Brownsword, eds., *Diary of Gideon Welles*, 1:29–30; and Nevins, *War for the Union*, 1:65 n.

61. Simon Cameron to Robert S. Chew, April 6, in *CWL*, 4:323–24; Simon Cameron to Theodore Talbot, April 6, in *OR*, 245.

62. See John Campbell, "Papers," 34–35.

63. Robert Anderson to L. Thomas, April 3, in *OR*, 236–38.

64. As I discuss in the Introduction, whether to interpret Lincoln's course regarding Fort Sumter as peaceable or manipulative has long bedeviled scholars. Specific debate has focused on when Lincoln made his final decision to relieve Sumter, but the larger question is how hard Lincoln tried to avoid war. As I discuss above, Lincoln claimed in his July 4 address to Congress that he deliberately held back the Sumter expedition until it had been determined that Pickens could not be reinforced in time. See Lincoln, "Message to Congress," July 4, 1861, in *CWL*, 4:424–25. Skeptics have pointed out that it was on April 4, two days *before* receiving definite word on Pickens, that the president ordered Fox to execute the relief mission and sent word to Anderson that it was coming. Charles Ramsdell and others have followed Confederates such as Jefferson Davis in accusing Lincoln of deliberately provoking war, while more moderate critics Kenneth Stampp and Richard Current argue that Lincoln recognized that war was inevitable and contrived to force the Confederates into beginning it. The harsher criticism can be found in Jefferson Davis, *Rise and Fall*, 1:290–95; Tilley, *Lincoln Takes Command*; Ramsdell, "Lincoln and Fort Sumter," 278–88; and Barbee, "Line of Blood." More moderate are Stampp, "Lincoln and the Strategy of Defense," 311–15; and Current, *Lincoln Nobody Knows*, 121–30, and *Lincoln and the First Shot*, 182–208. Lincoln's defenders argue that Fox's orders could have been rescinded at any time before the ships left New York harbor; the irrevocable act of informing Governor Pickens did not come until April 6, *after* Lincoln learned that Pickens could not be relieved in time. See Randall, *Lincoln the Liberal Statesman*, 94–117, and Potter, *Lincoln and His Party*, 358–75, xxxix–lii. The most balanced account is Stampp, "Lincoln and the Secession Crisis," 177–88.

As I argue above, Lincoln had never really embraced the idea that exchanging Sumter for Pickens would accomplish anything of value, but he was willing to maintain the option as long as possible. Thus final word about the reinforcements at Pickens, by taking away the last alternative means of maintaining federal authority in the seceded states, merely confirmed the decision he had already made. As to the larger question of whether Lincoln acted belligerently or peacefully, Lincoln acted as peacefully as he was able, given his ideological restrictions: he would not sacrifice the Union, which is what he thought losing Sumter would do and was convinced losing Sumter *and* Pickens would do, in order to avoid war. See the Introduction and further discussion in this chapter.

65. Lincoln, "Message to Congress in Special Session," July 4, 1861, in *CWL*, 4:424.

66. For the effect of Lincoln's announcement to Governor Pickens on the outbreak of hostilities at Fort Sumter, see the exchange of letters and telegrams among F. W. Pickens, P. G. T. Beauregard, L. P. Walker, and M. J. Crawford, April 8 to April 10, in *OR*, 289–91, 292–93, 297; P. G. T. Beauregard to L. P. Walker, April 11, with enclosures, in ibid., 300–302; G. V. Fox to Simon Cameron, April 19; Robert Anderson to Simon Cameron, April 18; and Robert Anderson to Lorenzo Thomas, April 19, with enclosures numbered one through five, in ibid., 11–14; and P. G. T. Beauregard to S. Cooper, April 27; James Chesnut, Stephen D. Lee, and A. R. Chisolm to D. R. Jones, April 11; and James Chesnut and Stephen D. Lee to D. R. Jones, April 12, in ibid., 30–31, 59–60.

67. Lincoln, "Reply to a Committee from the Virginia Convention," April 13, in *CWL*, 4:329–31.

68. Lincoln, "Proclamation Calling Militia and Convening Congress," April 15, in *CWL*, 4:331–32.

69. Crofts, *Reluctant Confederates*, 310–52.

70. Lincoln, "Message to Congress in Special Session," July 4, 1861, in *CWL*, 4:424.

Chapter Ten

1. Augustus B. Frey to Samuel L. Frey, April 16, Frey Family Papers, NYHS. Gus Frey would serve in the 110th New York Volunteer Infantry Regiment from 1862 to 1863. The Whangdoodle allusion is to a mock Bible passage found in William Penn Brennan's satire of a Hardshell Baptist sermon, "Where the Lion Roareth and the Wang-Doodle Mourneth," in Avery, *Harp of a Thousand Strings*.

2. *New York Herald*, April 19.

3. Ibid.; John Frey to Samuel L. Frey, April 17, Frey Family Papers, NYHS.

4. Johnson Diary, April 22, NYHS.

5. Ibid.

6. *Bangor Evening Times*, May 4, in *NES*, 2:756.

7. *New York Times*, April 5–6, 8–10; *New York Herald*, April 5–8; *GTS*, April 8–10 entries, 3:116–17; Tailer Diary, April 8, NYHS; Osborn, "Union or Slavery," 267–68; McKay, *Civil War*, 54.

8. *GTS*, April 12 entry, 3:118; Tailer Diary, April 12, NYHS; Lowenfels, ed., *Walt Whitman's Civil War*, 21; Abby H. Woolsey to Eliza W. Hoffman, April 14, in Bacon, ed., *Letters of a Family*, 1:37–38; Osborn, "Union or Slavery," 268.

9. *GTS*, April 13–20 entries, 3:119–27; Tailer Diary, April 13, 15, 17, NYPL;

Dunstan Diaries, April 13, 15, 18–20, NYPL; Lester Diary, April 15, NYHS; Turnure Diary, April 15–17, 19, NYHS; Henry Frey, April 18, and A. Hees, April 26, to John Frey, Frey Family Papers, NYHS; McKay, *Civil War*, 55–56.

10. *GTS*, April 19 entry, 3:126; Turnure Diary, April 19, NYHS; Dunstan Diaries, April 19, NYPL. Compare these accounts to Daly, *Diary of a Union Lady*, 13.

11. *GTS*, April 20 entry, 3:127; McKay, *Civil War*, 62–64 (quotations of medical student and woman on balcony on 62, 64). See also Dunstan Diaries, April 20, NYPL; Meade Diary, April 20, NYHS; and Bacon, ed., *Letters of a Family*, 1:39–44.

12. Osborn, "Union or Slavery," 287–88; Brummer, *Political History of New York*, 144–46. The call for the meeting can be found in *New York Herald*, April 18–19.

13. *GTS*, April 18, 19 entries, 3:124–26; Dunstan Diaries, April 18, 19, 22, 26, NYPL; *New York Herald*, April 17.

14. McKay, *Civil War*, 60–61.

15. On volunteer motivation and demographics early in the war, see Wiley, *Life of Billy Yank*, 17–21; McPherson, *For Cause and Comrades*, 16–26; Glatthaar, "Common Soldier," 123–25; Rorabaugh, "Who Fought for the North?" 695–701; Marvel, "Poor Man's Fight," 21–25; Vinovskis, "Have Social Historians Lost the Civil War?" 12–21; Kemp, "Community and War," 33–38, 58–70; and Teresa Thomas, "For Union, Not for Glory," 26–27.

16. McKay, *Civil War*, 65–72; Osborn, "Union or Slavery," 273; Ryan, *Women in Public*, 142.

17. Lincoln, "Message to Congress in Special Session," July 4, 1861, in *CWL*, 4:425.

18. Dunstan Diaries, April 13, NYPL; *GTS*, April 13 entry, 3:119. See also Turnure Diary, April 15, NYHS; Daly, *Diary of a Union Lady*, 11–12; *New York Evening Post*, April 10; and *New York Tribune*, April 15.

19. *GTS*, April 10 and 11 entries, 3:117. See also April 14 entry in ibid., 120.

20. *New York Times*, April 15.

21. *New York Evening Day-Book*, April 17, in *NES*, 2:718. See also *Brooklyn Eagle*, April 15, in ibid., 2:771. A variation on this theme is in *New York Herald*, April 5.

22. *New York Times*, April 16, 17; *New York Tribune*, April 16, 17; *GTS*, April 16 entry, 3:122.

23. Tailer Diary, April 17, NYPL; *GTS*, April 15, 17 entries, 3:123; Dunstan Diaries, April 17, NYPL; Turnure Diary, April 17, NYHS; Sidney Webster to Caleb Cushing, April 17 and 19, Cushing Papers, LC; *New York Times*, April 18; *New York Tribune*, April 18; *New York Journal of Commerce*, April 18.

24. Sidney Webster to Caleb Cushing, April 17 and 19, Cushing Papers, LC; Turnure Diary, April 16, NYHS. See also Sidney Webster to Franklin Pierce, April

19, Franklin Pierce Papers, LC, quoted in Wright, *Secession Movement*, 204; and Osborn, "Union or Slavery," 272–73.

25. Tailer Diary, April 12, NYHS; Tammany resolution quoted in Brummer, *Political History of New York*, 147. For remarks on the apparently unanimous support of the Democrats, see, for example, Lester Diary, April 12, NYHS; *GTS*, April 13–16 entries, 3:119–22; and G. B. Lamar to Howell Cobb, April 13, in Ulrich Phillips, ed., "Correspondence of Toombs, Stephens, and Cobb," 561. See also Osborn, "Union or Slavery," 269–77, 280–83, 288; and Wright, *Secession Movement*, 202–4.

26. Spinola's speech in *Brooklyn Times*, April 19, quoted in Osborn, "Union or Slavery," 282 (see also 271–72); Daly, *Diary of a Union Lady*, 12.

27. Amos A. Lawrence to John J. Crittenden, April 16, Crittenden Papers, LC; *Boston Evening Transcript*, April 27, quoted in Stampp, *And the War Came*, 288.

28. Caleb Cushing to John Andrew (draft), April 25, and William L. Williams to Caleb Cushing, April 24, Cushing Papers, LC. See also Anonymous to Caleb Cushing, April 24, ibid.

29. John Andrew to Caleb Cushing, April 27, Cushing Papers, LC; Schouler, *History of Massachusetts*, 1:48–50; O'Connor, *Civil War Boston*, 56–59; McGraw, "Minutemen of '61," 101–15.

30. Schouler, *History of Massachusetts*, 50–55; Ware, *Political Opinion*, 67–71; Everett Diary, April 19 (Everett did find flags being rented out at a dollar a day, but he refused to pay it); O'Connor, *Civil War Boston*, 57.

31. *JANY*, 1025–27; *JSNY*, 600; *Albany Atlas and Argus*, April 16–17; Brummer, *Political History of New York*, 139–43.

32. Nortrup, "Richard Yates," 188–89.

33. *Illinois State Journal*, April 17, 19; *Illinois State Register*, April 18; Stephen A. Hurlbut to Lincoln, April 23, AL.

34. *Jersey City American Standard*, April 12; *Hartford Daily Times*, April 13; *Providence Daily Post*, April 13; *Portland Eastern Argus*, April 15; *Trenton Daily True American*, April 15; *Buffalo Courier*, April 16; *Wilkes-Barre Luzerne Union*, April 17; *Salem (Ind.) Washington Democrat*, April 18; *St. Clairsville (Ohio) Gazette and Citizen*, April 18; *Kenosha (Wis.) Democrat*, April 19; *Joliet (Ill.) Signal*, April 23; *Concord (N.H.) Democratic Standard*, May 4, all in *NES*, 2:706, 709, 711, 767, 716, 769, 780, 782, 784, 787, 788, 793.

35. Talmadge, "Peace Movement," 306–13.

36. Barns, "Attitude of Illinois," 53–56; James Jones, *"Black Jack,"* 77–84; Etcheson, *Emerging Midwest*, 137–39; Krug, *Lyman Trumbull*, 185–86.

37. Talmadge, "Peace Movement," 313.

38. Dusinberre, *Civil War Issues*, 117–19; Wainwright, ed., *Philadelphia Perspective*, April 15, 18, 20 entries, 385–86.

39. Barns, "Attitude of Illinois," 61–62; Nortrup, "Richard Yates," 191–94; James Jones, *"Black Jack,"* 83.

40. Mrs. Charles F. Johnson Diary, April 28, NYHS; William H. Green to John A. Logan, April 28, Logan Family Papers, LC. See also Sam DeFord to Caleb Cushing, April 18, Cushing Papers, LC; and O. H. Browning to Lincoln, April 18 and 22, AL.

41. Barns, "Attitude of Illinois," 53–63; James Jones, *"Black Jack,"* 77–84; Etcheson, *Emerging Midwest*, 137–39; Krug, *Lyman Trumbull*, 185–86.

42. For sources on Douglas's course after Sumter, see below, notes 51–52. On Logan, see James C. Robinson, April 18, and Mary Logan, May 25, to John A. Logan, Logan Family Papers, LC; John A. Logan to editor, St. Louis *Missouri Republican*, June 18, and to Mary Logan, July 4, 6, 10, 16, ibid.; Long, ed., *Personal Memoirs of U.S. Grant*, 125; and James Jones, *"Black Jack,"* 77–103. For a more elaborate discussion of both leaders, see McClintock, "Shall It Be Peace, or a Sword?" 562–66. On the abortive Confederate recruitment, see Barns, "Attitude of Illinois," 61–62; Nortrup, "Richard Yates," 191–94; and James Jones, *"Black Jack,"* 83.

43. *Illinois State Register*, April 15, 18.

44. See, for example, *Brooklyn Eagle*, April 15; *Boston Herald*, April 15; *Boston Post*, April 16; *New Hampshire Patriot and State Gazette*, April 17 and May 8; *Milwaukee Press and News*, April 18; *Grand Rapids Daily Enquirer*, April 18; *Detroit Free Press*, April 29; *Daily Chicago Times*, May 6; and *New York Journal of Commerce*, May 6, all in *NES*, 2:771, 729, 739, 778, 830, 785, 744, 753, 881, 759; *Chicago Times*, n.d., reprinted in *Illinois State Register*, April 16. See also Cardinal, "Ohio Democracy," 32–33; and Wubben, *Civil War Iowa*, 31–32.

45. Douglas's speech is printed in *Illinois State Register*, April 27, and *Illinois State Journal*, April 26. For Douglas's letter, see Douglas to Virgil Hickox, May 10, in Johannsen, ed., *Letters*, 511–13, published in *Washington, D.C., National Intelligencer*, May 17. See also Douglas to Thomas E. Courtney, April 15, and James L. Faucett, April 17, both printed in *Illinois State Register*, April 22, and reproduced in Johannsen, ed., *Letters*, 510; *Illinois State Register*, May 3; and Johannsen, *Douglas*, 862–69.

46. Johannsen, *Douglas*, 870–72.

47. Accounts of such meetings can be found in most Northern newspapers between about April 17 and April 25. Summaries of numerous local Union rallies can often be found in larger papers of regional importance. See, for example, *New York Herald*, April 17, 19; *New York Tribune*, April 16–17; *Albany Atlas and Argus*, April 16–26; and *Illinois State Register*, April 17–18.

48. *Hudson (N.Y.) Star*, April 19, clipping in Van Ness–Philip Papers, NYHS; John Van Ness Philip to William H. Philip, April 22, ibid.

49. *Hudson (N.Y.) Star*, April 19; John Van Ness Philip to William H. Philip, April 22, Van Ness–Philip Papers, NYHS.

50. *Hudson (N.Y.) Star*, April 19.

51. Ibid. Philip confirmed that the meeting was successful in gaining recruits.

See John Van Ness Philip to William H. Philip, April 19 [misdated April 18], Van Ness–Philip Papers, NYHS.

52. John Van Ness Philip to William H. Philip, April 22, Van Ness–Philip Papers, NYHS.

53. Lincoln, "Message to Congress in Special Session," July 4, 1861, in *CWL*, 4:426.

54. Lincoln, "Address at Gettysburg," November 19, 1863, in *CWL*, 7:21.

Conclusion

1. Lincoln, "First Inaugural Address—First Edition and Revisions," March 4, in *CWL*, 4:261.

2. On Lincoln and Euclid, see McCoy, " 'Old-Fashioned' Nationalism."

3. See Potter, "Why Republicans Rejected," and Stampp, "Comment."

Bibliography

Note: Items marked with an asterisk (*) were accessed online at the Library of Congress's American Memory Web site, <http://memory.loc.gov/ammem>. Items marked with a double asterisk (**) are secondary works whose primary usefulness lies in the significant amount of contemporary material, usually letters, that they reproduce.

Manuscript Collections
Illinois
    Chicago Historical Society
        William Butler Papers
        David Davis Papers
        Joseph Gillespie Papers
        John Munn Diary
        Logan Uriah Reavis Collection
    Abraham Lincoln Presidential Library, Springfield
        (formerly the Illinois State Historical Library)
        Moses G. Atwood Papers
        John Courts Bagby Papers
        Bailhache-Brayman Papers
        David Jewett Baker Papers
        Nathaniel Prentiss Banks Papers
        Orville Hickman Browning Papers
        James C. and Clinton C. Conkling Papers
        Samuel R. Curtis Journal
        Stephen A. Douglas Collection
        Jesse K. Dubois Papers
        Ozias M. Hatch Papers
        William Jayne Papers
        Norman B. Judd Papers
        Charles H. Lanphier Papers
        John A. McClernand Papers
        Lyman Trumbull Correspondence
        Wallace-Dickey Papers
        Yates Family Papers
    University of Chicago
        Stephen A. Douglas Papers

Massachusetts
    Massachusetts Historical Society, Boston
        Adams Family Papers
        John Andrew Papers
        Edward Everett Papers
        Amos A. Lawrence Papers
        Winthrop Family Papers
New York
    New-York Historical Society, New York
        Beekman Family Papers
        Frey Family Papers
        Gilder-Lehrman Collection
        Mrs. Charles F. Johnson Diary
        Andrew Lester Diary
        William Creighton Meade Diary
        Samuel Lyman Munson Diary
        John Austin Stevens Papers
        Henry A. Stimson Papers
        Edward N. Tailer Jr. Diary
        David Mitchell Turnure Diary
        Van Ness–Philip Papers
    New York Public Library, New York
        John Bigelow Papers
        Bryant Family Papers
        Bryant-Godwin Papers
        Caroline Dunstan Diaries
        Alfred H. Satterlee Diary
        Samuel J. Tilden Papers
        Fernando Wood Papers
    New York State Library, Albany
        Edwin D. Morgan Papers
    University of Rochester
        William Henry Seward Papers
        Thurlow Weed Papers
Washington, D.C.
    Library of Congress
        Robert Anderson Papers
        Nathaniel Prentiss Banks Papers
        Simon Cameron Papers
        Salmon P. Chase Papers
        John J. Crittenden Papers
        Caleb Cushing Papers

Thomas Ewing Family Papers
Hamilton Fish Papers
Giddings-Julian Papers
Horace Greeley Papers
John Alexander Logan Family Papers
*Abraham Lincoln Papers
Franklin Pierce Papers
William Cabell Rives Papers
John Sherman Papers
*"The Washington Diary of Horatio Nelson Taft"
Lyman Trumbull Papers
Elihu B. Washburne Papers
Thurlow Weed Papers

Government Documents
Illinois
  Journal of the House of Representatives of the 22nd Assembly of the State of Illinois. Springfield, 1861.
  Journal of the Senate of the 22nd Assembly of the State of Illinois. Springfield, 1861.
Massachusetts
  Documents Printed by Order of the House of Representatives of the Commonwealth of Massachusetts during the Sessions of the General Court, A.D. 1861. Boston, 1861.
  Documents Printed by Order of the Senate of the Commonwealth of Massachusetts during the Sessions of the General Court, A.D. 1861. Boston, 1861.
  Journal of the House of Representatives of the Commonwealth of Massachusetts. Boston, 1861.
  Journal of the Senate. Boston, 1861.
New York
  Documents of the Assembly, State of New York, Eighty-Fourth Session. Albany, 1861.
  Documents of the Senate, State of New York, Eighty-Fourth Session. Albany, 1861.
  Journal of the Assembly, State of New York, Eighty-Fourth Session. Albany, 1861.
  Journal of the Senate, State of New York, Eighty-Fourth Session. Albany, 1861.
United States
  Congressional Globe. 36th Cong., 2nd sess., Washington, 1861.
  Journal of the House of Representatives. 36th Cong., 2nd sess., Washington, 1861.

Journal of the Proceedings of the Special Committee of Thirty-three under the Resolution of the House of Representatives of the United States of the 4th of December, 1860. 36th Cong., 2nd sess., House Report No. 31, Washington, 1861.

Journal of the Proceedings of the Special Committee under the Resolution of the Senate of the 18th of December, 1860. 36th Cong., 2nd sess., Rep. Com. No. 288, Washington, 1861.

*Journal of the Senate. 36th Cong., 2nd sess., Washington, 1861.

Report of the Joint Committee on Reconstruction. 39th Cong., 1st sess., House Report No. 30, Washington, 1866.

United States War Department. The War of the Rebellion: A Compilation of the Official Records of the Union and Confederate Armies. 128 vols. Washington, 1880.

Newspapers (all titles refer to daily editions)

Albany Atlas and Argus
Albany Evening Journal
Boston Advertiser
Boston Courier
Boston Traveller
Chicago Tribune
Illinois State Journal
Illinois State Register
New York Evening Post
New York Herald
New York Times
New York Tribune
Springfield (Mass.) Republican

Pamphlets and Broadsides

Appleton, Nathan. Letter to the Hon. Wm. C. Rives, of Virginia, on Slavery and the Union. Boston: J. H. Eastburn's Press, 1860.

Baker, J. L. Slavery. Philadelphia: John A. Norton, 1860.

Baldwin, J. B. Interview between President Lincoln and Col. John B. Baldwin, April 4, 1861: Statements and Evidence. Staunton, Va.: "Spectator" Job Office, 1866.

Boutwell, George S. An Address upon Secession. Delivered at Charlestown, Mass., on the Eve of the 8th of January, 1861. Boston: n.p., 1861.

Bowden, J. J. A Voice for the Union; a Plea for Conciliation. A Sermon, Preached in St. Stephen's Church, Pittsfield, Thanksgiving Day, November 29, 1860. Pittsfield, Mass.: n.p., 1860.

Circular. Concord, [New Hampshire], Feb. 1, 1861, Concord, N.H.: Fogg, Hadley & Co., 1861.

Clark, Bishop T. M. The State of the Country. A Sermon Delivered in Grace Church, Providence, on Sunday Morning, November 25, 1860. Providence, R.I.: n.p., 1860.

Eddy, Zachary. Secession:—Shall It Be Peace or War? A Fast Day Sermon Delivered in the First Church, Northampton, April 4, 1861, by the Pastor, Zachary Eddy. Northampton, Mass.: n.p., 1861.

Ely, Alfred. *The Revolutionary Movement. A Letter from Hon. Alfred Ely.* N.p.: 1861.

Furness, W. H. *Our Duty as Conservatives. A Discourse Delivered in the Congregational Unitarian Church, Sunday, November 25, 1860, Occasioned by the Threatened Secession of Some of the Southern States.* Philadelphia: n.p., 1860.

Haldeman, R. J. *Territorial Distractions Ignored as Now Immaterial, and a More Radical Issue Raised: Address of the National Democratic Union Club of Harrisburg, to the Democracy of Pennsylvania.* [Harrisburg?]: Lemuel Towers, 1860.

Johnston, William. *An Address on the Aspect of National Affairs and the Right of Secession, Delivered before the Literary Club of Cincinnati, Saturday Evening, March 16, 1861, by William Johnston, of the Cincinnati Bar.* Cincinnati: n.p., 1861.

Kettell, Thomas Prentice. *Southern Wealth and Northern Profits, as Exhibited in Statistical Facts and Official Figures Showing the Necessity of Union to the Future Prosperity and Welfare of the Republic.* New York: George W. and John A. Wood, 1860.

Lawrence, Edward A. *Speech of Hon. Edward A. Lawrence, of Queens County, in the Senate of the State of New York, on Friday, March 1st, 1861.* N.p., 1861.

Raymond, Henry J. *Disunion and Slavery: A Series of Letters to Hon. W. L. Yancey, of Alabama, by Henry J. Raymond, of New York.* New York: n.p., 1861.

Sanders, George N. *George N. Sanders on the Consequences of Southern Secession.* New York: n.p., 1860.

———. *George N. Sanders to President Buchanan.* New York: n.p., 1860.

Thomas, Benjamin Franklin. *A Few Suggestions upon the Personal Liberty Law and "Secession" (so called). In a Letter to a Friend.* Boston: n.p., 1861.

Tilden, Samuel J. *The Union! Its Dangers! And How They Can Be Averted.* New York: n.p., 1860.

Treadwell, Francis C. *Secession an Absurdity: It Is Perjury, Treason & War, by Francis C. Treadwell, Counselor at Law, Lecturer upon the Constitution of the United States.* 2nd ed. New York: n.p., 1861.

Union Meeting in Carlisle, Pa. N.p., 1861.

Published Primary Sources

[Adams, Charles Francis]. "The Reign of King Cotton." *Atlantic Monthly*, April 1861, 451–65.

Adams, Charles Francis, Jr. *Charles Francis Adams, 1835–1915: An Autobiography.* Boston: Houghton Mifflin, 1916.

Adams, Henry. "The Great Secession Winter of 1860–1861." In *The Great Secession Winter of 1860–1861 and Other Essays by Henry Adams*, edited by George Hochfield. New York: Sagamore Press, 1958.

Angle, Paul M., ed. *The Complete Lincoln-Douglas Debates of 1858*. Chicago: University of Chicago Press, 1991.

Avery, Samuel Putnam. *The Harp of a Thousand Strings, or, Laughter for a Lifetime*. New York: Dick & Fitzgerald, 1858.

Bacon, Georgeanna M. W., ed. *Letters of a Family during the War for the Union, 1861–1865*. 2 vols. New Haven: Tuttle, Morehouse & Taylor, 1899.

Baker, George E., ed. *The Works of William H. Seward*. 5 vols. New York: Redfield, 1853–84.

Bancroft, Frederic, ed. *Speeches, Correspondence, and Political Papers of Carl Schurz*. 6 vols. New York: Putnam, 1913.

**Barnes, Thurlow Weed. *Memoir of Thurlow Weed*. Boston: Houghton Mifflin, 1884.

Basler, Roy P., ed. *The Collected Works of Abraham Lincoln*. 8 vols. New Brunswick, N.J.: Rutgers University Press, 1953–55.

Beale, Howard K., ed. *The Diary of Edward Bates, 1859–1866*. Washington: Government Printing Office, 1933.

Beale, Howard K., and A. W. Brownsword, eds. *Diary of Gideon Welles*. 3 vols. New York: Norton, 1960.

Belmont, August. *Letters, Speeches, and Addresses of August Belmont*. New York: De Vinne Press, 1890.

Bigelow, John, ed. *Letters and Literary Memorials of Samuel J. Tilden*. New York: Harper, 1908.

——. *Retrospections of an Active Life*. 2 vols. New York: Baker & Taylor, 1909–13.

Botts, John Minor. *The Great Rebellion: Its Secret History, Rise, Progress, and Disastrous Failure*. New York: Harper, 1866.

Boutwell, George S. *Speeches and Papers Relating to the Rebellion and the Overthrow of Slavery*. Boston: Little, Brown, 1867.

[Buchanan, James]. *Mr. Buchanan's Administration on the Eve of the Rebellion*. New York: D. Appleton, 1866.

Burlingame, Michael, ed. *An Oral History of Abraham Lincoln: John G. Nicolay's Interviews and Essays*. Carbondale: Southern Illinois University Press, 1996.

——, ed. *With Lincoln in the White House: Letters, Memoranda, and Other Writings of John G. Nicolay, 1860–1865*. Carbondale: Southern Illinois University Press, 2000.

Burlingame, Michael, and John R. Turner Ettlinger, eds. *Inside Lincoln's White House: The Complete Civil War Diary of John Hay*. Carbondale: Southern Illinois University Press, 1997.

Campbell, John A. "Papers of John A. Campbell, 1861–1865." *Southern Historical Society Papers* 4 (1917): 3–81.

Chase, Salmon P. "Diary and Correspondence of Salmon P. Chase." *American Historical Association Annual Report, 1902*. 2 vols. Washington: Government Printing Office, 1903.

Chittenden, Lucius E. *Recollections of President Lincoln and His Administration.*
New York: Harper, 1891.

Coleman, Mrs. Chapman. *Life of John J. Crittenden.* 2 vols. Philadelphia: J. B.
Lippincott, 1871.

Coleman, Evan J., ed. "Gwin and Seward.—A Secret Chapter in Ante-Bellum
History." *Overland Monthly,* 2nd ser., 18 (November 1891): 465–71.

Coulter, Kenneth E., ed. "The Irrepressible Conflict of 1861: The Letters of
Samuel Ryan Curtis." *Annals of Iowa* 24 (1942–43): 14–58.

Crawford, Martin, ed. "Politicians in Crisis: The Washington Letters of William
S. Thayer, December 1860–March 1861." *Civil War History* 27 (1981): 231–
47.

Crawford, Samuel W. *The Genesis of the Civil War: The Story of Sumter, 1860–
1861.* New York: C. L. Webster, 1887.

Crist, Lynda Lasswell, and Mary Seaton Dix, eds. *The Papers of Jefferson Davis.*
11 vols. Baton Rouge: Louisiana State University Press, 1971–.

Daly, Maria Lydig. *Diary of a Union Lady, 1861–1865.* Edited by Harold Earl
Hammond. 1962. Reprint, Lincoln: University of Nebraska Press, 2000.

Davis, Jefferson. *Rise and Fall of the Confederate Government.* 2 vols. New York:
D. Appleton, 1881.

"The Diary of a Public Man: Unpublished Passages of the Secret History of the
American Civil War." 1879. Reprinted in Frank Maloy Anderson, *The Mystery
of "A Public Man,"* 191–249. Minneapolis: University of Minnesota Press,
1948.

Dickinson, John R., ed. *Speeches, Correspondence, Etc., of the Late Daniel S.
Dickinson, of New York.* 2 vols. New York: Putnam, 1867.

Dix, Morgan, ed. *Memoirs of John Adams Dix.* 2 vols. New York: Harper, 1883.

Doubleday, Abner. *Reminiscences of Forts Sumter and Moultrie in 1860-'61.* New
York: Harper & Bros., 1876.

Fehrenbacher, Don E., and Virginia Fehrenbacher, eds. *Recollected Words of
Abraham Lincoln.* New York: Harper, 1996.

**Fessenden, Francis. *The Life and Public Services of William Pitt Fessenden.*
2 vols. New York: Houghton Mifflin, 1907.

Foner, Philip S., ed. *The Life and Writings of Frederick Douglass.* 4 vols. New
York, International, 1950–75.

Ford, Worthington Chauncey, ed. *Letters of Henry Adams, 1858–1891.* New York:
Houghton Mifflin, 1930.

Graf, Leroy P., and Ralph W. Haskins, eds. *The Papers of Andrew Johnson.* 16
vols. Knoxville: University of Tennessee Press, 1967–86.

Gunderson, Robert G., ed. "Letters from the Washington Peace Conference of
1861." *Journal of Southern History* 17 (1951): 382–92.

**Hamlin, Charles E. *The Life and Times of Hannibal Hamlin.* 1899. Reprint,
Port Washington, N.Y.: Kennikat Press, 1971.

Hughes, Sarah F., ed. *Letters and Recollections of John Murray Forbes.* 2 vols. Boston: Houghton Mifflin, 1900.

——, ed. *Letters of John Murray Forbes.* Supp. ed. 3 vols. Boston: George H. Ellis, 1905.

——, ed. *Reminiscences of John Murray Forbes.* 3 vols. Boston: George H. Ellis, 1902.

Hunt, Gaillard, ed. "Narrative and Letter of William Henry Trescott, Concerning Negotiations between South Carolina and President Buchanan in December, 1860." *American Historical Review* 13 (1908): 528–56.

Johannsen, Robert W., ed. *The Letters of Stephen A. Douglas.* Urbana: University of Illinois Press, 1961.

Keyes, Erasmus. *Fifty Years' Observation of Men and Events.* New York: Scribner, 1884.

King, Horatio. *Turning on the Light: A Dispassionate Survey of President Buchanan's Administration, from 1860 to Its Close.* Philadelphia: J. B. Lippincott, 1895.

Koerner, Gustave. *Memoirs of Gustave Koerner.* Edited by T. J. McCormack. 2 vols. Cedar Rapids, Iowa: Torch Press, 1909.

Laas, Virginia Jeans, ed. *Wartime Washington: The Civil War Letters of Elizabeth Blair Lee.* Urbana: University of Illinois Press, 1991.

Lamon, Ward Hill. *Recollections of Abraham Lincoln, 1847–1865.* Edited by Dorothy Lamon Teillard. 2nd ed. 1911. Reprint, Lincoln: University of Nebraska Press, 1994.

Lowell, James Russell. "The Election in November." *Atlantic Monthly* 6 (1860): 492–503.

——. "E Pluribus Unum." *Atlantic Monthly* 7 (1861): 235–46.

——. "The Question of the Hour." *Atlantic Monthly* 7 (1861): 117–21.

Logan, John A. *The Great Conspiracy: Its Origin and History.* New York: A. R. Hart, 1885.

Long, E. B., ed. *Personal Memoirs of U. S. Grant.* 1952. Reprint, New York: Da Capo Press, 1982.

Lutz, Ralph Haswell. "Rudolf Schleiden and the Visit to Richmond, April 25, 1861." *Annual Report of the American Historical Association for the Year 1915.* Washington: Government Printing Office, 1917.

Magruder, A. B. "A Piece of Secret History: President Lincoln and the Virginia Convention of 1861." *Atlantic Monthly* 35 (1875): 438–45.

McClure, Alexander. *Abraham Lincoln and Men of War-Times.* Philadelphia: Times, 1892.

Meigs, Montgomery C. "General M. C. Meigs on the Conduct of the Civil War." *American Historical Review* 26:2 (1920–21): 285–303.

Moore, Frank, ed. *The Rebellion Record.* 12 vols. New York: Putnam, 1861–68.

Moore, John Bassett, ed. *The Works of James Buchanan: Comprising His*

Speeches, State Papers, and Private Correspondence. 11 vols., 1908–11. Reprint, New York: Antiquarian Press, 1960.

Nevins, Allan, and M. H. Thomas, eds. *The Diary of George Templeton Strong.* 4 vols. New York: Macmillan, 1952.

Nicolay, John G. *The Outbreak of Rebellion.* 1881. Reprint, New York: Da Capo Press, 1995.

Niven, John, et al., eds. *The Salmon P. Chase Papers.* 5 vols. Kent, Ohio: Kent State University Press, 1993–.

Palmer, Beverly Wilson, ed. *The Selected Letters of Charles Sumner.* 2 vols. Boston: Northeastern University Press, 1990.

Pease, Theodore, and J. G. Randall, eds. *The Diary of Orville Hickman Browning.* Springfield: Trustees of the Illinois State Historical Library, 1925–33.

Perkins, Howard Cecil. *Northern Editorials on Secession.* 2 vols. Gloucester, Mass.: Peter Smith, 1964.

Phillips, Ulrich B., ed. "The Correspondence of Robert Toombs, Alexander H. Stephens, and Howell Cobb." *Annual Report of the American Historical Association for the Year 1911.* Vol. 2. Washington: Government Printing Office, 1913.

Phillips, Wendell. *Speeches, Lectures, and Letters.* Boston: Lee and Shepard, 1884.

Piatt, Donn. *Memories of the Men Who Saved the Union.* New York: Belford, Clarke, 1867.

Pierce, Edward L., ed. *Memoir and Letters of Charles Sumner.* 4 vols. Boston: Roberts Brothers, 1878–93.

Richardson, James D., ed. *A Compilation of the Messages and Papers of the Presidents.* 18 vols. New York: Bureau of National Literature, 1897–1927.

Russell, William Howard. *My Diary North and South.* 1863. Reprint, New York: Harper, 1954.

**Salter, William. *The Life of James W. Grimes.* New York: D. Appleton, 1876.

Schouler, William. *A History of Massachusetts in the Civil War.* Boston: E. P. Dutton, 1868.

**Schuckers, J. W. *The Life and Public Services of Salmon Portland Chase, United States Senator and Governor of Ohio; Secretary of the Treasury and Chief-Justice of the United States.* New York: D. Appleton, 1874.

**Seward, Frederick W. *Seward at Washington as Senator and Secretary of State.* 2 vols. New York: Derby and Miller, 1891.

Stampp, Kenneth M., ed. "Letters from the Washington Peace Conference of 1861." *Journal of Southern History* 9 (1943): 395–403.

Sumner, Charles. *The Works of Charles Sumner.* 15 vols. Boston: Lee and Shepard, 1870–83.

Thompson, Robert Means, and Richard Wainwright, eds. *Confidential Correspondence of Gustavus Vasa Fox, Assistant Secretary of the Navy, 1861–*

1865. 2 vols. New York: Printed for the Naval History Society by the De Vinne Press, 1918.

Thorndike, Rachel S., ed. *The Sherman Letters: Correspondence between General and Senator Sherman from 1837 to 1894*. 1894. Reprint, New York: Da Capo Press, 1969.

Villard, Harold G., and Oswald G. Villard, eds. *Lincoln on the Eve of '61*. New York: Knopf, 1941.

Wainwright, Nicholas B., ed. *A Philadelphia Perspective: The Diary of Sidney George Fisher Covering the Years 1834–1871*. Philadelphia: Historical Society of Pennsylvania, 1967.

Weed, Harriet A., ed. *Autobiography of Thurlow Weed*. Boston: Houghton Mifflin, 1883.

Welles, Gideon. *Lincoln and Seward*. 1874. Reprint, Freeport, N.Y.: Books for Libraries Press, 1969.

Welling, J. C. "The Proposed Evacuation of Fort Sumter." *The Nation* 29 (1879): 383–84.

Williams, Charles Richard, ed. *Diary and Letters of Rutherford Birchard Hayes, Nineteenth President of the United States*. Columbus: Ohio State Archaeological and Historical Society, 1922.

Wilson, Douglas L., and Rodney O. Davis, eds. *Herndon's Informants: Letters, Interviews, and Statements About Abraham Lincoln*. Urbana: University of Illinois Press, 1998.

Secondary Sources

Abbott, Richard H. *Cotton and Capital: Boston Businessmen and Antislavery Reform, 1854–1868*. Amherst: University of Massachusetts Press, 1991.

Adams, Charles Francis, Jr. *Charles Francis Adams*. Boston: Houghton Mifflin, 1909.

Alexander, Thomas P. *Sectional Stress and Party Strength: A Study of Roll-Call Voting Patterns in the United States House of Representatives, 1836–1860*. Nashville: Vanderbilt University Press, 1967.

Altschuler, Glenn C., and Stuart M. Blumin. *Rude Republic: Americans and Their Politics in the Nineteenth Century*. Princeton, N.J.: Princeton University Press, 2000.

Ambrosius, Lloyd, ed. *A Crisis of Republicanism: American Politics during the Civil War Era*. Lincoln: University of Nebraska Press, 1990.

Anbinder, Tyler G. *Nativism and Slavery: The Northern Know Nothings and the Politics of the 1850s*. New York: Oxford University Press, 1992.

Anderson, Frank Maloy. *The Mystery of "A Public Man": A Historical Detective Story*. Minneapolis: University of Minnesota Press, 1948.

Angle, Paul M. *"Here I Have Lived": A History of Lincoln's Springfield, 1821–1865*. Springfield, Ill.: Abraham Lincoln Association, 1935.

Arieli, Yehoshua. *Individualism and Nationalism in American Ideology*. Cambridge, Mass.: Harvard University Press, 1964.

Auchampaugh, Philip Gerald. *James Buchanan and His Cabinet on the Eve of Secession*. Lancaster, Pa.: Privately Printed, 1926.

Baker, Jean H. *Affairs of Party: The Political Culture of Northern Democrats in the Mid-Nineteenth Century*. 1983. Reprint, Bronx, N.Y.: Fordham University Press, 1998.

——. *James Buchanan*. New York: Henry Holt, 2004.

Bancroft, Frederic. "The Final Efforts at Compromise, 1860–1861." *Political Science Quarterly* 6 (1891): 401–23.

——. *The Life of William H. Seward*. 2 vols. 1899. Reprint, Gloucester, Mass.: Peter Smith, 1967.

Barbee, David Rankin. "The Line of Blood: Lincoln and the Coming of the War." *Tennessee Historical Quarterly* 16 (1957): 3–54.

Barbee, David Rankin, and Milledge L. Bonham Jr. "Fort Sumter Again." *Mississippi Valley Historical Review* 28:1 (1941): 63–73.

Baringer, William E. "Campaign Techniques in Illinois in 1860." *Illinois State Historical Society Transcripts* (1932): 202–81.

——. *A House Dividing: Lincoln as President Elect*. Springfield, Ill.: Abraham Lincoln Association, 1945.

Barney, William L. *The Secessionist Impulse: Alabama and Mississippi in 1860*. Princeton, N.J.: Princeton University Press, 1974.

Barns, Julia Elizabeth. "The Attitude of Illinois on Secession, 1860–1861." M.A. thesis, University of Chicago, 1924.

Baum, Dale. *The Civil War Party System: The Case of Massachusetts 1848-1876*. Chapel Hill: University of North Carolina Press, 1984.

Baum, Dale, and Dale T. Knobel. "Anatomy of a Realignment: New York Presidential Politics, 1848–1860." *New York History* 65 (1984): 61–81.

Baxter, Maurice. *Orville H. Browning: Lincoln's Friend and Critic*. Bloomington: Indiana University Press, 1957.

Bearss, Edwin C. "Fort Pickens and the Secession Crisis: January–February 1861." *Gulf Coast Historical Review* 4 (1989): 6–25.

Benson, Lee. "Causation and the American Civil War." *Toward the Scientific Study of History: Selected Essays of Lee Benson*. Philadelphia: J. B. Lippincott, 1972.

——. *The Concept of Jacksonian Democracy: New York as a Test Case*. Princeton, N.J.: Princeton University Press, 1961.

Benson, Lee, Joel H. Silbey, and Phyllis Field. "Toward a Theory of Stability and Change in American Voting Patterns: New York State, 1792–1970." In *History of American Electoral Behavior*, edited by Joel H. Silbey, Allan G. Bogue, and William H. Flanigan, 78–105. Princeton, N.J.: Princeton University Press, 1978.

Berger, Mark L. *The Revolution in the New York Party Systems, 1840–1860*. Port Washington, N.Y.: Kennikat Press, 1973.

Berwanger, Eugene H. *The Frontier against Slavery: Western Anti-Negro Prejudice and the Slavery Extension Controversy*. Urbana: University of Illinois Press, 1967.

——. "Negrophobia in Northern Proslavery and Antislavery Thought." *Phylon* 33 (1972): 266–75.

Bestor, Arthur. "The Civil War as a Constitutional Crisis." *American Historical Review* 69 (1964): 327–53.

Bilotta, James D. *Race and the Rise of the Republican Party, 1848–1865*. New York: P. Lang, 1992.

Blight, David W. *Frederick Douglass' Civil War: Keeping Faith in Jubilee*. Baton Rouge: Louisiana State University Press, 1989.

Blue, Frederick J. *Salmon P. Chase: A Life in Politics*. Kent, Ohio: Kent State University Press, 1987.

Bonham, Milledge L., Jr. "New York and the Election of 1860." *New York History* 32 (1934): 124–43.

Bonner, Thomas N. "Horace Greeley and the Secession Movement." *Mississippi Valley Historical Review* 38 (1951): 425–44.

Bradley, Erwin Stanley. *Simon Cameron, Lincoln's Secretary of War: A Political Biography*. Philadelphia: University of Pennsylvania Press, 1966.

Brainard, Newton C. "The Saybrook Peace Flag." *Connecticut Historical Society Bulletin* 27 (1961).

Brauer, Kinley J. "Seward's 'Foreign War Panacea': An Interpretation." *New York History* 55 (1974): 132–57.

Brigance, William Norwood. *Jeremiah Sullivan Black: A Defender of the Constitution and the Ten Commandments*. Philadelphia: University of Pennsylvania Press, 1934.

Brooke, John L. *The Heart of the Commonwealth: Society and Political Culture in Worcester County, Massachusetts, 1713–1861*. New York: Cambridge University Press, 1989.

Brown, Charles H. *William Cullen Bryant: A Biography*. New York: Scribner, 1971.

Brown, Francis. *Raymond of the Times*. New York: Norton, 1951.

Brown, Jeffrey P., and Andrew R. L. Cayton, eds. *The Pursuit of Public Power: Political Culture in Ohio, 1787–1861*. Kent, Ohio: Kent State University Press, 1997.

Brown, Thomas J. *Politics and Statesmanship: Essays on the American Whig Party*. New York: Columbia University Press, 1985.

Brummer, Sidney D. *Political History of New York State during the Period of the Civil War*. New York: Columbia University Press, 1911.

Buenger, Walter L. *Secession and the Union in Texas*. Austin: University of Texas Press, 1984.

Burnham, Walter Dean. *Presidential Ballots, 1836-1892.* Baltimore: Johns
     Hopkins University Press, 1955.
Campbell, Mary Emily Robertson. *The Attitude of Tennesseans toward the Union,
     1847-1861.* New York: Vantage Press, 1961.
Cardinal, Eric J. "The Ohio Democracy and the Crisis of Disunion, 1860–1861."
     Ohio History 86 (1977): 19–40.
Carman, Harry J., and Reinhard H. Luthin. *Lincoln and the Patronage.* New
     York: Columbia University Press, 1943.
Carnes, Mark C., and Clyde Griffen, eds. *Meanings for Manhood: Constructions of
     Masculinity in Victorian America.* Chicago: University of Chicago Press, 1990.
Carwardine, Richard J. *Evangelicals and Politics in Antebellum America.* New
     Haven: Yale University Press, 1993.
——. "Lincoln, Evangelical Religion, and American Political Culture in the Era of
     the Civil War." *Journal of the Abraham Lincoln Association* 18:1 (1997): 27–55.
Catton, Bruce. *The Centennial History of the Civil War.* Vol. 1, *The Coming Fury.*
     Garden City, N.Y.: Doubleday, 1961.
Chalmers, Leonard. "Tammany Hall, Fernando Wood, and the Struggle to
     Control New York City, 1857–59." *New-York Historical Society Quarterly* 53
     (1969): 7–33.
Channing, Steven A. *Crisis of Fear: Secession in South Carolina.* New York:
     Simon and Schuster, 1970.
Clapp, Margaret. *Forgotten First Citizen: John Bigelow.* Boston: Little, Brown,
     1947.
Cole, Arthur C. *The Era of the Civil War, 1848-1870.* Vol. 3. *The Centennial
     History of Illinois.* Springfield: Illinois Centennial Commission, 1919.
Coleman, John. *The Disruption of the Pennsylvania Democracy.* Harrisburg:
     Commonwealth of Pennsylvania, Pennsylvania Historical and Museum
     Commission, 1975.
Collins, Bruce. "The Ideology of the Ante-Bellum Northern Democrats." *Journal
     of American Studies* 11 (1977): 103–21.
Cowden, Joanna D. "The Politics of Dissent: Civil War Democrats in
     Connecticut." *New England Quarterly* 56 (1983): 538–54.
——. "Sovereignty and Secession: Peace Democrats and Antislavery Republicans
     in Connecticut during the Civil War Years." *Connecticut History* 30 (1989):
     41–54.
Crofts, Daniel W. "James E. Harvey and the Secession Crisis." *Pennsylvania
     Magazine of History and Biography* 103:2 (1979): 177–95.
——. "The Public Man Revealed: William Henry Hurlbert and the Coming of the
     Civil War." Unpublished manuscript in author's possession, December 2006
     draft.
——. *Reluctant Confederates: Upper South Unionists in the Secession Crisis.*
     Chapel Hill: University of North Carolina Press, 1989.

——. "A Reluctant Unionist: John A. Gilmer and Lincoln's Cabinet." *Civil War History* 24 (1978): 225–49.

——. "Secession Winter: William Henry Seward and the Decision for War." *New York History* 65 (1984): 228–56.

——. "The Union Party of 1861 and the Secession Crisis." *Perspectives in American History* 11 (1977–78): 327–76.

Crouch, Barry. "Amos A. Lawrence and the Formation of the Constitutional Union Party: The Conservative Failure in 1860." *Historical Journal of Massachusetts* 8 (1980): 46–58.

Current, Richard N. *Lincoln and the First Shot*. Philadelphia: J. B. Lippincott, 1963.

——. *The Lincoln Nobody Knows*. New York: McGraw-Hill, 1958.

Curti, Merle. *The Roots of American Loyalty*. New York: Columbia University Press, 1946.

Curtis, George Ticknor. *Life of James Buchanan: Fifteenth President of the United States*. 2 vols. New York: Harper, 1883.

Cuthbert, Norma Barrett. *Lincoln and the Baltimore Plot, 1861: From Pinkerton Records and Related Papers*. San Marino, Calif.: Huntington Library, 1949.

Dalzell, Robert F., Jr. *Enterprising Elite: The Boston Associates and the World They Made*. Cambridge, Mass.: Harvard University Press, 1987.

Daniels, George H. "The Immigrant Vote in the 1860 Election." *Mid-America* 44 (1962): 146–62.

Davis, David Brion. *The Slave Power Conspiracy and the Paranoid Style*. Baton Rouge: Louisiana State University Press, 1969.

Davis, Stuart John. "Liberty before Union: Massachusetts and the Coming of the Civil War." Ph.D. dissertation, University of Massachusetts, 1976.

Davis, William C. *"A Government of Our Own": The Making of the Confederacy*. New York: Free Press, 1994.

Denman, Clarence Phillips. *The Secession Movement in Alabama*. Montgomery: Alabama State Department of Archives and History, 1933.

Detzer, David. *Allegiance: Fort Sumter, Charleston, and the Beginning of the Civil War*. New York: Harcourt, 2001.

Dew, Charles B. *Apostles of Disunion: Southern Secession Commissioners and the Causes of the Civil War*. Charlottesville: University Press of Virginia, 2001.

Dibble, Ernest F. "War Averters: Seward, Mallory, and Fort Pickens." *Florida Historical Quarterly* 49 (1971): 232–44.

Dick, Robert C. *Black Protest: Issues and Tactics*. Westport, Conn.: Greenwood Press, 1974.

DiNunzio, Mario. "Ideology and Party Loyalty: The Political Conversion of Lyman Trumbull." *Lincoln Herald* 79:3 (1977): 95–103.

——. "Secession Winter: Lyman Trumbull and the Crisis of Congress." *Capitol Studies* 1 (1972): 29–39.

Donald, David. *Charles Sumner and the Coming of the Civil War*. New York: Knopf, 1960.

———. *Lincoln*. New York: Simon and Schuster, 1995.

———. *Lincoln's Herndon*. New York: Knopf, 1948.

Donovan, Herbert D. A. *The Barnburners: A Study of the Internal Movements in the Political History of New York State and the Resulting Changes in Political Affiliations, 1830–1852*. Philadelphia: Porcupine Press, 1925.

Duberman, Martin B. *Charles Francis Adams, 1807–1886*. Boston: Houghton Mifflin, 1961.

Dufwa, Thamar E. "Lincoln and Secession." Ph.D. dissertation, University of North Dakota, 1948.

Dumond, Dwight Lowell. *The Secession Movement, 1860–1861*. New York: Macmillan, 1931.

Dunham, Chester F. *The Attitude of the Northern Clergy toward the South, 1860–1865*. Toledo, Ohio: Gray, 1942.

Dusinberre, William. *Civil War Issues in Philadelphia, 1856–1865*. Philadelphia: University of Pennsylvania Press, 1965.

Edwards, Rebecca. *Angels in the Machinery: Gender in American Party Politics from the Civil War to the Progressive Era*. New York: Oxford University Press, 1997.

Elliott, Charles Winslow. *Winfield Scott: The Soldier and the Man*. New York: Macmillan, 1937.

Ellis, Joseph J. *Founding Brothers: The Revolutionary Generation*. New York: Knopf, 2000.

Ellis, Richard E. *The Union at Risk: Jacksonian Democracy, States' Rights, and the Nullification Crisis*. New York: Oxford University Press, 1987.

Ellis, Richard J. *American Political Cultures*. New York: Oxford University Press, 1993.

Endres, Kathleen L. "The Women's Press in the Civil War: A Portrait of Patriotism, Propaganda, and Prodding." *Civil War History* 30:1 (March 1984): 31–53.

Etcheson, Nicole. *The Emerging Midwest: Upland Southerners and the Political Culture of the Old Northwest, 1787–1861*. Bloomington: Indiana University Press, 1996.

Fehrenbacher, Don E. *Chicago Giant: A Biography of "Long John" Wentworth*. Madison, Wis.: American History Research Center, 1957.

———. *The Dred Scott Case: Its Significance in American Law and Politics*. New York: Oxford University Press, 1978.

———. "Illinois Political Attitudes, 1854–1861." Ph.D. dissertation, University of Chicago, 1951.

———. "Political Uses of the Post Office." In *Lincoln in Text and Context: Collected Essays*, edited by Don E. Fehrenbacher, 24–32. Stanford: Stanford University Press, 1987.

———. *Prelude to Greatness: Lincoln in the 1850's*. Stanford: Stanford University Press, 1962.

———. *The Slaveholding Republic: An Account of the United States Government's Relation to Slavery*. Completed and edited by Ward M. McAfee. New York: Oxford University Press, 2001.

Fermer, Douglas. *James Gordon Bennett and the New York Herald: A Study of Editorial Opinion in the Civil War Era, 1854–1867*. New York: St. Martin's Press, 1986.

Feuss, Claude M. *The Life of Caleb Cushing*. 2 vols. New York: Harcourt, Brace, 1923.

Finkelman, Paul, ed. *His Soul Goes Marching On: Responses to John Brown and the Harpers Ferry Raid*. Charlottesville: University Press of Virginia, 1995.

Fischer, Roger A. "The Republican Campaigns of 1856 and 1860: Analysis through Artifacts." *Civil War History* 27 (1981): 123–37.

Fitzpatrick, Jody L., and Rodney E. Hero. "Political Culture and Political Characteristics: A Consideration of Some Old and New Questions." *Western Political Quarterly* 41 (1988): 145–53.

Flick, Alexander. *Samuel Jones Tilden: A Study in Political Sagacity*. Port Washington, N.Y.: Kennikat Press, 1939.

Floan, Howard R. *The South in Northern Eyes, 1831–1861*. Austin: University of Texas Press, 1958.

Florang, Donald Dean, Jr. "Political World Views, Realignment, and Political Culture in Illinois, 1840–1856." Ph.D. dissertation, University of Chicago, 1996.

Foner, Eric. *Free Soil, Free Labor, Free Men: The Ideology of the Republican Party before the Civil War*. New York: Oxford University Press, 1970. Reprint, 1995.

Foner, Philip S. *Business & Slavery: The New York Merchants & the Irrepressible Conflict*. 1941. Reprint, New York: Russell & Russell, 1968.

Forgie, George B. *Patricide in the House Divided: A Psychological Interpretation of Lincoln and His Age*. New York: Norton, 1979.

Formisano, Ronald P. *The Birth of Mass Political Parties: Michigan, 1827–1861*. Princeton, N.J.: Princeton University Press, 1971.

———. *The Transformation of Political Culture: Massachusetts Parties, 1790s–1840s*. New York: Oxford University Press, 1983.

Freehling, William W. *The Road to Disunion*. Vol. 2, *Secessionists Triumphant, 1854–1861*. New York: Oxford University Press, 2007.

Freeman, Jo. *A Room at a Time: How Women Entered Party Politics*. Lanham, Md.: Rowman & Littlefield, 2000.

Gara, Larry. "Slavery and the Slave Power: A Crucial Distinction." *Civil War History* 15 (1969): 5–18.

Gatell, Frank Otto. " 'Conscience and Judgment': The Bolt of the Massachusetts Conscience Whigs." *The Historian* 20 (1959): 18–49.

Gellner, Ernest. *Nations and Nationalism*. Ithaca: Cornell University Press, 1983.

Gendzel, Glen. "Political Culture: Genealogy of a Concept." *Journal of Interdisciplinary History* 28:2 (1997): 225–50.

Genovese, Eugene. *The Slaveholders' Dilemma: Freedom and Progress in Southern Conservative Thought, 1820–1860*. Columbia: University of South Carolina Press, 1992.

Gibson, Florence E. *The Attitudes of the New York Irish toward State and National Affairs, 1848–1892*. New York: Columbia University Press, 1951.

Gienapp, William E. "The Crime against Sumner: The Caning of Charles Sumner and the Rise of the Republican Party." *Civil War History* 25:3 (1979): 218–45.

———. "Nativism and the Creation of a Republican Majority in the North before the Civil War." *Journal of American History* 72:3 (1985): 529–59.

———. *The Origins of the Republican Party, 1852–1856*. New York: Oxford University Press, 1987.

———. " 'Politics Seems to Enter into Everything': Political Culture in the North, 1840–1860." In *Essays on American Antebellum Politics, 1840–1860*, edited by Stephen E. Maizlish and John J. Kushma, 14–69. College Station: Published for the University of Texas at Arlington, by Texas A&M University Press, 1982.

———. "The Republican Party and the Slave Power." In *New Perspectives on Race and Slavery in America: Essays in Honor of Kenneth M. Stampp*, edited by Robert H. Abzug and Stephen E. Maizlish, 51–78. Lexington: University Press of Kentucky, 1986.

———. "Who Voted for Lincoln?" In *Abraham Lincoln and the American Political Tradition*, edited by John L. Thomas, 50–97. Amherst: University of Massachusetts Press, 1986.

Ginsberg, Judah B. "Barnburners, Free Soilers, and the New York Republican Party." *New York History* 57 (1976): 496–99.

Glatthaar, Joseph T. "The Common Soldier of the Civil War." In *New Perspectives on the Civil War: Myths and Realities of the National Conflict*, edited by John Y. Simon and Michael E. Stevens, 119–48. Madison, Wis.: Madison House, 1998.

Glover, Gilbert G. *Immediate Pre–Civil War Compromise Efforts*. Nashville: George Peabody College for Teachers, 1934.

Goldschmidt, Eli. "Northeastern Businessmen and the Secession Crisis." Ph.D. dissertation, New York University, 1972.

Goodman, Paul. "Ethics and Enterprise: The Values of the Boston Elite, 1800–1860." *American Quarterly* 18 (1966): 437–51.

Goodwin, Doris Kearns. *Team of Rivals: The Political Genius of Abraham Lincoln*. New York: Simon and Schuster, 2005.

Graebner, Norman L. "Thomas Corwin and the Sectional Crisis." *Ohio History* 86 (1977): 229–47.

Grant, Susan-Mary. *North over South: Northern Nationalism and American Identity in the Antebellum Era*. Lawrence: University Press of Kansas, 2000.

Gulley, Halbert E. "Springfield Lincoln Rally, 1860." In *Antislavery and Disunion, 1858–1861: Studies in the Rhetoric of Compromise and Conflict*, edited by J. Jeffrey Auer, 212–24. New York: Harper & Row, 1963.

Gunderson, Robert Gray. *Old Gentlemen's Convention: The Washington Peace Conference of 1861*. 1961. Reprint, Westport, Conn.: Greenwood Press, 1981.

——. "William C. Rives and the 'Old Gentlemen's Convention.'" *Journal of Southern History* 22 (1956): 459–76.

Gunn, L. Ray. "Antebellum Society and Politics (1825–1860)." In *The Empire State: A History of New York*, edited by Milton M. Klein. Ithaca: Cornell University Press, 2001.

Gustafson, Melanie S. *Women and the Republican Party, 1854–1924*. Urbana: University of Illinois Press, 2001.

Hall, Wilmer L. "Lincoln's Interview with John B. Baldwin." *South Atlantic Quarterly* 13 (1914): 260–69.

Hansen, Stephen L. *The Making of the Third Party System: Voters and Parties in Illinois, 1850–1876*. Ann Arbor: UMI Research Press, 1980.

Hansen, Stephen L., and Paul D. Nygard. "Abraham Lincoln and the Know Nothing Question, 1854–1859." *Lincoln Herald* 94:2 (1992): 61–72.

——. "Stephen A. Douglas, the Know-Nothings, and the Democratic Party in Illinois, 1854–1858." *Illinois Historical Journal* 87:2 (1994): 109–30.

Hartman, William. "The New York Custom House: Seats of Spoils Politics." *New York History* 34 (1953): 149–63.

Herndon, William H., and Jesse W. Weik. *Herndon's Life of Lincoln*. Edited by Paul M. Angle. 1942. Reprint, New York: Da Capo Press, 1983.

Heslin, James J. "Peaceful Compromise in New York City, 1860–1861." *New York Historical Society Quarterly* 44 (1960): 349–62.

Hess, Earl J. *Liberty, Virtue, and Progress: Northerners and Their War for the Union*. New York: Fordham University Press, 1988.

——. "The Mississippi River and Secession, 1861: The Northwestern Response." *Old Northwest* 10:2 (1984): 187–207.

Hesseltine, William B. *Lincoln and the War Governors*. New York: Knopf, 1955.

Hesseltine, William B., and Larry Gara. "New Governors Speak for War, January, 1861." In *Antislavery and Disunion, 1858–1861: Studies in the Rhetoric of Compromise and Conflict*, edited by J. Jeffrey Auer, 360–77. New York: Harper & Row, 1963.

Hicken, Victor. "From Vandalia to Vicksburg: The Political and Military Career of John A. McClernand." Ph.D. dissertation, University of Illinois, 1955.

Higham, John. *From Boundlessness to Consolidation: The Transformation of American Culture, 1848–1860*. Indianapolis: Bobbs-Merrill, 1969.

Holt, Michael F. *The Fate of Their Country: Politicians, Slavery Extension, and the Coming of the Civil War*. New York: Hill and Wang, 2004.

——. *Forging a Majority: The Formation of the Republican Party in Pittsburgh, 1848–1860*. New Haven: Yale University Press, 1969.

——. *The Political Crisis of the 1850s*. New York: Wiley, 1978.

——. *Political Parties and American Political Development from the Age of Jackson to the Age of Lincoln*. Baton Rouge: Louisiana State University Press, 1992.

——. "The Politics of Impatience: The Origins of Know-Nothingism." *Journal of American History* 60 (1973): 309–31.

——. *The Rise and Fall of the American Whig Party: Jacksonian Politics and the Onset of the Civil War*. New York: Oxford University Press, 1999.

Hoogenboom, Ari. "Gustavus Fox and the Relief of Fort Sumter." *Civil War History* 9 (1963): 383–98.

Horn, Stuart Joel. "Edward Everett and American Nationalism." Ph.D. dissertation, City University of New York, 1973.

Horton, James Oliver, and Lois E. Horton. *In Hope of Liberty: Culture, Community, and Protest Among Northern Free Blacks, 1700–1860*. New York: Oxford University Press, 1997.

Howard, Victor B. "The Illinois Republican Party." *Journal of the Illinois State Historical Society* 64 (1973): 125–60, 285–311.

Howe, Daniel Walker. "The Evangelical Movement and Political Culture in the North during the Second Party System." *Journal of American History* 77 (1991): 1216–39.

——. *The Political Culture of the American Whigs*. Chicago: University of Chicago Press, 1979.

Hubbell, John T. "The Douglas Democrats and the Election of 1860." *Mid-America* 54 (1973): 108–33.

——. "Jeremiah Sullivan Black and the Great Secession Winter." *Western Pennsylvania History Magazine* 57 (1974): 255–74.

——. "Politics as Usual: The Northern Democracy and Party Survival, 1860–1861." *Illinois Quarterly* 36 (1973): 22–35.

Hummel, Jeffrey Rogers. *Emancipating Slaves, Enslaving Free Men: A History of the American Civil War*. Chicago: Open Court, 1996.

Huston, James L. *The Panic of 1857 and the Coming of the Civil War*. Baton Rouge: Louisiana State University Press, 1987.

Isely, Jeter A. *Horace Greeley and the Republican Party, 1853–1861: A Study of the New York Tribune*. Princeton, N.J.: Princeton University Press, 1947.

Jensen, Richard J. *Illinois: A Bicentennial History*. New York: Norton, 1978.

Johannsen, Robert W. "The Douglas Democracy and the Crisis of Disunion." *Civil War History* 9 (1963): 229–47.

——. *The Frontier, the Union, and Stephen A. Douglas*. Urbana: University of Illinois Press, 1989.

——. *Stephen A. Douglas*. New York: Oxford University Press, 1973.

Johnson, Michael P. *Toward a Patriarchal Republic: The Secession of Georgia.* Baton Rouge: Louisiana State University Press, 1977.

Johnson, Reinhard O. "The Liberty Party in Massachusetts: Antislavery Third Party Politics in the Bay State." *Civil War History* 28 (1982): 237–65.

Jones, James P. *"Black Jack": John A. Logan and Southern Illinois in the Civil War Era.* 1967. Reprint, Carbondale: Southern Illinois University Press, 1995.

Jones, Stanley L. "John Wentworth and Anti-Slavery in Chicago." *Mid-America* 36 (1954): 147–60.

Jordan, Winthrop D. *White over Black: American Attitudes toward the Negro, 1550–1812.* Chapel Hill: University of North Carolina Press, 1968.

Kamphoefner, Walter D. "St. Louis Germans and the Republican Party, 1848–1860." *Mid-America* 57 (1975): 69–88.

Katz, Irving. *August Belmont: A Political Biography.* New York: Columbia University Press, 1968.

Keene, Jesse L. *The Peace Conference of 1861.* Tuscaloosa, Ala.: Confederate, 1961.

Kelley, Robert L. *The Cultural Pattern in American Politics: The First Century.* New York: Knopf, 1979.

Kemp, Thomas R. "Community and War: The Civil War Experience of Two New Hampshire Towns." In *Toward a Social History of the American Civil War: Exploratory Essays*, edited by Maris Vinovskis, 31–77. New York: Cambridge University Press, 1990.

Keogh, Stephen. "Formal & Informal Constitutional Lawmaking in the United States in the Winter of 1860–1861." *Journal of Legal History* 8 (1987): 275–99.

Kersh, Rogan. *Dreams of a More Perfect Union.* Ithaca: Cornell University Press, 2001.

King, Willard L. *Lincoln's Manager, David Davis.* Cambridge, Mass.: Harvard University Press, 1960.

Kirwan, Albert D. *John J. Crittenden: The Struggle for the Union.* Lexington: University of Kentucky Press, 1962.

Klein, Maury. *Days of Defiance: Sumter, Secession, and the Coming of the Civil War.* New York: Knopf, 1997.

Klein, Philip S. *President James Buchanan: A Biography.* University Park: Pennsylvania State University Press, 1962.

Kleppner, Paul J. *The Cross of Culture: A Social Analysis of Midwestern Politics, 1850–1900.* New York: Free Press, 1970.

——. *The Third Electoral System, 1853–1892: Parties, Voters, and Political Cultures.* Chapel Hill: University of North Carolina Press, 1979.

Klingberg, Frank W. "James Buchanan and the Crisis of the Union." *Journal of Southern History* 9 (1943): 453–74.

Knupfer, Peter. "Aging Statesmen and the Statesmanship of an Earlier Age: The Generational Roots of the Constitutional Union Party." In *Union and Emancipation: Essays on Politics and Race in the Civil War Era*, edited by David W. Blight and Brooks D. Simpson, 57–78. Kent, Ohio: Kent State University Press, 1997.

———. *The Union as It Is: Constitutional Unionism and Sectional Compromise, 1787–1861*. Chapel Hill: University of North Carolina Press, 1991.

Kohn, Hans. *American Nationalism: An Interpretive Essay*. New York: Macmillan, 1957.

Krug, Mark. *Lyman Trumbull: Conservative Radical*. New York: A. S. Barnes, 1965.

Krummel, Carl F. "Henry J. Raymond and the New York Times in the Secession Crisis, 1860–1861." *New York History* 32 (1951): 377–98.

Lader, Lawrence. *Bold Brahmins: New England's War against Slavery, 1830–1861*. New York: Dutton, 1961.

Lankford, Nelson. *Cry Havoc! The Crooked Road to Civil War, 1861*. New York: Viking, 2007.

Larkin, Jack. "Massachusetts Enters the Marketplace, 1790–1860." In *A Guide to the History of Massachusetts*, edited by Martin Kaufman, 69–82. New York: Greenwood Press, 1988.

Lee, Alton R. "The Corwin Amendment in the Secession Crisis." *Ohio Historical Quarterly* 70 (1961): 1–26.

Lee, Charles Robert. *The Confederate Constitutions*. Chapel Hill: University of North Carolina Press, 1963.

Link, William A. *Roots of Secession: Slavery and Politics in Antebellum Virginia*. Chapel Hill: University of North Carolina Press, 2003.

Litwack, Leon. *North of Slavery: The Negro in the Free States, 1790–1860*. Chicago: University of Chicago Press, 1961.

Long, E. B., and Barbara Long. *The Civil War Day by Day: An Almanac 1861–1865*. Garden City, N.Y.: Doubleday, 1971.

Lowenfels, Walter, ed. *Walt Whitman's Civil War*. 1960. Reprint, New York: Knopf, 1971.

Lowrey, Lawrence T. *Northern Opinion of Approaching Secession, October 1859–November 1860*. Northampton, Mass.: Department of History of Smith College, 1918.

Luebke, Frederick C., ed. *Ethnic Voters and the Election of Lincoln*. Lincoln: University of Nebraska Press, 1971.

Luthin, Reinhard H. *The First Lincoln Campaign*. Cambridge, Mass.: Harvard University Press, 1944.

Maizlish, Stephen E. "The Meaning of Nativism and the Crisis of the Union: The Know-Nothing Movement in the Antebellum North." In *Essays on American*

Antebellum Politics, 1840–1860, edited by Stephen E. Maizlish and John J. Kushma, 166–98. College Station: Published for the University of Texas at Arlington, by Texas A&M University Press, 1982.

——. "Race and Politics in the Northern Democracy: 1854–1860." In *New Perspectives on Race and Slavery in America: Essays in Honor of Kenneth M. Stampp*, edited by Robert H. Abzug and Stephen E. Maizlish, 79–90. Lexington: University Press of Kentucky, 1986.

Marvel, William. "A Poor Man's Fight: Civil War Enlistments in Conway, New Hampshire." *Historical New Hampshire* 43 (1988): 21–40.

McClintock, Russell. "Shall It Be Peace, or a Sword?" Ph.D. dissertation, Clark University, 2004.

McCoy, Drew R. *The Elusive Republic: Political Economy in Jeffersonian America*. Chapel Hill: University of North Carolina Press, 1980.

——. "Lincoln and the Founding Fathers: A Reconsideration." *Journal of the Abraham Lincoln Association* 16 (1995): 3–13.

——. "An 'Old-Fashioned' Nationalism: Lincoln, Jefferson, and the Classical Tradition." *Journal of the Abraham Lincoln Association* 23 (2002): 55–67.

McGraw, Robert F. "Minutemen of '61: The Pre–Civil War Massachusetts Militia." *Civil War History* 15 (1969): 101–15.

McKay, Ernest A. *The Civil War and New York City*. Syracuse, N.Y.: Syracuse University Press, 1990.

McManus, Michael J. " 'Freedom and Liberty First, and the Union Afterwards': State Rights and the Wisconsin Republican Party, 1854–1861." In *Union and Emancipation: Essays on Politics and Race in the Civil War Era*, edited by David W. Blight and Brooks D. Simpson, 29–56. Kent, Ohio: Kent State University Press, 1997.

McPherson, James M. *For Cause and Comrades: Why Men Fought in the Civil War*. New York: Oxford University Press, 1997.

Meerse, David E. "Buchanan, Corruption, and the Election of 1860." *Civil War History* 12 (1966): 116–31.

Meredith, Roy. *Storm over Sumter: The Opening Engagement of the Civil War*. New York: Simon and Schuster, 1957.

Miers, Earl Schenck, ed. *Lincoln Day by Day: A Chronology*. 3 vols. Washington: Lincoln Sesquicentennial Commission, 1960.

Milton, George Fort. *The Eve of Conflict: Stephen A. Douglas and the Needless War*. New York: Houghton Mifflin, 1934.

Mitchell, Betty. "Massachusetts Reaction to John Brown's Raid." *Civil War History* 19 (1973): 65–79.

Mitchell, Reid. *Civil War Soldiers: Their Expectations and Their Experiences*. New York: Viking, 1988.

——. "Soldiering, Manhood, and Coming of Age: A Northern Volunteer." In

Divided Houses: Gender and the Civil War, edited by Catherine Clinton and
Nina Silber, 43–54. New York: Oxford University Press, 1992.

Mitchell, Stewart. *Horatio Seymour of New York*. Cambridge, Mass.: Harvard
University Press, 1938.

Morison, Elting. "Election of 1860." In *History of American Presidential
Elections, 1789-1968*. Vol. 2, *1848-1896*, edited by Arthur M. Schlesinger Jr,
1097–122. New York: McGraw-Hill, 1971.

Morris, Thomas D. *Free Men All: The Personal Liberty Laws of the North, 1780-
1861*. Baltimore: Johns Hopkins University Press, 1974.

Morrison, Michael A. *Slavery and the American West: The Eclipse of Manifest
Destiny and the Coming of the Civil War*. Chapel Hill: University of North
Carolina Press, 1997.

Mulkern, John R. *The Know-Nothing Party in Massachusetts: The Rise and Fall of
a People's Movement*. Boston: Northeastern University Press, 1990.

Murrin, John M. "A Roof without Walls: The Dilemma of American National
Identity." In *Beyond Confederation: Origins of the Constitution and American
National Identity*, edited by Richard Beeman, Stephen Botein, and Edward C.
Carter II, 333–48. Chapel Hill: University of North Carolina Press, 1987.

Mushkat, Jerome. *Fernando Wood: A Political Biography*. Kent, Ohio: Kent State
University Press, 1990.

Nagel, Paul C. *One Nation Indivisible: The Union in American Thought, 1776-
1861*. New York: Oxford University Press, 1964.

———. *This Sacred Trust: American Nationality, 1798-1898*. New York: Oxford
University Press, 1971.

Nevins, Allan. *The Emergence of Lincoln*. 2 vols. New York: Scribner, 1950.

———. "He Did Hold Lincoln's Hat." *American Heritage* 10:2 (1959): 98–99.

———. *The War for the Union*. 4 vols. New York: Scribner, 1959–71.

Nichols, Roy F. *The Disruption of American Democracy*. New York: Macmillan,
1948.

Nicolay, John G., and John Hay. *Abraham Lincoln: A History*. 10 vols. New York:
Century, 1890.

Niven, John. *Connecticut for the Union: The Role of the State in the Civil War*.
New Haven: Yale University Press, 1965.

———. *Gideon Welles*. New York: Oxford University Press, 1973.

———. *Salmon P. Chase: A Biography*. New York: Oxford University Press, 1995.

Nortrup, Jack Junior. "Richard Yates, Civil War Governor of Illinois." Ph.D.
dissertation, University of Illinois, Urbana-Champaign, 1960.

Nye, Russel B. *Fettered Freedom: Civil Liberties and the Slavery Controversy,
1830-1860*. East Lansing: Michigan State College Press, 1949.

Oates, Stephen B. *To Purge This Land with Blood: A Biography of John Brown*.
New York: Harper & Row, 1970.

——. *With Malice toward None: The Life of Abraham Lincoln.* New York: Harper & Row, 1977.

O'Connor, Thomas H. *Bibles, Brahmins, and Bosses: A Short History of Boston.* 3rd ed. Boston: Trustees of the Public Library of the City of Boston, 1991.

——. *The Boston Irish.* Boston: Northeastern University Press, 1995.

——. *Civil War Boston: Home Front and Battlefield.* Boston: Northeastern University Press, 1997.

——. *Lords of the Loom: The Cotton Whigs and the Coming of the Civil War.* New York: Scribner, 1968.

Olsen, Christopher J. *Political Culture and Secession in Mississippi: Masculinity, Honor, and the Antiparty Tradition, 1830–1860.* New York: Oxford University Press, 2000.

Osborn, David. "Queens County and the Secession Crisis." *Long Island Historical Review* 5 (1993): 132–45.

——. "Union or Slavery: Metropolitan New York and the Secession Crisis." Ph.D. dissertation, City University of New York, 1993.

Paludan, Phillip S. "The American Civil War Considered as a Crisis in Law and Order." *American Historical Review* 77 (1972): 1013–34.

——. *A People's Contest: The Union and Civil War, 1861–1865.* 1988. Reprint, Lawrence: University Press of Kansas, 1996.

——. *The Presidency of Abraham Lincoln.* Lawrence: University Press of Kansas, 1994.

Parish, Peter J. "American Nationalism and the Nineteenth-Century Constitution." In *The American Constitution: The First Two Hundred Years, 1787–1987,* edited by Joseph Smith, 63–82. Exeter, U.K.: University of Exeter, 1987.

——. "An Exception to Most of the Rules: What Made American Nationalism Different in the Mid-Nineteenth Century?" *Prologue: Quarterly of the National Archives* 27:3 (1995): 219–29.

Parks, Joseph Howard. *John Bell of Tennessee.* Baton Rouge: Louisiana State University Press, 1950.

Pearson, Henry G. *Life of John A. Andrew.* 2 vols. Boston: Houghton Mifflin, 1904.

Pendergraft, Daryl. "Thomas Corwin and the Conservative Republican Reaction, 1858–1861." *Ohio State Archaeological and Historical Quarterly* 57 (1948): 1–23.

Perkins, Howard Cecil. "The Defense of Slavery in the Northern Press on the Eve of the Civil War." *Journal of Southern History* 9:4 (1943): 501–31.

Phillips, Ulrich Bonnell. *The Course of the South to Secession.* New York: Appleton-Century, 1939.

Pierson, Michael D. *Free Hearts and Free Homes: Gender and American Antislavery Politics.* Chapel Hill: University of North Carolina Press, 2003.

Potter, David M. "Horace Greeley and Peaceable Secession." *Journal of Southern History* 7 (1941): 145–59.

——. *The Impending Crisis, 1848–1861.* Completed and edited by Don E. Fehrenbacher. New York: Harper & Row, 1976.

——. *Lincoln and His Party in the Secession Crisis.* 1942. Reprint, Baton Rouge: Louisiana State University Press, 1995.

——. "Why the Republicans Rejected Both Compromise and Secession." In *The Crisis of the Union, 1860–1861,* edited by George Harmon Knoles, 90–106. Baton Rouge: Louisiana State University Press, 1965.

Power, Richard Lyle. *Planting Corn Belt Culture: The Impress of the Upland Southerner and Yankee in the Old Northwest.* Indianapolis: Indiana Historical Society, 1953.

Preston, James R. "Political Pageantry in the Campaign of 1860 in Illinois." *Abraham Lincoln Quarterly* 4 (1947): 313–47.

Prucha, F. Paul. "Minnesota's Attitude toward the Southern Case for Secession." *Minnesota History* 24 (1943): 307–17.

Rael, Patrick. *Black Identity and Black Protest in the Antebellum North.* Chapel Hill: University of North Carolina Press, 2002.

Rainwater, P.L. *Mississippi: Storm Center of Secession.* Baton Rouge: O. Claitor, 1938.

Ramsdell, Charles W. "Lincoln and Fort Sumter." *Journal of Southern History* 3 (1937): 259–88.

Randall, James G. *Lincoln the Liberal Statesman.* New York: Dodd, Mead, 1947.

——. "When War Came in 1861." *Abraham Lincoln Quarterly* 1 (March 1940): 3–42.

Ratcliffe, Donald J. "Politics in Jacksonian Ohio: Reflections on the Ethnocultural Interpretation." *Ohio History* 88 (1979): 5–36.

Rawley, James A. "The Nationalism of Abraham Lincoln." *Civil War History* 9 (1963): 283–98.

Reid, Ronald F. *Edward Everett: Unionist Orator.* New York: Greenwood Press, 1990.

Reilly, Tom. "Early Coverage of a President-Elect: Lincoln at Springfield, 1860." *Journalism Quarterly* 50 (1972): 469–79.

Renda, Lex. "Credit and Culpability: New Hampshire State Politics During the Civil War." *Historical New Hampshire* 48 (1991): 3–84.

Rezneck, Samuel. "The Influence of Depression Upon American Opinion, 1857–1859." *Journal of Economic History* 2 (1942): 1–23.

Rich, Robert. " 'A Wilderness of Whigs': The Wealthy Men of Boston." *Journal of Social History* 4 (1971): 263–76.

Richards, Leonard L. *The Slave Power: The Free North and Southern Domination, 1780–1860.* Baton Rouge: Louisiana State University Press, 2000.

Rorabaugh, W. J. "Who Fought for the North in the Civil War? Concord,

Massachusetts, Enlistments." *Journal of American History* 73 (1986): 695–701.

Rosenberg, Norman L. "Personal Liberty Laws and the Sectional Crisis: 1850–1861." *Civil War History* 17 (1971): 25–44.

Roske, Ralph J. *His Own Counsel: The Life and Times of Lyman Trumbull*. Reno: University of Nevada Press, 1979.

Ross, Raymond A. "Slavery and the New York City Newspapers, 1850–1860." Ph.D. Dissertation, New York University, 1966.

Rotundo, E. Anthony. *American Manhood: Transformations in Masculinity from the Revolution to the Modern Era*. New York: BasicBooks, 1993.

Rozett, John M. "Racism and Republican Emergence in Illinois, 1848–1860: A Reevaluation of Republican Negrophobia." *Civil War History* 22:2 (1976): 101–15.

Ryan, Mary P. *Women in Public: Between Banners and Ballots, 1825-1880*. Baltimore: Johns Hopkins University Press, 1990.

Saum, Lewis O. *The Popular Mood of Pre-Civil War America*. Westport, Conn.: Greenwood Press, 1980.

Sears, Louis. "New York and the Fusion Movement of 1860." *Journal of the Illinois State Historical Society* 16 (1923): 58–62.

Sewell, Richard. *Ballots for Freedom: Antislavery Politics in the United States, 1837-1860*. New York: Oxford University Press, 1976.

Shanks, Henry T. *The Secession Movement in Virginia, 1847-1861*. Richmond: Garrett & Massie, 1934.

Shefter, Martin. *Political Parties and the State: The American Historical Experiences*. Princeton, N.J.: Princeton University Press, 1994.

Shortridge, Ray M. "Voter Turnout in the Midwest, 1840–1872." *Social Science Quarterly* 60:4 (1980): 617–29.

Siddali, Silvana R. " 'The Sport of Folly and the Prize of Treason': Confederate Property Seizures and the Northern Home Front in the Secession Crisis." *Civil War History* 48:4 (2001): 310–33.

Sibley, Joel H. *The Partisan Imperative: The Dynamics of American Politics before the Civil War*. New York: Oxford University Press, 1985.

———. *A Respectable Minority: The Democratic Party in the Civil War Era, 1860-1868*. New York: Norton, 1977.

———. *The Shrine of Party: Congressional Voting Behavior, 1841-1852*. Pittsburgh: University of Pittsburgh Press, 1967.

———. *The Transformation of American Politics, 1840-1860*. Englewood Cliffs, N.J.: Prentice-Hall, 1967.

Simon, Donald E. "Brooklyn in the Election of 1860." *New York Historical Quarterly* 51 (1967): 249–62.

Simpson, Brooks D. "Daniel Webster and the Cult of the Constitution." *Journal of American Culture* 15:1 (1992): 15–23.

Sitterson, J. Carlyle. *The Secession Movement in North Carolina*. Chapel Hill: The University of North Carolina Press, 1939.

Skinner, Quentin, et al. "Political Thought and Political Action." *Political Theory* 2 (1974): 251–303.

Smith, Anthony D. *National Identity*. Reno: University of Nevada Press, 1991.

Smith, Elbert B. *The Presidency of James Buchanan*. Lawrence: University Press of Kansas, 1975.

Smith, George Winston. "Ante-Bellum Attempts of Northern Business Interests to 'Redeem' the Upper South." *Journal of Southern History* 11 (1945): 177–213.

Smith, W. E. *The Francis Preston Blair Family in Politics*. 2 vols. New York: Macmillan, 1933.

Smith, Willard H. *Schuyler Colfax: The Changing Fortunes of a Political Idol*. Indianapolis: Indiana Historical Bureau, 1952.

Somkin, Fred. *Unquiet Eagle: Memory and Desire in the Idea of American Freedom, 1815–1860*. Ithaca, N.Y.: Cornell University Press, 1967.

Sowle, Patrick M. "The Conciliatory Republicans during the Winter of Secession." Ph.D. dissertation, Duke University, 1963.

——. "A Reappraisal of Seward's Memorandum of April 1, 1861, to Lincoln." *Journal of Southern History* 33 (1967): 234–39.

——. "The Trials of a Virginia Unionist: William Cabell Rives and the Secession Crisis, 1860–1861." *Virginia Magazine of History and Biography* 80 (1972): 3–20.

Stampp, Kenneth M. *And the War Came: The North and the Secession Crisis, 1860–1861*. 1950. Reprint, Baton Rouge: Louisiana State University Press, 1970.

——. "Comment to David M. Potter's 'Why the Republicans Rejected Both Compromise and Secession.'" In *The Crisis of the Union, 1860–1861*, edited by George Harmon Knoles, 107–13. Baton Rouge: Louisiana State University Press, 1965.

——. "The Concept of a Perpetual Union." In *The Imperiled Union: Essays on the Background of the Civil War*. New York: Oxford University Press, 1980.

——. *The Era of Reconstruction, 1865–1877*. New York: Knopf, 1965.

——. *Indiana Politics during the Civil War*. Indianapolis: Indiana Historical Bureau, 1949.

——. "The Irrepressible Conflict." In *The Imperiled Union: Essays on the Background of the Civil War*. New York: Oxford University Press, 1980.

——. "Kentucky's Influence Upon Indiana in the Crisis of 1861." *Indiana Magazine of History* 39 (1943): 263–76.

——. "Lincoln and the Secession Crisis." In *The Imperiled Union: Essays on the Background of the Civil War*. New York: Oxford University Press, 1980.

——. "Lincoln and the Strategy of Defense in the Crisis of 1861." *Journal of Southern History* 9 (1945): 297–323.

———. *The Peculiar Institution: Slavery in the Ante-Bellum South*. New York: Knopf, 1956.

———. "The Republican National Convention of 1860." In *Antislavery and Disunion, 1858–1861: Studies in the Rhetoric of Compromise and Conflict*, edited by J. Jeffrey Auer, 193–211. New York: Harper & Row, 1963.

Stewart, James Brewer. *Holy Warriors: The Abolitionists and American Slavery*. New York: Hill and Wang, 1996.

Stoler, Mildred C. "The Democratic Element in the New Republican Party in Illinois, 1856–1860." *Papers in Illinois History and Transactions for the Year 1942* (1944): 32–71.

Strickland, Arvarh E. "The Illinois Background of Lincoln's Attitude toward Slavery and the Negro." *Illinois State Historical Society Journal* 56 (1963): 474–94.

Summers, Mark W. " 'A Band of Brigands': Albany Lawmakers and Republican National Politics, 1860." *Civil War History* 30 (1984): 101–19.

Swanberg, W. A. *First Blood: The Story of Fort Sumter*. New York: Scribner, 1957.

Sweeney, Kevin. "Rum, Romanism, Representation and Reform: Coalition Politics in Massachusetts, 1847–1853." *Civil War History* 22 (1976): 116–37.

Talmadge, John E. "A Peace Movement in Civil War Connecticut." *New England Quarterly* 37 (1964): 306–31.

Thomas, Teresa A. "For Union, Not for Glory: Volunteers of Lancaster, Massachusetts." *Civil War History* 40:1 (1994): 25–47.

Tilley, John S. *Lincoln Takes Command*. Chapel Hill: University of North Carolina Press, 1941.

Tusa, Frank Joseph. "Congressional Politics in the Secession Crisis, 1859–1861." Ph.D. dissertation, Pennsylvania State University, 1975.

Van Deusen, Glyndon G. *Horace Greeley: Nineteenth-Century Crusader*. Philadelphia: University of Pennsylvania Press, 1953.

———. *Thurlow Weed: Wizard of the Lobby*. Boston: Little, Brown, 1947.

———. "Why the Republican Party Came to Power." In *The Crisis of the Union, 1860–1861*, edited by George Harmon Knoles, 3–20. Baton Rouge: Louisiana State University Press, 1965.

———. *William Henry Seward*. New York: Oxford University Press, 1967.

Varg, Paul A. *Edward Everett: The Intellectual in the Turmoil of Politics*. Selinsgrove, Pa.: Susquehanna University Press, 1992.

Vinovskis, Maris. "Have Social Historians Lost the Civil War? Some Preliminary Demographic Speculations." In *Toward a Social History of the American Civil War: Exploratory Essays*, edited by Maris Vinovskis, 1–30. New York: Cambridge University Press, 1990.

Voegeli, V. Jacques. *Free but Not Equal: The Midwest and the Negro during the Civil War*. Chicago: University of Chicago Press, 1967.

Walters, Ronald G. *American Reformers, 1815-1860*. New York: Hill and Wang, 1978.

Walther, Eric H. *The Fire-Eaters*. Baton Rouge: Louisiana State University Press, 1992.

Ware, Edith Ellen. *Political Opinion in Massachusetts during Civil War and Reconstruction: Studies in History, Economics, and Public Law*. New York: Columbia University Press, 1916.

Weatherman, Donald V. "James Buchanan on Slavery and Secession." *Presidential Studies Quarterly* 68:1 (1987): 66–92.

Weisberger, Bernard A. "Horace Greeley: Reformer as Republican." *Civil War History* 23 (1977): 5–25.

Welch, Stephen. *The Concept of Political Culture*. New York: St. Martin's Press, 1993.

Wells, Damon. *Stephen Douglas: The Last Years, 1857-1861*. Austin: University of Texas Press, 1971.

Welter, Rush. *The Mind of America, 1820-1860*. New York: Columbia University Press, 1975.

Westfall, William. "Antislavery as a Racist Outlet: A Hypothesis." *International Social Science Review* 61:1 (1986): 3–11.

Westwood, Howard C. "President Lincoln's Overture to Sam Houston." *Southwestern Historical Quarterly* 88 (1984): 125–44.

White, Laura A. "Charles Sumner and the Crisis of 1860–1861." In *Essays in Honor of William E. Dodd by His Former Students*, edited by Avery Craven, 131–93. Chicago: University of Chicago Press, 1935.

Wilentz, Sean, *The Rise of American Democracy: Jefferson to Lincoln*. New York: Norton, 2005.

Wiley, Bell Irvin. *The Life of Billy Yank, Common Soldier of the Union*. 1952. Reprint, Garden City, N.Y.: Doubleday, 1971.

Williams, Kenneth P. *Lincoln Finds a General*. 5 vols. New York: Macmillan, 1949–59.

Wilson, Bluford. "Southern Illinois in the Civil War." *Transactions of the Illinois State Historical Society* 16 (1911): 93–103.

Wilson, Major L. "The Repressible Conflict: Seward's Concept of Progress and the Free Soil Movement." *Journal of Southern History* 37 (1971): 533–74.

———. *Time, Space, and Freedom: The Quest for Nationality and the Irrepressible Conflict, 1815-1861*. Westport, Conn.: Greenwood Press, 1974.

Winkle, Kenneth J. "A Social Analysis of Voter Turnout in Ohio, 1850–1860." *Journal of Interdisciplinary History* 13 (1983): 411–35.

———. "Voters of Lincoln's Springfield." *Journal of Social History* 25:3 (1992): 595–611.

———. *The Young Eagle: The Rise of Abraham Lincoln*. Dallas: Taylor Trade, 2001.

Woldman, Albert A. *Lincoln and the Russians*. Cleveland: World, 1971.

Woods, James M. *Rebellion and Realignment: Arkansas's Road to Secession.*
Fayetteville: University of Arkansas Press, 1987.

Woodward, Isaiah A. "Lincoln and the Crittenden Compromise." *Negro History
Bulletin* 22 (1959): 153–54.

Wooster, Ralph A. *The Secession Conventions of the South.* Princeton, N.J.:
Princeton University Press, 1962.

Wright, William C. *The Secession Movement in the Middle Atlantic States.*
Rutherford, N.J.: Fairleigh Dickinson University Press, 1973.

Wubben, Hubert H. *Civil War Iowa and the Copperhead Movement.* Ames: Iowa
State University Press, 1980.

Zorn, Roman J. "Minnesota Public Opinion and the Secession Controversy,
December, 1860–April, 1861." *Mississippi Valley Historical Review* 36 (1949):
435–56.

Index

Butler, Benjamin, 264
Butler, William, 222

Cabinet, Lincoln's: movement for
Southern members in, 90–91, 92,
94, 125, 167, 192, 193, 196, 298
(n. 20). *See also* Lincoln: and cabi-
net selection/patronage; Lincoln:
and Southern unionism/unionists;
Lincoln: support of for conciliatory
gestures
Cairo, Ill., 266, 267
Cameron, Simon: selection of to cabi-
net, 122–24, 125, 161, 192, 193, 224,
279, 304 (n. 48); and Fort Sumter
crisis, 214, 218, 232, 233, 246
Campbell, John A., 215–16, 217–18
Cass, Lewis, 40, 63, 86–87, 106
Chandler, Zachariah, 55
Charleston forts, 62–64, 85–87, 104,
105–7. *See also* Anderson, Robert;
Fort Moultrie; Fort Sumter
Chase, Salmon P., 44, 71, 80, 244;
selection of to cabinet, 89, 90, 124–
25, 192, 193, 199, 223; and Fort
Sumter crisis, 214, 229, 231, 232–
33, 234, 247
Chicago Democrat, 46, 55
Chicago Tribune, 46, 47, 161, 163
Clark, Daniel, 121, 166
Clemens, Sherrard, 197
Cobb, Howell, 40, 62, 86
Cochrane, John, 323 (n. 68)
Colfax, Schuyler, 166
Collamer, Jacob, 184
Commissioners, Confederate. *See*
Seward, William H.: and Confeder-
ate commissioners
Commissioners, South Carolina, 107,
112, 207
Committee of Thirteen, Senate: forma-
tion of, 70, 72–73, 97; compromise

debates of, 97–98, 103–4; adjournment of, 103–4, 112, 113
Committee of Thirty-Three, House:
formation of, 70, 73, 97; compromise debates of, 79, 82, 101–3, 104,
117, 142, 160. *See also* Corwin-
Adams plan; Dunn resolution in
Committee of Thirty-three;
Republican Party: influence of rank
and file of on party leaders
Compromise: possibility of, 18, 69–70,
90, 132, 153; proposals for, 57, 66,
73, 92–93, 98, 116–17, 101–3, 121,
160, 162, 183; failure of, 135, 164,
185, 187; false rumors of, late January, 167–69. *See also* Border-state
plan; Committee of Thirteen, Senate; Committee of Thirty-Three,
House; Conciliationists; Corwin-
Adams plan; Crittenden, John J.;
Crittenden plan; Democratic Party,
Northern: and compromise; Douglas, Stephen A.: as conciliationist
leader; Lincoln, Abraham: support
of for conciliatory gestures; Personal liberty laws; Republicans,
conciliatory; Republicans, hard-
line; Slavery, westward expansion
of; Slavery in Southern states;
Washington Peace Conference
Conciliationists: views of described, 9,
56–57, 144–47, 148–50, 163; in
eastern cities, 74–76, 78, 152, 153,
154, 155, 219–20; public expressions of, 74–79, 142–43, 152–55;
support among for peaceable disunion, 75, 148–49, 153, 194, 220,
238; and panic of 1860, 75–76, 77;
support among for defense of government, late December and early
January, 109, 153–54; renewed
efforts of in January and early Feb-

for resistance to federal use of force, 138, 149, 157, 266, 267–68; opposition of to Republican antislavery agitation, 138, 149, 255, 268; and defense of the flag, 164, 263, 264, 265, 268; and Fort Sumter crisis, March–April, 220–21, 225, 226; groping of toward loyal wartime opposition, 254–55, 268–69, 274, 280. *See also* Anti-Republicans; Breckinridge Democrats: Northern supporters of; Conciliationists; Douglas, Stephen A.

Democratic Party, Southern. *See* Breckinridge Democrats

Democratic state conventions: in Illinois, 139–40; in New York, 155–58

Democrats, former, in Republican Party, 44–45, 124, 193, 232

"Diary of a Public Man," 319 (n. 24)

Dix, John A., 113, 175, 259, 272

Dixon, James, 167

Douglas, Stephen A.: in election of 1860, 21, 28, 32; and Democratic Party, 28, 32, 97, 99, 209–10, 239, 268–69; public silence of early in crisis, 30, 39; and Kansas-Nebraska Act of 1854, 32, 115; patronage battle of with Buchanan, 32, 37; and Lecompton Constitution, 32, 37, 70; and use of racism as political strategy, 35–36, 114; and the Union, 36, 97, 98, 115, 149, 209, 233, 239, 267, 268, 269; efforts of to attract Northern conservatives, 37, 69–71, 116, 156, 210, 239; and Southern Democrats, 37–38, 70; and popular sovereignty, 37–38, 98, 116; and the use of federal force, 38, 39, 70, 96–97, 115–16, 139, 148, 209, 238; New Orleans letter of, November, 39, 65; and secession,

39, 70, 115, 116; as conciliationist leader, 69–71, 74, 97–99, 114, 116, 140, 164, 185, 196, 268; and Southern unionists, 69–71, 168, 196, 209–10, 211, 212, 239; and Founders, 70; appeals of to antiparty spirit, 70, 115, 116, 268; alliance of with Crittenden, 70–71, 98–99, 114, 116, 164, 167–69, 174, 184–85, 211, 313 (n. 8); January 3 speech of, 114–16, 169; attitude of toward Republican Party, 115, 149, 209; emphasis of on maintaining peace, 115–16, 209; and the Constitution / law and order, 115–16, 238, 269; and Illinois, 126, 267, 268–69; and Seward, 167–69, 174, 209–12, 313 (n. 8); and Lincoln administration, 190, 210–12, 238; powerlessness/ desperation of, 209, 210–12, 238– 40, 253; efforts of to establish Democratic Party as loyal opposition, 211, 268–69; and Fort Sumter, 211– 12; and congressional Republicans, March, 223, 238; and peaceable disunion, 238; post-Sumter support of for the administration, 254, 267, 268–69; death of, 269; and the flag, 269. *See also* Conciliationists; Democratic Party, Northern

Douglass, Frederick, 79

Dred Scott decision, 26, 98

Dunn resolution in Committee of Thirty-three, 73–74, 82, 102

Economic recession. *See* Panic of 1860

Egypt. *See* Northerners, response among to attack on Fort Sumter: in southern Illinois

Election of 1860, 1, 15–16, 19–22, 23, 26, 28–29, 58, 69; fusion movement in, 30–39

Empire State. *See* New York

Etheridge, Emerson, 119, 159

Evangelical Christianity. *See* Northerners: influence of evangelical Christianity on

Everett, Edward, 110–11, 152–55, 156, 163, 164, 265

Fell, Jesse W., 224

Fessenden, William, 238

Fillmore, Millard, 1856 supporters of: in 1860 election, 23, 29, 45; as Republican conciliationists, 76–77

Floyd, John B.: and Charleston forts, 17, 39, 62–64, 86–87, 106; desire to avoid hostilities, 40; and secession, 40; threat to resign, 40–41; financial scandal of, 108–9; and transfer of arms from Pittsburgh, 109; and the South Carolina commissioners, 112; resignation of, 112, 302 (n. 19)

Fogg, George G., 89

Forbes, John Murray, 44

Force bill, congressional, 166, 174, 183, 206

Forsyth, John, 207, 211, 216

Fort Monroe, 107, 119, 135

Fort Moultrie, 16, 86, 106–7, 113, 254

Fort Pickens: Buchanan administration's truce over, 135; reinforcement of debated under Lincoln administration, 204, 227, 229–31, 234, 242, 335 (n. 64); reinforcement of attempted under Lincoln administration, 235, 236, 240–41, 243, 246, 247, 252, 334 (n. 60)

Fort Sumter: Confederate attack on, 1, 2–3, 249–50; Southern forces around strengthened, 119–20, 135; crisis of, March and April, 188,

200–201, 208, 212, 226, 248. *See also* Anderson, Robert; *Star of the West*

Fort Sumter, under Buchanan administration: policy toward debated, 86, 175–76, 201; reinforcement of attempted, 113, 119–20

Fort Sumter, under Lincoln administration, 11, 202–3, 323 (n. 67); March 15 cabinet meeting on, 212–15, 248, 252; and desire to avoid appearance of aggression, 213–14, 232–33, 243, 247–49; Lincoln's fact-finding missions to, 218, 227–28; Winfield Scott and, 229–31; March 29 cabinet meeting on, 231–33; and plan of announcing fort's resupply/reinforcement in advance, 232, 247–49; final decision, early April, 240–47, 252, 335 (n. 64); as comedy of errors, 246. *See also* Blair, Montgomery; Fox, Gustavus V.; Lincoln, Abraham; Republican Party; Seward, William H.

Forts, Southern coastal, 85, 205. *See also* Charleston forts; Fort Moultrie; Fort Pickens; Fort Sumter; Fort Sumter, under Buchanan administration; Fort Sumter, under Lincoln administration

Founders: secession crisis as failure of, 2, 5, 14. *See also* Anti-Republicans: and Founders; Lincoln: and Founders; Northerners: and Founders; Republican Party: and Founders

Fox, Gustavus V., 193–94, 233, 235; plan of for reinforcing Fort Sumter, 176, 247, 248; and Lincoln administration, 213, 214, 218, 227, 228, 252, 325 (n. 77); expedition of to reinforce Fort Sumter, 229, 240, 246, 249–50

240, 241–44, 249, 250, 251; and defense of federal authority in South, 51–52, 124, 127, 181, 182, 187, 196, 204–5, 242, 243, 248, 252, 275; contribution of to Trumbull's November speech, 51–53; and policy of balancing magnanimity with firmness, 52–53, 90, 170–71, 173, 195, 199, 243–44, 248; influence of on congressional Republicans, 79, 81–82, 83, 100, 134, 160, 183, 195, 279; opposition of to compromise, 79, 88, 92, 93, 94–95, 101, 124, 134, 161, 171, 172, 176, 189, 195, 199, 239, 275, 279, 314 (n. 15); and Republican principles / slavery in the territories, 79, 92–93, 94–95, 112, 171, 172–74, 187, 189, 196; and William Kellogg, 80, 161, 170, 171, 176, 314 (nn. 14–15); strain of crisis on, 87–88, 228–29, 230–31, 233–34, 237, 240, 252; and Winfield Scott, 88, 194, 201, 204, 215, 229–31, 233, 234; and office seekers, 88, 224, 228, 234; reluctance of to make important decisions, 89–90, 112, 123–25, 218–19, 225, 226, 233, 237, 252–53; and Lyman Trumbull, 90, 112, 123, 124, 190, 223–25, 312 (n. 68); support of for conciliatory gestures, 91, 92–95, 125, 170, 171, 177, 189, 195–97, 199, 206, 243; and Thurlow Weed, 91–93; response of to Buchanan's compromise overture, late December, 112, 122, 302 (n. 20); and *Illinois State Journal*, 147, 170, 171; desire of to avoid role of aggressor, 147, 173, 182, 195–96, 205, 233, 243, 247–49, 250, 251, 275; false rumors of support for compromise of, 168, 177; and rule of law and constitu-

tional system, 171, 172–73, 182, 189, 196, 275; February 1 letter of to Seward, 171, 174, 177; inaugural address of, 172–73, 175, 187, 189–90, 191, 195–96, 198, 199, 206, 210–11, 235, 250; blames secessionists for crisis, 173, 181–82, 249, 250, 251, 275, 276; and Southern revenue collection, 173, 187, 199, 216–17, 218, 229; and Southern mails, 173, 187, 205; and survival of self-government, 173, 242, 251, 273–74, 275; and Washington Peace Conference, 176, 177, 178, 315 (n. 33), 318 (n. 16); strategy of buying time with hard-line pronouncements, 177, 195, 206–7; desire of for peaceful resolution to crisis, 181, 182, 189, 226, 252, 335 (n. 64); speeches of along road to Washington, 181–83, 189, 206; inauguration of, 187, 188–89, 199–200, 210–11; and Fort Sumter, March–April, 188, 202–3, 212, 215, 217, 218–19, 225, 226, 227–31, 233–34, 240, 242–49, 252; and Baltimore assassination plot, 190, 193, 317 (n. 3); effect of Washington environment on, 194–95, 197, 199; offers of to evacuate Fort Sumter in exchange for Virginia's loyalty, 196–97, 198, 243, 319 (n. 19); concern of over Robert Anderson's loyalty, 202, 230; frustration of with military and political advisers, 214–15, 230, 233; disorganization of, 217, 234, 235, 236, 237, 325 (n. 76); fact-gathering missions of to Charleston, 218, 227–28, 246, 248, 325 (n. 77), 326 (n. 78); isolation of in Washington, 225, 233–34; and Lyman Trumbull's Senate resolution, 228, 230,

North Carolina. *See* Upper South

Northerners: common political culture of, 2–3, 7, 8–10, 148, 150, 255, 260, 271, 276–77, 279–80; responsible for final decision on war, 3, 14–15, 120, 132, 276; centrality of political system to, 5–7, 8–9, 26–28, 60, 68, 150, 152, 164, 276–77, 288 (n. 20); centrality of political leaders to, 6–7, 8, 9, 12, 59, 60, 68, 74, 83, 105, 108, 120, 132, 133, 134, 136, 150–51, 164, 186, 188, 189, 225, 227, 239–40, 253, 254, 269–73, 277, 278, 284 (n. 14); and Founders, 8, 28, 70, 126, 257, 258, 260, 270, 271, 276, 277; and the Union, 8, 28, 105, 111, 126, 127, 128, 130–31, 137, 145, 147, 148, 150, 156, 221, 259–60, 269, 270, 271, 280; and law and order / constitutional system of government, 8, 28, 105, 128, 129, 130–31, 144–45, 147, 221, 255, 257, 259–60, 269, 270, 271, 273, 276, 277; attitude among toward secession, 8, 131, 144–45, 147–48, 219, 221, 256, 257, 277; importance of parties among, 8–9, 60, 151–52, 239, 277–78; and public property / federal forts in the South, before the inauguration, 18–19, 67, 86–87, 109–10, 143, 144, 145, 254, 277, 279; free-labor ideals among, 24, 25; anti-aristocracy sentiment among, 24, 25, 26–28, 144, 163, 258; influence of evangelical Christianity on, 24, 27; racism among, 25; West as symbol to, 25; wait-and-see attitude of in November, 30, 68, 188; contempt of for Buchanan, 41, 67, 108–10, 182; public involvement of in political process, 60, 68, 74–79, 83, 133,

142; views of regarding possible outcomes of secession crisis, 67, 275–76; antiparty sentiment among, 70, 111, 121, 128, 129, 137, 155, 156, 157, 162, 221; majority of in favor of compromise, 104, 133, 146, 164; patriotic unity among in late December and early January, 105, 109–11, 114, 119, 130–31, 131–32, 133, 134, 142, 149, 254, 259–60; confusion and fear among, late December and early January, 110–11; support of for armed defense of federal authority, 110–11, 130–31, 133, 134, 136, 148, 279; support among for Southern unionists, 130–31, 133, 137, 145–46, 221, 272; and the flag, 133, 136, 147, 148, 255, 257, 259–60, 266, 270, 271; polarization of, 136, 137, 142, 149–50, 221, 252, 280; concern among with aggression, 136, 147, 149, 254, 261, 277; desire of for peaceful resolution, 145, 148, 166, 178, 221, 263; influence of new communications technology on, 150; attitudes among on Fort Sumter crisis, March and April, 188, 203–4, 219–23, 244–46; local and state elections among, March–April, 244–45; responsible for success of Lincoln's strategy, 253; unity of in wake of Fort Sumter attack, 254–55, 256–62, 263–66, 269–72, 274, 277, 279; military response/enlistments among, 255, 256, 257, 258, 259, 260, 263–66, 269, 270, 271, 279; concern of with national honor, 260, 270; response of to Lincoln's Fort Sumter strategy, 261–62, 266, 279; post-Sumter political repression among, 262–63, 266–68; influence of on political leaders, 269–73. *See also* Anti-Republicans; Conciliationists; Democratic Party, Northern; Republican Party; Republicans, conciliatory; Republicans, hard-line; Sectional tensions

Northerners, response among, to attack on Fort Sumter, 254–55; in New York City, 256, 257–63, 269; as local Union meetings, 256, 258–59, 269–72; in Boston, 264–65; in Albany, 265; in Springfield, Ill., 265–66; in Philadelphia, 266; in southern Illinois, 266, 267–68; in Hudson, N.Y., 270–72

Northern state legislatures. *See* Legislatures, Northern

Nullification crisis of 1832–33, 18, 48, 127

Old Hickory. *See* Jackson, Andrew

Opdyke, George, 77

Osborn, David, 220

Oswego, N.Y., 19–20, 255–56

Palmer, John M., 266

Paludan, Phillip S., 71

Panic of 1860, 22–23, 58, 69, 75–76, 84, 90, 109, 217, 260. *See also* Morrill tariff

Parties: relationship between state and national organizations in, 30, 43, 126, 160–63. *See also* North: importance of parties in; Party system

Party system: instability of in 1860–61, 30, 59, 85, 105, 111, 139, 140, 164, 185, 278; and federal system of government, 43; centrality of ideology to, 150, 278. *See also* Parties; Second party system

Pat's skunk, 49

Peaceable secession. *See* Conciliation-ists: support among for peaceable disunion; Republican Party: support within for peaceable disunion

Peck, Ebenezer, 46

Pendleton, George, 148

Pennington, William, 69, 70, 99, 184

Pensacola Navy Yard. *See* Fort Pickens

Personal liberty laws: repeal of as compromise proposal, 57, 66, 75, 78, 91, 93, 121, 140, 152, 153. *See also* Fugitive Slave Law of 1850; Slaves, fugitive

Philadelphia, 74, 75, 266

Philip, John Van Ness, 270–72

Pickens, Francis, 107, 120, 134, 175, 227, 229, 230, 247

Pine Street meeting (New York City), 74–75

Popular sovereignty, 117, 160. *See also* Douglas, Stephen A.: and popular sovereignty

Potter, David M., 11, 93

Railroads, Pacific: as compromise proposal, 121

Ray, Charles H., 140

Raymond, Henry J. See *New York Times*

Republican Party: attitude within toward compromise, 8, 57–58, 146, 151–52; attitude within toward Southern forts, 8, 87, 121, 140, 279; impact of on crisis, 8–9; faith in Southern unionism/skepticism within toward secession, 20, 41–42, 47–53, 58, 75, 79, 81, 101, 148, 179, 187, 205, 213, 243; origins of, 26–28; and the South, 33, 50; and Founders, 35, 51, 53–54, 187, 191, 244; transition of from opposition party, 43, 44, 279; Lincoln as leader of, 43–44, 53, 83, 164, 165, 192–93,

227, 239–40, 278–79; divisions within, 44–47, 53, 55–59, 60–61, 88–90, 92, 94–95, 122–25, 126, 129–30, 139, 140–41, 146–47, 149–50, 160–63, 164, 192–93, 198, 223–25, 232; 1860 efforts of to attract 1856 Fillmore voters, 45, 76–77, 146; connection of party radicals to former Democratic faction, 45, 232; concern within with manliness, weakness, and honor, 48, 49–50, 53–54, 80–81, 82, 100, 143–44, 145, 147–48, 163, 168, 244; on Northern Democrats, 48, 58, 60, 82, 140, 150, 151, 178, 276, 280; and policy of balancing magnanimity with firmness, 48–49, 52–54, 77–78, 100, 160, 178; resistance of to compromise, 48–49, 154; and law and order / survival of self-government, 54, 81, 82–83, 118, 121, 128–29, 130, 137, 140, 141, 142, 143, 150, 161, 222, 228, 244, 276; divisions among party moderates over response to secession, 54–55, 79, 85, 100–101; support within for peaceable disunion, 56, 77, 137, 149, 163, 310 (n. 36); instability of, 60–61, 69, 74, 75, 83–84, 93, 95, 124, 129, 137, 138, 141, 187, 227, 229, 230, 240, 278–79; influence of rank and file of on party leaders, 61, 68, 79–82, 83, 102–3, 118, 142, 159–60, 162–63, 195, 239, 244, 245–46, 303 (n. 31); and Buchanan, 66, 67, 244; strength of in Thirty-sixth Congress, 68–69, 95, 98–99; Washington's effect on with regard to compromise, 73, 183, 195; anti-compromise sentiment within in Congress, 73–74, 82–83, 95, 98–99, 101, 117–19, 120–21, 131, 166;

procompromise sentiment within in Congress, 73–74, 90, 102–3, 113, 121–22, 158–63, 165–66; pro-compromise sentiment outside of Washington, 76–78, 129, 136, 137, 139, 141, 146–47, 177; and the use of force to prevent secession, 77, 82–83, 119, 130, 138, 163, 178, 182, 244; and Southern unionists, 77–78, 80, 83, 99–102, 114, 117, 130, 139, 141, 159, 160, 161, 165–66, 178, 179, 181, 183, 195; survival of threatened by conciliation, 79, 81, 102, 103, 104, 118, 177, 178, 222, 227, 241, 279; anticompromise sentiment outside of Washington, 79–82, 128, 129–30, 141, 142, 143, 161–63, 177–81, 183–85; and the Union and the Constitution, 81, 121, 128, 222, 228, 245; in control of congressional compromise, 100, 146, 151–52, 154, 164, 165, 185, 239; and defense of the flag, 140, 147, 262; remained intact until inaugural, 151, 160, 164, 165, 185, 192; rumors of support for compromise among, 167–68; debate of over participation in Washington Peace Conference, 176–80; and Washington Peace Conference, 180–81, 183–84; response of to Fort Sumter crisis, March–early April, 203–4, 222–23, 225, 226, 227, 228–29, 231–33, 244–45; view of dissent as treason, 255, 263, 280; on Lincoln's Fort Sumter strategy, 261–62, 279. *See also* Adams, Charles Francis; Cabinet, Lincoln's: movement for Southern members in; Fort Sumter, under Lincoln administration; Kellogg, William; Lincoln, Abraham; Republicans, conciliatory; Republi-

22, 156, 160–61, 164, 169–70, 178, 233, 240; and radicals, 72–73, 88–89, 124, 198–99; and Southern unionists, 73, 93–94, 121, 125, 166, 167, 168, 169, 174–75, 181, 185, 190, 191, 196, 199, 205–7, 208, 209–10, 212, 217, 225, 234, 235–36, 239; selection of to cabinet, 88–90, 91–92, 93, 121, 123–24, 167, 192, 194, 198–99, 223, 319 (n. 24); power-lessness/desperation of, 91, 93–94, 121–22, 166–67, 168–69, 182–83, 190, 191–94, 209, 210, 217, 234–38, 238–40, 253; and Committee of Thirteen, 97, 103, 170; reluctance of to split the Republican Party, 103, 166, 168–69; and defense of Washington, 110, 169, 193; possible support of for Crittenden plan, 114; appeals of to Northern unionism, 121, 236; January 12 speech of, 121–22, 166, 170; call of for a national convention, 122, 167; desire of to create a national party, 154, 156, 170, 205–6, 239, 279; and William Kellogg, 161–62, 169; late-January compromise rumors of, 167–69; and Stephen Douglas, 167–69, 174, 209–10, 211–12, 239, 313 (n. 8); and Southern revenue collection, 169, 170; and the Southern forts, 169, 170, 191; late-January letter of to Lincoln, 169–70; belief of in latent Deep South unionism, 170, 174, 205, 213, 228; and Washington Peace Conference, 181; and Lincoln's speeches on the road to Washington, 181–83, 189–90; and Winfield Scott, 190, 193–94, 234; and Lincoln, late February–April, 190–94, 198–99, 203, 204–5, 205–7, 217–18, 234–38, 323 (n. 68);

and Lincoln's inaugural address, 191, 198, 199, 206, 235; and Fort Sumter, 202, 207–9, 213–14, 215–16, 217–18, 225, 232, 234, 235, 236, 247, 248; and Confederate commissioners, 207–9, 215–16, 217–18, 222, 225, 235; and Fort Pickens, 216, 231, 234, 236; and Sumter expedition flagship, 235, 246; April 1 memorandum of to Lincoln, 236–37, 240, 245, 331 (n. 30). *See also* Adams, Charles Francis; Cabinet, Lincoln's: movement for Southern members in; Republican Party; Republicans, conciliatory; Republicans, hard-line; Weed, Thurlow

Seymour, Horatio, 157, 220
Seymour, Truman, 15–17
Shaw Memorial, 78, 152, 153
Sheahan, James, 96
Sherman, John, 69, 73, 101
Slave codes, territorial, 37–38, 66, 67, 70, 98, 101, 117, 161, 183, 206
Slave Power, 25–26, 29, 44, 48, 50, 54, 58–59, 80, 90, 94–95, 163, 275, 276
Slavery: as cause of sectional tension, 14, 18, 23–28, 85; attitudes toward among Republicans, 44–45, 102, 120–21
Slavery, westward expansion of: opposition to, 24–25, 33–34, 36–37, 79, 91, 92–93, 94–95, 102, 112, 118, 120–21, 131, 142, 163, 171, 187, 303 (n. 31); support for, 24–25, 120, 131; as source of friction among Democrats, 37–38; conciliatory Republicans and, 76–77, 80, 92–93, 118, 146, 166, 206; as subject of compromise proposals, 98, 116–17, 146, 278. *See also* Lincoln: and Republican principles / slavery in the territories

Slavery in Southern states, 183; proposed amendment protecting, 103, 117, 121, 147, 173, 185, 189, 199. *See also* Corwin-Adams plan

Slaves, fugitive: as subject of compromise debates, 172, 183–84. *See also* Fugitive Slave Law of 1850; Personal liberty laws

Slemmer, Adam, 135

Smith, Caleb B., 193, 214, 224, 231, 232

Softshells. *See* Democratic Party: factional divisions within; Democratic Party, Northern

South Carolina, 15–17, 19, 85–86; secession of, 60, 73–74, 84, 90, 93, 101, 102, 104, 105–6, 107, 108, 113, 117; and *Star of the West* episode, 120. *See also* Deep South; Fort Sumter; *Star of the West*

Southern Illinois. *See* Democratic Party, Northern: in southern Northwest and eastern cities; Northerners, response among to attack on Fort Sumter

Southern unionists, 11, 14, 77; views of toward secession, 94, 150, 175, 185, 197; and compromise, 98, 146, 208; and the use of federal force to prevent secession, 133, 197, 208, 241, 243, 251; and the evacuation of southern forts, 215, 230, 234. *See also* Cabinet, Lincoln's: movement for Southern members in; Gilmer, John; Lincoln, Abraham: and Southern unionism/unionists; Republican Party: and Southern unionists; Seward, William H.: and Southern unionists; Union Party; Upper South

Sowle, Patrick, 10, 198, 237

Spaulding, E. G., 79

Spinola, Francis B., 129, 130, 137–38, 263

Springfield, Ill., 41–42, 51–55, 125, 265–66. *See also* Legislature, Illinois; Lincoln, Abraham

Stampp, Kenneth M., 3–5, 11, 66

Stanton, Edwin, 86

Star of the West, 167, 176; attempt of to reinforce Fort Sumter, 119–20, 226; Northern response to reinforcement attempt of, 121, 130–31, 131–32, 133, 134, 135, 136, 142, 145, 147, 149, 154, 159, 167, 254, 263

Stephens, Alexander, 90, 94

Stewart, A. T., 78

Strong, George Templeton, 20–21, 87, 106, 146, 258, 259, 261, 265

Summers, George, 196, 215, 217, 241. *See also* Southern unionists

Sumner, Charles, 27, 48, 154, 179, 197, 310 (n. 36), 316 (n. 35)

Swett, Leonard, 45–46, 91, 122, 160–61, 169

Tammany Hall, 157, 263

Tariff, protective, 124

Tennessee. *See* Upper South

Thayer, James S., 157

Thomas, Philip, 86, 112, 113

Thompson, Jacob, 40, 61, 62, 108, 112, 120

Tilden, Samuel J., 30–39, 50, 65, 66, 157, 220, 251

Toombs, Robert, 97

Totten, Joseph, 202

Toucey, Isaac, 40, 175, 176

Tremain, Lyman, 157

Trumbull, George, 147

Trumbull, Lyman, 85, 140, 163, 222, 244; and Republican factionalism, 44, 46, 124, 126, 223–24; speech of at Springfield Jubilee, 51–53, 291

not much just chillin'

not much just chillin'

the hidden lives of middle schoolers

LINDA PERLSTEIN

Farrar, Straus and Giroux

New York

Farrar, Straus and Giroux
19 Union Square West, New York 10003

Copyright © 2003 by Linda Perlstein
All rights reserved
Distributed in Canada by Douglas & McIntyre Ltd.
Printed in the United States of America
First edition, 2003

Library of Congress Cataloging-in-Publication Data
Perlstein, Linda, 1971–.
    Not much just chillin' : the hidden lives of middle schoolers / Linda
Perlstein.— 1st ed.
        p.   cm.
    Includes bibliographical references (p.   ).
    ISBN 0-374-20882-4 (hc : alk. paper)
    1. Middle school students.   2. Middle school students—Psychology.
3. Adolescent psychology.   4. Teenagers.   I. Title.

HQ796.P46157 2003
305.234—dc21

                                                            2003003705

Designed by Patrice Sheridan

www.fsgbooks.com

1   3   5   7   9   10   8   6   4   2

The names of the children and their families have been changed out of respect for their privacy. Everything else remains unaltered. The few conversations and situations presented that the author did not witness firsthand were related to her soon after by one or usually more participants.

For Lisa, David, Rachel, and Noah

contents

not much just chillin'

at least they can't
shove me in

You can eat french fries for lunch every single day, if you want. There's something really cool, too, about having a locker, your very own parcel of the earth to which nobody else knows the code. In middle school, you don't have to walk through the halls in hushed, prissy lines. You get to cook food and saw wood and still make it home in time for the end of *CatDog*.

What else the kids filing into the half-lit cafeteria have heard about middle school: If you stand in the long line for fries, you might not have enough time to eat them before recess. The teachers can be mean, and the homework so hefty it really cuts into your valuable time. You have to change for gym, in front of everyone. Barely any fun stuff, like the gingerbread house your fifth-grade class made last Christmas. Worst of all: The eighth graders like to jam sixth graders inside lockers.

As the two hundred almost-sixth graders—girls with wet ponytails or freshly knit braids, boys with gelled spikes and droopy shorts—find their friends and settle into rows of blue plastic chairs for Wilde Lake Middle School orientation the Thursday before school starts, they greet each other loudly and think silently:

After finally persuading Mom to replace my dorky snakeskin binder with the black kind you can write on with milky pens, will those all of a sudden be out of style, leaving me one step behind the school-supply trends yet again?

Should I risk getting my butt kicked in lacrosse this year, since all the other boys look like they gained four inches on me this summer?

Can I wear my American-flag shirt from Old Navy on Monday, even though Dale insists it really only works on the Fourth of July? "We have to go in looking cool," she said. "We have to go in with style."

Could I rig some sort of basket inside my locker door with suction cups, so my friends can drop notes in there? Will my friends be in my classes? Will my friends be my friends?

Am I really going to start thinking, "Eww, Mom, you're weird, go away"? Is middle school really my last chance to be a kid?

The parents share those last two concerns, and others. Their minds are filled with equal parts worry and nostalgia about their children's entrance into this baffling no-man's-land between child and teen. Most adults say the most humiliating experience of their lives took place in middle school (or junior high, as it was called then), and many parents in the cafeteria remember their own preadolescence as the worst time of their lives: The awkward changes of puberty and the obsessions that entailed. The fumbling steps toward independence. The cliques. Being too embarrassed to sneeze in public. Constantly checking the armpit. Thinking everyone else was smarter, happier, better.

The men remember the time they asked out a girl they didn't want to be seen with, and the women remember the time they showed up at school to find all their friends wearing matching jeans and matching sandals and matching blazers with matching patches on the elbows. "Guys," today's mothers pleaded, "why didn't you call me?" They remember blindly joining the boycott of the benevolent redheaded girl who went, in one school year, from eating lunch with the most popular clique to eating lunch with the special-ed students, for no reason she (or anyone, for that matter) could discern. They remember when they stopped doing homework for a month, because they discovered that in the all-important world that revolved around their friends, there was nothing cool about getting A's. They remember telling their classmates that they'd been sick for a week instead of the truth—that they'd been in Greece with their parents—because if you're eleven, there are seventy-three ways you can make fun of someone just because he went to Greece.

How strange they were then. When they were twelve, they couldn't believe Styx would ever be oldies music; they were appalled at the gauchos they wore even one year before but couldn't imagine that what they had on at the moment would ever go out of style; they actually wanted braces and glasses, until they had to have them.

Maybe they don't remember. Maybe they've blocked it out. But at the parent meeting in the spring, they heard Wilde Lake's principal, Brenda Thomas, warn, "There are some poor decisions made at this age. If anyone gets through unscathed—I don't know them." When puberty's all over, she said, you'll get back a person much like the one you used to know, in personality much the same as before. "Eventually that child is going to be exactly who you raise it to be," she told them. "But in the meantime . . ." The meantime. While her own daughter was in middle school, Thomas called her Regan, after the possessed child in *The Exorcist*. Horror-movie mood swings, sudden demands for privacy, defiance, pushing away. Each public hug the parents have gotten this week is, they fear, the last. Will kids be mean to their child? Or worse: Will their child be the mean one?

Most of these parents have read the newspaper. They've read that middle school is an "academic wasteland," the new ground zero for state and national school-reform efforts, the point at which a child has to start thinking about *college*. In some ways, America's twelve and a half million middle schoolers are growing up faster than ever, their workload piling on as quickly as their distractions.

A few of the parents have even read what little "literature" is out on middle schoolers. They've learned that their children are about to go through the greatest period of physical and emotional growth, after infancy, that humans experience—years during which no significant part of themselves will go unchanged. They've read that the irresponsibility, the selfishness, the boredom their kids are about to exhibit are signs of progression, not regression—no, *really*. They've read to expect contradictions: Children start to fix their values and figure out who they are independent of their families, at the same time they are too timid to set themselves apart as individuals. Twelve-year-olds are eager to turn everything into arguments but don't have the cognitive skills to win them. They are at once submissive and defiant, idealistic and materialistic. The titans of commerce have started rearranging their world around the shopping habits of "tweens"—who are thrilled to be targeted, except they don't make their own money. They want to be cuddled. Except when they don't.

More than anything, middle school pulls in children and pitches back teenagers. It is a time of change, which means, at this age, many things.

For Eric Ellis, an eighth grader, change means going from striving to please his teachers and mother to realizing that there's not much room in his life—what with skating and video games and dealing with his family—to aim for A's, and that if work is boring, which it often is, it is in his power to simply not do it.

For Jackie Taylor, a seventh grader, change means going from someone who not long ago invented a playground-wide inoculation against boy germs to spending a major chunk of time obsessing over and writing notes about her and her friends' serial crushes, recounting soap-operatic plot lines that are agonizing to them and utterly mystifying to everyone in their lives (usually over the age of thirteen) who thinks you actually have to *talk* to a boy to be his girlfriend.

For Elizabeth Ginsburg, also a seventh grader, change means going from chattering on about life's rich details in the car to swim practice and asking her parents for help with just about everything to all of a sudden shrugging off their suggestions, demanding to be left alone, invariably answering "Nothing" to the daily and now useless question, "What did you do at school today?"

For Jimmy Schissel, who is starting sixth grade, change means living through strange, uncomfortable alterations to the way his body works—inside and out, from sleeping to eating to thinking to sitting to running—and forever wondering both what is normal and what comes next.

For Lily Mason, also in sixth grade, change means experiencing a new intimacy with her friends and a new absorption in where she stands among them, such that to peek underneath her easygoing persona is to witness a constant effort to wear the right clothes and say the right things and not make one single move to stand out, lest she drop a notch in the eyes of the girl she considers her best friend.

The teachers in their matching white polos take the stage one by one to lay the first of a year full of transparencies on the overhead projector and lay down the laws of sixth grade: You may go to your lockers only before school, before lunch, and after school. No sticky book covers—they ruin the textbooks. Travel at all times with your agenda, a spiral-bound date book that serves as both assignment log and hall pass. Classes rotate every other day, four on A-days, four on B-days, eighty minutes each—don't worry, you'll get used to it. The kids are given orientation folders, and page through them.

"What's on the next page?" a mother says to her daughter, who clamps it shut. "What, is it a secret?"

One little brother, a third grader with a sitcom child's knack for one-liners, is not too young to sense the tension. "What if I skip middle school," he suggests, "and go straight to high school?" His mother is one of the many who linger at the sides and back of the cafeteria, clucking their tongues, shaking their heads, smiling frowny smiles: "It seems like *yesterday* he was graduating from *kindergarten*." They make mental notes to take a photo this weekend, in case their children grow that fast. They look around and are not quite able to picture gangs in this cafeteria, arson in the trash cans, like the rumors had it. Wilde Lake lies at the heart of Columbia, Maryland, a suburb between Washington and Baltimore created in the late 1960s as developer James Rouse's original planned community, a tree-thick, sidewalk-lined town made up of individual "villages" where people of all races and social classes would live in harmony and chat and swap tools at communal mailboxes. Even though it's relatively progressive, things haven't quite worked like Rouse envisioned; Columbia has been suffering from a nationally pervasive suburban white flight, whereby more prosperous residents flee the core for the outer, more pastoral, less eclectic villages. The parents who remain have heard that this place is a little "rough" for a suburban school in such an affluent county, and parents with children still uneasy about cooties wonder if this is where it all starts: Drinking. Smoking. Drugs. Sex.

Not to mention indifference to schoolwork.

"She's worked so hard," one mom tells her friend. "I don't want her to lose any gains."

"Is she going to get so defiant," the other says, "and not be my quiet, studious little girl anymore?"

Homerooms are announced by surname, and after packs of friends bless or curse the accidents of the alphabet that keep them together or separate them, they are sent to walk through their class schedules and—finally!—try their lockers. The lockers aren't even six inches wide, so everyone can't fit at once. Some parents crowd in, some force themselves to stay back. Kids bounce on their heels, trying their combinations ten times in a row. The parents stand mute, until they can't any longer.

"We'll stay here until you can do it five times by yourself." (Sucked teeth.)

"Abby, can I come in and help?" (No answer.)

"Why don't we walk your schedule and come back and try when there are fewer people here?" ("One more time.")

From inside a classroom, an eighth grader who came to spy on the new kids perches on a desk, swinging her long legs, and watches. As the kids in the hall talk about skateboards and locker combinations and summer camp and the 'N Sync concert—they look so *small*—she tilts her head side to side. "I've been waiting for this day for years," she says. "I'm going to own this school."

Lily Mason tries her locker combination several times as her best friend, Mia Reilly, sits next to her on a high ledge, paging through the papers they've been given. A newsletter called *Middle Years* gives instructions on Backpack Safety. *Please*, Mia thinks. Lily's face practically touches the dial as she spins slowly—right, left, right, stop—and each time she tugs on the little metal handle, nothing.

"My camera makes little sticky pictures," she tells Mia. If she ever gets her locker open, she can paste them inside. Her father, standing a few steps behind, asks, "Do you want me to help?" Since it's a matter of the locker being stuck, and not a matter of getting the combination wrong, Lily figures it's not immature to let him unjam it.

The girls make plans to meet right here the moment middle school starts for real, and Mia goes to open her locker. Eight times she tries, quiet and serious. The crisscross of her swimsuit straps shows above her tank top. Her mother, Leigh, would like to help but can tell Mia wants to do it herself—which she finally does. *Such an accomplishment*, Leigh thinks. A bigger accomplishment is when Mia tries to sidle into the locker. All that fits of her four feet nine inches is one tanned leg.

"Well," she announces, "at least they can't shove me in."

autumn

i can't believe the day's almost over

On Monday morning some mothers drive their children to the bus stop, where they achingly resist the urge to hug their babies. Instead they settle on forehead kisses so quick as to be nearly invisible. One boy stands slumped, breathing in the muggy air slowly, tired from being kept awake most of the night by lingering images from *The X-Files*. A mom rolls up in a Suburban and leans out the window: "Brittany, did you remember your keys?" Brittany scrunches her face, mortified, and rolls her eyes to Mia. Mia's got on a camouflage tank top, khaki shorts, two old string anklets, and white, silver-striped Adidas with the laces tied under the tongue. (White Adidas are the best shoes you can wear; Vans or Skechers are okay, too. If your Adidas are colored because your mom says white gets ruined too soon, you may as well be wearing Stride Rites.) Having decided that a sixth grader has to care more about her looks, Mia took a while to get ready today. She had her mom blow-dry her shoulder-length chestnut hair pouffy, but not too pouffy.

As Mia pushes her hair behind her ears, the seventh graders, weighed down by enormous backpacks, grill her:

"Do you like school?"

"Yes."

"Well, you won't by the end of sixth grade."

One of the most popular kids in her elementary school, Mia has the confidence that comes with having popular jocks as older brothers, plays soccer (the coolest sport), isn't afraid to try a never-before-seen hairstyle, and sasses just enough to crack the class up but still get away with it. She was the only girl not to cry at the end-of-fifth-grade pool party. So none of her classmates would guess that Mia Reilly has worries, too.

The only reason she didn't cry at the pool party was that she got it all out in private, the day before. She's anxious about middle school. If only she could wear her tall hidden-roller-skate shoes—then she might not be the shortest in the school. After being with the same group since kindergarten, she's looking forward to meeting new kids from the two other elementary schools, but that's also what scares her: "How will I know I can trust them?" She's concerned about times tables and about teachers "from the Black Lagoon."

Another huge issue: Mia has to broker peace between Lily and their friend Alexandra, who aren't speaking after a fight this summer. They ended fifth grade best friends—quite an accomplishment for Lily, who arrived, quiet and Southern and with no Adidas, in the middle of December. Lily and Alexandra spent practically all summer together, until one day Alexandra wanted to go outside to dance and Lily didn't. They argued and stopped talking to each other completely. "Alexandra has to be the boss of everything," Lily says. Seems to Mia like a stupid thing to fight over, but there it is. Getting them to make up "might take a little bit of time," she says, but "it's crucial, because I can't spend time with just one."

Dropped off by the buses but not allowed inside until the eight-forty-five bell, the students swarm outside the school building, a flat, cream-brick hexagon that lies in view of the big high school and the strip mall. A few eager boys peer through the front doors. They half shake hands or don't touch at all. The girls touch each other's hair. "Fine, don't say hi," one girl says to another. "I *did* say hi." The bell goes off and the students push their way inside, where Ms. Thomas snatches hats off heads. Teachers stand in the hall with homeroom lists, filtering kids down one hall or the other.

In homeroom Mia finds her assigned seat, up front. Lily sits in the back corner, wearing turquoise-plaid shorts, a white T-shirt, and a navy cardigan from The Children's Place. For an eleven-year-old she rarely slouches, conditioned from the discipline of ballet and gymnastics and a desire to one day be Miss America. Her dirty-blond hair spurts from a little ponytail; she hates the way it styles and wishes it were thinner. Her blue-gray eyes are always either cast down bashfully or (when she is sure they are not looking) studying the people around her, for clues on how to act. When her face is at rest, like now, it is inscrutable, but she will tell you she's pretty happy today. Last night she and Mia went to the Aaron Carter concert and screamed. Middle school all sounds interesting to her—the lockers, the teachers, getting to sew in home ec—and anyway, she doesn't fashion herself a worrier. Her answer to an annoyingly large number of questions is "I don't care," whether it's her mom asking what she wants for dinner or a friend asking what game she wants to play.

Split personalities are common among middle schoolers, Lily included. At home she is chatty and confident, not a hint of self-consciousness about her. She is an able caregiver to her siblings, nine-year-old Gabrielle, five-year-old Sean and the foster newborns who arrive one, two, three at a time without names. Among the neighbor kids she is something of a mother hen, leading the skit-writing and fort-building and chalk drawing. When she is alone with Mia, hyperactivity takes over. Heady with the companionship of a true friend, Lily gets wacky. She cannot stop moving, talking, touching, goofing. At school—in any large group, in fact—Lily rarely speaks, so her teachers would laugh if you told them this. Not Lily! Since she got to Maryland it's only every two months or so Lily figures she has something amusing to add to a lunch-table conversation. In the rare instances when, having appraised the sentence thoroughly in her head, she judges it worthy of emitting, everyone is like, "Uh, yeah."

Whereas Mia looks forward to meeting new kids, Lily's friends are set and she doesn't much care about making new ones. She learned the sign-language alphabet so they can communicate during class. Mainly, when Lily talks about friends, she is talking about Mia. "We're best friends," she's explained, "and we're the same height and same age. Our noses come up to the same place and so do our eyes. Her birthday is the day after my birthday. We were born twelve hours apart. So when my mom was having me, her mom was in labor. I call Mia 'M' or 'MM' or 'Mi' or 'Mia.' She calls me 'Lil' or 'Lily.' I have four names for her and she has two for me."

Lily has only one name for Alexandra—"Alexandra"—and though the two saw plenty of each other during orientation last week, she didn't use it once. When Alexandra came into the cafeteria that day, instead of seeking out Mia and Lily, she bounced over to Tamika, one of the few other black girls from their elementary school, which was somewhat of a relief to Lily, because she sees Alexandra as competition for Mia's attention. At the same time she was a little insulted. Today Alexandra is late; she is supposed to occupy the empty seat in front of Lily, who eyes it nervously.

The school computer has run Lily's first and middle names together: Lilyelise. During roll, when the rest of the kids are offering up corrections and nicknames to Mrs. Stokes, Lilyelise is too shy to say anything about it. The students are silent, and efficient Mrs. Stokes is already going over schedules—no warm "Hi!" or "Welcome to middle school!"— when Alexandra walks in, wearing a white button-down, a plaid miniskirt that wouldn't pass the fingertip test, and chunky black-heeled loafers. She finds her seat in front of Lily, who watches and then tilts her head down and keeps it there, through morning announcements, through Mrs. Stokes reviewing all the papers that need to be signed, through the questions about gym shoes and recess and what if my backpack doesn't fit in my locker, through the explanations of Homework Hotline and hall passes, until the bell finally rings and the kids set out on their favorite task of the day: unloading backpacks into lockers. The girls walk through the hall with Mia in the middle, Alexandra and Lily talking to her from either side, but not to each other.

When they walk into the cafeteria for lunch, the swim-team girls at one round table, already making progress on their bagels and sandwiches and Trix yogurt, call out for Mia. They've saved her a seat, but she leads the way to an empty table. Everyone there except Alexandra brings lunch from home; when she returns with fries, they are dispersed, and enthusiastically approved of. Lily listens as the girls discuss Mia's blue Kool-Aid, the classmate whose new house has closets the size of bedrooms, and Brittany's mother's bus-stop appearance. In the telling, "Did you remember your keys?" has become "*DID YOU REMEMBER YOUR KEEEEEEYS?*" but the girls still agree that this was preferable to a hug.

Ms. Thomas comes by the table and asks, "How was your first day?"

"Good."

"Did they stuff you in the locker?"

"Too small."

She laughs. New sixth graders are just the cutest. Later in the year they'll turn a corner, and the teachers will wonder, "Who are you?" But for now most of them are overwhelmed, sweet, taking it all in soundlessly. In the cafeteria they raise their hands for permission to use the bathroom. The noise is one-fifth what it will be during seventh-grade and eighth-grade lunch. When Ms. Thomas counts down from five into the microphone, the room falls utterly silent, for which she congratulates them. "Welcome," she says. "It's nice to see people from all the feeder schools, and all over the world."

At recess, some boys chase a shopping cart. Keith West, the assistant principal, quarterbacks a football game. Mia marches to the soccer field with the swimmers, where they play against the boys and her shoe keeps flying off. Alexandra and Lily are left alone on the blacktop to speak their first words to each other in a month.

"What do you want to do?" Lily asks.

"Nothing," says Alexandra.

"I can't believe the day's almost over."

"Like my new watch?"

"Don't tell me—you got it at Kohl's. I put the pink one on hold, but I can't decide." Maybe this isn't so hard.

When the whistle calls everyone inside, the boy who played Robin Hood in the fifth-grade play passes by. "Hey, Joel," Alexandra calls, "nice tights!"

Lily rolls her eyes—at the boy having worn tights once, at Alexandra taunting him, at all of it.

At eighth-grade lunch, Eric Ellis and his friends are discussing whether the plane crash that killed the R&B singer Aaliyah will affect the Video Music Awards and whether it's okay to cry if you're injured (only if there's blood involved), when Mr. West sits down and asks what grades they're going for this year. Liam, who always gets A's, says "A's." Chris, who wants to stop being the class clown so he can play football in high school, says "A's." Shawn, who thinks he's too dumb to get A's but is not too dumb to know what the right answer is here, says "A's."

Eric figures he could make A's if he really wanted to. But with skating and paintball and missing his mom and getting along with his dad's girlfriend and improving at saxophone, he says, "It's too hard to get A's. My brain is too full. I'm gonna get B's."

Sixth and seventh grade, Eric pretty much lay back, did what he was told. This year, there's a little excitement at being at the top of the school, an "I'm not a little kid anymore" feeling—for once, wanting to succeed not just for Mommy but for himself. This is a typical shift in attitude among eighth graders, as they prepare for the big league of high school. But in Eric and most of his classmates, it does battle with an equally strong attitude: ambivalence. The collective eighth grade of the United States could be labeled "Doesn't work to potential." Decline in motivation from elementary school to middle school is universal and documented. Thirteen-year-olds can't get interested in anything that bores them, no matter how many times they're told, *This is important, you'll see why in ten years.* In the preteen years, the brain's gray matter has almost fully thickened, but it is not yet pruned to its most efficient level of activity. All of a sudden there's a vast overproduction of brain cells and connections—by the time puberty is done, only some will have survived—and quantity trumps quality. It's not a particularly spectacular time to soak up information, because, even though emotional centers closer to the core of the brain have developed well by now, capacity for skills like logic, organization, and judgment, centered in the still-immature frontal lobes, is poor.

Eric's level of effort is typical for his age: Sometimes he does his work, sometimes he doesn't. Sometimes he pays attention in class, sometimes he doesn't. He likes school, and he doesn't like school. He likes his teachers, he thinks they're shrews. He thinks he's very bright compared to Chris and Shawn, and tells them, "You'll be sorry when you're out there asking for pennies on Route Forty." It's because teachers tell him so that Eric assumes he could get A's whenever he wanted, but when he's bored he can't pay attention, and when he's frustrated he can't either. "I want it to challenge me," he says, "but not to be too hard." He doesn't want to be too smart, "just a little intelligent." If you're too smart, people talk behind your back—"He thinks he's all that," and so on, like they do about Liam—and he's heard it's even worse if you're an adult. What would be best, he figures, is if everyone were born just smart enough so that school didn't have to exist.

Adults love Eric, who knows when to "sir" and especially when to "ma'am" and never curses above "Dag!" or "Snap!" In conversation Eric shows genuine interest, looking straight at them with his dark-ringed eyes and nodding and laughing along. He escapes the torture normally directed at a boy of his substantial weight, partly because his chubbiness doesn't prevent him from attempting the normal physical adventures of boyhood (as proved by the topography of scars on his legs) and partly because Eric is kind to everyone who doesn't cross him. He is black, but the racial divides of friendship don't apply to him. White boys in younger grades argue about who was friends with him first.

All in all, Eric does okay in school, particularly when his mother gets on his back about it, and when he has a teacher he adores, like Mr. Shifflett in seventh grade, who was really into sharks and always made science fun. Eric briefly had a 104 average in that class and once had all B's on a progress report. He was invited to the Most Improved pizza party, which felt good, though he didn't appreciate his friends calling him "Teacher's Pet" and "Egghead." There are always dozens of sixth graders at functions like that, but often by the time kids get to eighth grade they've banished A's to the same black hole where they keep their Backstreet Boys CDs. Despite the teasing, Eric really would like all B's again, although he has no idea how hard it's going to be this year to make that happen.

Last year he lived in a town house with his mother, Tenacious, and his half-brother on his mom's side, Tim, who's eighteen. They were evicted over the summer and Tim left for college, so Tenacious has moved in with friends in Baltimore, where she works as a health counselor in the jail. Eric has moved in with his dad, William, an over-the-road trucker; his fiancée, Beulah; and Eric's half-brother on his dad's side, nineteen-year-old Thomas. Their town house is only a half-mile from Wilde Lake Middle School and barely a mile from Eric's old place, but it may as well be in another state. Without a ride, he doesn't see his old neighbors. Nobody around here walks that far. His new neighbors—not that he wants to be friends with them anyway—go to a different middle school. (Eric is breaking the districting rules, but nobody will complain.)

More significant, Eric is separated from his mother for the first time ever. She still plans to stay in control of his schoolwork. She figures she'll be more lenient about his time now that he's in eighth grade. "I'd prefer he do his homework right away," Tenacious says, "because that frees his afternoon up, but if he calls and says he's getting a snack or needs to unwind, that's okay." Since Eric will be reading *Romeo and Juliet* this year in English, she has bought a copy.

"It's a great love story," she says.

"Yuck," he says.

On the days he comes home, Eric's father may ask if he's done his homework, but he never questions the "yes," is usually too tired to check, and doesn't make Eric talk about school. "I don't talk about work if I don't have to," William says. So Tenacious plans on driving a half-hour from Baltimore to Columbia each morning by six-forty-five, to check Eric's work and take him the half-mile to school. And she has made her expectations clear: "The absolutely lowest grade you can get is a C. B's are great, just as good as A's to me. C's are beneath you, but I'll accept them. D's are out of the question." William, too, says anything less than a C is unacceptable.

It's also unacceptable to the powers that be. Concerned that middle schoolers were allowed to coast in mediocrity for too long, last year the school-board members of Howard County, which encompasses Wilde Lake, implemented strict rules: A student can't move from eighth to ninth grade without passing state reading, writing, and math tests designed for high schoolers. If he has below a C average or even one F, the principal can hold him back, or bar him from sports and extracurricular activities in ninth grade. Ms. Thomas, the principal, is serious about helping kids over the bar, and it breaks her heart—and theirs—when they don't make it. Last year thirty eighth graders were put on the no-sports list, and eleven were held back. So far, Ms. Thomas thinks the new policy is working, that kids have seen enough classmates retained to focus far more on their grades. When she tells parents about the new policy, she says of the students, "They do understand that academics are number one—that's why we're here."

In Eric's mind, academics aren't number one. That spot is reserved for God. They're not number two. That's his mother. Music and the rest of his family—tied for third. Skating is fourth, paintball and video games are fifth. But Eric does know that, in order to satisfy the Lord, Tenacious, and the Wilde Lake High School marching band, he has to do his homework.

Eric's science class is two hallways and a universe removed from the hush of the sixth grade. The eighth graders have dropped their forbidden backpacks on the floor—they are supposed to be kept in lockers—and laugh and taunt and fiddle and compare who grew over the summer and who didn't. They keep finding reasons to go in and out of the room, and they ask things like, "Do I need to do all this?" Ian Garvey zips off a section of his cargo pants, tosses it in the air, and says, "Look, my leg came off."

Most kids arrive at Wilde Lake behaving just fine, but there are enough who are so inattentive to direction—enough Ians—that the whole first week is spent going over school rules and philosophies. Students take quizzes on the importance of their agendas, perform skits about the school motto, and answer questions like, "Which is the most important rule and why?" They highlight key sentences from an Ann Landers passage called "How to Fail" and parse the school's Mission Statement:

> WLMS staff, students, family, and community members will work together to create a supportive and stimulating school environment for all. This will enable students to achieve academic excellence, demonstrate cultural sensitivity, provide service for the community, and develop the skills for lifelong learning.

For the many children who have never acted up in class—who still respond to "Boys and girls, raise your hands if you're waiting quietly," or "Put your hand on your head when you have your name on your paper"—all this emphasis on rules is overwhelming, and boring, and they wonder how they'll ever finish the curriculum at this rate. To be told you have to raise your hand before answering is like being told you have to put the toilet lid up before you sit down. When they are debriefing over dinner after school the first night, the main thing Lily and her friends tell their parents, aside from which friends are in which classes and the unfairness of the no-spaghetti-strap rule, is that some of these kids are just plain *rude*. At Clemens Crossing Elementary, disobedient kids might talk in between what the teacher was saying, but not *over* it. And sometimes the teacher doesn't do anything about it!

Though Eric, too, finds these sessions numbingly tedious, this year he has decided to be Mr. Participation. So he alone volunteers to read aloud from the worksheet and to answer every question of today's lesson, positive and negative consequences.

"What would a negative consequence be?" Ms. Drakes asks.

With the pants leg balancing on his head—sending it there will get Ian no negative consequences—Eric raises his hand.

"Eric?"

"A negative consequence would be getting punished. I can't do nothing. I can't even play with Power Ranger toys," he jokes, and plucks the pants leg from his head.

"What's a positive consequence?" she asks.

Eric's hand is up again. "Get a piece of candy?"

"What's one positive consequence you want to earn? Eric?"

"Positive phone call home."

"What would you have to do to earn that?"

"Pay attention in class and keep up with homework and stuff."

Ian announces, "I was good once. I went to the Capitol. I still have the ticket in my wallet. It was free. See?" Next to him, Eric drums a sophisticated beat with his knuckles and fingers.

"Okay, Eric, stop." Ms. Drakes stands up front and folds her fingers down, one at a time. "Five, four, three, two, and one. One, two— You went two past my countdown. You shouldn't. Ian, turn around."

After the class has listed more positive consequences of doing schoolwork ("ice cream," "pizza party," "extra recess"), the students complete a worksheet. Eric fills in the blanks: "My goal for this year in order to *earn good grades* as a positive consequence is *to study and work hard*." When Ms. Drakes asks if anyone wants to share, Eric reads what he's written.

Good grades alone as positive consequence? He may as well have written "know a lot." Ms. Drakes suggests, "Maybe the consequence you would want is the honor-roll breakfast or something."

It doesn't take long to know what a class is going to be like for the rest of the year. By the second week at Wilde Lake, Eric's hand is already cramped from writing class goals and expectations, and he has made some assessments:

Science, she's no Mr. Shifflett. Too many worksheets, not enough labs.

Band should be good. The new teacher was visibly impressed when Eric, the best sax player in the school, said he had taught himself to play in only two years. Sometimes he gets bored with band, but Mr. Vega seems enthusiastic, and, anyway, his mom would be crushed if he quit. Music, she tells him, is his special gift, even at age two, when he would pull the pots and pans out of the cupboard and entertain himself for hours.

English might be cool, *Romeo and Juliet* notwithstanding. Mrs. Brown has set the bar high—"Eighty and above, that's success"—but she also lets them set expectations for *her*: Be prepared, don't pick favorites, don't go too slow, don't go too fast, don't punish the whole class for the misdeeds of a few, and, from Eric, make sure you understand a kid's question before you answer. Also, Mrs. Brown and Eric share a passion. One of the first days, she asks, "Does anyone like auto racing?" Eric, who has sweated with excitement each of the nine times he's watched *The Fast and the Furious*, shouts "Yes!" and stops tapping his pencil. Mrs. Brown tells about one of her favorite authors, who spent eight years studying auto racing for a novel, and she answers Eric's questions about NASCAR superstar Dale Earnhardt, even though they're irrelevant.

Eric's not sure about academic enrichment, a class where students who aren't taking a foreign language learn study skills and review subjects there's not time for in other classes. He likes that Mrs. Cook seems stern and caring at the same time, that it's instantly clear she's determined her students turn out good citizens. She already has the class totally under control. "When it's time to work in her class," Eric says, "you work." But he goes blank at the topics she announces they'll learn: Microstudio and PowerPoint and Hypertext and Concept Mapping, whatever all that is.

He has Mrs. Cook for reading, too. Reading and English classes are a lot alike, and for Eric the two just combine to mean too many books. Even though his mother tried to pass on her passion for books to Eric, and he fondly remembers their Peter Rabbit moments, officially Eric says that no book is good unless it's about cooking, cars, funny stuff, or skateboarding. Unofficially he really liked two books he read in sixth grade: *Freak the Mighty*, a novel about a midget kid and his grotesquely huge friend Max, whose dad killed his mom, and a biography of Langston Hughes. When they read how Hughes was treated poorly in his new all-white neighborhood, Eric says, "That related to me. When I lived in the city everybody was black, and then when I moved out here—aside from Shawn and James; they were like, 'What's up?'—everybody else was like, they already had their little cliques, and I had to find somebody else to be friends with." Eric's thinking he might not hate reading so much this year, because they're going to write a research paper on whatever they want, which for Eric is cars, and for class he has written a poem he's pleased with, called "I Am":

> *Soft, friendly sometimes, mamas boy, easy!*
> *Who discovered, that its hard to be popular in a variety of cultures in a*
>   *school*
> *Who feels alive, brainy, curious*
> *Who fears breaking another bone, failing, parent-teacher conferences*
> *Who loves my rollerblades, sportscars, and my parents*
> *Who wants 99.9 million dollars, a fully equipped car*

Eric thinks America is one of the best countries in the world, even though for its celebrations Africa has cool decorations like beads made from animal skin and "we just have that flag." But he's not pleased with American-history class. First of all, Eric hates the way Shawn copies from his homework. His classmates cheat a lot; there's a homework worksheet being copied at half the cafeteria tables every day. Eric doesn't have a problem with people copying off him, but only when he gives permission. He hates the way Mrs. Conroy capitulates to the girl who complains, "Obstruction of justice! I know my rights, and I have a right to go to the bathroom!" and the way she seems to just stand up there at the front of the room smiling, calling on them, and referring to the book.

Still, Eric raises his hand to answer all the time, as if a pulley attached to the ceiling were jerking his wrist.

Ms. Adams, the new, young math teacher, who wears a different pair of funky glasses practically every day, intrigues Eric; he touches her long blond ringlets and says, "Your hair is mad curly!" Sometimes her lessons are cryptic, though, or incomplete. The first day, in an attempt to interest the many black students in the class, she asks what "40 Acres and a Mule" means. After some guessing (Eric: "Oooh, did the slaves use mules to fight back?"), she explains. She adds, "Everything we do in here is not necessarily what you'd think is math," though why they're discussing forty acres and a mule, beyond the fact that forty is a number, never becomes clear.

Within days Eric realizes that when he's not in a math mood he can talk about Red Lobster or *Gridlock* with the kid sitting next to him, or watch the girls across the room stick tape all over a boy's ears and face. "Do you not know better?" Ms. Adams says. "Do you not know better? You owe me a roll of tape." Still, when Eric feels like working, he wants to get it right. One day in the second week of school, the drill for the day is written on the overhead:

1. What day followed the day before yesterday if two days from now will be Sunday?

Eric says to himself, "Wednesday. Yep, that's easy."

2. A math teacher drove by a playground that was full of boys and dogs. The teacher happened to notice that there was a total of 40 heads and 100 feet. How many boys and how many dogs were there?

Eric doesn't know where to begin on this one. He guesses fifteen dogs, in which case there's twenty-five boys. Too many. He shakes his notebook. There are kids working; there are kids talking. Eric picks some numbers randomly and figures them in his head, but they don't work. "I don't get number two, Ms. Adams, so I'm quitting because I'm getting frustrated and then I'll get mad." He pounds the desk: "How many legs on the goddamn dogs?"

3. Replace A, B, and C with numbers so that A × A = B, B − A = C, A + A = C.

Last year Eric's half-brother Tim, a college freshman, taught him tricks to figuring these kinds of expressions, but variables don't make sense to him. Can you own "A" CDs? Invite "B" people to your birthday party? Are there "C" days till Christmas? Ms. Adams tries A as one, then two, then three. Bingo. "I still don't get what you're doing," Eric says.

Ms. Adams, a twenty-five-year-old who spent the two years before teaching school as an exercise physiologist, doesn't totally get it either. In the last two weeks she's been learning the rules, too. Don't stand on a desk to put up your bulletin board. Check the duty map to see when you have hall patrol. Write comments to parents every week on the agendas, and phone if a grade goes down. Make sure kids don't fill out their hall passes in pencil. Keep your eye out for bandanas, hats, purses, Palm Pilots, spaghetti straps, pagers. Follow the official levels of discipline intervention laid out in this fat binder—don't make up your own system.

Last year Ms. Adams student-taught sixth graders in a prosperous middle school near Pittsburgh; here, the amount of time spent going over the discipline policy has made her fearful for what the teachers call "our population." She can't pronounce the foreign kids' names ("Give me a vowel, just one vowel"); she worries black kids will call her racist; she doesn't know much about geography, which she has to teach in addition to math; she doesn't know how to plan for an eighty-minute class, because she's used to fifty; she rear-ended a Cadillac on the Beltway and can't afford the five-hundred-dollar deductible (in addition to the five-hundred-dollar deductible from when she was rear-ended herself); she's already missed a day of school to fight a speeding ticket; her neck hurts; she can't find an affordable apartment that will take her dog and cat, so she's staying on her boyfriend's brother's girlfriend's couch; and she's realizing that eighth graders are way different from sixth graders, even when they're at the same place mathematically. They look ready to tear her apart. She wonders if she can help them.

"Eric," she says, "explain to me what's confusing."

"Everything."

chapter two

everyone else thinks it's a
stupid plane crash

On picture day, a Tuesday morning in September, students are called to the cafeteria, class by class. The sixth graders take the occasion very seriously, and several, on their mothers' request, wear collared shirts, which they change out of right after photos. Most of the eighth graders aren't buying their pictures. They can list every nonawful photo ever taken of them, and school photos are never among them. Just as well, since several eighth-grade boys made themselves pass out at recess yesterday (lean against the wall, take ten quick deep breaths, have someone press a fist into your chest), and their foreheads are bruised from hitting the asphalt.

Seventh graders still care about their pictures, but they care about having a half-hour out of class with their friends even more.

"Last year I looked retarded."

"Are there bags under my eyes?"

"Man, it stinks!"

"Eww!"

They all wave their order forms under their noses and eye a girl in a messy orange T-shirt, who says, "I did not fart, I swear."

One boy does a karate chop to another's neck, because his brother in the Army said you can stun someone that way. Onstage, in front of screens painted in some disco-cheesy way to look like they're emanating light, the photographers form their fingers into L's and angle them. But the kids remember how stupid their heads looked tilted in last year's photos, as if they were all going to topple off the yearbook page, so they resist.

As one boy settles into the stool, his friend grabs his crotch and says, "Go like this!"

"That's not funny," a teacher says.

"It *was*."

"But was it appropriate?"

"Last year I looked like an insane clown," Ann says. "My hair was all lumpy from the ponytail the night before."

"Are you going to go out with Adam?" Ann thinks Adam is cute and funny but is taking into account that the last time they went out, he dumped her.

Across the street Ms. Thomas is sitting in a room full of principals listening to a talk about emergency procedures when, shortly after nine, the assistant superintendent comes in and announces that an airplane has hit the World Trade Center. It's part of the meeting, they think, a sneaky practice drill. No, he insists, this is real, and the meeting is disbanded. Ms. Thomas's older daughter comes up from the train into the World Trade Center every morning on the way to work. Ms. Thomas goes home to check CNN: It's real, all right. Futilely she dials Ashley's cell phone, Ashley's friends, Ashley's work. She heads to school.

Just yesterday there was a staff meeting about the emergency-procedures manual: how to do a lockdown, how to evacuate, where the orange vests are kept. Clearly this is an emergency, but what kind? There may or may not be problems in Baltimore, a half-hour away. There may or may not be problems in Washington, forty-five minutes away. This isn't in the manual.

By late morning, the teachers have started to hear the news, and many parents show up for their children. Ms. Thomas wants to keep the kids out of this. She agrees to let them be released but makes parents wait outside; she tells the staff not to congregate in the halls; she pulls one who is crying into her office. She struggles to keep her composure, worried desperately about her daughter, and her six hundred other children too. Televisions next door at the high school play CNN, and the students watch and cry, but mass terrorism, Ms. Thomas decides, is something twelve-year-olds should hear about from their parents. The day will be as normal as possible.

So the sixth graders go to lunch oblivious. They talk about Round-wiches, those new packaged peanut-butter sandwiches without the crust; they talk about the truck accident they saw from the bus this morning; they talk about everything, nothing.

"Mia, I have another plum if you want it."

"You want to hear something traumatizing? I left my book in the eighth-grade pod and I can't get it back."

"This school is so cold compared to Clemens."

Ms. Thomas's daughter has finally called, so while Ashley is telling her, with sirens in the background, how she was in the towers just hours ago, how from where she stands blocks away "it looks like a nuclear disaster," Mr. West goes to the cafeteria to fetch the kids whose names come over the PA.

"If you hear me," he says from the center of the room, "raise your fingers. I need you to use elementary-school voices today, because there are important announcements I need to hear. Please whisper." When the names penetrate the buzz of lunchtime one by one, Mr. West finds each child and says, "Your parents are here to pick you up."

"Oh, cool," says one girl at the table as she fumbles with her Sprite and applesauce. "I get early dismissal." Onstage, the photographers roll up their screens, and the wondering grows loud.

"Maybe there's a bus broken down so they can't get home."

"What's going on?"

"Anyone named Jeff is a geek."

"My mom never packs me enough food. Does anyone have any money?"

"Something must be going on."

"Remember the snow days last year? Remember we did the snow dance?"

"Why are so many people leaving?"

"Maybe something happened at the high school."

"All voices off," Mr. West says. "I have a serious announcement. As you noticed, a lot of your classmates have had early dismissal. There is something taking place across the nation. It is a crisis including Washington, D.C., and New York City. We are confident that you are safe. You will be dismissed a half-hour early."

"YES!"

"Please. Today is the day to have your attention. Something has transpired across the nation. We don't have any information now. Trust us that we would tell you. Please act like the mature sixth graders that you are. You're not in elementary school anymore. I need voices to be *this quiet*. We're not going to have snack or recess today."

Groans.

Mia isn't concerned about snack or recess. She's concerned about her father, a college professor who, like many Wilde Lake parents, works in Washington. *Oh my God,* she thinks. Lily can't think of anyone she has to worry about, but most of the kids come up with someone—a baby cousin in Brooklyn, their moms at Fort Meade. They figure that if Mr. West knows "something has transpired across the nation," he knows exactly what it is, and he should tell them. Especially since Brittany is crying!

Softly, she says, "My grandma lives in Queens."

"Anyone want a Chewy Granola Bar? Hey—maybe the president was assassinated!"

"Yay!"

"Maybe it's World War Three!"

"I hope it's not the end of the world," says Lily.

"My dad's in Washington, D.C.," Mia says. Next to her, a girl shivers.

"I heard in health that a terrorist plane crashed into a building," Jonathan says. He is one of only two sixth-grade boys brave enough to sit with girls at lunch, but right now his eyes are red with fear.

By eighth-grade lunch many parents have picked up their kids, so the cafeteria is half empty. A guidance counselor told some of the boys what had happened, the little he knew. In the back corner Eric worries about his father, who drives between Baltimore and Washington all the time, and his brother, who plays college football. "They travel to the different states," he says, "and he might catch a plane."

"Death is my biggest fear," Malik says, and his friends nod. "Planes all around us crashed. Are you afraid they're going to hit us? They were saying the last one was eighteen miles away."

"Our humanity: lost!"

"Why are you sitting there? You didn't sign the paper."

"I wasn't here that day and Ms. Thomas said sit anywhere."

"Tara, I hope your boyfriend didn't die."

Mr. West tries to silence the room. "One, two," he says.

"Are we going to die?"

"Three."

"There's a rapist in the school."

"Four. Five. A lot of you have been hearing information. We're not going to share too much with you." But he's shared enough that even the tough boys have wide eyes. Mr. West continues, "This is not a drill. This is not fake. This is real. When you get home, ask your parents. There have been bits of information given to some of you—I don't know if that's factual. When you get home, you'll have all the information you need."

Eric's head is in his hands. Shawn comes up and asks, "Pal, you okay?"

"Everyone else thinks it's a stupid plane crash," says Liam.

Eric lifts his head, shakes it. "I wonder if it has to do with Aaliyah. Who are the idiots doing this? These people have no reason to live." He wants more from Mr. West, who says, "I'm sorry, Eric, this is all I can tell you."

When the bell rings for the day, Ms. Thomas herds the children right outside. She won't let them go to their lockers for books. Some of the kids have heard there's no homework, but Lily isn't sure. She asks the music teacher, who tells her to ask Ms. Thomas, who is standing in front of the office with a group of teachers. Lily can't get up the nerve, and leaves. She feels stupid.

It's quiet on the buses. Once home, kids dial their mothers' cell phones, with little success. Nobody's home at Eric's, where he flips through BET, *Rugrats*, MTV. It's practically impossible to find a channel without the World Trade Center footage, which is getting more explicit each time more video is found, so he rides his bike to McDonald's.

Mia watches with her dad, as one simple thought loops through her head: Oh my God. Oh my God. When the CD she is listening to before bedtime ends, the radio comes on, and a man with two five-year-olds pleads for someone to find their mother in the wreckage. At this she cries, and clings to her mom. Cartoons can't take her mind off the possibilities: What if it happened at BWI? What about Grandma and Grandpa, who are driving back to Ohio? Why didn't anyone ever tell me what a terrorist was before?

Howard County schools are the only ones in the Washington area open Wednesday, which Ms. Thomas is glad of—it sends the right message to terrorists. Although she hates dressing up, she wears the black suit she bought as a joke last year for a colleague's fiftieth birthday. "We don't know which of our kids will be affected," she tells the staff before school, "but there will be some for sure. No reaction is a wrong reaction. Allow them to go to guidance. I'm not going to say you can't discuss it, I'm not going to say you should discuss it. I just ask that you not tune in to TV, these tragic visions again and again. If kids are laughing, don't come down hard on them. Many of our students are Muslim; make sure they are not blamed. We are all here to support each other."

The kids arrive looking a little shell-shocked, tired, the hair not quite as neat as normal. A group of eighth graders waits under the half-staff flag for the doors to open.

"Doofuses. They were dumb. Do you think they'll rebuild the World Trade Center? It'll take a year or so."

"I bet they're going to Chicago—to the big tall one."

"The Sears Tower."

"I think the president is a stupidhead, putting a Christian spin on his speech. He should have said, 'Don't blame Muslims.' " Max and Malik, both Muslims, start to tussle. Max calls Malik "Bin Laden wannabe." Malik calls Max "Turbanhead." A teacher intervenes: "Not today, guys."

"Or tomorrow," one girl adds. "And the day after that? Not so good either. Oooh, there's a plane!"

The eighth graders, more mad than sad, want to get to the bottom of this. Today the students in Mrs. Conroy's gifted-and-talented class raise their hands at every question. A typical middle school has very little time—often none—to teach current events, and this is the most rapt they will be all year, meandering through not just the horror of the carnage but its geopolitics.

"We know this will be in the history books," Mrs. Conroy says quietly.

"Are they going to hit anyone else?"

"My guess is not at this time, because we are all on alert."

One after another, the students say where they heard the fourth plane was headed: Camp David, Baltimore's World Trade Center. "I heard on the news," one boy says, "that they got threats three weeks ago but nobody took it seriously."

"There are always threats we don't know about," Mrs. Conroy says.

"Lateshia's mom's co-worker's daughter was on the plane, and she called on her cell phone."

"I hear they might have killed people right away because none of the panic buttons were pressed."

"There is that theory," Mrs. Conroy says.

"Who bombed the World Trade Center a couple of years ago?"

"Bin Laden," she says. "He has openly said we are evil."

"They found a van in Boston with instructions on how to fly the plane."

"A news agency did an undercover test about whether you could get through security in the airport, and you could twenty percent of the time."

As always, a girl named Daisy pops her head in the door and says, "Hi, everybody!" For once she is ignored.

"My mom says someone in her office was in some religion that said Tuesday was War Day."

"The date was nine-one-one."

"It was exactly three months after McVeigh was executed."

"It could be Americans. After the Oklahoma City bombing they captured all Muslims, and it turned out not to be them."

"U.S. terrorists usually don't kill themselves," Mrs. Conroy says. "There's no glory or reward for Americans who kill themselves. How many people watched the president's speech?" Everyone. "Who else is he holding responsible?"

"Those who supported them."

"The news said the airport would be running at noon. Wouldn't that be a bad idea if they were working from within?"

"I suspect," Mrs. Conroy says, "they won't open them till they think they're safe."

"Why were they telling everyone where the president was?"

"Maybe," she says, "they wanted people to know the president was safe, that we are not going to hide. Girls," she tells a group in the back, "share with everyone."

"We both saw a plane flying over our neighborhood last night. Why was it flying there?"

Mrs. Conroy can't answer every question, she will never be able to, but she has always thought that eighth graders are ready to become engaged citizens and that her job is to get them there. "This has changed our culture now," she says before flipping on the overhead to reveal the daily drill question: "What document guaranteed all Christians the right to worship as they choose?"

"This has changed America. You have just lived through a historical event."

"Cool," the students say.

It is not, the way the eighth graders see it, about them—it is about the world beyond their own five square miles. This is a perspective most sixth graders aren't quite mature enough to grasp. They're not used to discussing current events, and in this case their loved ones are okay, so for many the news, and the sorrow, sit in their heads only briefly. If any time is spent dwelling on the tragedy, the thoughts are mostly about the personal losses, the broken families.

Mia, one of the hundred students absent today, believed her mother when she said it wouldn't happen again, because the FBI is on the case, but still she was too upset for school this morning. It didn't feel right yesterday, trying to kick a medicine ball over other people's heads in PE when what she really wanted to do was visit the guidance counselors for comfort. Had she known them, she would have. At home she cries, as hard as she tries not to, the plane crashing into the tower over and over in her head. She decides she'll find work around the house and in her mom's dental office so that she can sponsor a cute poor girl she saw on a TV commercial for eighty cents a day.

At school, her classmates are evenly divided between those who want to remember and those who want to forget. Last night three of the swimmers assembled in a bedroom lit with candles and sat around the best-smelling one, thinking, What are we supposed to do about this? They pulled out the big children's Bible and found the pages with the prettiest pictures and read aloud. They discussed forgiveness, and agreed to disagree. But today one of them says, "I just want to move on. This happened before, at Pearl Harbor, and they didn't get all worked up about it."

Her English class has voted to forget—to debate, as scheduled, whether the government should rate music. There is a boy in the class whose father, a Baptist pastor, came home warning of an apocalypse. Today the child wonders, to himself only, if a nuclear bomb is the size of his car, or his apartment building, or bigger. With low, brassy squawks coming from the band room next door, a sixth-grade music class discusses what the word "opera" makes them think of ("Opera Winfrey," "people breaking glasses," "fat ladies screaming at the top of their lungs"), and why in the old days sopranos were fat ("because the noise echoes in their stomachs," "they show up better," "they hold more air").

Those who have voted to remember—and avoid a math worksheet—discuss whether braces will set off an airport metal detector and who "that big terrorist guy" is. "The leader of Afghanistan," the teacher says, which is in either the Middle East or Asia, she's not sure. In another class they write to firefighters. "Can we draw fire in the background?" one boy asks, and his teacher says, "That's not appropriate. We want to get their mind off what they're doing and show how much we appreciate them." So they write things like "Dear Fireman, That was really sad what those guys did. Thanks for being brave," and "I know that because of the tragic things that happened Tuesday, you have been working hard. USA!"

Talk at lunch is about whether people are still buried in the rubble at the Pentagon, whether anyone has tried a turkey-and-ketchup sandwich, whose uncles worked in the World Trade Center, and whether you would rather die from a gigantic fireball or jump out a window on the hundredth floor. Lily found out last night that her cousin had flown one of the F-15's that accompanied President Bush, but she doesn't mention this. Jonathan pokes fries into his ears, then eats them, then says to Lily, "You're invited to my birthday party." Lily has worn a new knee-length maroon sweater from Candie's with a fake-fur collar, and she does a model's twirl for her friend Maddy. The rest of the girls are still immersed in talk about defenestration when Lily asks, "Is anyone going outside? Is anyone going outside? Is anyone going outside?"

Lily has an idea about identifying the terrorists, that you could pause the video of the plane crashing into the building and zoom in real close. After the sermon in church about what happened Tuesday, Lily's sister, Gabrielle, who is in fifth grade, is inspired to write a musical about patriotism and freedom. So the girls open the cover of Lily's binder, which is coated with photos of Britney Spears and Christina Aguilera even though she thinks they've gotten ugly, and go to work. In the play, George Washington declares war on the British, becomes president, and throws a party. "Food all over," the stage direction says. A soldier collapses. In death, he says, "I see a bright light."

Other than that, Lily doesn't have much time to think about global terrorism. She is too busy serving as the poster child for middle-school self-absorption.

When she thinks about anything—not like she stresses; nothing, she claims, gives her stress—she's thinking about Halloween. She doesn't want to trick-or-treat, since her sister already claimed the pale-blue pageant dress Lily wanted to wear, and anyway Mia has other plans. So Lily decides to set up a haunted house and Creepy Maze in the yard and starts by drawing diagrams and making to-buy lists: dry ice, red candle wax to drip for blood.

She's thinking about Wesley, one of the foster babies, whom the Masons are considering adopting.

She's thinking about Abigail Werner, who has a locker next to hers and, because it's too cramped for them to get their books at the same time, always stands there with her arms crossed over her chest, threatening to get inside Lily's locker and change the combination. "She knows how," Lily says.

She's thinking about the way that everyone in home ec, kids she barely knows, looks at her when Mrs. Brodian announces that Lily can help with sewing if anyone needs it. "Stop staring at me," she wants to tell her classmates, "and don't call me Miss Lily anymore."

She's thinking about how already Wilde Lake is harder than her school in Louisiana, and even though she pays attention, whenever teachers call on her she doesn't know the answer. She likes being quiet, because you never get in trouble and you never get made fun of and nobody much cares what you say or what you think, but it also means teachers call on you more, because they know you'd never raise your hand.

She's thinking about Eric Ellis's friend Chris, who pulls scrunchies out of girls' ponytails on the bus. He may not be trying to hurt anyone, but a kid who's six feet—"his Afro is, like, two feet tall"—can cause pain even when he's not trying. He gets Lily across her eye and bops her on the head, and she almost cries. Her mother, Avy, and two other moms call the school, and Chris is suspended from the bus. Lily just hopes he never finds out who tattled.

She's thinking about the way her mom will only let her wear lip gloss and a teensy bit of eye shadow, not that she cares about wearing it to school, because none of her friends do, but still. And her parents made her pay three dollars every time she butted into their conversation from the back of the van on the way to Niagara Falls—"Whatchou talking about, Mama? What'd you say?"—and when Avy calls "Lily!" up the stairs she has to respond with "Ma'am?" instead of "What?" or "Yeah?" like every other kid in the state of Maryland. Her parents can feel the changes coming on, the way a tickly swallow portends a sore throat. Cheekiness has started to seep through Lily ever since they moved from Louisiana six months ago. Avy—who tells her kids even the word "butt" is "ugly talk"—has a feeling that during middle school it's going to be some kind of struggle to preserve what's left of Lily's Southern gentility.

More than anything, Lily's thinking about her friends, a tiny bit about the ones she left in Louisiana and a lot about the ones here. Social scientists explain that being eleven means that you put friends number one on your list of priorities, that for the first time you perceive intimacy as a desirable state, not just within your immediate family but in your very own world outside it, that what you're doing is less important than whom you're doing it with. You pick your friends not just because they live near you or happen to be in your ballet class but because, well, *you pick them*. You want to share. You learn that making them happy makes you happy. Parents lately have read a lot about the vicious nature of schoolyard exclusion, and mean girls, and much of it is true. But even if a middle-school girl is as well situated as Lily—she hates nobody, and is hated by nobody—the ebb and flow of her friendships consume her to a mind-boggling degree.

So she's thinking about recess. Most of the girls follow Mia to play soccer, but Lily is terrified of "anything with the last name Ball." Alexandra double-dutches, switching easily between the black girls' jump rope and the white girls' jump rope, but Lily doesn't like jumping rope, and besides, she doesn't know those girls. She doesn't try to. On Friendship Day, during the scavenger hunt, when you find people in the class who share your birth month or favorite food or what have you, Lily is too shy to approach many people, and her sheet never fills up. The Masons go to her sister's friend's house for dinner, and a boy there asks, "Do I know you?"

"I'm in your homeroom," Lily says. Thanks a lot.

Lily is not, she insists, thinking about Alexandra. Or maybe she thinks about her, but she doesn't care, which are two different things. "I'm never mad at people," she says, "so it doesn't really matter." Still, she notices that Alexandra doesn't eat at their lunch table anymore; usually she eats with the tall girls, or the black girls.

More than anything, Lily's thinking about Mia and how to keep her close, how this new math class she's just moved up to seems hard but at least they're together, and how she really wants a double birthday party in February, in Mia's new basement, because you can wipe up spills easier on a concrete floor.

Jackie Taylor is thinking about her birthday party, too, but that doesn't mean she ever stopped thinking about death. A couple days after the attacks, Miss Colton writes on the overhead, "September 11, 2001 will prove to be an important day in American history. It will also be remembered by the writings of those who lived through it." "You can write a letter, poem, story, whatever," she tells the seventh graders. "But you have to write something, because your reflections are important. Each of you should have something to say about it, because it *did* affect your lives."

My life was affected because I got out of school a half hour early.

I was saying no more World Trade Center that is bad, but as long as I am okay, and my family.

Jackie's mom had just done some work at the Pentagon offices before they were destroyed. One of her acquaintances there had heard about the World Trade Center during her commute and phoned her colleagues with a premonition. "Please," she urged, "come out into the parking lot." They did, then the plane crashed, and Jackie fills up a whole page with this story, which Miss Colton asks to keep.

In the hall after class, her friend Judy keeps directing her hand downward like a crashing plane and saying "Zoom! Zoom! Zoom!" "That's not funny," Kelly tells her. The girls complain that they're the only county to have school today. Jackie tells how her mom worked at the Pentagon, and Judy demonstrates dominoes with her hand, the rooms collapsing.

The zooming, the dominoes: Though Jackie doesn't say anything in the hall, it's not funny to her either. Over and over she thinks, We're not safe anymore. Even before yesterday, Jackie had been thinking about mortality a lot, and though it doesn't take up quite as much space in her brain as wondering what other kids think about her, particularly the boys, particularly Jay Starr, it still feels like a lot. Too much. Sometimes she tells herself, "You're twelve, you don't have to worry about this now," but she can't help it.

Thoughts of death—their own and their loved ones'—weigh heavily on many children as they approach puberty, though they rarely let on. For some kids, like Jackie, these thoughts are part of a broader onset of spirituality and seeking. For all of them, it's about fear. They fear more than anything the death of a parent. When their parents are ill, they lie awake anxious. Those with older fathers grimly calculate how old they will be when their dads die. Sad, they know, but they are certain. One boy came to school the day after his mom died of a heart attack, and his classmates couldn't even imagine it. When Jackie is annoyed with her mother for not letting her walk to the Giant, she pictures her sick, with breast cancer maybe, like their next-door neighbor, and then she stops being mad, at least for a little bit.

Her father went through thoughts like that when he was Jackie's age, but her mother never did, and would be stunned to know that in her journal Jackie writes pages upon pages of questions about death. What if her soul can't escape her body? What if it does, and then winds up in some third grader's science project? What if heaven is a myth? Really, who can say "ribbis" and priests know any better than anyone else? What if she dies? If a genie floated down to grant Jackie a wish, she'd choose to live forever. If there were a giant question box in the sky, to which you could submit any query without fear of embarrassment, Jackie would ask two things: *How do you make out?* and *What happens after you die?* Jackie remembers what it felt like to be unborn. She wonders: Will it be like that? Will it be like heaven, or will it be black? She believes you are reincarnated until you fulfill your goals—not including your goals about Jay Starr.

chapter three

any girl will obsess over at least 1 guy in their life

After death, Jackie's biggest worry is whether Jay likes her, pretty much par for the course for a twelve-year-old. Jackie plays drums in the school band and has a good mind for canasta and imagines having a house with every room a different color, red and silver in the dance room and blue in the aquarium room. One day on the swings, she thinks, she'll flip clear over the top. Her parents love this sense of adventure—"spice and zing," her mom calls it—though they worry a little when she lies back on a skateboard and luges, fast, down the steep sidewalk.

"It's so great to be popular!" Jackie declares once at the lunch table, hands thrown in the air, apropos of nothing. She is at the less socially advanced end of the group, which means she is always the one dispatched to say, "So-and-so is mad at you." She doesn't get into fights and is proud that she can, and will, carry on a conversation with someone she doesn't even know, unlike her friends. They're always "in a band," though they never play music—just make up songs and band names over the phone, like "Obsession," the "i" dotted with a rose. Jackie's typical report card is one or two B's, the rest A's. Her shiny brown hair would fall straight down her back if she didn't tie it up all the time; in her wildest dreams it is streaked green, or at the very least it's thick and curly like the girl's in *The Princess Diaries*, or at the very, very least it's redder. Her orthodontist and her grandma and her friend Kristina's mom say she should

be a model, but her mother won't let her sign up on the Barbizon Web
site, "so I'm obviously not a model right now." Jackie is tiny, thin, flat;
even though her hips are lower than the hurdles, during gym class she
floats right over them, to her surprise.

In Jackie's house, her dad, Mike, stays home with the baby, and her
mom, Sara, an interior designer, drops Jackie at the bus stop, goes to the
office, and makes it home in time to be the boss. Mike and Sara have
raised Jackie to stand up for herself, and she was into the surface notions
of girl power even before the Powerpuff Girls told her to be. In third
grade she announced to the class that she wanted to be quarterback for
the Miami Dolphins, and when one boy protested that girls can't do that,
she hit him. It bugs her that there's never been a female president, that
women barely show up in her history textbooks, and that so many people
assume men are stronger, not just physically but mentally. She wears a
T-shirt that says, "Girls are the best. Boys are OK" and really wants this
calendar with a picture of a gingerbread man that says, "The perfect man:
He's quiet, he's sweet, and if he gives you any grief you can bite his head
off." On her mom's computer in the basement, Jackie has created a
PowerPoint presentation about boys that she calls her "Web site." It
urges, "Always remember to put your self ahead of your guy no matter
what!" and lists reasons girls are better than boys:

- They scream higher than we do.
- We get better test scores.
- We're better. Face it.

Sara said no to *CosmoGIRL!* magazine and its French-kissing tips,
and fortunately even Jackie disdains the concept of *BoyCrazy!* trading
cards and magazine—which doesn't even pretend to have articles about
anything else—but Sara yielded to pleas for a subscription to *YM*, which
promises better living and better boyfriends through low-rider jeans and
always knowing just the right thing to say. Sprawled on her waterbed,
surrounded by a kittens-in-a-basket poster and a slew of spent glow sticks
and Dolphins pennants and ink-on-loose-leaf pronouncements of her
musical tastes taped to the door (Sum 41, Linkin Park, Incubus) and
forty Beanie Babies piled on a shelf, Jackie loves to read the embarrassing
moments column. A twelve-year-old lives in perpetual fear of being em-

barrassed. She always feels like an audience full of people is watching and judging her, worries they'll think her outfit looks gay, and, in Jackie's case, even feels like someone's peeping through her window. Still, some sense of schadenfreude draws her to the magazine accounts of spilling punch in front of a crush, losing a bikini top after a dive, peeing in the pool and trailing an inky tail from the gotcha chemicals. The one that cracked Jackie up the most was the girl who was at her boyfriend's for dinner and the toilet clogged so she threw her poop out the window and went back to the table, where everyone was laughing because they saw it hanging off the telephone pole. Jackie always scores in the just-right realm on the quizzes—"Sincerely Yours" on the lying quiz, for example, instead of "Pants on Fire" or "The Truth Hurts"—and she gives her own advice to girls who write in:

"My guy friend puts his arm around me a lot—does this mean he likes me?"

"No! 'Cause Brad does that to me. Brad does that to me all the time and he's going out with Mimi."

What little most teen-girl magazines have to say about sidelines like school, they do through the prism of guys—"What do boys' lockers tell you about their personalities?" Jackie may say she likes *YM* for the horoscopes, which, she insists, "really work," and boast about owning only one dress, and express relief that her baby brother, Kyle, is not a girl, because then she might have to play tea party instead of army men, but for all her tomboyhood and feminism and independence Jackie exhibits a good share of the signs of preteen boy-craziness—and, like most girls her age, is not sure why. She says guys are the second-most-important thing in her life, after friends and before family, school, and shopping. Her girlfriends generally rank life the same way.

For most children, middle school is a time when the hormones bubble, when boys and girls notice each other *that* way. Some Wilde Lake girls, like Lily and Mia, are focused fully on schoolwork and girlfriends and hobbies and are not interested in boys at all. Some Wilde Lake girls have been put on the Pill by their worried mothers and are either having sex or very close to it. The majority of the girls are somewhere in between: simultaneously boy-crazy and boy-phobic, yearning for love but clueless about how to attain it. Their dramas are serious and absurd: Who can help laughing at the way a preteen girl obsesses over a "boyfriend" with whom she has never had a conversation? The way she writes "I ♡ Danny" on her hand in black marker and then hides it in her sleeve so nobody can see? And who can help feeling sorry for her pain when he ignores her, and worrying that her insecurities won't go away when the crush does?

A girl on the cusp of adolescence has this need to branch out from familiar, familial relationships and create an independent universe of allies and adversaries. She needs to test fidelity and see, in the starkest way, what others think of her. Although boys and girls may never be more fickle than at this age, they may also never have more capacity for devotion. Above all, according to what little research exists on the subject, having romantic relationships—even if the concept is used loosely—exalts boys' and girls' status among their peers, as long as they choose correctly. Crushes give girlfriends something to conspire about.

"It is a proven fact that any girl will obsess over at least 1 guy in their life," Jackie writes on her "Web site," and she's already got that covered. Last year she had a crush on the lead singer of Blink 182 and in real life went out with Dan Arnstein, who called her every day (she had to do the talking), then Dan Pryor, then Kevin Heneman. Kevin was three times, for a total of three months, which she'll never understand; she suspects all the milk she'd been drinking might have warped her brain. She started this year with a thing for the lead singer of Linkin Park, and all September, though Sara doesn't like Jackie to write on herself—it's one of those I-just-said-sos she tries not to mandate too often—the acronym of Jackie's longing is inked onto the fingers of each hand: J-A-B.

Jay Starr.

Anton James.

Brad Aronson.

Jackie's friends, at age twelve, span the spectrum from prim on one end to boy-crazy on the other, from well rounded to hobbyless, closely supervised to unbound, polite to mouthy, engaged to indifferent. Kristina and Celia say they got caught passing themselves off on the Internet as eighteen-year-olds from Las Vegas and another friend tells her dad, in a fit of peevishness, "Why don't you go sixty-nine Mom?" Jackie whines a lot, but it's doubtful she will ever instruct her parents to perform sex acts.

Even though they're not *doing* much, these girls talk all the time about boys and romance; lesbians come up a lot. They speculate that one female rabbi is gay and might hit on a girl while she reads the Torah at her Bat Mitzvah.

When Jackie meets Kristina and Celia at the mall, she hitches a Betty Boop beeper (no batteries, no phone number) to the back pocket of her sparkly jeans. She laughs with them at the key chains at Spencer's, especially the one that says "I'll be your 6 you be my 9." Jackie spots a pimp Halloween costume. "This is Anton! This is Anton!" She buys two stickers for her binder that say "Warning: HEARTBREAKER" and "I Recycle Boys." Over cookies in the food court, Kristina complains about how the terrorist attacks are on television all the time. "I don't really care about it, because it doesn't affect Maryland," she says, to which Jackie replies, "We're going to *war*, Kristina." Then they discuss Kristina's new boyfriend, for whom she has written on her hand, "I love Scott 4ever." "He has a nice personality and the nicest ass," she says. They compare numbers: Kristina has had twelve boyfriends, Jackie seven, and Celia five. Jackie has kissed one boy, though not French.

Jackie is in the norm for preteen sexual experience, or lack thereof, and has no plans to go further. Who has done what at this age can be discerned mainly from anecdotal evidence, since researchers are rarely permitted to ask children so young about sexual experience; it is, however, generally held that most girls and boys Jackie's age have been kissed, but nothing more. Barely a quarter have been on either end of breast-fondling, and far fewer have had intercourse, oral or otherwise—second base, third base, and a home run, respectively (it is either comforting or not that some lingo will never change). Nearly all middle schoolers have had some sort of crush, and one-quarter of twelve-year-olds report having had a "special romantic relationship," though at this age, given their psychological immaturity, that term doesn't have too much meaning. Generally they just realize the roles they are supposed to play and pretend to do so.

It's the sexually active minority that gets discussed, though, not just in the newspaper (for a while it seemed, from reading the papers, that you couldn't pass through seventh grade without participating in oral sex on the playground) but at the lunch table. Who's a slut, who's a player, who gave a hand job in the bathroom next to the band room: There are plenty of children who never get near this kind of talk, but in a popular crowd like Jackie's, sex and its accoutrements make up a large part of conversations. Girls that allegedly go all the way are looked down on; boys are not. Celia and Kristina enthusiastically list the kids at school they think have had sex, including an eighth grader who, supposedly, had two abortions and a miscarriage.

Eww. The way Jackie sees sex—well, she doesn't want to do it. Maybe when she's thirty, when she doesn't have the drive anymore. Or maybe she'll never do it and just adopt, which is probably better for the world's children anyway.

"You guys," she says, "we're too young to even think about that."

On a dare once at a party, Celia showed Jay her breasts and he showed her his penis, they say. This, Celia insists, was the worst day of her life; she took a knife, barely, to the soft white skin on her arms afterward; but still, her fingers read "J A Y." Jay knows there's a club called JSC but doesn't know it stands for "Jay Starr Crushers." If he did, he'd add it to his mental list of the weird ways girls obsess about boys. Jay hears about these crushes and doesn't quite understand what the fuss is about, why at a sleepover the biggest laugh of the night is when the girls kiss the wall, pretending it is him. Don't get him wrong—he thinks about girls and loves to flirt. But it's not like he is particularly nice to them or cares about his looks. "I don't even comb my hair in the morning," he says. He doesn't realize he exudes cuteness—his freckles are cute, his grin is cute, even his name is cute, the way it pops out all at once, like a spotlight. The girls call him the "pervertedest of the perverted," like how when they flirt on Instant Messenger he will write things like, "The fat rabbit is getting fatter."

"He used to be my best friend," says Celia, "and he was really nice then, and I just can't get over him." The thing she says she wants most in the world? "That Jay would at least think of me the way he thinks about Kristina."

A few days later, at school, two girls slip Jay a note in careful cursive, the "i"s dotted with hearts, the mistakes blotted out with Liquid Paper.

When I am with you, the caterpillars in my stomach turn to butterflies. I want to give you oral sex. I really want to suck on your head.

Love,
Daphne

Jay's shown it around, and when Daphne finds out, she's pissed. On the playground she points at Kristina and circles her. "You tell me who wrote this! You tell me! I did NOT write this. I will kick their ass! I'll wipe the floor with their ass. There will be blood."

A crowd has gathered. The girls who wrote the note stand off to the side laughing, then are scared away by bees. Jackie stands next to Brad, the "B" on her fingers, a little guy who serves as a sort of mascot for the girls. She leans on his shoulder, which is just the right height, and watches.

The girls appear to be the stars of middle school's romantic dramas. But the boys deserve equal billing. Even though they don't draw hearts on their tennis shoes, they occasionally draw them at home, when nobody's looking. There was more than mischief behind the forays they made a couple of years back across the playground, in order to shove a girl. They strut, they act ambivalent, but really they're anxious. They feel like girls know so much more about romance than they do. Boys certainly don't spend as much time with each other analyzing it; God forbid they admit their vulnerability . . . or *feelings*.

Because they aren't so comfortable with intimacy as a social skill, the romance thing can be more difficult for them and even, in the end, without as much of a support network to help them bounce back after rejection, more damaging. It's painful even thinking about girls, despite the lack of interaction. Strutting masks true emotion, which once in a while they go out on a limb and show. A sixth grader named Brendan was going out with one of the swimmers, and when somebody told her he liked someone else, she broke up with him. "She thought I didn't care," he says, but he did, he totally did, and he ached over the fact that all the girls, especially her, were mad at him. He spent many hours on Instant Messenger pleading for their respect. A seventh grader named Nathan beat up his best friend since kindergarten not because the kid tried to pants him in front of a girl but because he tried to pants him in front of a girl Nathan really, really likes. Some care about what girls think of them so much that in class they cannot keep their minds on anything else.

Many sixth-grade boys have learned that the crushes that would have lasted one day last year stick around for at least a week now, and the ones that once lasted a week now last a month, and, more often than one would imagine, their crushes last years. Jimmy Schissel has had a crush on Mia since third grade, even though the last time he asked her out she called him a freak. Last year he carved a wooden bird emerging from an egg to give her at the end-of-fifth-grade party. The whole night went by, the swimming, the food, the DJ, and when everyone was leaving, his mother finally said, "Aren't you going to give her the bird?" He did, then rushed off. His friend Will didn't fare any better with the stuffed otter he'd brought back from Alaska for Mia's friend Marnie. "Stop trying," she told him.

For the Wilde Lake magazine sale, Jimmy studies the prize catalogue with his dad, figuring out exactly what he wants—Spy Ears, the ten-foot snake, the Magic Ball—and how many subscriptions he has to flog to get it all. He sells $519.36 worth of magazines, the most in school, and in the end gravitates toward the bubble machine, because he heard Mia wanted it. "Here," he says by the buses, and hands it over.

By seventh grade, many boys have learned to protect themselves, fast withdrawing unreciprocated affections. Kristina liked a boy named Stephen for a while, but he didn't like her back "like that." Then he did, and she told him she only liked him a little bit, not enough to go out. So he instantly shut off his feelings for Kristina. A year ago, he says, he would have pined. If it sounds fickle, that's not how Stephen sees it. "It wasn't just, like, one day I like her like that and the next day I don't. It's just, two weeks I like her like that, then the other month I don't, then the other month I do."

Sometimes the stars converge and a boy and girl actually go out. "Out," these first times, would better be described as "in," either because of discomfort or lack of opportunities. A few awkward phone calls, a lot of empty instant-messaging, a mildly flirtatious note or two, a slow dance at the school social, no kisses, no dates. Still, the elation can be immense, and the heartbreak inevitable, rejection being the most miserable thing imaginable. Whether the romance includes actual involvement and ex-pressions of affection or it's just people passing each other in the hall, its importance is as massive as the planet. Especially for a girl less confident than Jackie, euphoria at being chosen can cloud her judgment. She offi-cially likes the guy even when he's an out-and-out jerk and ignores her.

She wonders, after they've broken up, why he's going around calling her a slut, when she wouldn't even do anything. He wonders, too. In a sense, the ways boys and girls try out romance and adulthood are fundamentally at odds, according to the enduring philosophy of the psychoanalyst Erik Erikson: Girls step toward womanhood by attaching themselves to others of the opposite sex; boys step toward manhood by breaking away from such ties.

It can be a brutal combination.

Jackie doesn't see it that way. Some sociologists contend that the selection process and image-obsession and stress involved in adolescent romantic relationships, particularly in breakups, is not worth the anxiety and depression it produces, whereas others conclude that the stress is motivating and the experience good for a kid's self-worth. Jackie sides firmly with the latter camp. To her, the breaking-up stuff is hard, but the going-out part, the "mmm, someone likes me," really makes her feel "self-esteemish," as she puts it. Somehow Jackie always manages to run into the cutest guys—her friend Leslie tells her to travel with a Polaroid—though she often displays an ability uncommon among her more boy-crazy peers to just not get too worked up.

Part of it can be attributed to her parents, who work nonstop to make sure Jackie doesn't grow up too fast, "cramming as much crap into her head as possible and hoping to God it sticks," as Sara puts it. Unlike her friends, Jackie doesn't have cable, so she can't watch throngs of bikini-clad dancers writhe around the gold-crusted rappers who call them ho's; she doesn't have the Internet, so she can't spend hours bantering with boys who ask her bra size; she's not allowed CDs with a "Parental Advisory" sticker, so she doesn't hear singers brag that they're "gonna tap that ass soon"; she can't watch any movie rated PG-13 for sexual content, so she has never seen a boy masturbate into a pie. Even on prime-time television, deviance has been defined down, way down, so Jackie's parents watch with her.

They are her authorities on values.

They don't allow her to walk to the Giant, where the other seventh graders meet at the fountain and flirt and ride bikes and get into trouble when a gym mat outside the high school is discovered aflame and buy condoms on a dare. ("Don't be embarrassed," the cashier says. "At least you're using protection.") Sara would never let Jackie wear a stretchy, deep V-neck like Celia's or a bra-strap-baring tank like Kristina's or fish-nets like Leslie's.

Jackie's body has a purpose: jumping, flying, spinning. When Celia and Kristina and Leslie walk around the track during gym class, she runs. She trampolines competitively, moving like an old-time movie speeded up, bouncing halfway to the gym ceiling, doing double tucks and layouts with tight, zippy twists. The very most popular girls in seventh grade, Jackie has noticed, don't do sports. "Maybe they think since they're pop-ular they don't need to do anything else," she says, "because they've already fulfilled their lifetime dream."

Her period, which she's been told she'll get when she's fifteen or six-teen, can wait: "I'm in no hurry to pee blood." Breasts, though—she'd like breasts. Her doctor says she's only in stage two, two stages away from actual breasts, but Jackie thinks she might be able to will them to grow, like this monk she heard of who changed her own eye color through meditation. Unlike Celia, who got her period at age eight, or Kristina, whose breasts surprised her in fourth grade, Jackie's body does not yet draw attention from boys, like when one guy calls to Kristina, "Omigod, you have a nice ass," and smacks it, or another guy tweaks Celia's breasts and says, "Squeeze squeeze!" Celia and Kristina respond with faux, flirtatious dismay.

Jackie doesn't get this. "I'd hit anybody who touched my boobs," she tells them.

The home-economics room is crowded, and Mrs. Brodian can never re-ally get control of the class. She's calling kids up one by one to discuss progress reports as the others laugh and argue at squished-together round tables. At Jackie's table, a boy named Kendall says, "Anton doesn't like you. He likes Amy. Do you know Amy?"

"Amy Anders?"

"Yeah."

"Shut up—you don't know anything about relationships because you've never been in one." Jackie absently runs a rubber band up and down her family-tree poster for French, which is rolled in a tube.

Justin raises his eyebrows. "I like the looks of that."

"Pervert!"

While Mrs. Brodian is still on the D's, Justin tosses Lauren's pen under the table so she'll look at his and Kendall's naked penises, which they've pulled over their low-slung pants and boxers. Jackie knows something's going on under the table but not that it's naked penises; Justin tells her to stomp her feet if Mrs. Brodian comes, but she never does. Lauren, Kendall, and Justin arrange to meet in the boys' bathroom at nine-fifty. When she goes there is groping, and over twenty minutes, she leaves and goes back twice. Through the wall, a friend in the girls' bathroom hears Lauren laughing. When they see each other in the hall, the friend tells her to come back to class, but Lauren says she's having fun. Afterward she says the boys pulled her into the bathroom, and her friends are appalled. "Uh, Lauren, that's rape!" they yell.

Jackie doesn't know exactly what went on in the bathroom. One minute she's saying of Lauren, "She didn't ask for that." Next minute she says, "She brung it on herself."

chapter four

stop! don't touch! get out!

When Jackie's mom drops her at the bus stop the next morning, another mother tells her that there might or might not have been a rape in the bathroom at school.

Horrified, Sara asks Jackie, "Do you know anything about this?" Jackie heard the gossip, she knows the players, she was practically *there*.

"No," she says.

These newly private middle schoolers are the same children who two years ago clogged the air in a room with detailed narratives of their day. All of a sudden a parent must develop the sensitive ears of a Kremlinologist, praying for emissions from accidentally loose lips. You learn of the change in your little girl, who not long ago said "Yech!" at any mention of kissing, the first time you hear her say, "He's hot!" about a guy who pops up on television. You pick up on pieces from your son's conversations in the back seat during car pool. They give, then take away: In sixth grade, when they tell their mothers whom they like, they use first names. Seventh grade, first initials. Eighth grade, "some kid," or nothing. Jackie used to reveal her "crush of the moment," as Sara calls it, but not so much this year. With Sara so good at "sucking the details out of me," Jackie finds it easier to stay mum.

Elizabeth Ginsburg, also a seventh grader, feels that way, too. In sixth grade, when Eugene bought her a bracelet and wrote her notes like,

"Let me express how much I love you," she asked her mother for advice on how to rebuff him. This year, she's getting unwanted attention from Mitch—Why, Elizabeth wonders, are all the guys who like me stupid?—but she doesn't bother asking her mom for advice. That might encourage a line of inquiry about whom Elizabeth "*like*-likes," which she hates, because why does everybody insist she has to like-like someone at all?

One of the other girls in the home-ec room saw the penises, and Ms. Thomas tells her that her mother has to know. The girl is worried about worrying her mom, who has enough on her mind. "She can't handle that," she says. Ms. Thomas thinks: And you can? She sends a note home to all the parents about the incident, saying that the parties were consenting but, still, it was totally improper. Wilde Lake has worked hard to improve its reputation, and this doesn't help. Moreover, she writes, it's disturbing the way some girls are flattered by the inappropriate attention boys give them.

At school that day, conversation is all about the rumors: A boy got beat up in the bathroom, according to Jonathan. A girl got raped in the bathroom, according to Jimmy. Eric believes that the boys forced her into the bathroom, which he calls "mean and desperate." Jackie's lunch table discusses the difference between rape and sexual assault and sexual harassment, though they really don't know. If something like this happened to her, Celia says, "my dad would stick a gun up their butt and pull the trigger." In art class an eighth-grade girl says, "Well, she wasn't screaming," and the teacher, Mr. Mitchell, listens to the kids' discussion—the anger and the sexuality, the old arguments about sluttiness and she-asked-for-it-ness alive and well—and is appalled. He wonders if he should ever reproduce.

Elizabeth, too, has been discussing what happened, how creepy it is that something like that could go on at their school. Her friends are scared, but she says that if two boys pushed her into the bathroom—this is the operative rumor at lunch table 6D—she would kick and scream. When her parents read the note from Ms. Thomas that evening, she is lying amid the stuffed animals on her big cloud-sheeted bed. "The letter," her dad says to her from the study, then comes into her room and sits on the desk chair. "What do you know about the letter?"

"I don't know," Elizabeth says. "Nothing."

He bends down and picks up an inside-out T-shirt from the floor.

"Stop! Don't touch! Get out!"
And he does.

For their only child, Joseph and Ellen Ginsburg hoped for a girl. They got what they wanted, and since then a sheepdog, Rosie, and a guinea pig with several names have joined them in their 1970s split-level, nestled in a wooded cul-de-sac. All of a sudden Elizabeth is taller than her friends, and catching up to her parents. Last year her skin had pimples, but now it's ideal, rosy and smooth. Everything about her face evokes roundness: her cheeks, the tip of her nose, her brown eyes, her arched hairline. Her long curly hair is always knotted into a sturdy brown braid—a rope you could climb up if you had to. If you compliment Liz on any of this, she'll tilt her head, smile her huge metal-filled smile, and say, quick and high-pitched, "I know." Her child's voice seems out of line with her developing face and form.

On Elizabeth's bedroom doorknob hangs a fuzzy pink sign that says GO AWAY on the side you see all the time and ENTER on the side you don't. On another sign Elizabeth has written KNOCK in huge letters and "please" in tiny ones. Ellen is good about knocking and waiting, but Joseph will knock and come right in; once Elizabeth was half naked. "I'm like, '*Daaad*, the whole point of knocking is so I can say "Come in." ' "

Elizabeth hides cookies in her underwear drawer and a mess of candy in a deep drawer of her night table, behind the organized piles of magazines, which range from *Disney Adventures* to *Seventeen*. Her dolls sit atop the bookshelves, including Emily, whose brown eyes have turned an eerie red over the years. Ellen hates the clutter covering up Elizabeth's newly painted lavender walls but indulges it: *Buffy the Vampire Slayer* posters, a Polaroid of Joseph with Santa, synchronized-swimming posters, ribbons from her meets.

On the wall of the study, Joseph and Ellen have hung writings from when Liz was little:

My mother is the most wonderful mom in the world. She's as pretty as me. She weighs 90 pounds and she's six feet tall. Her favorite food is lobster. I wish Mom would take me to school every day. I wouldn't trade my mother for my special stuff. Happy Mother's Day, Love, Elizabeth.

I like winter because I like when my daddy lets me play in the snow and make big snowballs. Weight 22 pounds height as tall as the swings. He makes pancakes for breakfast. Thank you for loveing and caring for me.

Ellen and Joseph are nostalgic for the days when Elizabeth would proclaim her affection in ways that could be hung on the wall, when she was fun and funny in wide swaths instead of unpredictable slivers, when she hobbled sympathetically the time Joseph broke his foot or offered a hug at just the right moment before he delivered his father's eulogy, when Ellen could win affection through a Fluffernutter sandwich cut in tidy triangles. They're nostalgic for the way they knew what Liz was thinking, the way they knew what they were doing, even when they didn't.

These days, not only does Elizabeth not thank Joseph for loving her, she doesn't talk to him when he drives her the fifteen miles to synchro practice three times a week.

"How was school?" he asks in the car one October evening.

"Fine."

"Anything you want to talk with me about?"

"No."

"Do you have chorus three days a week?"

"Two or three."

"And home ec? What do you learn in home ec?"

"I don't know."

"What do you learn—how to clean? Using the washing machine?"

"No. You're annoying." The pop station he let Elizabeth choose plays into the silence.

It stings. Joseph tries not to cross-examine Elizabeth like his parents used to do to him, but she thinks any question he asks is a cross-examination. It's better during car pool, because the girls gossip in the back seat as if he's not there. Ellen gets yelled at when she calls Elizabeth by the nicknames Liz Whiz or Lizilia, which Elizabeth liked just a year ago. She used to enjoy the preschool songs her mom sang, and now she thinks they're "weird-annoying," and in front of other people they're "weird-embarrassing." Elizabeth learned they were weird-embarrassing when she sang them to her own friends, who told her so.

As for any parents of a twelve-year-old, life for Ellen and Joseph is a constant quest to figure out what their child is thinking—what they would pay to know this—and to decipher their status in her ever-changing mind. After the chorus concert one autumn evening, Elizabeth finds her parents in the audience, squeezes her tall, swimmer-firm body onto Ellen's lap in front of the whole grade, and lets her mother quiz her on Latin American capitals for tomorrow's Spanish test. Then, after three capitals, she says, "You're annoying! Stop!" and wriggles away.

All of a sudden, it seems, arguments with Liz have gotten circular; any criticism, however minor, is met by, "I don't do *any*thing right." She shuts off conversation in a snap, like the other day in the car, when Elizabeth was going on and on about how badly she'd do at the swim meet and Ellen said, "I only want to hear positive thoughts."

"We're going to be first," Elizabeth said. "Does that make you *haa*ppy?"

Feels to Ellen and Joseph like they've been here before, ten years ago. Middle schoolers share the most endearing traits of two-year-olds but also the most frazzling ones—whining and forty-three others. The desire to be a big girl and a baby at the very same time. Mood shifts, growth spurts, minuscule attention spans, temper tantrums. Inflexibility, egocentrism, defiance.

It's as if children operate on a loop, child development experts point out, but this time around the immaturity is less expected. The Terrible Twos are written about, but nobody tells you about the Terrible Twelves, so they seem less justifiable, even though they're not. And the Twelves aren't nearly as cute—those horrible clothes choices are easier to chuckle over when they're made by a toddler rather than by a gangly preteen.

Middle school is when the "Get out!" starts in earnest, and the natural reaction among parents who feel helpless is to do so, in many ways. The last thing they want to do is alienate their child more—she seems so fragile. They indulge her new mood swings more than they'd like; they waffle; they bail her out. The Ginsburgs care about their daughter—lovingly, excruciatingly so. But they are beginning to learn that raising a middle schooler—a species that hungers for freedom as it lives on reliance, whose location on the continuum from "baby" to "grown-up" seems to change constantly, and not just in the direction you'd think—is not only about what they *should* do, but what they *can* do. They are beginning to learn that parenting a preteen is a daily series of tests of their ability to trust their choices, and their child.

The couple were hippies once, and moved to Columbia for its planned-city promise. They've read all the books. They've read *Reviving Ophelia* and are conscious of the concept of the self you have for others, that a baby learns to laugh not just because she's happy but because she knows that's what you want her to do. So, although they want to think Elizabeth does well in school because she cares about her education, they can't help also thinking it's because she wants to please them, which weirds them out a little. They want her to live with free will. Last year, every month or so Ellen would get on a kick where she checked Elizabeth's agenda a few nights in a row. They don't bother anymore; she always seems to be doing her work, of her own volition, and she'll say she hasn't done it yet if that's the truth. Ellen knows Elizabeth shares her dangerous ability to do nothing for hours, so occasionally she shoos her off the computer for homework, but in general they leave her alone about the work. Elizabeth is pleased they trust her "to do it good and correct."

Ellen, a preschool teacher, went to middle school at a small private academy in Manhattan where she was the class Fatty and the class Four Eyes, and her parents let her do as she pleased. She did well in the subjects she liked and got D's in those she didn't. Joseph, who works in computers for a government health agency, remembers getting hours of homework each night at his Coney Island middle school. "I studied a lot," he says, "but look where it got me"—still bitter about growing up a miserable nerd with demanding and chilly parents.

"I'm doing everything I can," he says, "to not be like my parents, to have a better relationship with Liz than they did with me, but it's hard. My parents just leak out of me. You have a kid and you're like your parents. There's something you can't do about it. Maybe I should just be happy that she's happy."

Right now she's not. Elizabeth's plan to get all A's is being thwarted by the "stupidhead" strings teacher, who, Liz announces one day, is giving her a B.

"Why are you getting a B?" Joseph asks.

"I don't want to talk about it right now."

"I'd like to talk with Miss Colyer," Joseph says, then asks Elizabeth, "Do you want to talk with her first?"

"I think she should talk to her first," Ellen says.

"I wasn't asking you," Joseph says, "I was asking Liz." And that starts a parental argument about interrupting, after which Ellen lies down with Elizabeth and asks, "Can I fall asleep in your bed?" Elizabeth, who can't even imagine why two people would fight over something so minor, shrugs, and sleeps next to her mom.

Joseph worries that he's too worried about the B-ness of the B. The time Elizabeth got three points off her social-studies project for using lined paper instead of unlined, he made himself drop it, decided that instead of getting caught up in Elizabeth's grades he should be more concerned about whether she's learning how to learn and feeling good about herself. That's why it bothers him that Liz hates strings. He wants to ask the teacher, "How are you making this fun for the kids?" because here Elizabeth is choosing to play the viola instead of going to an ungraded study hall, and if she gets a B she'll be disappointed she can't go to the straight-A breakfast. "Let's make it fun," he says. "Let's keep the kids interested in music. I want to talk about bonding with the kids, if I can do it gently."

At the elementary school, the parents could have gone en masse to the principal to complain about a teacher. Neither Ellen nor Joseph finds it easy to be involved the way they were there, where they knew the other parents, where it was more of a community, where they knew Elizabeth's friends. They worry that the work in middle school is dumbed down to the lowest kids, that they don't get enough homework, that teachers teach to some pointless standardized tests, but they're not sure what to do about it. Joseph sits on the parent-teacher committee that plans the school's academic goals, though he doesn't always show up for meetings, because he thinks the principal "shoves her agenda down people's throats."

He and 250 other parents went to Back to School Night, where he found out that Elizabeth will study renaissance art and algebra and eating disorders and needs a seventeen-dollar gym suit; learned that the fundraiser wrapping-paper rolls are twice as long as the ones from CVS; was offered a pamphlet entitled *Think College? Me? Now?*; heard a talk about how 20 percent of Howard County eighth graders used alcohol in the last month, and that being a "hands-on" parent cuts underage drinking by one-fourth; and listened to one teacher review the dress code and another tell them to check their kids' homework even though they will resist and Ms. Thomas say, "This is not an easy age. They're going through tremendous changes. You ask why they made a decision they did and they say, 'I don't know,' and they're telling you the truth. You send us your best," she told the parents, "and we love them."

"I sent 'em my only," Joseph murmured.

All evening, various teachers said, "Your child should have shown you such-and-such," and the dads looked at the moms and the moms looked at the dads.

"Have you seen that?"

"No."

Children this age have a lot of things on their minds, and notes to their parents are not one of them. They don't make it home anymore, or they make it home crumpled in a crevice of the backpack, to be excavated in months. The preteen mind is weak on logic, very selective on memory. It drives Joseph and Ellen crazy the way they spent twenty minutes deciding with Elizabeth that she'll only do one swim meet this weekend, and then, the next day, after practice, she says, "Coach wants me to swim Saturday." Joseph says, "We agreed you'd only do one event, remember?" and Elizabeth says, "When?" Constantly losing things, too. "How can Jackie remember every word to every song Linkin Park ever made," says Mike Taylor, "but she can't remember her gymnastics jacket?"

The section of the brain where thoughts about notes and gymnastics jackets once resided is now occupied by thoughts about themselves.

Which means that their parents' concerns are changing, too: Will I have to buy her another jacket? Will the kid eventually realize the world doesn't revolve around him? Once this year Avy Mason was so fed up with Lily's begging and me-me-me that she said, "For twenty-four hours, I don't want to hear about you." Five minutes later, as she headed out to the hairdresser, Lily asked, "Can you get me some mascara at Skinmarket?"

But the kids aren't always as clueless at it looks.

The day the back of the fish tank pops out in the Ginsburgs' family room, and everything is out of place when Elizabeth gets home from school, all she says upon seeing Joseph on the floor where the tank used to be is, "You're home?" Could she not have noticed the garage door up, the car and a weird vacuum machine in there, the sofa misplaced, the aquarium gone, *her father on the floor where the fish were?* Joseph is thinking, That's all she has to say? You're home?

He's right—Elizabeth didn't really notice the fish. What she was thinking is this: The last time her dad was in the family room when she got home from school, Ellen was at the hospital, sick.

chapter five

i'm scary enough as it is

Halloween night, Elizabeth comes downstairs in the hippie costume Ellen bought at Target, a snug halter and low-rider bell bottoms made of blue velvet and pink gauze. Ellen looks up from her salmon and says, as Liz covers it all with her bulky Adidas jacket, "Good thing I spent all that money on the costume." Elizabeth turns over her plastic witch's cauldron, and last year's gummed-up loot tumbles onto the sofa.

"Anyone want some candy?"

"Let me take a photo."

"No."

Every year Elizabeth goes trick-or-treating with her neighbor Laura, her best friend. With the neighborhood growing older, there are no other kids in the dark cul-de-sac. As they wait for Laura and her father, Joseph looks up and announces, "This is the first full moon on Halloween in forty-six years, and the only one in your generation."

"Who cares?"

Like every year, the girls talk about which kids from school used to live where, pass quickly by the house where someone died, ring doorbells, and eagerly plop candy into their cauldrons. Elizabeth holds up the orange box she got at Sunday school and asks, "Would you like to support UNICEF? You don't have to. It's, like, for kids all over the world." The dads fall back, talking about the return of the neighborhood skunk and school-system redistricting and whether this retired meteorologist Bob knows would make a good caterer for the girls' joint Bat Mitzvah in the spring.

Something, though, is different this Halloween. Usually the girls run from house to house through the yards as if there were a deadline, tripping over their costumes, and the dads can't keep up. This time everything's slower; the girls defer to driveways and sidewalks. "They must be getting older," Joseph tells Bob, glowing a bit from his lantern.

Eric spends Halloween in his living room, watching television.

Lily's plans to build a Creepy Maze disappeared into whatever Bermuda Triangle eleven-year-olds' elaborate plans disappear into. Instead she decorates her porch with cottony spiderwebs and eyeball candles and jack-o'-lanterns and a cauldron of dry ice. While her mother hands out special Baggies of treats for the kids she knows and regular candy for the others, Lily dresses as a witch and goes trick-or-treating with a neighbor. She returns looking a little disappointed, especially when her sister comes and goes with her big, laughing group.

At a Halloween party in Dustin Fried's basement, Jackie and Celia are dressed in costumes they call "PJ Ho's," though Jackie has explained to her mom that she's a baby. They wear pajama bottoms and white long-sleeved T-shirts and suck on lollipops. It took forever at the mall to find a white shirt, because first of all every one Jackie liked wasn't on sale and second of all, even though Jackie knows that with Dad taking care of Kyle instead of working they can't just buy on a whim even if she says, "I love you, Mommy," real sweet, she saw a zillion things she had to beg for—a Sagittarius necklace, fancy jeans, a plaid purse with a planner inside, an oversize yellow hooded sweatshirt. "I had to wear Anton's sweatshirt today," she told her mom. Anton, Sara wondered, and said, "Put it on your Christmas list." At the party, during truth-or-dare, Kristina kisses Scott, and Celia kisses Brad and Jay, and one girl even has to lick a boy on the cheek. Jackie doesn't play. "I'm not kissing anyone," she says.

Jimmy Schissel goes trick-or-treating with a friend, for the first time without a costume. "I'm scary enough as it is," he says, only half kidding.

*   *   *

Even though Jimmy has just-right pumpernickel hair that lightens in the summer, and skin that's creamy where it should be creamy and pink where it should be pink, and lovely brown eyes with lashes as thick and even as the fringe on a flapper's dress, he can't think of one thing he likes about the way he looks right now. After he went to bed the night he and his parents made a personal-culture poster for social studies, his parents glued a fifth-grade school picture smack in the middle of the neatly typed passages about his interests. At school, he ripped it off.

At eleven, Jimmy can feel hints of it ending: the little-boy years when he was slender and nearly bionic, able to leap and dive and dart easily, comfortable with the way he looked, even happier with the way he moved. He was Superman when he wanted to be. Now he doesn't know where his body's going. "Those videos in health class, the *Your Changing Body* ones where they say, 'Puberty is the best thing to ever happen to you!'—they're so stupid," he says, the way they try too hard, propagandizing something that just isn't that cool. He has no sense that this upheaval is temporary. How can he? Underneath his ultra-baggy jeans, ragged at the hem, are feet that have stretched four sizes in three years—they are size-ten paws and he is the puppy who hasn't grown into them yet. A typical eleven-year-old has reached four-fifths the height he'll attain by adulthood but only half the weight—so here it comes, to his surprise. Whose flesh is this? Underneath his T-shirts—often a Superman shirt—that hang past his butt is a small belly that wasn't there before, small enough that you can't see it when he's clothed but big enough that he thinks maybe he should diet, or jog. He weighs 110 pounds, perfectly healthy for his five feet two and a half inches, but if he lost five pounds he'd weigh the same as his older sister, Brianna.

It happens at different times for everyone, which is why there are kids in sixth grade who look eight and kids who look eighteen. These physical changes are the greatest they've experienced since they were babies. This mysterious force that visits preteen boys' bodies, which causes blond hair to darken and easy grace to disappear in a tangle of limbs and skin to pock with pimples, is objectively something wonderful—growth! change! maturity!—but it infuses them with a profound, unidentifiable sense of loss, as they start to see their childhoods fall. They're not so cute anymore, and they know it. Their smells outpace their awareness of them, feet and armpits and breath, such that sixth-grade teachers wonder if they can tell their first-period classes to brush their teeth, or should they have the nurse do it? Eventually muscles will form, visible through forearms when fingers are flexed, but for now the bones come alone, and arms and legs grow faster than the brain's ability to track them. A boy hits himself on corners of doorways, bangs his funny bone. So many times, as he races to get his gym clothes off to catch the bus home, Jimmy gets his head stuck in his shirt, the pants in the shoes, so he's started to wear his gym clothes home. Entering puberty, a child grows so fast (three inches a year, on average, for boys) and so unevenly that inactivity is actually painful. He squirms after sitting still for fourteen minutes, which makes eighty-minute classes excruciating. Why do the teachers make you sit up straight? They think you can learn only if your body is propped a certain way?

And how quickly a swimming-pool party has lost its allure. Nowadays boys are bombarded with body-image obsessions almost as much as girls. Muscles. It's all about muscles. Some of Jimmy's classmates have started to lift weights. Some have grown a tiny bit of hair on their chests, and though they've sort of been waiting for this, it's simultaneously maddening, because (as they see in the Abercrombie catalogue) body hair is just not cool. They shave their non-mustaches surreptitiously in the bathroom. I am twenty, they think, in a moment of pride. I am a man.

Jimmy's not quite there yet. But puberty is an aggregate of physiological changes—many less visible than mustache fuzz—and Jimmy is embarking on many of them. He is tired when he is supposed to be awake, and awake when he is supposed to be tired. His attentions have begun to scatter, his temper has begun to grow. Hobbies and intellectual pursuits that once captivated him to no end have begun to strike him as childish. Some of his friends are about to strike him as childish, too. How he appears to others is suddenly a subject of great concern and mortification. His thoughts on girls are still chaste, though strong. Peter Parker, also known as Spider-Man, has had his crush since fourth grade, too. "Maybe I should get bit by a spider," Jimmy says during the movie. That would help, wouldn't it? His belly would morph into a six-pack, he could jettison the glasses, his brown eyes would turn blue—not to mention the impressive superpowers. Imagine.

Jimmy has notions of romance. In English class, he has to write a new ending to the Ray Bradbury story where a group of kids lock a girl in the closet while they enjoy the hour of sun their planet gets every seven years. Jimmy's classmates' endings involve a lot of tears and apologies after Margot gets out of the closet. One boy plots a prank involving toothpaste and hot sauce. Jimmy writes that Margot beats up the boy who trapped her, runs away to the other side of the planet, and steals food that arrives on the landing pad: " 'I need to leave this planet. If only I could hijack a rocket ship,' Margot always says." Then she meets an astronaut who takes her to Earth, where she falls in love with the astronaut's son and marries him when they're old enough.

Jimmy figures he'll have a wife one day, but it's hard for him to imagine ever being as foolish as seventh graders on the subject of crushes. "Girls are all mean," Jimmy sometimes says, not just because of the way they treat him but because of the bratty way they treat each other, particularly since sixth grade started. First they'll set up a scenario to make someone look stupid; then, beyond the hurt of that, they'll call the person stupid for falling into the trap. Aside from his parents, he gets clues about what relationships are like from women on television, such as Anna Nicole Smith. "They use all their money to look good," he says. "Then they get a boyfriend and take all his money."

There's something comforting about a crush, like his on Mia, that is 100 percent unattainable. "What happens if they like you back and someone else likes you, too? Then you have a problem." There are a few girls in school he considers friends, kind of, girls he helps with homework or talks with during class. But he can't really have them over or anything, because then it's like, "She's your *giiiirlfriend*," which is what the boys say to Jonathan during lunch just because he eats with the girls.

The school bathrooms are locked for a while after the seventh-grade incident, and whereas he wouldn't have cared about it two years ago, Jimmy is too embarrassed to use the permissible toilet in the front office, so his bladder hurts, and his parents wonder why he has to pee the second he comes home. Jimmy now showers once a week, instead of taking a bath. Every day he washes his hair in the sink so it doesn't stand up, and if it's still sticking up when he's running out the door, he'll lick his hand and rub it down. (The comb is only for weddings and church.) He sometimes worries about clothes.

His parents worry about keeping him in clothes. With the growth comes an unbelievable appetite; like a dog, Jimmy would eat all the food in front of him until it was taken away. His favorite beverages are grape soda, orange soda, cream soda, Pepsi, Coke, root beer, Sprite, 7-Up, Sierra Mist, water, and the milk left over from a bowl of Apple Jacks. The food diary Jimmy keeps one day for home ec looks like this:

Breakfast—two Rice Krispie treats, milk
Lunch—peanut butter sandwich, pineapple, juice
Dinner—kielbasa, five carrots, sparkling water

Here's what he didn't mention: the venti-size caramel apple cider from Starbucks, two Cokes, three Hershey's kisses, two York Peppermint Patties, and seven handfuls of Doritos he ate after school. The cheese-filled Pillsbury rolls he tore through at dinner until his father said, "Enough croissants, Jimmy." And who knows when Jimmy ate the two puddings whose empty containers his mother found hidden behind the toilet in the downstairs bathroom, as if he weren't allowed the food.

The pineapple, too, is a white lie: Jimmy gives his fruit cup away every day. It's not uncommon, particularly among the girls, for middle-school lunches to go uneaten save four bites of apple. Even though the cafeteria teems with hungry, growing children, at least fifty parent-hours of slicing and spreading are dumped each day into the Wilde Lake Middle School garbage cans. Ms. Thomas figures that if the kids just handed over their sandwiches when they walked into school in the morning, she could give them to a soup kitchen and solve whatever hunger problem there is in Columbia.

When Jimmy ordered a large gym suit at the beginning of the year, the PE teacher said, "You're living dangerously. Bring it back if it's too big." Mr. Jackson scared the boys a bit that day when he warned that kids sometimes reach into the locker-room baskets and pick pockets or knot shoelaces together. Each day when the boys come out of the locker room, they tear around the gym in their baggy Wilde Lake shorts, chasing, sliding, jumping over one another onto the mat. Girls clump and talk. As the door shuts to separate basketball from field hockey, they run up and scream, "Bye!"

Some boys look surprised if their shot makes it into the basket; others get nothing but net. Jimmy is not a star, but he plays fine. He blocks Alexandra, who is good, forcing a turnover. Occasionally he bloops the ball errantly into the air, but just as often he makes it. When he does, his friend Will, who stands in the middle of the court picking his fingernails, calls out, "Nice shot, Schiss!"

Everybody ran around in elementary school, but in middle school kids clearly separate into jocks and not-jocks. Many of the not-jocks have mistaken their temporary clumsiness and weakness for permanent lack of ability, or they simply can't bear the taunts when they can't keep up. Children arrive at a point where they decide they are athletic, or they are not, and this dichotomy holds until adulthood, when they realize they can enjoy sports again even if they suck at them. For the moment Jimmy still sees himself as athletic; he doesn't notice what his parents are just starting to: that his growth is making him a little clumsier, weighed down. He enjoys PE even though the girls beat him, and most of the boys in his class, in running, sit-ups, and push-ups. He thinks he'll play lacrosse again.

In gym, Jimmy likes Ping-Pong best. "I sweat more in this than in basketball," he says as he hits the ball back and forth, hard, with Will. When Mr. Jackson says, "No smashes," they bounce the ball off the walls. "Oops," Jimmy says, "I caught it in my ding." The ball rolls away to two boys who play keep-away. Jimmy begins to push one of them into a tall stack of chairs but stops himself and instead says, "We're going to tell Mr. Jackson."

Last year Jimmy and his friends played four-square and freeze tag at recess, but now they mostly stand against the wall, because there's not enough time and not enough friends for games. Boys who used to spend recess throwing a Nerf football as hard as they could at each other now pelt each other with jokes and insults. Sometimes Jimmy plays tetherball, winner stands, with the hand that hits the ball tucked inside his long sleeve. "I play Jimmy even if he loses," the next boy in line says, "because he's bad."

Jimmy's parents make him play one team sport each season, and occasionally he shoots baskets or zooms around the cul-de-sac on his bike, but for the most part, as with many boys his age, inactive hobbies have replaced play and movement. For the dream bedroom he designs for a geometry project, Jimmy includes a DVD player, GameCube, VCR, and flat-screen Phillips television. Unfortunately, the Schissels only have the kind of cable that makes your reception better, not the kind that brings you the Cartoon Network, so during the week Jimmy mostly watches the cartoons on PBS, which he knows are babyish, but still. He's not allowed to watch his favorite show, *The Simpsons*, and, besides, almost every kid in school, whether or not he will admit it, still kind of likes PBS. At a recent assembly, a teacher started singing the theme song to *Blue's Clues*, and every kid in the sixth grade joined in, heartily—the only time during the year they did something in unison. Jimmy doesn't watch *Pokemon* anymore, but he still watches *Digimon*. He's critical of commercials; he knows their tricks. What if kids with mental disabilities decide they can do back flips just because they wear Gap jeans?

As for movies, he likes *The Matrix* and the old Bond films that come on Saturday nights, and ever since he watched a documentary about asteroids he thinks that *Deep Impact* and *Armageddon* might be more realistic than you'd think. He gets to see PG-13 now, but he yearns for R. "I'm not a baby anymore," he says. "I know not to see movies with a lot of bad language." Anyway, he figures, he hears those words in school all the time. Though Jimmy has read all the Harry Potter books and can parse them emphatically, when his friends talk about how excited they are for the movie, he says, "It's stupid. I have to take my cousin."

Though he still sneaks into the living room to check out his Christmas presents using a Fisher-Price stethoscope and occasionally plays with his Star Wars Legos, Jimmy has started to think toys are boring. He barely touches the seventy Beanie Babies hanging in plastic on his bedroom door, except for a battle he stages every blue moon before bed. He and his friends have crafted origami planes and weapons and even a terrain for a fantasy game called Warhammer, but they haven't played it yet, and never will. More than anything, Jimmy—like all his male classmates—is obsessed with video games. He could probably play eight hours in a row if nobody stopped him, cross-legged, feet over knees, or lying on his stomach. Jimmy can win at Super Smash Bros. even when he chooses the weakest character, Pikachu, and he has paged through his game primers so much that the ink has begun to rub off.

Jimmy has always been curious, an active thinker. Inside his head sits a store of vivid memories, all in black and white, of things that happened when he was exactly three: He fell down the stairs. He left a chocolate bar in the car for a year. He spilled eggs on his sister's tent during a camping trip. He zoomed around the family room delivering toys from a cart, saying, "I'm the mailman!" until he ran into his mother, making her spill hot tea down his arm, for which he went to the hospital. Three, Jimmy says, is when he first became good at vocabulary.

Used to be, Jimmy would sit up and wonder about how we had night and day, or whether Adolf Hitler might still be alive—or perhaps he has an equally evil twin none of us knows about. In the fall, a new invention is revealed, the Segway, a stabilized motorized scooter. This fascinates Jimmy; he also thinks magnetic sidewalks and jetpacks might be a good idea. He has concluded that Bill Clinton was a good president except that he lied about Monica Lewinsky and highway tolls. "He said he was going to lower them," Jimmy says, "but he highered them." He still wishes he had voted for Ralph Nader instead of Al Gore in last year's mock election, because of the environment, which he prioritizes right up there with sports and almost as high as video games. For a Chesapeake Bay conservation project, Jimmy and his father raise and study three thousand oysters out where they keep their boat, and cultivate bay grasses in a plastic tub on the family-room hearth. When he grows up he wants to work in 3-D animation or with lizards. In a cage in the kitchen live two green anoles, which eat crickets that chirp through dinner.

Boys and girls going through puberty swing madly from energetic to exhausted, and never get enough sleep to sate them. It's become more difficult lately. Jimmy is supposed to go to bed at ten, but often he's not tired—it's not known exactly why, but around age ten the circadian clock pushes back, keeping kids awake when they should be feeling sleepy. Experts have found that for preteens a good night of sleep doesn't just help the next day's learning but reinforces the previous day's lessons, and they recommend nine hours. Most kids never get that much, since they can't fall asleep when they're supposed to, even if they were exhausted all day, and the bus comes at seven-fifteen, whether or not you've had time to dry your hair. Sometimes Jimmy is on a sugar high from the candy he stashes near his trundle bed. With the sheets tangled and the mattress pad exposed from last night's tornado of sleep, Jimmy will stay up reading *Calvin and Hobbes* for two hours. This makes him feel out of sync with this world, like a comic he once saw that said, "My internal clock is on

Tokyo time." No problem getting up Saturday mornings for cartoons, but getting out of bed for school is another story.

Jimmy gets nightmares, too. The day before sixth grade started, he dreamed that he was going to get detention for being late and on top of that wasn't wearing underwear. Before September 11, he dreamed that a plane crashed into a skyscraper, there were screams, then everything went dim. After September 11, he dreamed that he was on top of a tall building, there was an explosion, then the building collapsed. His recurring nightmare, which makes him sweat, is this: He is hiding under his bed when a werewolf peeks into the room. The werewolf leaves, and reappears through a trapdoor in the floor. To escape, Jimmy skis down a mountain.

Then he falls off the edge.

chapter six

there's always next quarter

"Middle-school kids," Ms. Thomas says, "have to move around. They have to be able to talk, they want to be engaged in what they're learning, and you really can't do anything in the classroom for more than fifteen or twenty minutes without losing the class." A teacher learns at a middle-school seminar to divide his class into four segments: the teacher speaking, the students speaking, the students working alone, the students working in groups. When the teacher doesn't make movement a priority, the students fidget. They tap their feet. They sprawl. If you're Jimmy, "Sean, please stop tapping" doesn't have anything to do with whether you personally are barred from tapping. In class Jimmy makes origami cranes and arachnids and planes, the tinier the better. On the other side of the school, Eric drums with his pencil, hums, plays guessing games with the clock. What time will it be when he looks up? He always overshoots. If you say a word in your head enough times in a row, he discovers one day during class, it doesn't sound like a word anymore. *Accurate. Accurate. Accurate. Accurate?* When he can get away with it he studies the sheet of paper he carries everywhere, a printout from sk8house.com of the Rollerblades he wants for Christmas.

By preadolescence the brain has become quite adept at emotion, but the parts devoted to organizational skills—as well as reasoning and judgment—mature more slowly. The disorganization can be appalling. In sixth grade kids are enchanted by the orderly and proprietary cubbiness of their lockers; by eighth grade many, like Eric, stack their books on top of the lockers, wherever's convenient, science book in one place and binder in another. "Somebody stole my agenda," they tell Ms. Thomas when they lose it, as if this is an item with potential black-market value. Sixth graders' agendas are usually carefully tended, pages folded into shapes after each date has passed, boxes filled in dutifully. By eighth grade many agendas are, like Eric's in only the second month, a mess—pages gone, pages empty, except for notes like, "Dear Ms. Epps, NO home-work rec'd Geography of the Americas pgs. 36–44." They leave their names off papers. Why use an eraser or Wite-Out when you can cross out with a mess of marks? By the second day of school Eric's book covers are scrunched; by the second week they are missing.

He pulls the school directory out of his bag, crumples it, tosses it in the trash. His binder, instead of being divided into classes and subdivided into Warm-Ups and Vocab and Notes and Graded Papers, has become a sloppy heap of materials that matter to Eric (Grand Theft Auto 3 cheat codes, a printout of the blue Supra he wants) and missed opportunities: A permission slip to be on the leadership council for the aquarium club, which he would have liked to do, but he forgot to turn it in. Half-finished worksheets of scientific nomenclature. Entire folders of assign-ments he completed but didn't hand in.

If Eric doesn't hear the homework announced, he says, he won't stay after class to find out what it is, because then he'll be late for his next class, which means twenty minutes' time-out during the upcoming dance and an automatic detention. Except that Eric doesn't like the dance—and every teacher at Wilde Lake writes the next day's homework on the blackboard before class even starts.

Eric has taken an orange highlighter to a reading called "Instant Study Skills," which says to find a fixed place in your home for nothing but studying. Where he studies—the living-room sofa—is also where he watches TV, plays video games, eats fried rice from the Hunan Wok and chicken patties from the freezer, and sleeps, under a sleeping bag but without sheets. The room is small, square, dark. The venetian blinds, like his neighbors', always remain shut. Thomas's stereo is distracting, but Eric doesn't ask him to turn it down because he figures he wouldn't. His best stuff is in a storage shed off Route 99. Above the television is a painting of Jesus, flanked by Ms. Beulah's high-school diploma and his dad's GED. There is a framed poem titled "Don't Quit" on the wall, a shelf packed with the Grolier's Encyclopedia, and, all over the place, in plastic cracked frames and nice glass ones, studio shots and candids of Beulah's family and a few of Eric's two brothers. Eric appears in none of them.

"I don't care," he says. "Well, I used to. It's pictures, man. I wished they cared, but pictures is pictures."

He feels like he's living in someone else's home. Even though sometimes she makes him chicken, gives him thirty dollars for a hockey stick, Eric decides Ms. Beulah is snappish, the way she tells him to do chores, the way she spends so much time upstairs in the bedroom, the way she walks in and grunts "Fine" to his question "How are you, Ms. Beulah?"

Aside from his choice in women, Eric worships his father. When William told Eric that eating raw onion cures a cold, he carried one around school in his pocket, stinking up science class. Eric practices playing "In a Sentimental Mood" on the sax for the wedding in October. He loves to hit the road with his father in his truck, not just for the father-son time but because "I know there's more up there than I learn in social studies." He can tell you why Wisconsin is boring and how to read a map and which truckers are retiring and how his dad got the handle Frosty because of a runny nose during a winter freeze.

William is on the road most of the time. That Eric doesn't see his father every day isn't unusual, but most kids who don't at least see their moms. Eric misses his, painfully. She moved to Columbia because she didn't want her kids going to school in Baltimore, and she doesn't want him back there now. Especially since she saw that commercial, the one that says a sixth grader knows a roach as a bug and a seventh grader knows a roach as marijuana. When Eric lived in Baltimore, before fifth grade, he knew that you could get weed on the corner of Barclay and Greenhurst for twenty bucks. A child in the city knows too much.

A parent in the city, or the country, or Columbia, Maryland, doesn't know enough. The truth of a child's situation is generally one step worse than parents perceive. Or more: One study showed that middle schoolers were at least ten times as likely to engage in risky behaviors—drinking, having sex, attempting suicide, smoking—as parents thought. If you're fairly certain she's tried a cigarette, it's likely she's smoked several; if you know he hid his last F on a math test, there's a good chance he's forged a progress report, too. Eric watches his Wilde Lake friends smoke pot all the time in the corner of an empty ball field. But he has no interest in trying it himself. Because marijuana's a pure plant, Eric doesn't think it can hurt you bad—not like cigarettes, the rat poison he's heard they put in there, the urea, the tar, the ammonia—but he knows Tenacious would cut his lips off. "My family," he says, "we don't do that."

Sometimes he thinks about asking to move in with his godparents, where his mom is, but he figures there's not room and he doesn't feel like imposing. "I don't ask for anyone's help," Eric says, "unless it's mad critical." Eric learned this self-reliance—an admirable trait, perhaps, for an adult, but a lamentable one for a thirteen-year-old—from his mother. "All my life, I hear from people, 'Remember that time I helped you?' and they throw it all back in her face."

Tenacious was raised as an only child by foster parents. She always waited, in vain, for her mother to appear magically at important moments: graduation, the birth of her sons. Because of that, she always promised she'd never leave her boys. The separation slays her. She can't hug Eric as much as she wants. She picks him up for school most mornings but doesn't see much of his work in those short snippets of time. A few days she initialed his assignments in his agenda, but then her brakes failed and she couldn't get to Columbia. Tenacious feels like this is a turning point for Eric; she sees his interest in school fading.

When their children reach this age many parents, mothers especially, figure this is their chance to work more, since their kids can dress themselves, let themselves in the door, get themselves a snack. This is exactly the opposite of what psychologists and educators say should happen. Teachers as a whole would choose more active parents, combined with better-behaved kids, over higher salaries. While "active parents" is narrowly understood as those who help out at school, study after study has proved what teachers' intuition already told them: that the true measure of involvement, for families of all incomes or backgrounds, is something much more. It's tutoring one's children at home. Setting an example by turning off the television and reading for pleasure. Finding out when the newsletter comes each week and insisting it be dug out of the backpack. Setting high expectations and talking about college. Family "connectedness," feeling your parents care for you, improves academic achievement and protects against nearly every possible middle-school health risk and behavioral problem. Flunking, smoking, depression—to avoid these, merely spending time with your child is necessary but not sufficient; a family must participate in activities together and show warmth and love, every single day. Organizations across the country—and an entire office of the federal Department of Education—have been set up to help schools help parents help their children. "Being a whole family unit" is the way Ms. Thomas puts it, emphatically, to concerned parents, "and it has to start early."

Tenacious knows this, instinctively. She doesn't know what to do about it.

"I could lose him," she says. "I feel inadequate."

Halfway to his second-quarter report card, in October, Eric gets his interim report. A D in reading and C's in academic enrichment, social studies, and English, for missing assignments. He doesn't know how he's going to make it through the year in social studies. "It's up and down in her class," he says. "You're doing things one minute that everybody's into, then you go back to doing the gay crap." Wars, he likes. Anything that can be tied to September 11.

"Why were the British after the Sons of Liberty?" Mrs. Conroy asks as the class corrects a true-false quiz on the Coercive Acts.

"They were the head of all the protests and things."

"Think about today—are we looking for the leaders of something?"

"Bin Laden!" The questions pile on: "Why don't they just kill him?" "Wouldn't there be more terrorism than ever if they killed him?" "Isn't it true that if Bush doesn't catch Bin Laden he won't get elected again?"

"The election's in three years," Mrs. Conroy says. "It's hard to know what effect that would have."

Eric says, "If they came over and did more terrorism, wouldn't that threaten Bin Laden—wouldn't we kill him?"

"The U.S. is a democracy," Mrs. Conroy says, "and we think people have certain rights. Okay. We're moving back to colonial times."

Bev Conroy knows the diversions perk the students up and teach them something, too. Maybe she could indulge more of them if she had more time, if there were fewer standardized tests to prepare for, if stu-

dents did the assigned reading at night, if there weren't so many interruptions for kids to go to guidance or the library or wherever. If they
were used to reading and tuned in to the world—each year fewer kids
raise their hands when she asks whose families take the newspaper. If they
didn't need their hands held so much these days. The teachers who have
been around awhile say today's children show up with less of an independent work ethic than their predecessors. They are the beneficiaries
and victims of a new era of shortcuts: fancy calculators, spell check,
years of typing on computers that have precluded their cursive from ever
becoming legible. They won't read the instructions even when they
need to.

All this and a county curriculum to get through. Some teachers feel
like they're pushing new knowledge too fast, instead of making sure
the kids have better mastery of a smaller amount of information. But
you can't risk sending kids on to the next class without covering the last
two units.

So, back to colonial times.

"If you give me, like, the Bill of Rights and crap like that—man,"
Eric says later. "We're just sitting there, reading up the book, hearing,
'Class, c'mon now.' How you gonna be a kid, only thirteen years old, and
sit there in the class and listen to a teacher talk about nothing?"

"Nothing" means, for instance, Paul Revere. When Mrs. Conroy asks
what he was famous for before the British were coming, one girl says he
was "known for beautiful, elegant silver work." Mrs. Conroy corrects
her: "He was a talented silversmith and engraver."

This is one of the things Eric hates most—how some teachers look
for one right answer and only that answer. In science the other day, the
drill asked, "Charlie Chromedome went for a walk without an umbrella.
He did not wear a hat and he did not take refuge under a shelter: yet, not
one hair on his head got wet. How was that possible?" Eric doesn't know
why his answer—"He was wearing a hood"—or Robert's answer—"He
was bald"—was not just as right as "It wasn't raining." Who cares that
Paul Revere made tea sets and silverware anyway? At this point Eric's
head is buried in his shirt, to emerge only when Mrs. Conroy tells the
class that Paul Revere made false teeth, too.

In reading, Eric is supposed to have turned in journal entries for his
research project on street racing cars. The first bit of writing flowed so

well, all off the top of his head, that he couldn't believe how much was on the page—"What so great about its power is that it has 320 hp and 290 ft lbs of torque and that's good for racing because if the car has a faster start than the Shelby, the Shelby will catch the car and it pass the other car." Mrs. Cook wanted the completed journal Monday, but Eric didn't hand in any more than he had written in class.

In academic enrichment, Mrs. Cook urges the class to "transcend from elementary to approaching high school. You can tell the scholars, who use teachers as role models, *ex*ceed and *suc*ceed and *ex*cel. Look around. Not all of these people will be your classmates in ninth grade. As the teacher sets the example, so will you follow. Very traditional—it will last a lifetime." Eric doesn't understand any of what Mrs. Cook puts on the overhead. "Objectives: To develop representational thinking. To develop flexibility and plasticity by rapid transition from one perspective to another. To use several sources of information simultaneously to arrive at a conclusion." For practically the whole period they do a fancy connect-the-dots exercise, then fill out a "Take Time to Reflect" worksheet that prompts, "Today I learned." Eric fills in: "Nothing." Still, if he had to choose teachers to hug, Mrs. Cook would be one of them.

He hates doing the homework in English but feels cozy there. Sometimes Mrs. Brown lets him use television shows instead of books for his homework, so he draws a character web of SpongeBob SquarePants ("Helpful—will listen to what people have to say. Funny—his shoes squeak when he walks") and describes why Dragonball Z illustrates suspense ("because Goku and Vegeta finally got to fight for real then they restarted the series. That shows suspense because want to know who win."). Eric likes writing the journal entries Mrs. Brown assigns each day.

If I could buy anything I would buy a Toyota Supra—2002 white backs, loud pipes, high spoiler, 18 inch rims chrome, tinted windows, nitrus combustion kit, turbo kit, glowing chasis, glowing logo, racing sticker, lab top, big system, taz air freshener, waterproof seats, racing style seatbelts, hydrolics, twin turbo engine, with 430 hp, 4,300 rpm for tourque. 6 gear transmission, and fire breathing exhaust system. And a nice 3 room, 2 bathrooms, big basement, a yard and a brick kitchen and a half pipe.

I love winter because I can relax and stay to myself. I drink hot
chocolate with marshmallows that gooze from the heat. I have
snowball fights and after play video games and go snowboarding
with my friend James just chill.

Mrs. Brown has Eric read this one aloud and praises the sensory images, the detail. Eric likes hearing other people's entries, too, how Lena's
brother is annoying but a policeman, how Max fasts during Ramadan,
how Talia's friend was shot and recovered, then was hit by a drunk driver
and died. Mrs. Brown tries to get the quiet smart people to speak up—
"Sandi, I know you're around verbal people, but you have to fight for it,"
she'll say, or, "Let's listen to Sue. She talks softly and has a lot to say."
She has an orderly system of awarding points for participation, and Eric
likes to see the checkmarks accumulate next to his name on the overhead.
Once Mrs. Brown called his house. "Am I in trouble?" Eric asked. "No,"
she said, "I just wanted to tell your parents how hard you're working in
English." Eric was amazed a teacher would phone for a good thing, and
disappointed his father wasn't home.

Excellent in PE, excellent in band, of course. Eric's got a hundred in
math and a B in science, because, even when he doesn't get his homework problems correct, both teachers give full credit for trying. There are
some days in math where he has grasped the algebraic expression so well
that he gets to explain it to the rest of the class, step by step. "Yes!" he
says when this happens. "I was right! You know what you should do? Just
look closely at the parentheses next time."

He blames the bad grades on his lack of glasses, the way, when
he reads small print, a zingy pain shoots from the back of his head
straight out his eyes. Also, he says, it's because of the wedding, the day of
school he had to miss plus all that time picking out and practicing the
song. "Now that this wedding crap is over," Eric declares, "I'll get
straight A's."

Not exactly. When he opens the envelope on November 9, the wedding
long past and glasses living on Eric's nightstand, he has A's in music and
gym, D's in health and science, and C's in everything else. "But I'm awesome in science!" he says. The immaturity of middle schoolers' frontal

lobes causes a disregard for consequences, along with the impulsive be-havior. No surprise they often think grades fall from the sky. There they were on the spreadsheet all quarter, two F's on tests, a bunch of zeros on homeworks that brought down the hundreds, and then they ask, "Why did you give me a D?"

"Well, that's the most A's I ever had in this school," Eric says. "Oh well, there's always next quarter. Hopefully there's no distractions for second quarter. Hopefully."

After school he gets shrimp fried rice at the village center, then comes home, where Ms. Beulah, who works the very early shift, is asleep upstairs, and calls his mom. When he tells her about the D's, she is exasperated.

"Health?" Tenacious teaches inmates about health and is studying to be a nurse. That her son blows this stuff off drives her crazy. "You've got to do better in that class. Eric, you're not even putting forth the effort to learn, and learning is free. Why should I put down a hundred dollars for a paintball gun for two D's?" He rolls his eyes. Beyond that, she cannot muster more punishment, since she is not there to enforce it. "It's not the best report card in the world," she tells him, "but we'll do better next time."

Eric sits on the sofa and watches television all afternoon—cartoons, the new Busta Rhymes video, extreme sports, Emeril, an obstacle-course show. He gets a ride to the skating rink, where the cashier lets him in for free even though he forgot his ID card. Eric's charming that way. When he gets home, he says he's tired and tries to slip upstairs to the bathroom. His father asks to see his report card.

"You know you have to do better," William says. "I'm going to start checking your homework."

Over the PA a few days later, Eric is called into Ms. Thomas's office, where she meets one by one with every student with so much as one D. Eric sits in the chair in front of her desk and says, "I've only been in here two times."

"Hi, Eric. You probably know I've been seeing kids for grades this week. What did you think of your report card?"

"It's not as good as I thought it would be, but I know I can do better."

She asks about the D's.

"In science, I missed a lot of days and she wouldn't let me make up the work. In health, I'm just not interested, and when I'm not interested, I don't do the work."

"So you prefer D's."

"I don't prefer them, but when I'm bored, I don't do the work. I used to hand in homework, but with classwork, she would be collecting it and I would always be skipped because I sat in back, and I would call out for her to collect mine but she didn't listen. So then I just stopped trying."

"When I listen to you, you know what I hear? 'It's everybody's fault but mine.' "

"It *is* my fault."

"What do you have for related arts now?"

"Tech ed."

"You bored in there?"

"No, I'm close up in there, not just reading a book." This week he made a wooden lamp and sanded it smooth. "I need to have activities, not just reading a book. Because, if I'm bored, I disrupt class, I tap on my desk. But I don't want to be in GT classes, because that's too much homework."

"Are you that lazy, Eric?"

"Yep."

Eric hears all the time that he's smart enough for gifted and talented, that it would be more interesting for him. Every year he grabs the form for GT projects, thinking he'll show how to soup up cars, but he never fills it out. Too hard. "And I don't have the time," says the boy who spends at least three hours a day in front of the television.

Typically for his age, Eric often starts things he doesn't finish. At the end of September he got a new little notebook with colored paper, dated the first page, and wrote about going with his mom to Boston Market and the Laundromat and helping each other put quarters in the machines. "This day may not seem like a lot to others, but it ment alot to me." He doesn't write in it again. He plans to build a snowboard in tech ed, but the class ends and the snowboard never happens.

Getting a boy like Eric to follow through, meet his potential, is a constant struggle for Ms. Thomas and the teachers at Wilde Lake. There are plenty of kids who are thrilled to be moved into GT, where learning tends to be less rote, projects and field trips more common, discussion richer. But just as often, when teachers plead with a parent to move a student up the child doesn't want to, and the parent doesn't force it. It's particularly frustrating for Ms. Thomas with a black boy like Eric. Her late husband was black, her son is half black, and it tore her up when he worked below potential because that's what his friends did. The last thing she wants is a class you can tell is GT because it's filled only with white faces.

Schools have been tracking—assigning students to classes based on ability—for a century. Between one-half and two-thirds of middle schools have some form of tracking, under the theory that kids this age are at such different places intellectually and cognitively that to lump them in the same classes does them a disservice. A teacher with a homogeneous group of kids can teach at exactly the pace she needs to; there is less chance for boredom with the quicker kids, less chance for frustration with the slower ones. And kids who have an inkling to excel won't be held back among classmates who ridicule them for that.

Critics contend that tracking gives the best experiences, and often the best teachers, to the students who already have the most advantages, that it denies kids valuable role models: each other. They say it perpetuates lesser expectations for certain children, way before they are fully formed. They say getting shunted into a lower track is demoralizing, a self-fulfilling prophecy, the way Harry Potter's classmates whom the Sorting Hat sends to Gryffindor are slated for great things, while Slytherin kids are doomed to a life of malfeasance.

But for Ms. Thomas, the reality is that if a kid doesn't have GT at Wilde Lake he'll never get it in high school, and he'll never have the edge on the SAT. If he blows math in eighth grade, unless he plays a lot of catch-up he's blown his SAT scores totally, because, as Ms. Thomas puts it, "they're looking at math you're not going to be able to do. It's so sequential, but kids really don't understand that."

She says to Eric, "You have a lot of checks here for not coming prepared for class."

"I'm always losing pencils. I have a hole in my pencil case, so I have to keep them in my pocket. Here, I have them in my pocket right now."

"What are your goals for this year, Eric?"

"My goal is passing."

"That's a very minimal goal. You are capable of much more than that."

"Let's raise the stakes?"

"Yep. You're a very smart kid."

"I get bored and then I start tapping with my pencil . . ."

"I've seen it, and I'm not wild about that."

"Neither is my mom."

"The teachers will have to start making recommendations for high school very soon, the level courses you'll be at. And your teachers don't know you very well yet, do they?"

"Nope."

"So what can you do to let them know what you can do?"

"Study for tests. Do more homework, because that will prepare me for the tests. I should take my time more and focus more. I don't like to do homework, because it's no fun."

"Most people, if they were being honest, would say they don't like to do homework either. But in life there are always things we have to do that we don't want to do. In high school there are different tracks—GT, honors, on grade level, and review, which is below grade level. Where do you see yourself?"

"Probably on or above grade level. I'm going to get all B's."

"Do you want to go to college?"

"Yep, I want to go to Tennessee University. I want to be a Volunteer." Eric has seen the Tennessee Volunteers play football, heard they have a good culinary program.

"There are all sorts of things that happen soon that impact the university's decision to select you. SATs, PSATs, they look at the level of your classes, the activities you've been in—sports and band and even maybe student government—when they're considering what you can handle. I would like to see you taking honors-level classes."

"The work ain't hard."

"Not 'ain't.' We're not saying 'ain't.' " They laugh.

"My mom is my only motivation. No one else cares besides my mom, and my dad."

"Why are we sitting here? Do you think I care?"

"Yes."

"I care very much. You are a very smart boy. You are also a typical thirteen-year-old boy. You don't understand that what you do today affects your future. You don't have very long to show what you're capable of." She looks at his report card. "There are not many A's and B's here, and there should be. Next marking period I want you on the honor roll. That list outside on that wall should say 'Eric Ellis.' So what are you going to do about that?"

"When I go home, I usually turn on the TV, but instead I'll put on the radio, because that helps me concentrate. And I'll do my homework nice and neat and accurate—instead of rushed, like I normally do. And I'll buy a new pencil case."

"Yes, don't go into class without what you need."

"Yes, ma'am."

"If you need supplies, ask me. I always have some extra around here."

"All right."

If Eric were *really* screwed up—if he were blowing most of his classes instead of a couple, if he weren't such a "good kid," as everyone calls him, if his mother never showed up at school—maybe there would be a more thorough, more meaningful intervention to keep Eric from crumbling. But this one ends here.

"Got anything else to say?" Ms. Thomas asks.

"Thank you for . . . Thanks for . . ." He collects his thoughts. "Thank you for saying that I'm a good student. At least I know that somebody cares." Eric gets up to leave. "Do you want this chair pushed back closer to the desk?"

"Oh, that's okay," Ms. Thomas tells Eric, and he heads back to class, still for a moment meaning what he said.

chapter seven

it's not you it's me

Days after the girl and boys fooled around in the bathroom, posters fill the Wilde Lake hallways, decorated by the sixth-grade health class with teary-eyed stick-figures.

Sexual Harassment! What it really is! Unwelcome conduct of a sexual nature that interferes with a student's ability to learn, work, study, achieve or participate in school activities!

Ways to stop sexual harassment: Tell harasser how you feel—file complaint—talk to teacher/principal—write letter to harasser!

"Dear Mr. Harasser," the kids mock, "could you please stop harassing me? It makes me uncomfortable." They gather in the library, one class at a time, for a lesson on what constitutes harassment. Each group of six discusses a different form, and Jackie's gets Verbal. They watch a video they find hilarious, in which boys grab girls' butts, and decide if examples listed on a card are flirting or harassment.

The number of schools that educate students about harassment has increased greatly over the last decade. But incidents of harassment—comments and gestures in the hallway, flashing, groping—show few signs of abating. They're commonplace in schools even when they're hard to see, and they have an impact on what goes on in the classroom, where girls and boys who have been harassed have a harder time paying attention or participating.

At Wilde Lake, the kids come away from the library session with a few ideas: First, it can be harassment if two people are making out in front of you and you're uncomfortable. Leslie, whose favorite T-shirt is adorned with a glittered Playboy Bunny, does this on the bus with an eighth grader. Sitting behind them, Jackie says, "Stop making out and just hold hands," but the boys yell, "Kiss her again!" Second, the lines are hazy. "What if a little kid runs home and says, 'I'm gay,' " Jackie asks, "and someone hears? That could be sexual harassment." Third: "If you like it, it's not harassment." As for Lauren and the bathroom incident, Jackie now says, "No one really likes her."

The whole school takes an anonymous survey in homeroom asking if they've been harassed, or harassed anyone. Even though Jackie and her friends have all wound up on one boy's list of People Who Would Take Off Their Clothes for Money, all been grabbed—including Jackie, whose butt has come under increased attention from Adam—none of them check Yes. The boys write that they haven't harassed. At lunch they discuss the survey. Sometimes being grabbed bugs Kristina, sometimes it feels like her body is the only reason boys talk to her, and she's tried to stop it by ignoring, or getting mad, or at the very least not flirting in response. But she likes the attention—so does that count as harassment? Leslie figures she might just as well fudge on the survey. "Why not?" she says. "They'll just do it again." Then she leans on Adam's shoulder. "Right? You'd do it again?" Jackie approaches the table with her lunch tray. Kevin has stolen her chair, so she wallops him on the head with a carton of milk. "You got three boobs," he responds, and reaches toward one of them.

Jackie's parents would be horrified by such behavior; her father's response might well involve a baseball bat. Parents like them can be attentive (which they are), can model healthy patterns of sexuality (which they do), but they can't control their daughter's longings, they can't control the boys' boldness, they can't, as social scientists point out, infuse disgrace back into activities that are portrayed shamelessly on MTV. Nor, for that matter, can the teachers. And none of them can control what they don't know exists.

When it comes down to it, Jackie insists what happens at school is no big deal, even though she would never want her parents to find out about Adam grabbing her butt several times a day at recess, one hand on each cheek. She knows this is supposed to anger her, but she thinks, "Big deal, it's a *butt*." In a way, she's flattered, but "I wouldn't go out with Adam, because he likes too many girls."

Jay Starr, Jackie says immediately after Halloween, "is a fag. He stopped being perverted. He's not like, 'Hey, babe,' anymore. He doesn't even say hi to me anymore." She washes his name off her hand and writes instead, "HippieBabe629." "That's my screen name. My uncle says we're really close to getting the Internet." Now she is fixated fully on Anton, the "A" of "J-A-B." In the middle-teen years, social scientists have found, kids choose their mates based on more individual preferences, but at Jackie's age it's because the guy is someone her friends would approve of. For now, it's mostly about the superficial stuff: He's got the right look, he's got the right clothes. Jackie attempts her own explanation: "Anton's funny and—I can't explain it. He's not necessarily shy but he acts really—" Often she can't find the right word. "It's cute."

Jackie isn't sure how grown-up relationships start. "They wouldn't say, like, 'Do you want to go out with me?' like a little preppy person. I've always wondered that. What do they do?" In her world, the asking out and dumping are done through intermediaries, so at school, the first Friday in November, Kristina tells Anton that Jackie likes him and would he ask her out? He says yes. So they're going out, which is a concept that Jackie previously explained to Sara ("I'm not belittling you," she had told her daughter, "I just don't know what that means") as talking more to someone at school and on the phone. "It's just like saying, 'She likes him, he likes her.' They're just better friends." It's not like romantic status really changes anything, since the skating rink isn't cool at the moment and she's not allowed alone at the movies and without the Internet she can't even IM anyone. Jackie and Anton don't go anywhere together. They don't talk much, on the phone or at school. Mainly their relationship means Jackie checks herself in the bathroom every day after lunch and runs around Anton on the playground, except when she carefully ignores him.

He is pleased with her attentions but doesn't turn away those of other girls. Jackie and Anton are assigned to different days for the harbor field trip that week, so Celia sits with him on the bus, playing keep-away with his Red Sox hat and trying to snap the rubber bands on his wrist.

"You are the biggest flirt I've ever seen," says Martin, sitting across from them.

"I'm not," Celia says. "Anton's my best friend. I just like to annoy him. Anton is gonna keep me from falling off the boat. Anton calls me and never has anything to say. Look, Ravens Stadium!" She yanks his arm.

Martin tells Anton, "If I were you, I'd change seats right now."

"Somebody's gotta hold my hand so I don't get run over by a car." This is the girl writers like Mary Pipher and Peggy Orenstein explain, someone who tries to appear helpless around the guys she crushes on, submerging herself to make others feel bigger, better. You only have to meet Jackie to see this isn't always the case; if a boy doesn't want her bossy, brassy self, that's his problem. But even though twenty-first-century girls are supposed to be all about "empowerment," their self-esteem hasn't kept pace with expectations. And besides—this says as much about the boys as it does about the girls—baby talk works.

"You don't want me to get run over by a car, do you, Anton?"

"Why do you want to sit with Celia? Don't you already have a girl-friend?" Martin asks.

"I have, like, twenty girlfriends," says Adam.

"Yeah," says Martin, "whose names all end in at-aol-dot-com."

"Anton," Celia says, "you have a girlfriend."

Anton finally speaks. "So?"

"He goes out with Jackie," Jay says, and turns toward the window. "That's gross. Look, Gay Street!"

"Jay Starr," Celia announces, "is a homophobe."

"What's a homophobe?" he asks.

"Someone who hates gays and lesbians."

"But I don't hate *you*."

The boat ride captivates the seventh graders, who sit up in awe as their boat passes under a container ship and the largest cranes in the world scooping up coal. They steer the boat. They measure oysters to determine their health, and translate distances on a nautical map. They make tinfoil-and-Popsicle-stick vessels that are set in a tank of water and laden one by one with sinkers, to see which is most buoyant.

Walking up the pier to the bus at day's end, someone announces, "It smells like hamburgers." Jay says, "It smells like Anton's girlfriend." On the boat Anton was glad to be away from the taunting; now he is reluctant to get back on the bus. He thinks Jackie is nice, and funny, and he likes her, simple as that. They are, he says, "good friends."

The next day, Jackie, Lily, Mia, and sixty other kids stay after school to try out for *Peter Pan*. Jackie practices by herself in the hallway. Lily and Mia and five friends practice in a group outside the music room, tapping their white-stockinged feet, crowing through their rolled-up score sheets. They rub each other's heads, right above the ponytails, for luck. Lily is nervous and Mia is not. "I'm going to be real weird," she says.

At Jackie's turn in front of the teachers, she sings sweetly and does little movements she made up to match the lyrics. Jonathan flusters mid-song and leaves the room crying. Mia sings to the crowd, squawking goofily at the "I gotta CROW" part, and bounds into her chair when she's done. Then—Lily's turn. Even though she has a lovely voice and performs in ballet and shows off to everyone in the neighborhood how she can pedal her bike with one foot and may very well have to sing for millions at the Miss America Pageant, this is a different kind of performance: Her friends are watching. Just like she wouldn't dare raise her hand in class, she feels stupid here too. She keeps her eyes from the judges, tugs at the hem of her lavender T-shirt, forgets a line, sings softly, laughs uncomfortably. "I was horrible," she says later, when everyone compares how badly they did.

Back in the cafeteria, a few seventh-grade girls tell Mia, "Did you know Matt Grant likes you?" A group of boys appear on the other side of the room, the girls flock, and Mia and Lily roll their eyes: "Seventh graders." With Mia, Lily does cartwheels. Jonathan sits on a chair in the middle of the room, his head down. Jackie listens to her Discman, until Mrs. Bloom takes it away, announcing to the whole cafeteria that she's not allowed to have it here, even after school. Jackie didn't know.

She heads to the lobby and sees her dad's car idling outside. But she's not up for gymnastics. She doesn't think she auditioned well, she's stressed, she can't get her Discman back. She stews and glances at the car for fifteen minutes before heading out. Five days later, Jackie still hasn't gotten the Discman back, because a parent has to pick it up, and she hasn't mustered the courage to tell either of them. Sara will find a note on her dresser. It starts, "I got in trouble for no reason."

And Jackie doesn't get a part, not even a tiny one. The judges' eyes were down, she's certain, when she was doing her cute movements. And besides, "Ms. Drumm doesn't like me." Jonathan, despite his meltdown, is cast as a pirate. Mia is the only sixth grader to get a main part, little Michael, and Lily is the only other sixth-grade girl to make it in. She will play a Lost Boy.

Normally she would not be at all pleased to play a boy, she explains, "but the Lost Boys sit with Michael some of the time!"

"You'll do the 'freak' conversation?" Mr. West asks Ms. Thomas this November morning, hours from the first dance of the year. He's worked in elementary schools most of his career; it's strange for him to deal with such sexual stuff. So Ms. Thomas takes the mike at lunch and says: "I have a serious announcement. I need everybody tuned in here, everyone looking at me. We will wait." And she waits.

The freaking has been going on for several years with older teens and on MTV, and finally has crept down to middle school. Kids don't dance face to face anymore. A boy approaches a girl from behind and grinds his groin against her butt. At school and church dances the chaperones act as freak cops. But at teen dance clubs like the one a half-hour away in suburban Baltimore where a few Wilde Lake kids have gone, to the envy of several of Jackie's friends, children as young as eleven simulate sex on the dance floor as rappers bleat about oral gratification. (The lyrics made great use of the fact that "motherfucker" and "dick sucker" rhyme.) A mother may think her daughter is sleeping at a friend's house; that girl's father drops them off and thinks the place is okay, since kids are frisked at the door and no booze is sold. What they don't see is the security guard playfully slapping pleathered bottoms, girls bent at the waist with their heads nuzzling boys' crotches, girls not sure if they want these guys they don't know grinding fast as a coin-fed motel-room bed against their behinds, but what can they do?

At least Ms. Thomas can do something.

"We have had dances during the school day at Wilde Lake for almost twenty years," she tells the seventh graders. "We want to reward you, and we do it because very rarely do we have kids who don't know how to behave appropriately. Some people in this school almost ended this tradition two years ago by dancing inappropriately. When I go into that gym, I better not see one person dancing that way." Laughter. "You know exactly what I mean. I don't think it's funny. This is the grade I worry about most being able to handle this activity, and you are proving me exactly right."

Ms. Thomas and Mr. West aren't so worried about the sixth graders, who haven't coupled up yet. When the sixth graders on the playground talk about whom they're "going to the dance" with, Lily says Beth, the sweet girl whose locker is on the other side of her from Abigail Werner. They've become friendly. Someone asks Jonathan, who is sitting against the wall with three other boys, whom he's taking.

"Brittany."

"She just told us she's not going with you."

"She said sure. She said sure."

"Do you like her?"

"I like Melissa. I just need someone to walk in with me."

During recess, the seventh graders run wild. Middle schoolers, particularly on a big day like this, step on each other, shove each other—boys shove girls, and girls shove boys, and they all shove each other. For some kids it hurts, for others it doesn't; you can't always tell which. Everything has force, everything makes noise. Jackie organizes a game of duck-duck-goose. The girls, breathless and loud, hold cartwheel contests, and Jackie madly weaves in and out of groups of kids standing around talking. Some boys follow her, knocking everyone down. Others kick the soccer ball onto the roof, play three-on-three, give each other the finger every time someone makes a basket. Farther out on the field, the boys who like to throw trash have found trash to throw. Adam is wrestling, his pants to his knees, butt showing through thin white Hanes. Mrs. Brodian comes up to the group and says, "No pushing. Though I'm sure as soon as my back is turned you'll start again."

At twelve-thirty-five the students are released one grade at a time from the classes where they can no longer pay attention to the gym, where lights flash and music plays and fog spills across the floor. The sixth graders are excited about their first middle-school dance and enter the room slowly, unsurely. The seventh graders are excited to freak, or to see who else freaks, or at the very least to see their friends and request their songs. The eighth graders act like they aren't excited about anything. "Everyone cool has time-out," one says.

For the first twenty minutes, everybody clumps in groups and watches, moving almost imperceptibly to the music, lip-gloss wands emerging for duty. One fat boy break-dances and everyone laughs at his jiggle. In the corner, eighth-grade boys stand around a chair and look down on it. They swear it is moving by itself. Then the DJ calls out, "How many of you know the Booty Call?" Ah, the line dance: the perfect dance for middle school, since the Law of Preteen Dancing mandates that you cannot move your limbs in any way differently from everyone else. Here the steps and their exact-sameness are laid out for you.

The seventh-grade boys start a brief, hyper conga line. The Electric Slide gets just about everybody dancing. At "Clint Eastwood," things get slow, and six couples are urged together by their friends. They clutch each other awkwardly, boys shorter than girls, one bold enough to pet his partner's back. Nearly everyone else leaves the room, because "it's a gay song." There are rap songs that send all the white kids to the cafeteria, and power-pop songs that send all the black kids to the cafeteria; there are a few songs, like DMX's "Party Up," that hold everybody's attention, get them bouncing, get a few of them freaking. One bold person, usually a boy, goes for it: He grinds his butt into the behind of whatever girl is handy, or maybe he jokingly freaks his guy friend, or humps the floor. A few kids join in. A circle grows around the dancers, to protect them from the teachers who stream through the gym, sniffing out inappropriateness. But the teachers are swift at getting right in the middle of it, nipping the freak in the bud.

Eric watches from the gym mats against the wall, except for when he tries to cool down a bunch of his friends who are stalking each other and verging on fights (for dancing with another girl's boyfriend, for degrading skateboarding skills, and so on).

Elizabeth's friends teach her to dance to "Take It to the House," which essentially means jumping up and down, until the "Barney" song comes on, which she sings.

Lily's gang goes back and forth. In the gym, a bunch of them bounce to Blink 182 and sway to 'N Sync's "Gone," holding up silver barrettes like cigarette lighters, as Lily and Beth tentatively tap their feet. In the cafeteria, ten of them pose for group Polaroids they each buy for a dollar. Half the girls look goofy. Mia is front and center; part of Lily's face peeks from behind her.

Jonathan spends the dance in the classroom where *Shrek* is showing. Next door, the kids in time-out fill pages of paper: "Knowing full well chewing gum is against school rules, I will refrain from doing so in the future. Knowing full well chewing gum is against school rules, I will refrain from doing so in the future." Celia buys a heart tattoo that says "Love" and plants it at the top of her breast, visible down her tank top.

Jimmy occasionally comes into the gym to listen to a song, but since he can't dance, he spends most of his time at a corner table in the cafeteria, where a group of sixth-grade boys eat snacks and fold origami. They talk about Game Boy. They jump up and down with the idea that when they're off the ground they're farther from China. His friend John does a Russian dance with his fingers, and the other boys copy him. When the movie is done, Jonathan runs over, hiding from two seventh-grade girls he says want to dance with him, and the boys continue bragging, and interrupting, and arguing (as usual) about who's smarter and better.

"I can play saxophone better than you."

"I can play piano better than you."

"I can play trumpet better than you."

"That's because I can't even spell 'trumpet.' "

"Yes, you can."

"No, I can't. T-R-O-U-M-P-E-T-T."

"Exactly."

"No, I spelled 'troumpett.' "

"Exactly."

"I didn't spell 'exactly.' I spelled 'troumpett.' "

Jimmy tells Daniel a complicated fishing/cat joke that ends with the punch line, "If the fly drops four inches, there's bound to be a pussy involved." Daniel's freckled face is blank, his eyes scrunched behind his glasses, and Jimmy repeats the punch line. Ten seconds later, Daniel says, "I get it," which he either does or doesn't.

On a Saturday in early December, at Jackie's thirteenth-birthday party, six girls in various forms of bikini—from Jackie's tankini that barely shows her belly, to Kristina's and Celia's revealing strings—goof off in the humid swimming-pool bubble. Five of the girls carry Jay and Brad through the water. They call the boys babies and treat them as such, touching Jay's feet, holding him from behind, passing him around, dunking him. Sure, he likes being touched, but this is annoying. Jackie is cold and sits huddled into herself on the edge of the pool, near a group of seven-year-olds tossing a beach ball.

They get out to wait in line for the diving board, and Kristina rests her hands on Jay's shoulders. So do Meghan, Leslie, and Celia, who mock-strip for him. As this goes on, Jackie heads up the stairs to the top of the water slide, splashes down in front of them, and shouts, "Guys! Guys! I went down the tube backwards!" Her lips purple, she stands in line for the rope swing while the others disappear.

Over hot dogs and Pepsi, Leslie, whose hair is splotched violet, says, "I'm getting my eyebrow pierced next year, my belly button pierced the year after, and my lip pierced the year after that." Kelly says to Kristina, "If your mom was my mom, I'd have my eyebrow pierced already, but she's not, and my mom's a fag." Kristina says, "Anton says I'm going to hell," and "Anton says Celia's going to hell," and Leslie hears only a bit of this and says, "Where are you going? I want to go, too."

Jackie's lips are still purple as she opens her presents. "Watch me!" Jay gives Jackie a flowery card from his mom's drawer. She gets cash, fifteen dollars at a time, fruity glitter lotions and sprays, and a bunch of CDs. Her friends sing "Happy Birthday" but they're doing it off-key, on purpose, so Jackie says, "Shut up!"

When Jackie wrote invitations for her birthday party, she didn't have Anton's address, so she didn't invite him. A month after they started going out, they are still a couple, in a fashion. They don't hang out; they do write notes. "I'm not going out with u just for the hell of it," Anton writes, "I'm going out wit u cause I love you!!" The exclamation marks are punctuated at the bottom by a smiley face. Jackie is not so sure. He didn't ask her to dance at school, she's gotten ambivalent, going out with him has started to feel like a job: "You have to keep your eye on him all the time." Like how Celia told Jackie that Anton told her that he likes her instead. So, when Jackie sleeps over at the house of a friend who's on the Internet, she instant-messages him:

I can't go out with you anymore. It's not you it's me.

Anton responds,

WHY???

A pause, then he adds,

Fine. Be that way.

"It's not you it's me"? It *was* him, but Jackie doesn't want to be mean. "There's no point," she explains. "It's like revenge." She is, in a way, relieved—especially the next day, when Leslie passes her a note: "I'm glad u don go out w/Anton he was hitten on me online LOL." Jackie still has to sit next to him in social studies, and every time he opens his mouth she digs a little. When they have to pick Middle Ages personae Anton says, "I'm going to be a knight." Jackie snaps back: "More like you're gonna be *working* at night, as a blacksmith."

winter

chapter eight

i can't make her do anything

By this evening seventh grade has been going on for three months, but still Mr. Shifflett, waiting in the front hall for his next conference, is stumped. "Elizabeth Ginsburg," he murmurs to the gym teacher. "Elizabeth Ginsburg. I have to remember what she's like in class. I have no idea."

Joseph and Ellen never get too much out of conferences. Teachers always say they want parents to show up even when their children are doing fine, but what's there to say? They come anyway, searching the bulletin boards and teachers' recollections for clues, however small, into their daughter's psyche. Once in a while there is a surprise, like when they hear about this jokey sense of humor Elizabeth supposedly has.

"We'd like to know Elizabeth's strengths and weaknesses," Joseph says once they're seated in a rectangle of desks—Joseph, Elizabeth, and Ellen on one side, and Mr. Shifflett and Ms. Hammond, the math teacher, on the other.

"Okay," Mr. Shifflett says. "Liz is an absolutely stellar student in science. She had a ninety-seven percent this quarter, she's particularly well prepared, she gets right to work. For groups she picks people who will help her, and not those who she has to carry along." He asks Elizabeth, "What do you think your strengths are?" No answer. "Weaknesses?" She tucks her head into the crook of her arm.

"Look how red she is," Ellen says to Joseph. Elizabeth is in some ways easygoing, but also easily mortified. For example, her parents are the only people on earth who know she wears headgear at night. When Mr. West comes up to her lunch table and asks, "How you girls doing?" she starts giggling and can't stop. When she raises her hand in class, she tucks her fist into her sleeve and gives the answer in a mumble just this side of baby talk.

Ellen reaches over and rubs Elizabeth's shoulder, then quickly pulls away. Mr. Shifflett says he can't think of any weaknesses. "Have you caught her humor?" Joseph asks.

In math Elizabeth is doing ninth-grade algebra. If the problems aren't exactly like the examples in the book, Ellen can't help. Joseph grasps it—"It all just goes back to a = mx + b, distance equals rate times time, regression analysis"—but Elizabeth won't ask him for help. "I'll tell you," he says to Ellen, "and you tell her." Too shy to ask questions in class, when Elizabeth had problems she stayed after school with Ms. Hammond until she got it. She aced the test, best score in the class.

"You did a great job helping her," Ellen tells the teacher. "It was getting beyond where I could help."

"She did that by herself," Joseph says.

"What do you think about that?" he says proudly as they walk down the hall, hoping Elizabeth will share his enthusiasm. She does, inside. But she answers, "I don't know."

The next afternoon Joseph sits at a round table in the music room, across from Miss Colyer. Elizabeth got a B, she says, because she didn't practice enough—one week only twenty minutes, instead of the prescribed two hours. Other than that, she just says she enjoys having Elizabeth in class. That's not what Joseph wants to get at.

"Like I told you when I met you at Back to School Night," he says, "Elizabeth's the kind of kid who interacts with teachers. I don't think she's experiencing you the way you experience her. She says she's not having fun."

For soft-spoken Miss Colyer, this is the first year of teaching, the first year sitting across the table from discontented parents. "I tried to connect with her," she tells Joseph. "I'd love to do a better job, but I'm not sure how."

Miss Colyer asks for specifics, but all Joseph has is that one day Elizabeth came home in a tiff, saying she had had a fight with a teacher. She wouldn't say more.

"There was one day she had a small problem with another student," Miss Colyer explains. "It got worked out the best it could." Danielle had stolen Elizabeth's chair, they started yelling at each other and had to sit in the hall during lunch and write up behavior plans, but Miss Colyer stays short on detail.

"I hate to have her drop strings," Joseph says, rubbing his beard. "The dynamics in the class might be set. It's just something to be aware of. Sometimes she gets the sense you're not listening to her. Maybe it's the competition with other kids for attention."

"I can understand her feeling like I'm not paying attention. That class is a tough class."

"Why's it tough?"

"There are a lot of behavioral problems in that class. It's a lot of kids thrown together who don't mix well."

"Maybe that's what she's feeling. Isn't this class an elective in a sense? It should be fun. She should want to do it."

"I'm working on it."

"Sounds like you are. Basically, what I should tell her is she's doing a great job?"

"I know that there are certain disagreements. I can ask her if there's a way to talk about it without her feeling embarrassed."

"I just don't know. Her feelings are hurt easily. She's at the age she's not telling us much."

Joseph leaves the school with a feel for the class dynamics but no more feel for his daughter. He can't get her to practice viola. He can't get her to let him help with math. He can't get her to open up to him. Is this what he signed up for, twelve and a half years ago?

"I can't make her do anything," he says as he opens the door of his Celica. "I feel like a third wheel sometimes. I really want to help her do things, instead of just being a chauffeur."

Joseph and Ellen spend more time driving their daughter to various lessons—synchro three times a week, speed swimming once, Bat Mitzvah class, math tutor, Hebrew school—than they spend with her anywhere else. They shell out for the quickly outgrown swimsuits, including the tuxedo one with a fake red bow tie. Ellen applies Knox gelatin to Elizabeth's hair the nights before synchro meets so it stays glued in its bun, and carefully smooths it. Joseph and Ellen sit through long, steamy meets and cheer all Elizabeth's synchronicity while wearing their purple swim-team polos.

At speed practice Elizabeth cuts through the water on her back, doing a butterfly kick. Her body is graceful, grown, womanly almost. In her purple swim cap, her hair is a bubble of grape Bubble Yum. She uses this time, as she generally does, to think about problems at school and wonder why you don't choke when you open your mouth under water.

At seven o'clock, as a dozen girls swim laps around her, Elizabeth calls to her coach, "I want to go home."

"For that," he says, "you have to stay till seven-thirty-five."

"Nooooo!"

"I thought you wanted to be good."

"So?"

" 'So' is a child's answer."

"So?"

Children's sports are intense: In Elizabeth's grade there is a field-hockey player who runs two hours every morning so her coach won't move her from center forward, soccer players with chiropractors, swimmers with weekly massage appointments. Elizabeth wouldn't mind being in the Olympics but doesn't want to work too hard. At the speed meets, when she gets out of the pool with a time slower than the last, she does what kids her age do—with sports, with school, whatever. "That was the best I could do," she says, as if insisting she's happy with her performance means she doesn't have to be disappointed in herself. Ellen and Joseph don't like this, Elizabeth can tell. They don't congratulate her profusely enough, which she finds totally not right, especially since it's hard to swim fast with all this new *body*. It's not like Liz's parents want her to be an Olympian, or think she can, but if she's going to do competitive sports, she should be, well, competitive.

After practice, her wet hair as always soaking the back of her shirt, Elizabeth grabs her huge gym bag—stuffed with towels, affixed with key chains and laminated motivational quotes from her coaches—and gets in

Ellen's waiting car. While looking at herself in the lighted vanity mirror (she will do this the whole drive home), she complains, "Katie Dean got to go in lane four and I had to go in three. Pat made me stay late." Ellen wishes Elizabeth were tougher; the complaints about coaches are getting to her. "If you're going to do it," she says later, "be focused and do it. She's perfectly capable. She's definitely capable of improving, and she really hasn't improved very much in two years."

Elizabeth's interests in general shift quickly. This is part of the process of the evolving brain's testing out which cells and connections to shed or to keep, but to an adult it looks a lot like lack of ambition. "When she says she wants to do something like be an artist or an actress or be whatever," Joseph says, "she's not taking steps to try to do that. We can offer her art camp or a play or whatever, and for some reason she doesn't want to do that." Sure, a twelve-year-old may just say these things to try them on, but the way Joseph sees it, she's not leaving them on long enough to see if they fit.

The balance between encouraging and overbearing is so hard to master. A kid thrives on your high expectations for her, but those same high expectations feel a lot like pressure. If Ellen and Joseph try to boost Elizabeth by suggesting she might make it to finals at synchro nationals, she wigs out. "That's really hard! Sometimes they expect me to do so good at everything, even though I'm not that good at everything." If Joseph says, "You're great," at a moment when Elizabeth doesn't agree, "it's sometimes annoying, because it's not always true!" If they skip a meet, she gives them grief. This weekend they're missing regionals for a blues festival.

"You like your friends better than my swimming."

"No," Joseph says, "I like my blues better. You could have come, but you didn't want to." She used to like that sort of event. He remembers taking Liz to the Folk Festival when she was little, and she stripped to her diaper and danced around; it's the kind of thing about which he says, "Don't you remember?" and she never does.

If the Wilde Lake principal could have one wish, it would be for parents and teachers to resist a distance that seems inevitable and draw nearer to their middle schoolers instead. With parents of preadolescents immersed in their own worries—the rate of children living in two-parent house-holds is declining, for example, and more than three-quarters of children have mothers who work—it can be tempting to indulge the "Leave me alone."

But look close, Ms. Thomas says, and you'll see that these budding adolescents, for all their bluster, are still needy children. A better way to think of a preteen's changing relationship with her parents is as a reor-ganization, not a rejection. Wanting to be independent is not the same as wanting to be left alone. She wants to explore; she also wants a safe har-bor. She will admit—not to her parents, of course—that hibernating into the bedroom isn't ideal for her either, not all the time. She enjoys helping shape the rules and having responsibilities around the house, especially those that show off her talents—just not so much that it's a burden. She needs some meaningful independence, and if she gets it at home, she won't seek it in inappropriate places. She wants to talk—but, please, not just about chores. She wants to talk *more* about her schoolwork, in fact, though not her grades. She likes to hear about her parents' past, and hers. She cares what they think of her; family is by far a middle schooler's greatest source of self-esteem. She wants role models. Their affection means tons to her, and she wouldn't mind cuddling once in a while. (No, not in *public*.)

It may not look like it, but a middle schooler wants to be told no. If she hears it from an early age, she'll be used to it when the stakes are raised. She wants rules—which sometimes get her out of situations she isn't comfortable being in anyway. Okay, maybe she doesn't *always* want rules, maybe sometimes she despises the rules. But psychologists insist parents should persist anyway, because, in ten, twenty, thirty years, se-cure, successful adults say they appreciate their childhood rules, in retro-spect. Even if the kids whose parents set strong, reasonable ethical and moral limits may experiment, they're likelier to drift back eventually within the standards their parents tried to enforce. They turn out better, simply put. Even if she resists them outwardly, a child with strong con-nections to adult authority figures becomes stronger herself, more in control. Kids whose parents have distanced themselves are far more susceptible to peer pressure and more likely to misbehave in school.

Elizabeth doesn't tell it to Joseph and Ellen much anymore, but she does love her parents. They may not hear it for decades, but she does want their help.

She still wants to be tucked in bed, she still wants to be able to let her guard down and be comforted during storms. She hated the time Joseph insisted, "Don't be scared, calm down," which didn't make any sense to her, because how can you decide not to be scared?

She wants to be taken care of. She's kind of insulted that Ellen stopped making her lunches this year, even though she prefers what the bag contains when there are no adults involved: a candy bar, malted-milk balls, Doritos, chocolate-chip yogurt. The kids whose parents make their lunches are proud of this, even prouder when their mothers use napkins not to remind them "Homework club today!" but to profess their love or, better yet, once a week to scribble a trivia question for the whole lunch table, answer revealed in tomorrow's brown sack.

She wants their company. She wants them home, as long as they don't bug her. Like most middle-school students, Elizabeth does her homework in the family room, not in the bedroom, so that her mother is nearby. "We bought her this desk," Ellen complains. "Does she use it?" When Ellen was in New England with her mother-in-law, Joseph taped *Buffy the Vampire Slayer* so that he and Elizabeth could watch it together, even though it bores him, and she slept in his bed because she was scared. She wishes he brought her to the office for Take Your Daughter to Work Day, instead of saying, "You'd be bored."

She wants their rituals. Even though neither Elizabeth nor her dad likes baseball, she cherishes their yearly Orioles game. (When the vendors only had square boxes left for her autographed ball, she said she wanted the round case with the stand and would wait till next year if she had to. Joseph thought, That is just like me.) She likes the way her mother takes her to a five-thirty breakfast before summer swim team, and the way her parents treat her to golden rolls at Sushi King after good report cards, though she hates how Joseph sings "Sushi King, Sushi King" all week beforehand.

She wants her mom to be the swing vote when she can't decide between two pairs of jeans, and she wants her to shrink a few more T-shirts in the dryer so she can have them. She likes that Ellen is going to let her pick out her own clothes for Chanukah presents, because if her mom did

the picking, "I think that, like, only half of it would be right, I guess, because she got these shorts and they were, like, white, and I liked the
white part, but they had fireworks all over it and I didn't like that part."

She wants them to listen to her, sympathize with her, say how awful
something is that she thinks is awful, not spaz out over it or try to solve
it or anything, just say, "Oh, you poor thing," and mean it.

She wants her parents to pick up her hints that she cares. The only
time she releases her pounds of curly dark hair from the braid in public is
for school pictures, because she knows her parents like it that way. She
carefully selects gifts—a fancy marble for him, hair clips for her—at the
Chanukah bazaar. At the end of every phone call, and at the end of every
silent twenty-minute drive to swimming, Elizabeth says, "I love you,
Dad."

She wants them there forever. When she found out Will Meyer's
mom died of a heart attack, Elizabeth thought for a week straight about
her mom dying and couldn't imagine it. She knows she wouldn't be able
to come to school like Will did. As it is, her mother has pneumonia for
the second time and "bronchisimpatootie, I don't know." Elizabeth stays
up at night and worries with each cough that storms through the wall.

As stingy as Elizabeth is about showing her parents affection, like many
kids her age she clings to other adults. When her sixth-grade math
teacher, Ms. Jones, visits from maternity leave like a rock star in purple
sunglasses and a slick black trench coat, Elizabeth gets a pass out of
strings to see her. They walk through the hallway holding hands as Ms.
Jones says to the girls who pass, "How's my little mathematicians?" Elizabeth hugs her goodbye and says, "I got a cut on my finger from opening a calculator case. This wouldn't have happened if you hadn't put me
in GT math."

The list of people to whom Elizabeth sends every sentimental chain
e-mail she receives includes as many teachers, aunts, and coaches as it
does peers. She embraces her synchro coach Lorraine unabashedly and
calls her "Mommy" as a joke, ever since a waitress mistook them for
mother and daughter. She likes to tell Lorraine all about school. "Guess
what?" she'll say. "I think I failed." She always says this, but she never
fails. Seems to Lorraine that Elizabeth's a lonely kid. "Sometimes she's

talk talk talk talk talk"—Lorraine makes the gabby motion with her hand—"so I just have to shoo her away. I just want to talk with her about swimming."

At recess, Liz often wanders away from her friends toward whichever adult is monitoring the schoolyard. "Those boys took our court and they won't play half-court because they said they were here first," she tells Mr. Merrills, a guidance counselor. "And I'm scared of the ball." Mr. Merrills tells the boys to play half-court, then at the foul line tries to help Elizabeth conquer her fear. "I was hit in the stomach with a basketball when I was little," she explains. Her hands cover her face. She takes the ball and spins it, shoots. Shoots again. She's getting somewhere and then announces, "I'm scared of bees, too," and takes off. "The bees are attracted to you," Mr. Merrills calls, "because you're sweet. Your hair smells sweet."

"My hair doesn't smell sweet. It smells like chlorine. It's going to turn green."

Finally mature enough to deal in abstract thought, a kid like Elizabeth can see her parents as real, flawed people instead of mysterious, mythical characters. She can design in her mind the perfect parents—and determine that hers aren't it. She can compare them with whatever idealistic image she concocts in her head of the other adults in her life; not that she would trade, but, still, it kind of feels like she's outgrowing her mom and dad and needs to connect with other, less flawed adults who will treat her more like an equal, who don't know her baggage, who might give it to her straight. It's the same mechanism, child psychologists explain, that causes crushes on rock stars. It's healthy and normal— though more common among isolated children, and certainly among only children, who tend to be more comfortable with adults than with peers—unless the relationships become too thick with emotional attachment, turn into substitutes for those with parents and friends.

In this sense Elizabeth is on the edge. In some ways, the relationships she builds with grown-ups replace the relationships other kids her age have with their siblings or even their friends, when they're in tighter-knit friendship groups, or at least more dramatic ones. Elizabeth creates her own drama; she has a hard time rolling with the punches when she feels a chosen adult has let her down. She is trying to figure out who likes her and who doesn't, and, absent proof either way, she makes up the answers. For one, she is certain Miss Colyer has it in for her—with a seventh grader it is always, always personal; when you're twelve you're obsessed with justice—and therefore has engaged in a constant power struggle, a whining campaign that a teacher can shut down but never win. So, too, with Mrs. Rashid, the teacher who monitors lunch and always tells Elizabeth to stop playing with her food and get outside, which Elizabeth never wants to do, because it's cold and boring, or hot and boring.

"She singles me out," Elizabeth says. "She doesn't pick on anyone else the way she picks on me."

This is the unanimous complaint of middle schoolers, a scientific impossibility.

chapter nine

i barely ever have a chance to make fun of anyone

Dodgeball has been banned this year in the Howard County public schools—too violent, too humiliating. In a way, though, middle school is a game of dodgeball, except instead of a red ball you avoid annoying people. Nobody is immune: Jackie is teased for being short. Eric is teased for being fat. Elizabeth is teased for being Elizabeth. And so on.

Jimmy started sixth grade closely knit into his group of best friends from elementary school, boys who are clever, obedient, and not very popular. There's Daniel, who wants to be a band director like his dad and keeps a pen clipped to his shirt collar "because it's resourceful." There's John, who has secret stress stomachaches and natural, impeccable humor, a combination that makes it inevitable he'll quit premed one day to write sitcoms. And there's Will, who plans to apply to Harvard, Stanford, Yale, Princeton, MIT, and Caltech and become a biorobicist. For his eighth-grade science project, he wants to make an artificial hand.

The boys' favorite things to do together are play video games, talk about video games, and taunt each other. This sort of taunting is tolerable, a sign of affection almost, coming as it does from true friends. It's not unfathomable to Jimmy that when he grows up the nerdy guys will have become the cooler ones while the popular kids turn fat, bald, and boring. Maybe what adults say is true: Jimmy's type wins in the end. But that's not great comfort right now. "I'm not funny," he says. "I used to correct people too much, and I still do a little. It makes me feel better a little. I don't know what I like about myself. I don't like anything else."

Of the group, Will and Jimmy fight the most—practically all the time, it seems—mainly about friendship stuff. Girls' bickering gets most of the attention from teachers and parents and authors and so on, but they tend to deny their conflicts, let them fester under the surface. The sports and rule-based games boys choose are ripe for argument. In fact, boys actually report more conflict in their friendships than girls do. Jimmy keeps a framed photo of himself and Will in first grade on the shelf above his bed, the same photo Will has over his bed. Will is a loyal friend. But Jimmy hates the way Will makes him feel when he gets B's. And, concerned about Will's uncoolness, he is facing a common dilemma of the preteen years: balancing the benefits of a satisfying one-on-one friendship with the desire to negotiate a better place for yourself, popularity-wise. Deep inside, Jimmy thinks that maybe part of growing up is growing out of people, and perhaps Will will be the first.

The kids above their group socially act older, as if they have to be nasty to be popular. Will especially arrived at middle school worried about big mean kids, and it comes true when Chris Kopp lifts him up by his backpack on the bus, which chokes him and makes him cry. In telling the story, he mentions that Billy Mara saved him a seat on the bus. "Billy Mara? He's a geek," Jimmy says.

"I hate him," Will says, "but he saves me a seat."

You will never, all your life, forget the rank order of popularity in your sixth-grade class, or the rules of the middle-school food chain: You will prey upon anyone who appears remotely more vulnerable than you are. The people toward the bottom, rather than refrain from teasing because they know it is the single most painful thing about middle school, "get so mad they have to take it out on someone," Jimmy says. With nothing to lose, they make fun of everyone. They feel bad, but they feel good. Strong, kind of. For someone in the middle, like Jimmy, it's no use getting mad at the popular people, "because then a lot of people gang up on you."

"I barely ever have a chance to make fun of anyone," he says, "because they make fun of me."

*   *   *

By the time winter starts, though, he's getting his chance. He makes fun of Billy for keeping his school supplies in a Game Boy case around his neck. He makes fun of blue-haired Louis, turning around in science to call him an Oompah Loompah or say, "I finished three seconds ahead of you," or threatening to tattle when Louis hides in a banned cranny of the schoolyard. And he even has a seventh grader to make fun of.

At an after-school class called Engineering Challenge, Jimmy and his friends are building a shoe-size magnetic levitation racecar. Annoying Mitch, from seventh grade, is also on the team. "It's Engineering Challenge," John tells him, "not Engineering for the Challenged." As they use various instruments they find in the shop room—the vise, a string, a pencil—to shape foam for the car's body, they keep calling Mitch "M-Dog."

"That's not even funny," he says.

"The only not-funny thing here is your fricking face," says John. Mitch kicks the ground and stomps away. They call after him: "Girl! You're a girl!" Mitch can't stand it, collects his backpack, and leaves. "M-Dog got in trouble!" Jimmy says, and turns his attention to the pencil he's got in a vise. It heats up as he saws at it with a string. "Smell that. It smells like popcorn," Jimmy says, and smashes the pencil.

A little rejection isn't the worst thing—kids who are isolated in childhood tend to emerge as more self-sufficient adults, which might be why the coolest grown-ups were miserable in middle school. But there's a difference between rejection and humiliation, and teasing comes in degrees. On a scale from one to ten, Jimmy getting ribbed for missing a catch in gym class is maybe a four. It hurts, has a little truth to it, but is neither persistent nor insurmountable. Mitch in engineering club: more like an eight or a nine.

An adult who doesn't inspect extremely closely might never be able to figure out why certain kids merit the eights. For example, there is a sixth grader named Valerie who gets teased every day. Very few people want to be her friends. A grown-up would look at a lineup of middle schoolers and be unable to pick out this girl, who, despite a lack of physical defect or lisp or back brace, will elicit snickers and eye rolls no matter what she does or wears or says—the one whom classmates won't talk to, though they secretly wonder what would happen if they made her up like all the uncool-turned-cool kids in the movies. The adult would think,

"What a friendly girl. Those pigtails are adorable." To the kids it's obvious but hard to explain.

Something about how her bright-pink nail polish is always partially chewed off.

Something about how, when she's called on to read aloud, she orates.

Something about how she wears a Mickey Mouse T-shirt the day she presents her biography poster of Walt Disney.

Something about how she writes your name on her binder in milky pen as if you signed it yourself, when you're not even her friend.

Something about how you'll be talking at recess and she'll come and say, "Hi guys. What do you want to do?"

"Stand here and talk."

"Pick on people, or just talk?"

Something about how during the culture presentation in social studies she says she likes *Amelia* books and *American Girl* magazine, as if she were ten. "For transportation," she announces loud and clear, "I put a van. I'd like to have a van one day, when I have children." The idea of Valerie having children sends several kids into snickers.

"Valerie," a girl asks during health class, "do you know what a D-I-C-K is?"

"I know what it is."

"What is it?"

"I'll tell you later."

"We want to know if you know what it is."

Valerie mumbles.

"We can't hear you."

"Fine, I'll tell you what it is. It's the front part of the woman's—"

"No, it's a man's you-know."

"I knew that all along."

One time in art, Abigail tosses a crumpled paper towel in Valerie's face and says, "Oops, sorry, thought you were the trash can." The next period, her class searches reference books in the library to fill in various facts on a worksheet. One of Valerie's braids has come out of its pin, and dangles. Two boys and two girls sit at a table staring at her instead of at the books spread in front of them.

"Look at the back of her head when she walks," one boy says, loudly.

Valerie drops some books from the shelf and they laugh. The look on her face is half defiant, half scared. "You're a retard," the boy says. "*You're* a retard," she replies. Mrs. Stokes intervenes: "I thought I told you two to stop talking to each other. One more word and you're both going to the reinforcement room." The teacher walks away and the kids at the table laugh. The boy says, "Retard."

Back at her table, Valerie wonders what the crime is in self-defense. "I'm trying to protect myself," she mumbles. " 'If you say one more word.' I know I'm not a little kid."

Teasing, if some people had their way, would become a federal crime. Brightly colored pamphlets tout efforts like the National Education Association's National Bullying Awareness Campaign; "bullyproofing" schools is debated on the floors of Congress, with the idea that bullying is why angry teens turn guns on their classmates; Miss America takes it up as her platform. Just like with sexual harassment, schools teach prevention. In health class, Ms. Rouiller gives the middle schoolers "effective strategies" against bullying; in academic enrichment, Mrs. Stokes says you can choose not to give a bully the power to make you afraid. She teaches an acronym: CUE. "Check it out, Use your strategies, Evaluate." Ignore them, she recommends.

These trendy awareness programs, the laws and lawsuits, are predicated on a false, almost quaint notion: that the "them," the bullies standing ready to take your lunch money and your dignity, are a minority, vultures who can be ignored or disciplined into quiescence. In fact, though, the primary form of bullying in middle school is not shoving or threatening but excluding from the group. The bullied are the small number (usually the aggressive, or the withdrawn) and the bullies nearly everyone else, who—empowered by groupthink, tinged by guilt over abandoning their Do Unto Others values but not so much so as to trump the overwhelming desire to belong—poke and prod these chosen victims more often than not in subtle, gossipy, tiny ways, ways impossible to legislate away or even, often, to notice.

Besides, "ignore them" doesn't make you feel any better when you learn Andrew only asked you out because he was paid twenty dollars, when everyone laughs because you're fat and collide into the hurdle, when you hear a boy in gym class saying, not quietly at all, "That's ugly. She dyed her hair. She has a pointy nose. Point point," or when one of the popular kids' instant-message profile announces "RICH . . . YOUR A LOOSER . . . YOU THINK UR COOL BUT UR NOT, UR A FAGGET . . . UR SO FUCKING GAY."

Gay. Used to describe an activity, say, or a book, it's a simple synonym for "lame." Used to describe a person, it's the biggest insult in the male middle-school lexicon. If someone called you gay, a boy this age figures, it would be even more upsetting than if he spied on you in the shower or pulled your pants down or even made you touch him. A boy knows he can't deviate or he's a "fag." Not being a fag preoccupies him. Being normal preoccupies him. But there are no guidelines for whether you're normal or not. So he and his friends identify freaks at school, outliers, oddballs, to define themselves against. You can't know if you're normal, but if you've established that these other guys are freaky, you definitely have an edge on the competition.

Many kids at Wilde Lake think Jack is hilarious on *Will & Grace*, many have a gay aunt or uncle or cousin they enjoy, many would say they support gay rights, if asked, and many surely are curious about the whole thing. None of this, however, diminishes the horror, in their minds, of homosexuality encroaching on their own lives. Eric, for example, professes to be a huge proponent of the "live and let live" school of thought. But every time a certain mysterious boy shows up at the skating rink wearing his striped rugby shirt and knit scarf—it's unclear if this kid is actually homosexual or just enjoys the trauma pretending to be so creates—Eric and his friends spend the whole evening strategizing about how to avoid him.

"He's so faggy," Eric's friend says. "I asked if he was gay and he said, 'Yessssss.' "

"We gotta watch each other's back," says Eric. "One skates forward, one backward, and one sideways. All gays should go to the moon or something. I mean, no offense, but that is nasty."

"If I so much as smell his breath."

One boy the sixth graders have decided is gay—not to mention "Donkey," "Four Eyes," and "Metalmouth"—is Jeff Graff. His main crimes are whining, "Can I play with you? Can I play with you?" nonstop at recess, growing a little tail of hair down the back of his neck, and bringing an Icee to lunch one day after a doctor's appointment. Everybody likes Icees, but because Jeff has one, it is proclaimed a stupid thing to bring to lunch. In health class, Ms. Rouiller makes groups by drawing names from a box, and when the first group is completed without Jeff's name called, there are "phew"s.

"If you have a problem with who is in your group and make it verbal," Ms. Rouiller says, "you will work alone." Then she calls a group with his name.

"Oof."

"Ow."

"Ha!"

Ms. Rouiller freezes. This is her pet peeve. "Jeff, go ahead to the media center and start your work. The rest of you stay." He leaves the room. "Do you know why I let him go ahead and had the rest of you stay?"

Silence.

"Because he was the only one who wasn't talking?"

"That's not exactly it."

"Because people were making fun of him?"

You can hear the lights buzz. "How would you like to be the person singled out and laughed at?" Ms. Rouiller pauses long between sentences. "Do you think it feels good? I don't. Hopefully, he didn't hear what people were saying, because he was sitting in the front." Jimmy looks at his purple pen. "How do *you* feel? Do you feel bad? You should feel bad. I don't know what is allowed in the rest of the school, but this does not happen in my classroom. It does not happen in *your* classroom. What do you think I should do?"

"You should have us apologize to him?"

"What else?"

"You could call our parents if anyone makes fun of him again?"

"That's more what I was thinking. I'm not going to have you apologize, because if he didn't hear what was going on and then we apologize, he'll know. But if this happens again, I'll call in your parents and you can work it out then. If you can't work in a group with him, have your parents call me. Have them write me a note."

What would that note look like?

Dear Ms. Rouiller,

My son can't work with Jeff because he has a tail, and might be gay. Not like he has sex with other boys, just that my son knows he is supposed to dislike Jeff and can't articulate it any better. He isn't comfortable with himself, he thinks he might be kind of unpopular, but as long as he can make fun of Jeff he feels a little better about himself. At least he's not that bad.

Most often when you're teased there's no Ms. Rouiller to defend you. Another boy pegged as gay is a seventh grader named Petey, definitely show-offy and nasal and his jeans are all wrong, but he is kind and bright. He has friends, though they don't defend him, and are often the ones torturing him. Toward the back of the field-trip bus he is told, "I would have voted for no one for homeroom rep before I voted for you." The boys stone him with insults.

"If he were hit with a crowbar, fifteen minutes later he'd say 'Ow.' "

"You don't want to hire Petey for a freak show because he'd scare away all the freaks."

"Your momma's so dumb she climbed over a glass wall to see what's on the other side."

"Your momma's like a TV—even a two-year-old could turn her on." *Check it out.*

The insults are swiped straight from a crappy dollar-store joke book. Petey rolls his eyes at how lame they are, but still it hurts bad.

Use your strategies.

Petey tries to ignore his tormentors. He slouches and looks out the window, can't block it out. He tries clever sparring. "You don't even know what 'E equals MC-squared' stands for."

"Oooh."

"You just sit there. You three, no one listens to you, so you can say what you want."

Evaluate.

"Find one person here who hates me who's not on crack."

Several hands go in the air.

chapter ten

but what does this actually have to do with real life?

For the second day in a row, Eric refuses to do his work during math. He hums, hard. A4 is Ms. Adams's nightmare class, and Eric is usually a leader—raising his hand, telling the other kids to be quiet. She needs him for that. But at the beginning of the period he and David were throwing cookies at each other and one hit a girl. Even though David threw that particular cookie, and even though a few minutes before that she was throwing paper, and even though she was smiling and the cookie didn't mess up her shirt or anything, she blamed Eric, whom Ms. Adams threatened to send to the office. So—humming.

The humming drives the teacher crazy, it drives the kids crazy, and the louder the class gets, the louder Eric hums. Ms. Adams tells him to stop and he says, "I don't care. I don't care about any of this stuff. This is stupid." She squats next to his desk and speaks steady and slow, looking him in the eyes, which look elsewhere. "Do you hear me, Eric? You know, Eric, what you want to do is your choice. If you sit and tune me out, that's your choice. If you're disruptive, I'll have to ask you to leave. If you're disrespectful, you'll have to go to the office. Do you hear me? Eric, if you don't acknowledge me, I can't be responsible for you. Eric, you're not responding to me."

Eric doesn't bother talking—doesn't seem like anyone listens to him anymore anyway. "Why am I the only one she ever picks on?" he thinks.

He gets up and heads for the door. "Stop! What are you doing?" He goes right out of the room. She follows, and yells so the other teachers can hear, "Eric, stop! Stop!" He walks down the hall.

When Eric leaves school he doesn't have his homework and has no intention of asking Ms. Adams for it. If someone in his class were standing right in front of him, he'd ask for the assignment. But nobody is, so he heads home.

For the first two-thirds of the twentieth century, where junior-high schools existed they were seen mainly as dehumanizing, anonymous institutions in need of defrosting. They comprised seventh, eighth, and sometimes ninth grades and were, in essence, miniature high schools: the same content-divided structure, the same content-oriented teachers. By the time the midcentury baby boom had settled, elementary schools were crowded and adolescence had sneaked in earlier. In response, a new model emerged in the 1960s, in which sixth grade was moved up, and the name was changed, to "middle school."

Often the name and grades were all that distinguished this new school from the old junior high. But educators had developed a philosophy for middle school, based on the idea that brains change substantially during early adolescence. The human brain has two major growth spurts: in infancy and preadolescence. Though it's nearly full-size by this age, it is no longer thought to be fully formed. In fact, there is still enormous capacity for development. Right before puberty, brain cells grow extra connections, far more than are needed, like trees wildly putting out extra roots, twigs, and branches. This growth in the frontal cortex peaks at age eleven for girls and twelve for boys; the cells then fight it out for survival. The ones that are being used prevail. The rest will be shed.

Thus, it has been acknowledged, only during these years when the brain is so amazingly adaptable is it neither too early nor too late to fill the mind with its most important frameworks of ethics and knowledge. What a child learns and does at this point is crucial—sports, languages, typing, whatever—because those connections can last forever. And preteens are finally able to get themselves around the abstract as well as the concrete. They begin to see—in fact, need to see—the relationship between the self and the world the self lives in; they are unsatisfied simply to hold a fact in their heads. They have to know *why*.

So, in the ideal middle-school class, the theory goes, students would be challenged to use their newly acquired cognitive skills, with "Why" and "What if" questions that they might not have been able to tackle just a year ago, that don't have only one correct response, whose answers begin, "I think . . ." They would work collaboratively, and debate. Fact-finding would be emphasized over fact-memorizing. To overcome twelve-year-olds' fickle attention spans, information would be relevant to life as they see it, and the presentation hands-on. To address the vast diversity children display at this age, the curriculum would let students progress at different rates and to different depths, and explore their own interests. The kids would have some say in what happens at school.

There was also a consensus among educators that at this hormone-roaring point in children's lives—when they are searching for their selves, when moods swing wildly, when tossing a cookie leads to storming out of class in three minutes flat—they need more nurturing at school. Students at the ideal middle school would have a daily "advisory" period, so a specific adult checks in with each of them and teaches various coping skills. Teachers would team by grade rather than content area, so they could share knowledge about shared students and plan lessons that cross academic subjects. Schools would be better connected with their communities, the way elementary and high schools are.

Above all, middle-school teachers would be trained specifically to teach middle-school students, so they would deeply understand who these kids are—their mood swings on the one hand, their curiosity on the other.

"The great thing about kids this age," says Ms. Thomas, who taught social studies in high school for eight years and middle school for ten, "is that they're not jaded. They'll try different ways of looking at problems, and they can be very creative and out of the box. When I taught high school, the kids were just basically walking into the classroom and waiting for me to teach. Whereas these kids can be much more active learners—if they're tapped by the right teachers and right materials."

Several Wilde Lake teachers have mastered the perfect combination of serious and light; they know when to treat their students like adults and when to treat them like children. Group work is common. ("Can we work with partners?" is heard every day, in every class. Partners of their choosing, they mean, since preteens would rather clean latrines with their friends than ride roller coasters with people assigned to them.) When a girl is elected student-council president, some teachers notice, and joke, "Do I have to bow to you now?" One takes a role in the school play that includes crawling on the ground; another chants raps to help students remember math formulas.

The best middle-school teachers set high expectations and stick with them. They point out the good things a student does as much as—or more than—the bad ones. They can tell a child is having a cruddy day just by the cant of his shoulders. They hand back work promptly. (If not, kids bristle at the hypocrisy.) They explain why the right answer is right, and why it matters. They indulge questions about how banks work when the lesson is actually on the specific formulas for principal and interest, instead of saying, "Does anyone have any real questions?"

The right material is connected to students' culture and interests and lives. When one teacher surveys her class about what would help them write better, none of them say learning more mnemonic devices like CUPS (Capitalization Usage Punctuation Spelling) and ACE (Answer all parts, Cite all evidence, give Examples); most check "Writing about things that interest me." In the science fair, eighth graders studiously determine whether music affects your heartbeat (yes) and which type of pitch falls the most in inches (curveball) and which gum lasts the longest (Original Bubblelicious). Whenever kids relate history to something they've watched, there's one teacher who always says, "Remember, don't use movies for reference, because they're only for your amusement." But to teach probability, Mrs. Bloom brings up the Showcase Showdown wheel on *The Price Is Right*, and Ms. Knighten has her sixth graders create their own carnival games, which they play for prizes. For percentages they go to fast-food restaurants and calculate how much of a value the value meals are. She likes to say, "No matter what you're doing, it seems like math," and activities like these make the kids believe it. Mrs. Rashid's seventh graders create clever political cartoons: "Osama," one says, "I think we're losing Taliban support." "What makes you say that?" And there is a series of signs outside the hideout: OSAMA THIS WAY. To explain electrical charges, Mrs. Harris talks about static when you pull clothes out of the dryer, what lightning really is, how Saran Wrap works, and this makes sense.

The right material allows students to solve problems. In science seventh graders determine which teacher committed a murder by studying hair samples under a microscope, and in English they interview the principal and secretaries for a newspaper article about a fake anthrax scare. At outdoor ed the sixth graders figure out how to fit seven people on an eighteen-inch square by holding hands across and stepping on each other's feet, and keep the music teacher aloft on a wooden A-frame attached to red ropes like a Maypole. In science class, to show why bones are shaped the way they are, the kids experiment to see which shape of folded-up note card, rectangular prism or cylinder, will support more textbooks.

Middle-school reform has become its own industry, the subject of many research dollars and foundation studies, which all say this kind of learning is key. But it takes an unusual amount of determination and creativity to be able to turn the academic research—and the intuition each teacher has about what the kids really need—into connections strong enough to engage all students. The norm is lessons that fall flat. As it stands, according to one estimate, 70 percent of questions asked in middle-school classes are rote recall.

A large part of the problem is that most middle-school teachers learn what their students need only on the job, if at all. Even though educational researchers have concluded that middle schoolers learn best from those who were trained specifically to teach *them*, and in theory teachers should know as much about the students as they do about their subjects, very few teachers have had significant coursework on approaching young adolescents. Middle school was long neglected as a developmental phase unto itself, so at most universities students are turned into specialists in content with high-school certification or specialists in elementary education. And if you've heard enough horror stories about seventh graders, or remember your own, you're not apt to seek out the unmarked door for middle school.

The number of schools that offer middle-school specialization is growing, and as of 2002, twenty-two states required specific middle-school certification. But in some states that certification is preceded by only three or so specialized courses, and anyway "require" is a loose term during a teacher shortage, when many desperate school systems hire faculty with no training at all.

One of the largest educational reforms in the last half-century, President George W. Bush's No Child Left Behind Act, in many ways places content over pedagogy, which may push out any nascent moves toward educating aspiring educators on the nature of middle-school students. The law also makes things more difficult for middle-school teachers with majors in elementary education but not math or social studies or whatever. All teachers, new and old, will have to prove thorough knowledge of the content they teach, which will mean some veteran teachers sitting for a test or going back to school for the equivalent of another major— roadblocks that experts predict will make it even harder to keep good teachers in middle schools.

If they take the opportunity, teachers can still read up on the preadolescent brain, or attend a seminar in "hands-on" teaching strategies. Many schools across the country have aligned their classrooms with the prevailing philosophy to at least some degree, and their students have been shown to have significant academic and other advantages. In reality, though, in most school systems curriculum is king, and cannot be discarded in the name of self-directed learning. Been there, done that, got really bad test scores. When many middle schools transformed into more nurturing places in the 1970s and 1980s, their mission to cultivate good people sometimes overtook their mission to educate them. Middle school, many educators thought, simply needed to be a place to do no harm, just get those crazy kids through. And it showed, academically.

But now the balance has shifted. State and locally mandated assessments often dictate what is taught and how fast, making flexibility nearly impossible. Much attention is being paid to the fact that standardized test scores stagnate in middle school—experts call it an "intellectual wasteland," in which Americans start to fall behind other countries—at the same time that middle school is thought to set the stage for how well students will do the rest of their academic careers and even their lives. It's a time considered particularly make-or-break for poor and minority children. The standards-and-accountability movement that has overtaken the country's schools in general means that the academic demands on teachers and students are higher than ever. The push gives rise to tests about the tests:

> The Form-Audience-Tone-Purpose (Fat-P) can be found where
> in the prompt?
>   a. First paragraph only
>   b. Last paragraph only
>   c. Middle paragraph only
>   d. First and third paragraphs
>   e. Second and third paragraphs
>
> The Maryland Writing Test includes which of the following:
>   a. Narrative composition
>   b. Explanatory composition
>   c. Objective test
>   d. All of the above
>   e. A and B only

In an attempt to beef up a middle-school education that was considered too soft and nurturing, the pendulum has swung the other way, disturbing even those who agree that achievement should be measured, and must improve. "We're going backward thirty years," is how the head of the National Middle School Association puts it. The group work, "why" questions, and exploration too often fall victim to the quest for content, to the drive to get everything covered before the assessments, instead of serving to make the content all the more learnable, and real. Content versus rigor is a false debate: Both are necessary, and getting one right necessarily makes the other easier.

Teachers, however, are human; they differ in their ability to be interesting, to mediate debate, to manage a roomful of kids who aren't silent, to understand what is relevant, much less make it so. Students, Ms. Thomas says, "are never going to be in a situation where they have nine different teachers, and every single one of them is dynamic and thought-provoking. That just doesn't exist. Maybe it does exist in some places, but I've never seen it." So, in algebra, when one seventh-grade class is introduced to matrices, the example on the overhead is about how many boys and how many girls take various classes at fictional Kelly and Glenn middle schools.

"But what does this actually have to do with real life?"

"Okay, listen. I'm showing you the basics, and then I'll explain why information is sometimes organized this way."

"Today?"

"I'm going to add a homework problem for every time I get interrupted."

The teacher explains that Ms. Thomas presented the school's state test scores to the Board of Education in a matrix, and the kids would rather see *that* matrix, find out if the boys scored higher than the girls or the other way around, than figure out the enrollment for each class if the number of students at Kelly Middle School—wherever that is—triples.

Jimmy is annoyed when his science teacher says there's not enough room in school actually to fly paper airplanes, and instead they learn whether construction paper or notebook paper flies farther by copying data off the overhead. Jackie wonders why in home ec she has to plan for a randomly assigned career as photographer, instead of a fashion designer, her real-life goal of the moment. Elizabeth enjoys taste-testing cocoa cereals but wonders why they write To Whom It May Concern letters to the companies of the cereals they liked best. Who ever writes a letter that says, "Your cereal was the best bargain and surprisingly had the taste I liked the best"? Wouldn't you write to the one you liked least? Eric is happy to eat Snickerdoodle dough but wonders why they assemble the recipe from ingredients a girl has already measured and placed at their work stations. If he's going to be a chef, he figures, shouldn't he create dishes from his head?

Eric knows his teachers care. Then again, caring is necessary but not sufficient. Eric will tell you what the rest of the equation is: Understanding kids his age. Knowing how to control a roomful of unruly kids. Making the material interesting. Avoiding the touchy-feely goal-setting and "What I Have Learned" crap that just feels to him like a fat waste of time. When those pieces converge, he experiences the joy of discovery. With any of those pieces missing, the teacher's heart can be irrelevant. In science, Eric thinks a lot about Mr. Shifflett, like the way he turned a tragedy into a perfect project last year. When someone knocked over the dead little shark he kept in a jar, "instead of fussing around, talking about

'Nyah nyah nyah, everybody has extra homework,' he actually dissected the shark and let us look at the insides. 'Cause he was in love with that shark. Instead of getting mad, he made it into a project, where we had a packet, we filled out the different information about the certain parts of the shark."

"Ms. Drakes, she goes directly by the curriculum." He doesn't like her idea of "cooperative learning," in which pairs of students fill out a worksheet ("What is an ionic bond? What is chemical bonding?") and then switch partners for the next set of questions. It's not really a two-heads-are-better-than-one thing, because each kid just digs through the textbook for half the answers, then they swap. Eric works by himself, bored but productive.

And then there are the problems that no studies of effective teaching or organizational reform can solve: the problems that take place at home. They assume particularly great significance at this age, when the brain's emotional and logical control centers are engaged in a tug-of-war. The frontal lobes managing memory and learning also manage emotion, which, being the more developed skill at this point, wins this battle every time. If you're sad that you rarely see your mom or dad, those emotions literally shrink the space available for your science test.

After talking with Ms. Thomas in November, Eric got the pencil case, for a while even put the radio on during homework instead of the TV. When he told her he wanted to do better, he wasn't lying. "I really like to do well," he admits. Chris, who taunted Eric for going to the Most Improved party last year in seventh grade, is thrilled because, for the first time in his life, he is getting all A's and B's. His mom is so happy, his dad is so happy, and Chris himself never had any idea *good grades* could make him this happy. Eric doesn't say so, but he's envious. "To tell you the truth, I may be like 'I don't care,' but sometimes I really do care."

He blames his teachers, but that's not really fair: If you pay attention and follow directions and attempt your homework, no matter how unintelligent you are, you will get at least B's in middle school. Eric, however, can't be bothered. He'll do his math in pen instead of pencil, and turn down an opportunity to copy it over: minus fifty. Absences to him mean no homework. When he lived in his last neighborhood, Tenacious wouldn't let him go outside until he finished his homework. Many of his friends had the same rule, and they'd come around and hurry each other up. After homework Eric would go to Liam's house and ride bikes and eat his mom's famous cookies and play games. His report cards had lots of B's and even A's back then. Even if he had that rule at his dad's, there's nothing to go outside for—those kids aren't his friends.

A teacher can give students a dozen opportunities to retake a quiz they bombed—Come in before school! At study hall! At lunch! After school!—and they won't, either because they forget or because their time is too important to them. A kid who is sick on the day review worksheets are handed out will neglect to get one the next day, then blame the teacher for his bad test grade. A child can be asked again and again how her social-studies project is coming, and she'll say it's done; then, the day before it's due, she asks for help.

Mrs. Conroy doesn't understand why Eric's class has only 84 percent for homework. "You just have to try it and you'll get credit," she pleads. "It's easy. It's easy to do well." Mrs. Brown, too, practically begs her students to do homework, so she won't have to drop the grade three points for lateness. One day, as she hands back the graded homework, she tells the class, "People say, 'Oh, it's so easy,' then you don't get one hundred percent. You say, 'It's so easy,' then you get six out of eight." Eric, who said, "It's so easy," and then got six out of eight, raises his hand.

"Is six out of eight good, though?"

In life, Eric has been told over and over, we all have to do things that are boring, simple as that. But Eric thinks he's smart and isn't convinced he should have to prove it. "If I got judged in math for the quality of my work and not for whether I did it or not," he says, "I'd get a hundred percent. It's not like I'm a bad student, I just don't like school. I know what I can do. I've seen what I can do."

Too bad they don't learn clairvoyance in teaching school. Because he's heading toward a D in English. And in science, he's on his way to an F.

His very first F.

Tuesdays and Thursdays, Eric goes to after-school Homework Club. He gets to work right away and races through, according to his motto: Why do it good when you can do it fast? Occasionally, stopped up on an assignment, he will ask, "Anybody good in science here? Real good? Like teacher-good?" If someone can explain a concept one-on-one, he'll listen, and learn. If not, he writes down whatever.

"I don't care anymore," he says. "It's too hard not living with my real mom. My mom has just always been there. It just ain't the same. Everybody's 'Do this, do that.'" It feels like his brothers—one of whom is back from college and sharing the couch with Eric, and one of whom lives upstairs—think they're too cool to hang out with him. Close quarters in the four-room apartment are rubbing the luster off his father-worship. William's on the road half the time, and when he's back, it's never like, "Let's do something fun." He just goes upstairs and hangs out with his wife. Eric tells his teachers that he got a fifteen out of fifteen on a geometry worksheet but Ms. Beulah wouldn't let him put it on the re-frigerator, which is decorated with advertising magnets and a chore list, because it looks junky. "She's a witch," he tells them.

Worst of all, they're talking about having a baby. That can't happen—all that poop and crying. "Why are they going to have another kid? He don't have time for this one. He's not even home long enough to make a pot of beans. Not canned beans, but his homemade beans. Man, I love beans. I'll strangle the kid if it keeps me up." Eric's opposition isn't just logistical: "*I'm* the baby. But she's his wife, and what she wants, she gets." Tenacious suggested the baby idea recently, when her friend gave birth to the cutest little girl. Eric said, "Mom, I'm the baby," and that was that. He wishes his mother were married because she'd be happy, but, then again, "She wouldn't be all mine."

Eric still has goals—culinary school, the automotive program at Lincoln Tech, racing his own car, and running his own restaurant and jazz club in California called ETT (for Eric Thomas Tim), where he will conduct surveys to find out what people want to eat and drink. Sometimes Eric feels like, Hey, success is possible, I can always do better in high school. But more often these days he feels as if it's too late: The teachers will see his old report cards and say, "He doesn't look like a hardworking student."

What is success, anyway? Eric doesn't really know what it looks like; he doesn't feel he knows anyone settled, with a good job, who has what he wants and what he needs. The one day Eric spends in downtown Washington, he goes to the ninth floor of a building, sees all the office people on the sidewalks, and feels like this is as high as he'll ever get. He also wonders if neckties hurt.

Tenacious feels Eric's depression, his drastic change in attitude. He's withdrawing from her, too. He still answers "Great" to the question "How's school?" but she knows it's not. She doesn't see everything, but she did see that sheisty book report he did for Mrs. Cook, and wonders when the teachers will call.

When he tells her Ms. Thomas wanted him in GT but he didn't want to go, her skin crawls. His relatives always say, "Go go go, do do do. Do good, don't do what I did." His brother Tim always says, "Why settle for Lincoln Tech when you could go to MIT?" Sometimes Eric agrees. An MIT grad doesn't wind up with kids early and nothing to settle on, but a Lincoln Tech grad might, and if his dad had been more ambitious they'd have a house already. But sometimes he feels like he just wants to be ordinary, and ordinary, as far as he has seen, means being a mechanic or a truck driver, and Eric tells Tenacious he'd be content with that.

"Without truck drivers," Eric says, "you wouldn't have clothes, you wouldn't have food."

"Is that a copout for not working hard, not applying yourself? You're telling me you'd rather be mediocre than be extraordinary? It's okay to be ordinary," she tells her boy. "But it's also okay to be extraordinary."

"I don't get it," she says later. "I just don't get it."

When Eric walks out, Ms. Adams is frustrated and desperate, too. She doesn't know what to do about fourth period. "How do you remove the fact that they hate math because they did bad before because they didn't have the skills and they still don't have the skills? My mentor says, 'You're behind in the curriculum. Go faster.' Okay. I'll go faster, so they can hate math more, so they can hate me more, so I can hate teaching more, so I can hate kids more."

She can't find the right balance to let her students talk a little bit without getting wild. She incorporates their interests into classwork, like when they learn proportions by resizing Garfield and Boondocks comics and making scale drawings of skateboards, but at test time the grades are still low. She knows she is supposed to set high expectations, but how can kids meet them who can barely multiply? She tries the interactive teaching methods she learned in school. Once she paired off the kids to tutor each other, and Eric, who was a tutor, whispered in her ear, "Ms. Adams, this is great. Everyone gets to do things." But more often when she tries to do supposedly engaging activities like a math game show, all of a sudden a quarter of the class is going over to Malik to check on his latest bruise, a quarter is talking about how even if you don't like your dad it's okay seeing him on the weekends if he buys you stuff, a quarter is arguing about who spat on whom. A quarter is sitting there ready to go, ready to learn, ready to play, but Ms. Adams is so fed up she just makes the whole class sit and copy definitions from the book instead.

At the start of the quarter she'd announced new policies to the class: no late homework, no credit if you don't show your work, the whole class stays after if anyone is disruptive. And an incentive: homemade funnel cakes if there are no more than six D's or F's on a test. "It's your choice now—you're in a new quarter. It's your chance to shine. Many of you have shown great ability in the past, and I know you can do it."

But four weeks in, Ms. Adams doesn't see any difference. For the life of her she can't control the class. Eric feels for her; he wants to say to the kids around him, Stop talking, maybe you'll learn something. "Her bogus rules make it worse," he says. "She's just making good kids go bad." They don't get things the way Ms. Adams explains them, so they goof off instead, which results in her perpetual chant: "Please listen. Please listen. Please please please listen."

At first it saddened Ms. Adams. Now it just angers her—working hard all week preparing students for the quiz, pulling them out of study hall, e-mailing and calling at home to ask, "Are you doing your homework? Should we go over any problems?" Then eight kids do okay, and the rest just finish. One girl can remember exactly what page in her agenda the multiplication tables are on. Why can't she transfer that brainpower to remembering the actual multiplication?

"You can't teach," a kid told her once.

You can't learn! she thought.

And the funnel-cake bribe doesn't work: On one quiz most of the students get eight out of twenty; Eric gets thirteen, a D-minus.

"I'm surprised and confused," Ms. Adams says as she hands back the papers. "There is a correlation between homework and the grades you get on tests and quizzes. Homework is practice. When I go to run a race, do I sit on my sofa first all day and eat bonbons? No, I practice. I run, even when I don't feel like running. Are you perfect the first time you Rollerblade, the first time you do sports, the first time you draw?"

"Yeah," Eric blurts, "the first time I played Tony Hawk, my high score was forty."

"Some of you think, 'I can do this, but I'm lazy.' When you go to apply for a job, I'll give you a hint. Don't put on there, 'I'm lazy.' Lazy is not a quality that's admirable. This is a sixth-grade quiz. You're laughing. It's not a joke. You will be here this summer. You will be here next year. You're mature outside of class, social, kind, for the most part smart. But you are terrible students, because you're lazy."

"Why you blow up my self-esteem?"

"Don't talk about self-esteem or how you feel, because it's your choice." Eric is typing on his fancy calculator, which has letters as well as numbers. "You have the ability. I don't understand why you're choosing to fail. Shannon, if I may, has chosen to do her homework, and she got one of the highest grades on the quiz. Last quarter, what was your grade?"

"An F," Shannon says.

"Did you do your homework last quarter?"

"No."

"That book is pretty heavy," the girl next to her complains.

"You know how you only have PE a few quarters? Well, carrying the book is your exercise the rest of the time."

"Were we close to getting funnel cakes?"

"Not even close."

"Can we just have some of the powder?" one girl asks.

"Who invented funnel cakes?" asks another.

Teachers know that Tenacious Epps cares, that she comes when called, and the day after Eric walks out of class she sits for forty-five minutes with him and Ms. Adams. That Eric refuses to show his work or use pencil, doesn't raise his hand anymore, copies homework answers—this hurts. Who is this child?

"Eric, what's going on?"

"Nothing. I don't know."

They go back and forth, gently, as Ms. Adams thinks, They're friends.

"Why don't you show your work?"

"I don't know why I have to. I can do it in my head."

"You have to show your work. How do you think she knows how you got your answer? You could have cheated. You could have guessed. Eeny-meeny-miney-moe."

To Tenacious, Ms. Adams says Eric is one of her brightest students. To Eric, she says, "I cried when you left class yesterday. I care about your learning."

"Ms. Adams, I'm sorry I did that in class. I'll be more helpful from now on."

"I need you to be a leader," she tells Eric, and squeezes his big shoulder.

chapter eleven

purple. is that close enough?

Of course everyone has seen *Snow Day* already, but it's still irritating that the girls dangling their legs from the side table won't shut up. It's the day before winter break, Holiday Activity Day, and Lily sits between Mia and Beth in the front row of Mrs. Stokes's dark room. Between Mia and Beth is Lily's new favorite place to be. Beth, a girl with looks like Lily's and a manner just as serene, is her new second-best friend. She joined Lily at the last church dance when Mia wouldn't, and empathizes about Abigail Werner taking so long at the lockers, and might take gymnastics with Lily next month, and is the only girl she really, truly likes in PE and health. It's nice to have a friend in health class, with all the stress induced by the laminated line drawings of sex organs that make Lily gasp and whose names you have to actually *say*, and the boys who shoot rubber bands and pretend to smoke their pen caps when Ms. Rouiller is in the hall. When Beth shows off her newly decorated binder or a new hairstyle, Lily says, "You rock, girlfriend!" In her locker Lily has stashed two long tubes of neon-green lights, Christmas gifts for Mia and Beth.

One might think friendships get more stable as kids get older, but at this age they're not. A preteen has become more cognitively able to see the problems in her existing friendships and envision the potential for new ones. When you are eleven, the new is alluring; idealism is very powerful. This next friend will be better than the last—perfect, perhaps!

During the movie Alexandra sits with the talky girls, limbs entangled, and Lily's glad for the distance. "It's always me and Mia," Lily has explained, "and then Alexandra butts in. Alexandra more than anyone else, she has to be the number-one friend of Mia. We could be walking down the hall, and all of a sudden I'm in the back. And Alexandra's there talking with Mia. She used to seem kind, but then she started to get, I guess she started to realize me and Mia were closer than me and her were, so then she got snobby to me, and bratty and rude."

Alexandra and Lily are both wearing metal bangle bracelets from Mia. She asked Lily to wear hers today so that Alexandra will think it's the main Christmas gift she's giving out, when in fact she bought Lily a felt pencil case and glitter nail polish. Why should she get Alexandra a real gift with the way she's acting lately? When Alexandra's other friends are around, Mia says, "she acts like I'm trash, and then, when it's just her alone, she says, 'What's up, Mia?'—all friendly." This kind of thing didn't happen in elementary school, and Mia doesn't say anything about it, because what can you say? "Do you still like me?"

Alexandra is oblivious to this. In true eleven-year-old fashion, Lily and Mia tell each other she is rude but never say anything to Alexandra, who is just happy to have more friends. The black people tell her she shouldn't hang out with the white girls so much—now, that doesn't make sense to her. The children of Wilde Lake have grown up steeped in Columbia's multicultural sensibility, and whether they get along with each other has little to do with race. In high school, interracial dating is common and black kids and white kids both are elected to Homecoming Court. But most Wilde Lake Middle School kids grew up on streets or in buildings that were largely either black or white, and when it comes to choosing cafeteria tables in middle school, they stick with what, and whom, they know.

Research has always shown that race is one source of attraction to friends. Hanging more with the other black girls in middle school is a natural part of growing up, not born of prejudice but, rather, because in middle school race and income and all sorts of differences come into sharp focus and a child seeks out peers she can identify with on at least these basic levels. An eleven-year-old cares more about similarity than an eight-year-old, and her views on what makes people different or similar can be superficial, unnuanced.

One day Alexandra arrives at school with glitter still stuck to her cheeks from a cheerleading party and talks about how, because her squad won the last tournament, the coach gave out red, black, and white roses and made a toast over sparkling cider. Lily goes to one of Alexandra's tournaments and enjoys it, but she and her mom are both glad she quit the squad, what with the cute but sadistic coach who made them do push-ups and repeat the entrance eight times, until nobody turned her head, and the fake smiles, and the real tears, and the mothers on the sidelines who petted their Shih Tzus and chewed gum to calm their nerves and loud-whispered about the girls, things like, "She's got issues. She thinks she's in a beauty pageant."

The way Alexandra sees it, she acts the same with everyone. She likes being part of different groups. She still thinks Lily is a good friend, and Mia her best friend. Alexandra's been telling this to people, and when they relay it to Mia on the bus—where she sits with Lily every day—she says, "Lily's my best friend." This reassurance is especially important since Mia didn't agree to the double birthday party.

Alexandra's in a different world now, Lily thinks, but that's okay. She's the one Mia calls her best friend.

Over winter break, Lily dances as a lovely Snow Angel in *The Nutcracker*, eyes slathered in blue eye shadow and glitter. One night she falls during the curtain call, but she is not embarrassed. If that happened in the cafeteria, she'd die. She goes to Beth's, where they play with her baby sister, and Beth comes over to Lily's, where they play Outburst Jr. and model and dance. They put up a sign on her bedroom door offering free massages and makeovers: "Ask about it. You'll look cool in no time." A light-up mirror sits on a little table in the corner of the room, which is newly painted lime green. A pom-pom hangs from the mirror. Curlers from her Southern-belle days sit on the top bookshelf; propped on the shelf below are three picture frames and a paper on which she's written in bubble letters "Friends and Best Friends." In the center of a fuzzy star-shaped frame, Mia smiles with her lips closed, and Lily leans on her shoulder in the bottom right of the frame, a bigger smile. The other frames are empty.

When it comes time for Christmas services, Lily gets out of the bath and can't find her special red cardigan in the closet. She insisted on wearing it to a birthday party with no shirt underneath, even though her mother warned it would get dirty. Lily swears she put it in the laundry hamper. Boy, is she getting to be a pain, Avy and Jack think. When they tell her to do something, instead of saying "Yes, ma'am," she might say, "No, not right now," or "I don't think so." They wonder if her friends are making her this way. "Sometimes I think she was put on God's green earth to drive me crazy," Avy says as Lily searches the house for the sweater.

She eventually finds it in her bureau. For some reason this, like everything, is her mother's fault. "She's so stupid," Lily says, brushing out her wet hair.

The instant soulmate is a hallmark of middle school, and a month later Lily gets one, a third-best friend. After opening night of *Peter Pan*, Lily rides with Mia to Bennigan's for the cast party. With Ashley Schwartz, the bubbly seventh grader who plays Peter Pan, they squish into two chairs at the long, crammed table. Ashley took a big-sister interest in the girls during the play, and all of a sudden, as they share chicken fingers, Lily feels like she has a new lifelong friend and wonders if it's too late to invite her to her birthday party Friday. She rolls her eyes in the right places when Ashley tells about how a secret-admirer note for her fell out of a boy's pocket and then he denied he wrote it, and the three decide right then and there the world will end if they don't go to camp together. Ashley says they have to find a camp for less than three hundred dollars. "Maybe bowling camp or ice-skating. I'll think about it," Lily says, and she will, for several days.

"Are you friends with Katherine?" Ashley asks.

Lily is tentative, not knowing the right answer. "Sort of."

"Me, too."

Phew.

They talk about favorite colors.

"Pink," says Ashley.

"Pink, too," says Mia.

"Purple," says Lily. "Is that close enough?"

Six days later, on Lily's birthday, her parents take her, Mia, Beth, Ashley, Lily's sister, Gabrielle, and a girl named Nina to Port Discovery in Baltimore. There they solve mysteries about Egypt and spelunk through a giant model of a house's plumbing and race around an indoor play-ground. At Hard Rock Cafe, the waiters put Mia and Lily up on chairs—Mia's birthday is tomorrow—and the whole restaurant shouts, "Happy birthday!"

Ashley sort of has fun, except that these girls still laugh at dumb stuff like farts, and her three best friends went to see *A Walk to Remember* without her. Also, it feels to her like Lily ignores everyone else in favor of Mia, who in turn treats Lily as if she were her daughter, as opposed to an equal. Beth is polite but a little gossipy for Lily's parents' taste, whereas they are impressed that Ashley includes everyone and nudges the conversation away from anything nasty. Of course they wouldn't tell Lily how much they like Ashley, because that might ruin it. Ashley gives Lily a Build-a-Bear, Beth gives her a shirt and socks, Nina gives her a CD, and Mia gives her a shirt and eye shadow. Mia's party is coming up in three weeks, and her gift sends Lily into an intense mental quandary on how she'll ever reciprocate, when her mother has set the birthday-present limit at fifteen dollars.

Even though Lily thinks *The Diary of Anne Frank* should be banned because Anne wants her best friend "to be her girlfriend!"—she says this with eyes wide open and mouth scrunched tight—and, like all her friends, she signs yearbooks "LYLAS" ("Love You Like a Sister") instead of simply "Love," lest someone mistake her for a lesbian, the only way to describe Lily's affection for her own best friend is as a crush. It's a common though rarely studied phenomenon among girls this age: They crush on other girls, as much as on boys. Though there's generally no sexual component, it's a real romance, an attraction, a feeling that everything is better, brighter, warmer when this person is around.

Lily, like practically all the other sixth graders at Wilde Lake, thinks Mia is cool, kind, and brave. In fifth grade, popularity corresponded to athletic aptitude, mainly soccer and lacrosse. The middle-school formula hasn't been worked out yet, but it's clear Mia tops the list, and she is that one girl in every grade who has achieved popularity without being mean. When someone's binder comes apart during recess and papers fly all over the schoolyard, Mia chases them down as the other girls watch, and grabs sheets from the hands of boys who want to rip them. When she pats her hair at her locker and the boy next to her says, "Who puts a mirror in her locker?" Mia says, "Me. You got a problem with it?" Lots of boys want to go out with her, and to Lily's dismay she finally says yes to one of them, a gymnast named Ricky.

At game time in study hall, Mia and two other girls make a dollhouse out of Jenga blocks. Mia and Anna make people for the house, and Abby makes the furniture, and all the other girls, barred from participating, lean in and observe. Mia is the first to embrace designer Paul Frank's monkey T-shirts. Within weeks, everybody tries to draw the monkey, Julius. "Julius is the coolest," their binders say. Mia shows up with a shoelace tied in her hair, and for one day, every girl wishes she'd thought of that, although, of course, if any of them had thought of it, it wouldn't be impressive at all. Once, in Mia's absence, the girls are talking about soft shirts, and one girl says that when Mia has fluff on her sweater they blow it off their fingers. "Mia?" asks Anna, as if this sweater-fluff girl has no claim to her. Before gym, Mia and Anna play with a purple nylon book cover, swatting it at each other and putting it on their heads. Three girls look on, wishing for the intimacy.

When school is out one winter conference day, Lily and Mia eat cereal out of the box in Lily's kitchen and try to choose between ice-skating and bowling. They decide to vote, but Lily won't until she hears what Mia wants. She is totally hyper—now and until Mia leaves—dancing all over the floor. She occasionally reaches to touch Mia, or bumps into her. Lily tears slips of paper for the vote. Mia writes, "I would like to go ice-skating *and* bowling because it seems fun." Lily doesn't write anything.

They wind up at the rink, and though Mia hasn't skated much, she's a natural. Lily lags behind. "Mia!" "Mia!" "Mia, watch this!" Mia figures Lily says "Mia" a million times a day.

"No, I only say it three times a day. Except today."

"I only say 'Lily' three times a day."

They make up a dance routine. Lily keeps falling into Mia. She pats her butt—just kidding! Mia tries to teach Lily to spin, but she can't really let herself go.

Back home, Lily asks Mia to sleep over and Mia says yes. When the adults go to sleep, the kids go down to the basement and make up a skit. Mia sings, and Lily, with unbelievable energy, dances to S Club 7 on the boom box. She crawls on Mia—just kidding!

Her little brother shouts, "Shake your thing, Lily!"

And she does. She has no inhibitions. She is having a blast.

Mia is having fun, but she's a little weirded out, too. She knows she wouldn't get much sympathy complaining about the downside of popularity, but "it kind of freaks me out," she says, the way girls go and buy *her shoes*, the way she never knows who likes her for her popularity and who likes her for her, the way people sometimes get into fights in her name when she just wants everyone to get along, the way Lily talks to other friends about Mia this and Mia that, the way she always has to be so close to her, clingy even. It can feel threatening, invasive.

It's not like Mia's this supersocial dynamo anyway—over break, when Lily was hanging out with Beth, Mia mostly redecorated her bedroom, and the one time she had plans, to meet some elementary-school pals at the mall, they switched the time without telling her, and Mia found herself all alone. So—to be, supposedly, the object of everyone's affection? Mia, who thinks of herself as a big dork, doesn't really get it.

chapter twelve

i don't care about the
snack pass

At seventh-grade lunch, Elizabeth isn't wiping the cafeteria tables well enough to please Mrs. Rashid, who tells her so. Elizabeth swings her fat braid and protests in her grinding whine, which turns one word of each sentence into a weapon:

"I *waaaaashed* that one already. I did it *gooood*!"

"Elizabeth, you're not washing this one well either." Mrs. Rashid points to a wet spot. "It's not going to be dry there."

"Yes, it *wiiiilll*! I'm giving it time to *dryyy*."

They go back, they go forth, until Mrs. Rashid says, "Well, if you're not going to wash the tables, then just go outside and don't get a snack pass."

An hour later, heading to English and thinking about the lunch table, Elizabeth all of a sudden breaks down—absolutely breaks down. With every other Wilde Lake student walking to class around her, she slumps her newly grown body to the ground underneath the awards bulletin board, right beneath a slip of paper announcing, "Elizabeth Ginsburg was caught helping out Mrs. Rashid!" She wails, and only if you have a clue what's on her mind can you decipher what she's wailing: "I hate Ms. *Raaaaashid*!!!" Two teachers bend down to try to talk with her, and Eric, walking by, asks, "What's her problem? Is she having a nervous breakdown?" This makes Liz cry louder. Mr. West helps her up and into his office to calm down. Middle schoolers wear their hearts on their sleeves, and this surfeit of emotion is what so many of their teachers love about them. But it's also what drives them mad. Elizabeth sits at Mr. West's table with her head on her binder for fifteen minutes, sobbing and snuffling. He tries to coax her out of her misery, saying he'll get her a snack pass, but finally she breathes in deep enough to speak:

"I don't care about the snack pass."

It's not about the snack pass. It's never about the snack pass. It's about practicing her Torah and Haftarah portions every day with the tape recorder so she can chant in front of hundreds of people in just two months, and about the thing she said about a girl at synchro that got back to her so now everyone's acting all weird, and about Elizabeth's dad obsessing about every little thing for the upcoming Bat Mitzvah, and her mom obsessing about every little thing for the upcoming swim meet, and though her parents wouldn't call it fighting, more like discussing in naturally loud voices, that's what it sounds like to Elizabeth.

It's about how, even though she was nice for a while, now Miss Colyer is "poopy," as Elizabeth puts it, making her lower her music stand even though she likes being eye-level with the music; making her cut her fingernails, which Elizabeth likes to keep long, especially the pinky; telling Elizabeth she might have to go to the principal's office when Liz swears all she did was get a tissue; announcing that she and Molly can't sit together "for the rest of the year—understood?" When Elizabeth is the only one who has the pizzicato down pat, why does Miss Colyer have to say, "Whoa, *some people* have been practicing very well," instead of naming her specifically? The injustice infuriates Elizabeth so much that she vents in Spanish class, where Mrs. Bloom yells at her for talking.

It's about how Elizabeth never remembers the good dreams and never forgets the bad ones, like when her math teacher dropped the ring from *Lord of the Rings* and turned evil, or when she had to leave in a rush for synchro nationals and forgot to pack her clothes. Fortunately, the car turned into her bedroom, so all the clothes were there, but she left her toothbrush and hairbrush behind, and it was very stressful in the meantime.

It's about Mitch teasing her in social studies, when maybe she'd like him back if he were half as annoying, and homework that seems as if it never ends, and this self-induced quest for not just straight A's but also perfect attendance, which is hard when you have a sore throat.

And it's about one of her least favorite things in the world: being told she didn't do something well that she's sure she did.

When her mother gets home and asks what happened at school today, Elizabeth says, "Nothing."

When her father gets home and asks what happened at school today, Elizabeth says, "Nothing."

And then it storms. Used to be, on nights when Elizabeth was scared from the thunder that boomed through her window and the witch who scowled in her dreams, stressed out about schoolwork, or sad about an argument, she'd crawl into her parents' bed. Their room is in the back of the house, protected by trees, and nestling between them is particularly snug.

She considers telling her parents about Mrs. Rashid, but lately when worries spill into her nights, instead of climbing in bed with her parents—instead of mentioning her problems to her parents at all—Liz writes.

> now i hate ms. rashid and shes sssssssssssssoooooooooooo annoying so thats y i cryed and i didn't like her that much b4 anyway. i felt stupid it was stupid to cry like that about something like that its just she hurt my feelings she told me i was acting like a brat and stuff and i just felt really bad and all this stuff is happening

Then Elizabeth lies under a pile of old blankets, resting her head on the soft, worn butt of her doll Rebecca and wondering how she'll face all those kids who saw her crying, until she finally falls asleep.

Ellen used to think it was her job to sniff out the source of every one of Elizabeth's bad moods. If she asked the right question, maybe she'd find the problem, and solve it. Now, she's decided, Elizabeth's bad moods are her own. Her daughter often holds the secret that's upsetting her like a little gold nugget and at bedtime is generous enough to share it before she goes to sleep.

"It'll be like nothing—'Hanna looked at me funny' or something—so I've learned not to panic. She'll tell me when she wants."

When she wants, it's usually the little things, which they connect about comfortably in the car, or on the rare afternoons Elizabeth stays downstairs to talk with Ellen instead of heading right up to instant-message the friends she left twenty minutes before.

"How was school?" Ellen asks one day as she sits down on the couch, arm around her daughter's shoulder.

Elizabeth takes her binder from her backpack. That's kind of a hard question to answer—the specific ones usually work better. "Boring. I missed the strings picture."

Ellen looks at the worksheet. "You're learning how to tell time? Is this advanced math? Oh, Spanish. Do you have any tests before the end of the marking period?"

"No."

"No projects? I ordered your Bat Mitzvah invitation."

"But I wanted to see it! We played a game in math. Can I see it sometime? I don't remember what it looks like."

"It's just like the one in the book. We can see it on the Internet. There's a response card, too, and a separate invitation that says the party's at seven. And there's thank-you notes that say Elizabeth Nicole."

"Did you do the thing with the Hebrew name? 'Cause Dad was like 'Nyah nyah nyah.' "

"No, I didn't think you'd want that. I forgot to bring Fuzzy home." He's the guinea pig at the preschool where Ellen teaches.

"I want to see Fuzzy. I miss him."

"We can bring Fuzzy home for the weekend. So you'll have your nice thank-you notes so you'll be motivated to write them. Everything cost extra. The lining, changing the ink color."

"How much does it cost?"

"Guess."

"A thousand dollars?"

"No, three seventy-five."

"Three thousand seventy-five?"

"That would be an expensive invitation. No, three hundred seventy-five. We were going to put the brunch invitation and the directions in there, but we knocked off almost two hundred dollars—we decided to go to Giant and get cards for that. Nancy from swim team can do the calligraphy for the envelopes. She charges a dollar an envelope. Or we can find a nice font on the computer, if we can figure out how to feed the envelopes."

"Calligraphy—I want to do that."

Elizabeth starts her math.

"You woulda had fun today," Ellen says. She often shares quotidian details she knows won't be boring to a kid. "A kid threw up. Remember when you threw up?"

"Yeah, Danielle walked on it. I want cookies."

"I'll get you some. I'll be nice. Do you want one or two?" She brings back a Keebler elf. "So are you done with sex ed? Because I haven't been signing anything lately."

"Mmmmm."

"You don't know?"

"Mmmmm." Elizabeth nods, and returns to her Spanish worksheet. "Mommy, do you think 'leaving for school' would be what time I leave for the bus stop or what time I get on the bus?"

"What time you leave the house, probably."

"What time do I do my homework? It's different on different nights. This is hard."

"Liz, you can make up a time. No one's gonna come over and check."

"Mommy, what time do I watch TV?"

"Nine."

"I'm not even supposed to watch TV."

"What do you want for dinner?"

"Sketti. Do I go to bed at ten or ten-thirty?"

"Liz, why don't you know what time you do all these things? We learned about different types of learners today. You're an interpersonal-intelligent learner. You like to do things in groups and discuss them."

"I do? How do you know? I have to call Hanna."

"That's how I know. You call Hanna every day."

"Oh, I got a hundred on my math quiz!" Elizabeth says, and pulls it out to show her.

*　　*　　*

When Joseph comes home, Ellen tells him about the quiz. He asks Elizabeth, "Aren't you going to show me your math?"

"Show him," Ellen commands. Elizabeth puts the quiz under his
nose and flicks it back. He wants to look at the equations. She gives him
two seconds: "One. Two."

"That's great! Congratulations!"

There must be, Joseph thinks, some vast conversational world Elizabeth shares with her friends. If he eavesdropped at lunch, however, he'd
hear the girls talk about how cold the cafeteria is, which is their favorite
Powerpuff Girl, how stale the taco shells are, and how if you go to the
nurse she always just says, "I can't do anything for you." Not that Joseph
wouldn't take those scraps, were they offered.

"When did you get that coat?" she asks him on the way to swim
practice.

"Last year. You like it?"

"Yeah. I don't remember it."

"I got it when you got that other stuff that time."

Pause.

"You want to have your Hebrew name on your invitation?"

"I don't care. It doesn't make that big a difference."

"The scrolls have to stay blue."

"Why?"

"She said the lettering can change. Between the scrolls you can have
your Hebrew name on the top."

"I don't care."

Elizabeth puts her elbow on the armrest and leans her head on her
hand and turns up the radio.

Joseph looks at his daughter. He has an idea for a Bat Mitzvah gift,
passing on the thirteen silver dollars his grandfather gave him on his thirteenth birthday. "She won't understand," Ellen has warned—not that she
thinks it's a bad idea, she just doesn't want Joseph to be disappointed if
Liz is ambivalent. It didn't use to be like this; he used to know what she
wanted, she used to tell him things.

Car time is valuable time, Joseph knows, Quality Time. If he had an
idea what he was doing, he could use these trips to instill some values in
his daughter; if things had turned out the way he imagined, they'd spend
this time talking about blues or photography.

Instead there's silence for the next fifteen minutes.

They pull up to the swim center, and as Elizabeth gets out she says, "Love you, Dad."

At least he has that.

While Elizabeth swims, Joseph drives back to school for a School Improvement Team meeting. Plied with Snapples, the parents and students on the committee page through packets that explain, for one, the difference between "milestone" and "benchmark," watch a PowerPoint presentation about standardized test scores, hear that office referrals have gone down but the seriousness of offenses has gone up, and learn that school-improvement goals should be Specific, Measurable, Attainable, Results-Oriented, and Timebound (SMART!).

When he picks Elizabeth up at eight-thirty, she asks, "How was the meeting?"

"Better than when Ms. Thomas goes on and on."

"Ms. Thomas is annoying."

"What about her?"

"I don't know. She's just annoying."

"Is there anyone there you like?"

"You mean, like, a teacher?"

"Yeah. We have to get Ms. Jones's address. Do any of your friends have her address?"

"Noooo."

Ten minutes later: "Wanna go to Subway?"

Elizabeth nods. "What did you do at the meeting?"

"Listened to Ms. Thomas talk. They seem to be doing better with discipline, academically. It's all about goals, goals, goals. Do you have to write complete sentences in each class? Read and understand? They're having someone come do experiments in the fish tanks. They're getting more computers, PCs for the eighth graders."

"We had to do a survey about computers."

"About what exactly?"

"Computers," Elizabeth says, and escapes the car in search of dinner.

Once, when Liz was two, Joseph told her Mommy was out running. Wearing only a diaper, Elizabeth toddled unnoticed out the front door, through the parking lot, down the path, and to the curb on Columbia Road, where she stood watching cars whiz by. When a frantic Joseph finally found her, she wasn't scared at all. In her two-year-old way, she said she knew he would come get her.

Now being rescued is not so simple.

Joseph has been expending a lot of energy trying to ensure Elizabeth's happiness in strings, a task that's become more difficult. Elizabeth dreads the class. She fights with the other viola players and laughs in the middle of her scales; she is dawdly; Molly makes raspberry noises, borrows her viola, and breaks a string on the bow. Elizabeth talks back, which is new. She's always asking her reading teacher, "Don't you have more work for me? Isn't there something I could do for you next period?"

"You have a hundred-five average," the teacher says. "Go to strings."

Joseph and Miss Colyer have talked on the phone regularly these last two weeks, and they're no closer to solving the mystery. Some days Elizabeth's fine, and some days she's not.

"That probably means she really likes you and wants the attention," Joseph says.

"That's what I'm assuming."

In one call Miss Colyer tells Elizabeth's father that she has been making weird noises, sighing, asking, "Why do we have to *dooo* this?" Maybe, she says, it's because they switched to a boring practice book.

"She's under a lot of pressure," Joseph says.

One day Elizabeth doesn't play because Molly says she's messing her up, and the next day she doesn't play because Molly borrows her music.

"Is there a reason you're not playing?"

"I don't have my music."

"Share with Stu and Karen, then." But Elizabeth hates sharing. Miss Colyer e-mails Joseph: "Today Elizabeth didn't play, she just sat there." Joseph and Ellen don't tell Elizabeth about the e-mail—they figure they'll give it another week—but Elizabeth sees it anyway while playing on the computer. Excuse me? This is my life you're whispering about.

That night Joseph and Ellen ask Elizabeth if she's too stressed, if she wants to give up swimming until the Bat Mitzvah is over, but she says no, and stomps upstairs to the computer.

"You're not in trouble now," Ellen calls after her, "but get it together."

Later she sees another e-mail, about the "weird noises," and doesn't think she did that. "It's not fair. She didn't ask me about it. She didn't even know what was going on. Stu plays all the time, Molly talks, and she never gets mad at them. If she's going to call my parents, she could tell me." Joseph has taken notes on the computer from a phone call: "Liz is not following directions (slow to get started?)." "Oh my gosh, I hate her. That is so not true."

Ellen suggests that Elizabeth have a talk with Miss Colyer, but she won't. Joseph suggests Miss Colyer go to the source. She sends an e-mail.

Hi Elizabeth,
I noticed that you seemed upset today in class. Are you doing ok? Are you frustrated with Stu or is it something else? Sorry I didn't get a chance to ask you today after class. See you tomorrow.
Miss Colyer

hi
well its just that molly said she was squished and she had more room then me also i'm always at the end and really far over and a lot of things have been going on and i have been very annoyed and frustrated and upset and mad etc. lately so . . . . .
elizabeth

Once, when Elizabeth looks particularly upset, Miss Colyer tries to talk with her after class. She ticks off a list of things Elizabeth might be mad about, and Elizabeth shakes her head no to each. Finally, "Are you stressed?" A shrug, then "Yes." "Friends? School?" Elizabeth won't elaborate. "Sometimes," Miss Colyer says, "when I'm stressed, I journal," so Elizabeth does that in Miss Colyer's office for twenty minutes, well into English time. "Is it me?" Miss Colyer asks, and Elizabeth shrugs. Miss Colyer trusts Elizabeth to be open with her and figures that if she's not saying the problem is her, it isn't.

In general, teachers, particularly the more experienced ones, don't allow themselves to be drawn into their students' moods; they have learned that power struggles are unwinnable, whining unanswerable. But Liz's way of developing relationships with adults sometimes sucks in the unwary.

Miss Colyer wants to figure out how to please Elizabeth. Just as much, she wants to figure out how to end the tension, tiny but nagging. She tells Elizabeth that she knows she has problems with some of the kids in the class but that "you have to compromise, too."

Why doesn't she see that it's bigger than that?

Elizabeth is sick of Miss Colyer calling her parents. She is sick of Miss Colyer. She is sick of being this character in a novel like the ones she has to read in school, except her parents are the students, talking about her in the third person and figuring out symbolism in her every move and finding interesting ways to discuss her inner struggles.

Elizabeth is scared of getting in trouble. She wonders if her parents will make the situation worse, or better.

She instant-messages a swimming friend about how mad she is.

tell ur teacher.
NOOOOOOOO.
CHICKEN!
its scary. y dont u try, FRUITCAKE
if you dont tell her how u feel itll just get worse
u dont no that so there. anyway i cant
wwwwhyyy
bbbeecauuuse im scared ☺
then write a note Shes just trying to help you
i know but thats annoying
then tell yr parents to do something
no its scary
LIZ, if u dont tell and make up the escuse that it is scary then
   i don't want to ever hear u complain about a teacher!
i will . . . later . . . maybe.
i don't understand u i mean i would tell!!!
yeah rite i bet and ud b as scared as me just meet her. u can
   tell her 4 me. i g2g!!!!
fine
bye
bye be strong
whatever

chapter thirteen

not much just chillin'

In the nineteenth century people came calling, in the twentieth century they phoned, and now preteens communicate on the Internet. They type to each other fast as thirty-dollar-an-hour secretaries (except that secretaries can spell), one instant-message box on the screen for each conversation.

Wus ˆˑ
NMJC.

What's up? Not much just chillin'. If not much is up and they're just chilling, you wonder why they don't have time to type out the words. But anyway. Parents have become familiar with the sounds of IM, the arpeggios of acceptance twinkling every time the person on the other end of the line has something to say.

Or nothing to say:

Starlett89:..........
KT2001: ....
Starlett89: dont copy me! find ur own system of dots!
KT2001: no thanks
BABEXOX: GO BONGUESHA!

BABEXOX: LMAO*

Starlett89: ROTFLMAO†

Starlett89: ah! somethings under my desk!

KT2001: is there a reason for me to be here?

Starlett89: oh, its just my shoe...

BABEXOX: CAUSE WE KNOW WHO U ARE...BUT U DON'T KNOW WHO WE ARE

KT2001: yes i do

KT2001: catherine

BABEXOX: WRONG!

Starlett89: do u know her?! r u her mother?!

Starlett89: i think not!

KT2001: no but i no her

BABEXOX: NO YOU DON'T

KT2001: and i wasnt tlkaing to u so fuck off

Starlett89: fuck urself

BABEXOX: ...YOUR BETTER AT IT

BABEXOX: HAHA

KT2001: okay bye

BABEXOX: ISN'T THIS SUCH A NICE CONVERSATION?

Starlett89: extremely!

BABEXOX: DAMN, I WISH KELSEY WAS HERE

Today's calling card is the IM profile, a box you click on to read a kid's explanation of himself, updated every possible moment. The moment a girl returns from an event, she uses her profile to evaluate it:

> Hiya this is Traci! I just got back from the best dance in my life! CHA CHA SLIDE!!!!!!! and the booty call..... (put your butt in it!) I had the best time slow dancing with Andrew (he didn't go for the butt) The CHICKEN DANCE! Well thanks to Jen, Jen, Cubby, Dina, MM, and Dave for making this the best dance of my life!

Boys make lists like "Whos most likely 2 suck dick rite now" and announce their favorite phrases ("Bonermobile," "chillin shit!," "poo

---

*Laughing my ass off

†Rolling on the floor laughing my ass off

fuck!") and their favorite sports teams and their least favorite teachers ("dont u just wanna kill mrs weinstein i mean bitch") and their philosophies ("Remember it takes 42 muscles in the face to frown but only 4 in your arm to bitchslap that asshole who pissed you off"). Kids create quizzes about themselves: "What is my favorite sk8? What is my favorite color? What is my dog's name?" They self-publish:

> why is it that when we are mad at someone we tend to wait right by the phone for them to call us tell us that they are ok but they never call and you get mad at them and you worry about them and you start to fall in love with them and you realize that they dont love you back and you are so sad and angry and you want to cry and cry until they see you curled up into a corner crying and you just sit there and wait for him to say its ok and for him/her to put there arm around you and then you feel better like there is a god like someone is up there praying for you and that is the best feeling you can ever have in the whole world

Each of the swim-team girls has her own Web site (the introduction on one: "Hi I'm Adrienne. I am 11 and single") and they have a collective site:

Dolphins Gossip! Ex-tra Ex-tra! Read all about it!
More good news has arrived! The couples still out there:
** Sarah & Kendall
** Lia & Peter (maybe/almost. if you want to vote about this go to the mini quiz)
** Abby heard that Henry likes Dale! But Dale does NOT like Henry back (she is not trying to be mean she just doesn't like him).
** At the dance, Noel asked Tina to slow dance! And guess what she said! NO WAY!!! You won't believe this, NOEL LOVES TINA!

Middle school is when most kids start to truly immerse themselves in the worlds of communication, culture, and consumerism—the Internet is only the latest manifestation. Fads—short-lived, by definition—have always been a big part of being eleven: Twenty years ago at Wilde Lake girls affixed safety pins to their Docksiders, last year they simultaneously fished glittery plastic kindergarten barrettes from their bathroom drawers, this year they stick rhinestones on their upper arms and pass out rubber bands they've popped from their braces so everyone can chew on them.

But even spheres that have always interested the preteen have become more and more centered on them. Now the promoters of popular culture—like *CosmoGIRL!* and the Delia's catalogue and ABC Family Channel—focus to an overwhelming degree on a girl like Lily, whose every penny spent is the result of a calculated decision about what CD or shirt or lip gloss will help her fit in. What they watch on television, whether they drink, what they want to be when they grow up—for preteens, parents influence these decisions more than any other source. But for music and clothes, the biggest influence is friends. Lily's ballet and sewing skills don't matter so much as these things, because at this age children define themselves by what they have. Or what they don't: What agony when the girls arrange themselves on the schoolyard according to shirt color—purple, white, purple, white—and Lily's wearing a black vest.

Middle-school kids no longer crib their older siblings' cultural identity—they've got their own—and retailers are seizing on this like never before. It's partly because the preteen population is growing so fast. It's partly because kids, beneficiaries of a flush economy and victims of busy-or-otherwise-guilty-thus-indulgent parents just have so much money to blow. (One study found that someone between twelve and fifteen spends, on average, fifty-nine dollars a week, about one-third on clothes, the bulk of the rest on entertainment. And that doesn't even count what their parents spend on them.) It's partly because kids are growing up faster. And it's partly because retailers, having saturated every small town, every other market, simply have nowhere else to go.

Thus there are more teen magazines on the newsstand than ever, more teen lines of adult clothing brands. One by one, grown-up retailers in the Columbia Mall are closing, replaced by stores or, at other malls, entire wings for preteens and teenagers, with Skinmarket and Limited Too and Aeropostale and Journeys and the Piercing Pagoda and Viktor Viktoria and PacSun and Stickerz. Parents drop their kids off a little jealous. When they were that age, there weren't any stores for them—just the kids' department, which you couldn't wait to get out of. But they're also a little wary: The styles have grown up. This year the small of the back is everywhere, as shirts for girls stop short of the belly and make announcements across the chest: "Trouble," or "How Hot Am I." The jeans ride tight and low, real low, so flowered cotton underpants—these are still children, after all—bunch up above the belt loops. The boys wear pants low, of course, and baggy, and the girls like to mock the way this forces them to run, grabbing their waistbands and bowing their legs out, almost a waddle.

The consumerism that is such a big part of young adolescence these days is, truly, a big pain for parents, many of whom reasonably think those pants look stupid. But they can, and should, pay attention to the school dress codes and exercise some control at the mall, even when they hear, "But it's *my* money!" Giving in is easier in the short run, but a kid who gets used to hearing "no" might stop fighting it after a while.

Insensitivity to the importance of fitting in, however, is unforgivable. By all means, a boy in the year 2001 should not be made to wear snug slacks. But he *can* be denied any jeans where a basketball could pass through the leg. A girl who wants a message to crawl across her chest? A mother can tell her which messages are too slutty and why, and let her choose from the others.

A parent's control is limited—nothing's changed on that score. An aspiring punk-rocker might be forbidden from wearing that raggedy skull wristband, but he will keep it in his backpack and put it on at school. A girl whose parents ban eyeliner applies it, shakily, on the bus. That doesn't mean parents shouldn't forbid what they truly feel is untoward. They should, however, think carefully about just how dangerous that ratty wristband really is. Because growing up, after all, is in large part about creating a style.

Or, rather, choosing from among a small range of options.

It's one of the biggest contradictions of preteenagerhood: The kids see clothes and music as their chance to shape their own personae, but that identity needs to be as much as possible like everyone else's. That's why stores like Hot Topic and Urban Outfitters, meccas for nonconformist conformists, are so popular. Or clothing stores that are a socially safe brand but offer enough choices and accessories so that kids can feel they're creating their own look. At American Eagle Outfitters, for example, you can customize the jeans you buy with rhinestones and studs. They're your very own creation—but they're still American Eagle, so you're okay. Your phone has a pink faceplate nobody else's does—but it's still a Nokia, so you're okay. You've concocted your own gold-glitter Supersmooch Lip Gloss at Club Libby Lu—but you're still wearing lip gloss, so you're okay.

Middle-school kids have their own sitcoms, at once treacly and ironic, usually starring the Olson twins or some facsimile. The music industry, too, has begun to capitalize on the vast buying power of preteens, who used to listen to their older siblings' records (or even their parents'!) but now have genres all to themselves. They are sick of hearing their baby-boom parents brag about how great their music was. They are sick of what they listened to last week, and thank goodness, because, with the music-production process sped up, there's always something new right around the corner. They begin to realize music can be their own and at the same time a way to connect with their friends, which means they all like the same stuff, give or take. Jimmy started the year listening to his sister's boy bands, but by the middle of the year he has developed his own favorite groups and written their names in silver pen on his backpack: Blink 182. Kid Rock. Bands with an attitude go over well with middle schoolers, bands that they consider "outsider" and "punk" and "underground" but that the music industry considers pop. "When a band becomes popular, they get shallow," one eighth grader puts it, without realizing that once Good Charlotte's music has made its way to the thirteen-year-olds in Columbia, Maryland, it's no longer "outsider," and the group's first album went quickly gold, what with every other girl just like her at every other school in the country feeling the same way.

chapter fourteen

it's the jackie show!

The night after Christmas, just after his first birthday, Kyle Taylor has a fever. Sara gives him baby Tylenol in the living room, and moments later he throws it up, aspirates on the vomit, stops breathing. Jackie watches as her father carries the purple-lipped baby like a big fish to the kitchen table and begins CPR. To her mother Jackie says, though she's not sure why, "I'm sorry. I'm sorry." Her mind goes blank; she goes to her room and can't cry but prays, a prayer that mostly goes, "Oh my God. Oh my God. Oh my God." Her baby brother, whose poops, cries, and giggles she jokingly charts on the computer, whose noises she's listed ("argglgle," "hahhahooo"), whose cuteness she is certain he gets from her even though he looks exactly like his dad and she like her mom, whose peanut allergies she carefully tends, whose crawling body she crab-walks over as he laughs, looks like he's dying. Jackie's sure that he's dying.

But he does not die.

Kyle is breathing again as the ambulance wails to a stop in front of the house. On his way into the house one of the paramedics says to Jackie, "How you doing today?"

She doesn't know what else to say but "Fine."

*   *   *

Preadolescent passion flits. Just when you think a child will never detach from an obsession, her attentions take off and alight elsewhere. For Jackie, her brother's crisis is the first gust that lifts her off the rock she was sitting on, thinking of boys. Crushes slip to number five on her priority list, or even six, as Jackie lands firm-footed on a new fixation: identity. She will spend the rest of the winter immersed in the vital preteen exercise of figuring out and then creating the Jackie Taylor *she* wants to be. This is common for a thirteen-year-old, to pause for a moment to question her values, her life-style, her hobbies, her wardrobe.

The first stop on Jackie's inner journey is religion. Her mother is Jewish and her father Lutheran; her religious practice mostly consists of holiday dinners and gifts, but with everything happening in Israel it feels like she should go to synagogue. Maybe, if enough people talk to God at the same time, it will help. So her mother takes her, four Friday nights in a row, until Jackie decides she'd rather have friends over. In temple Jackie looks up at the stained glass, listens to the beautiful songs she doesn't understand, feels safe. As well, she writes letters for her mother to deliver to the cemetery, where her grandfather has been buried two years. "I miss you Grandpa. I love you. Love, Jackie." He was her biggest fan and gave her a gymnastics jacket that makes her think of him every time she puts it on.

Jackie has been spending a lot of time in the basement playing Sims, a massively popular computer game in which the players create characters and decorate their homes and find them jobs and control their levels of comfort and hygiene and energy and so on. It pretends to simulate real life, except that in real life bragging doesn't always cause couples to like each other more and you can't earn spending money simply by typing shift-control-C and then !;!;!;!;. Jackie likes to be in charge of her own world of characters, which never happens otherwise. She and her neighbor Jenny have created the Sexy family and the Pimp family (their mansion is P-shaped, a swimming pool tucked into the hole in the P), the Lovers' Castle, the J Squared House, and a Japanese pagoda where the band members from System of a Down live.

Beyond Sims, Jackie is sick of everything there is to do in her house and, able to do some serious imagining, has begun to wonder incessantly why she doesn't have a cooler life, the life her mental Jackie Taylor—hipper, older, freer—is entitled to. "My life is so boring. If we had cable my life would be so much better," she says. "We'd be watching MTV right now." There are no stricter adherents to the grass-is-always-greener conviction than thirteen-year-olds; Jackie is certain all her friends have more exciting lives. But when she tests her theory with a phone survey one day, three girls, all of whom have cable, are doing chores, and the fourth is visiting her grandma.

Sometimes, it seems to Jackie, life is just a collection of things she cannot do or have. Mr. Acie won't let her sit at the back of the bus anymore, because he said she was bouncing when she really wasn't, and Jackie wants her mom to get him fired for this and other grave injustices, but Sara points out that Mr. Acie probably has a family, and do you really want to put him out of a job, and besides, she likes to hear he's strict and doesn't let the kids dangle their limbs out the window.

Already Jackie is bargaining for a car in three years. You pay for the car and insurance, Jackie offers, and I'll pay for the gas. Sara suggests the opposite. If Jackie were the mother, she would let her kid walk to Giant in the daytime with friends she knew and trusted. "I'm just like, 'Why can't I do this?' and they're like, 'Because I said so.' The thing that gets on my nerves—it plucks my last nerve—is when my mom says, 'I'm the parent, you're the child.' "

A reason, *please*.

She thinks that her dad is so laid-back that if he made all the decisions she could go wherever she wanted, especially Giant, but she is wrong.

Jackie can never pass notes in math because, even though Ms. Hammond once overlooked a spin-the-binder game in the corner during study hall, she knows a note's a note, wherever in the room she's standing, whatever work she's immersed in. A hawk, that woman is, and there's just something unconstitutional about it. Doesn't she know that a seventh-grade girl's need to communicate with her friends is as fundamental as her need to breathe and bathe? In English, Mrs. Gayle, however, thinks that when they toss crumpled paper across the room they're just trying to hit each other, so, as the class does a worksheet about the characters in "The Monsters Are Due on Maple Street," Jackie passes a note back to Stephen.

wassup? do you like any 1? (i dont know y, do you wanna pass notes?)

Stephen's wiggling the black Bic in his mouth, squiggling in his seat.

i don't know why but i wanna. yes i like someone actually i like 3 people!
3! tell me 1. or 3.
okay i'll tell you 2 but u gon tell . . . please don tell.

He hides the note under his worksheet as he writes.

i promise on my grandfathers grave i wont tell
i sorta like Kristina. i think Ann is hot.
i know you ass wipe.
who do you like
you have to tell me the 3rd person because i already know the other 2 and never talk to me again like that. Bonge moi pat garcon.

For some reason, Jackie thinks this means "Bite me, dough boy." She turns around and asks, "Kate?"
"She's ugly! You and Ben. You and Eugene."
"That's nasty."
"You and Dante."
"That's nastier. Why are you picking on me? Because I'm short?"
Stephen writes another note:

lets talk about something else. i read the note you gave 2 Leslie on friday.
what note? how did u get it?
that said you might have cancer.

Jackie is going to explain that the cancer thing was a joke on Leslie—who got quite pissed about it—but instead she crumples the paper.
"Jackie. Jackie. Write back."

But Jackie is finishing her worksheet. "What's that word, a small word, one little thing that's wrong with you? It starts with an 'f.' " She looks in the glossary. "It's not in here." And then the thesaurus: "Flaw! That was it! I feel better now. I feel complete." Jackie loves thesauruses, the way they take you from mad to angry to infuriated, or nettled, or splenetic. Stephen wants another note. "I'm trying to do my work," Jackie tells him. "I'm sorta trying to pass this class"—she bounces her head from side to side and smiles—"even though I have a ninety-six-point-one."

Jackie knows she's a good scholar, so she figures New Jackie should play on Old Jackie's strengths. In reading, she's been raising her hand so much, ramrod-straight, almost always with the right answer, that the teacher announces, "It's the Jackie show!" In math, they're graphing inequalities, which she loves. In science, Jackie watches the crabs mate and does all her experiments with Leslie. Jackie has seen this salinity experiment before on *Zoom*, where you pour three candy colors of orange, blue, and green water into a beaker to see how they layer. "You put the one with less salt in first," she says. Jackie likes *Zoom*, although ("not to be clique-racist") she doubts any of the kids on that show are popular. Jackie draws the beakers on the worksheet and shows Leslie how. She tells Mr. Shifflett that the orange on top is fresh water, the green is brackish, and the blue is salt water. She sets up beakers with different water levels and taps them to play "When the Saints Go Marching In."

Science is so easy that sometimes Jackie wants to move into GT, which her mother would love. Sara has always envisioned her daughter in an outdoor, exploratory kind of job, though she hopes not Greenpeace. But Jackie doesn't want her grade to go down. Also, she figures Leslie would get a C without her around. Jackie is selected to go on a field trip with other girls who are good at science, to a place where computer chips are made. She looks at a display of how the chips have gotten smaller over the years, and puts on a spacesuit and booties and gloves to enter the disinfectant chamber. She keeps the gloves.

It sounds corny, she knows, but Jackie really enjoys school right now. Not just the seeing-your-friends part, but the work. The surge in enthusiasm is due in part to her brand-new career goal, one she thinks good grades might make possible, one shared by Lily and Elizabeth and probably half their peers: Jackie now wants to be an actress when she grows up. That way she can buy a yellow convertible Dodge Viper and be remembered after she dies. She hasn't told her mom, who would suggest something more practical, and she hasn't told her dad, who would say it's not realistic. But Jackie knows it can happen—"TV, movies, commercials, whatever I can get my hands on." Though she often imagines herself a Casey or an Elissa, she's not going to change her name, because it's a pain to redo all those documents and she's already practiced her signature. She zips "Jackie Taylor" across the page, over and over, like she used to do two months ago with "Jackie Starr."

As for trampolining, Jackie wavers. Since she started at age eight, the tramp has gone a long way toward teaching Jackie how to take turns, sit still, focus. "A Mexican jumping bean," Sara calls her. At the gym, Jackie waits tidy and cross-legged on the mat. She loves the social part, goofing off with her teammates between routines. When it's her turn for the double mini, she mouths "Watch me" across the gym to her mother, runs as if toward a vault, performs a series of tricks on two small tramps, and dismounts onto a mat. "I did back tuck back tuck!" When she jumps, with the thick practice harness or without it, her arms swing in the air, and at each bounce her left knee bends for momentum.

Jackie loves speed—when she was little, Mike had to wear roller skates to keep up with her Big Wheel—and as the Olympics play on television, she wonders if she should bobsled instead, or maybe figure-skate. She goes to the rink for the first time and is amazingly at ease. She teaches herself to do triple spins and pull her arms in fast. A man who used to teach skating tells her she is phenomenal, and a group of girls her age watch, looking impressed despite their best efforts not to be.

Right before trampoline sectionals there's a stretch when Jackie's not doing well on the double mini and always complaining before practice. On the way to the meet, Jackie, in her purple warm-up suit, keeps saying she's not going to do well. If she has that little confidence, Sara says, she can choose not to compete, just like that. Jackie goes ahead and warms up, but you can see from her hard face that she's miserable—she blew her new trick two practices in a row, and the equipment in this gym sucks, and she's going to screw up. Her coach comes up to Sara and says, "She's a headcase."

"She said she had a couple of bad days this week."

"She has fifteen bad days and one good day. She has twenty-five bad days and one good day. She convinces herself she can't do it, then she can't."

Jackie aces the double mini and the tramp and wins first place in both.

Looks-wise, Jackie's in a good groove these days. In sixth grade, when she didn't care what people thought, she wore a turtleneck with a vest. "Eww," she says, "I can't believe I wore that. I have no idea how I got so many boyfriends wearing that." Her look, she has decided, should be dark colors and black, though not Goth. She proudly coordinates tops and bottoms from different stores even though they're not made to go together. Her aunt bought her new shirts, all long-sleeved variations of navy blue, with messages of course: "Angel to Devil in 3.5 Seconds." "I Know I'm Cute So Keep Trying." "Samurai Princess." She's pleased with her new style, and even if someone she admired criticized her favorite shirt, she'd keep wearing it. (If it was just something she got because it was on sale, though, she'd save it for weekends only.)

"All my neighbors think I'm beautiful," Jackie says. "They're like, 'Oh my God, she's so beautiful.' Then they look at Kyle and then nobody talks to me, but that's okay." Jackie wears a tiny bit of makeup, a little liner mostly, to frame her eyes, which she thinks are amazing, the way they change color. She has just started shaving the nearly invisible blondish hair on her legs. Aside from the tricky ankle area, she's doing pretty well. Though Jackie wishes she weren't so skinny and her legs weren't so bruised from gymnastics, she is proud of her abs, a baby six-pack. Her eyebrows she has started to find "thick and manly—I have one. I have *one*." So she asks, "Mommy, can I use your tweezers?" Sara approves of the action but not quite of the result: The brows are plucked so glamour-girl thin that Sara says they need to grow out so Jackie's grandma can fix them.

Jackie thinks Leslie is pretty, too, but is a little worried about (1) her style and (2) her family life, in which she argues with her mom and thinks her dad considers her an embarrassment to the family and only her cat really loves her and (3) her forwardness with boys. Jackie is totally in line with Leslie on checking out the guy across the street at the high school who rates a "Cole," the highest rating on their scale of hotness, named after the bad-boy character on *Charmed*. But she is creeped out by how many boys Leslie will "make out with." Kristina tells Leslie she's acting like a ho, changing who she likes every day, and Leslie says that she knows she can act a little ho-like sometimes but she'll try to change. "Everyone has a flaw," she says, "and that must be mine, I'm sorry." It's not like any of those guys are into her anyway, she's just seeing who likes her. She wonders, Is that acting like a ho?

Although *YM* tells Jackie that a "forward Leo" wants to be her Valentine, on February 14—when the boys at her table eat candy hearts their moms put in their lunches, and the girls wear red and have hearts on their hands or pink stars glued to their eyelids or Valentines to pass out to friends (and to other girls who ask for them, because what can you do, say, "You're not my friend"?)—Jackie shows no signs of holiday spirit. Maybe she doesn't need Valentine's Day. Maybe she doesn't need boys.

She goes that week to the skating rink, where as usual she rules on the car-racing video game and cannot resist the opportunity to not win a stuffed animal from the crane. As she skates around the rink, Dan Arnstein, her ex, watches from the penalty rink. As she passes, he says: "Dan likes you."

"Which Dan?"

"Dan Pryor."

Next time around the ice: "I heard you're going out with Adam."

"Which Adam?"

"Adam Buchman."

"No."

When she gets home, she says to Sara, "Dan Arnstein was there."

"Oh, he's such a cutie."

"No, he isn't."

"Sure he is. I think he's such a cutie."

"Mooooooom," Jackie says, and that's that.

Nobody's asked Jackie out since Anton, whom she is way over. On his IM profile he pays homage to the women of the world by posting the lyrics of Timbaland and Magoo's "All Y'all," in which the rappers feel "like a pimp," plump with cash and class and "a gat loaded for that ass."

This has never made sense to Jackie, the way rappers are like, as she puts it, "I love you ba-a-by. I'll show it with a shotgun! Baby, I love you, but you're a BLEEP!" Celia doesn't mind it, and for a while goes out with Anton. But she grows tense from the instant-messages she gets from a girl in New York who calls her a bitch and says she stole Anton away from her; besides, she wants to be single, "because then you can have fun, and Stephen and I always like to put our arms around each other, and Anton would get all jealous, and also the whole school would know, since our school is so involved in everyone's relationships." So she breaks up with him at Kelly's Bat Mitzvah and then cries, because she still likes him. Jackie is glad she can enjoy the dancing at the party and not have to cry about anyone. For the record, the supposedly lesbian rabbi doesn't hit on anyone.

Jackie attributes her sudden ambivalence about boys in large part to her horrible pickiness. She will only eat Burger King fries, not McDonald's. It takes her forty-five minutes to choose one movie at Blockbuster. Even though it's a bad age for movies when you have a strict mom—everything is either too adult or too babyish—there are a thousand that would be acceptable. Jackie doesn't want any of them, especially if they were made before 2001. And the boys: "In sixth grade, you're like, 'Omigod, I'm in a new school, I'm so cool—ah!' You didn't know the people in sixth grade. But now that you know they're big butt-munchers and jerks, you're like, 'Eww, I don't want to go out with them.' I can't believe I went out with them."

She doesn't want anyone who likes her just for her looks—if someone asks her out, she makes him explain in a note or through a friend why he likes her, to make sure "funny" and "smart" are in there and not just "hot." All the seventh-grade boys, she figures, only care about big boobs. "They all just like Ann," Jackie says, "because she's hot and she can do a roundoff back handspring.

"Some people think they're, like, the most beautiful person in the world and they can go out with anybody, and they say it in front of the world: 'I want to go out with this person, I'm so beautiful and lovable, look at me.' Some people are just like, 'I'm so ugly, no one will want to go out with me.' And I'm just like, Okay, whatever. If someone likes me, that's cool.

"If you like somebody, think about it. If it's not going to happen, reality-check."

Even if she did like someone right now, she'd think twice before writing on her hand again. It's embarrassing if someone finds out you like him but he doesn't like you back. She would confide in Leslie only.

She is keeping that prospect open; it's not like she's joining a convent. Brad broke up with Mimi, and she'd go out with him if he wanted. There are a few others she'd consider, too. Plus, the last few months her horoscope has mentioned an "exuberant Aries who smiles a lot."

Who, Jackie wonders, could that be?

chapter fifteen

i'm not that curious anymore

Jimmy calls out his bedroom window into the clouds, "Do we need a notebook?"

"Three years we've been going to the oysters," his father says, slamming the trunk, "and you still ask that?"

Jimmy shuffles out on the cold driveway in his holey-toed socks, holding his boots, one pair of many. *Independence Day* was on last night, loud and intense, so he had trouble sleeping.

"Do you have a ruler? A pencil? The Game Boy is going in the trunk." Jimmy goes back upstairs, then downstairs, and finally they are off, toward Annapolis and the oysters they raise. At the pier next to the family sailboat, Paul lifts four metal baskets from under the dock with a long hook and hauls them, dripping, onto the wood. The three thousand oysters, small as poppy seeds, are crusted onto dead oyster shells. Jimmy hoses off the dirt and mud so the bacteria wash away and the oysters can grow. He absently wipes muck onto his jeans.

"Watch what you're doing here," Paul says, bending to pick something off the pier. "Those are your good boots."

"Dad, stop showing your underwear." Jimmy thinks nothing of embarrassing his parents in public, returning the favor. Over pasta and candlelight and a big loaf of crusty bread being passed at Will's house one recent night, Jimmy told his mother loudly, "You're wearing too much eye shadow."

Paul hitches up his jeans. "Jimmy, how's the oysters?"

"The thing I've really wanted to try all my life is giving an Alka-Seltzer tablet to a seagull to see if it really explodes."

"Is that how we treat living things?"

While the oysters dry in the sun and the flatworms on them die, Jimmy and Paul go for lunch in tourist Annapolis and browse the stores. At the Discovery Channel store, each next item Jimmy sees is the one he has to have. Back at the dock, Jimmy holds the oysters up to the ruler and calls out measurements: "Twenty millimeters. Forty-three. Sixty-four." He's really not into this anymore. There are four hundred things he'd rather be doing, but Paul always says, "No, Jimmy, you have to keep on going for years. It's a major job." If it's so important, Jimmy wants to say, why don't you do it yourself?

Just like that, Jimmy has stopped sitting up in bed wondering about the universe. "I'm not that curious anymore," he says. This, too, is part of the changes engulfing him as he enters adolescence. Though these changes take place in the brain, he has no more control over them than he does over the growth of his feet. And they happen so fast. All of a sudden Jimmy gets bored more easily, his temper slips from his grasp—full self-control won't come until the brain's frontal lobes are pruned—and, like Jackie, he is contemplating seriously whether maybe what made up the old Jimmy should not make up the new Jimmy. No longer is pleasing his parents a major factor in the equation of how to spend his time. Just the contrary: For reasons he cannot figure out even while it's happening—and not like he loves them any less—Jimmy, like his peers, finds great sport in contradicting his mother and father.

A preteen has plenty of interests, they just rarely sit still for long. Jimmy's theory is that school used to teach you less stuff, so you had to be curious on your own, but now, in sixth grade, the material is more interesting, so there's less room for extracurricular curiosity. Occasionally he digs up his backyard, where among the archaeological detritus of his childhood he might find something cool, like Jefferson salamanders. He looks up their habitat on the Internet and creates a home for them in his sister Brianna's old frog tank, but the next day he opens the lid and lets them disappear. Mostly he plays on the computer or GameCube. You could say he's a big reason the video-game industry has grown so massive in the last decade—except that his parents only let him own five games at a time. It's alluring, the totally captivating, passive yet active, out-of-this-world experience of a video game, a place Jimmy can excel. Boys today can't imagine their counterparts of three decades ago, who didn't have video games to play at home, who spent money on music (now downloadable right from PCs), who spent more time outside, when that was considered a safer option. Two decades ago home-video games became popular, Atari and the like, but even one decade ago they weren't nearly as big a deal as they are right now—new, better, faster, sexier games arriving on the shelves each week, easily accessible on the computer, affordable to kids with a whole different level of spending money.

Scientists have varying theories on the impact of so much gaming, but in general they're cautionary. "Hand-eye coordination," Jimmy protests, but he doesn't realize what's going on in his brain. Whatever brain cells he's using at this phase of his life are the ones that will survive. Video games may help you maneuver in a fast-paced, info-saturated society, but if you're perpetually playing them instead of something more physical, the development of your cerebellum may be delayed. And one theory posits that the rapid pace of video games triggers irrational fear responses, so out of line with how you should respond in the real world that the development of rational thought is at risk.

At school Jimmy has been spacing out a lot. He especially tunes out whenever the lesson revolves around reading the textbook (often) or filling out a worksheet (which takes up one-fourth of a middle schooler's classroom time) or anytime the overhead projector is turned on. God, how these kids hate copying from the overhead: definitions of the jobs required to put on a play ("director," "stage manager"), definitions from high school ("SAT," "elective," "graduation requirement"), definitions from the school mission statement ("community," "stimulating," "lifelong"). Jimmy likes learning new words but sometimes feels like only a vessel filling up with vocab, vocab, vocab.

He's playing with his calculator when Ms. Knighten says, "What's the principal, Jimmy? Page two seventy-four." "Plains and plateaus, Jimmy," Mrs. Graves tells him in social studies, but he's writing instead of following the textbook, and it takes a few seconds to focus, as air drones through the vents. He is flipping his miniature skateboard from one desk to another when the squeaky-voiced substitute in academic enrichment hands out a crossword puzzle. "I'll take that, please," she says. As everyone else copies the science answers from the overhead—"Magma cool slowly → called intrusive rocks. Ex: granite"—Jimmy doodles. The aide directs his head to his worksheet and pats his shoulders. He yawns, audibly. In music, when he's supposed to be underlining "aria," "duet," "quartet" in the reading, it's "Jimmy, put your chair down, please." Four seconds later, he leans back again.

"School is the worst thing that ever lasted six hours in a kid's life," Jimmy says. And homework is the worst thing that ever lasted three hours. It's an endless struggle between Jimmy and his parents.

Today, as soon as he gets home from school, he turns on the radio in the family room, plops on the rose-colored rug in front of the entertainment center, and starts playing Super Smash Bros. Melee. At three-thirty his dad looks in from the kitchen. "Homework, Jim."

"No."

"You made the choice to wait till the last day. You know the rule. Do I have to take the game away?"

Silence.

"The game is done."

"You promised me thirty minutes of free time! Good job, Dad."

Paul sets a kitchen timer for thirty minutes and places it on the floor between Jimmy and the television. "When this goes to zero, the game goes off."

God, Jimmy thinks, when will Dad get out of the house? Paul lost his job at a dot-bomb last year, the same time Marie was laid off from a telecom company. At first Jimmy was worried about the money, but Marie assured him there was plenty in the bank. He likes that his mom isn't working, that she's around more, that he doesn't have to worry every time she's on a plane or wait at the babysitter's for her two-hour commute to be over. For a child, one study says, having a parent travel for work is as stressful as having a close relative die. Now it's just that his dad is around *all the time*.

Four-twenty. The timer beeped when Paul was upstairs, and when his mother comes home, Jimmy has just switched from GameCube to cartoons. "Jimmy, come on," Marie says. It feels like his parents call his name three hundred times a day.

"Only seven or ten minutes till *Dragon Tales* are over," he says, and she goes upstairs. Four minutes later she comes back down, and Jimmy is trying to download the Starship Troopers game from the Internet. "You can look up one more thing," she says from the kitchen, "and then it's homework time."

Four-twenty-seven. "Your show is over. TV off."

"I'm not turning it off. Brianna got to do her homework in front of the TV."

"Jimmy, I'd like to see you." Pause. "Jimmy, I'd like to see you. Now."

He switches the radio to 99.1, which his dad calls the "cussing, swearing station," for its profligate use of not just "hell" (which Jimmy doesn't consider a swear anyway) but also "bitch" and "effing."

"I wish to see you now." Pause. "I wish to see you now." Seven times she says it, until the phone rings and she answers. Jimmy can't get Starship Troopers to work. He finds three slices of cheese in the refrigerator and fills a bowl to the rim with Peanut Butter Crunch cereal and milk.

"You're stalling, Jimmy. Jimmy, I asked you to take the trash out. Please do so."

Four-fifty. "Homework, please?"

Four-fifty-six. The phone rings again. Jimmy changes the screen color on the computer.

Five-oh-four. He goes outside to check the birdhouse. He turns the latch, lowers the side, and peeks in: four or five babies snuggling up to a very fluffy mom. He goes back inside, gets the old cutting board he puts his papers on, and flops it onto the ground. The best time to get information from your child is when he is trying to procrastinate; Jimmy will talk about anything to avoid his work—the skunk in the neighbor's backyard, how much he likes babka. "The baby birds are in there," he tells Marie. The television is still on.

"JIMMY!"

"Yes, I AM!"

"You show me you can get it done, and in a half-hour you'll have time for TV."

"What are you thinking? I'll finish and then I'll have no time for TV." He fetches a strawberry-cheesecake granola bar.

"Oh, I see, Jimmy. You're avoiding again?"

"I'm hungry."

"That's called avoiding. Jimmy, you're dawdling. Jimmy, you're dawdling. You may have one. That's it."

Five-oh-nine. He lies on his stomach on the rug, kicking up his left foot, staring into space, eating the granola bar. He takes his shoes off; his feet smell like old apple peels, or a filled garbage disposal left too long.

"Jimmy, go upstairs and change those socks RIGHT NOW."

"If I finish this, can we go to the mall to get a present for my communion?"

"Your father and I already got one."

"But I want Starship Troopers."

"We already picked something out, and maybe you'll get it, after the communion."

Five-eleven. He goes upstairs to change his socks and, while there, counts his money. He goes back downstairs.

Five-sixteen. He goes back upstairs to get paper.

At five-twenty-three, Jimmy starts his homework. He cuts out a bookmark for reading class, and swirls a paper shred that came off onto the scissors.

"See what my parents do?" Jimmy says. "They overemphasize." The way his dad makes him go into "overtime" when he screws up homework problems, how before a quiz his mom makes him go over not just the sample questions but also the key concepts and definitions, how they don't understand that he can't make a drawing without his favorite mechanical pencil, how when he gets a C for the quarter they make him do extra credit, even though *that* quarter is over and he's doing fine in this one. When he gets a seventy-seven on a math quiz, he fears his father's reaction. "Don't tell him," a classmate says. "Say you got an A and Ms. Knighten kept it."

"He'll call her. He's strict."

At school the Schissels are known as intense parents, "Active" with a big fat "A." Jimmy doesn't mind having them around school or on field trips; he's glad when they drop off Chick-Fil-A or cookies in the cafeteria for special occasions. He likes it when they guide him on projects, and he was grateful for his dad's mnemonic device to remember the countries of Africa.

But their checking his homework so carefully every day aggravates him: "They look at the *one* thing I did wrong." Even if they didn't check, he says, "I would do it and all. If they laid back on it—like, did it every couple of days instead of every day—maybe I'd do better in school. It stresses me out." Don't they trust him? Would it kill them—would it kill *him*—if it was good enough, instead of perfect?

The homework fights have been leading to tantrums ever since fourth grade, ever since grammar got serious and math passed division. Two or three times a year, Jimmy gets too obstinate and the argument ends in a smack. Jimmy thinks a kid his age should be "old enough to take the pain" and tries to save the tears for things like thinking about his great-grandma, who died before he got to know her, or cutting himself when he was affixing aluminum-can pieces to his bike tires so it would sound like a motorcycle. Really, when you're a sixth grade boy, you're not supposed to cry even if an inch-long splinter lodges in your finger or a hockey puck nails your crotch, because that's sissy, and sissy is gay. But when his dad hits him Jimmy always cries, half for the pain and half for the sadness.

Paul isn't proud of that; he blames himself. Like most middle schoolers, sometimes—much of the time—Jimmy can be so fun, so lovable. But, also like most middle schoolers, Jimmy has mood swings, and he can swap his lovableness, without warning, for something unimaginably frustrating. His tiny handwriting—you really do need a magnifying glass. The humming and whistling and singing ("Rudolph the Red-Nosed Reindeer" in March?) while he studies. His insistence on always using the exact long procedures he learned in class instead of his own logic, which might yield the same answer faster. When the instructions say to use resources from the worksheet, he won't accept Marie's suggestion to look on the Internet, too, because the instructions say "worksheet," not "Internet," duh. The way he can hear, over Paul clicking at the computer to his right and Marie slicing potatoes to his left, the faintest hint of music coming from Brianna's room. He marches to the stairs. "Brianna, turn it down!"

And above all when he completes his homework—they watch him finish—and it never makes it into the teacher's hand. The English assignment forgotten in between pages of the math book, the English assignment remembered in between pages of the English book but never passed up front: It is one of the largest mysteries of middle school. Solving it would have to merit some sort of Nobel, teachers figure. After Marie found out about five completed assignments never handed in, she bought Jimmy clear plastic sheets to organize his work in. It didn't make much difference, and she tries to pull back and concern herself with the important things: "Is he having fun? Is he happy? Is he learning? Is he increasing his vocabulary? Can he sustain an argument?" (An emphatic yes to that one.)

Marie is trying to get Jimmy out the door for the orthodontist, but he keeps playing piano, "Für Elise" and then "Star Wars." "He needs to listen to your mother," Brianna's friend says as the girls lie on the family room floor doing homework in front of cartoons. Jimmy grabs a twenty-ounce bottle of red Gatorade and downs it in the quarter-mile between the house and the orthodontist.

After one minute in the orthodontist's back chamber, Jimmy comes out and announces they've come on the wrong date. He takes a pack of chewy Jolly Ranchers from his pocket, unwraps one, and pops it in his mouth.

"We can take him anyway," the receptionist says.

"No, next week," Jimmy protests.

"He's already got candy in his mouth," Marie says.

"He's not supposed to do that," the receptionist says.

"The candy just turns up." It disappears at home; it appears from school. Jimmy and his friends all have this need these days, sugar every half-hour, or more. Marie found four Reese's Peanut Butter Cup wrappers in the bookshelf behind his bed the other day. Marie is glad Jimmy got braces at age eight, when he was too young to really fight it. He goes back to the chair, and she writes the check, eighty dollars for the month.

The receptionist pokes her head through the window to the waiting room. "Jimmy has a loose appliance today. This is his sixth. We start charging after five, but we won't count this one."

"This candy thing. He must have gotten it off the counter. I found it in a suitcase."

"He didn't get a star either. And I know he likes stars." The stars add up to prizes, but when your mouth literally waters for Jolly Ranchers, who can think of stars? All that effort Marie makes to follow the rules, cutting his apples into pieces. He doesn't understand that the candy does harm even when it doesn't pop out the bracket, that it bends the wires, pushes your teeth in directions they're not supposed to go.

Jimmy isn't even out the door when he pops in another Jolly Rancher.

"No candy."

"Just if I suck it! He said I can suck it."

"Jimmy."

"I'm not chewing!"

"What's the homework situation?"

"Some English, I have to finish these chapters, and math, some polynomials. They're easy."

"How many problems?"

Chewing sounds from the back seat of the Lexus.

"Give me the candy."

"I'm not chewing!"

"Give me the rest of the candy. I didn't put it on the counter so you could take it."

God, Jimmy thinks, it is like his parents are trying to rule his life. Jimmy is big into the concept of "my time," and he doesn't feel like he's getting a lot of it these days, what with the oysters and homework and his stupid teeth. He plays hoops with a neighbor in his driveway but otherwise doesn't see a lot of his friends anymore outside of school.

One afternoon a few days later, when Jimmy is supposed to stay after for aquarium club, Paul is surprised to see him walk in the door at three. Jimmy says he forgot about Aqua Havens, though really he just doesn't want to go. Paul gets mad, talks about honoring commitments, and drives him back to school. The next day Jimmy refuses to go to the Engineering Challenge contest. He doesn't tell his reasons: that he doesn't want to give an oral report and, anyway, he's sure they'll lose. Then, the same week, Jimmy won't budge from the sofa as the clock ticks toward the time of his dentist appointment, then past it. What can I do, Marie thinks, carry him there?

It was embarrassing to call the engineering teacher and apologize, and call the receptionist and apologize, and he'll have to go to the dentist eventually, and now his dad is talking about the video games "being taken out of your life." Jimmy figured his pertinacity would result in all that fighting, and afterward he says his weeklong strike "was worth it one hundred percent. I know he'll get mad. I just have to take the risk." He had to show, just for a little bit, who is in charge of Jimmy and of Jimmy's time.

Besides, the magnetic levitation car only got sixty out of a hundred points.

"Ka. Boom. That. Is. What. You. Heard. On. October. Four. Teenth. Nineteen. Forty. Seven. If. You. Lived. Near. Mur. Oc. Army. Base." Today the students in English are presenting their biography posters. After Aaron finishes stuttering about Chuck Yeager and his cheeks cannot get any redder, it's Jimmy's turn. Going through old *Calvin and Hobbes* cartoons for a poster on Bill Watterson was fun, but reading aloud is misery. Jimmy's shirt is misbuttoned at the collar; his broad shoulders and eyes point almost at the side wall. The other kids gave their presentations out in the open, but Jimmy talks from behind the teacher's counter, rubbing a roll of masking tape, sure he'll blow it. Since he has no notes, the teacher, who is holding his poster, prompts him. His eyes are scrunched a little, he looks down at the table and pauses big. He reluctantly puffs the words out of his mouth.

Last year Jimmy had little problem putting on a kilt and ruffled collar for the elementary-school production of *Macbeth*. Now he wonders if he was insane. Not even his bold classmates are immune from such nerves. Lily has been pleading with Mia to do an act together at the outdoor-ed talent show, and even though they did one last year, Mia says no way. "This is middle school," she says. "People look for the littlest thing to pick you apart."

Jimmy so hates getting up in front of people lately that he dreads his first communion, even though he doesn't have to say one word during the whole ceremony and only has to walk down the aisle in a line with the other kids. His parents held off on communion until Jimmy was old enough to really understand, but now everybody walking with him will be half his age and half his size, and he doesn't care about what it stands for anyway. Jimmy believes in God, whom he used to ask for a million dollars, but he doesn't feel like a churchy person. Maybe a private communion would be okay. "What happens if someone I know is there and doesn't like me very much and makes fun of me?"

At least, he says, he wants a sports jacket. Marie takes him to JCPenney, where, for the first time in his life, he doesn't fit into boys. Even the biggest size, twenty, is short in the torso. So they try the men's department. The men's department! A little old man takes one look at Jimmy and says, "Thirty-six short." And he's right.

The blazer is navy blue, with three smooth gold buttons at each wrist that Jimmy rubs with his thumbs as the priest speaks. The gray pants are a little tight, the blazer a little roomy, and the Looney Toons tie a little short, but Jimmy looks great. Throughout the service, he leans on his dad, bored, as his parents and sister sing out. He works on his cuticles. On his white felt banner, which hangs alongside the others on the platform of the interfaith center, the sun and goblet and host and cross are cut out perfectly, thanks to some help at home. He likes the wheat stalks the best, since they are real. For his sermon the priest goes into the aisle Oprah-style. He singles out Jimmy and asks what Jesus wanted them to learn. All he wanted was not to be embarrassed, and in front of the hundreds of parishioners he squeaks out, "I don't know."

As the parents sang "One Bread, One Body" and the children walked the aisle during rehearsal the other day, Jimmy slouched and studied the floor. When he was back on the plastic chair, feet in the aisle, leaning into his father's arm and neck, Paul told him, "Life's more interesting if you look up"; then they nuzzled, and he kissed Jimmy's head. They were the oldest parent-communicant combo, the tallest by far, and also the cuddliest. When the teacher asked, "Do you want to try again?" all the little kids said yes, except for Jimmy, who said, "No!" This time, the real thing, Jimmy walks in a straight line, military corners, faster, head down—

please, don't look. Though cameras have been banned during the service, everyone else is photographing, so Paul extends a lens the size of his forearm and shoots.

Jimmy grimaces at the wine in the chalice but toward the end of the service whispers to his mother, "It's a special occasion. Can we have Asti Spumante tonight?" Though he'd rather go home and play his new Spider-Man game all night, he knows that's out of the question, so he approves an outing for barbecue. By night's end, his legs kill from all that sitting.

i love you more than words
can say

For the first time in twelve years, Joseph oils the kitchen table, so it will look nice for the brunch the Ginsburgs are hosting the day after the Bat Mitzvah. He leaves the green turtle sandbox in the backyard, though, for another thirteen years perhaps, because he doesn't want to know what's under the plastic lid. Over the Internet he orders his favorite sour pickles from New Jersey. He hangs the photographs he used to take all the time, including one in the dining room called *Fire* that Elizabeth doesn't think looks like fire or anything else.

As long as Joseph is on this hanging kick, Elizabeth asks him to put up the crayon-shaped coat rack she made in tech ed. So he does, and while he's at it he putties the nail holes in the door and paints over them. This freaks Elizabeth out. He's not a professional! You can see streaks! They argue over whether repainting the door was part of her work request, leaving Elizabeth dreading the rest of the week. "I just know we're going to get into a big fight about something annoying," she says.

Ellen and Joseph sense Liz's stress, but they're stressed, too. Frenzied, even. At least the dress shopping goes fine: At Teens 'n Up Elizabeth picks out a lilac knee-length dress with a long matching coat that ties in front for the Bat Mitzvah service. For the party she gets a black dress with sparkly flowers and a zigzag hem. It's cocktail-length, Ellen tells her. Ellen and her neighbor Kay Stern—their daughters are having their Bat Mitzvah together—are making the centerpieces themselves, which seemed like a good idea, once.

Two weeks before the Bat Mitzvah, the Sterns come over for a wine tasting on the screened-in porch. As everyone sips from tiny Dixie cups, Laura says she's been studying every day.

"That's better than me," Elizabeth says.

"Aren't you supposed to practice two hours a day?" Ellen asks.

"No."

"Yes."

"No."

"Now I know the truth."

Elizabeth works on her Bat Mitzvah speech, but the part about her parents gives her trouble. Who knows what to say? She'll ask her Bat Mitzvah tutor. Then she works on her science. "Daddy, do you know what 'experimental group' and 'control group' means?"

Saturday morning, before the Ginsburgs leave for synagogue, Joseph gives Elizabeth the silver dollars his grandfather gave him, which date as far back as 1878. There are nine tarnished ones plus, to replace those his father spent at the market long ago, four shinier ones. She shrugs and says "Thanks." In fact, she is touched; this is her favorite gift. Later Elizabeth tells this to Ellen. Ellen tells it to Joseph.

Liz has been a wreck all week, as nervous as they've ever seen her. In the rabbi's office before the service, he tells Joseph and Ellen that, while a lot of kids in the Bat Mitzvah class were disdainful of the whole thing, acting like it wasn't cool, Elizabeth showed enthusiasm. She took it seriously.

In the same room of the interfaith center where Jimmy had his communion, Elizabeth and Laura sit in chairs next to the bimah, so poised. Elizabeth has invited several teachers—though not Miss Colyer—to the service, and this is the first time they have seen her hair down, pounds of it spiraling down her back. Laura looks at ease but Elizabeth is shivering. Joseph is telling people where to sit. "This is the day she made me a man," he says. "Look at those shoes." They are black sandals, platform; they make a tall girl taller than her father.

Ellen is amazed at how her daughter looks. So grown up. So grown up and glorious. Times like these, Joseph feels a tiny bit of selfish pride: Except the nose, Elizabeth looks like him, everyone says that. He never thought he was beautiful, but there's no doubt she is, always has been. "Oh my God," he says as he looks at her. "I'm a little nervous." Ellen is concerned about the parade of the Torah: "Do I kiss, then touch—or touch, then kiss?"

"Mom, I'm scared," Elizabeth says.

But she reads Torah and Haftarah flawlessly; her baby voice morphs almost completely into something more teenager. At the point in the service where she reads, "You shall each revere his mother and father," she exchanges smiles with Joseph. When she parades the Torah by, navigating well in her heels, Ellen kisses it. Then she reaches for her daughter's hair, but Liz is gone.

Elizabeth looks at her nails as Laura gives her speech, which is thoughtful and well written. Then Elizabeth's turn. Hers is standard Bat Mitzvah speech issue, complete with the jolty transition from "what my Bat Mitzvah means to me" to the thank-yous.

> I would like to thank many people for helping me to achieve this day. First I would like to thank you, Mom and Dad. I would like to thank you for loving and caring for me and supporting me through the ups and downs of my life. You have not only helped me prepare for my Bat Mitzvah but you helped me with school, swim team, and becoming my own person. I love you more than words can say.

When she gets to the last line, Joseph and Ellen look relieved. They are relieved. As much as their daughter has grown apart from them in all the superficial ways, she is still theirs. They are still hers. Joseph's eyes are closed, and nearly teary. Much of it, including the "I love you more than words can say," was suggested by the Bat Mitzvah tutor. But Ellen and Joseph don't know this, and to two people who haven't been thanked for loving and caring for Elizabeth since that kindergarten proclamation, the speech is no less touching for being formulaic.

Elizabeth will say later that she screwed up, because of the one time she said "all" instead of "those," but to her parents she is perfect. After all her anxiety, they are shocked by her poise. It's magical. Thirteen years down, not bad, and a long time to go.

"I never had two such girls in all my life," the rabbi says.

Between the ceremony and the party, Joseph's car runs out of gas, and he trudges along the road until an uncle picks him up, but everything else runs perfectly. Under the party tent there's a buffet, and a kiosk where you can get rainbow-colored wax molded around your hand, and a disc jockey named Jumpin' John who orchestrates line dances and a mummy-wrapping contest to "Walk Like an Egyptian," which drives the thirteen-year-olds into a determined frenzy and wastes enough toilet paper to accommodate the bathroom needs of a moderately sized village for a week. Stu, one of the few boys there, works up the courage to ask Hanna to dance. He chucks bread at Elizabeth, and she sticks out her tongue. In a couple of days the routine will take over, the intense flash of love and pride from her parents will fade, it will become all about whether Elizabeth will ever sort her presents and write thank-you notes, the science project, getting to swim practice.

But for now her dress sparkles all night long.

chapter seventeen

sometimes i wanna say stuff,
but i don't wanna say stuff

Tenacious showed up one morning before school and Eric had already left the house, after a fight with Tim. Another morning he introduced her to a rubber glove filled with water and knotted on the bottom, a face drawn on, his new friend Buddy. After work on New Year's Eve, Tenacious made it over with fifteen minutes to spare and Eric was fondling his Rollerblades, waiting with a bottle of sparkling grape juice as his dad and stepmom hung out upstairs in the bedroom.

"I feel like a bump on a log in here," he says one day.

"C'mon, Mr. Bump, let's go to school," Tenacious says, giving Eric a cheerful hug, wounded that a boy can feel like a bump on a log at his own father's house.

In middle school, who really feels like he fits in? Eric has seen one of the high schoolers flying through the parking lot with wavy blond hair and a skateboard. He's got on a maroon-plaid shirt and a red mismatched tie with his baggy cords. There's something about the guy that says Cool even though there is, probably, nobody else like him. Nothing about middle school makes Eric cool. Band doesn't make him cool. But Liam, who has older siblings, tells him that in high school band is more like a club than a class, where all sorts of people can fit in. Popularity is flexible;

there are far more niches in which to find acceptance. This, to Eric, is what high school is about.

It's not about the fat packets that sit on the desk in front of him, explaining the course options for ninth grade. They have to make a four-year plan. Pick honors classes, Mrs. Cook warns. The on-level classes, "they're a bunch of dummies. You go out there and cut the fool with the rest of them." Eric has been placed in Intro to Algebra and the Reading Acceleration Program—does this make him a dummy?—and the rest on-level classes. No room for the Italian he wanted.

The high-school stuff brings Mrs. Cook to full form. "Try to keep your binder organized—that's a good sign of becoming a scholar." "This is just a dress rehearsal." "Knowledge is contagious." "They're not going to say how cute you are and give you a good grade. They'll say, 'Did you do the work? Did you do the work? Did you do the work?' " Teray is at the shut door: "You're late," Mrs. Cook tells him, and says that, just like in high school, he'll have to wait.

One boy asks, "In high school, failing is a D, right?"

"No, you pass unless you have an F."

"Whoo-hoo," Eric says, "I'm gonna make it!"

The guidance counselor comes to talk about how they can be kept in eighth grade if they don't have at least C's in all their core subjects, but how Ms. Thomas will consider whether they come to school each day, seek extra help, work to the best of their ability. She explains the mathematics of grade-point averages, which Eric can do in his head, and when she says that an F is below 0.75, Eric says, "You must be helluv stupid to get that." Fresh sheets of paper are handed out: Write your goals for fourth quarter and how you'll get there.

"My goal is to pass," Eric says, and writes nothing.

Mrs. Cook has invited three Wilde Lake High School boys to talk about clubs and sports. Eric raises his hand when they ask who's trying out for football and then takes out his calculator and types. He shifts in his chair and knocks his instructions on class scheduling to the floor, where they'll stay. "Anyone worried about high school?" the football captain asks. "Do you worry about getting stuffed in lockers?"

"I'll be stuffing people in lockers," Eric says to himself. He has heard about Freshman Fridays, when the upperclassmen beat on the ninth graders, and about the huge essay assigned the first day of school, but Eric's not worried—the rumors about sixth grade didn't come true, did they?

The high schoolers give advice: Jog before showing up for fall sports, or else you might get a full-body cramp like this one guy who couldn't move and had to be taken to the hospital. Drink Gatorade before the game and water during. Don't turn in your permission form more than one day late. They tell about the kid who was the first to do band and football at the same time, and Eric says he'll be the second. The captain talks about what a blast Spirit Week and pep rallies are, and all the while Eric is typing SCHOOL SUCKS SCHOOL SUCKS SCHOOL SUCKS SCHOOL SUCKS.

They head to the gym for an assembly, and while they are settling on the floor Eric hears the high-school marching band. "Hey, a euphonium! That's going to be me someday." He chants with the fight song: "Go, Wilde Lake! Go, Cats!" He smiles, hums along. For a small moment he is delighted. "That's the drum major. Man, I know that whole rotation. I've been listening to it four years in a row. Four years!" Liam is typing patterns of zeros and ones into Eric's calculator.

As the assistant principal talks about schedules and orientation, as model students talk about how much freedom there is in high school and how everything is handed to you on a silver platter freshman year and how to get into the Letterman Club, as the guidance counselor explains you need twenty-one credits to graduate and you can't be in activities if you get F's this year, Eric lies on his side and lah-dee-dahs.

"How many years of social studies do you need to take?" she calls out, hoarse but cheery, arm cocked to toss a foam Wildcat paw to the eighth grader who answers right.

"Three!"

"What do you think makes the difference between students who get A's and students who get F's?"

"Nerds," Eric mutters.

"My lizard's leg is rotting away," Liam says. "We're going to leave him outside when it's below freezing. He'll fall asleep and die. It's painless."

"Man, this is gay," Eric says.

Liam shows Eric the sign-language alphabet he made up. Chris raises his hand. "If there were a girls' football team, do you think they could beat our team?"

The counselor laughs. "Any other questions?"

"I have a question," Eric says, not so quietly. "When is this bullcrap over?"

"What is the one most important thing to succeed in high school?" Another foam paw at the ready.

"Popularity," says Eric.

"Homework," says the kid who gets the paw.

The next day, the girl on Eric's side in doubles Ping-Pong lets a lot of balls past, and his street clothes have somehow gotten wet, and there's a dollar missing from his pocket. He keeps his clothes in Mr. Jackson's office, a three-dollar lock being yet another thing he doesn't want to trouble his mother for.

To add to the misery, every other day for the next three months the whole band has to go to Mrs. Bloom's classroom to prepare for the state standardized tests—in math, English, social studies, and science—in May. The grade in test-prep will count toward band—before today, Eric's only sure A. Last year's scores have just been released; they dropped significantly for Wilde Lake. The highest score in the county was seventy-eight ("those rich preppies," Eric says), and Wilde Lake's eighth graders had forty-nine, third from the bottom. Fine with them, as long as they beat Harpers Choice.

Teachers rarely explain why students have to take a given standardized test, what the scores mean, but in Eric's review session Mrs. Bloom does elaborate on the "rewards and opportunities" that come on testing week in May: no academic classes, no homework all week, daily treats like ice cream and doughnuts.

"You have to think on this test," she says, and the class groans loudly. She explains that it's "really, really, really important," and Eric has his head in his hands. Because all the feeder elementary schools have much higher grades than the middle school, it looks like Wilde Lake's teachers are doing something wrong, she says. *So this is about the teachers?* The

Maryland School Performance Assessment Program gives scores for a whole grade, not for each kid, so the students know their personal performance is never evaluated. If it's the teachers being judged, who cares? Mrs. Bloom tells them what they already know: "In elementary school, the teacher tells you something, you believe. In middle school, you start to make your own choices about these sorts of things."

Between the test prep and Ping-Pong and the gym clothes, Eric's in a really lousy mood when he gets to social studies. He's supposed to search the Constitution to see which chamber—House, Senate, or both—is granted each of the powers listed on the worksheet.

Eric hasn't been Horshak with the eagerly raised hand lately, but this is something else entirely. He's not moving at all. Mrs. Conroy makes it to the back corner of the room to check homework and asks him, "Do you have the terms?"

He shakes his head no.

"Why?"

"I didn't know we had to do it."

"Let me see your agenda." She points. "It's right there. I suspect you forgot to look." Tapping. Shrugging. "What are you going to write with? You've broken both your pencils. Want to sharpen one?" No response.

She moves on, and when she tells the class they can work with partners, Shawn comes over. "I could be in GT," Eric says while setting Shawn's watch. Shawn copies the worksheet into his notebook in case he loses one or the other. Ever since all the D's on his last report card and the nightmare he had one night about still being stuck in eighth grade at age thirty, he has cracked down on himself.

Eric writes a capricious series of letters down the answer column— B S H B how about an H here S's are cool all in a line S S S—until Shawn takes his shredded pencil away. "Stop tapping, man." The rest of the students are working. "C'mon, let's do this."

"I'm done."

Shawn puts his head in his hands. "Why me? Here, Eric, I found number four."

"Whatever. Mrs. Conroy, I'm finished."

"I'll be there in a second." She comes over, checks. "How did you do that?"

"I looked in the book."

"How did you do it so fast? Eric, what's going on?"

Eric chews on his calluses. "I'll get at least one of them right."

"Show me where you found these."

"Why?"

"Because the teacher instructed you to."

"Why?"

"Because that's the assignment."

"Why?"

"I'll be back when you're ready to succeed."

Mrs. Conroy, too, has read all about middle schoolers' being just like toddlers. She knows how a class with them can feel more like managing than teaching. She knows that when teachers get into power struggles with middle schoolers the kids never give up, and nobody wins. When teachers' frustrations get the better of them and they stop trusting the kids and focus above all on keeping them docile, the class is doomed.

Another thing she has noticed: Behavior has deteriorated over the years, especially when there are family problems but even when there are not. So, six months after the positive-and-negative-consequences sessions, six months after the sixth graders were stunned to see classmates talking back to the teacher and getting away with it, the way the misbehavior of the recalcitrant minority changes the tone of a classroom is part of the landscape. The kids have become acutely aware of the teachers whose threats are empty, who when a boy shouts "Piss!" say, "You can't use that type of language in this class," but he does, again and again. Even when the obstruction doesn't involve cussing, it can be equally insidious, like Eric's at the moment, in the amount of teacher attention it sucks up.

In Eric's case, he is just pissed off. But many middle-school boys know what research has proved: that the more aggressive and defiant they are, the more popular their peers will perceive them to be. More than anything in the world they want to look cool, and doing extra credit and paying attention in class instead of goofing off do not win points with their pals. Class schedules at Wilde Lake are assigned by a secretary with a click of the mouse—"Too many there, I'll move some here"—so tinderbox combinations occur, of kids who might behave fine when apart.

By this late in the year, it has gotten to the point where, even if an event demands audience participation, the immediate instinct of the teachers is to shush everyone.

After misbehaving and being sent to the principal to fill out action forms, which ask, "Why do you think you were sent to the office?" students write things like, "Because Mrs. Wright blamed me for talking and I wasn't even talking." The most commonly uttered sentence at Wilde Lake Middle School? "But I didn't do anything!" If you believe the kids, teachers have made up 95 percent of the infractions out of thin air. Sometimes parents back the teachers; just as often, they don't. "It's like *Divorce Court*," one guidance counselor says. "It's never anyone's fault."

The teachers love their kids, love their jobs at the core. But for many it has become beyond hard. After thirty-three years at this, Mr. Wolfe, a seventh-grade social studies teacher, sums it up: "I'm tired of the kids' talking back, the parents' talking back, the lack of interest in learning. It used to be fun. I'm not having fun anymore." And he's one of the teachers the kids really like, and behave for.

In math, Ms. Adams starts a lesson on surface area, but Eric and David are talking on their calculators:

> *Wassup*
> *Nottin*
> *I want to go home*
> *That's always*
> *I broke the kingpin on my back trucks*

Ms. Adams is filling out a sheet on the overhead: How many sides does a cylinder have, how many faces, what's the formula for area. David says, "My stomach hurts." "Mine, too." "What did you have for lunch?"

> *I got peperroni*
> *Pepporoni*—delete. *Pepperoni*
> *Uuuhh*

Ms. Adams holds up the wooden cylinder and a ruler. "What's the diameter of this circle? The radius is two-point-five."

Dude I hate school

While half the class is making its way to $SA = 2B + 2H = 19.63$, Eric tells David, "I bought this new CD yesterday, it's so cool. Slipknot. I'm going to make chicken patties and chicken-flavored Oodles of Noodles when I get home." Prisms make their way across the room, and kids measure and calculate, while Eric and David's side conversation segues to looks. Except for his toes, Eric thinks he's "ugly as heck," and it's not low self-esteem to say so if it's true. Most of the class is figuring out the formula at hand, but Eric is typing the alphabet, forward and back. David types the lyrics to "Paranoid" by Green Day.

"What are we supposed to do?" Eric asks David.

David shrugs.

"I can't go to Homework Club today, because I can't stay in school another minute. It's only two o'clock!"

Ms. Adams catches them talking. "This is worth twenty points of classwork," she warns.

"Well, I just lost twenty points."

"Eric, look at what I just wrote."

"That's, like, half the song." Eric and David think about doing the problem the other groups did four problems ago, but then they'd have to erase the song. They try calculating on paper, but they think the diameter is the circumference and the radius is the diameter.

"Two and a half is the circumference, so half of that is one and a half."

"No, 'cause one and a half and one and a half is three, so it's one-point-five." They demonstrate skateboarding moves with the rectangular prism. "Man, I was so close to a kickflip yesterday. Then my truck broke while I was ollieing off the curb."

Eighteen minutes of this, then the bell rings.

Beulah has just found out she's pregnant, and Eric, who has no idea how he'll ever get any work done with a baby around, enjoys coming home to a quiet house while it lasts. Well, if not quiet, at least the kind of noises he is used to. Rap booms from upstairs as Eric sits on the sofa with his math book; Thomas's stereo is so good and so loud, it sounds like there's a live show up there. It's distracting, but Eric figures there's no use asking him to turn it down. *Hey Arnold!* is on TV. "Aw, Jesus, man," Thomas shouts upstairs, as something falls to the ground. Eric writes the answers to eight of his math problems quick and tiny across two lines of torn-out loose-leaf, and skips the other two.

He doesn't know his science assignment and doesn't know the number of Homework Hotline, so he lies down for a while. When he gets up, he calls Shawn for the hotline number and hears page 159, numbers one to nine. One fifty-nine doesn't have any questions, though, so he does the ones on 172. Thomas yells down that he's getting in the shower and leaves instructions on what to say if various girls call. Eric drinks Kool-Aid and eats wings. The phone rings; Thomas comes downstairs and says nobody's coming home tonight. Beulah's gone out with their dad to spend the night in his truck.

Eric plays with his skate, which is missing the middle wheel, and decides to go outside. He blades back and forth across the same seven squares of sidewalk. His skates are so strong, he says, that the only way they'd break is if you landed on them after doing five somersaults from the roof. He likes to fall, because falls are "learnable," meaning they tell you what to do better next time. He likes to do a Macchio, in which he skates to the stoop, jumps, and stops himself on the edge of the first step. Hockey practice starts Saturday. It will be the best day of his life.

Behind the building, as the light fades, younger kids play kickball with a squashy old soccer ball, rutted patches of dirt for bases. Eric joins in, but the kids argue after every other play, and he wearies of trying to defuse the anger. Inside, he soaks up the peace of nobody's-home. He rings his mom at work, gets through after three tries, three times lowering his voice: "Yes, may I have extension seventy-seven, please? May I speak with Tenacious Epps, please?"

He tells her about the Ping-Pong and the gym clothes. "We'll buy a lock," she says. "Mr. Jackson has better things to do than watch your stuff." He tells her how he likes Ms. Drakes but she's boring, and Tenacious says, "I know. You've just got to deal with it. Middle school is over. This is preparation for high school." When he says, "Ma, it's eighth grade," she says, "Yes, a stepping-stone to ninth grade." "Trust me," she always says, about algebra, English, whatever. "I know you don't see the connection, but there is one."

This morning, when Tenacious saw the A+ Eric had gotten on an English vocab quiz, she said, "Great! That's awesome. Why can't you do work like this all the time?" She's the best encourager of all time. After he gets off the phone, Eric sees a Hot Wheels commercial and imagines the house they're going to live in one day, maybe as soon as his mom has her next paycheck. He's going to collect Hot Wheels in the basement. Catonsville, he imagines, near his friend James, who says it's a good school even though, after there was a food fight once, lunch was like a prison—no snacks, no fries. If he can't move, Eric at least wants a bomb to blow up Wilde Lake, or, rather, every Howard County school, so they can't find another place to transfer everyone.

Before he walked home today, Eric told Mrs. Conroy about the locker-room incident, and she said he could finish his worksheet at home. But instead he watches *As Told by Ginger* and *Rocket Power* and wrestling, and at eight goes to Safeway for a Three Musketeers. When he returns, he sees the kickball boys pushing each other hard and spinning out in an abandoned red plastic toddler-car. The red looks extra good illuminated by the parking-lot lights. Eric takes a turn. Somewhere there is a sad two-year-old without his wheels, but these boys are thrilled.

After Eric got a second-quarter report card with an F in science, Tenacious said hockey would be over if he didn't bring his grades up. So he starts doing his work, simple as that—not the research paper due in May ("due in May": that means "do in May," right?) but at least what's due the next day. Plus, for the last month Eric's brother Tim, who's taking a semester off from college, has been staying on the couch with him. Whether Eric wants to or not, Tim brings him in the kitchen every night to go over homework. He explains why certain answers are wrong and makes Eric explain why other answers are right. Especially in math, Tim is a good explainer. This feels good, both the doing it right and the doing it with someone.

"I know I should do my work anyway," Eric says, "but it's nice to have somebody care." And it makes a difference. It says so right there on the awards bulletin board:

> Ms. Adams' March Student of the Month is Eric Ellis because he has found that working hard—and persevering—has rewards both academically and personally.

For third quarter he gets A's in gym and band and a B in math and brings his English and academic-enrichment grades up, too. Eric jumps around, proclaiming this the best report card ever, though it isn't, and science is still an F. There are GT kids who cry over 89.7's, but most of Eric's classmates say they did well even if they didn't. One girl, bummed about one C, takes a look at Eric's report card and can't believe he's all excited about *that*. "My mom is going to be so happy!" Eric says.

But as quickly as it started, Tim gets into an argument with William and has to move out. Eric starts tagging along with Ms. Adams as she packs up after class, sitting in her office as she marks grades, sitting in the computer lab as she enters them in the computer, sometimes as late as seven. He still does the work—enough so that roller hockey won't be at risk—but he goes back to doing it sloppily, incompletely, not showing his work. "I don't care," he tells Ms. Adams as he eats her snacks, " 'cause no one else does."

"You've got to do the work," she says, and even lets him do makeup work, against her policy. She doesn't want to tell parents they're making unwise decisions or butt in, but as soon as Eric leaves one evening at six, Ms. Adams calls Tenacious.

"Eric seems really sad about not living with you. He seems very unhappy."

Tenacious says she knows; she wants to change it but doesn't know how. She suggests that Ms. Adams set up a meeting with William. The social worker, whom Eric has told recently that people are teasing him about his weight, comes to the meeting. His seventh-grade reading teacher is there, too.

It's no mystery to the staff that Eric's home situation has a huge amount to do with his academic problems and his behavior, and that worse problems could emerge soon if it doesn't improve. Eric feels cared for at school right now, which helps—and it's because he feels that way that he spends so much time at school when he doesn't have to—but that's no replacement. At home Eric does not feel at all "connected," to use the experts' word.

"He used to always talk about you," the teachers tell Eric's father. The social worker says she's impressed by Eric's maturity, his openness, how family means a lot to him. "Eric is grieving," the teachers tell William. He misses his mom and is sad that he doesn't get one-on-one time with his dad anymore. William says he travels a lot and because of company policy can no longer take Eric with him in the truck on weekends, though that might change back. He says his Masons time and motorcycle time are sacred, his only pure indulgences.

William has sensed Eric's mood changing, but at the same time, he has always figured Eric tells him everything and would say if something was wrong. Whenever William calls home from the road, he asks whoever answers, "Is everything okay?" The answer's always yes, so he has no idea the tension is building. Eric feels deserted by his dad and deserted by his mom and deserted by his brothers, but he loves them too much to get mad at them—so he gets mad at Beulah. He complains in the meeting that Beulah doesn't want to cook or clean. He scrubs the floor, doesn't feel important, doesn't feel like his housework is acknowledged. Eric talks about a recent time when he asked Beulah for a hug and she wouldn't give it, and about the assignment he wanted to put on the refrigerator.

"Sometimes I wanna say stuff," Eric says, "but I don't wanna say stuff, 'cause I don't want to hurt anyone's feelings."

William feels caught in the middle. "Son, you can tell me anything."

"But I can't tell *her* anything. Sometimes I don't get her."

It's not like anything is solved, but it feels good to open up. Oh, the teachers tell William, one other thing. Eric really wants to be taken to skating. And so the conversation moves to the logistics of driving Eric on Friday nights, as if a ride to the roller rink will solve his problems.

chapter eighteen

another survivor of the woods

Even though at his house Jimmy and Will play MechWarrior 4: Vengeance and SSX Tricky, and at Will's house they tell ghost stories with flashlights under their chins and wrestle, even though whoever's the guest always fights his parents when it's time to go home, even though they can discuss for ages whether you can drown in your own spit and whether your balls can pop while you climb the rope in PE, even though the photo of the two of them still smiles over both boys as they sleep, Jimmy doesn't put Will on his cabin-request form for the sixth-grade camping trip.

After all, Will still brags that he knows where Andorra is and makes Jimmy feel bad about his grades and stuffs his gray binder so fat and heavy that he spends all day scooching it up with his right thigh. Jimmy has added Will to his teasing list at school, while he himself has discovered that a well-timed belch in music class makes popular boys laugh.

"I'm not going to be friends with Will," he says, "because he's not going to be cool. Unless he's the first person to go up on one of those rocket things, and he's on TV and famous."

Jimmy does get Rich Stoessel in his cabin. Bad enough the boys have found out Camp Ramblewood is a nudist colony in the summer, but to have to spend two nights in a cabin with someone they're sure is gay? Because they don't want Rich taking pictures of them naked, the group makes a rule: no going in the bathroom while someone is showering.

As they stand around a science-room table the day before the trip, gluing felt letters to their cabin banner, one of the boys announces, "Rich has no dick."

"He probably has a dick," Ben says.

"But a small one," Jimmy says. "I'm so much taller than you it's, like, not even funny."

"You're so much *what*?"

"I'm so much taller than you it's, like, not even funny. Stand up."

"No."

"Why not?"

"I don't like being made to feel short."

"You can't take any pain. You can't even take a spider bite." He pinches Ben's skin with his thumb and middle finger and presses his index finger in.

"Don't!"

In the room next door, a tube of fabric paint squirts all over Mia's pants leg. Her eyes tear up, and Lily comes to the rescue with her gym shorts. Of course she put Mia and Beth on her cabin-request form. Mia told her friends she put them all down, even though the teacher said to list only two, and winds up with Alexandra and not Lily. Lily is unhappy about this, but she's glad at least to be with Beth, and glad to see Mia out on the soccer field wearing her very own shorts.

The next morning there are four buses for kids and two for luggage, which includes many hair dryers and stuffed animals and Jimmy's Batman pillow and even some blankies. Lily and Beth are first in line, and behind them is Mia, who has decided to sit by herself. They take the very last seats, which they never get to do when eighth graders are around. They make HELLO signs on loose-leaf and press them to the back window, so Jimmy and his friends can see. The boys sing "Ninety-Nine Bottles of Beer," but the health teacher stops them, so instead they strum air guitars and make up goofy rhymes and get truckers to honk.

When they arrive at Camp Ramblewood, nobody is nude, fortunately, and the activities begin right away. Two dads lead Jimmy's group down a path to the confidence course and explain: Cross a wobbly log suspended between two trees, hug the tree, and scooch around to a rope, cross that while holding on to a more flaccid rope, swing through a set of five tires suspended just far apart enough to be tricky but not impossible, traverse a series of ropes hung like U's and then another set of loose double ropes, walk a very high log (this one at least secure), then scale a rope web to a platform way up in a tree. If your feet touch the ground, start over.

Two boys and a girl go before Jimmy, and from his perspective they have no trouble. Some people scooch across the first log on their butts, Colin dashes across it, and Jimmy crawls on his tummy, getting it on his first try, along with stains on his long white T-shirt. He makes it through the first rope okay, nicks the ground twice from the tires but nobody sees, struggles through the U's, then gets to the ropes crossed like an X.

He freezes. He leans backward, his belly slight but visible under his shirt. "I'm scared," Jimmy tells the dad. "I can't do it. I'm scared."

It looked so easy for everyone else. It always looks easy for everyone else.

Times like this, it's clear to Jimmy that God all of a sudden has anointed a privileged section of the sixth-grade jocks, and he is not one of them. The second he misses a catch in kickball he's yelled at, and the second he misses a kick the pitcher says, "You can't kick!" "You can't pitch!" he shouts back. Flag football gives him cramps, and when he misses a high spiral off the tip of his fingers, a girl—a girl!—says, "Bum!"

"I'm not a bum."

"You should be glad I'm making you something."

Jimmy quit his lacrosse team last month because he didn't like getting hit or hitting back, and went to Play It Again Sports to trade his stick and pads for a skateboard. In floor hockey there's always this one boy who appoints himself center forward, plays the whole court, yells at everyone who does anything minutely wrong, which often enough includes Jimmy. As for his plan to start running, it turns out Jimmy is dog-tired when he gets home from school. And, typical of a boy in puberty, lazy in ways he never used to be. At soccer, he's not bad but isn't aggressive, is only half in the game. Before practice he prays for rain and, though he is afraid of storms, blesses the lightning that eventually arrives.

It's not like he wants to be a jock. There's something appealing about how comfortable they are in their bodies, but you know what's sad about them? They're so cocky that they drive crazy. "A lot of them die in car accidents," Jimmy says. "It pisses me off."

Still and all, it would be nice to be able to cross these goddamn ropes, since everyone's watching.

"Yes, you can," the dad says.

I'm gonna fall, Jimmy thinks, I should start lifting weights and doing curl-ups. Out loud, barely, he says, "I can do it. I can do it."

He inches across the low rope, gripping the high rope tight, wobbling. Wobbling. His arms feel weak. The lighter boys had it easier, the lacrosse boys had it easier, maybe he never should have quit the team.

"I can do it."

Even though Jimmy Schissel may never be a Jock with a capital "J," there is a part of him that can take his blue Mongoose around the cul-de-sac three times in 27.4 seconds. There is a part of him that once in a while magically catches passes in the end zone. There is a part of him that, when the spiky-haired little neighbor boy mouths off, takes chase, sending the eight-year-old tearing away in fear. There is a part of him that last week couldn't keep himself from checking with his lacrosse stick in gym class. When Darnell checked back, Jimmy kept going, and when Darnell said "Fuck you, stupid," even though he knew it might turn every black kid in the school against him, Jimmy took a swing.

On the ropes a part of Jimmy still wobbles. And the other part impels himself across.

Then—the tall log. "I'm scared," he announces, and inches forward on his stomach, his blue surf shorts riding up. Slowly, he makes it across, and leaps to the unsteady web of ropes. If I drop, he thinks, nothing will be holding me but the net, and that will hit the ground, too. Some kids scaled this in four swift scampers, but Jimmy Schissel has not yet been bitten by a magic spider, and it takes him a while.

"Another survivor of the woods," he declares from atop the platform, a thicket of leaves crowning his head.

The buzzword for outdoor education is "team-building." Remove students, teachers, and parents from the normal school atmosphere, let them unify into a cohesive group, and in the meantime have some educational fun in a world some kids never get to explore. In several ways, the planned bonding takes place. But, just like in a Victorian costume drama, being in the country lays everything bare, and inhibitions collapse. Some teams fall apart.

At the arts-and-crafts table Lily is knotting pink, blue, green, and purple embroidery floss into a bracelet for Mia. Mothers sit in the shade nearby, sharing snippets of love that their boys have allotted—he hugged me in front of everyone at the buses this morning! he made pancakes with me! "Last week," one mom says, "I came home and there was a bouquet of roses on the kitchen table from my eighth grader, and he wrote a note. He said, 'Mommy, thank you for helping me on *The Odyssey.*'"

"Awwww," the other moms say, jealous of the note, not the flowers.

One mother says that her boy, Joe, has gotten moodier, that "he is the one on the outside now," but she doesn't want to be one of those mothers who call and complain, and anyway, "they're nice boys." On the other side of camp, on a rolling green lawn, the nice boys play tag with Joe around an old blue metal swing set.

"One two three NOT IT!"

"You're It."

"No fair. I heard Paul last."

"You're It. Just be It. I swear I will beat you up."

During freeze tag with movie titles, they quickly run out of options, after everyone has tried *Star Wars Episode II: Attack of the Clones* at least twice. (Memories don't go far past *The Sandlot*, and *The Lion King* is as old-fashioned as it gets.) Jimmy drops to a squat with a movie title every time It nears, rather than run. The boys trap Joe on the slide and decide he's It. Every time he tags someone, they change the rules to somehow invalidate the tag. A dad watches from a porch nearby, but from the middle distance the torture is invisible.

"Get Joe!" Jimmy says. "You're not It yet." Somebody bangs the slide, and the metal reverberates under Joe's feet. "You're not It yet."

"I didn't know."

"You didn't know? That's brilliant."

"You have to count, stupid. You can't catch him really fast. It's not hide-and-seek, it's freeze tag."

"Oh my gosh, Joe, you're going in the wrong area."

"He can't even get up the slide!"

"I'm not playing," Joe says.

"Yes, you are."

"No, I'm not."

"You're a wuss."

Joe heads off and bumps Jimmy on the way.

"He kicked Jimmy!" Joe goes off to his cabin. "Did you guys see Joe last year in the music room? He was yelling, 'I quit everything!' He was crying and throwing stuff."

Lily's cabin, which they've named "The Bubbles," is stuffy, but the girls don't want to open the wooden shutters because then ghosts will come through the window screens. Not ghosts "like *wooo-hoooo*," one girl explains, wiggling her fingers, but, rather, "like spirits." Not ghosts that will kill you, just ghosts that will possess your body and loot your belongings. There has got to be some reason for the blood on the ceiling.

Bugs—they're creepy, too. The girls ask each other to stand sentry by the shower in case of spiders—"I'll wear my swimsuit, don't worry." By day's end the stories about what's transpired in the cabins have intensified in the telling: the cockroaches that sallied forth from the drain during someone's shower, the frog that jumped from the toilet drain, one girl's nosebleed oozing from her eyes so bad they were going to pop out of their sockets, the tarantula as big as a saucer that Mrs. Lewinsohn killed.

Besides Lily and Beth, the five swimmers are in the cabin, all of whom Lily likes. It might be that, it might be a sugar high from the warehouse-club sacks of Jolly Ranchers and Twizzlers Beth's mom and the other chaperone brought—whatever the reason, she is a cyclone whenever she's inside these wooden walls. When visitors eye the loot splayed out on the cots, Lily says, "Hey, our candy, not yours!" When the girls do the cancan and sing, "We're the Bubbles, the slippery sticky Bubbles," as Beth and Lily blow soap bubbles, Lily stops and says, "I stink like shit." She puts scented lotion in her armpits. When she changes, she declares, "Close your eyes, Lily's going down!"

That night at the assembly, the talent-show acts—a rock trio, a Britney Spears dance, two piano solos, a long skit about a birthday party, a house-stopping dance to "Thriller," a soul trio—receive honest and sustained applause, though each group rushes off the stage when done, embarrassed. The teachers don clown suits and wigs and goofy shoes for a completely zany version of *Cinderella*, which brings the kids to the edge of their seats. They say they are glad they didn't have to make "idiot fools" of themselves, but that's exactly what they loved so much about their teachers for one night.

Back in the cabin Lily nurses her sunburn. "This lotion has no freakin' aloe!"

"Lily," Beth's mom says, "I'm gonna spank you."

Beth says, "Lindsey thinks Lily's a lesbian, because she saw her giving me a piggyback ride."

Lily marches around the cabin comparing her legs with everyone's: "Mine are sexier." On Beth's bed, the two sing, "Apples and bananas in my soup, loopdy loopdy loopdy loop." Lily lies on her back with a pillow between her knees, kicking her legs, clapping her hands. She lets out a huge belch. She flips back and forth. She stomps to the other side of the cabin. "Bethie said I peed in the bed!" She leaps from bed to bed.

"Don't bounce on the beds," Beth's mom says.

"I didn't bounce, I leapt. Oh, pillow, how I love you, pillow. I could kiss you, pillow."

"Please, Lily."

She bangs her leg. "Shit."

"She just said the 's' word!"

"Lily, stop cussing."

Lily gives another sturdy belch. "Belches are loud and burps are silent. Farts are loud and poots are silent."

"I'm going to get dressed," Maddy says. "That means if my towel falls don't look at my butt."

"Drawers have two holes in them," Lily continues, "for the boy's thing to go through. Underwear has elastic around the waist."

"What's the difference between Lily and Beth?"

"Lily's much more politer and Beth's more bossier."

"What's the difference between boys and girls?"

"Boys have one thing that sticks out straight and two things that"— Lily cups her hands.

"What's the difference between socks and shoes?"

And on and on, until the chaperones shut it down. Lily announces good nights around the cabin: "Good night, Abby!" "Good night, Lily."

"Good night, Beth!" "Good night, Lily." "Good night, Dale!" "Good night, Lily." Six more times, until finally she is silent, though far from asleep.

Four cabins away, Alexandra and a girl named Lynn won't shut up. "Be quiet!" girls yell from the other side of the cabin partition. "We're trying to go to sleep!" Finally, after a half-hour, one of the mothers says, "Cut it out, you guys." In the morning, their side of the cabin tries to sleep in and the other side makes noise. They tell them to shut up, as if they have that right, and Mia goes over to make a truce. She is shooed away.

The second night, things get bizarre. One girl says another girl took her bandana, as if there is no possibility in the universe they could own the same bandana, and tensions are so high the teachers separate them at dinner. Someone started a rumor that Valerie said she was going to dump her boyfriend and go out with Devon, and her friends are desperate to defuse the situation before she gets beaten up. Devon would have killed for this kind of attention last year. "But now," he says, "you don't know how annoying this is." Valerie keeps her eye out for anyone who looks like she's flirting with Devon ("Oh no, not Alexandra!"). In one cabin a boy is dancing and another boy says, "That's my move." "No, it's mine." Poom, there's a punch, and the kid who did the hitting packs up and heads into the dark, where a teacher sees him during a cabin check and he is sent home. Abigail Werner's cabinmates had left her out of their talent-show act, saying the dance steps were too confusing. She stews over it and when she gets back to the cabin tries to hold it in as long as possible, which isn't that long, and says, "You didn't let me in the cabin song because I'm white."

"Are you calling me racist?" asks Felicia, her best friend since second grade.

"Yes."

Whoops. She's mad at herself for saying that and winds up crying all night, and her mom, who is chaperoning, doesn't feel comfortable stepping in, and on the other side of the cabin the girls listening to the fight complain of stomachaches and headaches, cry because there is no night-light, beg to go home. Ms. Thomas sends three girls from Abigail's cabin to Mia's, where Alexandra has moved out because she felt like being with

Tamika ("I guess she doesn't like me that much now," Mia tells her mom), and Carla's crying because she's never been away from her mom, much less in a place like this, and Lynn's leaving, too, because she was pretending she was struck blind, even though a chaperone who happened to be an ophthalmologist said she was fine, and she miraculously regained her sight for the talent show and lost it again afterward, at which point everyone, including Mia's mom, Leigh, had to help her around. The teachers told her if she was blind she should lie down in the infirmary, and she said that would give her a headache, so they said, "Okay, you're going home." At ten-thirty Leigh Reilly is packing Lynn's bags in the dark, and Mia is wondering if her cabin situation could be any worse.

When Lily arrives home the next day, her mother asks how the trip was.

"Fine."

"How was your cabin?"

"Fine."

"How was Mia's cabin?"

"Better."

spring

she started humping me!
and i was like :-o

It comes in the spring sure as tulips, the time when sixth graders turn into middle schoolers. The dramas that unfolded on the camping trip weren't a simple case of cabin fever; they were a harbinger of things to come.

It takes Mr. Vega, who student-taught last year only in the fall, by surprise: the snobbiness, the cattiness, the spleen. They'll just announce, "I don't like Jordan, Mr. Vega." A girl comes up to him after school and says, "Mr. Vega, the rumors are true." Please, he thinks, don't let someone be pregnant. "Alicia and Julie and them are talking about me behind my back." One girl issues Mr. Vega an ultimatum: Let me switch from clarinet to sax, or I'll quit. He kinda wishes he'd said, "Okay, quit band," for all the trouble it's caused. After making the switch, she gets to practice in the hall with another girl, and they goof off for the first fifteen minutes, at least. When he calls her on it she shoots back, "Not fair," or "Whatever."

At least fifteen kids ask to go to the bathroom during each half-hour practice. They stand up as if sleepwalking and head across the room; they stop in the middle of a song while the other fifty kids play and say, "My folder is broken," or "Can I show you my practice chart?" The trombones are suddenly paranoid that someone is moving their music. "I guess their hormones are changing so fast," Mr. Vega says, "they can't remember anything."

"They're getting crazy," Ms. Thomas says. The last two months of the year, fights break out, physical and emotional. Friendship groups split apart—for the moment, anyway. Your supposed best friend invites you to her lake house and then the weekend comes and she's at the lake with two other girls. Another friend is mad because you both thought to bring cupcakes for the reading teacher's birthday, another friend is mad because you said you do the Cha-Cha Slide better, and another friend is all of a sudden saying you insult her too much, even though you've been insulting each other all your lives, as a joke. This girl has removed you from the "I wanna say hi to all my friends" part of her IM profile, and you get so mad you can't remember why.

"It seems like everyone is ganging up on me these days and taking sides, like I'm a nobody," one seventh grader says. "Like, one day we'll be really cool and hanging out, and the next day one of them is all mad at me for saying the wrong thing." The girls are wondering if it's worth it to be popular, if having thirty "friends" they talk to only in school but who always pull them into some sort of drama is any better than the way it used to be, when they each had three good friends, three true friends. It seems small to an outsider, but these spells are huge to the girls who suffer them. They will make up in weeks, days, hours; the friendships are restored and the cruelty disappears. The anxiety, however, is there to stay. Even if a girl makes new friends, it doesn't compensate for the intense crisis of confidence she's endured, a crisis that her athletic skills or her intelligence or her good relationship with her family can mitigate but not erase. Her mother, who used to know all her daughter's friends, who orchestrated their play dates, may ask why those girls don't call anymore. She shrugs. "They're just jealous of you," her mom says. "You're so wonderful." This means nothing to her in the scheme of things, and she kind of wants to explain the whole thing to her mom, but at the same time she doesn't, because she wants to handle it on her own.

God, this sort of thing drives Ms. Thomas nuts. "Best friends one day and the next day they hate each other. And the girls just don't let it go. Boys, if they have an issue, they get it out and it's over. Girls, it can linger for quite a while. So dramatic. Ugh. They're looking for ways to be more independent, they see slights that aren't there, they're overly sensitive. That can be a bit wearing." Girls and their meanness are all over the literature right now, the subject of the hottest sessions at educational conferences and the hottest books in stores (with diagrams and code names for where people stand in the social web). Consultants visit schools to help with "clique-busting." Ms. Thomas attempts her own clique-busting, but the effort is Sisyphean. For example, she convenes what she thinks is a successful meeting of a group of seventh-grade girls who are getting in each other's business and yelling at each other for getting in their business, but an hour later, at lunch, one of the girls is ragging another about a fight her little sister got in and she storms out of the cafeteria yelling, "Shut! The! Fuck! Up!"

Chaos like this isn't Mia's or Lily's style. Their modus operandi, when they are annoyed, is gossip, though only so much as they consider good-natured and harmless. Gossip is the glue that holds together many middle-school friendships, a conflict-avoidant way to let people know what bugs you about them—word almost always gets back, after all—but in such an indirect fashion that the gossiper remains protected, and so does the friendship. Alone, Mia and Lily discuss which of their friends are mean and which are posers, in that they copy everyone else (as if they'd be spared a hard time if they didn't).

Mia spends as many as four hours a day on the Internet, instant-messaging the two hundred kids on her buddy list. Usually kids' profiles include lists of inside jokes, and many are meant for Mia:

Mimi~DOGS DOGS . . . lol . . . chic yet humorus, sophisticated yet sexy. . . . 123456 . . . u ripped my jacket!! . . . say it like u mean it. . . . im a bluie!!! . . . she grabbed ur butt @ da rink! ooooo we have soo many more insides.

Mia's insides:

lisa and alexandra—Cheerleading! Dancing! Guuurls! haha lylas!*
lisa—oh too many insides!!:-/ lylas!
Lunch table—the most beautiful pringle display i have seen in my WHOLE life!!
alexandra—she started humping me! and i was like :-O

If Lily ever went online—she rarely does; she has several girls on her IM list, "but they don't even talk to me"—she might see that her affections for Mia have become an inside joke among the girls: "She started humping me!" "She grabbed ur butt . . . !" This revelation serves as a litmus test: In elementary school we goofed all over each other, but we're in middle school now, we're being watched, is this okay? And in some way it's not about Lily at all. It's about appearing to know a lot of good juice without appearing to be the one who spread it. It's about discovering who stands where in the organizational chart of life. It's about turning something uncomfortable into a joke. It's about the seductive power of having people listen to you, of having this thing you started become an *inside*!

This kind of gossip could wreck a girl for good—it doesn't take much at this age—but it never gets back to Lily, it's not really about her anyway, and nobody shuts her out. Mia and Lily are true friends, after all, and Mia has no desire to ruin that.

Lily knows that her best friend has several worlds she will never be a part of, that Mia doesn't *need* the relationship as much as she does, but that's the price of friendship with the popular girl. With her other friends Mia plays sports, she kicks around the neighborhood, she talks online. She had thirty people—twice as many as Lily even *knows*, she figures—to the roller rink for her birthday party in February. The present Lily carefully picked out, a stuffed bunny with buck teeth and a pink T-shirt that says HUGS in little rhinestones, looked so insignificant on the huge gift-wrapped pile. Tonya was there, a girl from Clemens who goes to a different middle school, skating around loud and bossy. Mia doesn't quite comprehend that she's popular, but Tonya, she knows, *she's* popular. Lily avoided her, because a few weeks earlier they all went to the mall and Tonya wouldn't go to the store Lily wanted to, so she practically cried until Mia went with her, and then they were late for their ride home. Alexandra said she'd be at the party but she didn't show up, which happens with her sometimes. Even though two months ago Mia agreed with Lily that no sixth-grade boys are cute, four boys were at her party, though they stayed away from the girls. Lily and Beth kept to themselves, too, without much to say, and during cake time watched as the other girls noisily plunged sporks in their hair.

When school lets out early, Mia sometimes goes to the Giant with her other friends. They never invite Lily, so she misses out on teasing the boys by the dried-up fountain, gossiping about whose hair is ugly, dancing with stuffed Easter Bunnies in the Seasonal aisle, going back to Mia's rec room to watch a man discuss his diaper obsession and a woman practically rape her sister on *Jerry Springer.*

"We live less than a mile away from the Giant," Lily says. "But if I'm not invited, then I won't ask."

Another other world of Mia's is that all of a sudden Alexandra is back in the picture as if she never disappeared. Lily barely acknowledges her. "I couldn't come to *Peter Pan,*" Alexandra nicely tells Lily, who turns the other way. At lunch Alexandra says, "I'm going to Bingo Night with my mom and Mia." Lily says she already invited Mia, who turned her down for a soccer game, and later rolls her eyes and tells Mia, "*Alexandra* said you're going to bingo." The way Lily sees it, she's been paying her dues all year with Mia, and Alexandra hasn't. How fair is that for her to hop right back in? The way Mia sees it, she's friends with both, and she and Alexandra had a lot of fun together playing stupid-dress-up not long ago, purple lipstick all over their mouths and dresses hanging from their legs. At the end of the play date, Alexandra lent Mia her best teddy bear. In math, when they can work with partners, Mia never moves and Alexandra and Lily come to her, one on either side.

Lily realizes maybe she needs to be accepting of Alexandra. Not just because of Mia, but because of one of the life lessons you start to learn when you're twelve: Sometimes, *not* being friends with a person can take up as much of your psychic energy as being friends with her. She may resent Alexandra, but Lily, less emotionally sophisticated than her friends, less aware of what her values are and how to stand by them, is a pleaser. If it pleases Mia for her to get along with Alexandra, she'll suck it up. At lunch Lily offers Alexandra her chocolate chips, and at recess they practice a cheerleading routine. Mia invites both Lily and Alexandra to sleep over one night, and they're all excited, but then her dad makes plans over hers, so she has to cancel.

Avy doesn't get it. "I can't imagine Mia chose to be friends with

Alexandra again," she says. She and Jack are not subtle about letting their daughter know what they find irritating about Alexandra, mostly reflecting what Lily tells them and how she always comes home cranky after spending time with her. But Avy realizes that it wouldn't be productive to invade, that Lily's friendship choices may be annoying but they're not dangerous.

Parents have to accept that their kids will shed some friends, gain others, and their best role is to help their children figure out what's motivating their choices and remind them of that. You don't want to manipulate a child's friendships, turn her into a hothouse flower too precious to grow on her own, become part of the problem. You don't want to get upset over your kid's friendships, because your kid, upset to see you upset, will stop sharing. And you certainly don't want to choose ignorance.

The middle ground is to act as a supportive coach, on her team but never part of the game yourself. Sneak through windows of opportunity to help your child see patterns and connections ("Didn't Andrea blow you off like that last summer?"), discuss what she does and doesn't like about her friends, let her know what are okay ways to be treated and what are not. Rather than discourage the friendships that feel wrong, which backfires, encourage the ones that feel right. "Do you think Dana wants to come to Six Flags with us?"

Remembering all the while that you don't see everything, so you don't have a perfect read on who's worthy and who's not.

As a goal, trying to improve your status in a social group isn't always complementary to nurturing the most rewarding friendships. Lily's affections for Mia don't abate—she will always think Mia's cabin is better, no matter how much fun she has in hers—but she's realizing she'll never win that contest. Nobody will win; Mia is too kind to alienate any of her many best friends. The asymmetry Mia and Lily have in their relationship is commonplace, but it's good for a child, less stressful, to have friendships that are as close as theirs but more reciprocal. Reciprocity, knowing you are both committed to each other, is the hallmark of friendship, after all. Which is why it's nice to see her friendship with Beth blossom. "We didn't know each other at all," Lily says, "and now we're like best friends." She corrects herself: "We're really good friends."

In Lily's eyes Mia is still first, then Beth, then her instant third-best friend, Ashley, though she hasn't spent time with Ashley since her birthday party, and never one-on-one. Lily still asks people, "Do you like my haircut? It reminds you of Mia," and at the spring dance has a Polaroid taken only with Mia, and on the playground hangs out with Beth only as a second resort. But her new, equal friendship is causing some change: When Mia's not around, Lily has been coming out of her shell, acting more like she does in the neighborhood, emboldened, like the way she took over the cabin on the camping trip.

It's hard to say if how a child interacts with her friends at age twelve has much to do with how she will when she's thirty, but certainly experiences have impact. A shy girl can find a niche and hide, but the fact that Lily has learned to cope with people of higher social status, watched them operate at a higher level of social skill, will help her later, and is helping her now. She has more people to hang out with than at the beginning of sixth grade, far more than in Louisiana, and is more comfortable opening up. Her confidence has grown (albeit not always the most pleasant kind). While doing BigTop Math in the computer lab, she narrates, "What's seven times seven? Okay. Six times nine. I'm stupid right now. What's four times eight? Isn't that thirty-two? What's eight times seven? Isn't that fifty-six? What's eight times eight? How many do you have, Maddy?"

She gets back at Abigail Werner by taking her sweet time at her locker, talking with Beth.

"Hurry up," Abigail says.

"I don't have to hurry up. You always talk at your locker, so why can't I?"

Abigail says, "If I get five late notes I have to go to Saturday school."

"It's your problem that you get late notes."

With Beth, "I can talk to her whenever I need," Lily says, "because her friends, they don't bug her or hang around her when I talk to her." At recess Lily and Beth do dances Lily made up and one-handed cartwheels. She looks forward to swimming in Beth's outdoor pool when it gets warm. "It used to be 'Mia' all the time," Avy says. "Now it's 'Mia and Beth.'" Which is fine, nice even, except for the fashion obsession that seems to have rubbed off. Clothes are one thing Lily loves about Beth, who can fit into extra smalls at Forever 21. The Children's Place doesn't cut it anymore. Lily comes home from school and tells Avy, "We have to go to Limited Too—there's this shirt I saw in the catalogue and it's like this, thick right here on this strap, and it goes to here, and it has a tiny strap right here that's removable, and it has American flags—"

"Who had the catalogue?"

"Beth." Always Beth now, setting the trends, on top of it all. Beth has two sets of parents, and Mia's dad is a professor and her mom a dentist, Avy tells Lily, so that's why Beth can shop from catalogues and Mia can buy new sneakers even though her old ones are still very white and too big, kicked off easily on the playground.

When Avy's underwires snap in her only two bras, Lily accompanies her to the mall, and, walking by the shoe store, she says, "I need sandals," even though she left five pairs of shoes by the stairs the other day, including three pairs of sandals.

"I just bought you sandals."

"You didn't buy them—I paid for some," Lily says, having chipped in for one-quarter of one pair. "How many pairs are you buying me for back to school?"

That's four months away, and anyway, Avy says, it's not a matter of how many they're buying but, rather, how many she needs. As opposed to Gabrielle, who says, "I don't need everything fancy name-brand, but could I have just one pair of Gap shorts?" Lily wants a new tankini from Limited Too, because her one-pieces from Sam's Club "aren't in fashion." Lily has six short-sleeved shirts, but she wishes they didn't fit, because there's a new style this year. "Roxy—their shirts are more like classic modern. They look better—funkier. And not just plain. 'Cause my clothes sorta stick out from everyone else."

Beth doesn't have any problem with Lily's clothes. What she does think is strange is how Lily and Mia say they're best friends even when she's the one who plays with Lily all the time these days. "I don't care," Beth says, "but it's weird, because Mia barely talks to Lily, and then she says I'm her second-best friend." When they get together, though, Lily is just as spastic as she is with Mia, and though she wouldn't admit it later, has just as much fun.

One day at recess, Lily tells Beth, "My brother's friend Matt is coming over and my sister's friend Mara is coming over and she's annoying, so my mom said I could invite someone, and I invited Mia and she's busy, so I'm inviting you." At Lily's house they dress up her neighbor

Rick in a skirt and blue eye makeup. Lily decides he has a crush on Mia because of the way his lips tauten when she shouts her name in his face: "Mia Reilly! Mia Reilly! Mia Reilly!" Inside, Lily belches loud and Beth says, "That's all you ever do." They turn the video camera on and dance, take close-ups of butts, giggle, wrestle, tangle themselves up in each other, do their special handshake (wave a hand around your head, grab hands, jump up and down like maniacs), sing the H-A-P-P-Y song, and after they've tumbled to the ground in exhaustion, they face the camera, which is propped up on a chair.

"This is Lily."

"And her old pal Beth."

chapter twenty

now you have the persentage
of your love

When kissing games escalate from peck to French, Jackie begs out. Still, by the end of seventh grade, she has come to love the boy-girl party and its rituals: movies she could never watch at home, junk food the girls will only eat once the boys have left, so they don't look like pigs, post-party dishing about spin-the-bottle. The other girls discuss whose tongues were slow and whose fast, whose moved horizontally and whose vertically. "I felt dirty," one usually says, and the rest agree. There's something distasteful about making out with guys you don't even like, or have never even talked to. Watching is better than kissing, sort of. Couples are allowed to opt out with impunity, but there's always one single boy who won't play, which gets him teased (and makes him wonder why it appeals to everyone but him). The guys crack the lesbian joke every time the bottle lands in a girl-girl combo. How can boys like the idea of two girls kissing when *they* don't like the idea of two boys kissing? Maybe, just maybe, they could deal with three-way kisses if it were two boys.

By the time you're thirteen, some very grown-up concepts have probably started to tumble around in your mind. In Jackie they don't take full shape, she is not a sexual being yet, but her sexuality is emerging. She has some of the vocabulary, less of the knowledge, and even less of a desire actually to partake in the activities she and her peers joke about constantly. Still, phrases float in the air, and from listening to other people she knows what some mean ("giving head"), though not others ("blow job"). Before social studies, Anton asks what he could put on his penis when he gets head, and Jackie makes suggestions. While Jackie is playing at her friend Meghan's, they come across a videotape called *Amazing Penises*. For five minutes it plays, and Jackie sees what she's never seen before, things being done that almost nobody has seen before. She's neither intrigued nor exactly grossed out. Her mind just goes blank.

At the same time, Jackie's behavior is changing some, and as spring blossoms, Sara Taylor can see fourteen coming. Five minutes before she needs to leave for a trampoline meet, Jackie knocks on the bathroom door, clutching a crusty old tube of purple mascara. "Mom, because it's the Cherry Blossom Invitational, can I put purple streaks in my hair?" Sara says no. The next week, Jackie comes home from school with purple streaks Leslie gave her, and Sara gives her the "What the hell were you thinking?" look. Whether it's renewing *YM* or her strange pleas to take cheerleading, which she hated ten minutes before, or wearing Leslie's stud collar—Leslie is trouble, they think, but what can they do?—Jackie's parents are suddenly always having to shut her up with, "Jacquelyn, you're on the gray line."

"Sometimes," her mother says, "she just doesn't know when to stop."

Jackie's teachers are getting that idea, too. In reading she gets all goofy during her presentation, and her teacher has to tell her to stop running chalk lines back and forth across the blackboard. By day's end the social-studies teacher wishes Jackie wore a muzzle. In science the kids get in partners to cut out little ghost monsters, flipping coins to determine their recessive and dominant traits and genotypes and phenotypes, then breed them with each other. Jackie tap-dances. She bounces. She has named her ghost thing Joe.

"Nobody likes Joe," she says. "Joe was on *Blind Date*. He was rejected on *Blind Date*."

"He's so sexy," Leslie says.

Trista comes up to breed, and they squish their monsters together. Leslie does, too.

"Hey, Mr. Shifflett," Jackie says, "we started mating but Leslie put hers on top. Joe likes to be on top."

"They're standing up. Hey, they're taking a shower."

"Ladies!"

"They're taking a shower because they're *dirty*."

"No!"

As the spring dance starts, on the one hand Jackie is scared boys are going to freak her, and on the other hand she hopes boys will freak her. She likes that little circle that forms, the way everyone says, "Go, Jackie! Go, Jackie!" and she thinks, "Go, me! Go, me!" Who would want to dance the old way anyway? "Do the Monkey"?

Teachers approach each group from time to time, trying to diffuse the magnetic force pulling the kids together, stopping the mosh pit from taking casualties, but the sentries are imperfect. When Lil' Bow Wow sings, "You run through my mind like all the time," Jackie's got her groove on. Her hair runs down her red T-shirt and her hands run through her hair, top to bottom. She piles it atop her head, lets it fall, twirls her hands in the air. You wouldn't have thought she had hips until you see them swivel, getting closer and closer to the ground, her jeans tight and pocketless, this nonsexual body looking for a quick moment very sexual. A nearby couple get their freak on, fast, and Jackie says, "Oh my God," hand to her braces. After the shock, she smiles.

One boy has six girls freaking on him, including Leslie and Kristina. Then the music switches and the children become children, clapping and stamping to "If You're Happy and You Know It." Adam appears, sweaty from the effort of pushing his way into groups of dancing girls. He's not having much luck or much fun: "I can't get any ass or I'm in trouble."

Truth be told, Adam doesn't actually ever "get ass"; by his own admission, 90 percent of his boasts are empty. And Jackie feels no more inclined to make out with anyone than she did before getting her groove on. But it's still worrisome, what this supposed freeing of sexuality for girls and boys portends as they grow older, as they actually do get involved in relationships. *If* they get involved in relationships. The idea that a boy can practically hump any one of a large group of girls from behind on the dance floor, that he can call her a ho with impunity, that she thinks it's funny to be flashed, that she unthinkingly indulges his conversations about blow jobs, that they both agree that blow jobs aren't really sex, gives lie to the conventional wisdom that somehow girls have the power now. When they finally do get together, will boys and girls meet face-to-face? Or will the girls be on their knees?

Plenty of social scientists study teenage sex, but few study romance—too frivolous, too fickle. So little is known of how relationships affect development, whether the crushes you have in middle school say anything about your romantic adulthood. The kids themselves think that it all could be just a phase, that it doesn't predict anything, though they occasionally speculate on who will become a stripper and who will become gay.

Studies have shown that kids who initiate dating earlier are more likely to become sexually active sooner and have more partners; those with lots of sexual partners misbehave more in other ways, too. But researchers haven't discovered anything predictive about crushes per se. Some girls who are totally boy-crazy in middle school remain overly focused on boys, but others become very self-possessed by high school. Usually these are the kids with solid family structures; research has shown that the stability of a child's relationship with his parents predicts the stability and quality of his romantic relationships in adolescence.

And the quality of the relationship makes a difference in how much stress it induces. The girls with the most unhealthful attachments to boys tend to be the ones who developed early, the ones whose parents don't have real authority in the house—even if they think they're strict on the small things, they don't pay attention to the hours she spends online with strangers. They tend to be the ones whose parents aren't married, who bring boyfriends or girlfriends around, who engage in needy romantic relationships themselves, giving the idea that it's all about courtship, about pleading, about conflict.

The most romantically balanced of Jackie's friends are the ones, including her, whose parents keep track of whom they hang out with and control their time. They have close, realistic marriages; they don't delude themselves into thinking that "he's such a nice boy, he wouldn't do anything," or that coed sleepovers are okay because "nothing could happen when they're all together." At this age, when they're all together is precisely when things happen.

As a parent, you can't control the crushes and the obsessions; you might never know about them, and that's okay. It's productive, at this age, for boys to get to know girls, and girls to know boys; kids who can navigate a healthy romantic relationship feel more competent. Mom and Dad shouldn't freak out over spin-the-bottle—it takes some of the mystery out of kissing and can be harmless, especially if Mom comes downstairs occasionally to replenish the soda.

Most of all, adults should be careful not to belittle their children's crushes, and should show sympathy when it's needed. Romance can exacerbate depression in adolescents: They're sad or ashamed when things don't work out; they're let down when things do work out but fall short of their expectations; even being the subject of someone else's crush can be difficult. And rejection, simply put, is never fun. Jackie sees this all the time with her friends. Even if you want the freedom to flirt, and you're not allowed to hang out with the guy anyway, when you hear he wants to break up with you, you are miserable. And even if you are one of the few couples at Wilde Lake who are actually comfortable together, who actually talk to each other regularly about your lives, you hide in the bathroom stall, too scared to say anything, as your friends bombard you: "Are you gonna break up with him first? When?"

Despite this, Jackie has found it impossible to go without a crush. That's what makes up at least 60 percent of your friends' conversations, and, well, you just *should* have one. "When you have a crush on someone," Jackie says, "even them saying 'Bye' makes you feel special." Besides, at recess Adam keeps poking Jackie—and Jackie alone, she is certain—in the side.

"Don't touch me."

"What you say?"

"Don't touch me."

"What you say?"

"Don't touch me."

"What you say?"

"That's unwanted touching. Sexual harassment!"

Adam stretches a girl's elastic necklace two feet, to demonstrate how long his penis is, and simulates masturbation with a Lipton Brisk bottle. But Jackie knows he is all talk. Leslie tested it once, by offering him a blow job after school. At first he said okay, but in two minutes he came back and said, "Nah, I don't like you like that."

QED.

So, when Jackie overhears Anton behind her in social studies saying to Adam, "You'd be lucky if she says yes," she swings around.

"What did you say?"

"Adam wants to know if you'd go out with him."

"Did you say that?"

Adam shrugs, smiles.

"Yeah," Jackie says, "sure."

At lunch, she asks Adam, "What you said during social studies, did you mean it?"

"Sure."

She hugs him and spends the afternoon jumping around Leslie's bedroom listening to Staind, yelling, "I have a boyfriend!" The two of them go to the roller rink and wait for Adam, who said he would be there.

Each Friday night, Columbia's middle schoolers line up outside the door to enter the one place that is, for the moment, *theirs*. Girls wear the spaghetti straps they can't wear in school; bellies see the light. Boys wear pants so baggy it's an insult to physics that they stay up while in motion. A Rollerblade under each arm, a girl says to her father, "I need money." "I gave you money." "Whatever." "Do you have it? Take it out." "I *have* it. *Dad*, leave." "Are you sure you have it?" A kid in a Redskins jersey gets his wrist run over—he shakes it and stomps his feet but he will not cry. The lone mother, a woman who has never left her boy without a parent, watches from behind the glass, and she and her son wave to each other as he skates by. A group of eighth-grade girls with O-rings up their arms plot a secret mission to Wendy's.

Adam has a history of being not exactly the most fulfilling roller-skate date. Ann, a subtle, big-eyed princess who tosses her hair and fends off all comers with a straight line of closed lips, would eventually hook Jay Starr, but in the fall Adam, her boyfriend at the time, blew even her off at the roller rink. She spent couples skate sitting on the bench crowded with shoes as Adam begged off with a supposedly hurt ankle and then trolled the parking lot for a ninth grader named Jennifer. Tonight, as Jackie circles the rink with her eye toward the entrance, Adam never shows up. He is "studying" in the bedroom of a girl from church, a girl with boobs.

And so it ends much as it began, as these things do. During social studies on Monday, Anton tells Jackie that Adam cheated on her. She had an idea something was up, because at recess one of her friends asked Adam why he liked Jackie and he said, "I don't." After Anton opens his big mouth Adam hits him in the head, three times. Jackie is sad, but not so much so that she has to cry.

Jackie has created a compatibility test on the computer:

Boys And Thier Love for You

THIS IS THE SURVAY TO SEE HOW GOOD OR HOW BAD A GUY IS FOR YOU. JUST FILL OUT A CARD TYPING HOW YOU THINK THAT GUY RATES FROM A SCALE OF 1–10, THEN ADD UP HIS SCORE.

Looks
Personality
Athletic Ability
Things in Common With You
Favorite color (red, orange, yellow = 10, green, blue, purple = 9, all others like black = 5)
The gifts he gives you
Kisses
Hugs

Now subtract these next questions points to your total from the top questions for the total score.

Times he forgets you
Times he doesn't like your friends
Times he has cheated (on anyone)

Now take this score (that you have subtracted from the top) and put it over 90 and divide and now you have the persentage of your love.

Part of the reason that Jackie is so resilient—that she doesn't cry over boys, as some of her friends do—is that she's taken the time to figure things out for herself. She's getting to know who she is, what she wants.

Aside from "favorite color," the criteria in her formula make sense. This is the kind of thing a parent can discuss with a child. "What do you like about him?" "What would make a good girlfriend?"

Jackie still sits next to Adam and in front of Anton in social studies, which is in one way a pain, because "I hate all my ex-boyfriends," but in another way not a pain, because she doesn't really. She and Adam whisper all the time, and Mr. Wolfe talks to them sternly about not paying attention. They are filling in maps of the United States. Jackie has colored the Rockies brown and the Great Plains green and the East Coast Megalopolis red and labeled all the rivers and cities. Adam's map is blank, and he wants the answers from Jackie.

"What have you done for me lately?"

"He bought you a toothbrush for your birthday," says the boy next to Anton.

"Yeah, I bought you a toothbrush. Your breath stinks. You need a Tic Tac."

That is not the way to get the answers. Jackie continues her work, hands it in, gets an extra-credit word search of cities around the world, and Adam continues to pester her for help.

"Take back what you said."

"Okay, your breath doesn't stink, you don't need a Tic Tac, you don't smell," he murmurs.

"Say it like you mean it."

He says it again, clearer.

"You're lucky I'm nice." She puts aside the word search. "Okay, look on the map. Missouri. Do you see the state of Missouri? Do you see the Missouri River anywhere near there?" She goes through the map like this, nudging him to search the book for the Mississippi, the Rio Grande, until Adam says, "There's only seventeen minutes left. I don't have time to look in the index."

By the time Jackie gets to the St. Lawrence River, she just shows him where it is.

she's lost to us

When the buses arrive at Wilde Lake in the morning, the kids are supposed to stay aboard until the school doors open. Sometimes the drivers let kids off anyway, and this is what Elizabeth's driver does one day, until the art teacher notices and heads to the bus—just as Elizabeth is getting off.

"Get back on the bus," Mr. Mitchell tells her. "Hey, don't let people off the bus yet," he tells the driver.

The bus driver says Elizabeth was getting off the bus because she has diarrhea. The word amplifies in Elizabeth's head as she stands in limbo on the bus stairs—diarrhea—Diarrhea!—DIARRHEA!!—**SHE HAD DIARRHEA!!!**—to the point where she figures the jerk couldn't have yelled it louder if he had a megaphone in his hand.

If he had said, "Don't get off the bus because I don't want to get in trouble," she wouldn't have, and anyway why is she being singled out, and double anyway he doesn't have to keep calling her "bad girl" after Mr. Mitchell walks away, and triple anyway why would she even come to school if she had diarrhea? By the time she arrives late to first period, after spending ten minutes tearfully explaining herself to Mr. Mitchell, the kids on her bus have spread the word, and now *everyone is asking about it*, which makes her cry.

"Look," Mrs. Rashid scolds, "now you made her cry." If anyone on earth ever felt more pathetic than this, Elizabeth can't imagine.

The kids talk about making a petition to get the bus driver fired, but it goes nowhere, like all the petitions about getting bus drivers fired. Elizabeth doesn't bring the issue home, except to write:

> omg, my bus driver is a jerk an idiot and should b fired.
> he is such a lier
> he imbarresed me so much
> he needs 2 go back 2 school and learn responsibility

Days later, on the way to her math tutor, she and Ellen fight, Ellen angry that Elizabeth left her math book at school the night before a quiz. It escalates into screaming and crying, and sullenness sets in for the whole afternoon. Seems to Elizabeth—this is the way it looks when you become a teenager—that her mom is the one changing, becoming more irritable, harder to manage. When Joseph gets home and sees them both upset, he offers to take Liz to Starbucks for a Frappuccino. He watches Elizabeth's eyes tear up as she drinks, Ellen's strategies running through his head: Don't micromanage. Don't ask questions. Be patient. Just listen. So, even though Joseph is dying to know what this is all about, he doesn't say a word. He listens, and what he hears is his daughter sipping through a straw, sniffling occasionally.

He is so proud of himself for keeping his mouth shut.

What can a parent do, besides keeping quiet sometimes? Well, that's a start. So is whisking the kid off to a neutral territory, especially one as cool as Starbucks. He can acknowledge the pain inherent in her problems without trying to fix them, without overreacting. He can accept that she isn't totally grown up yet, which affects not just her sometimes babyish television choices but her ability to stay sane in the face of the small annoyances that seem so huge. All the while, he can't be insulted about what she doesn't share; he needs to realize that his attempts to help just increase her anxiety, and what may seem like absence of action *is* doing something after all.

At the last strings concert of the year, Joseph asks Mr. Shifflett about Elizabeth's science project, testing the effect of vinegar on swimsuit fading. "They've found out how to do the tanks of water, and Elizabeth found a chemist. Is she supposed to be a mentor-type person? Because maybe you could tell Elizabeth that. Could you write something down for her? Because she doesn't listen to me." Supposedly she's in the middle of a three-year experiment, but the science department drags these things out, and a year and a half into it, she hasn't soaked one swimsuit. It's the most difficult thing about parenting a thirteen-year-old, Joseph thinks: deciding when to hold her close and when to let her solve her own problems. If she waits till the last minute, like last year, she'll freeze. She won't take any guidance this year, which is good in the maturing sense, "but at the same time we could talk a little bit about the design or something," Joseph says. "A give-and-take."

The schoolwork thing is particularly hard for fathers, who want to teach their children how to do the work, the facts, of course you can do it, it all goes back to mx + b. But that's not what Liz needs sometimes; it's not really about the facts of the homework but about her insecurity over it, in which case she needs to be reassured that her struggles are normal, that he understands how she's feeling, that he had a hard time with this kind of project once, too.

After the concert, the children emerge from backstage and hook up with their parents, except Liz. Joseph and Ellen sit at the bottom of the staircase, waiting. Backstage, Elizabeth begs for an end-of-year party and no more practice charts for the year. It bewilders Miss Colyer the way a kid who supposedly disliked her so much all of a sudden cleaves to her, is now saying, "I'll bring you flowers next year."

"Have things gotten better with Miss Colyer?" Joseph asks in the car.

"I don't want to talk about it."

With Joseph, it's all about Miss Colyer and the science project and swimming. The more he makes it about sushi and *Buffy the Vampire Slayer*, the more he meets his daughter on her turf, the better his luck will be.

"She's lost to us," Joseph keeps saying. Months after Elizabeth's Bat Mitzvah, her supposed entry into adulthood, as far as her parents can tell she hasn't changed at all, responsibility-wise. The brush-offs continue, and feel massively significant. She seems to have more secrets.

But really—hard as it is for them to see—Elizabeth isn't lost to them.

Ellen and Joseph are her biggest influence, maybe not on whether she likes blues, but on the things that matter. They never give up. They provide the activities she wants, and insist on the ones that she needs. They always, always put her first. She knows when they're arguing, which is fine to a degree, because it shows parents can have conflicts and work them out, but they never, ever weigh her down with their burdens. They don't toss out rules when it's hard to enforce them. Liz cares, still, about their approval. She likes herself, in large part because they like her, too. In her Mother's Day cards—Elizabeth couldn't decide on which, so she bought both—she gives credit to Ellen. "I don't know about you Mom, but I think I turned out pretty good . . . Especially considering I had fifty percent of Dad's genes to overcome," and "Mom, it's because of you that I turned out the way I did. . . . Cheer up. That was supposed to be a compliment."

Elizabeth keeps a lot from her mom and dad, but at least they know that. Plenty of her peers have parents who think their kids are their best friends, who are deluded into thinking that "she tells me everything" and that easy banter and the erasing of generational lines are somehow good for a child. But a child needs her parents to be her parents, not her best friends, and if that means there will always be somewhat of a disconnect, so be it. The important thing is not that Joseph and Ellen are her best pals—they will never be that, at least not in her adolescence—but that they keep providing the combination of warmth, control, and expectations that raises good people. And that they have faith that, in the mystery world Elizabeth navigates without them, she is truly growing up, and making good decisions for herself.

The Sterns next door are divorcing, and though Elizabeth isn't one of the kids whose parents threaten divorce in front of them or stomp out on each other, the news sends Elizabeth into extreme sensitivity every time her own parents argue. Mitch, the boy in her social studies class who shows his affection by teasing her, is getting more aggravating, if that is even possible. Worst of all, she receives a note to be signed by her parents warning that she has been tardy too many times; the next time, she'll have to go to the reinforcement room. Elizabeth only remembers being late twice. Once was excused, and the other time was in the very beginning of the year, "when I didn't know." As she walks out of school, Elizabeth feels the tears in the corners of her eyes, feels Hanna trying to get a look at the note, which is really none of her nosy little business. Reinforcement room? That's where the bad kids work when they're sent out of class. Never in her life.

She ponders quickly. Maybe her parents could call the principal, tell her how she really wasn't late those two times. Maybe she'll get more Frappuccino out of it. Then Elizabeth thinks back to the way Ellen asks her, "How was strings?" every single afternoon, the never-ending e-mails between Miss Colyer and Joseph, how even though the Frappuccino was very delicious, after she drank it she was still crying inside and no less pissed at her mom.

She decides that being thirteen means her problems are her own. On her way to the bus, she crumples the note and tosses it in the trash.

And Elizabeth isn't late to class again.

this is the most i ever typed in one day!

If Eric were the boss of school—well, if Eric were the boss of school, he would abolish it. But if Eric were realistic about being the boss of school, "kids would have some power to say how they would like to have some projects done. 'Cause some kids have very creative talents. And if they gave ideas to their teachers the teachers would be like, 'Yeah, whatever. We can't do that. It's not part of the curriculum.' But if the kids had some say, then the school might actually be interesting to them, and there wouldn't be so many dropouts."

If Eric were the boss of school, American-history students would re-enact battle scenes, and at least half the class would be spent learning the story of African Americans.

In May, like just about every eighth-grade social-studies teacher in the state, Mrs. Conroy races through the Civil War. If she had the luxuries of time and student attentiveness, she would like to explain more social aspects of history, families split apart, espionage, riots in the North. Her classes would do activities she tried long ago, skits and a mock *Meet the Press.* "A lot of things I'd like them to *discover*," she says, "instead of me saying, 'This happened.'" During the Reconstruction video, Eric sleeps, he reads a magazine article called "Tony Hawk's Pro Skater 4: The Spine-Tingling Sequel," he watches the kid next to him draw Mrs. Conroy with a fireball heading toward her skull. In the video, a Northerner is

teaching a black child when a man approaches on a horse. "Do you realize the harm you're doing to that child? That colored child will lose his
desire to work." Eric looks up. "This child's parents see the value in education," the teacher says. The man on the horse shoots the place up,
yelling, "Leave, Yankee scum!"

"That was part of my history," Eric says later. "I don't know, that
might be my great-great-great-grandmoms and -dads. It's always interesting to see people on that TV screen who could be somebody that's in
your family. Somebody that you knew come back to life."

If Eric were the boss of school, teachers would choose more books
like *Beowulf*. He likes it not because he relates to the themes, although he
could. He's got a mother as loyal as Grendel's, he feels as abandoned as
Beowulf. Mainly, it's catchy: "Tore him limb from limb and swallowed
him whole, sucking the blood in streams, crunching the bones." But,
still, disorganization intrudes. One day, after school, Eric asks Mrs.
Brown his grade on the quiz. A seventy-two, she says.

"Yes! I passed!"

"A C isn't enough for you."

"Why?"

"Because you're you." Mrs. Brown looks in her grade book. "You
have only a sixty percent, darling." The *Beowulf* Part I quiz a parent was
supposed to sign and his Gilgamesh essay are missing. "You've gotta do
this stuff!"

"Can I just have my dad sign a piece of paper with the information
on it?"

"Yes, but that'll only be three out of five—a sixty! It's sixty!"

"As long as you don't call my mom."

"That's what I need to do!"

"Please don't give her a call, because then I'll be punished."

"I'm not trying to get you in trouble, I'm trying to get you to do
your work. Eric, did you do the Gilgamesh paragraph?"

"Yeah, you were sitting right there."

"What did you do with it?"

"I probably cleaned my binder," he says. "Can I do makeup? Can I
do extra credit?"

"You're an enigma, Eric."

"I'm an egg man?"

"Enigma. E-N-I-G-M-A. Look it up."

He doesn't.

But he shows up for the after-school study group to prepare for the next test, nine kids sitting in a small circle of desks. The conversation is gentle. It ranges from vocab ("Unswert calls him a what? And what does 'braggart' mean?") to plot ("What's the point of the whole thing with Brecka the sea monster?" "How do they know he made it back to the lair?") to language (" 'Bolts burst apart'—what's that?" " 'Torch flaming in his eye'—is there really a torch in his eye?") to form ("What do we see here that makes him an epic hero?"). Eric listens, he participates—"the more you participate," he says, "the more you remember"—and exudes a joy of mastery.

With Mrs. Brown, Eric is finally learning that onomatopoeia is more than just a stumbling block in spelling bees. He learns about metaphor. And he learns words, some of them big and some of them little, but all of them juicy: Unfettered. Torrent. Keening. Gluttonous. Clamorous.

He likes it when Mrs. Brown explains words. For "turret": "Like in some of the video games you play." For "round": "Remember in the movie *Back to the Future*—I watched it this weekend with our niece—when he turns around and says, 'Nobody calls me chicken!' He's *round-ing* to his enemy." All of a sudden this feels important to Eric, and he studies. His vocab quizzes come back with a huge *A+* written on the top, and when he can remember he squeezes the words into conversation later. He defines them—"Tyrant, that's an unjust, harsh ruler"—in case you didn't know.

Sometimes in music it seems all they do is fill out worksheets, but one day, after labeling the parts of a guitar, they finally take down the in-struments from the rack, and discover the magic moment when you find the one string that turns your hapless, dissonant chord into something lovely. They are picking out "Ode to Joy" and Eric gets it first. "I did it! That sounds good!" His grin is huge. "Good thing I play sax! I got rhythm!"

Ms. Drumm asks if anyone plays bass. "I do!" Eric says. "I'm learn-ing it now." He has been tooling around on the bass in the band room after school—students who hate school and students who don't all hang out there every afternoon, jamming and getting Mr. Vega to teach them drums. "Man, I kill at bass! I bought a little book. I'm saving money to buy a bass—I'm gonna get one that's two hundred or three hundred dollars."

"Come up here. Would you be willing to show everyone how it works? In two weeks we're doing a special song for the grade."

"Oh yeah, that would be cool!"

This is the middle-school philosophy in play: Yes, Eric is learning the parts of a guitar, which is part of the curriculum. He's also getting to explore, try something self-directed, and this makes him feel great. Learning works best when these elements happen together. Too often the false debate between content and self-concept, academics and self-esteem, turns middle school into a muddle, where students bounce back and forth from useless goal-setting and what-kind-of-learner-am-I exercises to cram sessions for standardized tests. Instead, present the material in a way that gets kids enthusiastic about learning it, and enthusiastic about their lives, and you will be amazed at how well they absorb it.

When music class is over, Eric is reluctant to put the guitar away. He is so excited about the bass demonstration that when he leaves Ms. Drumm has to chase him down the hall: He forgot his guitar-part worksheets.

It's no surprise that this surge in enthusiasm coincides with smoother sailing at home. The pregnancy has cheered up Beulah, he thinks. One day at home it's just the two of them, and she says, "Wanna go see a movie?" They do, and laugh. He is starting a band with two friends, called Beef. The football coach at the high school says he has shoulder pads awaiting Eric. With the help of his mom, he's gone on a diet. Sick of the teasing, he eats apples and Lean Cuisine instead of junk all the time, milk instead of juice, and Tenacious and Eric walk-run around the track, two miles each time. The weight disappears like that, ten pounds in a month. For Mother's Day he buys his mom an outfit and takes her to Pizza Hut and *Spider-Man*. She drives him each week to roller hockey, where he has started playing goalie, a position that feels like it was made for him. After getting paintballs at Dick's Sporting Goods with his old friend James, James pushes him in the shopping cart through the parking lot. The world zooms by, and it is good.

The study-skills packet Eric highlighted in the fall had it only partly right: Sure, it's important to have a dedicated, well-lit place to study each day. But that's not nearly so important—for kids from affluent, stable families as well as those from poorer ones, as much for Jimmy as for Eric—as having at least one person in your family who consistently takes an interest in you and your schoolwork. That means "schoolwork," not "grades." Bribes and threats work—like Tenacious's roller-hockey/science-grade contingency—but only for the short term, and they don't help a child become a learner, just an achiever. When Eric's brother stayed with him and sat him down at the kitchen table for study sessions every day, his grades improved. When his parents show up not just for concerts and conferences but also at home, his grades improve. Now, at the end of the year, when his mother has more time for him, when he feels part of something, he is getting somewhere.

To a degree.

If Eric were the boss of school, he wouldn't change a thing about his research project for Mrs. Cook. "That's giving the kid his time to go ahead and pick a subject he wants to do a project on. Can't get any better than that. It's your choice; you ain't gotta read what you don't want to. I'd read tons of books on cars if there was a lot of books on them."

That doesn't means Eric does the assignment thoroughly, or promptly. It was assigned in November, but the week in May before it's due, Eric hasn't started. The class is in the computer lab, some students studiously typing the What I Learned and Questions I Asked sections of their reports on karate or teen pregnancy or what you must do to become a lawyer. Some students are checking out e-mail, or mtv.com, or rampage.com, which interests Mrs. Cook, because she wants a new black shirt. Eric aimlessly searches car sites: King of the Street, Fastest Street Cars (¼ Mile) in the USA, bakersfieldstreetracing.com. "Look at that cobra look on that Civic. That's the way my car is going to be—the brake pedal. Mrs. Cook, wanna see the world's fastest truck? It goes three sixty-five mph. It has thirty-six thousand horsepower."

On Saturday he goes to work with his dad, then to Baltimore for a haircut with his mom, then to hockey (where he scores twice), then to Josh's for the night, where they play video games. He stays at Josh's till nine Sunday night, eleven hours before his six-month project is due. At

Josh's he hears a stale rumor that his favorite skateboarder died. He has the same skates as him! Once home, Eric stays up all night watching cartoons and thinking about the news. When Tenacious arrives to pick Eric up Monday and finds out his paper isn't done—isn't started, even—she's exasperated. Instead of searching the Internet for roller skates and paintball guns, why can't he use that time to start his research paper? They rush into Mrs. Cook's room late, Tenacious says something about the computer, and Mrs. Cook gives Eric an extension.

After school, and after playing drums in the band room, he goes to the computer lab. It is quiet in there, nearly dark, and the seats down the rows and rows of blue Macs are empty save for a girl named Mary. Mary has arranged fifty note cards for her research project, a PowerPoint presentation on Civil War photographers. Deep in Eric's reading folder, untouched, are a series of reminders and checklists for the research paper. First is this note: "Your product is up to you. This counts as a major grade for the third quarter. Use your time wisely and do a fantastic job." Then the requirements: an outline, a timeline, note cards gathered with a rubber band, a daily journal about your research, the explanation at the outset of the questions you wanted answered, the explanation at the end of how you did your research. If Eric did that part, it might go like this:

> Most of the stuff about cars I knew off the top of my head. I didn't actually open a book or do any interviews like you told us to. But I found some car Web sites last night using Google. And Mrs. Brown happened to be in the computer lab at the time, so she suggested where you can keep your nitrous oxide so the cops don't find it and how to explain what racing-style tires are for.

A bibliography with five or more sources. Final copy typed and double-spaced, with a clear plastic cover and a creative design. The paper itself is worth fifty points, all the other things together worth one hundred.

In the lab, the many things Eric knows about race cars want to spill out of his head through his fingers. But he doesn't use a computer much—too much of a bother to ask his way into his dad and Beulah's room, where it's kept at home—and when academic-enrichment class meets in the computer lab for Mavis Beacon Teaches Typing, Eric selects Beginner and taps A-S-D-F exercises, "fad daff dad ada sad," eleven words per minute, while kids nearby zip through the advanced exercises about squawking gorillas and weightlifters quipping jovially, well practiced from all that instant-messaging.

Eric does frequent word counts, stopping occasionally to consider which photo in a sheaf he's printed out would be good for the cover. He doesn't know how to insert text in Microsoft Word, he doesn't know that if you type a paragraph the paragraph below it will push down by itself, but to Eric this feels like cruising. He writes and writes and writes about the specs of the best possible quarter-mile race car in the land.

"Mrs. Brown, can you come read this and tell me how it sounds from a car person's point of view?"

"It looks good. It looks professional. I think it's one of the best pieces you've written all year."

"Four hundred and ten words! This is the most I ever typed in one day! And I still have homework. Oh, man. I'll write a paragraph about turbo exhaust. Then I feel like Rollerblading."

Which he goes home to do, the paper still unfinished.

Does it do Eric any good that, when he hands in the assignment a day later, mediocre and incomplete, he gets a B? Certainly it boosts his mood, but the good grade is clearly charitable. Teachers and administrators like Eric, they know his circumstances aren't ideal, they know his mother tries hard, very hard. They want him to succeed. They give him a million breaks. Absent true success, absent true academic progress, you can't help feeling the teachers are manufacturing the success for him, relaxing their standards and expectations so that this lovable boy can stay afloat. His parents do the same: "D's are out of the question," Tenacious said in September, and William agreed. Since then, D's, and even an F, have arrived without consequence. Perhaps he'll always be so buoyed by those around him. Or perhaps the sinking is merely being delayed.

On his fourth-quarter interim, Eric gets a C in science. This sends him over the moon but clearly does not impress Ms. Thomas, who calls him in for a meeting. With a mother who cares like his does, Ms. Thomas figures he'll be fine in high school, so she tells Eric he's going to pass. But, she says, the extracurricular activities are still in question, pending improvement in science. Eric says he doesn't care: "There ain't nothing new there. I know the whole marching band's songs before they start playing them." Band or no band, Eric knows for the sake of his mother he has to keep his science grade up so he doesn't get an F for the year. Hearing he's passing middle school is a huge relief. Now, he figures, he doesn't have to make up all the work his teachers are bugging him for.

"Next year," he says, "will be totally different. I'll be with my mom, and I'll be doing good in school." The plan is for an aunt to sell Tenacious her house in Baltimore, and she'll drive him a half-hour to school every day, and William will move into the city, too.

Ms. Thomas thinks his indifference to the band is a cover for insecurity. Insecurity about high-school work, about not having his hand held, not getting the same kind of nurturing. For someone who hates school so much, he sure spends a lot of time there, even walking back after going home. Often the students who most frustrate the teachers during the school day are the most pleasant company once the bell rings; Wilde Lake Middle School is a refuge, and they don't know if high school can take its place. At a jazz-band concert later that week, Tenacious snaps photos and worries about Eric worrying about high school. At the concerts she always stands at the side, often in her nursing uniform, with a small, proud smile. Eric sees her and winks. She's glad that he feels so nurtured here, that in the sea of feeling alone he chooses school as his island instead of one of many bad choices.

She's spoken with Ms. Drakes on the phone and knows Eric is teetering on the edge. A D, please. Just a D. Ms. Drakes thinks only an A would pull up his F's to a D for science for the year, but she won't let him do makeup work; she only lets seventh graders do that. "You've got to prepare them for high school," she says. Along those lines, she hasn't really gone to Eric; he comes in for help occasionally, and after all, "he knows what he has to do. He didn't care. He cares now."

One morning Eric wakes up sick, and Tenacious tells him to stay home with his Kleenex and orange juice and chicken soup. But he wants to go to school, because he stayed home yesterday. *He wants to go to school.* First period, in science, his eyes run, his nose runs; he makes his way back to the sink for paper towels every seven minutes, sticks wads of it out his nostrils, then trudges up front to the trash can to throw it all away. He emits noises that disgust his classmates and make them laugh, which brings him to hang his head low. Maybe then all this gunk will clear out. He coughs into the neck of his T-shirt. He can't focus. He is under water.

"Five, four, three, two, one. If you're talking, you're not listening." The class is going through the steps of mitosis, sketching cells on paper and using playing cards as chromosomes. They draw spindle fibers and simulate the fibers' shrinking and pulling the chromatids apart. Eric wipes his hand under his nose. His mouth is open. A haze coats his eyes.

Eric manages to fill out the mitosis worksheet and hand it in. "For the quiz," Ms. Drakes says, "you might want to take home your activity sheet and index cards so you can study. It's going to be a ridiculously stupid quiz."

The F flashes before Eric's eyes, but so does Ms. Thomas telling him he's passing. He is dizzy. He asks to go to the nurse, and on the way there to be sprung from school stows his binder on top of the lockers. Eric has a quiz in reading and a quiz in science, but he goes home bookless. His policy is that he doesn't have homework tonight, since he won't be around to get it. He walks home, enters the dark apartment, flops on the couch, and searches for the remote.

chapter twenty-three

why do people always take sex
as a play thing?

Dear Mia,
I hope you know you extremely sexy. The way you walk your legs look so sexy.
The way you look blow my. Your legs must be tired because you are running
through my mind all the time. Bye Bye my love.

Love,
Jimmy S.

Mia has received this note from a messenger named Nicole. Something
smells; the text is written in a light, scrawly hand, whereas the signature is
heavy. Mia asks Jimmy if this is his work.

"Yes," he says. "So—will you go out with me?"

"No way."

In the principal's office, Ms. Thomas meets with a girl suspected of leaving science class to smoke, one of a small group of eighth graders who are
appalled that a year ago they wore Abercrombie shirts, and now etch
their pain lightly on their forearms with steak knives and ink it on their
binders: "I always knew looking back on tears would make me laugh,

but never knew looking back on laughs would make me cry." They cut school to hang out with their nineteen-year-old boyfriends, read up on Wicca at the library, and sneak cigarettes. Just as with sexuality, there is a broad range of experience in a middle school regarding substance abuse, and Dawn, the girl in Ms. Thomas's office, is particularly fond of poems like, "Weed is a seed that grows in the ground. If God didn't like it it wouldn't be found."

She picks at a long skinny scab on the white of her forearm, pulling down the sleeve of her T-shirt to dab at the blood, and explains that she was not out smoking, just getting a tampon from her locker. Ms. Thomas begs—gently, kindly—that, if Dawn wants to finish the last nineteen days of middle school and avoid the Saturday-morning smoking-cessation program with its revolting slide show, she not bring cigarettes to school. Ms. Thomas asks about the small round scar on Dawn's cheekbone, which she says she got wrestling with her boyfriend while smoking. Dawn goes on: Her father put her in a choke hold until all she was aware of was her big sister screaming for him to stop; her sister ignores her, because she has stolen from her too many times; Zoloft makes her so tired that all she wants to do after school is sleep, except for the one day she didn't take the pill and got all her homework done.

"I'm glad you're getting help."

"I'm getting everything there is," Dawn says—everything working for nothing, as far as she can tell.

Like all Wilde Lake students, Dawn takes health class every year, but she can be told a million times that cigarettes are poison and still smoke. Then there are the kids like Jimmy, who wouldn't touch the stuff even without the never-ending series of overheads and quizzes. As Ms. Thomas meets with Dawn, Jimmy sits down the hall in health. The room is filled with boys who wear DARE T-shirts without irony and girls who run inside proclaiming an emergency when they find an empty cigarette pack in the backyard. Health class is where middle-school students who don't eat breakfast and are handed only carbohydrates and fat by the lunch ladies and wash down the brownies and pizza they make in home ec with pink Country Time lemonade learn about a well-balanced diet and heart disease. "It doesn't cost you any more to put that orange on your tray," Ms. Rouiller pleads, "to put that salad on that tray, to take your milk and drink it." What wall space there is—this cramped, odd-angled room was once a storage space—is covered by posters cautioning against peer pressure, pregnancy, HIV, anorexia, smoking ("tumor causing, teeth staining, smelly, puking habit"). Most of the sixth graders, Jimmy included, can't imagine why anyone would smoke.

The antismoking poster Jimmy is creating says, in green and orange bubble letters, "Tobacco makes you a wacko!" The dot of the exclamation point is a frowny face of a dead smoker, "X"s for eyes. Next to him Jacob draws blood dripping down cigarettes: "Smokers Are Jokers. Don't add yourself to the pile of bones." "I love Joe Camel," Jimmy says as he draws. He sings: "Tobacco, tobacco, I love ya, tobacco!"

Under the surface of Jimmy's cheekbones, begging to emerge, are pimples the same color as his skin. Jacob's nose has broadened since the year started, and he's got a little fuzz over his lip, which you can see from certain angles. Jimmy tells him, "Did you hear about the kid who was walking down the hall, he scratched his balls, they stuck to the wall? His girlfriend screamed, his thing turned green, and that was the end of his rubber ding-a-ling."

Jacob smiles, and Jimmy glimpses his mouth. "Your teeth are yellow. You're smoking."

"Maybe all those people in the World Trade Center died from smoking."

"It should say smoking supplies terrorists with money."

"That's drugs."

"Smoking is a drug."

Will asks Jimmy if he's going to the aquarium-club barbecue and Jimmy says no, he has homework and piano. "But they have a huge yard, and this train that goes around the whole yard."

"A baby train? Sounds like fun."

Jimmy turns back to Jacob and says, "Don't smoke! No dope!"

"Just say no, unless you want to be a ho!"

The students have learned that Americans lose five million years of potential life to cigarettes each year; they've searched in the textbook for tobacco's ill effects on each body part and copied it all onto a line drawing of a woman (when Jimmy sees "bladder" he thinks about the pee he's holding in, and says to no one in particular, "My bladder hurts"); they've learned that to Just Say No effectively you should use "proper body language, tone of voice, and repetition." Discussion then takes off, as it always does in health class, smoking and sex and their bodies far more interesting and mysterious than the Bill of Rights.

"I saw some high-school students who were late for school," Devon says, "and they were smoking, and one guy wanted a cigarette, but the other guy said no because he didn't want to share."

"That's not the kind of 'no' we're talking about."

"What if they're teenagers, and they ask if you want to smoke and you keep saying no and you can't really run away from them?"

"It doesn't ever really happen like that," Ms. Rouiller says.

"I saw it in a movie."

"My neighbor, her friend stopped being friends with her because she didn't smoke."

"I have some friends who smoke," Ms. Rouiller says, "but they know I'd never smoke."

"How come people in movies smoke?"

"Is it true that secondhand smoke is worse than firsthand smoke?"

"If you just put a cigar in your mouth and don't light it, is it still bad for you?"

"If someone is smoking weed in front of you and they exhale, can you get high?"

"That's not a good question," Alexandra says.

"Why not?" says Ms. Rouiller. "She can ask that. We don't really get into marijuana in this class because it's illegal. You shouldn't put yourself in a situation like that, because it's illegal."

"What if your mom and dad smoke? What do you do?"

"I suggest you talk to them, discuss it with them—how it makes you feel. Show them information and ask them, 'Did you know this? Did you know what smoking does to you?' "

"I have a friend, his dad used to smoke. He hid his cigarettes, and it worked."

"For the record, I'm not telling you to take their cigarettes."

"I ask people why they smoke, they say it relaxes you."

"In reality it doesn't. It's a stimulant. Those people it relaxes because they're addicted. They need the nicotine."

"Are you married, Ms. Rouiller? Rick thought you like Mr. Juliano."

"What does this have to do with nicotine?"

"Well, if one of you smokes, and you kiss, you'll get nicotine in the other person's mouth."

Jimmy raises his hand halfway, elbow bent.

"Could kids have heart attacks?"

Though the topic of health class is an eleven-year-old's favorite—himself!—Jimmy says he hates it. Every year it's Your Changing Body, Drugs Are Bad, Breakfast Is Good, blah blah blah. He says he knows it all. His classmates say they know it all. On the first day of the family-life unit, one boy says, "My mom kept asking me, 'What do you know?' I said, 'I don't know. What *do* I know?' More than she does."

Even if there were something Jimmy was curious about, if he wanted to look at a pamphlet from the rack he'd have to ask Ms. Rouiller's permission. Before embarrassment set in last year, he asked his parents whatever he wanted to know about sex. Now he'll just talk about the clinical things. His mother will creep further, things like, "Do girls sit on boys' laps on the bus?" Jimmy says no, but even if the answer were yes he wouldn't say, "because then they would think the school is really bad," and they might call, and his teachers might take it out on him.

Marie sat in on the sex ed Jimmy had at religious school earlier in the year, saw the explicit pictures of diseases the kids were shown, and on the ride home clarified her morals on certain points the minister made, like when he said gays are okay but not gays having sex. Gays having sex, she said, was okay, too. It felt to her like Jimmy was comfortable enough with this conversation, more than if Paul were trying. Jimmy doesn't discuss this kind of stuff with his dad at all.

A lot of what he needs to know he now asks his sister. Brianna is three years older and a better confidante than a parent would be. She tells Jimmy to eat with his mouth closed at the dinner table in a not-very-polite way and says, "That's so pointless," when he's playing GameCube, but at least is over her Valley Girl phase, when she would tell him, "Get a-waaaay!" Now he comforts her when she's sad. When a friend of hers committed suicide in the winter, Jimmy himself didn't cry, because he had only played with the guy three or four times, but he put up with Brianna's crying for an hour and a half, even though he couldn't hear the TV. She hugged him, which he was cool with, though eventually he felt squished and thought, "Okay, enough." In return for his empathy, she tells him about what she does with her boyfriend, which to Jimmy sounds "kind of funky," but, still, there is a limit, he feels, to what he can find out from other people and what he'll just have to come to know himself one day—whenever that day may be.

Jimmy hears girls talk about their puberty. But his friends talk about their physical changes in such coded and macho ways, mainly with mistruths about sex and jokes about penises and homosexuality. Any remotely related topic brings a boy Jimmy's age to giggles. In the library one day, when he and John have to look up Michelangelo, they get to the page in *The History of Art* with the statue of David—naked!—and begin laughing. They slam the book shut. They crack it open just enough to get the info they need without seeing the genitals they don't. He and his friends make up words like "dickonary" for "dictionary" and derive great humor from the fact that Australians say "fag" when they mean cigarette and that Billy Mara's uncle's middle name is Gay.

In middle school, everyone is changing at such different rates that there's little indication of whether the same thing is happening to anyone else. Some of Jimmy's friends have entered the lust phase. Jacob, for example, has testosterone running and pubic hair and the erections they giggle over in class. A boy at Jacob's stage thinks constantly about sex, as much as an adult times ten. *American Pie* wasn't so unreal: Every object and every female is sexualized, in his mind, a potential outlet for his energies. He wonders if he is the only one in the world who thinks these thoughts.

Jimmy wonders if he's the only one who doesn't. Why, he thinks, does Jacob look at porn all the time on the computer? Jimmy tried once. He typed in www.sex.com, and what came up was a tiny bit interesting, but mostly gross. As for the lurid note to Mia: Though he owned up to it, Nicole wrote it. In fact, Jimmy never even read it—he just signed it. His grammar and spelling would have been better, and for sure he would have been less explicit. It's not like he thinks Mia's legs are sexy, it's not like he even knows what it is to think someone's legs are sexy, it's not like he thinks about what it would be like actually to touch her. He just thinks she's cute. It's more like Nicole put *him* up to the note, not the other way around.

What Jimmy knows: The ovaries produce estrogen and progesterone, and puberty is triggered by hormones secreted by the pituitary gland, and the pituitary gland is the size of a pea, and testosterone causes body hair to grow, your voice to deepen, your sex organs to develop (as well as your sexual desire, which Ms. Rouiller explains as the "development of romantic feelings toward others"), and when such desire exists, semen enters the female's body through sexual intercourse and travels through the vagina and fallopian tubes to fertilize the egg. Jimmy raises his hand to give these answers as he folds tiny bright-pink origami in the back of the room, laughing occasionally with his classmates at a hilarious term such as "pelvic region" or "testes" or "uterus."

What Jimmy really wants to find out is buried with the rest of life's great mysteries in the daily Question Box, from which Ms. Rouiller plucks questions one by one, to answer or not.

Why do only women have their period, and why does it hurt?

"My mom, when she gets her period, she gets really agitated."

"My friend says it's called PMS."

"My teacher said it's like a roller coaster: Sometimes you're happy and sometimes you're sad."

"That roller coaster," Ms. Rouiller says, "is something you're all going to be riding the next few years. The boys, too."

Can you die if you have a baby?

"Yes, but it's not common."

If the baby's too big will it pop the uterus?

How does the baby come out of the vagina if it's so small?

What is masturbation?

"When a person handles their own genitals. That's all I'm allowed to say. You'll have to ask your parents."

"I can't ask my parents that! I'd get in trouble."

"I don't think you would. I think you'd be surprised. Tell your parents this question came up in health class and the teacher couldn't answer it."

Yeah, right.

What if sperm is injected into another male what would happen?

"It's kind of hard to inject sperm into a male," Ms. Rouiller says. "You can't do that."

"But on the *Men in Black* cartoon, Will Smith gets pregnant with an alien's baby."

Jimmy has just begun knotting a bracelet he started at outdoor ed when Ms. Rouiller picks his folded-up question from the box. She opens it, looks, and places it on the pile next to her without answering. *Why do people always take sex as a play thing instead of a life thing?* Jimmy's question is the same one he asked in health last year, when the teacher at least gave it a try. "It's different for everybody," she said then.

The increasingly influential proponents of abstinence-only sex education insist that in other forms of sex ed, in which teachers give technical information about contraception, they also enter the realm of morals (bad morals, it's said). In fact, sex ed teachers typically aren't allowed anywhere near such topics, so Ms. Rouiller can't answer Jimmy's question. What would she say, anyway? Could she explain why so many of the kids who are having sex these days (or a facsimile thereof) have no idea there's supposed to be meaning to it, not just about making babies but about making connection and love? Could she explain why they do it not just outside of marriage but outside of any relationship at all? Could she explain why a group of girls from a rival middle school were caught recently in the back row of a movie giving oral sex to a group of boys? These are the kinds of activities and attitudes that get written up in front-page newspaper stories, that shock politicians into pushing for abstinence-only sex ed, and that still produce a refreshingly sweet sentiment once in a while in a child like Jimmy.

Why do some people have sex every single day, he wonders, like it's just something for their pleasure?

As for Jimmy, he knows about the ideas, but it will be a small while before his body instructs him to feel the desire. His mother tells him it could happen any day now, but Jimmy is counting on more like two years.

All of it, come to think of it, seems further off than it really is. It's hard to imagine being a man, shaving, wet dreams. He's not too worried about those, since his neighbor's well into puberty and hasn't had one yet; Jimmy can't scream like a girl anymore, though, so he figures a voice change isn't far away. He hopes his goes smoother than Peter's did in that *Brady Bunch* special.

there's nothing to be scared of in middle school

If the students of Wilde Lake Middle School could select their own awards for the end-of-year assembly, Jimmy Schissel would get Most Creative in Social Studies. Barring that, Best at Origami.

Lily Mason would get Best at Sewing.

Jackie Taylor would get Most Willing to Go on Any Roller Coaster in the World.

Eric Ellis would get the Good Person Award, signifying a kid who was nice to everybody unless someone teased him and five minutes later came begging for a dollar. Better yet, Most Improved in English.

But for Most Improved you have to have started out super-lousy. Other than that, there are a couple of Citizenship Awards for effort and attitude, but it's mostly Academic Achievement Awards, for the boy and girl with the top final averages in each class. It's repetitive, the same kids over and over. For most students this ceremony is very boring. They expect the Award for Kids Who Got Awards to be next.

If that prize existed, Elizabeth Ginsburg would win it. She gets Academic Achievement for reading and English and Spanish, and Perfect Attendance, too. "They should just give all the straight-A students awards and let the rest of us go home," Jackie says from the back of the cafeteria, where she's sitting with her friends making a gel-pen tattoo on her arm that says "I LOVE _ _ _ AND _ _ _ _ _" (Jay, of course, and Danny);

across from her, a clot of nonawarded boys draw Japanese anime characters. But Jackie gets Perfect Attendance, too, and bounces to the front of
the room, Leslie whooping.

The jazz band in the front corner is supposed to provide entertainment—when Mr. Vega asks the eighth graders in band to stand, Eric
smiles and lifts his sax over his head—but as they get ready to play "Louie
Louie," the awards assembly ends. "For those of you who know in your
heart that you tried hard, that's award enough," Mr. Wolfe says, and the
students head back to class, unconvinced.

The band plays to an empty cafeteria, and ends halfway through the
song.

Eric leaves his binder on top of the lockers and his book bag under a
table and didn't buy a yearbook, so he can't leave that anywhere. Holding only an old birthday card he salvaged from his locker, he meets his
mother outside, to shop for a shirt for the graduation ceremony tonight.
Waiting for Eric, Tenacious sees Ms. Drakes, and they exchange hugs.

"We made it through another year," Tenacious says, and Ms. Drakes
says, "Sure did," but no word from either about Eric's science grade.

That night, the gym is packed for the ceremony, themed "Stars of
Tomorrow." Onstage with the jazz band, Eric picks out Tenacious in her
usual side spot with her camera, Thomas and Tim tall in their ball caps,
William and Beulah in the back. "Wow," Eric thinks. "Everyone's here.
Together even, kind of." The jazz band gives its best performance ever;
Eric plays like mad. He doesn't appear in the slide show and officially
doesn't care, but unofficially he does a little. One by one the teachers
come up to the podium to say how much they liked the eighth-grade students. "School may suck," Eric thinks, "but some of these teachers are
really nice." First and foremost Eric is contemplating how glad he is that
this is *it*, this is over, no more Ms. Thomas, a middle-school career without any suspensions, why are these girls crying when they're going to see
each other, like, next week? "I would not cry for nobody at this school."

But there's this other feeling, a tiny pea under the mattress: pride.

Eric was going to skip the dance, but he has time to kill, and in spite
of himself he has fun. The cafeteria is dotted with the glittered stars
the kids made in class with their names on them. The girls' dresses are

all clingy shimmers and flowers; the boys dance with sombreros and plastic top hats on their heads. The huge sheet cake and snacks in the fluorescent-lit hallway go largely uneaten. Besides the line dances, the kids mostly clump in the middle of the room, playing with toys the DJ gives out. "Baby Got Back" comes on, and it's all jiggling near-naked butts on the video screen, and Ms. Thomas alternately laughs and cringes. Parents will arrive soon to pick up their kids, and it's a few of the longest minutes of her life.

Then Mandy Moore's "I Wanna Be With You" comes on. Eric approaches a girl named Anna, pulls her close, a gray ball cap on his head, and for some reason a balloon inside his gray long-sleeved T-shirt. They dance, arms around each other, Eric's second slow dance in his life, not that you can tell. When the song is over, more balloons—a million, it seems—are released from a net in the sky and tumble down, knocking the last bits of middle school out of their heads.

William is waiting in a car outside, with Eric's pillow and bag in the back seat. "Congratulations," father tells son, and they drive without words to where William's semi awaits. The little refrigerator has drained the truck's battery, and they jump it, *er-er-er-er*, Eric in charge of gunning the gas in the car.

Once on the road, Eric stays awake through Maryland and a quarter of the way into Pennsylvania, then he falls asleep.

The light comes up, and Eric is still on the road when the last day of the school year begins. Ms. Thomas is crying, not because of the boy who cursed the nurse or the vandalism in the boys' locker room or the rash of fistfights this week—boys and girls, two in sixth grade, three in seventh, and two in eighth, over some fake slapping in class, a brownie, whatever, victory determined when the other person cries, gets a black eye, or falls to the ground—or even the remnants of today's brawl, three high schoolers and police and ice packs crowded right this moment into Mr. West's office. She is crying because of the typed letter she has gotten signed, "Mara Zall aka Bubbles."

Mara, a seventh grader, has been quite a source of stress for Ms. Thomas this year, starting with a notebook filled with writings about sucking dick and ending with notes that said much the same thing, so what the girl has written this time stuns her. Although it seems strange coming from her, Mara writes, Ms. Thomas should be proud of what she has accomplished as principal and with her family, and though Mara can't change the mistakes she herself has made, she wishes she could, and "I think you are the best principal ever, even though I didn't show it."

"You just never know who you're getting through to," Ms. Thomas says, through tears. "That's middle schoolers for you."

In the sixth-grade wing, Lily puts her head down as her teachers sign her yearbook. Most of the kids dart from room to room, but Lily and Beth, wearing light-blue T-shirts and matching ponytails, linger in Ms. Knighten's, the quietest room. Lily has written to Beth, "You're like a third sister to me. Hope I see you over the summer. LYLAS, Lily." She has signed her name on Mia's and written "BBFE" (Best Buds Forever), "but I haven't finished writing in hers. I don't want Alexandra to." Mia has written in Lily's book, "Mia Reilly LYLAS BBFE."

In the cafeteria, Ben comes up to Jimmy: "You're right. Yoda is eight hundred seventy-four years old, not eight hundred forty-seven."

"I knew it was near nine hundred."

"How does he live so long?"

"He waddles."

"He uses the Force to keep his heart beating."

"In *Episode II*, Luke is thirty-two," Jimmy says.

"No, he's in his twenties."

"In *Episode III*, he's going to be forty."

Jimmy has finished his lunch. He gets up from the table, burps, and heads outside. On the way out he sees Joe, who earlier in the day was tussling with another boy over some paper torn from a binder. Jimmy looks down at him—way down, farther down than even a month ago—and says, "I can't believe you were fighting over a blank piece of paper."

On the playground, Alexandra poses for photos with the new friends she's made this year. Mia is on the field practicing a new high-five with Marnie, and when she spots a man shirtless in the distance, she runs back and forth and shouts, "There's a guy running in his underwear! There's a guy running in his underwear!" Lily and Beth stand on the edge of the blacktop, kicking their Skechers and talking about amusement parks and pools.

At recess, Jackie tries to write "LOSER" on Dan Pryor's forehead, but the ink pen doesn't work well on his sweaty skin, and she only gets through "LOS." Kevin has drawn a penis on Dan's cheek. Dan doesn't know what's on his face, but whatever it is makes everyone laugh, so he rubs hard.

Jackie had decided that on the last day she was going to have everyone sign her jeans. She would save the butt for Adam and Jay. But when the time came, her mom wouldn't let her, so she settled for a white T-shirt instead.

Elizabeth has been going out with a boy named Dillon for a week because she didn't want to hurt his feelings by saying no, and she is trying desperately to get back inside the cafeteria to deliver him a note:

> *Hey wat's up? I am writing to say I think we should break up because we never talk or do ne thing. Don't be upset because you shouldn't get upset over me. We can still be friends.*

She's left his name off so her nosy friends won't figure out who it is, since everyone on the planet thinks Dillon is ugly and utterly gross. Except her—ugly, sure, but sweet, and only sort of gross.

"I have to give someone something," she says to Ms. Rouiller.

"Is it life-threatening?"

"Yes."

"This is Elizabeth," Mrs. Rashid says. "Everything is life-threatening with her."

Denied a pass inside, Elizabeth decides she'll break up on IM later, and now she's shoving Mr. Juliano toward Ms. Rouiller so she can take a photo of them together. "Go ask her," Mr. Juliano tells Elizabeth, who says, "I'm scared."

"There's nothing to be scared of in middle school," Mr. Juliano says. "Except all the teachers, and half the students."

In the eighth-grade wing, kids are screaming, signing yearbooks, eating leftover cookies from graduation, watching last night's slide show again, and singing along to its soundtrack. Chris pushes a toy cop car down the hall and says, "I'm a little kid." Dawn sits on a counter in the corner of the math room, thinking of how mean people were here, but she's a tiny bit sad to leave.

When the bell rings, the sixth graders yell and run out the door. The seventh graders are a little more huggy, and slow. Then the eighth graders emerge, through an arbor of clapping staffers. Dawn runs out with her hands up: "I'm free!" Some kids slap the teachers' hands. Some girls hold hands and cry. Liam tosses a tennis ball as he passes down the hall, Chris claps back at those who are applauding him. Some kids hug so hard they won't let go.

And somewhere in southern Michigan, in the silent cab of a truck, Eric tosses sunflower seeds at his father, who tosses them back. The Slip-knot CD is coming through his headphones. Eric smiles, and sits back. He thinks for a very small moment about how certain teachers at middle school were really cool, and he'll miss them.

But mostly he thinks about the music.

you get good at something and then you move on

The F comes in the mail, eventually—Eric's report card having been held up a month because he didn't turn in a textbook. At the bottom of the page it says PROMOTED, and Eric thinks, "Yes. They wanted me out of there, so they passed me." The F is supposed to mean no band, so Eric figures that's a good excuse to quit sax and focus on playing bass with Beef. "You get good at something," he says, "and then you move on. It's like skating, how the good bladers become skateboarders."

But when high school starts, Eric's on the list for band. The county F rule goes unenforced. So Eric sticks with the sax and tries out for All-State, waits for his baby brother to be born (there is no new house with a basement for Matchbox cars), hangs with his friends, old and new. He is impressed that kids can fit in all different ways in high school—he doesn't feel like an outsider. He visits his old teachers at Wilde Lake, except for Ms. Adams, who's gone to teach in a school with a supposedly easier "population." He tells Mr. Shifflett about his new science teacher, who has a real piece of lava rock and is giving him a B. Other than that, his first-quarter interim grades are all C's, which doesn't concern him in the least.

"If I were, like, 'Oh my God, I'm a dummy,' " he says, "I might be worried. But I'm smart."

*   *   *

Over the summer, Jackie develops a crush on Vin Diesel, and finally gets the Internet. In her instant-message profile, she muses that she is so bored—apparently the Internet hasn't cured this—that she is dipping her Frosted Flakes into milk one flake at a time. She puts the call out for a boyfriend. "If u r single give me a im n i will talk to u," Jackie writes.

Days later, at another of Dustin Fried's parties, she's sitting on the couch, damp from the hot tub, when Kevin says, "Adam likes you." Jackie asks Adam if he wants to go out, and he says okay. During truth-or-dare, she gives him a peck.

Four days later, she sees Adam at the pool. She says hi; he says nothing back. He is conferring with Kristina, one of those "You tell her" / "No, you tell her" conversations.

"What is it?" Jackie demands.

"I don't like you anymore."

Jackie is confused, yet sanguine. "He likes you a lot one day and you don't talk with him for a few days and all of a sudden he doesn't like you anymore. Hello? Oh well, there's a million guys out there, and by the time I'm twenty-one, a million more will be born."

Then again: "The one for you could be two years old right now, or ninety. My soulmate could have been Benjamin Franklin."

Elizabeth and her parents go to Seattle for the synchronized-swimming nationals, a fact Joseph tells even to the cashier at Subway, driving Elizabeth mad. Then a family vacation to British Columbia. It's the first time Elizabeth doesn't show interest in a family vacation—she'd prefer to be back east with her friends. She worries every time her mother mentions low cash flow.

"Are we going to be poor?"

"No, sweetie, we have a lot of money in the bank, we just don't have any with us."

The trip turns out to be not so bad, especially the restaurants. While taking pictures of the salmon running at the locks, Elizabeth mentions she might want to be a photographer, and Joseph's heart leaps a tiny bit but he keeps his mouth shut, lest he turn her off. He promises to bring her for Take Your Daughter to Work Day, and she is glad.

Later in the summer, they tour Switzerland, where, although her dad is embarrassing, there is a cute fourteen-year-old boy to talk to, and a group of twenty-year-olds who take her out one night and buy her a bottle of wine. She takes only three sips, because she doesn't want to come back drunk. When Joseph takes Elizabeth's film in to be developed, there are some photos of Miss Colyer, which he finds odd, but "she won't talk to me about it. They got along better, or something."

When eighth grade starts, Ellen assigns Liz one night a week to cook dinner. The first few times she grumbles, and they suffer through spaghetti with hot dog chunks, but she starts to enjoy it, and the meals get more palatable, too.

Over the summer, Lily starts to organize a campaign with the neighborhood kids to rescue pound puppies. She creates a newsletter on the computer, makes plans to alert the local newspapers and television stations, then drops it. Her mother has taken a job as the office manager of Mia's mom's dental practice, which at first seemed like a good way for the two girls to hang out, but it doesn't really happen. She sees a lot of Beth and not as much of Mia, who's pretty busy.

When school starts up, however, the three take gymnastics together on Fridays, at Lily's urging, and Beth and Mia become friends in their own right. Alexandra continues to do her own thing, but during French class she and Lily bond over their dislike of Abigail Werner, who sits at their table. Lily becomes a regular on Instant Messenger and, despite her avowal that she had no interest in speaking to boys for at least a decade, gets herself caught in the middle of online dramas with the boys who like Mia.

"Timothy is mad because I said Beth wasn't online but really she was—she was with me at my house—and then he found out. And so I'm trying to apologize but he won't answer me back so will you apologize to him for me?"

No, it doesn't make sense to her either, but she's enjoying herself.

Jimmy showers every day now, sometimes twice. While he's sailing and camping and swimming and practicing with his magician handbook (so he'll be comfortable getting up in front of groups) and playing with his new friends the Miller twins (no battle of egos), Jimmy is growing. He adds three inches in three months, and ends the summer at five six and a half.

After clearing off his bedroom floor, Jimmy starts doing thirty crunches a night, plus ten or twelve curls with eight-pound weights— stuff he saw in his father's *Men's Health* magazine. Cheese and crackers have replaced much of the junk regime: "After a while, cookies get old." His belly has flattened. His arms have muscled. Peach fuzz has started to emerge—not like Jacob, who has hair dangling under his arms, but still.

When school starts, his temper, as his parents see it, gets worse. They refrain from checking his homework and only help when asked—and Jimmy does well. The brick wall no longer appeals to Jimmy during recess; he plays football instead, and comes home and tells his mom about the touchdown he makes.

It took a while, but Jimmy has started to see many of his bodily changes as a good thing. He feels like he's not just getting bigger but getting stronger, too. He realizes that this is what makes him more like those older boys he watches, who seem so well adjusted and happy.

He misses what he left behind, but he wants to get there, soon.

notes

4   *The most humiliating experience of their lives:* Giannetti and Sagarese (2001).

5   *They've read to expect contradictions:* Some of these examples, and more, are found in Giannetti and Sagarese (1997, xiv) and Freud (1936).

5   *Children start to fix their values:* The British philosopher Alfred North Whitehead called preadolescence "the years during which the lines of character are graven." According to Albert Schweitzer, "The most important years in life are those between nine and fourteen. This is the time to plant the seeds of knowledge in the mind—afterwards it is too late. This is the time to acquaint the young with the great spirits of mankind."

6   *Middle school pulls in children:* An excellent source on children's changes from sixth to seventh to eighth grade is Judith Baenen, author of several pamphlets on middle schoolers and president of St. Mary's Academy in Englewood, Colo.

7   *James Rouse's original planned community:* The early years of Columbia were explored beautifully by the novelist Michael Chabon (2001), who grew up there at its inception.

16   *Thirteen-year-olds can't get interested:* Douglas MacIver, principal research scientist at the Center for Social Organization of Schools at Johns Hopkins University, which helps schools implement what he calls "minds-on" learning practices, has found middle schoolers less likely than third- through fifth-graders to display high-interest, active engagement and high effort, and to think what they're taught is valuable. As well, they are less convinced teachers care about their learning.

18   *Anything less than a C is unacceptable:* Temple University Professor Laurence Steinberg (1997, 161) found that black students thought a C-minus

was the grade threshold at which they'd get in trouble; for white students, the threshold was a full letter grade higher.

35   *Means that you put friends number one:* Sullivan (1953, 245–46) and Gesell (1956). Sullivan's work on the nature and importance of these formative friendships, what he calls "chumships," remains the prevailing philosophy today.

42   *Never have more capacity for devotion:* Freud (1968).

43   *Jackie is in the norm:* Data on young adolescents' romantic activity are scarce, thanks in part to a Bush-administration decision in 1991 rescinding funding for such research, on the grounds that asking children questions about sexual behavior might encourage it. While Thompson and Grace (2001, 191) report data from the Sexuality Information and Education Council of the United States (SIECUS) that 73 percent of girls and 66 percent of boys thirteen and younger had been kissed, a 2003 Henry J. Kaiser Family Foundation study found that 52 percent of thirteen- and fourteen-year-olds had been kissed romantically. According to the SIECUS data, 20 percent of thirteen-year-old boys had touched breasts, and 25 percent of girls that age had had their breasts touched.

In 1999, the federal Centers for Disease Control and Prevention reported that 12 percent of boys and 4 percent of girls had had intercourse by age thirteen. The National Campaign to Prevent Teen Pregnancy analyzed data from several 1990s studies to conclude in 2003 that 2 to 4 percent of twelve-year-old girls and 6 to 8 percent of boys, depending on how the question was asked, said they were sexually experienced. The analysis concluded that about one in five children had had sex by age fifteen, and that the parents of about two-thirds of experienced fourteen-year-olds did not know that their children had had sex.

45   *Because they aren't so comfortable:* Darling et al. (1999, 476).

47   *Not worth the anxiety and depression:* Both schools of thought are summarized in ibid. Among boys and girls in eighth grade, the study reports, comfort with the opposite sex is a consistent predictor of self-esteem.

47   *To make sure Jackie doesn't grow up too fast:* For more on the value and difficulty of holding on to childhood—and the media's role—see Postman (1994) and Elkind (2001). Pipher (1994, 66–67) writes on media influence and parents as "the enemies of the cultural indoctrination." Although movies, video games, and music are rated, the entertainment industries disregard their own ratings and market to young children products for people seventeen and up, according to a Sept. 2000 study by the Federal Trade Commission.

54   *The most endearing traits of two-year-olds:* Erikson (1963) and Caplan (1983). Some sentences from Caplan could be taken just as easily from a middle-school handbook: "They like to talk even if they have nothing to say." "He wants exactly what he wants when he wants it, cannot adapt, give in, or wait even a moment, perhaps because he is not able to think ahead."

61   *Four-fifths the height he'll attain by adulthood:* Gesell (1956, 72).

71 *Ten times as likely to engage in risky behaviors:* Young and Zimmerman (1998).

72 *Teachers as a whole would choose more active parents:* Public Agenda, 2000.

73 *Protects against nearly every possible middle-school health risk:* Resnick et al. (1997, 823–32). Pollack (1998) also cites research that correlates boys' behavior to both their relationships with their parents and their parents' relationships with each other.

73 *Organizations across the country:* They include the National Coalition for Parent Involvement in Education in Fairfax, Va., the National Network of Partnership Schools in Baltimore, and the National PTA in Chicago.

77 *A disregard for consequences:* Restak (2001) and Gesell (1956).

82 *Show few signs of abating:* American Association of University Women (2001). According to a study of eighth- through eleventh-graders, seven in ten students said their schools had harassment policies in 2000, compared with one-quarter in 1993. Eight in ten girls reported experiencing harassment at some time in their school lives, the same as in 1993. Fifty-six percent of boys said they'd been harassed, compared with 49 percent in 1993.

83 *Sometimes it feels like her body is the only reason:* "Being beautiful can be a Pyrrhic victory. The battle for popularity is won, but the war for respect as a whole person is lost" (Pipher [1994, 55]).

83 *They can't . . . infuse disgrace back into activities:* Ibid., 66.

85 *Tries to appear helpless:* Orenstein (1994, 22).

90 *The boys continue bragging:* Pollack (1998, 16) posits that boys brag to hide a lack of confidence, more pronounced in boys than girls.

100 *Children living in two-parent households:* The number of children living in two-parent households decreased from 77 percent in 1980 to 69 percent in 2001, according to the Department of Health and Human Services. In 1999, 78 percent of mothers of children age six through thirteen worked, according to the U.S. Department of Labor Bureau of Labor Statistics.

100 *She wants to talk* more *about her schoolwork:* Seventy-two percent of children age ten to thirteen said this was the case, compared with 48 percent of high school students (National Commission on Children [1991, 13]).

106 *Boys actually report more conflict:* Wyndol Furman, "The Measurement of Friendship Perceptions: Conceptual and Methodological Issues," in Bukowski et al., eds. (1996).

106 *You will prey upon anyone:* On insulting as a developmental achievement, see Thompson and Grace (2001, 106).

106 *Single most painful thing about middle school:* According to one thousand students surveyed by Giannetti and Sagarese (2001).

107 *Tend to emerge as more self-sufficient adults:* Pipher (1994, 266).

109 *Empowered by groupthink, tinged by guilt:* On the power of groupthink, see Thompson and Grace (2001, 103 and 177).

110 *More upsetting than if he spied on you in the shower:* American Association of University Women (2001, 11).

114 *For the first two-thirds of the twentieth century:* For more on the origins and

purposes of middle school, see Dickinson, ed. (2001), and David, ed. (1998).

114   *Able to get themselves around the abstract as well as the concrete:* The Swiss psychologist Jean Piaget originated the concept that children in preadolescence move from concrete thinking to formal operations, in which they can think abstractly and hypothetically for the first time. Donald Eichhorn, one of the fathers of the modern middle school, said in a 1972 speech printed in David (1998, 57), "It is vital that emphasis be placed on higher cognitive processes such as hypothesizing, generalizing, synthesizing, and evaluating" as well as recalling, recognizing, and copying. Good sources on the changes needed in middle schools include Jackson and Davis (2000); Scales (1996); Erb, ed. (2001); Carnegie Council on Adolescent Development (1995); and the 1997 vision statement by Joan Lipsitz of the Lilly Endowment, M. Hayes Mizell of the Edna McConnell Clark Foundation, Anthony W. Jackson of the Carnegie Corporation, and Leah Meyer Austin of the W. K. Kellogg Foundation, which all study middle-school reform.

115   *Curriculum would let students progress at different rates:* John Lounsbury, a founder of the middle-school movement, noted in 1977, "At this level when young people exhibit greatest diversity, we often present them a more standardized and common program than any other time in the educational process" (in George, ed. [1977]).

117   *70 percent of questions:* Alfred Arth, chairman of the middle-school program at the University of Nebraska School of Education.

117   *Learn what their students need only on the job:* In a 1992 study of middle-school teachers, only half said they had received specific middle-school preparation, and half said it was inadequate or poor. Most had not intended to teach middle school. Nearly a third of respondents had professional preparation that did not include coursework on young-adolescent development, 40 percent didn't include coursework directly on appropriate teaching methods for young adolescents, and nearly 60 percent did not include fieldwork in grades five through nine. The situation has improved since then, to some degree (Scales and McEwin [1994]).

118   *Shown to have significant academic and other advantages:* Lee and Smith (1993).

119   *The pendulum has swung the other way:* "The once-heralded argument for making a more humane and humanistic institution in the 1960s and 1970s was turned aside by the Conservative Restoration of the 1990s," "rolled back by neo-Puritan critique favoring schools that were less joyful, more stressful, focused almost solely on academics, and less concerned about young adolescents as people" (Dickinson [2001, xviii]).

121   *Those emotions literally shrink the space:* O'Neil (1996).

129   *Hanging more with the other black girls:* "As children approach adolescence, they seem to become more selective in their choice of same-race friends," write Frances E. Aboud and Morton J. Mendelson, "Determinants of Friendship Selection and Quality: Developmental Perspectives," in Bukowski

et al., eds. (1996, 91). Black girls, they found, have the most other-race friends, white girls the fewest.

148   *The biggest influence is friends:* The 2002 Roper Youth Report, conducted by Roper ASW, asked eight-to-seventeen-year-olds what is their biggest influence in making such decisions. For music, 64 percent said friends and 28 percent said parents; for clothing, 47 percent said friends and 42 percent parents. For television, however, only 26 percent said friends and 43 percent parents; for alcohol use, 20 percent friends and 71 percent parents; and for career plans, 18 percent friends and 53 percent parents.

148   *Spends, on average, fifty-nine dollars a week:* Teenage Research Unlimited, Glenbrook, Ill.

163   *And one theory posits that the rapid pace of video games triggers irrational fear responses:* Sylwester (1997).

164   *Having a parent travel for work:* Elkind (2001, 184).

178   *There are far more niches in which to find acceptance:* On how high school's wide range of activities and subcultures benefits children who didn't fit in during middle school, see Eder and Kinney (1995) and Kinney (1993).

182   *The more aggressive and defiant they are:* Rodkin et al. (2000, 14–24).

204   *Her best friend has several worlds:* For more on what each girl gets from an uneven friendship, see Thompson and Grace (2001, 60).

205   *Lily . . . is a pleaser:* The term "pleaser" is from Wiseman (2002). For more on the organizational chart of middle-school cliques, see Giannetti and Sagarese (2001).

206   *It wouldn't be productive to invade:* On what children want from parents regarding friendships, see Thompson and Grace (2001, 8–11).

210   *She has some of the vocabulary:* On the difference between having vocabulary and having knowledge, see Pipher (1994, 245).

214   *You just should have one:* One study found that the norm for middle-school girls is to think "one should always be in love" (Simon et al. [1992]).

223   *"kids would have some power":* On the value of self-directed learning and why some teachers feel threatened by it, see Pitton, in Dickinson, ed. (2001, 23): "As adults, we know we work harder on things we enjoy, we learn more when we choose to do something and are involved in the decision making, and we strive to do our work well when it means something to us." See also Richard R. Powell, "On Headpieces of Straw: How Middle Level Students View Their Schooling," in ibid. (117–52); and William Alexander's 1966 speech at the Mount Kisco Conference, reprinted in David, ed. (1998, 21).

selected bibliography

American Association of University Women Education Foundation. "Hostile Hallways: Bullying, Teasing, and Sexual Harassment in School." Washington, D.C.: American Association of University Women, 2001.

Asher, Steven R., and John D. Coie, eds. *Peer Rejection in Childhood*. Cambridge, UK: Cambridge University Press, 1990.

Blum, Robert William, and Peggy Mann Rinehart. *Reducing the Risk: Connections That Make a Difference in the Lives of Youth*. Report of the National Longitudinal Study of Adolescent Health. Minneapolis: University of Minnesota Press, 1997.

Bukowski, William M., Andrew F. Newcomb, and Willard W. Hartup, eds. *The Company They Keep: Friendship in Childhood and Adolescence*. Cambridge, UK: Cambridge University Press, 1996. Reprint, 1998.

Caplan, Theresa and Frank. *The Early Childhood Years: The 2 to 6 Year Old*. New York: Bantam Books, 1983.

Carnegie Council on Adolescent Development. *Great Transitions: Preparing Adolescents for a New Century*. New York: Carnegie Corporation, 1995.

Chabon, Michael. "Maps and Legends." *Architectural Digest*, April 2001, p. 46.

Coles, Robert. *The Moral Intelligence of Children*. New York: Random House, 1997.

Darling, Nancy, Bonnie B. Dowdy, M. Lee Van Horn, and Linda Caldwell. "Mixed-Sex Settings and the Perception of Competence." *Journal of Youth and Adolescence*, vol. 28, no. 4 (1999): pp. 461–80.

David, Robert, ed. *Moving Forward from the Past: Early Writings and Current Reflections of Middle School Founders*. Columbus, Ohio: National Middle School Association, 1998.

Dickinson, Thomas S., ed. *Reinventing the Middle School*. New York: Routledge-Falmer, 2001.

Eder, Donna, and David A. Kinney. "The Effect of Middle School Extracurricular Activities on Adolescents' Popularity and Peer Status." *Youth & Society*, vol. 26, no. 3 (March 1995): pp. 298–324.

Elkind, David. *The Hurried Child: Growing Up Too Fast Too Soon*. Cambridge, Mass.: Perseus Books, 3rd ed., 2001.

Erb, Thomas Owen, ed. *This We Believe: And Now We Must Act*. Columbus, Ohio: National Middle School Association, 2001.

Erikson, Erik H., ed. *Youth: Change and Challenge*. New York: Basic Books, 1963.

———. *Identity: Youth and Crisis*. New York: W. W. Norton, 1968.

Freud, Anna. *The Ego and the Mechanisms of Defense*. New York: International University Press, 1936.

———. "On Certain Difficulties in the Preadolescent's Relation to His Parents." In *The Writings of Anna Freud, Vol. 4*. New York: International University Press, 1968.

Furman, Wyndol, B. Bradford Brown, and Candice Feiring, eds. *The Development of Romantic Relationships in Adolescence*. Cambridge, UK: Cambridge University Press, 1999.

George, Paul, ed. *The Middle School: A Look Ahead*. Columbus, Ohio: National Middle School Association, 1977.

Gesell, Arnold, Frances L. Ilg, and Louise Bates Ames. *Youth: The Years from Ten to Sixteen*. New York: Harper & Row, 1956.

Giannetti, Charlene C., and Margaret Sagarese. *The Roller-Coaster Years: Raising Your Child Through the Maddening Yet Magical Middle School Years*. New York: Broadway Books, 1997.

———. *Cliques: 8 Steps to Help Your Child Survive the Social Jungle*. New York: Broadway Books, 2001.

Hersch, Patricia. *A Tribe Apart: A Journey into the Heart of American Adolescence*. New York: Ballantine Books, 1998.

Jackson, Anthony, and Gayle Davis. *Turning Points 2000: Educating Adolescents in the 21st Century*. New York: Teachers College Press, 2000.

Kinney, David A. "From Nerds to Normals: The Recovery of Identity Among Adolescents from Middle School to High School." *Sociology of Education*, vol. 66 (Jan. 1993): pp. 21–40.

Lee, V., and J. Smith. "Effects of School Restructuring on the Achievement and Engagement of Middle-Grades Students." *Sociology of Education*, vol. 64, no. 3 (1993): pp. 190–208.

Lipsitz, Joan, M. Hayes Mizell, Anthony W. Jackson, and Leah Meyer Austin. "Speaking with One Voice: A Manifesto for Middle-Grades Reform." *Phi Delta Kappan*, vol. 78, no. 7 (March 1997): p. 533.

National Commission on Children. *Speaking of Kids: A National Survey of Children and Parents*. Washington, D.C.: National Commission on Children, 1991.

O'Neil, John. "On Emotional Intelligence: A Conversation with Daniel Goleman." *Educational Leadership*, Sept. 1996, pp. 6–11.

Orenstein, Peggy. *Schoolgirls: Young Women, Self-Esteem and the Confidence Gap.* New York: Doubleday, 1994.

Pipher, Mary. *Reviving Ophelia: Saving the Selves of Adolescent Girls.* New York: Ballantine Books, 1994.

Pollack, William. *Real Boys: Rescuing Our Sons from the Myths of Boyhood.* New York: Random House, 1998.

Postman, Neil. *The Disappearance of Childhood.* New York: Delacorte Press, 1982. Reprint, New York: Vintage Books, 1994.

Public Agenda. *A Sense of Calling: Who Teaches and Why.* New York: Public Agenda, 2000.

Resnick, Michael D., et al. "Protecting Adolescents from Harm: Findings from the National Longitudinal Study on Adolescent Health." *Journal of the American Medical Association,* vol. 278, no. 10 (Sept. 10, 1997): pp. 823–32.

Restak, Richard. *The Secret Life of the Brain.* Washington, D.C.: Dana Press and Joseph Henry Press, 2001.

Rodkin, Philip C., Thomas W. Farmer, Ruth Pearl, and Richard Van Acker. "Heterogeneity of Popular Boys: Antisocial and Prosocial Configurations." *Developmental Psychology,* vol. 36, no. 1 (Jan. 2000): pp. 14–24.

Scales, Peter C. *Boxed In and Bored: How Middle Schools Continue to Fail Young Adolescents—and What Good Middle Schools Do Right.* Minneapolis: Search Institute, 1996.

———, and C. Kenneth McEwin. *Growing Pains: The Making of America's Middle School Teachers.* Columbus, Ohio: National Middle School Association, 1994.

Simmons, Rachel. *Odd Girl Out: The Hidden Culture of Aggression in Girls.* New York: Harcourt, 2002.

Simon, R.W., Donna Eder, and C. Evans. "The Development of Feeling Norms Underlying Romantic Love Among Adolescent Females." *Social Psychology Quarterly,* vol. 55, no. 1 (1992): pp. 29–46.

Steinberg, Laurence, with B. Bradford Brown and Sanford M. Dornbusch. *Beyond the Classroom: Why School Reform Has Failed and What Parents Need to Do.* New York: Touchstone, 1997.

Stepp, Laura Sessions. *Our Last Best Shot: Guiding Our Children Through Early Adolescence.* New York: Riverhead Books, 2000.

Sullivan, Harry Stack. *The Interpersonal Theory of Psychiatry.* New York: W. W. Norton, 1953.

Sylwester, Robert. "Bioelectronic Learning: The Effects of Electronic Media on a Developing Brain." *Technos: Quarterly for Education and Technology,* vol. 6, no. 2 (Summer 1997): pp. 19–22.

———, ed. *Student Brains, School Issues: A Collection of Articles.* Arlington Heights, Ill.: SkyLight Training and Publishing, 1998.

Thompson, Michael, and Catherine O'Neill Grace, with Lawrence J. Cohen. *Best Friends, Worst Enemies: Understanding the Social Lives of Children.* New York: Ballantine Books, 2001.

White, Emily. *Fast Girls: The Myth of the Slut.* New York: Scribner, 2002.

Wiseman, Rosalind. *Queen Bees and Wannabes: Helping Your Daughter Survive*

Cliques, Gossip, Boyfriends and Other Realities of Adolescence. New York: Crown Publishers, 2002.

Young, Thomas L., and Rick Zimmerman, "Clueless: Parental Knowledge of Risk Behaviors of Middle School Students." *Archives of Pediatric and Adolescent Medicine*, vol. 152 (Nov. 1998): pp. 1137–39.

I have also benefited from the expertise of these authorities:

On brain research, Jay Giedd of the National Institute of Mental Health.

On relationships with parents, Robert Billingham of Indiana University.

On relationships with friends, William Bukowski of Concordia University, Montreal, and Jeffrey Parker of the Pennsylvania State University.

On romance, W. Andrew Collins of the University of Minnesota.

On materialism, Michael Wood of Teenage Research Unlimited, and Marvin Goldberg of the Pennsylvania State University.

On motivation, Douglas MacIver of Johns Hopkins University, and Judith Baenen of St. Mary's Academy, Englewood, Colo.

On teacher preparation, Kenneth McEwin of Appalachian State University.

On middle school education, Sue Swaim of the National Middle School Association.

acknowledgments

This book would be nothing without the honesty and guts of the Wilde Lake children, especially those I wrote about in depth. Thanks for sharing, being fun, tolerating me. Thanks, too, to their warm families, who opened their homes and didn't put on an act. Brenda Thomas not only let me into her school but encouraged me to explore freely, and the staff was one hundred percent helpful. In the Howard County school system, thanks to John O'Rourke, Mike Hickey, Alice Haskins, Ken Gill, and Patti Caplan.

Gail Ross, my agent, took this project beyond where I imagined, and talked me off the ledge. Becky Saletan, my editor, let me tell the story I wanted to, then made it better. I couldn't have asked for any better than the FSG team. At *The Washington Post*, more people than I can name have supported this effort, and my career. The Ucross Foundation provided a beyond-marvelous place to write.

My friends helped in many ways, especially Hanna Rosin, Susan Gates, Marilyn Thompson, Amy Joyce, David Plotz, Lucy Spelman, Hank Stuever, Amy Argetsinger, Cabot Orton, Marina Walsh, Beverly Solochek, Gail and Bill McNulty, Heather Block, Annette Friedman, Paula McLain, Jennifer Starkweather, Angela Schaeffer, Rene Sanchez, David Finkel, Scott Shapiro, and John Miller. Thanks also to Team Meldrom, Madonna Lebling, Karen Sigel, the Fenland Field kids, and the loving Block-Perlsteins.

The devotion and humor of my parents, Sandi and Jerry Perlstein, enriched my own middle-school years. Thank you for that, and much more. My brothers Rick and Ben are my models of creativity and ambition. My grandparents, Celia and Harry Perlstein and Bernie and Sarah Friedman, have given me more than they know.

Thanks to my cousins, Rachel and Noah Friedman, for being empathic, hilarious, and still huggy after all these years. Last, I am indebted beyond words to Lisa Schneider-Friedman and David Friedman, my aunt and uncle, who epitomize goodness—and keep me in tuna.